Who Married Figaro?

A BOOK OF OPERA CHARACTERS

Who Married Figaro?

A BOOK OF OPERA CHARACTERS

Joyce Bourne

OXFORD

UNIVERSITY PRESS

OXFORD
UNIVERSITY PRESS

Great Clarendon Street, Oxford OX2 6DP

Oxford University Press is a department of the University of Oxford.
It furthers the University's objective of excellence in research, scholarship,
and education by publishing worldwide in

Oxford New York

Auckland Cape Town Dar es Salaam Hong Kong Karachi
Kuala Lumpur Madrid Melbourne Mexico City Nairobi
New Delhi Shanghai Taipei Toronto

With offices in
Argentina Austria Brazil Chile Czech Republic France Greece
Guatemala Hungary Italy Japan Poland Portugal Singapore
South Korea Switzerland Thailand Turkey Ukraine Vietnam

Oxford is a registered trade mark of Oxford University Press
in the UK and certain other countries

Published in the United States
by Oxford University Press Inc., New York

British Library Cataloguing in Publication Data
Data available

Library of Congress Cataloging in Publication Data
Data available

Typeset by SPI Publisher Services, Pondicherry, India
Printed in Great Britain on acid-free paper by
Clays Ltd., St. Ives plc.

ISBN 978–0–19–954819–4

1 3 5 7 9 10 8 6 4 2

For Michael with love and gratitude
Prima la musica, dopo le parole

Du meines Herzens heiligster Stolz (*Die Walküre*, Act 3),
Grand Theatre, Leeds, April 1976.

Foreword

This book is to be dipped into for enjoyment, for elucidation, for explanation and—of course—for education. It is a reference book for operaphiles who read synopses, but feel short-changed about information on the characters touched upon in such potted accounts. It gives in various degrees flesh and blood to these operatic characters.

Dr Bourne's stated intention is 'not to analyse anything musically, but rather to concentrate on the people in the operas—how they relate to each other, how they affect the events in the opera, what happens to them, how they develop throughout the work....', and at the same time to provide a brief description of the operas by way of context.

She has set about a formidable task covering something a little short of 280 operas and over 2,500 characters with clarity and sensitivity which should serve the needs of every level of enquiring mind delving for information about opera.

It is going to be the answer to a prayer for those who attend operas without doing their homework properly, or those attending performances which are incomprehensible for such unprofessional reasons as the prevalent disregard of singers to get the dramatic message of their roles across by articulation of the words.

It is also going to be the answer to a prayer for those who dabble in opera quizzes. Indeed, it may put an end to such quizzes, given the ease with which the answers will be found in this volume.

My advice to readers is to dip or riffle in Dr Bourne's work and simply enjoy the fruits of her researches—with the bonus of coming out considerably better informed and much the wiser.

GEORGE CHRISTIE

Glyndebourne, 1998

Contents

List of Contributors' Articles

Aaron
Philip Langridge

Don Alfonso
Sir Thomas Allen

Brünnhilde
Dame Anne Evans

Billy Budd
Theodor Uppman

The Composer
Sena Jurinac

Cressida
Susana Walton

Elektra
Susan Bullock

Hanna Glawari
Adèle Leigh

Peter Grimes
Michael Kennedy

Maximilian Hauk-Šendorf
Nigel Douglas

Herod
Robert Tear

Isolde
Christine Brewer

Kostelnička
Sir Charles Mackerras

Leporello
Bryn Terfel

Mandryka
The Earl of Harewood

Matthias Grünewald
Peter Sellars

Meg
Joyce DiDonato

Mélisande
Joan Rodgers

Norma
Andrew Porter

Otello
Plácido Domingo

Pilgrim
Ursula Vaughan Williams

Poppea
Sylvia McNair

Prospero
Simon Keenlyside

Rigoletto
Frank Johnson

Rodrigo, Marquis de Posa
Thomas Hampson

Hans Sachs
Sir John Tomlinson

Scarpia
Sir Jonathan Miller

Christine Storch
Dame Felicity Lott

Mary Stuart
Dame Janet Baker

Tito
Martin Isepp

Violetta
Marie McLaughlin

Preface to the Second Edition

This edition has enabled me to make a few minor corrections and, in some instances, to add the names of interpreters who have come to the fore in the past ten years. Two of these international artists have contributed new articles: Christine Brewer (Isolde) and Susan Bullock (Elektra), both of whom I thank most sincerely. The major additions are an appendix of web links and an appendix discussing operas which have been composed since the book was published in 1998. New operas often come—and go. They are given an initial run of performances by the company which commissioned them and then, for various reasons, fade from the repertoire. The twelve operas included in this appendix are all works which have, so far, shown signs of standing the test of time: they have received more than one production—in many cases there have been ten or more new productions—and they have travelled and succeeded outside their country of origin. I am most grateful to Joyce DiDonato (Meg in Mark Adamo's *Little Women*) and Simon Keenlyside (Prospero in Thomas Adès's *The Tempest*) for agreeing to put into words their experience in working with the composer in creating a new role.

I appreciate the help given to me by various people, especially Rita Grudźien at The Royal Opera House, Covent Garden; Jane Livingston at English National Opera; Joanna Townsend at Glyndebourne; and Libby Rice (LSO Archivist) and Dvora Lewis for their help in supplying synopses and original cast lists. I have been encouraged all along by Judith Wilson at OUP and also by the book's dedicatee, my husband Michael Kennedy.

Joyce Bourne

Manchester 2008

Preface to the First Edition

After twenty years working with Michael Kennedy on his *Oxford Dictionary of Music* and the *Concise* version, I caught the 'lexicography bug'. Also, I became aware of gaps on the reference bookshelves—for instance, it was extremely difficult to find cast lists for world premières. So the idea for this dictionary took root.

There are many books available in which may be found synopses of operas and, understandably, they dwell primarily on the musical aspects. This book does not—there are no musical analyses, no biographies of composers, no details surrounding composition, etc. The opera synopses are very brief, giving only sufficient outline of the plot to set the participants in context. I have concentrated on the opera characters, their place in the plot, their relationships with each other, and how they influence the outcome of the story. Some notable performers are mentioned, as are important arias or ensembles, all with English translations. If I felt that literal translations could only cause confusion, the words as sung in English have been used. Where it has been possible to ascertain it, I have included the name of the artist who created each role and the year of first performance.

For the most part, the operas are indexed under their original-language titles, but there are exceptions where I felt they were better known in their English form, e.g. *The Merry Widow* instead of *Die lustige Witwe*. Where these give rise to doubts, I have inserted cross-references. The characters themselves are given under their surnames whenever these are known, for instance Eva in *Die Meistersinger* is *Pogner, Eva*, as I felt this would make relationships between characters clearer, but again there are anomalies if I thought this would cause more confusion than it would cure. Sometimes the decision was not easy and I used instinct as much as logic in deciding the best path to follow. Within the opera synopses I have put an asterisk next to each character for whom an entry will be found, and usually this will be sufficient to indicate their position in the book. I have not used asterisks within the character entries—the whole book would have been spattered with stars and this seemed unhelpful. Abbreviations have been kept to a minimum and are generally accepted forms of words. A list of these is appended.

I felt it would add immense interest to have the views of various artists who have been involved in some way with a particular role—as interpreter, conductor, producer, administrator, or writer. For their willingness to find time in their busy schedules to write for me, I am deeply indebted to the contributors of all the special articles. Their generosity is in every case typical of them both as artist and person. I am sure readers will find their views as fascinating as I have done.

Every effort has been made to provide a cross-section of the repertoire which will appeal to both the casual opera-goer and the 'buff'. Whilst I have tried not to let my personal prejudices show through too clearly, I fear they will not be too hard to detect. Inevitably there are omissions—another author would include different rarities and have different emphases.

I am most grateful for the encouragement and enthusiasm of Angus Phillips and Nicola Bion at OUP, and for the tolerance and understanding of my oft-neglected family and friends. My thanks are due to many who have been so helpful in tracking down people and facts, saved me from howlers, and helped me with translations. They include my diligent copy-editor Rowena Anketell; Sally Groves and Rachel Oakley (Schott Music Publishers); Robert Rattray (Lies Askonas Ltd., London); Peter Alward and Anne Armes (EMI Classics, London); Elka Hockings (Universal Edition (London), Ltd.); Helen Anderson and Ann Richards (The Royal Opera, Covent Garden); Jane Livingstone (English National Opera); Marie McLaughlin; Susan Bamert (Boosey & Hawkes); Paul Dewhirst; Valentina Ilyeva (Bibliographer, Moscow Conservatoire); Mrs Judy Arnold; Sir Charles Mackerras; Dr Alena Němcová (Leoš Janáček Foundation, Brno); Charles Osborne; Lina Re (Istituto Nazionale di Studi Verdiani, Parma); Dr Olga Mojžíšová (Smetana Museum, Prague); Dr Ulrike Hessler and Detlef Eberhard (Bayerische Staatsoper, Munich); Edgar Vincent (Vincent & Farrell Associates Inc., New York); Christopher Underwood; Staff of the Theatre Museum, Covent Garden, London; Pierre Vidal, Musée Biblio Opéra, Paris; Joan Rodgers; Jan Austin-Hicken (School of Music, Florida State University, Tallahassee); Mrs Shelagh Yospur (Baylor College of Medicine, Houston, Texas); Gerald Hagan; B. Menard (Bibliothèque Nationale de France, Paris); David Cairns; Rhea Pliakas and Holly Haswell of Columbiana and Nick Patterson of the Music Library, Columbia University, New York; Humphrey Burton; Mrs Julie Goodwin; Kevin Higa; Sarah Williams (Music Section, Bodleian Library, Oxford); Dr Peter Nics (Österreichisches Theater Museum, Vienna); Brian Dickie (European Union Opera, Baden-Baden); Elizabeth Mortimer (Salzburg); Gerald Larner; Dr Anna Pia Maissen (Stadtarchiv, Zürich); and Dr Rosemary Williamson and her patient staff of the library, Royal Northern College of Music, Manchester.

The book is dedicated to Michael Kennedy, who has carried out his duties as consultant editor by constantly adding to the list of operas he thought I should include. He has, from the time the first idea for this book started to take root, given me every encouragement. Even when I have been late in processing his own work, he has remained patient (most of the time). But then I suppose he had to—after all, it was from him that I caught the 'bug' in the first place.

JOYCE BOURNE

Manchester 1998

Abbreviations

Amer.	American	Mass.	Massachusetts
b	*born*	mez.	mezzo-soprano
bar.	baritone	Mlle	Mademoiselle
bass-bar.	bass-baritone	Mme	Madame
Brit.	British	Mons.	Monsieur
Calif.	California	Nat.	National
c.	*circa* (Latin = about)	NY Met	Metropolitan Opera House
CBE	Commander of the Order		(or Company), New York
	of the British Empire	nr.	near
cent.	century	OBE	Officer of the Order of the
CG	Covent Garden (Royal		British Empire
	Opera House), London	Orch.	Orchestra
CH	Companion of Honour	Penn.	Pennsylvania
ch.	chorus	perf.	performed
co.	company	Pres.	President
comp.	composer/composed by	prin.	principal
cond.	conductor/conducted by	prod.	production/produced by
counterten.	countertenor	prof.	professional
d	*died*	prol.	prologue
DBE	Dame Commander of the	*R.*	Wagner, *Das Rheingold*
	Order of the British Empire	RAM	Royal Academy of
dir.	director		Music
ed.	editor	rev.	revised
edn.	edition	RNCM	Royal Northern College of
ENO	English National Opera		Music
ens.	ensemble	S.	San
epil.	epilogue	*S.*	Wagner, *Siegfried*
excl.	excluding	Sig.	Signore
Fest.	Festival	Sig.a	Signora
Fr.	French/Frau	SO	Symphony Orchestra
Frl.	Fräulein	sop.	soprano
f.p.	first performance	Sw.	Swedish
	(sometimes separated e.g.	SW	Sadler's Wells
	f. Amer. p. = first American	ten.	tenor
	performance)	trans.	translated
G.	Wagner,	Univ.	University
	Götterdämmerung	US	United States
GTO	Glyndebourne Touring	vers.	version
	Opera	*W.*	Wagner, *Die Walküre*
incl.	including	WNO	Welsh National Opera
Ind.	Indiana		
KBE	Knight Commander of the		
	Order of the British Empire		
lib.	libretto		

* An asterisk before a character's name within an opera synopsis indicates that a separate entry may be found for that character.

A

Aaron 1. (Aron) (Schoenberg: *Moses und Aron*). Ten. Brother of Moses, who asks him to use his powers of oratory to convince the Israelites to follow Moses out of bondage. Aaron is unable to accept the idea of a god which he cannot see in person. While Moses is away collecting the tablets of stone from the Lord, Aaron builds a golden calf for the people to worship. When Moses returns, he smashes the stone tablets in frustration and chides his brother for being so sceptical. Aaron, having been put in chains, is released on Moses's orders, but dies as soon as he is freed. Created (1954, concert) by Helmut Krebs; (1957, stage) by Helmut Melchert. It is interesting that in the title of the work, this character is spelt with one 'a', but as the character, there are two 'a's. There is a theory that Schoenberg was superstitious—to spell it with two 'a's in the title would have resulted in that title having thirteen letters. Therefore, one of the 'a's was dropped, but retained for the character. *See also* ARTICLE BY PHILIP LANGRIDGE, p. 2.

2. (Aronne (Elisero)) (Rossini: *Mosè in Egitto*). Ten. Finds his niece hiding with Pharaoh's son. Created (1818) by Giuseppe Ciccimarra.

Abaris (Rameau: *Les Boréades*). Ten. Son of Apollo. Brought up by the High Priest Adamas, his identity has remained a secret. In love with Queen Alphise, he is only able to marry her when his royal blood is revealed. Created (f. stage p. 1982) by Philip Langridge.

Abigaille (Verdi: *Nabucco*). Sop. Elder but illegitimate daughter of Nabucco. She is in love with the Hebrew Ismaele who rejects her in favour of her younger sister Fenena. She attempts to replace her father as ruler of Babylon, but later, as an act of remorse, commits suicide. Aria: *Ben io t'invennï, o fatal scritto!* ('Happy chance I found you, o fatal document!'). Created (1842) by Giuseppina Strepponi (who became Verdi's wife).

Abimélech (Saint-Saëns: *Samson et Dalila*). Bass. Satrap of Gaza. He taunts the subjugated Hebrews for praying to their God who is not helping them in their distress. Their leader, Samson, slays him. Created (1877) by Herr Dengler.

Achilla (Handel: *Giulio Cesare*). Bass. General and Counsellor to Tolomeo, who cheats him. Achilla defends Cleopatra against Tolomeo and is mortally wounded. Created (1724) by Giuseppe Boschi.

Achille(s) 1. (Gluck: *Iphigénie en Aulide*). Ten. Greek hero betrothed to Iphigénie. Defends her against her father, Agamemnon, who is about to sacrifice her. Created (1774) by Joseph Legros.

2. (Tippett: *King Priam*). Ten. Greek hero who takes pity on King Priam and returns the body of his eldest son Hector. He is killed by Priam's second son, Paris. Created (1962) by Richard Lewis.

Acis (Handel: *Acis and Galatea*). Ten. A shepherd, in love with Galatea. Killed by the giant Polyphemus. Galatea transforms him into a stream. Creator (1718) unknown.

Acis and Galatea (Handel). Lib. by John Gay and others; 2 acts; f.p. Cannons, Edgware, nr. London, 1718, possibly dir. by Johann Christoph Pepusch. Better defined as a masque or pastoral.

Mythological times. *Galatea, a sea-nymph, is in love with the shepherd *Acis, but their love is threatened by the jealous giant *Polyphemus. The lovers ignore warnings of danger. Polyphemus kills Acis. Galatea transforms him into a stream.

AARON   (*Moses und Aron*—Schoenberg)

by Philip Langridge

I have to confess that the first time I looked at the part of Aaron with a view to singing it, I thought it much too difficult to learn. It was not so much the rather angular vocal writing—I had seen music written in a much more aggressive way than this—it was more a question of tuning. The flow of the vocal line in many places is very lyrical, but when you look at the detail of the accompaniment, the chords written beneath almost every note, you find that some notes fit exactly with that of the singer and some absolutely do not. I began by learning each phrase, one note following the other, so that each note was exactly in tune. Then each of these notes had to be sung, whistled, or hummed while playing the notes of the chord underneath it. If there was an exact match with the note I was singing, I put a ring round it. On the other hand, a note which was 'challenged' in the accompanying chord was very firmly crossed out. I know it sounds very long and laborious, but actually it did save time in the end because I was aware of the sounds around me when I sang it and that gave me a great sense of security.

I first performed the role in 1984 in a concert performance under Sir Georg Solti with the Chicago Symphony Orchestra and we recorded it at that time. I feel now that the character of Aaron was not thought out as it would have been on stage and I had to wait until I met the late Jean-Pierre Ponnelle for the Salzburg Festival production (1987) before I understood how this could be achieved. The first thing he said (with his wonderful French accent) was 'Sportin' Life' [the 'spiv'-like dope-peddling character in Gershwin's *Porgy and Bess*] by which I thought he must have meant eloquent and persuasive. This gave me a great starting point for Aaron, who had to be extremely persuasive to get the multitudes to forget their troubles and march off to the promised land!

My next production was with Herbert Wernicke at the Châtelet Theatre in Paris (1996). This was a very different reading altogether. The chorus were at the back of the stage standing in square holes designed to appear as if their occupants were looking down on the proceedings from a high-rise building. Moses sat on a huge pile of Bibles at the front and this left me with the whole stage to play with. My only problem was to 'persuade' the chorus (at the back) while I was singing to the front over that huge orchestra! I felt very lonely out there, almost like a comedian dying on his feet. Then I realized that Schoenberg had originally written this piece as an oratorio and only later had he put in all the stage directions.

This actually made the whole situation clearer and I was able to see the dilemma of the Multitude (imprisoned in their 'Plight') and Moses trapped with his ideals, unable to express them, while Aaron tries to sort everything out. This still called for lots of persuasion and guile and a great deal of eloquence, but above all it called for immense energy and concentration. From the singing-actor's point of view then, this was an even better solution, and we performed the piece with real understanding. After all, this work is somehow a recreation of a bit of biblical history and it needs to be told with a certain amount of truth—which is what we should always be doing on the stage, whether in comedy or tragedy. If we play truthfully to each character, then we can speak to the heart from the heart.

Adalgisa (Bellini: *Norma*). Sop. (but often sung by mez.). An acolyte of the temple. Pollione's love for her makes him reject Norma, the High Priestess. Adalgisa is horrified to realize that Pollione was Norma's lover and determines to send him back to her, but fails. Duet (with Norma): *Mira, o Norma, ai tuoi ginocchi* ('See, Norma, at your knees'). Ebe Stignani, Fedora Barbieri, Giulietta Simionato, Fiorenza Cossotto, and Christa Ludwig all sang the role opposite Maria Callas's Norma. Created (1831) by Giulia Grisi.

Adamas (Rameau: *Les Boréades*). Bass. High Priest of Apollo, entrusted with raising Apollo's son Abaris. Created (f. stage p. 1982) by François Le Roux.

Adams, Rev. Horace (Britten: *Peter Grimes*). Ten. Rector of the Borough. Suspecting Grimes of being responsible for the death of his apprentices, he leads the men as they march to Grimes's hut to investigate his treatment of his latest Apprentice, John. Created (1945) by Tom Culbert.

Adelaide (Strauss: *Arabella*). *See* WALDNER, GRÄFIN ADELAIDE.

Adele 1. (J. Strauss II: *Die Fledermaus*). Sop. The Eisensteins' maid. With her sister Ida, she goes to Prince Orlofsky's party, wearing a dress she has 'borrowed' from her mistress. At the ball she meets another guest—Eisenstein. Later that night she visits the governor of the local gaol, whom she has also met at the ball, and again bumps into Eisenstein. It all ends good-humouredly. Aria: *Mein Herr Marquis* ('My dear Marquis'—known as the 'laughing aria'). Created (1874) by Karoline Charles-Hirsch.
2. (Adèle) (Rossini: *Le Comte Ory*). Sop. The Countess of Formoutiers. She has been left at the castle while her brother is away fighting in the Crusades. The amorous Count Ory disguises himself in unsuccessful attempts to win her hand. She marries Ory's page, Isolier. Created (1828) by Laure Cinti-Damoreau.
3. (Bellini: *Il pirata*). Mez. Imogene's companion and lady-in-waiting. Created (1827) by Marietta Sacchi.

Adina (Donizetti: *L'elisir d'amore*). Sop. Wealthy young lady who owns a farm. She finds the courting of the peasant Nemorino rather slow and in order to tease him she flirts with the soldier Belcore. When she sees other girls running after Nemorino, she becomes more aware of his attractions and confesses that she loves him. Duet (with Nemorino): *Chiedi all'aura lusinghiera* ('Ask of the welcoming breeze'); duets (with Dulcamara): *Io son ricco, tu sei bella* ('I am rich and you are lovely'); *Quanto amore* ('What great love'). Created (1832) by Sabina Heinefetter.

Admetus (It. vers. **Admeto**; Fr. vers. **Admète**) (Gluck: *Alceste*). Ten. Husband of Alceste. He is dying and can be saved only by somebody else being sacrificed in his place. Created (1767 vers.) by Giuseppe Tibaldi; (1776 vers.) by Joseph Legros.

Adolar, Count of Nevers (Weber: *Euryanthe*). Ten. Betrothed to Euryanthe. His rival, Lysiart, convinces him of her unfaithfulness and he plans to kill her. When the truth is revealed, they are happily reunited. Created (1823) by Anton Haizinger.

Adorno, Gabriele (Verdi: *Simon Boccanegra*). Ten. A Genoese nobleman (patrician), in love with Amelia Grimaldi, not knowing she is the daughter of the Doge, Simon Boccanegra, who was responsible for the death of Gabriele's father, a death Gabriele has sworn to avenge. Amelia and Gabriele persuade her guardian to bless their union immediately. Gabriele suspects Boccanegra of lusting after Amelia and determines to kill him, but is stopped by Amelia and the truth about their father-daughter relationship is revealed. The Doge promises they can marry if Gabriele can bring about a peaceful settlement between the warring plebeians and patricians. Before he dies, poisoned by Paolo, Gabriele and Amelia are married and Boccanegra names Adorno as his successor. Duet (with Amelia): *Angiol che dall'empireo* ('Angel who from heaven'). Created (1857 vers.) by Carlo Negrini; (1881 vers.) by Francesco Tamagno.

Adriana Lecouvreur (Cilea). Lib. by Arturo Colautti; 4 acts; f.p. Milan 1902, cond. Cleofonte Campanini.
   Paris, 1730: The actress Adriana *Lecouvreur tells director *Michonnet that her feelings are for the cavalier *Maurizio who, unknown to her, is the Count of Saxony. Maurizio comes to see her and she gives him a bunch of violets. The Prince

de *Bouillon intercepts a note from his wife, making an assignation with Maurizio. The Princess de *Bouillon is jealous that Maurizio may love another woman. He gives her the violets. Maurizio asks Adriana to help the Princess avoid being caught by her husband. The two women each suspect the other of being her rival for Maurizio's love. The Princess recognizes Adriana's voice and shows her the violets. In retaliation, Adriana alludes to the Princess's promiscuity. On her birthday, Adriana receives a box of violets, which she hopes are from Maurizio. But they are from the Princess, and are soaked in poison. Adriana dies.

Aegisth (Strauss: *Elektra*). Ten. Husband of Queen Klytämnestra. He became her lover while her husband Agamemnon was away fighting in the Trojan War. On his return, Aegisth helped Klytämnestra to murder Agamemnon. He now lives with her in the palace and is murdered with her by her son Orest. Created (1909) by Johannes Sembach.

Aeneas 1. (Énée) (Berlioz: *Les Troyens*). Ten. Trojan hero, urged by the ghost of Hector to create a new Troy in Italy. He leads the Trojans on this quest and, washed ashore in a storm, enters Queen Dido's palace in Carthage and falls in love with her. Reluctantly he leaves her to continue his journey. Aria: *Ah! quand viendra l'instant des suprêmes adieux* ('Ah! when the moment comes for the last farewell'); duet (with Dido): *Nuit d'ivresse et d'extase infinie!* ('Night of unending ecstasy and rapture!'). Created (1863) by Jules-Sébastien Monjauze.
2. (Purcell: *Dido and Aeneas*). Ten./high bar. Trojan prince. He lands at Carthage on his way to Italy to found a new Troy and falls in love with Queen Dido. The Sorceress sends her 'trusty elf' to tell him to leave Carthage at once and proceed to Italy. Created (1683/4) by an unknown schoolgirl.

Afron, Prince (Rimsky-Korsakov: *The Golden Cockerel*). Bar. Son of Tsar Dodon. Killed in battle. Creator (1909) not traced.

Agamemnon 1. (Gluck: *Iphigénie en Aulide*). Bar. Husband of Clitemnestre and father of Iphigénie, whose sacrifice is demanded by the goddess Diana before she will allow the Greeks to continue to Troy. Agamemnon is torn between love for his daughter and the need to appease his troops and the gods. Created (1774) by Henri Larrivée.
2. (Strauss: *Elektra*). Agamemnon does not appear in the opera, but his presence is felt from the onomatopoeic opening bars. He was Elektra's father, murdered in his bath by her mother Klytämnestra and her lover Aegisth, and vengeance for his death is the theme of the opera.

Agathe (Weber: *Der Freischütz*). Sop. Daughter of Cuno, in love with Max. Arias: *Und ob die Wolke sie verhülle* ('Even when the clouds hide it'); *Wie nahte mir der Schlummer ... Leise, leise* ('How could sleep come to me ... Softly, softly'). Created (1821) by Caroline Seidler.

Agave (Henze: *The Bassarids*). Mez. Daughter of King Cadmus of Thebes, mother of Pentheus, who succeeds to the throne. Hypnotized by Dionysus and his world, she leads the Bacchantes who kill Pentheus when he comes to their Mount Cythaeron, failing to recognize him as her son. Created (1966) by Kerstin Meyer.

Agrippina (Handel). Lib. by Vincenzo Grimani; 3 acts; f.p. Venice 1709.
Rome, about AD 50: *Agrippina, wife of *Claudio, Roman emperor, wants *Nerone, her son by a previous marriage, to succeed her husband to the throne, but Claudio names *Ottone as his successor. Ottone loves *Poppea, but Agrippina tells Poppea that he has been bribed by the offer of the throne. At Agrippina's instigation, Claudio orders Poppea to marry Nerone. But Ottone renounces the throne in order to claim Poppea as his bride, thus leaving the throne open for Nerone and satisfying all Agrippina's ambitions.

Agrippina (Handel: *Agrippina*). Sop./mez. Wife of the Roman emperor Claudio and mother of Nerone by a previous marriage. Wants her son to succeed to the throne and plots to discredit Ottone, her husband's choice as his successor. Created (1709) by Margherita Durastanti.

ägyptische Helena, Die (*The Egyptian Helen*) (Strauss). Lib. by Hugo von Hofmannsthal; 2 acts; f.p. Dresden 1928, cond. Fritz Busch.
Aithra's palace, on an island in the Mediterranean, after the Trojan War: *Helen of Troy

was seduced by King Priam's son Paris. On board a ship, her husband *Menelaus, having killed Paris, is about to kill his wife. In her palace, the enchantress *Aithra is bemoaning the absence of Poseidon, her lover. She is told by her Omniscient Seashell (the All-Wise *Mussel) of the murder which is about to take place. Aithra causes a storm and the wrecked ship is washed ashore. Menelaus enters the palace, dragging Helen with him. Helen wants Menelaus to forget the past, but he vows she shall pay for the men killed in the Trojan war and asserts that their child, *Hermione, shall never see her mother again. Aithra gives Helen some lotus-juice to drink, which will make her forget all the unpleasantness of the past. Aithra convinces Menelaus that it was not Helen who was unfaithful to him—she has been asleep in this palace all the time. But Menelaus, who has been distracted by Aithra's Elves, thinks he has killed Helen—his dagger is still in his hand—so this must be someone else. However, he sees his beautiful Helen again and Aithra transports them into a bedroom, giving Helen a supply of the 'forgetfulness juice'. Aithra summons *Altair, a chieftain, and his son *Da-ud. They and their followers all treat Helen with reverence. Menelaus mistakes Da-ud for Paris and kills him. Helen asks Aithra to give her a 'remembrance potion' that she can give to Menelaus to convince him that she really is Helen. She gives him the draught, drinking some of it herself. Aithra prevents Altair trying to separate Helen and Menelaus. Hermione is brought to see her beautiful mother and Helen and Menelaus are reunited and start a new life together.

Aida (Verdi). Lib. by Antonio Ghislanzoni; 4 acts; f.p. Cairo 1871, cond. Giovanni Bottesini (a double-bass virtuoso).

Egypt, the time of the Pharaohs: *Aida, daughter of the Ethiopian King *Amonasro, is a slave of *Amneris, daughter of the *King of Egypt. *Radamès wants to lead the Egyptian forces—he wants to see Aida, the woman he loves. Amneris is also in love with Radamès and, when he is crowned victor, the King offers him Amneris in marriage and whatever he desires. Radamès requests liberty for the prisoners. The night before the wedding, *Ramfis the High Priest accompanies Amneris to the temple where she will spend the night in

prayer. Aida is to meet Radamès for the last time near the river, but is suddenly faced by her father. He knows the Ethiopians can defeat the Egyptians if she will help by extracting from Radamès the army's plans. When Radamès arrives, she does her best to persuade him to elope with her. Amonasro shows himself as Amneris and her father emerge from the temple. Radamès prevents Amonasro killing Amneris and offers himself as prisoner as Aida and Amonasro escape. Radamès is sentenced to be buried alive under the temple altar. When he is entombed, he finds Aida has hidden there in anticipation. They will die together.

Aida (Verdi: *Aida*). Sop. Daughter of Amonasro, King of Ethiopia. She was captured when the Egyptians defeated Ethiopia and is now a slave to the Egyptian princess Amneris. Aida is torn between her love for Radamès, captain of the Egyptian army, and loyalty to her own country. She is urged to use Radamès to secure for her father the plans of the Egyptian army, so that the Ethiopians can defeat them. She tries to persuade Radamès to elope with her—this will avoid the marriage which is planned for him with Amneris and at the same time will remove the need for her to deceive him on behalf of her father. As they plan their departure, Amonasro appears. He tries to kill Amneris, his daughter's rival. Radamès foils his attempt and allows him to escape with Aida, offering himself as captive in their place. Knowing this will mean certain death for the man she loves, Aida secretes herself in the tomb beneath the altar where Radamès is to be incarcerated, and joins him to face death together. Arias: *Ritorna vincitor!* ('Conqueror return!'); *O patria mia* ('O my native land'); *O terra addio...* ('Farewell, O land'). Among well-known singers of Aida we can note Emmy Destinn, Rose Bampton, Leonie Rysanek, Birgit Nilsson, Ingrid Bjoner, Amy Shuard, Zinka Milanov, Maria Callas, Gré Brouwenstijn, Renata Tebaldi, Martina Arroyo, Leontyne Price, Montserrat Caballé, Ghena Dimitrova, Aprile Millo, Elizabeth Vaughan, Jessye Norman, Rosalind Plowright, Josephine Barstow, and Mechthild Gessendorf. Created (1871) by Antonietta Pozzoni-Anastasi (who was a second choice—the theatre director wanted Teresa Stolz, whom Verdi wanted for the Milan première six weeks later, but her demands for an outrageous fee made it impossible for Cairo to engage her and Verdi settled for Pozzoni. Verdi did not go to Cairo for the première).

Aithra (Strauss: *Die ägyptische Helena*). Sop. An enchantress who lives in a palace on an island in the Mediterranean, where she is served by a group of Elves. Her lover, Poseidon, is away and she is missing him. Her Omniscient Seashell (the Mussel) tells her that in a ship nearby a man (Menelaus) is about to kill his beautiful wife (Helen of Troy). Aithra summons up a storm and the ship is wrecked, Menelaus and Helen arriving at her palace. Menelaus is still determined to kill Helen, having already killed Paris who seduced her. She asks Aithra for help. Aithra gives her some lotus-juice to give to Menelaus to make him forget the past. Aithra transports them to a bedroom. However, now Menelaus does not remember Helen, whom he thinks he has killed, and assumes this is some other woman. Aithra commands the desert chieftain Altair and his son Da-ud to come to her palace, and they both fall in love with Helen. On a hunt, Menelaus kills Da-ud. Aithra gives Helen an antidote to the lotus-juice and she gives this to Menelaus, who now recognizes his beautiful wife. Arias: *Das Mahl ist gerichtet* ('The meal is prepared'); *Ihr grünen Augen* ('Your green eyes'). Created (1928) by Maria Rajdl. The first Vienna Aithra was Margit Angerer and the Munich creator was Hildegard Ranczak. In the 1997 British première by Garsington Opera, Oxfordshire, this strange character was sung by Helen Field.

Akhnaten (Philip Glass). Lib. by composer, Shalom Goldman, Robert Israel, and Richard Riddell; prol., 3 acts, epil.; f.p. Stuttgart 1984, cond. Dennis Russell Davies.

Egypt, 1375 BC: *Amenhotep III has died and his widow, Queen *Tye, and their son, *Akhnaten, join the funeral procession. Akhnaten is crowned. He builds a temple fortress, Akhetaten, and as he and his wife *Nefertiti gradually withdraw to worship the sun and become more and more isolated from their people, the pharaohs are overthrown. Visitors come to see the remains of Akhetaten. The ghosts of Akhnaten and Nefertiti are seen amidst the ruins of the city.

Akhnaten (Glass: *Akhnaten*). Counterten. Son of the recently dead Amenhotep III, and husband of Nefertiti. After his coronation, builds the temple of Akhetaten, into which he and his wife withdraw. Their city is overthrown and razed to the ground. Created (1984) by Paul Esswood.

Akhrosimova, Maria Dmitrievna (Prokofiev: *War and Peace*). Cont. Aunt who tries to persuade Natasha to part from Anatol who is already married. Creator (1945 vers.) not known; created (1946 vers.) by O. N. Golovina.

Aksinya (Shostakovich: *Lady Macbeth of the Mtsensk District*). Sop. Cook in the Ismailov household. Creator (1934) not traced.

Albazar (Rossini: *Il turco in Italia*). Ten. A young Turk who has saved Zaida from the death sentence imposed on her by her fiancé, Prince Selim, and taken her to Naples. She and Selim are reunited and leave Italy to return to Turkey. Created (1814) by Gaetano Pozzi.

Alberich (Wagner: *Das Rheingold*; *Siegfried*; and *Götterdämmerung*). Bass-bar. A Nibelung dwarf, brother of Mime and father of Hagen. This is the character that sets the whole four-part *Ring*-drama in motion—he steals the gold from the Rhinemaidens and makes from it a Ring which will give him the power to rule the world.

Das Rheingold: Alberich lustfully chases the Rhinemaidens at the bottom of the river. He sees the gold which they guard and they tell him that whoever makes a Ring from the gold will rule the world, but that to achieve this he must forswear love. Alberich curses love and grabs the hoard. He takes it to his brother Mime, an able goldsmith, who makes from it a magic helmet (Tarnhelm) and a Ring, which Alberich puts on his finger. The helmet bestows on the wearer the ability to turn into any form he desires, big or small. Alberich dons it and makes himself invisible, beating-up Mime who cannot see him. When Wotan and Loge visit him, Alberich proves to them how powerful he now is by turning himself into a serpent. He accepts their challenge to make himself into a very small animal, murmurs the spell and emerges as a toad. The gods capture him, tie him up, and take him away with them. Back on their mountain, they force Alberich to hand over the hoard of gold, and as the Ring is torn from his finger he puts a curse on it—whoever owns it will die. Arias: *Der Welte Erbe gewänn' ich zu eigen durch dich?* ('The world's wealth I could win through you?'); *Die in linder Lüfte Wehn da oben ihr lebt* ('You who aloft in the soft zephyr's breeze'); *Bin ich nun frei?* ('Am I free now?').

Siegfried: Alberich does not appear in *Die Walküre* but resurfaces in *Siegfried*. He first appears hiding behind a cliff in a forest near the cave in which Fafner, in the form of a dragon, is sleeping guarding the gold. Wotan (as the Wanderer) approaches and tells Alberich that Mime will bring a young boy to kill the dragon and will seize the gold. Alberich wakes up the dragon and tells him that if he gives him, Alberich, the gold, he will save him from being slain, but Fafner is not interested. He is killed by Siegfried. Mime and Alberich argue about the rightful heir to the gold. Siegfried emerges from the cave with the Tarnhelm and Ring, causing more curses from Alberich.

Götterdämmerung: Alberich's son, Hagen, is plotting to gain the Tarnhelm and Ring from Siegfried. In his sleep he hears Alberich encourage him to kill Siegfried and seize the Ring. Father and son can then bring about the downfall of the gods and they will be left as rulers of the world.

Created (*R.* 1869) by Karl Fischer; (*S.* and *G.* 1876) by Carl Hill.

Albert 1. (Massenet: *Werther*). Bar. [If the role of Werther is sung in the baritone version (*see* WERTHER), then Albert is sung by a tenor.] A young man engaged to Charlotte. After their marriage he suspects that Werther is in love with his wife. He lends Werther pistols, with which he kills himself. Created (1892) by Franz Neidl.

2. (Halévy: *La Juive*). Bass. Sergeant in the Emperor's army, friend of Prince Léopold. Created (1835) by Ferdinand Prévôt.

Albert Herring (Britten). Lib. by Eric Crozier; 3 acts; f.p. Glyndebourne 1947, cond. Benjamin Britten.

Loxford, a small market-town in East Suffolk, 1900: A meeting is held at Lady *Billows's house to elect a new May Queen. All candidates are rejected on various grounds of immorality. Supt. *Budd suggests a May King—Albert *Herring, son of Mrs *Herring who owns the greengrocer's. *Nancy and *Sid tell Albert he misses all the fun. Sid spikes Albert's lemonade at the May King ceremony. Albert decides to try sowing some wild oats and leaves home while his mother is out. She reports him missing and he is presumed dead. All now sing in mourning, in the midst of which Albert walks in. He has spent some of his prize money at the pub and had a wonderful time. The members of the village see him in a new light.

Albert Herring (Britten: *Albert Herring*). *See* HERRING, ALBERT.

Albiani, Paolo (Verdi: *Simon Boccanegra*). Bar. A goldsmith, a plebeian who helps Boccanegra to be elected Doge. He wants to marry Amelia Grimaldi (who is Boccanegra's daughter, although neither she nor Boccanegra realize it at first). She is in love with the patrician Gabriele Adorno. Paolo kidnaps her, but she escapes. Boccanegra curses the villain who attacked Amelia, and is determined to find and punish him. Paolo resolves to kill Boccanegra and puts poison in his drinking water, which the Doge drinks. When it is revealed to them all that Amelia is Boccanegra's daughter, the Doge gives Amelia and Gabriele his blessing. Paolo is sentenced to death, but has the satisfaction of knowing that Boccanegra will also die. Created (1857 vers.) by Giacomo Vercellini; (1881 vers.) by Federico Salvati.

Alceste (Gluck). Lib. by Ranieri da Calzabigi; 3 acts; f.p. Vienna 1767; Fr. vers. f.p. Paris 1776, cond. Pierre Montan Berton.

Mythological times. *Admetus is dying. The Oracle of *Apollo states that he can live only if somebody is sacrificed in his place. His wife, *Alceste, offers herself to save her husband. Apollo ultimately decides that they both can live in the original It. vers. In the rev. Fr. vers. (1776) it is Hercules who comes to the rescue, overpowering the infernal deities of the underworld to return Alceste to Admetus.

Alceste (Gluck: *Alceste*). Sop. Wife of Admetus, who offers herself as a sacrifice to save her husband's life. She is reprieved by Apollo in the original It. vers. and rescued by Hercules in the Fr. vers. Created (It. vers. 1767) by

Antonia Bernasconi; (Fr. vers. 1776) by Rosalie Levasseur in Paris.

Alcina (Handel). Lib. by Antonio Marchi; 3 acts; f.p. London 1735.

On Alcina's magic island: *Bradamante, engaged to *Ruggiero, comes (disguised as her brother Ricciardo) with her guardian *Melisso to the island where the sorceress *Alcina has him isolated. They are found by Alcina's sister, *Morgana, who is attracted by 'Ricciardo'. When Bradamante reveals who she is, Ruggiero does not recognize her and tries to persuade his rescuers to return home, as he fears that Alcina will lose interest in him. Melisso gives him a magic ring which returns him to his normal self. Alcina is prevented by Morgana from turning Ruggiero into a beast. *Oronte, in love with Morgana, is about to leave the island with the new arrivals. Alcina tries to detain Ruggiero, but the ring provides protection. Before they leave, Ruggiero uses the ring to break Alcina's spells and restore her various captives to normal life.

Alcina (Handel: *Alcina*). Sop. A sorceress in love with Ruggiero, whom she has isolated on her enchanted island, putting him under a spell. When her lovers tire of her she turns them into streams, animals, or trees. Created (1735) by Anna Maria Strada del Pò.

Alcindoro de Mittoneaux (Puccini: *La bohème*). Bass. An old, pompous, but wealthy state councillor, an admirer of Musetta. He escorts her to the Café Momus, where she immediately attracts the attention of her old lover, Marcello. On the pretext that her shoe hurts, Alcindoro is sent to the cobbler to have it adjusted. He returns, his mission completed, to find that not only has she left with Marcello and his friends, but that they have left the bill for their meal for him to pay. Created (1896) by Alessandro Polonini (who also created the landlord, Benoît, the two bass roles frequently being taken by the same singer).

Alcmene (Alkmene) (Strauss: *Die Liebe der Danae*). Mez. One of the Four Queens, previous lovers of Jupiter. Created (1944) by Maria Cornelius; (1952) by Georgine von Milinkovic.

Alexis (Sullivan: *The Sorcerer*). *See* POINDEXTRE, ALEXIS.

Alfio (Mascagni: *Cavalleria rusticana*). Bar. Village teamster, husband of Lola, who resumes her earlier affair with Turiddu. In a duel, Alfio kills Turiddu. Created (1890) by Gaudenzio Salassa.

Alfonso, Don (Mozart: *Così fan tutte*). Bar./ bass. A cynical bachelor who bets his two friends (Guglielmo and Ferrando) that, given the right conditions, all women will be unfaithful. They agree to allow him 24 hours in which to prove his theory. This he does with the assistance of their fiancées' maid and with the men's full co-operation. He does win his bet, wreaking havoc on their relationships as his machinations bring together the 'wrong' pairs of lovers. Aria: *Vorrei dir* ('I'd like to tell you'). Created (1790) by Francesco Bussani (whose wife created the maid, Despina). *See also* ARTICLE BY SIR THOMAS ALLEN, p. 9.

Alfred (J. Strauss II: *Die Fledermaus*). Ten. Singing teacher of Rosalinde, wife of Gabriel von Eisenstein. While her husband is serving a brief prison sentence, Alfred takes advantage to spend the evening with Rosalinde. Found in the house by the prison governor, Frank, he is assumed to be Rosalinde's husband and is escorted to gaol. Aria: *Trinke, Liebchen, trinke schnell!* ('Drink up, darling, drink up quickly!'). Created (1874) by Herr Rüdinger.

Alfredo (Verdi: *La traviata*). *See* GERMONT, ALFREDO.

Alhambra del Bolero, Don (Sullivan: *The Gondoliers*). Bass-bar. Grand Inquisitor who took the baby Prince to Venice and knows his identity. Aria: *I stole the Prince*. Created (1889) by W. H. Denny.

Alice Ford (Verdi: *Falstaff*). *See* FORD, ALICE.

Alidoro (Rossini: *La cenerentola*). Bass. Tutor to Prince Ramiro. A rather shadowy figure, he first arrives at Magnifico's home disguised as a beggar and Cenerentola is the only one who is kind to him. When she is left behind while the rest of the family go to the royal ball, Alidoro arrives and takes her to the ball. Aria: *Là del ciel nell'arcano profondo* ('In the secret depths of Heaven'). Created (1817) by Zenobio Vitarelli.

Aline (Sullivan: *The Sorcerer*). *See* SANGAZURE, ALINE.

DON ALFONSO   *(Così fan tutte*—Mozart)*

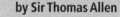

by Sir Thomas Allen

Cynicism may be present at various stages of an individual's development, but we tend to assume that the knocks and setbacks of life cause an increased encrustation of the cynical skin, becoming ever more severe as the years go by. And for that reason one normally associates the role of Don Alfonso with someone of more mature years and experience.

But one of the greatest problems for the singer taking on this role is to know how to manage the *longueurs*: the many moments when not occupied with singing or being an active participant in whatever is going on—in other words, the silent observer. I consider this to be the most forceful argument in favour of an artist of wide experience being cast in the role, as it would be rare indeed to find a bass, baritone, or bass-baritone of more tender years with sufficient confidence to appear happy doing nothing, *seemingly*, on stage.

The role of observer is in itself extremely interesting. With the proper concentration—and it is immediately obvious to an audience when an artist is 'coasting', or switching off from something with which he appears not to be involved—the character of Alfonso takes on much more interesting aspects than one has traditionally associated with the man. He is the *agent provocateur*, the puppet-master of his two arrogant pupils, and, at the end of the opera, the butt of the rage and accusations of five individuals in their realizations and recriminations.

Vocally, too, there may be one or two misconceptions of the role. The choice of a lower, older voice has usually more to do with the need to have a contrasting colour to that of the baritone singing Guglielmo. The tessitura is not particularly low-lying, not like a Figaro or a Leporello, for example, much less so in fact than might be assumed from the way in which the part is traditionally cast. (A similar case could be made for the character of Dulcamara in Donizetti's *L'elisir d'amore*. Here again the nature of the part conveys a certain heavy *buffo* quality in contrast to Belcore, but the actual 'lie' of the vocal line is in the area more easily managed by a higher voice than a *buffo* bass.)

For Alfonso, my memories go back to a season spent in the Glyndebourne chorus. There the role was sung and played most beautifully by the Frenchman Michel Roux [*Così fan tutte*, 1969]. It fascinated me to watch the man in his 18th-century deportment, the elegant use of his cane, and the feminine waft of his lace handkerchief in his moment of mock despair revealing, to their more than gullible fiancées, the impending perils about to befall his two young gentlemen friends. That gullibility has been my own stumbling block from the start with *Così fan tutte*, as it has been, I believe, for many of us. Many of the propositions we are asked to accept in the opera annoy, but there is no denying the beauty and correctness of every note of the music, even the rather dull—by Mozartian standards—finale to the second act, a Salieri-like composition in C major [Antonio Salieri (1750–1825), a composer and contemporary of Mozart's in Vienna], lacking (deliberately on Mozart's part) the champagne sparkle, as he tells us that, though six people are singing of a resolution, there is no joy here and the lacklustre nature of the orchestral writing tells us that, for these characters, nothing will ever be the same again. What other composer could suppress his brilliant best to convey such a point so vividly? A final word in favour of the baritone Alfonso—is it not worth having that voice, for the easier approach to the first line of that sublime Act 1 trio with Fiordiligi and Dorabella, *Soave sia il vento* ('May the wind be gentle')? Many the bass Alfonso who has perspired at that moment!

Alisa (Donizetti: *Lucia di Lammermoor*). Mez. Lucia's old nursemaid and companion. One of the famous sextet (with Edgardo, Enrico, Lucia, Raimondo, and Arturo), her first line being *Come rosa inaridita* ('Like a withered rose'). Created (1835) by Teresa Zappucci.

Aljeja (Janáček: *From the House of the Dead*). Sop. (can be ten.). A (usually) *travesti* role. A young Tartar prisoner in the Siberian camp, he is befriended by the political prisoner, Gorjančikov, and taught to read and write. He is very upset when the older man is released from the prison. Created (1930) by Božena Žlábková.

Almaviva, Count 1. (Rossini: *Il barbiere di Siviglia*). Ten. A Spanish nobleman, he presents himself as a student, Lindoro, in order to woo Rosina, ward of Dr Bartolo. He is helped by Figaro, Bartolo's barber. He enters Bartolo's house disguised as a drunken soldier and is recognized by Rosina. He is arrested but released when the officer realizes who he is. His second entry to the house is in the guise of Basilio's pupil, come to give Rosina a music lesson. Unfortunately, the real Basilio arrives in the middle of the lesson and has to be ushered out again. Figaro manages to secrete the balcony-window key, but the young couple's efforts at eloping are frustrated. However, Figaro has found a notary willing to marry them. Arias: *Ecco ridente in cielo* ('Lo, in the smiling sky'); sextet (with Rosina, Bartolo, Figaro, Basilio, and Berta): *Freddo ed immobile* ('Awestruck and motionless'). This is always a popular tenor role and has been sung by, among others, Dino Borgioli, Fernando De Lucia, Heddle Nash, Giuseppe Di Stefano, Luigi Alva, Peter Schreier, Ryland Davies, Nicolai Gedda, and Bruce Ford. Created (1816) by Manuel García.
　　2. (Mozart: *Le nozze di Figaro*). Bar. Married to Rosina (the Countess), whom he has neglected in favour of various amorous relationships. He attempts to seduce her maid Susanna and when almost caught in the act, has to hide behind a chair. He accuses his wife of having an affair with Cherubino and gives the young soldier a commission which means he must leave at once to join his regiment. He remains suspicious and continues to try to catch the Countess with a lover, while he himself still hopes to seduce Susanna. She plots with her mistress and Figaro to teach the Count a lesson and they prove the Countess's innocence and Almaviva's fickleness. He has to beg his wife's forgiveness. Aria: *Vedrò, mentr'io sospiro...* ('Must I live to see'); ens. (with Countess and others): *Contessa, perdono!* ('Countess, forgive me!'). This has remained one of the most popular bar. roles and among its best-known exponents are Roy Henderson, Matthieu Ahlersmeyer, George London, Sesto Bruscantini, Paul Schöffler, Gérard Souzay, Eberhard Wächter, Dietrich Fischer-Dieskau, Hermann Prey, Gabriel Bacquier, Tom Krause, Thomas Allen, James Morris, Dmitri Hvorostovsky, and Anthony Michaels-Moore—a veritable roll call of famous baritones. Created (1786) by Stefano Mandini (whose wife created Marcellina).
　　3. (Corigliano: *The Ghosts of Versailles*). Ten. Twenty years after the marriage of Figaro and Susanna, Count Almaviva and Rosina are still together. He has an illegitimate daughter who is loved by Rosina's son from her affair with Cherubino. His help is enlisted by the author Beaumarchais, to rescue Marie Antoinette. Created (1991) by Peter Kazaras.

Almaviva, Countess 1. (Rossini: *Il barbiere di Siviglia*). *See* ROSINA (1).
　　2. (Mozart: *Le nozze di Figaro*). *See* COUNTESS (1).
　　3. (Corigliano: *The Ghosts of Versailles*). *See* ROSINA (2).

Aloès (Chabrier: *L'Étoile*). Sop. Wife of Hérisson, ambassador to King Mataquin. Created (1877) by Mme Luge.

Alphise, Queen (Rameau: *Les Boréades*). Sop. Queen of Bactria, who must marry a Boread, but is in love with the unknown Abaris. She abdicates rather than lose his love. His royal identity is eventually revealed and they are then able to marry. Created (f. stage p. 1982) by Jennifer Smith.

Alphonse XI, King of Castile (Donizetti: *La Favorite*). Bar. He wants to divorce his wife and marry his mistress Léonore, who is also loved by Fernand. The King is threatened with excommunication if he divorces, and therefore agrees to Fernand marrying Léonore. Aria: *Léonore, viens, j'abandonne* ('Come, Leonore, before thee kneeling'). Created (1840) by Paul Barroilhet.

Altair (Strauss: *Die ägyptische Helena*). Bar. A desert chieftain, father of Da-ud. Summoned by the sorceress Aithra to her palace, they both fall in love with the beautiful Helen of Troy. Altair invites her husband Menelaus to join them on a hunt, in the course of which he kills Altair's son. When they return to the palace, Altair attempts to prevent the reunion of Menelaus and Helen, but Aithra interferes and stops him. Created (1928) by Friedrich Plaschke.

Altoum, Emperor (Puccini: *Turandot*). Ten. Father of Princess Turandot. When an Unknown Prince successfully answers the riddles, Altoum refuses to release her from her promise to marry him. Created (1926) by Francesco Dominici.

Alvaro, Don (Verdi: *La forza del destino*). Ten. A half-caste South American prince in love with Leonora, daughter of the Marchese di Calatrava. Her father has forbidden their marriage and they decide to elope. The Marchese interrupts their departure and Alvaro throws his gun down in surrender, but it goes off, killing the old man. Leonora's brother vows vengeance. The young lovers become separated during their escape. Thinking Leonora must be dead, Alvaro joins the Spanish army, fighting in Italy in the war between Spain and Napoleon. He is injured and cared for in the camp by his new friend, who is Leonora's brother Carlo under an assumed name. Alvaro gives Carlo his private papers to look after, and Carlo finds his sister's portrait among them, so revealing Alvaro's true identity. Their duel is interrupted by an army patrol. Alvaro enters a monastery as Padre Raffaele. Found there by Carlo, they again fight and Carlo is seriously wounded. Calling for a hermit in the nearby caves to give absolution to the dying Carlo, Alvaro recognizes Leonora. As she gives her brother the last rites, he stabs her and she dies in Alvaro's arms. (In the original version, Alvaro then threw himself over a precipice, but Verdi toned this down in 1869 for the Milan version, as above.) Aria: *O tu che in seno agli angeli* ('You who rose to the bosom of the angels'); duet (with Carlo): *Solenne in quest' ora* ('In this solemn hour'). Created (1862) by Enrico Tamberlick.

Alvise (Ponchielli: *La gioconda*). *See* BADOERO, ALVISE.

Alwa (Berg: *Lulu*). Ten. A composer, son of Dr Schön; he marries Lulu. Said to be based on Alban Berg himself. Created (1937) by Peter Baxeranos.

Amahl (Menotti: *Amahl and the Night Visitors*). Treble. A crippled boy, aged about 12 years. He watches the bright star in the sky as the Three Kings, on their way to seek the Christ Child, ask for hospitality. He offers his crutch as a gift for the Holy Child and is miraculously healed. Created (1951) by Chet Allan.

Amahl and the Night Visitors (Menotti). Lib. by composer; 1 act; f.p. NBC Television, USA, 1951 (the first opera written specifically for television), cond. Thomas Schippers.

Biblical times: *Amahl, a young cripple, watches the brilliant star. The Three Kings (*Kaspar, *Melchior, and *Balthazar) are taking presents to the Christ Child and stop off on the way, asking for shelter. In the night, Amahl's *Mother tries to steal from the men and there is a struggle. Amahl offers his crutch as a gift for the Holy Child. He is healed and joins the Kings (the Magi) on their journey to deliver their presents.

Amaltea (Rossini: *Mosè in Egitto*). *See* SINAIS, QUEEN.

Amanda (previously **Clitoria**) (Ligeti: *Le Grand Macabre*). Sop. In love with Armando. They spend most of the opera in a tomb making love, unaware of the momentous events taking place around them. Created (1978) by Elisabeth Söderström.

Amaranta (Haydn: *La fedeltà premiata*). Sop. An arrogant lady who aids the evil Melibeo in his attempts to sacrifice a loving couple to the sea monster. Is won by Count Perruc- chetto. Created (1781) by Teresa Taveggia.

Amastre (Handel: *Serse*). Alto. Heiress to Tagor, betrothed of Serse. Created (1738) by Maria Antonia Merighi.

Amelfa (Rimsky-Korsakov: *The Golden Cockerel*). Cont. Housekeeper to Tsar Didon. Creator (1909) not traced.

Amelia 1. (Verdi: *Un ballo in maschera*). (Amelia also in Amer. vers.) Sop. Wife of Cap- tain Anckarstroem, the King's secretary and friend. King Gustavus is in love with Amelia. In a field near Stockholm, she eventually admits that the feeling is mutual, but they must sacri- fice these feelings and she will remain faithful to her husband. Their meeting is interrupted by the arrival of Anckarstroem and Amelia covers her face with a veil. Anckarstroem offers to escort her back to the gates of the city. They are interrupted on the way by conspirators plotting against the King and Amelia's veil is pulled off, revealing her identity to her shocked husband. She accompanies him to a masked ball at the palace where he kills Gustavus. Arias: *Come avrò di mia mano quell'erba* ('When the herb is in my hand'); *Consentimi, O Signore* ('Grant me, O Lord'—known as Amelia's Prayer); *Morrò, ma prima in grazia* ('Before I die, one last wish'). Created (1859) by Eugenia Julienne-Dejean.

2. (Verdi: *Simon Boccanegra*). *See* GRIMALDI, AMELIA.

Amenhotep III (Glass: *Akhnaten*). King of the Pharaohs, husband of Queen Tye and father of Akhnaten. He has died just before the action begins.

Amenophis (Osiride) (Rossini: *Mosè in Egitto*). Ten. Son of Pharaoh. He is in love with Anaïs, daughter of Moses's sister Miriam, though his father wants him to marry an Assyr- ian. Anaïs offers to die if Pharoah will free the Israelites. Amenophis lifts his sword to strike Moses, but is killed by a bolt of lightning. Cre- ated (1818) by Andrea Nozzari.

Amfortas (Wagner: *Parsifal*). Bass-bar. Son of Titurel, who was the first ruler of the King- dom of the Grail. When Titurel became too old to care for the Grail and Spear, his son succeeded him. After inheriting the crown, Amfortas decided that it was his responsibil- ity to destroy the power of the evil Klingsor who threatened the Grail and he went to Klingsor's nearby castle, armed with the Holy Spear which had pierced Christ's side on the Cross. But he fell under the spell of Kundry and while she seduced him, Klingsor stole the Spear and used it to stab Amfortas. His wound will not heal and Amfortas is in constant agony, relieved a little only by his daily bath in the lake. When the opera opens, Amfortas has had a vision that only an 'innocent fool' who has been 'made wise by compassion' will be able to relieve his suffering by regaining the Spear from Klingsor and using it to heal the wound. The Knights of the Grail await the coming of this youth while Kundry brings Amfortas some balm to put on the wound (which she has allowed to be inflicted on him). Titurel tells Amfortas to uncover the Grail, but weakened by his wound he cannot find the strength to do this and begs his father to carry out the sacred office himself, and leave him to die. Titurel refuses, pleading old age, and Amfortas sug- gests leaving the Grail uncovered, to avoid the agony of having to move repeatedly to do it daily. The young knights place the Grail in front of Amfortas, who with great difficulty and pain, raises it and blesses the bread and wine before these are shared among the Knights. Amfortas is too weak himself to par- take of the ritual and is carried out on his litter. After Titurel has died, Amfortas feels respon- sible for his father's death—his own refusal to uncover the Grail each day has deprived Titurel of the nourishment he needed. Amfortas wants only to die and asks the dead Titurel to plead for him with the Lord. The Knights urge Amfortas to carry out his office at his father's funeral. He jumps up and rips the bandages from his bleeding wound, begging them all to kill him. Parsifal appears, the Holy Spear in his hand, and with this he touches Amfortas's wound which is at once healed. Amfortas kneels before Parsifal, the new King of the Grail. Arias: *Nein! Lasst ihn unenthüllt!* ('No! Leave it uncovered!'); *Ja, Wehe! Weh' über mich! … Mein Vater! Hochgesegneter der*

Helden! ('Yes, alas! Alas! Woe be on me! … My father! Most blessed of heroes!').

Amfortas is, from the beginning of the opera, in the most holy of positions, responsible for caring for the Grail and offering the Knights Holy Communion. But he knows that he has sinned and that this is the reason he has a wound which will not heal. His physical agony and despair are matched by his guilt, which is further felt when he feels responsible for the death of his father. Famous portrayers of Amfortas include Carl Perron, Anton van Rooy, Walter Soomer, Theodor Scheidl, Heinrich Schlusnus, Jaro Prohaska, Georg Hann, Herbert Jansen, George London, Hans Hotter, Dietrich Fischer-Dieskau, Eberhard Wächter, Siegmund Nimsgern, Thomas Stewart, Norman Bailey, Donald McIntyre, Bernd Weikl, and Thomas Hampson. Created (1882) by Theodor Reichmann.

Amida (Cavalli: *L'Ormindo*). Ten. Friend of Ormindo, former lover of Sicle. Creator (1644) unknown.

Amina (Bellini: *La sonnambula*). Sop. An orphan, raised by the mill owner, Teresa, she is the sleep-walker of the opera's title. She is to marry the farmer Elvino and during their civil wedding Rodolfo returns to the village. Sleep-walking, Amina is seen in Rodolfo's room at the inn and Elvino cancels the wedding. Only when he sees her sleep-walking across the mill roof does he believe her innocent. Aria: *Ah! non credea mirarti* ('Scarcely could I believe it')—the sleepwalking aria. In recent times the best known singers of this role have been Maria Callas, Joan Sutherland, and Renata Scotto. Created (1831) by Giuditta Pasta.

Aminta (Strauss: *Die schweigsame Frau*). Sop. Wife of Henry, the nephew of Sir Morosus. She and her husband run a troupe of travelling singers and actors. Morosus has disinherited Henry and disapproves of Aminta. When Morosus announces his intention of taking a wife, the young couple realize they must intervene or they will lose their inheritance. Aminta poses as 'Timida', a quiet and demure young woman, and Morosus decides to marry her. A mock wedding is arranged, but as soon as they are safely 'married', 'Timida' turns into a noisy, bossy, and inconsiderate wife and Morosus becomes desperate. Aminta feels guilty about deceiving the old man in this way and causing him so much distress. Eventually, she and Henry throw off their disguises and admit it has all been a deception. Fortunately for them, Morosus is able to see the joke. Created (1935) by Maria Cebotari.

Amneris (Verdi: *Aida*). Mez. Daughter of the King of Egypt. She is in love with Radamès, captain in the Egyptian army, but has guessed that he is in love with her Ethiopian slave, Aida. Amneris pretends to be a friend to Aida, and the girl confesses her feelings for Radamès. When Radamès returns triumphant and is crowned victor, the King of Egypt offers him Amneris's hand in marriage, an offer he cannot refuse without offending the King. The eve before her wedding, Amneris enters the temple, intending to spend the night there in prayer. As she emerges from the temple with her father, she sees Radamès, who has had a last meeting with Aida, and Aida's father Amonasro, who lunges forward to kill his daughter's rival, but is prevented from so doing by Radamès. Radamès is entombed below the temple, where he finds Aida waiting, ready to die with him. Amneris prays that the man she loves, and for whose death she is responsible, will find peace in Heaven. Aria (with slave-girls): *Ah! Vieni, vieni amor mio* ('Ah! Come to me, come to me my love'); duets (with Aida): *Vieni, o diletta* ('Come, dearest friend'); *Trema, vil schiava!* ('Fear me, slave!'). Popular as the role of Aida is with sopranos, so mezzo-sopranos flock to sing Amneris. In recent years these have included Giulietta Simionato, Constance Shacklock, Ebe Stignani, Irina Arkhipova, Oralia Dominguez, Fedora Barbieri, Jean Madeira, Grace Bumbry, Fiorenza Cossotto, and Sally Burgess. Created (1871) by Eleonora Grossi.

Amonasro (Verdi: *Aida*). Bar. King of Ethiopia and father of Aida. Since their defeat by the Egyptians, Aida has been slave to the Egyptian Princess Amneris and Amonasro is a prisoner, disguised as a common soldier. Amonasro knows his daughter is in love with the young Egyptian captain Radamès. The King of Egypt has offered his daughter Amneris as bride to Radamès. When Amonasro attempts to kill Amneris, his daughter's rival, Radamès intervenes, allowing Aida and her father to escape, and offering himself as prisoner in their place. Aria: *Ma tu, Re, tu signore possente* ('But thou,

O King, thou mighty lord'). This is always a popular role and there are few famous baritones—of all nationalities—who have not essayed it at some point of their career. These include Rolando Panerai, Giuseppe Taddei, Lawrence Tibbett, Leonard Warren, Ettore Bastianini, Tito Gobbi, George London, Hans Hotter, Robert Merrill, Cornell MacNeil, Sherrill Milnes, and Piero Cappuccilli. Created (1871) by Francesco Steller.

Amor 1. (Gluck: *Orfeo ed Euridice*). Sop. The God of Love, who restores Euridice to Orfeo because he is so moved by his sadness and the intensity of his lament. Created (It. vers. 1762) by Lucia Clavareau; (Fr. vers. 1774) by Rosalie Levasseur.

    2. (Monteverdi: *L'incoronazione di Poppea*). Sop. He and the goddesses of Fortune and Virtue discuss their various successes and failures, Amor claiming superiority over the others: love will always win in the end, as the opera which follows will prove. Creator (1643) not traced.

Anaïs (Elcia) (Rossini: *Mosè in Egitto*). Sop. Daughter of Miriam and niece of Moses. She is in love with Pharaoh's son. She offers to die in exchange for Pharaoh allowing Moses and the Israelites to leave Egypt. Created (1818) by Isabella Colbran (who was married to Rossini 1822–37).

Anastasia, Countess (Kálmán: *Die Csárdásfürstin*). See STASI, COUNTESS.

Anatol (Barber: *Vanessa*). Ten. Son and namesake of the man who deserted Vanessa twenty years ago. His father is now dead and Anatol comes in his stead to visit Vanessa. He first seduces her niece Erika and then deserts her when, like his father before him, he falls in love with Vanessa. He marries her and takes her to Paris. Created (1958) by Nicolai Gedda.

Anchise, Don (Mozart: *La finta giardiniera*). Ten. The Podestà (Mayor) of Lagonero. He is secretly loved by his maid, Serpetta, but falls in love with the gardener's assistant, Sandrina, not knowing she is the Marchese Violante in disguise. Created (1775) probably by Augustin Sutor.

Anckarstroem, Capt. (Verdi: *Un ballo in maschera*). (Renato in Amer. vers.) Bar. Secretary and loyal friend of King Gustavus III.

Married to Amelia, whom the King secretly loves. He uncovers a plot to overthrow the King and goes to warn him. He finds him with a lady who immediately covers her face with a veil. Advising the King to return safely to his palace, he himself escorts the veiled lady. They are accosted by conspirators and the lady's veil is removed. To Anckarstroem's horror, it is Amelia. Despite her protests of faithfulness, he vows to avenge himself by killing the King. He and his wife attend a masked ball at the palace. Under the pretext of needing to warn the King of enemies present, he persuades the pageboy Oscar to tell him which costume the King is wearing. He shoots Gustavus who, as he dies, swears that Amelia has remained faithful to her husband. Arias: *Alla vita che t'arride* ('To our life with which you are favoured'); *Eri tu che macchiavi quell'anima* ('It was you who stained that soul'). Nearly all famous Italianate baritones sing this role, and these have included Leonard Warren, Ettore Bastianini, Tito Gobbi, Robert Merrill, Cornell MacNeil, Sherrill Milnes, Piero Cappuccilli, Ingvar Wixell, Dietrich Fischer-Dieskau, Renato Bruson, Leo Nucci, Giorgio Zancanaro, and Thomas Hampson. Created (1859) by Leone Giraldoni.

Andrea (Verdi: *Simon Boccanegra*). *See* FIESCO, JACOPO.

Andrea Chénier (Giordano). Lib. by Luigi Illica; 4 acts; f.p. Milan 1896, cond. Rodolfo Ferrari.

    Paris, late 18th cent. (before and after the French Revolution): At a ball given by the Contessa di *Coigny, her servant *Gérard recounts his hatred of the aristocracy. He is secretly in love with Maddalena di *Coigny, the Contessa's daughter, who arrives with her maid *Bersi. Among the guests is the poet Andrea *Chénier. Five years later, his friend *Roucher tries to persuade Chénier to leave Paris, where he is being spied on by *Incredibile. But Chénier has received a letter from an unknown woman (Maddalena) asking for his protection. Gérard is now a member of the revolutionary government and tries to kidnap Maddalena, but Chénier wounds him. Chénier is arrested and Maddalena pleads with Gérard to save him. Despite defending himself, Chénier is sentenced to death as a counter-revolutionary. Gérard helps Maddalena enter the prison so that she can die with Chénier.

Andrea Chénier (Giordano: *Andrea Chénier*). *See* CHÉNIER, ANDREA.

Andres (Berg: *Wozzeck*). Ten. A soldier, friend of Wozzeck. Created (1925) by Gerhor Witting.

Andromache 1. (Andromaca) (Rossini: *Ermione*). Mez. Widow of the murdered Hector and mother of his son, Astynax. She is bribed into marriage with Pyrrhus (husband of Hermione). Created (1819) by Rosmunda Pisaroni.

  2. (Tippett: *King Priam*). Sop. Daughter of the King of Thebes, she becomes Hector's wife. After Hector is killed she is captured and married to Achilles' son Neoptolemus (also called Pyrrhus—*see* (1)). Created (1962) by Josephine Veasey.

Andronico (Handel: *Tamerlano*). Cont. *Travesti* role (originally castrato). A Greek prince. Ally of The Emperor of the Tartars, Tamerlano. Falls in love with Asteria, daughter of the defeated Turkish Emperor Bajazet. Despite competition from Tamerlano, he and Asteria are finally united. Created (1724) by Senesino (the castrato Francesco Bernardi).

Angel, The (Messiaen: *Saint François d'Assise*). Sop. *Travesti* role. Escorts St Francis on his spiritual journey (although the Angel is often seen by the audience and not by St Francis or other characters in the opera). Created (1983) by Christiane Eda-Pierre.

Angelica (Handel: *Orlando*). Sop. Queen of Cathay, in love with Medoro whom she now prefers to Orlando. Orlando is so distressed he loses his reason, but with the help of the magician it is all resolved and Orlando blesses Angelica and Medoro. Created (1733) Anna Maria Strada del Pò.

Angelica, Suor (Puccini: *Suor Angelica*). Sop. From a noble family in Florence, Angelica had an illegitimate child. To hide from the shame this brought on the family, she entered a convent, but she longs to know what has happened to the child she left behind. After seven years she has a visitor—the Principessa La Zia (her aunt, the Princess). Angelica asks for news of her son, and her aunt bluntly tells her that the child died two years ago. After the Princess has left, Angelica takes poison—she wants to join her son in heaven—but she then realizes that suicide is a mortal sin. She prays to the Virgin Mary for forgiveness, and has a vision of the Madonna bringing her dead son towards her. He will lead her into heaven. Aria: *Senza mamma* ('Without your mother'). Created (1918) by Geraldine Farrar.

Angelina (Rossini: *La Cenerentola*). Cont. Stepdaughter of Don Magnifico, known as Cenerentola (Cinderella). His daughters make her life a misery. The prince and his valet arrive at the house, having swapped clothes. Magnifico's daughters are introduced to the 'prince' (the valet in disguise) and invited to the royal ball. Cenerentola is attracted by the 'valet', but excluded from the invitation. When the rest of the family have departed, the prince's tutor arrives and escorts Cenerentola to the ball, where she creates a sensation and she and the 'valet' fall in love. But she has to leave at midnight. She gives the 'valet' a bracelet, keeping its identical partner herself. The real prince, by now in love with her, comes looking for her and they recognize each other and match up their bracelets. At their wedding, Cinderella asks the Prince to forgive her stepfather and stepsisters. Aria: *Un a volta c'era un re* ('Once upon a time there was a king'); duet (with Ramiro): *Un soave non so che* ('A sweet something'); aria with ens.: *Non più mesta* ('No longer sad'). Created (1817) by Geltrude Righetti-Giorgi. *See also* CENDRILLON.

Angelotti, Cesare (Puccini: *Tosca*). Bass. Former Consul of the Roman republic. He has been a political prisoner but has escaped and come to the church of Sant' Andrea where his sister, the Marchese Attavanti, has left a key for him. This opens a door to a side-chapel in which he hides. When Tosca leaves the church, he reveals himself to his old friend, the painter Cavaradossi, who gives him food and suggests he hides in the well in his garden to evade Baron Scarpia's troops. Tosca betrays his hiding-place when she is unable any longer to listen to the sound of Cavaradossi's screams as he is tortured. When he is discovered, Angelotti kills himself. Created (1900) by Ruggero Galli.

***anima del filosofo, L'* (*The Spirit of Philosophy*)** (Haydn). *See* ORFEO ED EURIDICE (HAYDN).

Anita 1. (Krenek: *Jonny spielt auf*). Sop. An opera singer, for whom Max writes a new work.

She has an affair with the violinist Daniello, but is reunited with Max as they all head for a new life in the USA. Created (1927) by Fanny Eleve.

2. (Bernstein: *West Side Story*). Mez. (and dancer). Girlfriend of Maria's brother Bernardo. Created (1957) by Chita Rivera.

Anna 1. (Strauss: *Intermezzo*). Mez. The family maid. She helps her mistress Christine Storch to pack her husband's things before he leaves to conduct in Vienna. Created (1924) by Liesel von Schuch (and based on the Strausses' maid, Anna Glossner, who was very cross about it).

2. (Marschner: *Hans Heiling*). Sop. Bride of Hans Heiling. She is frightened of him and meets and falls in love with Konrad. Created (1833) by Therese Grünbaum.

3. (Berlioz: *Les Troyens*). Cont. Sister of Dido. She urges Dido to remarry. Created (1863) by Mlle Dubois.

Anna Bolena (Donizetti). Lib. by Felice Romani; 2 acts; f.p. Milan 1830.

England, 1536: *Enrico (King Henry VIII) is losing interest in Anna *Bolena (Anne Boleyn) in favour of Giovanna (Jane) *Seymour. At a hunting party, Anna meets her first love, Lord Riccardo (Richard) *Percy, who has heard about her unhappiness and questions her brother, Lord *Rochefort. *Smeton, himself in love with Anna, overhears Rochefort arranging for Anna to see Percy. When she admits to Percy how unhappy she is, he confesses he still loves her. The King, finding them together, accuses her of infidelity and commits her to the Tower to await trial. Giovanna tells her that the King will spare her if she admits her guilt. Percy offers to die in her place, but Anna is led to the scaffold, together with Percy and Rochefort, as the wedding of Enrico and Giovanna is announced.

Anna Bolena (Donizetti: *Anna Bolena*). *See* BOLENA, ANNA.

Anna, Donna (Mozart: *Don Giovanni*). Sop. Daughter of the Commendatore, she is betrothed to Don Ottavio. Her father is killed by her seducer, Don Giovanni, and she determines to avenge him. She and Ottavio plot with Donna Elvira, whom the Don has won and then deserted, to prove he is the murderer and they come to a banquet costumed and masked. They accuse Giovanni of murder, but he escapes. He is later damned to hell by her father's statue. She asks Ottavio to wait for her until she has got over her father's death. Arias: *Or sai chi l'onore ...* ('Now you know who tried to steal my honour'); *Non mi dir* ('Do not tell me'). All Italianate sopranos of all nationalities sing this role. Over the years these have included Pauline Viardot-García, Ina Souez, Rose Bampton, Marianne Schech, Ljuba Welitsch, Elisabeth Rethberg, Gundula Janowitz, Elisabeth Grümmer, Sena Jurinac, Hilde Zadek, Suzanne Danco, Teresa Stich-Randall, Birgit Nilsson, Margaret Price, Joan Sutherland, Anna Tomowa-Sintow, Cheryl Studer, Karita Mattila, Christine Brewer, and Anna Netrebko. Created (1787) by Teresa Saporiti.

Ännchen (Weber: *Der Freischütz*). Sop. Cousin of Agathe (who is to marry the forester Max). Created (1821) by Johanne Eunicke.

Anne Trulove (Stravinsky: *The Rake's Progress*). *See* TRULOVE, ANNE.

Annina 1. (Strauss: *Der Rosenkavalier*). Mez. Partner of the Italian intriguer Valzacchi. She helps to compromise the Baron and leave the way clear for Sophie and Octavian. Created (1911) by Eraa Freund.

2. (Verdi: *La traviata*). Sop. Violetta Valéry's maid. She tells Alfredo how her mistress has had to sell her own possessions to keep them in comfort. When Violetta is dying, she is nursed by Annina. Created (1853) by Carlotta Berini.

Annio (Mozart: *La clemenza di Tito*). Mez. *Travesti* role (occasionally ten.). Young Roman nobleman, in love with his friend Sesto's sister, Servilia. Aria: *Tu fosti tradito* ('You were betrayed'); duet (with Servilia): *Più che ascolto i sensi tuoi* ('The more I hear your words'). Created (1791) by Carolina Perini.

Antenor (Walton: *Troilus and Cressida*). Bar. Capt. of the Trojans, he is captured by the Greeks and returned in exchange for Cressida. Created (1954) by Geraint Evans.

Antonia (Offenbach: *Les Contes d'Hoffmann*). Sop. A singer in Munich, daughter of Crespel. Because she is ill, he keeps her hidden for protection. Forced to sing by the evil Dr Miracle, she dies. Created (1881) by Adèle Isaac.

Antonida (Glinka: *A Life for the Tsar*). Sop. Daughter of Ivan Susanin, engaged to Sobinin. She thinks her father is betraying the Tsar, but later tells the people of his heroic death. Created (1836) by Mariya Stepanova.

Antonio 1. (Mozart: *Le nozze di Figaro*). Bar. The Almavivas' gardener, father of Barbarina and uncle of Susanna. He sees Cherubino escape from the Countess's bedroom by jumping through the window. Created (1786) by Francesco Bussani (who also created Bartolo; his wife created Cherubino).
   2. (Donizetti: *Linda di Chamounix*). Bar. A poor tenant farmer, husband of Maddalena and father of Linda. He follows his daughter to Paris where he thinks (wrongly) that she is living as the mistress of Carlo. However she returns to the family home and Carlo follows her and they are married. Created (1842) by Felice Varesi.

Antony (Barber: *Antony and Cleopatra*) Bass-bar. Encouraged by the Romans to prove his loyalty to the empire by marrying Octavia, sister of the Roman Emperor Octavius Caesar, Antony leaves his bride to return to the Egyptian Queen Cleopatra. When the Romans approach to capture him, Antony hides in Cleopatra's palace, but believing Cleopatra to be dead, he stabs himself. He dies in her arms. Created (1966) by Justino Díaz.

Antony and Cleopatra (Barber). Lib. by Franco Zeffirelli; 3 acts; f.p. NY 1966, cond. Thomas Schippers.
   Egypt and Rome, AD 43: *Antony leaves *Cleopatra in Egypt and returns to Rome. He is encouraged by the Romans to marry *Octavia, sister of *Octavius Caesar. After their marriage, he decides to return to Cleopatra, whom he really loves. Angry at his betrayal of his sister, Octavius declares war on Antony. As the Romans approach Alexandria, Cleopatra declares her intention of sharing her lover's fate. Antony, defeated in battle, urges his troops to beg for mercy from Octavius, and takes refuge in Cleopatra's palace. Cleopatra goes down to her tomb, and Antony believes she is dead. He stabs himself, is carried to her tomb and dies in her arms. As Octavius arrives to capture her and take her back to Rome, Cleopatra dies from the bite of an asp.

Anubis (Birtwistle: *The Second Mrs Kong*). Bar. A jackal-headed boatman / Death of Kong. He rows the dead to the World of Shadows and bids them relive their memories, thus setting in motion the rest of the plot. Created (1994) by Steven Page.

Apollo 1. (Strauss: *Daphne*). Ten. He first appears to Daphne's family as a herdsman who has been rounding up his cattle. Her father, who has forecast that Apollo will come to them, tells Daphne to take care of the stranger in their midst. Dazzled by her beauty, Apollo falls in love with Daphne but greets her as a brother. She is startled by his compliments, but looks after him as her father ordered, and tells him how important to her is nature and the sun. He promises her she will always have the sun in her life. He declares his love but she is frightened and cannot understand the change in his attitude to her. When she dances with the disguised Leukippos, Apollo reveals who he is and kills Leukippos. Realizing that Daphne will never love him as he wants, Apollo asks Zeus to allow him to have Daphne in an immortal form, as one of the trees she worships. She gradually changes into a laurel tree. Arias: *Ich grüsse dich …* ('I greet you'); *Was erblicke ich?* ('What do my eyes behold?'). One of two tenor roles in this opera of almost *Heldentenor* proportions. Among famous exponents are Set Svanholm and James King. Created (1938) by Torsten Ralf.
   2. (Monteverdi: *Orfeo*). Father of Orfeo, who takes his son to Heaven to see Euridice in the stars. This character did not appear in the cast of the première (1607), although he is in the printed score.
   3. (Birtwistle: *The Mask of Orpheus*). Electronic voice who, present at Orpheus' birth, gives him the gifts of speech, poetry, and music.
   4. (Gluck: *Alceste*). The Oracle of Apollo tells Admetus that he can live only if somebody is sacrificed in his place. Creator (1767 vers.) not traced; created (1776 vers.) by Mons. Moreau.

Apprentice (Britten: *Peter Grimes*). Silent. A boy, John, Grimes's new apprentice. He falls to his death from Grimes's hut. Created (1945) by Leonard Thompson.

Arabella (Strauss). Lib. by Hugo von Hofmannsthal; 3 acts; f.p. Dresden 1933, cond. Clemens Krauss.

Vienna, 1860: *Arabella is the elder daughter of Count *Waldner and his wife Adelaide Countess *Waldner. They are hard up and live in a hotel in Vienna. *Zdenka, the younger daughter, is kept dressed as a boy, as they are unable to afford to 'bring out' two daughters. Arabella must make a suitable marriage to rescue the family fortunes and a *Fortune-Teller tells Adelaide that he will be a foreigner. Among Arabella's admirers are three Counts— *Elemer, *Dominik, and *Lamoral—and an officer, *Matteo, but she rejects them all in favour of the wealthy Croatian landowner *Mandryka, who has come to court her after seeing her photograph. Mandryka overhears Zdenka arranging an assignation with Matteo on behalf of Arabella and in his distress he flirts with the mascot of the Cabbies' Ball, the *Fiakermilli. But Zdenka, who is in love with the young officer, takes Arabella's place with him in the darkened bedroom. After much misunderstanding, Zdenka confesses her scheming, whereupon Matteo realizes it is Zdenka he really loves and Arabella and Mandryka are reunited.

Arabella (Strauss: *Arabella*). Sop. Elder daughter of Count Waldner and his wife Adelaide, and sister of Zdenka. She is supposed to marry a wealthy man to help her impoverished family, but is determined to wait for 'Mr Right' (*der Richtige*). She rejects various counts who are in love with her and dismisses Matteo, a young officer (whom her sister secretly loves). She is attracted by a stranger she sees from the window and wonders if this might be the man she has been waiting for. It is the wealthy Croatian landowner, Mandryka, who has come to woo her, having fallen in love with her photograph. At the annual Cabbies' Ball, they declare their love for each other and she then goes back to the hotel to rest. Mandryka misunderstands an overheard conversation and thinks she is meeting Matteo, but Zdenka sorts out the situation and Arabella and Mandryka reaffirm their love. Arias: *Aber der Richtige* ('But the right one'); *Mein Elemer!* ('My Elemer!'); *Das war sehr gut, Mandryka* ('It's a good thing, Mandryka'); duet (with Mandryka): *Und du wirst mein Gebieter sein* ('And you will be my lord'). Created (1933) by Viorica Ursuleac (future wife of Clemens Krauss, conductor of the première). Among the most famous

singers of this enchanting role are Lotte Lehmann, Margarete Teschemacher, Maria Reining, Maria Cebotari, Lisa Della Casa, Eleanor Steber, Gundula Janowitz, Caterina Ligendza, Lucia Popp, Felicity Lott, Ashley Putnam, Julia Varady, Kiri te Kanawa, Karita Mattila, and Orla Boylan—a veritable galaxy of Strauss sopranos.

Arbace (Mozart: *Idomeneo*). Ten. Confidant of Idomeneo. He brings the news that the king's ship has been sunk and Idomeneo feared drowned. Created (1781) by Domenico de Panzacchi.

Arbate (Mozart: *Mitridate, re di Ponto*). Sop. *Travesti* role (originally castrato). Governor of Nymphaea, loyal to Mitridate. Created (1770) by Pietro Muschietti (sop. castrato).

***Ariadne auf Naxos** (Ariadne on Naxos)* (Strauss). Lib. by Hugo von Hofmannsthal; 1st vers. 2 acts and linking scene; 2nd vers. prol. and 1 act; f.p. 1st vers. Stuttgart 1912, cond. Richard Strauss; 2nd vers. Vienna 1916, cond. Franz Schalk. [NOTE: In the 1st version (1912) the work begins with a Molière play (*Le Bourgeois Gentilhomme*), there is a linking scene followed by the opera *Ariadne auf Naxos*. This proved impracticable and Strauss and Hofmannsthal devised a second version (1916): the play was jettisoned; the linking scene was lengthened and converted into the Prologue; and the revised opera again follows. This is the version now described.]

Vienna, 17th cent.: In the house of a nouveau-riche man, entertainment is being prepared for his guests. An opera company and a *commedia dell'arte* troupe are both rehearsing. The *Music Master complains to the *Major-Domo that the *Composer's opera is going to be followed by such a vulgar act. The scene is one of typical back-stage chaos—the Composer wants more rehearsal, the Tenor who is singing *Bacchus dislikes his wig, the Prima Donna (who will be *Ariadne) refuses to rehearse, the *Dancing Master is trying to teach the comedians their movements. The leader of the comedians is *Zerbinetta, whom the Composer finds attractive. The Major-Domo returns: to be sure the entertainment is over in time for the firework display, the two companies must perform simultaneously. The Composer is devastated at the thought of his

music being interrupted by a harlequinade—
music is the holy art. Zerbinetta mocks the
plot of the opera—nobody dies for love.

The Island of Naxos, mythological times:
Ariadne has been deserted by Theseus. She
sleeps, guarded by *Echo, *Dryad, and *Naiad.
She wakes and weeps—only death can end her
misery. Zerbinetta and the rest of the troupe
fail to cheer her up. Zerbinetta tries to make
Ariadne see things differently—off with the
old, on with the new, is her motto. Ariadne retreats to her cave. The young god Bacchus
arrives. Ariadne mistakes him for Theseus
and then for Death. She gradually abandons
the idea of death, happy to go with Bacchus to
find love.

Ariadne/Prima Donna (Strauss: *Ariadne
auf Naxos*). Sop. In the Prologue, the Prima
Donna is refusing to rehearse the role of
Ariadne, which she will sing in the *opera seria*.
She cannot accept that such a noble work will
be followed by anything as vulgar as the comedians' act. The Music Master does his best to
convince her that by performing the role, she
will best show up the differences between
herself and those to follow. After it has been
announced that the opera will have to be
shortened, the Prima Donna quietly tells the
Music Master that it is the tenor's role which
must be cut—people do not want to listen to
him trying to reach all his high notes. In the
opera seria, Ariadne has been deserted by
Theseus. All she wants to do is die—there can
be no other love for her. Zerbinetta propounds
her own philosophy of life and love—off with
the old, on with the new. When Bacchus arrives
on the Island of Naxos, Ariadne at first thinks it
is Theseus returning to her, then assumes it is
the god of death. Gradually, she gives in and
prepares to leave with Bacchus in order to find
new love—just as Zerbinetta said she should.
Aria: *Es gibt ein Reich* ('There is a land'). Since
its creation, many great Strauss sopranos have
been heard in this role, among them Viorica
Ursuleac, Germaine Lubin, Maria Reining,
Lisa Della Casa, Christa Ludwig, Claire
Watson, Gundula Janowitz, Jessye Norman,
Heather Harper, Anna Tomowa-Sintow, Anne
Evans, Christine Brewer, Anne Schwanewilms,
Deborah Voigt, and Orla Boylan. Created (1912
vers.) by Mizzi (Maria) Jeritza; (1916 vers.) by
Maria Jeritza.

Aricie (Rameau: *Hippolyte et Aricie*). Sop.
Beloved of Hippolyte and protected by the
goddess Diana. She agrees to share Hippolyte's
exile, but their union is eventually blessed and
celebrated. Created (1733) by Marie Pellissier.

Ariodante (Handel). Lib. by Antonio Salvi;
3 acts; f.p. London 1735.

Medieval Scotland: *Ginevra, the *King of
Scotland's daughter, is in love with Prince
*Ariodante. She is loved by *Polinesso but has
rejected him. *Dalinda, her lady-in-waiting,
would be happy to respond to his love, although she is already loved by Ariodante's
brother *Lurcanio. Polinesso tries to convince
Ariodante that Ginevra is unfaithful. He persuades Dalinda to dress up as the princess and
let him into the royal apartment. This is observed by a distressed Ariodante. Lurcanio
persuades him to avenge himself. As the King
pronounces Ariodante as his heir, *Odoardo
announces that the prince is dead and that
Ginevra has been unfaithful. In hiding,
Ariodante hears from Dalinda how Polinesso
deceived him and now wants to marry Ginevra.
Polinesso is killed by Lurcanio and confesses
his crime before he dies. Dalinda is pardoned
by the King and agrees to accept Lurcanio's
proposal. Ariodante returns to Ginevra.

Ariodante, Prince (Handel: *Ariodante*).
Mez. *Travesti* role (originally castrato). He is in
love with Ginevra, the King of Scotland's
daughter. Falsely convinced by Polinesso of
her betrayal, he pretends to be dead, but the
dying Polinesso confesses the truth and
Ariodante and Ginevra prepare for their wedding. Aria: *Dopo notte* ('After night'). Recent
famous interpreters of the role include Janet
Baker, Ann Murray, and Sarah Connolly. Created (1735) by Giovanni Carestini (castrato).

Ariodate (Handel: *Serse*). Bass. A Prince,
leader of Serse's army. Created (1738) by
Antonio Montagnana.

Aristaeus Hero (Birtwistle: *The Mask of
Orpheus*). Mime role. Created (1986) by Robert
Williams.

Aristaeus Man (Birtwistle: *The Mask of
Orpheus*). High bar. Makes love to Euridice
and later tells Orpheus of her death. Is killed
by his own bees. Created (1986) by Tom
McDonnell.

Aristaeus Myth/Charon (Birtwistle: *The Mask of Orpheus*). High bar. Rows Orpheus across the Styx. Created (1986) by Rodney Macann.

Arkel (Debussy: *Pelléas et Mélisande*). Bass. King of Allemonde, father of Geneviève and grandfather of Golaud and Pelléas. Created (1902) by Feliz Vieuille.

Armando (previously **Spermando**) (Ligeti: *Le Grand Macabre*). Mez. *Travesti* role. In love with Amanda, the two of them spend most of the time making love in a tomb, ignorant of the events taking place nearby. Created (1978) by Kerstin Meyer.

Armed Men, Two (Mozart: *Die Zauberflöte*). Ten. and bass. They guard the door of the Temple where Tamino must undergo his trials. Created (1791) by Johann Michael Kistler and Christian Hieronymus Moll.

Armide (Gluck). Lib. by Philippe Quinault; 5 acts; f.p. Paris 1777, cond. Louis-Joseph Francœur.

Damascus, 1099, during the First Crusade: The sorceress *Armide has seduced many knights but has failed with the most heroic, *Renaud. With the help of her uncle *Hidraot (a magician), Renaud is put to sleep. Armide cannot bring herself to kill him and uses her powers to make him fall in love with her. Fellow knights break Armide's spell using a diamond shield and he leaves with them, as *Hatred had warned her he would. Distraught, Armide destroys her enchanted palace and sets out to seek Renaud and take her revenge.

Armide (Gluck: *Armide*). Sop. A pagan sorceress, Princess of Damascus. Desires the valiant knight of the crusades, Renaud, and, aided by a spell put on him by her uncle, she makes him fall in love with her. He is rescued and leaves her. She determines to seek vengeance. Created (1777) by Rosalie Levasseur.

Arminda (Mozart: *La finta giardiniera*). Sop. Niece of the Podestà, admired by the knight Ramiro. Created (1775) possibly by Teresa Manservisi (who created either this role or that of the maid Serpetta).

Arnalta (Monteverdi: *L'incoronazione di Poppea*). Cont. Poppea's nurse. Creator (1643) not known.

Arnheim, Arline (Balfe: *The Bohemian Girl*). Sop. The girl of the title, daughter of Count Arnheim. Kidnapped as a child and brought up by gypsies, she falls in love with a soldier in the camp. The Queen of Gypsies has her arrested on a false charge and at her trial she is recognized by the judge, who is her father. Created (1843) by Miss Rainforth.

Arnheim, Count (Balfe: *The Bohemian Girl*). Bar. Father of the Bohemian girl, Arline, who has been kidnapped. Many years later, at her trial on a false charge, he rescues his daughter. Created (1843) by Mr Borrani.

Arnold 1. (Rossini: *Guillaume Tell*). Ten. Son of Melcthal. He loves the Princess Mathilde, sister of the Austrian governor who dominates his country. After his father has been held hostage and killed, he helps Tell rid their country of Austrian domination. Created (1829) by Adolphe Nourrit.

2. (Henze: *The English Cat*). Bass. Nephew of Lord Puff, frightened he will be disinherited if Lord Puff and his new bride have offspring. Created (1983) by Roland Brecht.

Aroldo (Verdi). Lib. by Francesco Maria Piave (adapted from *Stiffelio*); 4 acts; f.p. Rimini 1857, cond. Angelo Mariani.

England and Scotland, c.1200, during the Crusades: *Aroldo, a Saxon knight, returns from the wars to his wife *Mina. Her father, *Egberto, will not allow his daughter to confess to Aroldo that she had an affair with a soldier, *Godvino. Egberto challenges Godvino to a duel, which is interrupted by Aroldo. Realizing the truth, he insists on fighting Aroldo himself, but is reminded that his religious oath as a Crusader forbids him to do so. He offers Mina a divorce, but she insists she loves him and was seduced by Godvino. Determined to seek out Godvino and kill him, Aroldo finds his body—he has been murdered by Egberto. Aroldo goes into 'exile' with his friend from the wars, the holy man *Briano. Egberto and Mina are outlawed. In their wanderings, they come upon Aroldo's hut and he and Mina are reconciled. [NOTE: Italian audiences found Verdi's earlier opera *Stiffelio* difficult to accept: it contained a married priest, an adulterous wife, and a husband (the priest) prepared to forgive the adultery. So many difficulties were put in the way of productions that its performance was often impracticable. In 1856 Piave suggested setting the opera in medieval times, changing Stiffelio the Priest to Aroldo the Crusader and altering the final scene considerably. Verdi altered some of the orchestration and wrote some new music and in this form it achieved success. Nowadays, both *Aroldo* and *Stiffelio* are produced.]

Aroldo (Verdi: *Aroldo*). Ten. A Saxon knight married to Mina. He returns from fighting in the Crusades and learns that his wife has had an affair with a soldier, Godvino. Her father kills Godvino. Aroldo insists on divorcing Mina, despite her protestations of love for him. He goes into exile with the holy man, Briano, the friend he met during the wars. They live in a primitive hut on the banks of Loch Lomond in Scotland. There Mina, outlawed and wandering, finds him, and the two are reconciled. Created (1857) by Emilio Pancani. *See also* STIFFELIO.

Arsace (Rossini: *Semiramide*). Cont. *Travesti* role. Commander of the Assyrian army. The ghost of the murdered king, Nino, tells him that he is the son of Nino and Semiramide and must avenge his father, who was killed by the Queen and her lover Assur. He attempts to kill Assur, but Queen Semiramide throws herself between them and is killed by the blow. Created (1823) by Rosa Mariani.

Arsamene (Handel: *Serse*). Mez. *Travesti* role. Brother of Xerxes, in love with Romilda. Despite his brother's machinations, he and Romilda are married. Created (1738) by Maria Antonia Marchesini.

Arthur (Birtwistle: *Gawain*). Ten. King of Logres, from whose court Gawain sets out to meet the Green Knight. Created (1991) by Richard Greager.

Arthur/Officer 1 (Maxwell Davies: *The Lighthouse*). Bass. A lighthouse keeper, a Bible-thumping religious maniac. Created (1982) by David Wilson Johnson. *See also* ARTURO.

Arturo 1. (Bellini: *I Puritani*). *See* TALBOT (2).
   2. (Donizetti: *Lucia di Lammermoor*). *See* BUCKLAW, ARTHUR.

Arvidson, Mme (Verdi: *Un ballo in maschera*). (Ulrica in the Amer. vers.) Cont. A negro fortune-teller, she is accused of sorcery and is to be exiled, but the pageboy Oscar begs the King to show mercy. The King goes in disguise to her quarters to see for himself what she does. She reads his palm and tells him he will soon die, slain by the first man to shake hands with him. Arias: *Re dell'abisso, affrettati* ('King of the abyss, make haste'); *Dunque ascoltate* ('Then listen to me'). In this role, in 1955, Marian Anderson became the first black singer to appear on the stage of the New York Metropolitan Opera. Created (1859) by Zelinda Sbriscia.

Ascanio (Berlioz: *Benvenuto Cellini*). Mez. *Travesti* role. Cellini's apprentice. Created (1838) by Rosine Stoltz.

Aschenbach, Gustav von (Britten: *Death in Venice*). Ten. A novelist who has lost his creative urge and travels to Venice in the hope of renewing it. There he sees a young Polish boy, Tadzio, to whom he is strongly attracted. He meets a variety of strange characters, many of whom make him very uneasy and apprehensive. When a cholera epidemic breaks out in Venice, most people leave, but his love for Tadzio keeps him there, although he is unable to bring himself to speak to the boy. The writer, sitting on the beach watching Tadzio and his friends playing, dies from the disease. Arias: *My mind beats on; Ah Serenissima!* It is thought that Aschenbach could be based on Britten himself—the fear of a creative block being one aspect of both their characters, and the other obvious one being the attraction of young boys, neither of them apparently doing more than admiring them at a distance. Among tenors who have succeeded in this role are Donald Grobe, Anthony Rolfe Johnson, Philip Langridge, Robert Tear, and Ian Bostridge. Created (1973) by Peter Pears.

Ashby (Puccini: *La fanciulla del West*). Bass. Agent of the Wells Fargo Transport Company. It is Ashby who breaks the news that the bandit Ramerrez is somewhere in the vicinity and provides a photograph (sent by an old girlfriend of the bandit) which the sheriff can use to convince Minnie of Dick Johnson's real identity. Created (1910) by Adamo Didur.

Ashton, Lucy (Lucia) (Donizetti: *Lucia di Lammermoor*). Sop. Sister of Enrico, she is the Lucia of the opera's title. She is in love with Edgardo, but to save her brother's financial and political future, she is forced into marriage with Arturo, having been deceived into believing that her loved one has been unfaithful. As soon as she signs the marriage contract, Edgardo appears, and believing she has betrayed him he curses her. Lucia loses her senses, kills her new husband, collapses, and dies. Arias: *Quando rapita in estasi…* ('When, lost in ecstasy'); the famous 'mad scene': *Il dolce suono mi colpì di sua voce!* ('I was struck by the sweet sound of his voice!'); sextet (with Edgardo, Enrico, Raimondo, Arturo, and Alisa): *Io sperai che a me la vita tronca avesse il mio spavento* ('I hoped that terror would cut short my life'). This is one of opera's most famous coloratura show-roles, and the one in which Joan Sutherland burst on to the international scene at Covent Garden in 1959. Created (1835) by Fanny Tacchinardi-Persiani.

Ashton of Lammermoor, Lord Henry (Enrico) (Donizetti: *Lucia di Lammermoor*). Bar. Brother of Lucia. He has become embroiled in political movements against the King and has also lost most of the family fortune. To save himself on both scores, he arranges his sister's marriage to Arturo. Discovering her love for his old family rival, Edgardo, he conspires to prove to Lucia that Edgardo has been unfaithful. When Edgardo appears just after the wedding, Lucia goes mad. Aria: *Cruda, funesta smania* ('A cruel, deadly frenzy'); the famous sextet (with Edgardo, Lucia, Raimondo, Arturo, and Alisa), which he opens in duet with Edgardo: *Chi raffrena il mio furore* ('Who checks my fury?'). Created (1835) by Domenico Cosselli.

Aspasia (Mozart: *Mitridate, re di Ponto*). Sop. Betrothed to Mitridate. Loved by his son Farnace, she loves his other son, Sifare. Created (1770) by Antonia Bernasconi.

Assur, Prince (Rossini: *Semiramide*). Bar. Lover of Semiramide, he has been her accomplice in the murder of her husband. Created (1823) by Filippo Galli.

Asteria (Handel: *Tamerlano*). Sop. Daughter of Bajazet, Turkish Emperor defeated by Tamerlano. In love with Tamerlano's ally Andronico. Tamerlano attempts to win her for himself, but is unsuccessful and she and Andronico are united. Created (1724) by Francesca Cuzzoni.

Astradamors (Ligeti: *Le Grand Macabre*). Bass. An astrologer, married to Mescalina, a highly sexed lady who does not find him a satisfactory partner. Created (1978) by Arne Tyrén.

Astrologer (Rimsky-Korsakov: *The Golden Cockerel*). Sop. A *travesti* role. Gives Tsar Didon a cockerel to warn him of enemies, but later demands the Tsar's betrothed for his reward. Is killed by the Tsar who in turn is killed by the cockerel. Created (1909) by Ivan Altchevsky.

Astynax (Rossini: *Ermione*). Silent. Young son of Hector and Andromache. The Greeks want him dead so there will be no chance of his trying to avenge his father's murder.

Atalanta 1. (Handel: *Serse*). Sop. Sister of Romilda, in love with Arsamene. Created (1738) by Margherita Chimenti.
2. (Maw: *The Rising of the Moon*). *See* LILLY-WHITE, ATALANTA.

Athamas (Handel: *Semele*). Alto. Prince of Boeotia, betrothed to Semele, but loved by her sister Ino, whom he ultimately marries. Creator (1744) unknown.

Attavanti, Marchese (Puccini: *Tosca*). This lady does not appear in the opera but is referred to on several occasions. She is the sister of Angelotti, the escaped political prisoner who is hidden by Cavaradossi. The painting of the Madonna on which Cavaradossi is working is noted by the Sacristan to look like the Marchese who visits the church. This likeness is also commented on with great jealousy by Tosca.

Aufstieg und Fall der Stadt Mahagonny (The Rise and Fall of the City of Mahagonny) (Weill). Lib. by Bertolt Brecht; 3 acts; f.p. Leipzig 1930, cond. Gustav Brecher.

A modern American city, precise time unspecified: Leokadia *Begbick, Trinity *Moses and *Fatty are on the run from the police when their lorry breaks down. They decide to found a new city in the desert where there will be no unpleasantness—no one will have to work and the most important thing will be enjoyment. It will be the city of Mahagonny. In response to their propaganda, people flock to live there, including Jim *Mahoney and his friends.

Jenny *Smith and other girls arrive and Jim fancies Jenny. Gradually they all demand more and more pleasures and Mahagonny becomes the scene of debauchery. Jim, unable to pay his drinking debts, is imprisoned and Jenny deserts him. He is tried and as a result of the charges brought against him, including seduction of Jenny, is sentenced to the electric chair. He advises them all to think about what has happened to their 'ideal' city. Fire envelops Mahagonny and as Jim dies the city burns.

Auntie (Britten: *Peter Grimes*). Cont. Landlady of 'The Boar'. Trio (with Boles and Keene): *Grimes is at his exercise*. Created (1945) by Edith Coates.

Autonoe (Henze: *The Bassarids*). Sop. Sister of Agave, and aunt of Pentheus. Created (1966) by Ingeborg Hallstein.

Avis (Smyth: *The Wreckers*). Sop. Daughter of the lighthouse keeper and in love with Mark, who has abandoned her. Created (1906) by Luise Fladnitzer.

Azema, Princess (Rossini: *Semiramide*). Sop. In love with Prince Assur. Created (1823) by Matilde Spagna.

Azucena (Verdi: *Il trovatore*). Mez. A gypsy woman living in a gypsy encampment in Biscay. Her mother was burnt as a witch for putting the evil eye on the younger son of the old Count di Luna. Azucena snatched the Count's other son. She threw a baby on to her mother's funeral pyre, but she was demented and it is not known if she threw the noble baby or her own son. She tells Manrico that he is her son and nurses him when he is wounded in battle by the young Count di Luna. Manrico and Azucena are both arrested and she is made to watch Manrico's execution. She then reveals that it was her own child she threw on the pyre many years ago, so di Luna has executed his own brother. Aria (in which she tells how her mother died): *Stride la vampa!* ('Upwards roll the flames') (the famous Anvil Chorus surrounds Azucena's solo); duets (with Manrico): *Non son tuo figlio?* ('Then am I not your son?'); *Ai nostri monti ritorneremo* ('Let us go back to our mountains'). Created (1853) by Emilia Goggi.

Baba the Turk (Stravinsky: *The Rake's Progress*). Mez. A bearded lady in a circus, she is helped by Nick Shadow to become Tom Rakewell's wife. She does not reveal her beard until after they are married. Because her non-stop chatter drives him crazy, he repulses her and, furious, she storms around smashing various possessions. To stop her tirade of criticism and complaint in mid-word, he covers her face with a wig. When the wig is removed much later, she continues exactly where she left off. But Baba has a gentler side, and realising Anne is Tom's true love, encourages her to save him, herself returning to continue her circus career. Arias: *Come, sweet, come; Scorned! Abused! Neglected!* Created (1951) by Jennie Tourel.

Babette (Henze: *The English Cat*). Mez. Sister of Minette, later chased by Tom. Created (1983) by Elisabeth Glauser.

Bacchus/Tenor (Strauss: *Ariadne auf Naxos*). Ten. In the Prologue, the Tenor, who will sing Bacchus in the *opera seria*, is complaining about his wig, which he refuses to wear, aiming a kick at the Wigmaster. When he learns that the opera is to be shortened, he tells the Composer it is the Prima Donna's role which must be cut—nobody wants that woman on stage more than necessary. In the opera proper, he arrives on the Island of Naxos, thinking he will find Circe. He sees Ariadne and assumes she is the goddess he is seeking, and invites her to leave with him and go on his ship. Now life will begin for them both, he assures her. Aria: *Circe, kannst du mich hören?* ('Circe, can you hear me?'); duet (with Ariadne): *Das waren Zauberworte!* ('That was a magic spell!'). Too many tenors see this as *Heldentenor* territory, and it all too rarely receives the lyrical singing the role requires. Among the most famed of Bacchuses are Richard Tauber, Peter

Anders, Rudolf Schock, Torsten Ralf, Helge Roswaenge, Jess Thomas, James King, and Johan Botha. Created (1912 vers.) by Hermann Jadlowker; (1916 vers.) by Bela von Környey.

Badoero, Alvise (Ponchielli: *La gioconda*). Bass. One of the heads of the State Inquisition, married to Laura, who is in love with Enzo. Created (1876) by Ormondo Maini.

Bailli, Le (Massenet: *Werther*). Bass. The Magistrate, a widower, father of Charlotte, Sophie, and other children. Created (1892) by Herr Forster.

Bajazet (Handel: *Tamerlano*). Ten. Emperor of the Turks, defeated and captured by the Tartar leader Tamerlano. Commits suicide by drinking poison. Created (1724) by Francesco Borosini.

Baker, Steve (Kern: *Show Boat*). Spoken. Husband and partner of Julie La Verne on board the Cotton Blossom. Created (1927) by Charlie Ellis.

Balducci (Berlioz: *Benvenuto Cellini*). Bass. Papal treasurer, father of Teresa, who he wants to marry Fieramosca, Cellini's opponent. Created (1838) by Henri Etienne Dérivis.

ballo in maschera, Un (*A Masked Ball*) (Verdi). Lib. by Antonio Somma; 3 acts; f.p. Rome, 1859, cond. Eugenio Terziani. [NOTE: The libretto was based on the assassination in 1792 of the Swedish King Gustavus III at a masked ball. The censor found this offensive and refused to allow the opera to take place, so Verdi and Somma transferred the action to colonial Boston. Modern productions usually revert to the Swedish version, described below—the equivalent American names are given in the character entries.]

In and near Stockholm, late 17th cent.: Counts *Ribbing and *Horn plot to overthrow

*Gustavus III. The King's friend and secretary *Anckarstroem is married to *Amelia, whom the King loves. The page boy *Oscar begs clemency for Mme *Arvidson, who is being banished as a sorceress. The King, in disguise, asks this fortune-teller to read his palm. She warns him of death at the hands of the first person to shake his hand. Anckarstroem arrives and the friends shake hands. Amelia and Gustavus meet in a field and she tells him they must sacrifice their love and he must remain loyal to his friend. Hearing Anckarstroem arrive, she covers her face with a veil. He warns the King of a conspiracy, and advises him to take a safe route back to the city while he himself escorts the veiled lady. Amelia's identity is revealed en route and her husband is set on revenge. He and Amelia are invited to the palace to a masked ball. Oscar warns the King of an assassination plot, but he ignores the warning, anxious to see Amelia one last time. Unintentionally, Oscar reveals which costume the King is wearing. Anckarstroem kills the King.

Balstrode, Capt. (Britten: *Peter Grimes*). Bar. Retired merchant skipper. One of Grimes's few friends. He helps Grimes to haul in his boat and prevents Boles from attacking him in the Boar. Balstrode, accompanied by Ellen Orford, advises Grimes to take his boat out to sea and sink it to avoid the angry mob who think he has deliberately caused the death of his Apprentice. Aria: *We live, and let live, and look*. Created (1945) by Roderick Jones.

Balthazar 1. (Donizetti: *La Favorite*). Bass. Superior of the Monastery of St James. Father of Fernand, a novice in the monastery. Balthazar goes to see the King with an excommunication order from the Pope. He tells Fernand of Léonor's position as the King's favourite. Created (1840) by Nicolas-Prosper Levasseur.

2. (Menotti: *Amahl and the Night Visitors*). Bass. One of the Three Kings seeking the Christ Child. Created (1951, TV) by Leon Lishner.

Banquo (Verdi: *Macbeth*). Bass. An army general. The Witches having informed Macbeth that Banquo will never be king, but will father future kings, he has to be disposed of. He is killed, but his son, Fleance, manages to escape and so the succession is guaranteed. At a banquet in his castle Macbeth, now declared king, is horrified to see Banquo's ghost occupying

his customary position at the table, covered in blood. Created (1847) by Michele Benedetti.

Barak's Wife (Strauss: *Die Frau ohne Schatten*). *See* DYER'S WIFE.

Barak the Dyer (Der Färber) (Strauss: *Die Frau ohne Schatten*). Bar. A poor dyer who lives with his wife in humble surroundings. His three brothers live with them. He and his wife have been married for over two years but are childless. Barak is good natured and patient and works hard at the markets. In his absence, the Empress arrives with her Nurse and offers to buy the Wife's shadow (her symbol of fertility) in return for a life of luxury. When Barak comes home, he finds he has been banished to a single bed. As the Nurse persists in trying to force the Wife to sell her shadow, Barak becomes more sad, thinking his wife no longer loves him and when she tells him (untruthfully) that she has actually sold her shadow, he threatens to kill her. His Wife then admits that she was lying. Barak's feelings are apparent to the Empress who finds it impossible to accept the shadow at the cost of so much unhappiness. In a subterranean chamber, Barak and his Wife are separated. After the Empress and her Nurse leave and return to the spirit kingdom, Barak and his Wife are reunited and she is seen to cast a shadow. The voices of their unborn children are heard. Aria: *Mir anvertraut* ('Entrusted to me'). Among acclaimed Baraks are Friedrich Plaschke, Josef von Manowarda, Paul Schöffler, Ludwig Weber, Dietrich Fischer-Dieskau, Walter Berry, Gustav Neidlinger, Donald McIntyre, Bernd Weikl, Norman Bailey, and Franz Grundheber. Created (1919) by Richard Mayr.

Barbarina (Mozart: *Le nozze di Figaro*). Sop. Daughter of the gardener Antonio and cousin of Susanna. In love with Cherubino. Responsible for delivering a note, supposedly arranging an assignation with Susanna, to Count Almaviva. Aria: *L'ho perduta, me meschina!* ('I have lost it, unhappy me!'). A role in which many sopranos have first made their mark. Created (1786) by Anna Gottlieb (aged 12!).

Barber (Schneidebart) (Strauss: *Die schweigsame Frau*). Bar. Barber to Sir Morosus, he has learnt how to handle the old seaman. He offers to find him a wife, a quiet woman who will be a suitable bride for a man who cannot bear any noise. Created (1935) by Matthieu Ahlersmeyer.

barbiere di Siviglia, II (Rossini). Lib. by Cesare Sterbini; 2 acts; f.p. Rome 1816, cond. Gioachino Rossini.

Seville, 17th cent.: Count *Almaviva, disguised as Lindoro, a poor student, sings outside *Rosina's window. She lives with her elderly guardian, *Bartolo, and *Berta, her governess. The Count is recognized by *Figaro, who tells him that Bartolo wants to marry Rosina. Almaviva enters the house in disguise and is recognized as Lindoro by Rosina. He poses as a pupil of her music teacher, *Basilio, come to give Rosina a music lesson. When Bartolo falls asleep during the lesson, they admit their love for each other. In the house to shave Bartolo, Figaro acquires the key to the balcony window, to help Lindoro and Rosina elope. Their plans are frustrated and the Count admits his real identity to Rosina. Figaro coaxes a notary to marry Almaviva and Rosina. Bartolo, acknowledging defeat, gives them his blessing.

Bardi, Guido (Zemlinsky: *Eine florentinische Tragödie*). Ten. Son of the Duke of Florence, he is having an affair with Bianca, wife of the silk-merchant Simone. When her husband catches them together, the two men fight a duel and Guido is killed. Created (1917) by Rudolf Ritter.

Bardolph (Bardolf) (Verdi: *Falstaff*). Ten. A follower and drinking companion of Falstaff. Created (1893) by Paolo Pelagalli-Rossetti.

Barena (Janáček: *Jenůfa*). Sop. A servant at the Buryja mill. Created (1904) by Marie Tůmová.

Barnaba (Ponchielli: *La gioconda*). Bar. A spy of the Inquisition. Wants to possess la Gioconda, who rejects him. Tricks the nobleman Enzo into meeting his lover Laura, now married to Alvise. Gioconda helps the lovers escape, and rather than fulfil her promise to give herself to Barnaba in return for Enzo's life, she kills herself. As she dies, Barnaba screams at her that he has strangled her old blind mother. Created (1876) by Gottardo Aldighieri.

Baron (Massenet: *Chérubin*). Bar. Suspects Chérubin of having an affair with his wife and challenges him to a duel. Created (1905) by Mons. Chalmin.

Baroncelli (Wagner: *Rienzi*). Ten. A Roman citizen supporter of Rienzi, who turned against him and encouraged the people to fight against him and plot his death. Created (1842) by Friedrich Traugott Reinhold.

Baroness 1. (Barber: *Vanessa*). Cont. The Old Baroness, mother of Vanessa. Created (1958) by Regina Resnik.

2. (Massenet: *Chérubin*). Cont. Forces Chérubin to admit to her husband that he has not had any relationship with her. Created (1905) by Blanche Deschamps-Jehin (whose husband conducted the première).

Bartered Bride, The (*Prodaná Nevěsta*) (Smetana). Lib. by Karel Sabina; 3 acts; f.p. Prague 1866 (with spoken dialogue), cond. Bedřich Smetana; Prague 1870 (definitive vers., sung throughout).

Bohemia: *Mařenka tells her lover *Jeník that her father may force her to marry *Vašek, son of *Micha and *Hata. They swear eternal love, though she is curious about Jeník's past. Mařenka's parents, *Krušina and *Ludmila, discuss with the marriage-broker, *Kečal, their daughter's proposed husband. Mařenka confesses her love for Janík and Kečal tries to bribe him to give her up. Vašek meets Mařenka but does not realize this is his prospective bride. She takes advantage of the opportunity to tell him that 'Mařenka' loves someone else and will make sure he dies if she is forced to marry him. Meanwhile, Jeník has agreed not to marry Mařenka, but on condition that she marry only 'Micha's son'. The circus arrives. The dancer *Esmeralda and the *Circus Master persuade Vašek to take over the part of their star turn, who is drunk. Mařenka, thinking Jeník has rejected her, considers marrying Vašek, whose parents are astonished to hear Jeník claiming his right, as 'Micha's son', to marry Mařenka. In truth, he is Micha's son, who left home after his own mother's death, when Micha married Hata. Jeník and Mařenka receive his father's blessing.

Bartley (Vaughan Williams: *Riders to the Sea*). Bar. A fisherman, last surviving son of Maurya, his brothers having all drowned. He insists on crossing the sea at low tide to take horses to Galway Fair. He, too, is drowned. Created (1937) by Alan Coad.

Bartolo, Doctor 1. (Rossini: *Il barbiere di Siviglia*). Bass. Guardian of Rosina, who wants to marry her and tries to prevent her eloping with Count Almaviva. Admitting defeat, he gives them his blessing. Aria: *A un dottor della mia sorte* ('For a doctor of my standing'); sextet (with Basilio, Figaro, Count, Rosina, and Berta): *Freddo ed immobile* ('Awestruck and motionless'). One of the great roles for a *buffo* bass. Created (1816) by Bartolomeo Botticelli.

2. (Mozart: *Le nozze di Figaro*). Bass. Previous guardian of Rosina, now the Countess Almaviva. He turns out to be Figaro's father and agrees to marry the mother of his son, Marcellina. Aria: *La vendetta* ('Revenge'). Created (1786) by Francesco Bussani (who also created Antonio; his wife created Cherubino).

Basilio, Don 1. (Rossini: *Il barbiere di Siviglia*). Bass. Rosina's music-teacher. He suggests to Bartolo, Rosina's guardian, that one way of discouraging the Count, who is wooing Rosina, would be to spread rumours about his character. Aria: *La calunnia è un venticello* ('Calumny is a little breeze'); quintet: *Buona sera, mio signore* ('Goodnight, dear sir'). Created (1816) by Zenobio Vitarelli.

2. (Mozart: *Le nozze di Figaro*). Ten. The music-teacher. Aria (usually omitted): *In quegl'anni, in cui val poco* ... ('In those years when reason, little practised'). A famous Russian Basilio was Igor Stravinsky's father, Fyodor Stravinsky. Created (1786) by Michael Kelly (who also created the lawyer Don Curzio).

Bassarids, The (Henze). Lib. by W. H. Auden and Chester Kallman; 1 act (4 movements); f.p. Salzburg 1966, cond. Christoph von Dohnányi.

Greece, ancient times (the Bassarids, or Bacchae, are the worshippers of Dionysus): *Cadmus, King of Thebes, abdicates in favour of his grandson *Pentheus. Despite Pentheus' fury, his mother *Agave, her sister *Autonoe, and the blind *Tiresias all worship *Dionysus. Pentheus orders his guards to arrest them all, but learns nothing from them about the Dionysian way of life. The disguised Dionysus enables Pentheus to recognize his own subconscious sexual fantasies. Disguised in women's clothes, Pentheus goes to Mount Cythaeron to see for himself the Dionysian mysteries. The Bacchantes, led by his mother who does not recognize her son, tear him limb from limb. Cadmus and all his family are banished from Thebes, their palace burned to the ground.

Bastien (Mozart: *Bastien und Bastienne*). Ten. A shepherd in love with Bastienne, he is unfaithful. To bring him to heel, the magician Colas tells him that she no longer loves him. In despair, Bastien threatens to drown himself. Colas brings them together again. Creator (1768) not traced.

Bastienne (Mozart: *Bastien und Bastienne*). Sop. A shepherdess, distressed at her lover's infidelity, consults the village magician, Colas. He tells her that she should show equal indifference and this will bring Bastien to his senses. When they meet, they argue, but Colas reunites them. Creator (1768) not traced.

Bastien und Bastienne (Mozart). Lib. by Friedrich Wilhelm Weiskern and Johann Heinrich Müller, rev. by Johann Andreas Schachtner; 1 act; f.p. Vienna 1768.

A pastoral opera. *Bastien has been unfaithful to *Bastienne. The village magician *Colas uses his magic powers to bring them together again. (The première was probably given in the garden of the hypnotist Dr Anton Mesmer. *See* DESPINA.)

Bayan (Glinka: *Ruslan and Lyudmila*). Ten. A minstrel, who sings of the trials Ruslan will undergo but of his ultimate success in winning Lyudmila. Creator (1842) not traced.

Bear, The (Walton). Lib. by Paul Dehn and comp.; 1 act; f.p. Aldeburgh 1967, cond. James Lockhart.

Russia, 1888: Widowed for some months, the attractive young Mme *Popova has decreed that she will mourn her husband for the rest of her life. Her servant, *Luka, announces the arrival of *Smirnov, a landowner to whom her husband owed money for the oats he purchased for their horse, Toby. She is unable to pay him immediately and Smirnov, at first aggressive, is gradually attracted to the spirited young widow and challenges her to a duel to settle their argument. As he demonstrates to her how to hold the pistol, she realizes she has fallen in love with him.

Béatrice (Berlioz: *Béatrice et Bénédict*). Mez. Niece of the Governor of Messina, Léonato. She is in love with a young army officer, Bénédict, but will not admit it—they constantly mock each other. It is arranged that she 'overhears' a discussion in which it is said that

Bénédict is in love with her. The ruse works, and they acknowledge their feelings for each other. Created (1862) by Anne Charton-Demeur.

Béatrice et Bénédict (Berlioz). Lib. by composer; 2 acts; Baden-Baden 1862, cond. Hector Berlioz.

Messina, after the Moorish Wars: The governor *Léonato's daughter *Héro is to marry *Claudio, returning with the victorious army from the Moorish wars. *Béatrice will not admit she is equally delighted to see *Bénédict return. Don *Pedro and Claudio plot a way of tricking the couple into acknowledging their love for each other. Bénédict overhears a discussion in which it is said that Béatrice has fallen in love with him. Héro and her companion *Ursula are amused when Béatrice overhears a similar conversation, stating that Bénédict has fallen in love with her. The conductor *Somarone rehearses the bridal march he has written for Claudio and Héro. After they have signed the marriage contract, the registrar offers a second contract for whosoever would like to use it. Béatrice and Bénédict reluctantly admit their feelings for each other.

Beaumarchais (Corigliano: *The Ghosts of Versailles*). Bar. The author of the plays on which are based the operas *Le nozze di Figaro* and *Il barbiere di Siviglia*. His ghost is in love with that of Queen Marie Antoinette and he enlists the help of Figaro, his favourite character, and the entire Almaviva household from his plays to help him change the course of history through his art. He will write a third play and through it will prevent the execution of the Queen he loves. But it all goes wrong, and in the end he is forced to stage Marie Antoinette's trial. He fails to rescue her, but through his art she has seen the way to love him, so her execution can go ahead—they will be reunited in Paradise. Created (1991) by Håkan Hagegård.

Beaumont, Cornet John Stephen (Maw: *The Rising of the Moon*). Ten. Wanting to join the 31st Royal Lancers, he is set various tasks as his initiation, one of which is to seduce three women in one night. He succeeds with the wives of two officers, but as he is about to enter the room of young Atalanta, daughter of the camp adjutant, he is prevented by the arrival of an officer accompanied by the Irish

Cathleen, who fancies him. The next day he is able to announce his successes, but to save the honour of all involved he resigns his commission and the regiment has to leave Ireland. Created (1970) by John Wakefield.

Beccavivi (Mozart: *Così fan tutte*). Name used by Despina when disguised as a lawyer.

Beckmesser, Sixtus (Wagner: *Die Meistersinger von Nürnberg*). Bar. The Town Clerk, he is also the official 'Marker' at the Masters' Guild song contests, a post he is determined to keep. He would like to marry Eva, whom her father, Veit Pogner, has promised as a prize to the winner of the contest and he is going to enter the competition against the young visiting knight Walther. Walther wants to become a Master so that he can marry Eva, as they love each other. At Walther's audition, Beckmesser is shut into the marker's box, but the sound of his chalk heavily scratching on his slate to mark all Walther's errors, can be heard throughout the knight's song. Before the song is finished, Beckmesser emerges from his box and gleefully displays his slate while recounting a list of Walther's faults in style and content. The assembled Masters have to admit that Walther has failed the audition and Beckmesser is angered at Sachs's obvious support for the young fellow. That evening Beckmesser comes to serenade Eva beneath her window but finds himself constantly interrupted by the sound of Sachs hammering on his last as he makes the town clerk's new shoes. Magdalene and Eva have changed places and while Eva attempts (unsuccessfully) to elope with Walther, David catches Beckmesser apparently serenading his Magdalene and gives him a thrashing. The next morning, bruised and battered, Beckmesser visits Sachs. Finding the cobbler's shop empty, he looks around and sees on a table Walther's song for the contest. He presumes it to be Sachs's song and jumps to the conclusion (wrongly) that Sachs is going to enter the contest for Eva's hand. When Sachs returns, Beckmesser thrusts the song at him, accusing him of deliberately foiling his own attempts to marry Eva. Sachs neither admits nor denies these charges, but tells Beckmesser he can keep the song and Beckmesser can't wait to rush home to memorize it, having had Sachs's word that *he* will never again sing it. He effusively thanks Sachs, telling him fawningly what a great poet he is and hurriedly departs. At the contest, Beckmesser keeps looking at the piece of paper—he is clearly having trouble trying to make sense of the whole thing and even asks Sachs to help him. The poet comments that no one is *making* him sing it—it is his own decision. Beckmesser takes the competitors' stand. As he sings, the words come out as total rubbish because of his inability to grasp the meaning of them, and soon everyone is laughing at him. He leaves the stand, blaming Sachs for his humiliation, and slinks away. Because Wagner was well known as a hater of the critics, and his original name for the character who became Sixtus Beckmesser was Veit Hanslich, not unnaturally it was assumed that this was Wagner's way of getting his own back on Eduard Hanslick, the famous Vienna music critic who was a champion of Brahms rather than Wagner. It has also been suggested that Beckmesser is a manifestation of Wagner's anti-Semitism, but there is really nothing in the character or music to suggest this, although a producer determined to portray Beckmesser in this way can always make it stick. The role is a lovely character-part but, like many comic roles, there are elements of tragedy as he reaps what he has sown. There have been many excellent portrayers of this role, including Richard Mayr, Benno Kusche, Geraint Evans, Thomas Hemsley, Hermann Prey, Derek Hammond-Stroud, and Thomas Allen. Created (1868) by Gustav Hölzel.

Begbick, Leokadia (Weill: *Aufstieg und Fall der Stadt Mahagonny*). Mez. One of three people on the run from the police. She and her friends Trinity Moses and Fatty decide to found a new city in the desert where the most important thing will be enjoyment. It will be the city of Mahagonny. Creator (1930) not traced.

Bégearss (Corigliano: *The Ghosts of Versailles*). Ten. A friend of Count Almaviva, who has promised him his own illegitimate daughter in marriage, unaware that Bégearss is a Revolutionary. Created (1991) by Graham Clark.

Beggar's Opera, The (Gay/Pepusch). Words (lib.) by John Gay, music arranged by John Christopher Pepusch; 3 acts; f.p. London 1728.

Polly *Peachum's mother, Mrs *Peachum, discovers that Polly and the highwayman *Macheath have been secretly married. Because her father wants to have him hanged, Polly tells Macheath to leave and hide. In a tavern he meets two young ladies who take his guns. *Peachum and his men arrive and arrest him. He is confined in Newgate Prison where the gaoler's daughter, Lucy *Lockit, is an old conquest he seduced and deserted. He now agrees to marry her. Polly arrives in search of her husband and she and Lucy quarrel. Lucy helps Macheath escape but he is recaptured and returned to Newgate. Peachum and *Lockit escort him to the Old Bailey where he is confined in the condemned cell. He is reprieved and reunited with Polly.

Belcore (Donizetti: *L'elisir d'amore*). Bar. A sergeant who woos Adina until she agrees to marry him. However, at the wedding-feast she keeps postponing the signing of the contract, as she is really in love with the poor peasant Nemorino. Created (1832) by Henri-Bernard Dabadie.

Belfiore 1. (Mozart: *La finta giardiniera*). Ten. Count Belfiore, a somewhat mad young man, lover of the Marchesa Violante. He had stabbed her and fled, believing her to be dead. She is disguised as a gardener's assistant at the mayor's house. Belfiore arrives to be presented as the prospective bridegroom of the mayor's niece. He is accused of murdering the Marchesa, who saves him by admitting her identity. Created (1775) probably by Johann Walleshauser.

2. (Verdi: *Un giorno di regno*). Bar. Cavalier di Belfiore is a friend of the Polish King Stanislao, whose right to the throne is being challenged. To draw attention from the monarch, Belfiore poses as king and travels to France as a guest in Baron Kelbar's castle. On arrival he finds his sweetheart very angry—thinking he has deserted her, she is about to wed a local dignitary. He forbids the wedding—after all, he is king and they must do his bidding. News reaches the castle that the Polish crisis is over, the king is safe, and Belfiore can reveal his true identity and marry his Marchese. Created (1840) by Raffaele Ferlotti.

Belinda (Purcell: *Dido and Aeneas*). Sop. Lady-in-waiting and confidante to Queen

Dido. Created (1683/4) by an unknown schoolgirl.

Bella (Tippett: *The Midsummer Marriage*). Sop. Secretary to King Fisher. She and her fiancé Jack have an uncomplicated and down-to-earth relationship. Created (1955) by Adèle Leigh.

Belle Hélène, La (Beautiful Helen) (Offenbach). Lib. by Henri Meilhac and Ludovic Halévy; 3 acts; f.p. Paris 1864, cond. ? Lindheim.

Mythical Greece: *Menelaus' wife *Helen is unhappy with her weak husband and has heard that Venus has promised *Paris that he will win the most beautiful woman on earth—who else but herself? *Calchas meets a shepherd (Paris in disguise) and arranges for him to win the contest which will allow him to be alone with Helen. Menelaus returns earlier than expected and finds Helen and Paris in bed. Paris makes a quick getaway. On the beach, Helen and Menelaus quarrel and *Orestes thinks they have offended Venus. A priest approaches and orders Helen to atone for her sins by sailing with him to Cythera. When they have left, the priest throws off his disguise—it is Paris. The Trojan War is about to begin.

Belmonte (Mozart: *Die Entführung aus dem Serail*). Ten. A Spanish nobleman in love with Constanze. When she is kidnapped, together with her maid, he sets off to find her in Pasha Selim's house. With the help of his servant, he enters the palace and the two ladies are rescued. Arias: *Hier soll ich dich denn sehen* ('Here I shall see you again'); *O wie ängstlich, o wie feurig* ('Oh how fearfully, oh how fervently'); *Wenn der Freude Tränen fliessen* ('When tears of joy flow freely'). Created (1782) by Valentin Ademberger.

Ben (Menotti: *The Telephone*). Bar. Boyfriend of Lucy, his attempts to propose are frustrated by the constant ringing of her telephone. In the end he goes out and telephones from a public call-box. Now he proposes and she accepts—on condition that he never forgets her telephone number. Created (1947) by Paul Kwartin.

Bénédict (Berlioz: *Béatrice et Bénédict*). Ten. A young officer returning from the wars. He is in love with Béatrice, but they always tease and mock each other and he maintains that he will remain a bachelor. His friends arrange for him to overhear a conversation during which Béatrice admits her love for him. It works—they acknowledge their mutual love. Created (1862) by Mons. Montaubry.

Benny, Ben (Britten: *Paul Bunyan*). Bass. One of two Bad Cooks. Everyone complains about the food, and he and his partner walk out. Duet (with Sam Sharkey): *Sam for soups, Ben for beans*. Created (1941) by Eugene Bonham.

Benoît (Puccini: *La bohème*). Bass. Landlord of the house in whose attic live four bohemians. On Christmas Eve, as they celebrate with meagre rations and a bottle of wine, he calls to ask for his rent, which they cannot afford to pay. They ply him with wine and he boasts of his extra-marital conquests. They feign disgust at such behaviour in a married man and throw him out—the rent still unpaid. Created (1896) by Alessandro Polonini (the creator also of Alcindoro).

Bentson, Mistress (Delibes: *Lakmé*). Mez. English governess living in India. Created (1883) by Mme Pierron.

Benvenuto Cellini (Berlioz). Lib. by Léon de Wailly and Auguste Barbier; 2 acts; f.p. Paris 1838, cond. François-Antoine Habeneck.

Rome, mid-16th cent.: Pope *Clement VII has asked the Florentine Benvenuto *Cellini to make a statue of Perseus. *Balducci, papal treasurer, wanted his future son-in-law *Fieramosca to have the commission. Balducci's daughter *Teresa and Cellini plan to elope, overheard by Fieramosca who, with his friend *Pompeo, plans to stop them. During Shrove Tuesday revels there is a fight and Cellini kills Pompeo. He is arrested, but escapes and returns to his studio, where he, Teresa, and *Ascanio (Cellini's apprentice) plan to leave for Florence, but they are prevented by the arrival of Balducci and Fieramosca. The Pope, anxious to see his statue of Perseus, will grant Cellini absolution and allow him to marry Teresa if the statue is finished that day. The casting begins. When they run out of metal, Cellini throws into the foundry all his previous completed works of art. The statue is finished on time.

Benvenuto Cellini (Berlioz: *Benvenuto Cellini*). *See* CELLINI, BENVENUTO.

Benvolio (Gounod: *Roméo et Juliette*). Ten. Nephew of the Montagues, friend of Romeo. Created (1867) by Mons. Laurent.

Beppe (Leoncavallo: *Pagliacci*). Ten. A player in Canio's troupe. Harlequin in the play. Created (1892) by Francesco Daddi.

Berenice (Mozart: *La clemenza di Tito*). She does not appear in the opera; she is the daughter of Agrippa of Judaea and is the intended bride of Tito. She is therefore the source of Vitellia's jealousy, although by the time Vitellia has organized an attempt on Tito's life, Tito has another bride in view.

Bernardo (Bernstein: *West Side Story*). Bar. Leader of the Sharks gang, brother of Maria, who marries Tony, one of the rival gang, the Jets. Tony kills Bernardo. Created (1957) by Kenneth LeRoy.

Bersi (Giordano: *Andrea Chénier*). Mez. Mulatto maid of Maddalena di Coigny. Created (1896) by Maddalena Ticci.

Berta (Rossini: *Il barbiere di Siviglia*). Sop./mez. Rosina's governess. Aria: *Il vecchiotto cerca moglie* ('The old man seeks a wife'). Created (1816) by Elisabetta Loyselet.

Bertarido, King (Handel: *Rodelinda*). Cont. *Travesti* role (originally castrato). King of Lombardy, husband of Rodelinda and father of Flavio. He is reported killed in battle, and his enemy Grimoaldo wants to marry Rodelinda. Bertarido is helped by his old friend Unulfo to be reunited with his wife. Grimoaldo has him arrested and imprisoned. Unulfo helps him escape. When Garibaldo tries to kill Grimoaldo, supposedly his friend, Bertarido intervenes and kills Garibaldo. Grimoaldo renounces all claim to the throne and marries Bertarido's sister. Created (1725) by Senesino (the castrato Francesco Bernardi).

Bertha (Weir: *Blond Eckbert*). Mez. Wife of Blond Eckbert. She describes to their friend Walther her earlier life, brought up by an old woman. Bertha becomes ill and dies. The old woman reveals to Eckbert that Bertha was really his sister, abandoned by her father in childhood. Created (1994) by Anne-Marie Owens.

Bervoix, Flora (Verdi: *La traviata*). Mez. Close friend of Violetta. It is to Flora that Violetta runs when she agrees to leave Alfredo. And at a party at Flora's, Alfredo insults Violetta by throwing his gambling winnings at her feet. Created (1853) by Speranza Giuseppini.

Bess (Gershwin: *Porgy and Bess*). Sop. Girlfriend of Crown, who deserts her. She is given a home by the crippled Porgy. She visits the widowed Serena, whose husband Crown has killed. Bess gradually falls in love with Porgy, but Crown tries to win her back. In a fight with Porgy he is killed. While Porgy is being questioned by police, Bess leaves for New York. Aria: *I loves you, Porgy*. Created (1935) by Anne Brown.

Bezukhov, Count Pierre (Prokofiev: *War and Peace*). Ten. A friend of Natasha's aunt, he is himself in love with Natasha. He tells her that Anatol, for whom she has fallen, is already married. After the fall of Moscow to the French, he searches for her in the city. Creator (1945 vers.) not known; created (1946 vers.) by Oles' [Olexander] Semenovych Chishko (who was also a composer of some note).

Bianca 1. (Britten: *The Rape of Lucretia*). Mez. Lucretia's old nurse. Quartet (with Lucretia, Lucia and the Female Chorus): *Their spinning wheel unwinds*. Created (1946) by Anna Pollak.

2. (Zemlinsky: *Eine florentinische Tragödie*). Sop. Wife of the silk-merchant Simone, she is having an affair with Guido, son of the Duke of Florence. Simone finds out and the men fight a duel. Guido is killed. Bianca realizes she loves her husband and needed him to show how dominant he could be. Created (1917) by Helene Wildbrunn.

Bidebent, Raymond (Raimondo) (Donizetti: *Lucia di Lammermoor*). Bass. Raimondo, the Lammermoor chaplain. He reminds Lucia of her responsibility to her family and her duty to marry Arturo. He later announces to the wedding guests that Lucia has killed Arturo and gone mad. Takes part (with Edgardo, Enrico, Lucia, Arturo, and Alisa) in the famous sextet, his first words being *Qual terribile momento!* ('What a terrible moment!'). Created (1835) by Carlo Porto(-Ottolini).

Billows, Lady (Britten: *Albert Herring*). Sop. An elderly autocrat in whose house a meeting is held and the decision made to elect a May King. She puts up a prize of 25 sovereigns. Aria: *We bring great news to you upon this happy day*. Created (1947) by Joan Cross.

Billy Budd (Britten). Lib. by E. M. Forster and Eric Crozier; 4 acts (rev. to 2 acts 1960); f.p. London 1951, cond. Benjamin Britten.

On board *HMS Indomitable*, 1797, during the French Wars: In a short Prologue, Capt. *Vere, now an old man, reviews his career, and especially the summer of 1797. On board the *Indomitable*, a boat is seen returning from a press-ganging operation. The new recruits are questioned by the evil master-at-arms, *Claggart. They incl. Billy *Budd, who has a stammer. Billy leads a chorus of praise for the captain, Starry Vere. A fight breaks out when Billy finds *Squeak apparently stealing from his kit-bag—in fact, Squeak has been ordered by Claggart to spy on Billy. Claggart reports to Vere and accuses Billy of trying to rouse the men to mutiny. Vere questions Billy, whose stammer prevents him explaining what happened. In his frustration, he strikes out at Claggart who falls down dead. Although Vere knows in his heart that this was an accident, he nevertheless feels obliged to court-martial Billy, who is sentenced to death. As Billy is about to be hanged from the yard-arm, he pleads with the men not to mutiny on his behalf. His final words are in praise of Vere—who knows he could have saved Billy.

Billy Budd (Britten: *Billy Budd*). *See* BUDD, BILLY.

Birkenfeld, Marquise de (Donizetti: *La Fille du régiment*). Sop. The Marquise claims to be the aunt of Marie, the adopted daughter of the regiment, and takes her to live in her château, intending to find her a suitable husband. When the regiment arrive at the château, the Marquise confesses that Marie is really her own illegitimate daughter. She sees how much Marie loves the soldier Tonio and consents to their marriage. Created (1840) by Marie-Julienne Boulanger.

Biterolf (Wagner: *Tannhäuser*). Bass. A knight, one of five *Minnesingers*, who takes part in the singing contest. He is Tannhäuser's greatest opponent but, like all the Minstrels, he has nothing but respect for Elisabeth. Created (1845) by Michael Wächter.

Blanche 1. (Poulenc: *Les Dialogues des Carmélites*). Sop. Daughter of the Marquis and sister of the Chevalier de la Force. Enters a convent to find peace of mind. She escapes when the convent is ransacked and returns to her father's house. When she learns that the nuns are all to die by the guillotine, she joins them on the scaffold. Created (1957) by Virginia Zeany.

2. (Sullivan: *Princess Ida*). Lady Blanche. Cont. Professor of Abstract Science, in charge of the Castle Adamant, the ladies' college where Ida has taken refuge. Created (1884) by Rosina Brandram.

Blankytný (Janáček: *The Excursions of Mr Brouček*). Ten. A character Brouček meets on the Moon. He is a poet and is engaged to Etherea. His earthly counterparts are Mazal (Prague 1888) and Petřík (Prague 1420). Created (1920) by Miloslav Jeník.

Blazes/Officer 2 (Maxwell Davies: *The Lighthouse*). Bar. A lighthouse-keeper, short-tempered and having no time for his colleague's religious mania. Created (1982) by Michael Rippon.

Blind Ballad-Singer (Britten: *Gloriana*). Bass. Sings to the people in the street, reporting that Essex has escaped from custody and is inciting the citizens of London to rebellion. Aria (ballad): *To bind by force*. Created (1953) by Inia te Wiata.

Blind, Dr (J. Strauss II: *Die Fledermaus*). Ten. Eisenstein's lawyer. Created (1874) by Herr Rott.

Blitch, Rev. Olin (Floyd: *Susannah*). Bass-bar. A visiting preacher who finds Susannah attractive. He encourages her to attend church service and confess the 'sins' of which the village Elders accuse her, but she runs out, not prepared to confess to something of which she is innocent. He calls at her home to comfort her and, when she breaks down, he takes her to bed. Finding she is a virgin, he tries unsuccessfully to convince the village Elders of her innocence. He is shot by her brother Sam. Created (1955) by Mark Harrell.

Blondchen (Mozart: *Die Entführung aus dem Serail*). Sop. The English maid of Constanze. In love with Pedrillo. Captured with her mistress and held in Pasha Selim's house until rescued by their men. Arias: *Durch Zärtlich-keit und Schmeicheln* ('With tenderness and pretty words'); *Welche Wonne, welche Lust* ('What bliss, what delight'). Created (1782) by Therese Teyber.

Blond Eckbert (Weir). Lib. by comp.; 2 acts; f.p. London 1994, cond. Sian Edwards.

A bird tells a story to a dog: *Eckbert and his wife *Bertha live in the Harz Mountains. Bertha tells their friend *Walther of how she left her parents, who had been cruel to her, and went to live with an old woman who had a magic bird and a dog. Walther is able to tell her the name of the dog, causing her husband to be very suspicious. Out hunting, he kills Walther. Bertha becomes ill and dies. Eckbert leaves the mountains and meets *Hugo, but fancies he looks like Walther. In the wilderness Eckbert finds the old woman Bertha had described. The old lady tells him that she, Walther, and Hugo are all one person—and that Bertha was really Eckbert's sister. The news kills Eckbert.

Bluebeard (Bartók: *Duke Bluebeard's Castle*). Bass. He has married Judith and brought her to his gloomy castle. Behind various doors she discovers signs of torture and blood. He tries to dissuade her from opening the last door, from behind which come his former wives. Judith has to follow them back through the door to her fate. Bluebeard is left alone. Created (1918) by Oszkár Kálmán.

Blumenmädchen (Wagner: *Parsifal*). See FLOWER MAIDENS.

Bob Boles (Britten: *Peter Grimes*). See BOLES, BOB.

Boccanegra, Simon (Verdi: *Simon Bocca-negra*). Bar. A plebeian buccaneer, later doge, and father of Maria (known as Amelia Grimaldi). Amelia's mother was the daughter of the patrician Fiesco, who disapproved of her relationship with Boccanegra. She died and Fiesco blamed Boccanegra and would forgive him only if he handed over their child. However Boccanegra had left his little daughter in the care of an old lady. He returned from one of his trips to find the lady dead and the child gone. Meantime, Boccanegra has been elected doge, mainly due to the efforts of Paolo Albiani.

Twenty-five years on, Boccanegra visits the Grimaldi palace and sees the Count's daughter, Amelia. Through her mother's portrait, which she wears in her locket, Boccanegra recognizes Amelia as his long-lost daughter. She is being cared for by her guardian 'Andrea' (who is Fiesco living under another name) and she is betrothed to Gabriele Adorno (for whose father's death Boccanegra was held responsible). Paolo, who lusts after her, kidnaps her but she escapes. Boccanegra swears vengeance on the abductor and curses him (not knowing who it is). Boccanegra drinks water into which Paolo has put poison. Finding him drowsy and at his mercy, Gabriele is prevented from killing Boccanegra by Amelia, who then reveals that he is her father. As Boccanegra succumbs to the poison, he is reconciled with Fiesco, who now has his granddaughter back and the young couple are married. As he dies, Boc-canegra names Gabriele as his successor, the new doge. Aria: *Figlia! a tal nome io palpito* ('Daughter! ... I tremble at that name'). Created (1857 vers.) by Leone Giraldoni (who two years later created Anckarstroem/Renato in *Un ballo in maschera*; his son, Eugenio Giral-doni, in 1900 created Scarpia in Puccini's *Tosca*—notwithstanding their names, they were Fr., not It.); (1881 vers.) by Victor Maurel.

bohème, La (*Bohemian Life*) (Leoncavallo). Lib. by comp.; 4 acts; f.p. Venice, 1897, cond. Alessandro Pomé (who in 1893 had cond. the f.p. of Puccini's *Manon Lescaut*).

The major difference between this and Puccini's version is that the main male character is *Marcello: The friends all gather at the Café Momus on Christmas Eve. *Musetta has a wealthy lover who throws her out because of her attraction to Marcello. *Mimì accepts the proposal of Count *Paolo and leaves *Rodolfo; and Musetta, weary of being poor, leaves Mar-cello. Next Christmas they are all reunited, but Mimì, now sick, dies.

bohème, La (*Bohemian Life*) (Puccini). Lib. by Giuseppe Giacosa and Luigi Illica; 4 acts; f.p. Turin 1896, cond. Arturo Toscanini.

Paris, 1830: It is Christmas Eve. *Rodolfo and *Marcello are in their attic room. *Colline and *Schaunard arrive, bringing wine and meagre rations. They dine and celebrate Christmas. Their landlord, *Benoît, attempts to extract rent from them. Rodolfo decides to finish his poetry while the others set off for the Café Momus. As he writes, Mimì knocks on the door—she lives in a nearby room and her candle has gone out. She is about to leave, but starts to cough and has to rest. The candle blows out again and she drops her key. As they try to find it in the dark, their hands touch. They tell each other of their lives and aspirations, declare their love, and leave to join the others at the café. There, Marcello's old love, *Musetta, enters with the wealthy *Alcindoro. She makes sure Marcello notices her—clearly they still love each other. After sending Alcindoro on an errand, she and Marcello reavow their love and she joins the rest of them for supper. They depart, leaving their bill for Alcindoro to pay on his return. Two months later Mimì, frail and wracked by coughing, seeks out Marcello at a tavern. She and Rodolfo must separate—his jealousy is making their life impossible. Rodolfo emerges from the inn and regretfully he and Mimì agree to part. As they sing their farewells, Musetta and Marcello quarrel. Back in the attic some months later, Rodolfo is missing Mimì and Marcello longs for Musetta. The four friends try to cheer themselves up by playing the fool. They are interrupted by the arrival of Musetta—downstairs is Mimì, who is dying from consumption. They help her up to the attic and on to a bed. Their friends leave Rodolfo and Mimì together to reaffirm their love. They return and Rodolfo goes to speak to them. He is the last to realize that Mimì is dead.

Bohemian Girl, The (Balfe). Lib. by Alfred Bunn; 3 acts; f.p. London 1843, cond. Michael Balfe.

Pressburg (now Bratislava), late 18th cent.: Count *Arnheim's 6-year-old daughter Arline *Arnheim is kidnapped. She grows up in a gypsy camp and, aged 18, falls in love with *Thaddeus, a Polish soldier who has taken refuge in the camp. The *Queen of the Gypsies loves Thaddeus and has Arline arrested on a false charge. The judge at her trial is Count Arnheim, who recognizes his daughter. He welcomes Thaddeus and all ends happily.

Boisfleury, Marquis de (Donizetti: *Linda di Chamounix*). Bar. Uncle of Carlo, the young vicomte who is in love with Linda. Created (1842) by Agostino Rovere.

Bolena, Anna (Donizetti: *Anna Bolena*). Sop. Second wife of Enrico (King Henry VIII), she is being discarded in favour of Giovanna (Jane) Seymour. She confesses her unhappiness to Lord Percy, her first love, and he declares his love for her. The King, anxious to find a treasonable offence with which to accuse Anna, finds them together and commits her to the Tower to await trial. Giovanna tries to persuade her to save herself by saying that she is guilty and begging the King's pardon, but she will not do so. As the King and Giovanna's wedding is announced, Anna is led to the scaffold. Aria: *Cielo, a' miei lunghi spasimi* ('Heaven grant an end to my long agonies')—the tune of this aria is easily recognized as a decorated version of Henry Bishop's *Home, sweet home*). This long-neglected opera was revived in 1956 at Bergamo, Donizetti's birthplace. That performance was seen by Gianandrea Gavazzeni, conductor at La Scala, Milan, who recognized it as an ideal vehicle for the talent, both vocal and dramatic, of Maria Callas. It was staged for her at La Scala the following year. Created (1830) by Giuditta Pasta.

Boles, Bob (Britten: *Peter Grimes*). Ten. Methodist fisherman. An aggressive man, especially under the influence of drink. He is the chief instigator of the witch-hunt against Grimes. He tries to attack him in the Boar and is prevented by Balstrode. Created (1945) by Morgan Jones.

Bolkonsky, Prince Andrei (Prokofiev: *War and Peace*). Bar. Son of Prince Nikolai. He is a widower who falls in love with Natasha Rostova. His father disapproves and insists they spend a year apart. During that time Natasha falls for Prince Anatol. Her aunt and their friend, Pierre Bezukhov, tell her Anatol is already married and Pierre declares his own love for her. Napoleon crosses the border. Moscow is occupied and Natasha's family flee, taking the injured Andrei with them. He dies. Created (1945 vers.) by A. P. Ivanov; (1946 vers.) by L. E. Petrov.

Bolkonsky, Prince Nikolai (Prokofiev: *War and Peace*). Bass-bar. Father of Andrei. Created (1945 vers.) by N. D. Panchekhin; (1946 vers.) by P. M. Zhuravlenko.

Bonze, The (Puccini: *Madama Butterfly*). Bass. Uncle of Cio-Cio-San (Butterfly). He curses her for changing her religion in order to marry Pinkerton and rejects her, encouraging the rest of her family to do likewise. Created (1904) probably by Paolo Wulmann.

Boréades, Les (The Boreads) (Rameau). Lib. attrib. to Louis de Cahusac; 5 acts; f.p. Paris radio, concert extracts, 1964; f. stage p. Aix-en-Provence 1982, cond. John Eliot Gardiner.

Ancient kingdom of Bactria: Queen *Alphise must marry one of the Boreads, descendants of Boréas, God of the North Wind. Two Boreads, *Calisis and *Borilée, try to win her, but she loves the young foreigner *Abaris, not knowing he is the son of Apollo, entrusted as a child to the care of *Adamas, and therefore of royal blood. Alphise decides to abdicate, but is carried off by the winds. Abaris begs Apollo to help him find his love, and is given a magic arrow, which he uses to calm the winds. Apollo reveals the truth and the lovers are able to marry.

Borilée (Rameau: *Les Boréades*). Bar. A Boread who unsuccessfully woos Queen Alphise. Created (f. stage p. 1982) by Gilles Cachemaille.

Boris 1. (Janáček: *Katya Kabanová*). *See* GRIGORJEVIČ, BORIS.
　2. (Shostakovich: *Lady Macbeth of the Mtsensk District*). *See* ISMAILOV, BORIS.
　3. (Musorgsky: *Boris Godunov*). *See* GODUNOV, BORIS.

Boris Godunov (Musorgsky). Lib. by comp.; prol. and 4 acts; f. (complete) p. St Petersburg 1874, cond. Eduard Napravnik.

Russia, 1598: Tsar Fyodor has died. The people persuade his regent, the boyar Boris *Godunov, to accept the crown. He does so, but is very apprehensive. Six years later: the old monk *Pimen recalls the murder of the Tsarevich Dimitri, son of Ivan the Terrible and brother of the dead Tsar Fyodor. The young novice *Grigori realizes he is the age Dimitri would have been. Accompanied by *Varlaam and *Missail, he flees to Poland to raise an army to defeat Boris, so he can become Tsar. In the Kremlin *Xenia, comforted by her young brother *Fyodor and her nurse, still mourns the death of her husband the Tsar. Prince *Shuisky, rival to Boris, announces the arrival of a pretender who calls himself the resurrected Dimitri (Grigori, disguised). Boris is haunted

by the memory of his murder of the young Tsarevich. In Poland, Princess *Marina has fallen in love with 'Dimitri'. Her Jesuit confessor *Rangoni reminds her it is her duty, if she mounts the throne with 'Dimitri', to convert Russia to Catholicism. (This is the 'Polish act', added when the composer revised the opera, and is omitted in some performances.) Outside St Basil's Cathedral, Moscow, the starving people beg Boris to give them bread. A Simpleton accuses him of murder. As the boyars meet in the Kremlin, the deranged Boris arrives. Pimen announces that Dimitri is alive. Boris collapses. Left alone with the boy Fyodor, Boris bids him farewell as he dies. The crowds greet the false Dimitri and follow him to Moscow.

Boris Godunov (Musorgsky: *Boris Godunov*). *See* GODUNOV, BORIS.

Borromeo, Cardinal Carlo (Pfitzner: *Palestrina*). Bar. Cardinal of Rome. Persuades Palestrina to compose a Mass to convince the Pope of the devoutness of the new polyphonic music. Created (1917) by Fritz Feinhals.

Bottom 1. (Britten: *A Midsummer Night's Dream*). Bass-bar. A weaver, one of the rustics who rehearse and perform a play for Theseus and Hippolyta. Wearing an ass's head, he is loved by Tytania under the influence of a magic juice given to her by Puck on Oberon's orders. Arias (as Pyramus): *O grimlook'd night; Sweet moon, I thank thee for thy sunny beams*; ens. (with Tytania and the Fairies): *Hail, mortal, hail!* Created (1960) by Owen Brannigan.
　2. (Purcell: *The Fairy Queen*). Spoken. Similar to the role in (1). Creator (1692) unknown.

Bouillon, Prince de (Cilea: *Adriana Lecouvreur*). Bass. An amateur chemist who discovers the poison which his wife later uses to kill her rival, the actress Adriana Lecouvreur. Created (1902) by Edoardo Sottolana.

Bouillon, Princess de (Cilea: *Adriana Lecouvreur*). Mez. In love with Maurizio. Jealous of his relationship with the actress Adriana Lecouvreur, she sends her rival violets soaked in poison which kill Adriana when she sniffs them. Created (1902) by Edvige Ghibaudo.

Boum, General (Offenbach: *La Grande-Duchesse de Gérolstein*). Bar. Commander of Gérolstein's army. Created (1867) by Mons. Couder.

Boy Apprentice (Britten: *Peter Grimes*). *See* APPRENTICE.

Bradamante (Handel: *Alcina*). Mez. Ruggiero's future wife. Disguised as her 'brother Ricciardo', she comes to rescue Ruggiero from the powers of the sorceress Alcina. Created (1735) by Caterina Negri.

Brandenburg, Cardinal Albrecht von (Hindemith: *Mathis der Maler*). Cardinal-Archbishop of Mainz. Art-loving and a supporter of Mathis. However, the archbishopric has no money and the Cardinal's assistant tries to persuade him that he should renounce his oath of celibacy and marry Ursula, wealthy daughter of the Lutheran Reidinger. Impressed by her willingness to marry him for the sake of her religion, although she admits to being in love with Mathis, the Cardinal blesses her and makes the decision to withdraw from the world. Created (1938) by Peter Baxevanos.

Brangäne (Wagner: *Tristan und Isolde*). Sop. (but usually sung by mez.). Isolde's attendant and companion. She accompanies Isolde in the ship in which she is being taken by Tristan to meet and marry King Mark. Knowing nothing of Tristan's history (he killed Isolde's previous fiancé), Brangäne is puzzled by her mistress's obvious antagonism to Tristan. Sent to summon Tristan, she has to deal with Kurwenal, Tristan's loyal friend, and returns to tell Isolde that she has not been able to get a straight answer—he seems reluctant to come. At this point Isolde tells Brangäne the whole story, but fails to mention that, despite everything, she and Tristan have fallen in love. Brangäne is asked to fetch a box of potions and is horrified when Isolde takes out a death-potion. Isolde asks her to prepare this for her to drink, but Brangäne substitutes a love-potion: she at last knows that Isolde and Tristan love each other but cannot admit it, for she is the King's intended bride and he is the King's loyal nephew. Isolde shares the drink with Tristan and the two declare their love. As the ship arrives in Cornwall and King Mark's presence is imminent, Brangäne admits to her mistress what she has done. She now realizes that she has only made matters worse, as Isolde is not interested in the King. The lovers arrange to meet secretly while the King is out hunting. The signal that it is safe will be the extinguishing of a light at the door to their apartment. Brangäne is reluctant to extinguish the flame—she is worried a trap is being laid for the lovers and that Melot, Tristan's supposed friend, is at the bottom of it. She tries to warn her mistress, who will have none of it, and puts out the torch herself. While the lovers are together, Brangäne keeps watch, but when she tries to warn them that Mark and his men are arriving, they ignore her. Melot and Tristan fight and Tristan is badly wounded. He is taken back to his home by Kurwenal. Isolde is sent for and goes to join them. Brangäne realizes that the only way to make amends is to admit to Mark what she has done. He forgives everything. He will go with her to Tristan's estate and bless the couple's union. They set off for Brittany. On arrival, they find Isolde unconscious across Tristan's body. Aria: *Einsam wachend in der Nacht* ('Keeping solitary watch in the night').

Brangäne can be regarded as responsible for most of the action of the opera, for she it is who exchanges the potions, although only with the best of intentions, as she knows that the love between Isolde and Tristan should be fulfilled. And it is Brangäne who realizes that Melot is going to betray his master and inform on the young lovers to the King. She does her best to sort things out by confessing her actions to King Mark, but the damage has been done and all ends in tragedy. The role of Brangäne has attracted an impressive array of singers, including Anny Helm, Margarete Klose, Maria Olczewska, Grace Hoffman, Kerstin Thorborg, Constance Shacklock, Blanche Thebom, Kerstin Meyer, Regina Resnik, Christa Ludwig, Yvonne Minton, Della Jones, Jane Henschel, Hanna Schwarz, Petra Lang, and Katerina Karneus. Created (1865) by Anna Deinat.

Brétigny, de (Massenet: *Manon*). Bar. A rich nobleman. He coaxes Manon away from Des Grieux with promises of the wealth and luxury he can offer her. Creator (1884) not traced.

Briano (Verdi: *Aroldo*). Bass. A holy man who becomes a friend of the knight Aroldo during the Crusades. He accompanies Aroldo into exile after the knight divorces his adulterous wife. Created (1857) by G. B. Cornago. *See also* JORG.

Brighella (Strauss: *Ariadne auf Naxos*). *See* COMMEDIA DELL'ARTE TROUPE.

Bris, St (Meyerbeer: *Les Huguenots*). *See* SAINT-BRIS, COMTE DE.

Brogni, Cardinal de (Halévy: *La Juive*). Bass. President of the Council. After Eléazer's 'daughter' Rachel has been put to death for breaking the commandments, Brogni is revealed as her real father. Created (1835) by Nicolas Levasseur.

Brook, Master (Verdi: *Falstaff*). The name (in Eng., in It. Signor Fontana) used by Ford when, disguised, he offers to 'help' Falstaff seduce Alice Ford, i.e. Ford's wife.

Brouček, Matěj (Janáček: *The Excursions of Mr Brouček*). Ten. A landlord, he drinks heavily at the local inn, gives his lodger Mazal notice, and flirts with Mazal's fiancée Malinka, daughter of the Sacristan. Brouček dreams of a life on the moon, free from all worries about lodgers and taxes. He falls asleep, drunk, and when he wakes up he is on the moon. Everyone he meets there is identical to one of his earthbound acquaintances. However, he soon realizes life on the moon is not all sweet—to start with, they don't eat decent food, only flowers from which they can absorb the smell. He soon decides to return to earth, but when he does, Prague has gone back to the 15th cent. It is the time of the Hussite Wars and once again everyone he comes across resembles those he knew before. Charged with cowardice for refusing to fight in the war, he is sentenced to death by burning in a barrel. As the barrel burns, he wakes up: he really is in a barrel—the one into which he fell in a drunken stupor at the inn. Created (1920) by Mirko Štork.

Brown, Lucy (Weill: *The Threepenny Opera*). Sop. Daughter of Tiger Brown. Essentially the same character as Lucy Lockit in *The Beggar's Opera*. Created (1928) by Kate Kühl.

Brown, Tiger (Weill: *The Threepenny Opera*). Bar. (doubles the role of the Street Singer). Commissioner of Police and father of Lucy. He arrests Macheath and is really the same character as Mr Lockit in *The Beggar's Opera*. Created (1928) by Kurt Gerron.

Brünnhilde (Wagner: *Die Walküre*; *Siegfried*; *Götterdämmerung*). Sop. One of nine Valkyries, daughters of Erda and Wotan (and his favourite).

Die Walküre: Brünnhilde makes her first appearance in the *Ring* when her father, Wotan, instructs her to protect Siegmund in his fight with Hunding, after Siegmund has fled with Hunding's wife Sieglinde. With the arrival of Wotan's wife Fricka, goddess of marriage, Brünnhilde beats a hasty retreat, leaving her father to face by himself the forthcoming 'violent storm'. When Brünnhilde returns, Wotan rescinds his previous instructions, but she perceives that something is troubling him and asks him to tell her what it is. Wotan then uses his favourite daughter more or less as a sounding-board, explaining to her who her mother is and recounting the story of how he comes to be in possession of the accursed Ring. Now he is forced to betray Siegmund, his mortal son. Brünnhilde quickly understands that it is Fricka's idea that Siegmund be killed, but when she tells her father she will protect Siegmund, he becomes very angry and she is forced to agree to do his bidding even though she knows it is not his true wish. Sadly, she leaves to meet the fleeing Siegmund and Sieglinde. She tells Siegmund that she will lead him to Valhalla, castle of the gods, and there he will find his father, but Sieglinde must remain on the mortal earth. Without Sieglinde, Siegmund refuses to follow Brünnhilde, even though she explains that he is in danger, his sword doomed in battle, because his father has so decreed. Still he obstinately sticks to his vow. Now Brünnhilde makes her most important decision—she will defy her father and save both Siegmund and Sieglinde. Telling him to rely on his sword, she promises she will see him again on the battlefield. Hunding catches up with the lovers and he and Siegmund fight, Siegmund watched over by Brünnhilde. As he is about to thrust his sword into Hunding's breast, a furious Wotan appears, places his own spear in front of Siegmund, and the sword shatters on the spear. Hunding kills him (and Wotan kills Hunding). Brünnhilde sweeps Sieglinde on to her horse and gallops off to the Valkyrie mountain. There she is greeted by her sisters, the other eight Valkyries. She begs them to protect her— she has defied their father and he will be unforgiving—and to save Sieglinde who, she has realized, is pregnant. They are all too frightened of Wotan to risk helping her or

BRÜNNHILDE (*Der Ring*—Wagner)

by Dame Anne Evans

It is doubtful if any other role in the operatic repertory demands as much of a singer as does Brünnhilde in *The Ring*. For a start it has an extraordinarily wide tessitura. Apart from the opening 'Hojotohos', with their high Cs, much of the *Walküre* Brünnhilde lies easily within a mezzo-soprano's compass. *Siegfried*, on the other hand, is a true soprano role, particularly in the final, joyous pages where the phrases lead inexorably to the sustained, climactic C. The *Götterdämmerung* Brünnhilde embraces elements of both the other two operas and calls for huge vocal and physical stamina. Few, if any, sopranos find all three Brünnhildes equally easy to sing; every singer of this role that I know finds the *Götterdämmerung* Brünnhilde the most rewarding, both dramatically and vocally. (On one occasion at least, Bayreuth employed a different Brünnhilde for each opera, but it did not prove satisfactory from a dramatic point of view.)

Not only must a Brünnhilde be master of the actual notes, she must also be master of the text—written by Wagner himself—so that she can use it to make the character live, because in Wagner the drama must come out of the words as well as the music: the two are inseparable. A Brünnhilde must be able to colour her voice to match the changes of mood and situation, which are often reflected in the change of harmonies. For example, when in the *Todesverkündigung* ['prophecy of death'] from Act 2 of *Die Walküre* Brünnhilde comes to tell Siegmund of his impending death, she must adopt a grave, dark tone. Then, as she begins to understand the nature of Siegmund and Sieglinde's great love for each other—an emotion she has never known before—she has to sing with the utmost tenderness and warmth. In *Siegfried*, Brünnhilde experiences love herself, though, strictly speaking, the long Act 3 scene between Siegfried and Brünnhilde is not a love duet as such, but rather a falling-in-love duet, in which the two characters gradually discover one another.

At the end of *Götterdämmerung* Act 1, Brünnhilde has to switch almost instantly from sheer joy to whispered terror as she beholds not the expected Siegfried, but a complete stranger—Siegfried disguised as Gunther. Once Siegfried/Gunther has snatched the Ring from her hand, she feels raped—she has assumed, wrongly, that the Ring would protect her from a mere mortal. At the beginning of the next act, Brünnhilde is drained of all life. Harry Kupfer, in his Bayreuth production [first seen in 1988], underlined her humiliation by having her carried on in a net, like an animal that had been hunted down and captured. Only when Gunther announces the impending marriage of Siegfried and Gutrune does she burst into life. Her first reaction is one of alarm, which turns into terrible rage. By the end of the cycle, Brünnhilde has changed from the immortal hoyden of *Walküre* Act 2 to the wisest of mortal women as she leaps on to the funeral pyre to join Siegfried in death. Together, the music and text are infallible in guiding the singer through the twists and turns of the plot. I have sung Brünnhilde now in nine productions, all of them very different. If I had to choose just one it would have to be Kupfer's. His characters were not cardboard cutouts, but real people involved in real situations. Not everyone liked the result, but I was stimulated and excited by it. Such was the strength of the production dramatically that I always felt that if the music were to stop suddenly the play would continue unhindered, so believable were the relationships between the characters. For me the role of Brünnhilde is the Everest of the soprano repertoire. It never fails to fill me with awe.

Sieglinde, and Brünnhilde orders Sieglinde to escape alone, for the child she bears will be the greatest hero of them all. She will await her father's return—she is ready to face the consequences of her actions. Wotan arrives, as furious as they knew he would be, and the Valkyries beg him to forgive their sister. He points out that she is the one who has defied him and she will have to be punished. Brünnhilde comes face to face with her father. Wotan announces to them all that she is to be banished—cut off without the proverbial shilling. She will be put to sleep on a rock, and will belong to the first man who finds her and wakes her. He is deaf to all their pleas for clemency. Left alone with her father, Brünnhilde asks him to explain what she did that was so wrong. She knows that he changed his mind about her protecting Siegmund, but she also knows—and so does he—that the change of heart was entirely at Fricka's bidding. She really only carried out what her father, in his heart, wanted her to do, but he reluctantly insists she must pay for her misdeed. Accepting her fate, Brünnhilde asks for one favour—that she should, when asleep, be surrounded by fire so that she can be reached only by a brave hero who will risk coming through the fire. This he grants her. They bid each other a long and tender farewell, before Wotan places her on the rock and summons Loge to encircle her with fire. Arias: *Hoïotoho! Hoïotoho!* ('Hojotoho! Hojotoho!'); *War er so schmählich, was ich verbrach?* ('Was it so shameful, what I did?').

Siegfried: As predestined, Brünnhilde is found on her rock by Siegfried, the son of Sieglinde and Siegmund. Removing her armour, he wakens her with a kiss, and joyously she greets the sun. She wants to know who has woken her and he tells her he is Siegfried and they declare their love for each other. However, noticing her armour and her horse, she becomes a bit confused about the mixture of her feelings as a woman and her previous existence as a goddess. Nevertheless, she assures Siegfried she will always love him. Gradually she yields to his passionate words and bids farewell to Valhalla—she will always belong to Siegfried and he to her. Aria: *Heil dir, Sonne! Heil dir, Licht!* ('Hail to thee, sun! Hail to thee, light!'); *Ewig war ich, ewig bin ich* ('I always was, I always am'); duet (with Siegfried); *O kindischer Held!* ('O childlike hero!').

Götterdämmerung: Siegfried sets off on his adventures on Grane, Brünnhilde's horse, giving Brünnhilde the gold Ring. In his absence she is visited by her sister Waltraute, who asks her to throw the Ring back into the Rhine and lift the curse from the gods. But Siegfried gave her the Ring as a token of his love, and she will not part with it. She hears his horn approaching and rushes to greet him, only to see a stranger—it is Siegfried disguised as Gunther by use of the magic Tarnhelm. He has been at the hall of the Gibichungs, home of the siblings Gunther and Gutrune and they have given him a potion to make him forget Brünnhilde and marry Gutrune. At the same time, their plan is to bring Brünnhilde to their dwelling so Gunther can marry her—this is the purpose of Siegfried's mission. In this way the Gibichungs gain the Ring. Siegfried then leads the unwilling but defenceless Brünnhilde to meet the real Gunther. They arrive at the Gibichungs' hall, Siegfried wearing the infamous Ring so coveted by Gunther's half-brother Hagen. Brünnhilde is handed over to Gunther, but when he addresses Siegfried by name, Brünnhilde is horrified, staring at this man who led her here and seems not to recognize her. He cannot understand what is troubling her and gestures to Gunther as her prospective bridegroom. As he points with his finger, Brünnhilde sees the Ring on it, which she thought was taken from her by the stranger, Gunther. She wants to know how the Ring comes now to be on Siegfried's finger. Clearly Gunther knows nothing of it, and at this moment Brünnhilde realizes it was indeed Siegfried—disguised as Gunther—who pulled it from her finger. To learn that it is Siegfried, who will not even acknowledge her, is more than she can bear. Knowing nothing of the reason for his treachery, she is furious—as far as she is concerned, Siegfried has totally betrayed her for another woman. Raging with jealousy, she tells Gunther that Siegfried cannot marry his sister, as he is already married to her, Brünnhilde, and she equally cannot marry Gunther. The mystified Siegfried recounts how he took the Ring from the dragon's lair and he will swear on oath that he has done nothing dishonourable. Mortified, Brünnhilde calls on the gods to bear witness to her humiliation. On Hagen's spear Siegfried swears he was never wed to Brünnhilde. She snatches his hand from the spear and replaces it with her own, vowing the spear will bring about his destruction. Siegfried suggests to Gunther that he calm his overwrought bride, and leads everyone to the wedding feast. Brünnhilde denounces Gunther for using Siegfried to win her for himself and the innocent Gunther turns to his half-brother Hagen—instigator of all the plans—for advice. Hagen unequivocally deems that Siegfried must die. They will arrange it to look like a hunting accident, so neither of the brothers can be blamed. With thoughts of nothing but revenge, Brünnhilde agrees to the plan. Out hunting with Gunther and Hagen the next day, Siegfried drinks from a horn into which Hagen has put an antidote to the previous potion. He then remembers the past and knows that Brünnhilde is right—he has betrayed her. He turns round to look at two ravens flying overhead and Hagen thrusts his spear into Siegfried's back. As he dies, Siegfried tells the absent Brünnhilde that he will come to her again. His body is carried back to the Gibichung hall. There Brünnhilde has learned from the Rhinemaidens how she and Siegfried have both been cheated by Hagen. She orders a funeral pyre to be built, takes the Ring from Siegfried and places it on her own finger. She mounts her horse and rides into the flames surrounding her beloved hero. The Rhine overflows and the Rhinemaidens swim to Brünnhilde and remove the Ring from her finger. At last it is back where it started and where it belongs. Through a glow of smoke and flames Valhalla is burning—it is the twilight of the gods. Arias: *Zu neuen Taten, teurer Helde* ('You long for new adventures, dear hero'); *Wie Sonne lauter* ('Like pure sunlight'); *Grane, mein Ross, sei mir gegrüsst* ('Grane, my steed, I greet you').

Brünnhilde is a marathon role for any soprano, requiring physical as well as vocal stamina, especially when the four-part cycle is performed in a week as it should be. It is one of the three major roles in *Der Ring* (the others being Wotan and Siegfried). The role has fared well over the hundred or so years since it was written, each generation providing memorable exponents both in the theatre and the recording studio. These include (many of them Bayreuth stalwarts) Katharina Klafsky, Ellen Gulbranson, Olive Fremstad, Nanny Larsén-Todsen, Frida Leider, Florence Austral, Marta Fuchs, Anny Konetzni, Florence Easton, Martha Mödl, Kirsten Flagstad, Astrid Varnay, Birgit Nilsson, Ludmila Dvořáková, Rita Hunter, Gwyneth Jones, Hildegard Behrens, Anne Evans, Deborah Polaski, and Susan Bullock. Created (*W.* 1870) by Sophie Stehle; (*S.* and *G.* 1876) by Amelia Materna. *See also* ARTICLE BY DAME ANNE EVANS, p. 38.

Bucklaw, Lord Arthur (Arturo) (Donizetti: *Lucia di Lammermoor*). Ten. Lucia agrees to marriage with him to save her brother's fortune and political skin. Takes part (with Edgardo, Enrico, Lucia, Raimondo, and Alisa) in the famous sextet, his opening line being *Qual terribile momento* ('What a terrible moment'). Created (1835) probably by Achille Balestraccii.

Budd, Billy (Britten: *Billy Budd*). Bar. A press-ganged able seaman who has a stammer. He is delighted to be serving Capt. Vere on board *HMS Indomitable* during the French Wars in 1797. The evil Master-at-Arms, Claggart, unfairly suspects Billy of trying to rouse the men to mutiny and orders Squeak to spy on him. Billy finds Squeak searching his kitbag, accuses him of stealing, and fights with him. Claggart is determined to prove to Vere that Billy is a bad influence. When Billy tries to defend his actions, he stammers and can't get the words out. In frustration he strikes out at Claggart who hits his head as he falls and dies. A court-martial is held and Billy is sentenced to death. He is put into chains and while awaiting hanging he sings of the life he loved as a sailor and tells of his admiration for Capt. Vere. He knows his fellow-sailors want to avenge him, and he insists they must not mutiny on his behalf but must respect their captain, who he knows is a good man, even though Vere did not intervene to save him from the death sentence—'Starry Vere', he calls him, just before he dies. Arias: *Billy Budd, king of the birds!*; *Look! Through the port comes the moonshine astray*. There have been some outstanding exponents of this role, such as Peter Glossop, Thomas Allen, Simon Keenlyside, and, of course, its creator. Created (1951) by Theodor Uppman. *See also* ARTICLE BY THEODOR UPPMAN, p. 41.

Budd, Supt. (Britten: *Albert Herring*). Bass. Police Superintendent. He suggests that, in the

BILLY BUDD (*Billy Budd*—Britten)

by Theodor Uppman

It was just six weeks before the première of *Billy Budd*, scheduled for 1 December 1951, that I was chosen for the title role. Britten nearly always wrote leading roles in his operas for singers whom he knew and admired, but by early October of 1951 he had not found one he felt was right for the role of Billy. Auditions were held throughout Great Britain and the Continent without success. Britten and Pears then turned to the United States, where they had spent three years during the early part of World War II. They telephoned two friends and asked them to start searching. One of the friends was Alfred Drake, the original Curly of *Oklahoma!*

During the previous summer I had sung a small role in a Broadway show, directed by Drake. When the musical closed in August, I returned to my wife and two small children in California, and took a job in an aviation plant, rolling 700lb barrels of oil and acid to various departments. With my shirt off, the California sun tanned me and bleached my already blonde hair, thus preparing me well visually for the role of Billy.

Britten wanted a lyric baritone for the young sailor, with an appearance of innocence and youthful enthusiasm. Alfred Drake immediately thought of me and telephoned to ask me to come for the auditions. I flew to New York at once. A recording of me singing was made, Sir David Webster [general administrator of the Royal Opera House, Covent Garden, 1944–70] came for the second audition and returned to England, with photographs, to report to Ben. A week later I was in London to begin learning the role for the première.

Soon after my arrival, Britten and Pears gave a recital at the Victoria and Albert Museum. When I went to introduce myself afterwards, Britten took one look at me and said 'Well, you certainly *look* like Billy!' I worked day and night in the following weeks with several répétiteurs. I was not a quick learner and it was a struggle, but I accomplished it with the help of the various coaches.

One afternoon, Ben and Peter picked me up and drove me to their flat and talked over the opera and the role of Billy. 'Inner radiance' is what Ben emphasized. 'You must never be negative. Keep the positive feeling throughout, even when you know you are about to die. Even under the worst conditions, you must be able to smile. Never feel sorry for yourself. You love your ship and your shipmates, and you don't believe for a minute that anyone would want to hurt you. Keep your head up and your back straight—never droop'. These were words which I always remembered when I sang the role. Ben was an inspiration to work with—he was so human, simple, and patient.

On 21 November an announcement confirmed what had been rumoured—that Josef Krips, who was to have conducted, had found the handwritten score too difficult to see and bowed out because he didn't have time to learn it. To the delight of the cast and orchestra, Britten took over. He was considerate and helpful, and the rehearsal atmosphere was ideal. Hearing the orchestration was an inspiration and the excitement grew with each rehearsal.

Opening night was a wonderful dream. Ben was tremendously happy and everyone in the cast was aware he had participated in the world première of a masterpiece. I will never forget the overwhelmingly beautiful sound of the applause at the end!

Perhaps the most gratifying comment from Ben came later, when my wife Jean and our children were finally able to join me for later performances. He said: 'I can't believe that the whole time I was writing *Billy Budd*, Ted was in California and that we were going to find him!' What more could a singer ask?

absence of suitable candidates for the post of May Queen, they should elect a May King, and proposes Albert Herring. Created (1947) by Norman Lumsden.

Bunthorne, Reginald (Sullivan: *Patience*). Bar. A poet in love with Patience, who does not love him and marries another poet, Archibald Grosvenor. Created (1881) by George Grossmith.

Bunyan, John (Vaughan Williams: *The Pilgrim's Progress*). Bass-bar. The writer. He is in Bedford Gaol, finishing his book, *The Pilgrim's Progress*. Arias: *So I awoke, and behold it was a dream; Now, hearer, I have told my dream to thee*. Created (1951) by Inia te Wiata.

Bunyan, (the voice of) Paul (Britten: *Paul Bunyan*). Spoken. A figure of American folklore—he was born when the moon turned blue and grew as tall as the Empire State Building. He married and had a daughter, Tiny. He runs a camp for lumberjacks and tries to teach them that America has much to offer—it is what you make of it that counts. As it was clearly impossible to portray on stage a man 'as tall as the Empire State Building', Britten wisely made the decision to present Paul Bunyan as a voice only—he is heard, but never seen. Created (1941) by Milton Warchoff.

Buonafede (Haydn: *Il mondo della luna*). Bar. Father of Flaminia and Clarice and opposed to their marriages. He is fooled into giving his consent by their consorts and forgives them all for tricking him. Created (1777) by Benedetto Bianchi.

Buryja, Grandmother (Janáček: *Jenůfa*). Cont. Owner of the local mill, grandmother of stepbrothers Števa and Laca and mother-in-law of the Kostelnička. Both her sons are dead: her elder son married a widow who already

had a son (Laca) and they then had their own son (Števa). Her younger son (Toma) married and his wife bore him a daughter (Jenůfa). After his wife's death, he married the lady now known as the Kostelnička. Created (1904) by Věra Pivoňková.

Buryja, Jenůfa (Janáček: *Jenůfa*). Sop. Stepdaughter of the Kostelnička (who married Jenůfa's widowed father). She loves Števa and is expecting his baby, but he does not want to be tied down in marriage. Her stepmother, to avoid the shame and scandal of an illegitimate birth, keeps Jenůfa hidden away until she has had the baby. She then gives her a strong sleeping-draught, takes the baby, and drowns it in the icy river. Jenůfa awakes to find the baby gone—her stepmother tells her the baby died. Laca declares his love and Jenůfa agrees to marry him. When the ice melts, the baby's body is found. She expects Laca to leave her now he knows the truth, but he remains and, for the first time, Jenůfa admits she loves him. Aria (Jenůfa's Prayer): *Zdrávas královno* ('Salve regina'). At the end of this opera, we see that, through her suffering, Jenůfa has attained a depth of understanding which enables her to forgive her stepmother. She realizes that the older woman's actions have been undertaken out of love and a wish to save Jenůfa from an unhappy marriage such as she herself had endured. Jenůfa is able to accept Laca's love and love him in return—they have both seen the depths to which humans can sink and have been able to rise above them. Maria Jeritza was the first Vienna Jenůfa and also the first to sing the role at the NY Met. In England one remembers Josephine Barstow (who sang it opposite Pauline Tinsley's superb Kostelnička and later took over the older role herself). Other exponents include Tiana Lemnitz, Gré Brouwenstijn, Libuše Domanínská, Gabriela Beňačkova, Lorna Haywood, Ashley Putnam,

Roberta Alexander, Amanda Roocroft, and Karita Mattila. Created (1904) by Marie Kabeláčová.

Buryja, Števa (Janáček: *Jenůfa*). Ten. Half-brother of Laca Klemeň, grandson of Grandmother Burya. Like his half-brother, Števa is in love with Jenůfa (his cousin) and she is pregnant with his child. He is being interviewed with a view to going in the army, but is rejected, much to his relief. Jenůfa hopes this means they can marry, but Števa is in no hurry—he likes being free and attractive to women. The Kostelnička forbids any thought of their wedding until Števa has remained sober for a full year. After Jenůfa has given birth to their child, he makes it clear to her stepmother that he has no intention of marrying her and being responsible for the baby. Indeed, he is now engaged to Karolka, the Mayor's daughter. Created (1904) by Bohdan Procházka (usually known as Theodor Schütz).

Buryjovka, Petrona (Janáček: *Jenůfa*). *See* KOSTELNIČKA.

Butterfly (Puccini: *Madama Butterfly*). Sop. Known as Butterfly, her real name is Cio-Cio-San and she is a 15-year-old geisha. She is about to be married to an American, Lieut. Pinkerton, a contract arranged by a marriage-broker. For Pinkerton it is a light-hearted arrangement, but Butterfly takes it very seriously. She has fallen in love with him and renounced her own religion in order to have a Christian wedding, bringing down the wrath of her uncle who has led the family in rejecting her. This distresses her greatly, but after the wedding Pinkerton consoles her as, to a passionate duet, they retire for the night. The next time we see Butterfly it is three years since Pinkerton returned to the USA, promising her he will come back. Her maid, Suzuki, has no faith in his promise, but Butterfly believes him and prepares for his arrival. Pinkerton is indeed coming back, but he now has an American wife and has asked Sharpless, the US Consul, for help in preparing Butterfly for the truth. Sharpless visits Butterfly bringing a letter for her explaining the position. As soon as she sees the letter, she assumes her husband is returning to her, and all Sharpless's efforts to convince her otherwise are foiled, either by interruptions from others or by Butterfly's own

excitement. When she produces her son, born after Pinkerton departed, Sharpless realizes he cannot tell her the truth. The cannon sounds to announce the docking of Pinkerton's ship and Butterfly and Suzuki rush round cleaning and decorating the house for his return. As night falls, her son and her maid sleep, but she continues to watch for her husband—in the distance wordless voices can be heard (the Humming Chorus). Next morning Suzuki sends her for a rest. Pinkerton and Sharpless arrive and Pinkerton at last realizes how much heartache he has caused. Unable to face Butterfly, he again leaves Sharpless to deal with things. Gradually the truth dawns on Butterfly—Pinkerton wants to take their son back to America to be brought up by him and his American wife. He can have his son, she says, but he must come himself to collect him. Left alone with her child, Butterfly blindfolds him so that he cannot see what she is about to do. She then kills herself with her father's ceremonial sword. Arias: *Un bel dì vedremo* ('One fine day he'll come'); *Che tua madre* ('That your mother'); duet (with Pinkerton): *Vogliatemi bene* ('Love me a little').

Of all Puccini's heroines, Butterfly is probably the most developed character-study. She changes totally during the course of the opera, from a 15-year-old girl to a passionate and vulnerable woman, to a caring mother, and finally to a tragic self-sacrificing heroine. Maria Callas sang Butterfly only three times on stage, and John Ardoin described her portrayal as combining 'Amina's [*La sonnambula*] innocence..., Gilda's [*Rigoletto*] metamorphosis and betrayal and Violetta's [*La traviata*] passion and sacrifice'—a description of the role which I cannot better. Any soprano who undertakes this role must be able to act as well as to sing. A long line of Italianate sopranos have excelled as Butterfly, including Emmy Destinn, Geraldine Farrar (who sang it at the NY Met première in 1907, opposite Enrico Caruso's Pinkerton, and between then and 1922, when she left the company, sang the role nearly 500 times), Elisabeth Rethberg, Toti dal Monte, Maggie Teyte, Maria Cebotari, Joan Cross, Joan Hammond, Licia Albanese, Victoria de los Angeles, Sena Jurinac, Renata Scotto, Mirella Freni, Yoko Watanabe (who had an obvious advantage in looks and deportment), Susan Bullock, Amanda Roocroft, and Anne

Sophie Duprels. Created (1904) by Rosina Storchio.

Bystrouška, Vixen (Janáček: *The Cunning Little Vixen*). Sop. Literally, Vixen Sharp Ears (Bystrouška; she was originally called Vixen Lightfoot [Bystronožka] but this was misread at the printers and her originator, Rudolf Tešnohlídek, accepted the new name). A young cub, she lives in the forest among all the birds, insects and other animals. Caught and taken home by the Forester, she is treated as a family pet, but is miserable. As the hens are feeding, she bites off their heads and escapes back to the forest. She meets a Fox, they fall in love, and she becomes pregnant. They marry, the animals joining in their celebrations. The poulty-dealer Harašta chases the Vixen in the forest, her cubs running to hide. She trips him up and kills his chickens. He shoots her. At the end of the year, the Forester, again on his way home, starts to fall asleep in the forest. He sees a young fox cub playing—is it the daughter of the Cunning Vixen? This role requires a soprano of vocal and physical agility. She develops from an innocent cub at the beginning of the opera, through love, marriage, and parenthood to death. Because, despite what befalls individuals, in the larger pattern life goes on, Nature renewing itself as the seasons pass. Impressive performances as the Vixen have been given by Norma Burrowes, Lillian Watson, Lesley Garrett, Lucia Popp, and Rebecca Evans. This opera was put on the international map by the famous production in Berlin (sung in German) by Walter Felsenstein in 1956. Created (1924) by Hana Hrdličková.

Cadmus 1. (Handel: *Semele*). Bass. King of Thebes, father of Ino and Semele. Created (1744) by Henry Reinhold.

2. (Henze: *The Bassarids*). Bass. Founder of Thebes, he abdicated in favour of his grandson Pentheus. Created (1966) by Peter Lagger.

Caius, Dr 1. (Verdi: *Falstaff*). An elderly gentleman whom Ford has chosen as a husband for his daughter Nannetta. Created (1893) by Giovanni Paroli (who had created Cassio in *Otello* in 1887).

2. (Nicolai: *Die lustige Weiber von Windsor*). Bass. See (1) above.

Calaf (Puccini: *Turandot*). Ten. Son of the Tartar King Timur. He sees Princess Turandot when she has come to witness the execution of a Persian prince who has failed to answer her three riddles—the penalty for failure is death. The prize for the prince who succeeds is Turandot's hand in marriage. Calaf falls in love with Turandot as soon as he sees her and is determined to win her. Because he fears for his life from his father's enemies, Calaf announces himself as the Unknown Prince and strikes the gong to indicate his intention of taking part in the contest. His father and the slave-girl Liù beg him to desist, but he will not be deterred. He answers the first two riddles put to him by Turandot. She asks the third question: 'What is the ice that sets you on fire?'. He answers: 'Turandot'. Now that he has won, Turandot is anxious to be released from the obligation to marry him. He offers her one last chance—she must before morning discover his name. If she succeeds, he is prepared to die. If she fails, she is his. He knows that only he will eventually reveal his name to her. He refuses bribes from her ministers and even threats leave him unmoved. His only concern is when he sees his blind father, who was seen speaking to Calaf, arrested and threatened by Turandot with torture. However, Liù intervenes, telling everyone that she alone knows the answer, and then killing herself with a dagger. Calaf blames Turandot for the slave-girl's death, and then kisses the princess. She responds to his kiss, overcoming her coldness. He tells her his name—now his life is in her hands. The crowds assemble and Turandot addresses them—the Unknown Prince's name is Love. Arias: *Non piangere, Liù* ('Do not weep, Liù'); *Nessun dorma* ('None shall sleep'). This is the last of Puccini's great tenor roles and all the famous Italianate tenors have sung it, including Giovanni Martinelli, Richard Tauber, Giacomo Lauri-Volpi, James McCracken, Franco Corelli, Mario del Monaco, Jussi Björling, José Carreras, and Plácido Domingo. The lovely aria *Nessun dorma* became world-famous even to those who had never heard an opera in their lives, when it was recorded by Luciano Pavarotti as the theme song for the football World Cup in Italy in 1990. Created (1926) by Miguel Fleta.

Calatrava, Marchese di (Verdi: *La forza del destino*). Bass. Father of Leonora and Carlo. He has forbidden his daughter's marriage to Alvaro, a half-caste. As the young couple try to elope, Alvaro's gun accidentally goes off, killing the Marchese. Created (1862) by Sig. Meo.

Calchas 1. (Gluck: *Iphigénie en Aulide*). Bass. The High Priest who encourages Agamemnon to sacrifice his daughter Iphigénie. Created (1774) by Nicolas Gélin.

2. (Offenbach: *La Belle Hélène*). Bass. High Priest of Jupiter, who arranges for Paris to win Helen in a contest. Created (1864) by Pierre-Eugène Grenier. *See also* CALKAS.

Calisis (Rameau: *Les Boréades*). Ten. A Boread who tries to woo Queen Alphise. Created (f. stage p. 1982) by John Aler.

Calisto, La (Cavalli). Lib. by Giovanni Faustini; prol. and 3 acts; f.p. Venice 1651.

Legendary Greece: *Callisto is a follower of *Diana. To win her for himself, *Jupiter follows *Mercury's advice to come down to earth disguised as Diana. However, the real Diana is in love with *Endymion. Pan, himself in love with Diana, captures Endymion. Jupiter's wife *Juno turns Callisto into a bear. Endymion is rescued by Diana. Jupiter cannot undo his wife's spell, but places Callisto among the stars as the constellation Ursa Minor.

Calkas (Walton: *Troilus and Cressida*). Bass. High Priest of Pallas, father of Cressida. He admits to his daughter that he is going to desert to the Trojans. Once there, he encourages Cressida to marry the Greek prince Diomede, keeping from her Troilus's letters of love. When Troilus arrives at the camp and fights Diomede, Calkas stabs him in the back. Created (1954) by Frederick Dalberg.

Callisto (Cavalli: *La Calisto*). Sop. A nymph, follower of Diana. Jupiter falls in love with her and in revenge his wife, Juno, turns Callisto into a bear. Unable to break his wife's spell, Jupiter places Callisto among the stars as the constellation Ursa Minor. Creator (1651) not known.

Camille (Lehár: *The Merry Widow*). *See* ROSILLON, CAMILLE DE.

Canio (Leoncavallo: *Pagliacci*). Ten. Husband of Nedda. Leader of a troupe of strolling players. One of his players, Tonio, himself in love with Nedda, tells Canio that she is having an affair with a villager, Silvio. During a performance of their play, Canio (as Pagliaccio) orders Nedda (as Columbine) to reveal the name of her lover. When she refuses, he stabs her. Silvio tries to save her and Canio kills him also. Canio tells the audience: *La commedia è finita* ('The comedy is ended'). Aria: *Vesti la giubba* ('On with the motley'), sung as he prepares to play the clown, despite his desolation over his wife's affair. Created (1892) by Fiorello Giraud.

Capellio (Bellini: *I Capuleti e i Montecchi*). Bass. Head of the Capulets, father of Giulietta, whom he has promised to the Capulet partisan Tebaldo. Created (1830) by Gaetano Antoldi.

Capito, Wolfgang (Hindemith: *Mathis der Maler*). Ten. Counsellor to the Cardinal, whom he tries to persuade to renounce his oath of celibacy and take a rich wife. Created (1938) by Simons Bermanis.

Capriccio (Strauss). Lib. by comp. and Clemens Krauss; 1 act; f.p. Munich 1942, cond. Clemens Krauss.

Paris, about 1775: At a house party in her château, *Countess Madeleine and her brother the *Count listen to a sextet which *Flamand has composed for her birthday. *La Roche is to produce a play written for the occasion by *Olivier. The Count is attracted to *Clairon, an actress who is to take part. As La Roche rehearses the play, Olivier reads to the Countess a sonnet he has written for her. Flamand at once sets Olivier's words to music and sings it to Madeleine. Poet and musician quarrel as to whose work it now is. Flamand expresses his love for the Countess and his wish to marry her. She promises to give him an answer—at 11 o'clock the following morning in the library. She orders hot chocolate to be served. La Roche introduces a ballerina and *Italian Tenor and Soprano to entertain the guests. All discuss the relative importance of words and music, in two octets (the first known as the 'Laughing Octet', the second the 'Quarrelling Octet'). La Roche speaks about the work of a theatre director and today's lack of great artists. Madeleine suggests that Flamand and Olivier write an opera for him to direct. Her brother proposes a subject—the events of that day. The company departs for Paris. The Countess's *Major-Domo and the servants tidy up and prepare supper for her. Mons. *Taupe, the prompter, wakes up—he fell asleep some hours ago. The Major-Domo brings a message to the Countess from Olivier—he will meet her in the library at 11 o'clock next morning to be told how the opera is to end. Madeleine debates with her reflection in a mirror the relative merits of Flamand (music) and Olivier (words) and wonders how she can make a choice between them.

Captain 1. (Berg: *Wozzeck*). Ten. Capt. in the army. Wozzeck is his soldier-servant. The Captain likes to moralize and philosophize. He taunts Wozzeck for being a father without being married. Created (1925) by Waldemar Henke.

2. (Adams: *The Death of Klinghoffer*). Capt. of the cruise ship *Achille Lauro* which is hijacked by terrorists. He bargains with the terrorist leader—they can leave the ship peacefully if they allow it to return to port. On arrival in Alexandria he has to break the news to Mrs Klinghoffer that her husband has been killed. Created (1991) by James Maddalena.

Capulet, Count (Gounod: *Roméo et Juliette*). Bar. Father of Juliet. Leader of the Capulets, rivals of the Montagues. Created (1867) by Mons. Troy.

Capulet, Juliet 1. (Juliette) (Gounod: *Roméo et Juliette*). Sop. Daughter of Count Capulet. She meets and secretly marries Romeo, son of a Montague, long-standing rivals of her father. After killing Tybalt in a duel, Romeo is exiled. Juliet's father plans her marriage to Count Paris, and in order to avoid this, she drinks a potion which renders her unconscious, and her family believe she is dead. She is taken to the family crypt. Romeo, seeing her apparently dead, swallows poison. She awakens to find him dying and stabs herself with his sword. Duet (with Romeo): *Nuit d'hyménée, O douce nuit d'amour* ('Night, Hymeneal, sweetest night of love'). Created (1867) by Maria Caroline Miolan-Carvalho.

2. (Giulietta) (Bellini: *I Capuleti e i Montecchi*). Sop. Daughter of the Capulet leader. She is in love with Romeo but her father insists she marry Tebaldo. To avoid this wedding, she takes a sleeping draught to put her in a coma. Romeo thinks she really is dead and takes poison. She regains consciousness to find her lover dying. Aria: *O quante volte* ('O how many times'). Created (1830) by (Maria) Rosalbina Caradori-Allan.

Capuleti e i Montecchi, I (The Capulets and the Montagues) (Bellini). Lib. by Felice Romani; 2 acts; Venice 1830, cond. Vincenzo Bellini.

Verona, 13th cent.: To avoid war, it is suggested that the *Capulet Giulietta (Juliet) should marry the *Montague Romeo, whom she loves. Her father *Capellio (Capulet) refuses, wanting her to marry *Tebaldo (Tybalt). Romeo tries to persuade her to elope, but she cannot disobey her father and her wedding is planned. Sympathetic to the young lovers, the Capulet doctor *Lorenzo gives Giulietta a sleeping potion which will put her into a coma, so everyone will think she is dead. She will be taken to the family vault and Romeo will be brought to her. When Romeo sees her, he thinks she really is dead and swallows poison. She revives to find that Romeo is dying and throws herself on his lifeless body.

Cardinal (Maxwell Davies: *Taverner*). Ten. Not named, but presumably Wolsey. Reprieves Taverner after he is sentenced for heresy, because he wants him to remain as court musician. Created (1972) by John Lanigan.

Carlino (Donizetti: *Don Pasquale*). See NOTARY.

Carlos, Don 1. (Verdi: *Don Carlos*). Ten. Infante of Spain, son of King Philip II. He is engaged to Elisabeth de Valois of France, and it is hoped their union will bring an end to the wars between their countries. When they meet, they fall in love, but his father decides that he will marry Elisabeth himself. Carlos's closest friend, the Marquis of Posa, urges him to come to terms with the situation by going to Flanders to help the people oppressed by Spanish rule. Carlos asks to see the Queen— he wants her to persuade his father to let him go to Flanders. Philip is suspicious of the relationship between his wife and his son. Eboli, in love with Carlos, meets him when she is dressed in the Queen's clothes and, thinking it is Elisabeth, he expresses his love. He is mortified when he realizes it is Eboli and she swears to expose them to the King. At the auto-da-fé, Carlos defies his father and is arrested. Fearing he will be killed, Posa puts himself in front of Carlos and is shot. Eboli helps Carlos escape. At his grandfather's tomb, he bids Elisabeth farewell before his intended departure for Flanders. As the King and the Grand Inquisitor arrive to arrest him, the Emperor's tomb opens and Carlos is pulled inside. Aria: *Je l'ai vue, et dans son sourire* ('I have seen her, and in her smile'); duet (with Posa): *Dieu, tu semas dans nos âmes* ('God, you have sewn in our spirits'); duet (with Elisabeth): *O bien perdu ... Trésor sans prix!* ('O lost blessing ... Priceless treasure!'). Created (Fr. vers. 1867) by Jean Morère; (It. vers. 1884) by Francesco Tamagno.

2. (Verdi: *La forza del destino*). See VARGAS, CARLO DI.

3. (Verdi: *Ernani*). King Carlo V of Spain, he is passionately in love with Elvira, who is also loved both by her guardian Silva and by Ernani, whom the King outlawed after he had ordered the slaying of Ernani's father. Elvira refuses to elope with the King, who decides to arrest Ernani. He is helped to escape. When Carlo is elected Emperor, he forgives Ernani for plotting against him and agrees to the marriage of Ernani and Elvira. Aria: *Vieni meco, sol di rose* ... ('Come with me, a brighter dawning awaits thee'). Created (1844) by Antonio Superchi.

4. (Verdi: *Luisa Miller*). Ten. 'Carlo' is the name Rodolfo is using to hide his true identity from Luisa's father. *See* WALTER, RODOLFO.

Carlotta (Strauss: *Die schweigsame Frau*). Mez. Member of a troupe of travelling actors and singers, run by Morosus's nephew Henry. She poses as a possible wife for Morosus, but her unsophisticated personality and broad country accent are enough to make him discount her as a suitable bride. Created (1935) by Marion Zunde.

Carmen (Bizet). Lib. by Henri Meilhac and Ludovic Halévy; 4 acts; f.p. Paris 1857, cond. Mons. Deloffre.

Seville, *c*.1820: As *Carmen and the other girls emerge from the cigarette factory where they work, Don *José, a corporal in the dragoons, arrives with Capt. *Zuniga. *Micaëla, in love with José, brings messages from his mother. Carmen is accused of cutting another girl's face and José is ordered to take her to prison but he allows her to escape. In Lillas *Pastia's inn, Carmen, *Frasquita, *Mercédès, and *Morales sit smoking. The toreador *Escamillo enters and is attracted to Carmen. The smugglers, *Rémendado and *Dancaïre, urge her to persuade José to join them, and he reluctantly agrees. Escamillo arrives at their mountain camp, looking for Carmen and he and José fight. Micaëla tells José his mother is dying. He leaves with her. Outside the bullring the crowds wait to greet Escamillo, who enters with Carmen. José wants Carmen to go with him again. When she refuses, as she now loves Escamillo, he stabs her to death.

Carmen (Bizet: *Carmen*). Sop. (but usually sung by a mez.). A gypsy who works in the local cigarette factory, she regards love as a game. During a break from work, the girls all gather outside. Carmen notices a young dragoon corporal, Don José, who is in town with a battalion of soldiers. She flirts with him and throws him a flower and he falls in love with her. The women rush out of the factory—Carmen is accused of cutting another girl's face and José is ordered to take her to prison but on the way he allows her to escape. At an inn, Carmen and her friends drink and talk with soldiers. The toreador Escamillo arrives and is attracted to Carmen but she is waiting for José. He arrives but Carmen is cross when he says he must return to his regiment. If he loved her, he would stay with her and come to the mountains with her and her friends. Thus she persuades him to desert and join her band of smugglers. In their mountain camp, Carmen and José argue a lot. Reading fortunes in a pack of cards, Carmen is upset to see death for herself and her lover. Escamillo comes looking for her. Carmen prevents the two men fighting and then leaves with the toreador for the bullring to watch him fight. José, still in love with Carmen and jealous of Escamillo, hides in the crowd, watching their arrival at the bullring. When he reveals himself, Carmen tells him she no longer wants him and is in love with the bullfighter. José kills her. Arias: *L'amour est un Oiseau rebelle* (the *Habanera*) ('Love is like a rebellious bird'), *Près des remparts de Seville* (the *Séguidille*) ('By the city walls of Seville'); duet (with Escamillo): *Si tu m'aimes* ('If you love me'). Because the opera first met with real success in Vienna, the earliest performances of *Carmen* were in German and many German-speaking singers have undertaken the leading roles. In the title role these included the sopranos Emmy Destinn and Marie Gutheil-Schoder. However, in the past 50 years it has been more usual for Carmen to be sung by Spanish or Italian—or certainly Italianate—sopranos and mezzo-sopranos (there have been surprisingly few famous French Carmens, those who spring to mind being Emma Calvé and Régine Crespin). These have included Minnie Hauk, Giulietta Simionato, Jean Madeira, Risë Stevens, Victoria de los Angeles, Leontyne Price, Maria Callas, Grace Bumbry, Teresa Berganza, Sally Burgess, Maria Ewing, and Waltraud Meier. Created (1875) by Célestine Galli-Marié.

Carolina 1. (Cimarosa: *Il matrimonio seg-reto*). Sop. Younger daughter of Geronimo, secretly married to Paolino. She is loved by Count Robinson who is supposed to marry her elder sister Elisetta. Created (1792) by Irene Tomeoni.

  2. (Henze: *Elegy for Young Lovers*). Cont. The Gräfin von Kirchstetten, unpaid secretary of the poet Mittenhofer. Created (1961) by Lilian Benningsen.

Carruthers, Dame (Sullivan: *The Yeomen of the Guard*). Cont. Housekeeper of the Tower of London. Arias: *When our gallant Norman foes; Night has spread her pall once more*. Created (1888) by Rosina Brandram.

Casilda (Sullivan: *The Gondoliers*). Sop. Daughter of the Duke and Duchess of Plaza-Toro, she was married as a baby to the infant heir to the throne of Barataria. He is thought to be one of the gondoliers, but is shown to be Luiz, the Duke's drummer-boy, with whom (fortunately) Casilda is already in love. Created (1889) by Decima Moore.

Caspar (Weber: *Der Freischütz*). Bass. A for-ester who has sold himself to Samiel, the wild huntsman, and wants to give Max in his place. Gives Max magic bullets and is killed by the last one, guided by Samiel. Created (1821) by Heinrich Blume.

Cassandra (Cassandre) (Berlioz: *Les Troy-ens*). Mez. Daughter of the Trojan King Priam, she foretells the destruction of Troy. Rather than risk capture by the Greeks, she urges the Trojan women to join her in mass suicide. She stabs herself. Aria: *Malheureux Roi!* ('Unhappy King!'). Created (1890) by Luise Reuss-Belce.

Cassio (Verdi: *Otello*). Ten. Otello's young lieutenant, hated by Iago because Otello has promoted Cassio in preference to himself. He encourages Cassio to drink too much and in the ensuing drunken brawl Cassio injures Montano and is dismissed by Otello and replaced with Iago. Iago now contrives to per-suade Otello that Desdemona is attracted by Cassio. First he suggests that Cassio asks Desdemona to intercede on his behalf with Otello. Then he arranges for Otello to overhear Cassio talking and laughing about his latest mistress, which Otello believes (wrongly) to be Desdemona; and finally to support Otello's

suspicions, shows him the handkerchief sup-posedly seen in Cassio's hand, which was Otello's gift to his wife. Convinced, Otello plots to kill both Cassio and Desdemona. Created (1887) by Giovanni Paroli.

Castor (Rameau: *Castor et Pollux*). Ten. Son of Tyndareus and Leda and twin of Pollux. Beloved of Télaïre, he has been killed in battle and has descended to Hades. He cannot accept Pollux's sacrifice in taking his place, and agrees to return to earth for one day only. Jupiter relents and grants the brothers eternal life. Created (1737) by Denis-François Tribou.

Castor et Pollux (Rameau). Lib. by Pierre-Joseph Bernard; prologue and 5 acts; f.p. Paris 1737.

  Sparta and the Elysian Fields: *Castor is dead, killed in battle, and *Télaïre weeps for him. She persuades his twin, *Pollux, to beg his father *Jupiter to bring Castor back to life. Be-cause he loves Télaïre, Pollux agrees. Jupiter consents, but only if Pollux will take Castor's place in Hades, which he agrees to do. *Phébé, who loves Pollux, tries to prevent him entering Hades, but he completes his mission. Castor, much as he wants to return to Télaïre, cannot accept his brother's sacrifice, and agrees to re-turn to earth for one day only. Jupiter relents and restores the brothers to life, granting them both immortality.

Castro, José (Puccini: *La fanciulla del West*). Bass. A member of the gang headed by the bandit Ramerrez. He is captured and offers to lead the sheriff to the bandits' camp. Created (1910) by Edoardo Missiano.

Cathleen 1. (Vaughan Williams: *Riders to the Sea*). Sop. Daughter of Maurya. She identifies clothes from a drowned man as belonging to her brother Michael. Created (1937) by Jane Smith-Miller.

  2. (Maw: *The Rising of the Moon*). See SWEENEY, CATHLEEN.

***Cavalleria rusticana* (Rustic Chivalry)** (Mascagni). Lib. by Giovanni Targioni-Tozzetti and Guido Menasci; 1 act; f.p. Rome 1890, cond. Leopoldo Mugnone.

  Sicilian village, Easter Day, 'the present': After an affair with *Lola, *Turiddu departs with the army, and the fickle Lola mar-ries *Alfio. When Turiddu returns he seduces

*Santuzza, who becomes pregnant and is excommunicated by the Church. He then resumes his relationship with Lola. While the villagers are in church, Santuzza tells Turiddu's mother, Mama *Lucia, the whole sad story. When Turiddu returns, Santuzza again expresses her love, but he repulses her. In revenge, she tells Alfio of his wife's unfaithfulness. Alfio challenges Turiddu to a duel and Turiddu is killed.

Cavaradossi, Mario (Puccini: *Tosca*). Ten. A painter and republican sympathizer in love with Tosca. While he is in the church of Sant' Andrea painting a picture of the Madonna, Angelotti emerges from one of the side-chapels. He is an escaped political prisoner and if caught will be executed by Baron Scarpia's men. Cavaradossi gives him food and suggests he hide in a well in the garden of his villa, where he will come to him later. Tosca arrives to visit her lover and scolds him for making the Madonna look like the Marchese Attavanti (sister of Angelotti), of whom she is needlessly jealous. He reassures her and she leaves. The old Sacristan enters and announces the defeat of Napoleon—to celebrate victory, a *Te Deum* will be sung in the church and Tosca will sing that evening at Baron Scarpia's residence, the Farnese Palace. Scarpia has Cavaradossi arrested for aiding a political prisoner. Tosca is brought to Scarpia's apartments to witness her lover's torture. Cavaradossi begs her to say nothing of Angelotti's whereabouts and his torture continues. In the last hour before his planned execution, he is allowed to write to Tosca, and as he does so she appears. She tells him that his execution will only be a mock affair—Scarpia has promised them a safe passage from Rome. Guessing that she must have promised herself to Scarpia in return for this favour, Cavaradossi is distraught, until Tosca tells him she has killed Scarpia and they will be able to escape, but first he must pretend to fall as he is shot and he must lie perfectly still. As soon as the firing-squad departs Tosca will tell him and they can leave. They discuss how he will fall in a realistic manner and will not move until she says so. The firing-squad march in, line up, and shoot. Cavaradossi falls and the soldiers depart. Tosca rushes to his side—but Cavaradossi is dead. Arias: *Recondita armonia* ('Oh hidden harmony'); *E lucevan le stelle* ('And the stars were

shining'); duet (with Tosca): *O dolce mani* ('O sweet hands'). Created (1900) by Emilio de Marchi (a fragment of whose performance at the NY Met in 1903 has been preserved on a Mapleson cylinder). This is one of Puccini's most lyrical and popular tenor roles. Among those notable in the part since its creation have been Fernando de Lucia, Jan Kiepura, Alfred Piccaver, Beniamino Gigli, Helge Roswaenge, Giuseppe di Stefano, Jussi Björling, Ferruccio Tagliavini, Mario del Monaco, Carlo Bergonzi, Franco Corelli, Giuseppe Giacomini, Plácido Domingo, José Carreras, Franco Bonisolli, and Luciano Pavarotti.

Cecco (Haydn: *Il mondo della luna*). Ten. Servant to Dr Ecclito. In love with Lisetta, the maid of Buonafede. Helps his master trick Buonafede into giving his blessing to the marriage. Created (1777) by Leopoldo Dichtler.

Cecil, Robert 1. (Lord Burleigh) (Donizetti: *Maria Stuarda*). Bass. Urges Elizabeth I not to trust Mary Stuart and accompanies her to Fotheringay Castle to visit her cousin and rival. He encourages the Queen to sign Mary's death warrant. Created (1834 as Lamberto) by Federico Crespi, (1835) by Pietro Novelli.

2. (Lord Cecil) (Donizetti: *Roberto Devereux*). Ten. Together with Raleigh, informs the Queen that a silk scarf was found next to Essex's heart when he was searched. The Queen recognizes it as belonging to Sara, Duchess of Nottingham. Created (1837) by Timoleone Barattini.

3. (Sir Robert Cecil) (Britten: *Gloriana*). Bar. Secretary of the Council. Warns the Queen against her friendship with the Earl of Essex. Aria: *The art of government*. Created (1953) by Arnold Matters.

Celia (Haydn: *La fedeltà premiata*). Sop. Beloved of Felino, threatened with being sacrificed by the evil priest Melibeo who tries to force her marriage to various gentlemen. Felino attacks the monster and the goddess Diana blesses his union with Celia. Created (1781) by Maria Jermoli.

Cellini, Benvenuto (Berlioz: *Benvenuto Cellini*). Ten. Florentine goldsmith and metal-worker, in love with Teresa, daughter of the papal treasurer in Rome. Commissioned by Pope Clement VII to cast a statue of Perseus. Kills a man in a fight. The Pope will grant him absolution only if the statue is finished that day. When he runs out of metal, Cellini throws all his previous works of art into the foundry and succeeds in producing the statue on time. Created (1838) by Gilbert Duprez.

Cendrillon (*Cinderella*) (Massenet). Lib. by Henri Cain; 4 acts; f.p. Paris 1899, cond. Alexandre Luigini.

The fairy-story of Cinderella: *Pandolfe and his wife, Mme de la *Haltière, depart for the royal ball, taking her daughters *Noémie and *Dorothée with them but leaving *Cendrillon behind. She falls asleep. A *Fairy Godmother appears, gives her glass slippers and sends her to the ball, but tells her she must leave at midnight. *Prince Charming falls in love with Cendrillon. As midnight strikes she leaves, losing a glass slipper. Prince Charming searches the country for the lady whose foot fits the slipper. All ends happily. *See also* CENERENTOLA, LA.

Cendrillon (Lucette) (Massenet: *Cendrillon*). Sop. Her real name is Lucette, but she is known as Cendrillon. Daughter of Pandolfe and stepdaughter of Mme de la Haltière. Stepsister of Noémie and Dorothée. Loved by her father, who is dominated by his second wife, Cendrillon is excluded from the arrangements for the royal ball and left at home when the rest of the family depart in all their finery. She falls asleep by the fire. A Fairy Godmother appears and arranges for Cendrillon to be dressed for the ball, including a pair of glass slippers— these have a magic quality so her family will not recognize her, but she must leave the ball at midnight. At the ball the Prince falls in love with her. At midnight she departs, losing one of her glass slippers as she runs. The Prince searches for his lost 'princess', ordering all princesses to come and try on the glass slipper. When she steps forward and the slipper fits, there is general rejoicing. Aria: *Vous êtes mon Prince Charmant* ('You are my Prince Charming'). Created (1899) by Julia Guiraudon (who married the opera's librettist, Henri Cain).

Cenerentola, La (*Cinderella*) (Rossini). Lib. by Jacopo Ferretti; 2 acts; f.p. Rome 1817.

The age-old story of Cinderella: *Clorinda and *Tisbe despise their step-sister *Angelina (known as Cenerentola). The Prince arrives with his valet, *Dandini, the two of them having swapped clothes. Cenerentola falls in love with the 'valet' (in reality the prince). Clorinda

and Tisbe are introduced to the 'prince', but their father, Don *Magnifico, refuses to allow Cenerentola to join the rest of the family at the royal ball. When they have all left the house, the Prince's tutor, *Alidoro, appears and takes her to the palace. After the ball, the real prince sets out to find her. At the house he and Cenerentola recognize each other. At their wedding, she asks the prince to forgive her stepfather and stepsisters. *See also* CENDRILLON.

Cenerentola (Rossini: *La Cenerentola*). *See* ANGELINA.

Ceprano, Count and Countess (Verdi: *Rigoletto*). Bass and mez. Guests of the Duke of Mantua. At a ball in the ducal palace, the Duke is much taken with the Countess. The Duke's jester, Rigoletto, comments on this and the Count's jealousy is aroused. His determination to take revenge on Rigoletto by abducting the girl believed to be the jester's lover (but in reality his daughter) sets in motion the rest of the opera. Created (1851) by Andrea Bellini and Luigia Morselli.

'Chagrin, Chevalier' (J. Strauss II: *Die Fledermaus*). The name used by the prison governor Frank, to hide his real identity at Prince Orlofsky's party. This means he has to speak in very poor French. *See* FRANK.

Charlotte 1. (Massenet: *Werther*). Mez. Daughter of the Magistrate (Le Bailli) and sister of Sophie and six younger siblings. She promised her dying mother she would wed Albert, but she falls in love with Werther. He continues to visit her after her marriage, and she has to ask him not to come any more. When he borrows pistols from her husband she is frightened. In his study, she finds Werther dying from gunshot wounds. She admits her love for him and he dies in her arms. Arias: *Werther ... Werther* (letter aria); *Va! laisse couler les larmes* ('Go! let my tears flow'). Created (1892) by Marie Renard.

2. (Zimmermann: *Die Soldaten*). *See* WESENER, CHARLOTTE.

Charmian (Barber: *Antony and Cleopatra*). Mez. Attendant on Queen Cleopatra. Created (1966) by Rosalind Elias.

Charon 1. (Caronte) (Monteverdi: *L'Orfeo*). Bass. The boatman who refuses to row Orfeo across the Styx. Creator (1607) unknown.

2. (Birtwistle: *The Mask of Orpheus*). *See* ARISTAEUS MYTH/CHARON.

Chekalinsky (Tchaikovsky: *The Queen of Spades*). Ten. An officer and friend of Hermann. Created (1890) by Vasili Vasilyev.

Chelio (Prokofiev: *The Love for Three Oranges*). Bass. A magician, protector of the King. Created (1921) by Hector-Robert Dufranne.

Chénier, Andrea (Giordano: *Andrea Chénier*). Ten. A poet. At a ball at the home of the Contessa di Coigny, he reads a poem expressing his feelings about the selfishness of those in authority. After the start of the Revolution, Chénier is spied upon and his friend Roucher advises him to leave Paris. But Chénier wants to find the identity of the woman who has written asking him for protection. It is Maddalena di Coigny. Gérard, an ex-servant of the Contessa, has become a leading Revolutionary and supporter of Robespierre. Gérard tries to abduct Maddalena, but is wounded by Chénier. Swayed by his secret desire for Maddalena, Gérard denounces Chénier as a Counter-Revolutionary and the poet comes to trial. He passionately defends himself but, despite Gérard's intervention, he is sentenced to death. Gérard brings Maddalena to the prison to be with Chénier—she will die with him and so they will be together for ever. Aria: *Un dì, all'azzurro spazio* ('One day, in the blue heaven'); *Come un bel dì di Maggio* ('Just as a fine day in May'); duet (with Maddalena): *Vicino a te* ('Close at your side'). Created (1896) by Giuseppe Borgatti.

Chernomor (Glinka: *Ruslan and Lyudmila*). Mime role. A dwarf, an evil magician who puts a spell upon Lyudmila. His strength lies in his long beard, which Ruslan is able to cut off when rescuing Lyudmila. Creator (1842) not traced.

Chérubin (Massenet). Lib. by Henri Cain and Francis de Croisset; 3 acts; f.p. Monte Carlo 1905, cond. Léon Jehin.
  Spain, 18th cent.: *Chérubin (Cherubino in *Le nozze di Figaro*) gives a party—he is 17, an adult, no longer under the guidance of the *Philosopher. Various guests swear to keep him away from their ladies. Chérubin leaves a love-letter hidden for the *Countess but the *Count finds it and wants to kill Chérubin.

*Nina, the *Duke's ward, announces that the letter was for her. Rumour has it that the dancer L'*Ensoleillad, who is to dance at the party, may marry the King. Chérubin meets the dancer in the garden. He is challenged to duels by the Count, the *Baron, and the Duke, all suspecting him of a relationship with their ladies. The Countess and *Baroness force Chérubin to confess that it was the dancer he was with in the garden. The duels can be cancelled. The King claims L'Ensoleillad for himself. Chérubin realizes that it is Nina he really loves.

Chérubin (Massenet: *Chérubin*). Sop./mez. *Travesti* role. The post-*Figaro* Chérubin (Cherubino) is celebrating his 17th birthday and freedom from his guardian, the Philosopher. His reputation for flirting with all women lands him in difficulties, as the male guests suspect him of having a relationship with their ladies and challenge him to duels. The ladies force him to admit that it was the dancer L'Ensoleillad that he met in the garden, so duels are not necessary. When the dancer is summoned to marry the King, Chérubin realizes that his true love is Nina, ward of the Duke, who relents and gives his consent to their marriage. Created (1905) by Mary Garden (who in 1902 had created Debussy's Mélisande; she liked singing in Massenet's operas but found him a weak and insincere person, describing in her autobiography how he would pay gushing compliments to someone's face and then make disparaging remarks behind their back. She thought he did not have the 'genius' of Debussy).

Cherubino 1. (Mozart: *Le nozze di Figaro*). Sop. or mez. *Travesti* role. A youth infatuated with the Countess Almaviva and sent to join the army by the Count. He jumps out of the Countess's bedroom window to avoid being discovered by the Count and his escape is noticed by the gardener, Antonio, who complains to the Count about his damaged plants below the window. Cherubino is loved by Barbarina (Antonio's daughter). Arias: *Non so più* ('I no longer know ...'); *Voi che sapete* ('You who know'). Among well-known exponents of this role, the most notable have been Giuditta Pasta, Luise Helletsgrüber, Sena Jurinac, Hilde Gueden, Suzanne Danco, Christa Ludwig, Edith Mathis, Tatyana Troyanos, Teresa

Berganza, Frederica von Stade, Anne Sofie von Otter, Susanne Mentzer, Barbara Bonney, Susan Graham, Angelika Kirchschlager, and Magdalena Koženà. Created (1786) by Dorotea Sardi-Bussani (whose husband created Bartolo and Antonio).

2. (Corigliano: *The Ghosts of Versailles*). Mez. *Travesti* role. He and Rosina (Countess Almaviva) had an affair many years ago and she bore him a son, Léon. They are all enlisted by Beaumarchais to help him rescue Marie Antoinette from her historical fate. Created (1991) by Stella Zambalis.

Chiang Ch'ing (Mme Mao Tse-tung) (Adams: *Nixon in China*). Sop. Wife of the Chinese President, she devises a revolutionary ballet which the Americans are taken to see. Created (1987) by Trudy Ellen Craney.

Child (L'Enfant) (Ravel: *L'Enfant et les sortilèges*). Mez. Naughty and rude to his mother, he is punished. Cross about this, he has a tantrum and throws and kicks furniture and other objects around the house and garden—and the cat. All these items come to life and torment him. He becomes very frightened. When his pet squirrel is injured, he bandages its paw. Amazed and touched by the gesture, the various animals and furniture help him find his Mother. Created (1925) by Marie-Thérèse Gauley.

Choregos (Birtwistle: *Punch and Judy*). Low bar. The operator of the Punch-and-Judy booth who comments on the action. One of Punch's victims, he returns as the hangman Jack Ketch and is tricked into putting his own neck in the noose. Created (1968) by Geoffrey Chard.

Chou En-lai (Adams: *Nixon in China*). Bar. The Chinese Premier who meets Pres. Nixon on his arrival in Peking for his historic visit to China. Aria: *I am old and I cannot sleep.* Created (1987) by Sanford Sylvan.

Christine (Strauss: *Intermezzo*). See STORCH, CHRISTINE.

Chrysopher (Strauss: *Die Liebe der Danae*). The name used by King Midas when he arrives in disguise to meet Danae for the first time.

Chrysothemis (Strauss: *Elektra*). Sop. Daughter of Klytämnestra and the murdered

Agamemnon, sister of Elektra and Orest. She lives at the palace with Klytämnestra and Aegisth, her mother's lover and accomplice in the murder. She is the weaker of the sisters, and wants to live a full life and have children. She keeps seeing other women having children and the children growing up, while she sits with her sister like a caged bird. She wants to leave this place which is like a prison—she is so frightened that her knees shake, and she knows they would let her go if it were not for Elektra's hatred. She warns Elektra that Klytämnestra and Aegisth plan to throw her into a tower. She knows their mother is in a foul mood after having one of her bad dreams. When news (false) reaches the palace of Orest's death, Chrysothemis is terrified at the thought of having to help Elektra murder their mother. Aria: *Ich kann nicht sitzen und ins Dunkel starren wie du* ('I cannot sit and stare into the dark like you'). Created (1909) by Margarethe Siems (who also created such diverse roles as the Marschallin in *Der Rosenkavalier* (1911) and Zerbinetta in the 1912 version of *Ariadne auf Naxos*).

Cieca, La (The Blind Woman) (Ponchielli: *La gioconda*). Cont. Old blind mother of Gioconda. Gives a rosary to Laura in gratitude for protecting her from a mob. Murdered by Barnaba. Created (1876) by Eufemia Barlani-Dini.

Cinna (Spontini: *La vestale*). Ten./bar. A Roman centurion, friend of Giulia's lover Licinius. Created (1807) by François Lays (bar.).

Cio-Cio-San (Puccini: *Madama Butterfly*). *See* BUTTERFLY.

Cipriano, Marquis (Thomas: *Mignon*). The real name of Lothario, father of Mignon. *See* LOTHARIO.

Circus Master (Smetana: *The Bartered Bride*). Ten. Ringmaster of a troupe of circus artists who come to the village. Created (1866) by Jindřich Mošna (a celebrated actor).

Civry, Magda de (Puccini: *La rondine*). Sop. In her Paris salon Magda, mistress of Rambaldo, is entertaining guests including the poet Prunier. Despite all her lover's gifts and pleas, she will not marry him, and explains how once, when she was young and innocent, she had danced at Bullier's nightclub with a young man whose name she did not know. But she had gazed into his eyes and known that this was the sort of love she must find before agreeing to marriage. A young man, Ruggero, son of an old friend of Rambaldo, arrives to see him. As it is Ruggero's first night in Paris, it is decided he should go to Bullier's nightclub. When all her guests have left, Magda decides to go there too, but in disguise. She meets and dances with Ruggero and the two fall in love. She tells Rambaldo that she will not go home with him now or ever and she and Ruggero leave together and settle in a cottage in Nice. They are very happy together, but Magda worries about Ruggero's reaction when he learns about her past life when she sold herself for money. He tells her he has written to his parents asking permission to marry her and is sure they will welcome her as a daughter, but Magda knows differently. Her maid Lisette, having failed in her attempts to make a career on the stage, asks for her job back. Magda tells Ruggero that she has been living a lie and can never marry him. Heartbroken, she leaves the only man she has ever truly loved, and with Lisette she returns to her former existence in Paris. Aria: *Forse come la rondine* ('Perhaps, like a swallow'); duets (with Prunier): *Chi il bel sogno di Doretta poté indovinar?* ('Who can interpret Doretta's beautiful dream?'); (with Ruggero): *Ma come puoi lasciarmi?* ('But how can you leave me?'). Created (1917) by Gilda Dalla Rizza.

Claggart, John (Britten: *Billy Budd*). Bass. Master-at-Arms on board *HMS Indomitable*. He is a suspicious and brutal character, jealous of Billy Budd's good looks and popularity among the crew. Claggart does his best to ingratiate himself with Capt. Vere. He is determined to belittle Billy in Vere's eyes, and to this end he orders one of the sailors to spy on him. When Billy interrupts the man searching his belongings and accuses him of stealing, Claggart reports to the captain that Billy is rousing the men to mutiny. The two men face Vere together. Billy tries to defend himself to Vere, but stammers and cannot get the words out. In frustration he strikes out at Claggart who, striking his head as he falls, collapses and is found to be dead. Billy is sentenced to death. Aria: *Would that I never encountered you.* Successful portrayers of this role have included Forbes Robinson, Michael Langdon, John

Tomlinson, and Richard Van Allan. Created (1951) by Frederick Dalberg.

Clairon (Strauss: *Capriccio*). Cont. Actress friend of the Count, who brings her to his sister Madeleine's birthday celebration. She has previously had an affair with the poet Olivier. She takes part in the entertainment being rehearsed for the Countess's birthday. This includes the love sonnet written by Olivier and then set to music by Flamand. Despite the fact that in the score Clairon is designated a contralto, she was created (1942) by Hildegarde Ranczak, a soprano who also sang the role of Salome. However, she is usually sung by a mez., famous among whom have been Elisabeth Höngen, Christa Ludwig, Kirstin Meyer, Tatiana Troyanos, Trudeliese Schmidt, Anne Howells, and Brigitte Fassbaender.

Clara 1. (Gershwin: *Porgy and Bess*). Sop. Wife of a fisherman, Jake—he dies at sea in a storm, leaving her with their young baby. Aria: *Summertime*. Created (1935) by Abbie Mitchell.

2. (Zemlinsky: *Der Zwerg*). Donna Clara. *See* INFANTA.

Clarice 1. (Prokofiev: *The Love for Three Oranges*). Cont. Princess, niece of the King, who hopes to inherit the throne. Evil accomplice of the witch Fata Morgana. Created (1921) by Irene Pavlovska.

2. (Haydn: *Il mondo della luna*). Sop. Daughter of Buonafede, who disapproves of her future husband. She helps to trick him into giving his consent. Created (1777) by Catharina Poschwa (or Poschva).

Claudio 1. (Berlioz: *Béatrice et Bénédict*). Bar. An officer returning safely from the Moorish wars, to marry Héro, daughter of the Governor of Messina. Created (1862) by Jules Lefort.

2. (Handel: *Agrippina*). Bass. The Roman Emperor and husband of Agrippina. Names Ottone as his successor, although his wife wants it to be Nerone, her son from a previous marriage. Created (1709) by Antonio Francesco Carli.

Claudius (Thomas: *Hamlet*). Bass. Brother of the late King of Denmark, he is now marrying Gertrude, the widowed Queen and mother of Hamlet. Claudius had conspired with Gertrude and Polonius, the chief minister, to poison the King in order to gain the throne. When the King's ghost tells Hamlet the truth, Hamlet exposes his uncle and snatches the crown. Created (1868) by Jules-Bernard Belval.

Clement, VII, Pope (Berlioz: *Benvenuto Cellini*). Bass. Commissions Cellini to cast a statue of Perseus. Created (1838) by Mons. Serda.

clemenza di Tito, La (*The Clemency of Titus*) (Mozart). Lib. by Caterino Tommaso Mazzolà; 2 acts; f.p. Prague 1791.

Rome, AD 79–81: *Vitellia is jealous of Emperor *Tito's intention to marry *Berenice. She plans with *Sesto, who loves her, to kill Tito. *Annio wants to marry *Servilia, Sesto's sister, but Tito, deciding against marriage to Berenice, now wants to marry Servilia himself. When she tells him of her love for Annio, he gives them his blessing and decides to marry Vitellia. She is unaware of this decision and continues with her plot to assassinate him but plans go awry and Tito escapes death. *Publio arrests Sesto for his part in the plot and he is condemned to death. Tito tears up the death warrant, wanting his people to know he is not a dictator but a compassionate ruler. Vitellia, thinking Sesto will die, is overcome by guilt and confesses her own part in the plot. She is also favoured by Tito's clemency.

Cleopatra 1. (Barber: *Antony and Cleopatra*). Sop. Queen of Egypt, in love with the Roman Antony. After Antony has been forced to marry Octavia, sister of the Emperor, he leaves her and returns to Cleopatra. As Roman troops approach, Cleopatra hides in her tomb monument. Believing her dead, Antony kills himself and dies in her arms. Created (1966) by Leontyne Price (at the opening night of the new Metropolitan Opera House in the Lincoln Center, New York).

2. (Handel: *Giulio Cesare*). Sop. Queen of Egypt, sister of Tolomeo. When her brother has Pompey murdered, she goes to Cesare to join him in defeating Tolomeo. She is taken prisoner by her brother's troops but Cesare rescues her. Aria: *V'adoro, pupille* ('I adore you, eyes'). Created (1724) by Francesca Cuzzoni.

Climene (Cavalli: *L'Egisto*). Sop. In love with Lidio, from whom she is separated when kidnapped. He is moved by her loyalty and despair and they are reunited. Creator (1643) unknown.

Clitemnestre (Gluck: *Iphigénie en Aulide*). Sop. Wife of Agamemnon and mother of Iphigénie. Tries to defend her daughter when Agamemnon agrees to sacrifice her as demanded by the goddess Diana. Created (1774) by Mlle du Plant. *See also* KLYTÄMNESTRA.

Clitoria (Ligeti: *Le Grand Macabre*). *See* AMANDA.

Clori (Cavalli: *L'Egisto*). Sop. Loved by Egisto, from whom she is separated when they are all kidnapped by pirates. Falls in love with Lidio. Pity for Egisto, who goes mad with despair, makes her return to him and they are reunited as lovers. Creator (1643) unknown.

Clorinda (Rossini: *La Cenerentola*), Sop. Daughter of Don Magnifico, sister of Tisbe and stepsister of Angelina (Cenerentola) (one of the traditional 'ugly sisters'). Created (1817) by Caterina Rossi.

Clotilde (Bellini: *Norma*). Sop. Norma's confidante. Created (1831) by Marietta Sacchi.

Coigny, Contessa di (Giordano: *Andrea Chénier*). Mez. Mother of Maddalena. Created (1896) by Della Rogers.

Coigny, Maddalena di (Giordano: *Andrea Chénier*). Sop. Daughter of the Contessa. She is secretly loved by her mother's servant, Gérard, a leading Revolutionary. She falls in love with the poet Andrea Chénier, and asks him for protection. He wounds Gérard and is arrested and tried as a Counter-Revolutionary. He is sentenced to death. As he is held in prison awaiting execution, Maddalena pleads with Gérard to save him—she will even give herself to Gérard in return. He is unable to intervene, but helps Maddalena enter the prison and allows her to take the place of a condemned female prisoner so that she can die together with Chénier. Aria: *La mamma morte* ('My mother's death'); duet (with Chénier): *Vicino a te* ('Close at your side'). Created (1896) by Evelina Carrera.

Colas (Mozart: *Bastien und Bastienne*). Bass. The village magician. He advises Bastienne how to win back the unfaithful Bastien and ensures their reconciliation. Creator (1768) not traced.

Collatinus (Britten: *The Rape of Lucretia*). Bass. A Roman general, husband of Lucretia.

He is not surprised to hear she is the only wife to remain faithful to her soldier husband. Tarquinius wants to prove that she, too, can be tempted, but succeeds only in raping her. Collatinus, summoned home to the distressed Lucretia, forgives her, but she kills herself. Aria: *Those who love, create*. Created (1946) by Owen Brannigan.

Colline 1. (Puccini: *La bohème*). Bass. A philosopher, one of the four bohemians who live together in a garret in Paris. Although he has no money, he is fond of expensive clothes and his most prized possession is his old but elegant overcoat. When Mimì is dying, he bids the coat farewell, thanking it for being faithful to him, before going out to sell it to buy medicine for her. This short aria has become justly famous. Aria: *Vecchia zimarra, senti* ('Listen, my old coat'). Created (1896) by Michele Mazzara.

2. (Leoncavallo: *La bohème*). Gustavo Colline. Bar. A similar role to that in (1) above. Created (1897) by Lucio Aristi.

Colonna, Adriano (Wagner: *Rienzi*). Mez. *Travesti* role. Son of Stefano Colonna who is the leader of the noblemen in their battle with the people of Rome, led by Rienzi. Adriano is in love with Rienzi's sister, Irene, and his loyalties are divided between his father and Rienzi. He supports Rienzi, but when his father is killed in a fight between the nobles and the people, he swears to avenge his death. However, he warns Rienzi of a plot to kill him, but is too late. The people, roused by the plotters, set fire to the Capitol and Rienzi and Irene are seen in the flames. Adriano attempts to rescue them but they are all killed when the building collapses. Aria: *Gerechter Gott* ('Righteous God'). Created (1842) by Wilhelmine Schröder-Devrient (who caused a fair amount of havoc during rehearsals, as she was used to singing the heroine and didn't take too kindly to the *travesti* role: at one rehearsal, when she was having difficulty with some of the music, she threw her copy at the composer and stormed out, but was coaxed back to continue).

Colonna, Stefano (Wagner: *Rienzi*). Bass. A nobleman, father of Adriano. He leads the Roman noblemen against Rienzi and his followers, and is killed in a battle in the city. Created (1842) by Wilhelm Dettmer.

Columbine **(Columbina)** (Leoncavallo: *Pagliacci*). *See* *NEDDA.

Commandant (Strauss: *Friedenstag*). Bar. Commandant of a besieged city and husband of Maria. In the Citadel the soldiers are gathered. They have run out of ammunition. The townspeople are all starving. An officer suggests that they bring up more ammunition from the cellars down below, but the Commandant has other ideas. He has received a message from the Emperor, asking them to resist at all costs. The people send a deputation begging him to surrender and put an end to their hunger and misery. He tells them he agrees to their demands, but in reality he knows that rather than surrender to the enemy, he will blow up the fortress in which they are gathered, even if it means they will themselves die. His wife, Maria, joins him. She is much younger than he and loves him dearly. He does his best to persuade her to escape to safety, but she is determined to stay with him. As a soldier brings him the fuse to set fire to the arsenal below, bells ring out as a sign of peace. The enemy commander, the Holsteiner, leads his troops into the citadel. Thinking they come as the enemy, the Commandant draws his sword, but Maria intervenes to prevent any more fighting. Peace now reigns as the two commanders embrace and the rejoicing begins. Aria: *Ihr Alten habt ... mir treu gedient* ('The oldest of you ... have served me faithfully'); duet (with Maria): *Maria, du?* ('Maria, is it you?'). Created (1938) by Hans Hotter.

***commedia dell'arte* troupe** (Strauss: *Ariadne auf Naxos*). A troupe of comedians, hired by one of the richest men in Vienna to entertain his guests. They are led by Zerbinetta. Her male colleagues are Harlequin (bar.), Brighella (ten.), Truffaldino (bass), and Scaramuccio (ten.). The men were created (1912 vers.) by (respectively) Albin Swoboda, Franz Schwerdt, Reinhold Fritz, and Georg Meader; and (1916 vers.) by (respectively) Herr Neuber, Adolph Nemeth, Julius Betetto, and Hermann Gallos. *See also* ZERBINETTA.

Commendatore (Mozart: *Don Giovanni*). Bass. Father of Donna Anna. Killed by Don Giovanni after the latter has seduced his daughter. His graveyard statue comes to life and accepts an invitation to dine with

Giovanni. At the banquet he drags the unrepentant Don into the flames of hell. Created (1787) by Giuseppe Lolli (who also created Masetto).

Composer (Komponist) (Strauss: *Ariadne auf Naxos*). Sop. (or mez.). *Travesti* role. Pupil of the Music Master, he has written *Ariadne auf Naxos*, an *opera seria*, to be performed after dinner for the guests of one of the richest men in Vienna. The host's Major-Domo announces that the opera will be followed by the *commedia dell'arte* troupe's entertainment. This horrifies the Music Master—how can serious art be followed by such vulgar buffoonery? The Major-Domo points out that his master is paying for the opera, and will therefore decide how it will be performed. The Composer is already upset—he has learned that the musicians who are to play his music are currently playing for the guests as they dine, so he is unable to talk to them, the Prima Donna refuses to rehearse her role as Ariadne, and the Tenor needs to have it drummed into him that Bacchus is a god, not a 'conceited clown'. He sees Zerbinetta, leader of the comedians, and finds her most attractive—until he is told that her act will follow his opera. He is shocked when the Dancing Master suggests that as parts of the opera are dull and boring, his troupe will liven things up and keep the audience awake. The Composer's instinct is to withdraw his opera altogether, but he is convinced by his teacher that it is better to have it produced, albeit mutilated, than not performed at all. So he sets about cutting his masterpiece, prompted by the Tenor and the Prima Donna, each suggesting that the other's part is the one which needs reducing. Zerbinetta, overhearing the Composer discussing how Ariadne, deserted by her lover, will welcome death, explains to him that women are not like that—not even Ariadne. She will convince her that life must be lived, and if deserted by one lover, the answer is to find another. But for the Composer, music is a holy art and, as the entertainment is about to begin, he leaves the stage in despair, wishing he had not allowed his opera to be used in this way. Arias: *Du, Venus' Sohn* ('You, Venus-son'); *Musik ist eine heilige Kunst* ('Music is a holy art'). In the 1st vers. of the opera, the Composer (spoken) appears only briefly in the linking-scene. In the 2nd vers., 'he' is on the stage for about 40 minutes,

and singing for only half that time, but this role has nevertheless become a favourite with Strauss sopranos. Created (1916) by Lotte Lehmann (who later graduated to Ariadne), and sung memorably by Irmgard Seefried, Christa Ludwig, Sena Jurinac, Trudeliese Schmidt, Tatyana Troyanos, Ann Murray, Maria Ewing, Angelika Kirchschlager, and Sophie Koch. *See also* ARTICLE BY SENA JURINAC, p. 58.

Comte Ory, Le (Count Ory) (Rossini). Lib. by Eugène Scribe and Charles Gaspard Delestre-Poirson; 2 acts; f.p. Paris 1828, cond. François-Antoine Habeneck.

Touraine, *c*.1200: Count Formoutiers has gone to war, leaving his sister *Adèle in the castle with its custodian, *Ragonde. The ladies have taken a vow of chastity until the men return. Count *Ory, disguised as a hermit and aided by his friend *Raimbaud, attempts to win Adèle, not knowing that his page, *Isolier, is also in love with her. Having been recognized and exposed by his *Tutor, Ory arrives at the castle disguised as a nun, together with his band of 'sisters'. The 'nuns' get drunk on the contents of the castle's cellar. The men return from the war and Ory is again exposed and has to make a quick getaway. Adèle decides to marry the faithful Isolier.

Concepción (Ravel: *L'Heure espagnole*). Sop. Wife of the clockmaker Torquemada. While her husband is out of the house she is visited by her lovers. To keep them from him, she suggests they hide in large clocks and when he finds them she passes them off as customers. Created (1911) by Geneviève Vix.

Constable (Vaughan Williams: *Hugh the Drover*). Bass. Father of Mary, whom he wants to marry the wealthy butcher, John. He puts Hugh in the stocks when he is accused of being a spy. Created (1924) by Arthur G. Rees.

Constance 1. (Poulenc: *Les Dialogues des Carmélites*). Sop. Sister Constance, a young novice who prophesies that she and Blanche will die together. Created (1957) by Eugenia Ratti.

2. (Sullivan: *The Sorcerer*). *See* PARTLET, CONSTANCE.

Constanze (Mozart: *Die Entführung aus dem Serail*). Sop. A Spanish lady, in love with

THE COMPOSER (*Ariadne auf Naxos* (1916 vers.)—Strauss)

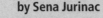

by Sena Jurinac

The Composer, in Strauss's second version of *Ariadne auf Naxos*, is different from his other soprano roles in that the character appears only in the Prologue and there are barely twenty minutes of singing. So why do sopranos so much like to perform it?

Well—it is wonderfully satisfying to sing and act. Like the *Rosenkavalier* Marschallin, in a different way, the character gives something to the singer on the stage due to the wonderful words which Hofmannsthal provided. It gives scope for a vast range of emotions. I think of him as a young Schubert, an idealist, rather than a young Mozart, who was totally practical and knew what would sell and make him a living. The Composer knows no middle-path—he is either fully up or fully down, in heaven or in hell, one might say. When he first appears, he is full of enthusiasm—he is writing an opera (*Ariadne auf Naxos*) to entertain the guests of one of the richest men in Vienna. When he is told his opera and the entertainment by the *commedia dell'arte* troupe will have to be given simultaneously so as not to interfere with the fireworks which are to follow, and that he must reduce the length of his opera, he is immediately downcast. The Music Master tries to explain to him that in art, as in life, one must make compromises if one is to survive. When the Composer meets Zerbinetta, leader of the *commedia dell'arte* players, he initially dislikes her, but gradually he forgets his dislike and falls in love with her, so all is happy again. But when he meets the singers who are to take part in his opera, he falls to pieces and wants to be turned to stone. The beauty of music and love make him leave the world; when he comes down to earth again he is unhappy. This can be quite humorous—one can smile at this young man, but always in a sympathetic way. He is not a ridiculous character and one must feel sorry for him as well as amused.

I first sang the Composer in Vienna in 1947 under Josef Krips, being given the opportunity of taking over, with no orchestral rehearsal, from Irmgard Seefried (for whom I was the understudy). Seefried remained, for me, the supreme interpreter of the part. She gave every role everything she had—she didn't worry about using too much energy on stage, her only concern was to get it right. I last sang it, again in Vienna, in 1980, a span of 33 years. Between those occasions the role took me all over Europe and to America, and I particularly remember the performances at Glyndebourne in 1953 and 1954, in Salzburg in 1964 and 1965 and in my home town, Zagreb, in 1970. I was lucky enough to sing opposite some excellent Music Masters and Zerbinettas, who are the main two characters to whom the Composer relates and responds, and to work with great conductors and producers. They worked differently, but all strived to interpret the action through the music, so my interpretation of the Composer did not need to vary greatly for different productions, although the producers and conductors had different ways of working. This wouldn't do today, the producers wouldn't like it! I think they make up their minds about a role in their brain disconnected from the music and the composer's intentions. Carl Ebert, at Glyndebourne, was able to show one exactly how he wanted it done. Günther Rennert, in Salzburg, 'organized' me—I could alter my interpretation from rehearsal to rehearsal and he would then make up his mind which way he wanted it. Tempi varied with the conductor, and a singer had to be able to sing at all tempos—sometimes faster, sometimes slower.

It is, of course, a trousers-role, and for that one has to learn how to move on a stage. There is a great difference between playing the Composer or Cherubino (*Le nozze di Figaro*), who are 'boys', and playing Fidelio, who is a woman *disguised* as a boy. One has to acquire the technique—the walk, the straight back, the definite and firmer movements of a young man. Vocally, there are pitfalls. I know the Composer is sometimes sung today by mezzo-sopranos, but it really does require a good high register. The singer must feel the music as in Strauss lieder: the words and music are so well combined that even though there are often difficult words on high notes, the rhythms and the beat are such that it is possible to sing it as Strauss intended. I only liked to sing parts where I could identify with the character. This was always one of my favourite roles.

Belmonte. She is kidnapped and held captive, with her maid Blondchen and Belmonte's valet Pedrillo, in Pasha Selim's house. The Pasha has made overtures to Constanze, who has resisted him, and his harem-keeper, Osmin, has lewd designs on Blondchen. Belmonte attempts to rescue them. Aria: *Martern aller arten* ('Torture of every kind'). Created (1782) by Katharina Cavalieri.

Consul, The (Menotti). Lib. by comp.; 3 acts; f.p. Philadelphia 1950, cond. by Lehman Engel.

Somewhere in Europe, after the Second World War: John *Sorel has to leave the country to escape the secret police, leaving behind his wife Magda *Sorel and their baby with Magda's *Mother. Magda tries to see the Consul to get a visa to join him, but all her efforts are frustrated by the bureaucratic *Secretary. Magda is watched by the secret police. Her baby dies. When this news reaches her husband, he risks his life by returning to be with his wife. He is arrested. Knowing what this means, Magda kills herself.

Contes d'Hoffmann, Les (The Tales of Hoffmann) (Offenbach). Lib. by Jules Barbier; 5 acts; f.p. Paris 1881 (excl. the Venice act), cond. Jules Danbé.

Nuremberg, Munich, Venice, 19th cent.: In a Nuremberg tavern, *Hoffmann and *Nicklausse, are drinking. The poet's beloved diva *Stella is also loved by *Lindorf, who plots Hoffmann's downfall. Hoffmann tells of his love affairs and how they were thwarted by Lindorf. First was *Olympia, whom he presumed to be the daughter of the inventor *Spalanzani. The inventor tried to buy off *Coppélius, inventor of eyes for dolls. As

Olympia sang, Spalanzani repeatedly wound up her mechanism. Hoffmann thought she was human and was enchanted by her, but Coppélius destroyed her. In Munich lived *Antonia. Because of her illness, her father *Crespel kept her protected and hidden. But she and Hoffmann fell in love. The evil Dr *Miracle made Antonia sing. The effort exhausted her and she collapsed. The doctor pronounced her dead. In Venice Hoffmann found wine preferable to women. Nicklausse and *Giulietta sang together. The sorcerer *Dappertutto offered Giulietta a diamond if she obtained for him Hoffmann's soul, but Hoffmann fell in love with her, fought a duel with his rival *Schlemil, and killed him. He took from Schlemil the key to Giulietta's room. But she had floated away in a gondola with *Pittichinaccio. Having heard all these stories, Nicklausse points out that all Hoffmann's loves were manifestations of Stella. She enters, but leaves the tavern with Lindorf. Nicklausse assures Hoffmann that his poetry will be all the better for his sad experiences in love.

Coppélius (Offenbach: *Les Contes d'Hoffmann*). Bar. Scientist and inventor of dolls' eyes, including those for Olympia, with whom Hoffmann falls in love. Cheated by his rival Spalanzani, he destroys Olympia. Created (1881) by Alexandre Taskin.

Corcoran, Capt. (Sullivan: *HMS Pinafore*). Bass-bar. Capt. of *HMS Pinafore* and father of Josephine, whom he wants to marry off to the First Lord of the Admiralty. It is revealed that the captain has been swapped as a baby and is in reality a simple sailor. Created (1878) by Rutland Barrington.

Corcoran, Josephine (Sullivan: *HMS Pinafore*). Sop. Daughter of the captain commanding the ship. She loves Ralph, a simple sailor. Her father opposes their relationship because he wants her to marry the First Lord of the Admiralty. Aria: *O joy, O rapture unforeseen*. Created (1878) by Emma Howson.

Cornelia (Handel: *Giulio Cesare*). Cont. Widow of Pompey. She and her son Sesto want peace with Cesare after he has defeated her husband, but Tolomeo, King of Egypt, has her husband slain and she is sent to Tolomeo's harem and her son arrested. When Tolomeo is defeated by Cesare, she and Sesto are welcomed by Cesare and Cleopatra. Created (1724) by Anastasia Robinson.

Coroebus, Prince (Prince Chorèbe) (Berlioz: *Les Troyens*). Bar. Fiancé of Cassandra, daughter of King Priam. Killed in battle. Creator (1890) not traced.

Così fan tutte (All women behave like this) (Mozart). Lib. by Lorenzo da Ponte; 2 acts; f.p. Vienna 1790.
   Naples, 18th cent.: *Ferrando and *Guglielmo boast to Don *Alfonso of the faithfulness of their fiancées, the sisters *Dorabella and *Fiordiligi. Alfonso bets them that all girls are unfaithful. He bribes their maid, *Despina, to help him prove it. Enter two Albanian suitors (Ferrando and Guglielmo in disguise). Fiordiligi and Dorabella gradually weaken and the 'wrong' couples pair off and sign their marriage contracts. The men are in despair at the result of Alfonso's machinations. The band is now heard announcing the 'return' from battle of the girls' fiancés. The new 'bridegrooms' are hidden in a side-room and emerge in their own uniforms to greet their loyal lovers. Alfonso shows the men the marriage contracts and the girls try to explain the situation. The men raise their swords and rush off to find their rivals, to emerge wearing part of their Albanian costumes. All is revealed, Alfonso has won his bet—but who will now be united with whom?

Costanza (Haydn: *L'isola disabitata*). Sop. Wife of Gernando, who has left her and her sister Silvia on a desert island for thirteen years. They are reunited when he comes to rescue her, having himself been a prisoner of pirates. Created (1779) by Barbara Ripamonte.

Count 1. (Strauss: *Capriccio*). Bar. Brother of the Countess Madeleine. He has organized a group of friends to perform a play for his sister's birthday, and they gather at her château to rehearse. The guests include the well-known actress Clairon, to whom the Count is attracted. Aria (with Clairon): *Ein Oper ist ein absurdes Ding* ('An opera is an absurd thing'). Created by Walter Höfermayer.
   2. (Massenet: *Chérubin*). Bar. He finds a letter from Chérubin to the Countess and determines to kill Chérubin. Created (1905) by Mons. Lequien.

Count Almaviva 1. (Rossini: *Il barbiere di Siviglia*). *See* ALMAVIVA, COUNT (1).
   2. (Mozart: *Le nozze di Figaro*). *See* ALMAVIVA, COUNT (2).
   3. (Corigliano: *The Ghosts of Versailles*). *See* ALMAVIVA, COUNT (3).

Countess 1. (Mozart. *Le nozze di Figaro*). Sop. Rosina, Countess Almaviva. She is, of course, the Rosina of Rossini's *Il barbiere di Siviglia*, now married to her Count. She feels very unhappy because of neglect by her husband. He suspects her of having an affair with a younger man, to which he objects, while at the same time he attempts to seduce other girls, especially her maid Susanna. The Countess plots with Susanna to teach him a lesson. In a complicated garden scene, she swaps clothes with Susanna and the Count accuses her of a relationship with Figaro. When the truth dawns, he has to apologize to her and they are reconciled. Arias: *Porgi amor*… ('Grant, love …'); *Dove sono i bei momenti* ('Where are the golden moments'). Most of the great sopranos of each generation want to sing this role, which gives opportunity for a range of emotions, from sadness to humour and, in the final scene, loving forgiveness. In the 20th century, these have included Margarete Teschemacher, Aulikki Rautawaara, Elisabeth Schwarzkopf, Lisa Della Casa, Sena Jurinac, Maria Stader, Hilde Gueden, Gundula Janowitz, Elisabeth Söderström, Ava June, Montserrat Caballé, Margaret Price, Kiri te Kanawa, Felicity Lott, Karita Mattila, and Joan Rodgers. Created (1785) by Lucia Laschi.
   2. (Strauss: *Capriccio*). Sop. Countess Madeleine, a young widow. Unable to decide between her two suitors, the poet Olivier and the musician Flamand. Her brother arranges

for an entertainment to be written and performed for her birthday and the two admirers come to represent 'words' and 'music'. Which will she choose? The subject of words versus music occupied Richard Strauss all his composing life, and in this opera he let the Countess Madeleine's two suitors represent those two aspects of opera. Her final choice will give the answer—she arranges to meet both Flamand and Olivier in the library the next morning. Alone and bathed in moonlight, she sings a long aria arguing with her reflection in the mirror the various merits of her two suitors. However, the audience is left guessing—or is there a hint in the orchestral postlude to her aria, with its reference to a Flamand theme? Aria: *Morgen mittag um elf! ...Kein andres, das mir so im Herzen loht* ('At eleven o'clock! ... Your image in my ardent bosom glows'). For the last of Strauss's great soprano roles, all in some way representations of his wife Pauline, this closing aria lasts nearly twenty minutes. Greatly admired Countesses have included Lisa Della Casa, Maria Cebotari, Gundula Janowitz, Dorothy Dow, Elisabeth Schwarzkopf, Anna Tomowa Sintow, Lucia Popp, Elisabeth Söderström, Kiri te Kanawa, Felicity Lott, and Renée Fleming—a roll-call of great Strauss sopranos, many of whom have also shone as Mozart's Countess—see (1). Created (1942) by Viorica Ursuleac (future wife of the conductor Clemens Krauss, who conducted the first performance).

3. (Tchaikovsky: *The Queen of Spades*). Mez. Grandmother of Lisa, the old Countess was, in Paris in her youth, a heavy gambler who lost a great deal of money. A Count told her the secret of three cards which would always win. She revealed this secret to her husband and later to a lover. A ghost then told her that she would die if she revealed it a third time. When threatened by Hermann, she dies of shock at the sight of his gun. She later appears to him as a ghost and tells him 'Three, seven, ace'. But she has tricked him and he loses. Aria: *Je crains de lui parler la nuit* ('I fear to speak of him in the night'). This aria was copied by Tchaikovsky from Grétry's *Richard Cœur-de-Lion*. Created (1890) by Mariya Slavina.

4. (Massenet: *Chérubin*). Sop. Godmother of Chérubin, who writes her a love-letter, found by the Count. Created (1905) by Mme Doux.

Coyle, Mrs (Britten: *Owen Wingrave*). Sop. Wife of Spencer Coyle. She is the only person who supports Owen's sticking to his principles. Created (TV 1971/stage 1973) by Heather Harper.

Coyle, Spencer (Britten: *Owen Wingrave*). Bass-bar. Head of a military cramming establishment. Tries to persuade Owen to continue as a soldier. Created (TV 1971/stage 1973) by John Shirley-Quirk.

Crawley, Frank (Josephs: *Rebecca*). Ten. Estate agent of Maxim de Winter at Manderley. He befriends the Girl who has become the second Mrs de Winter. Created (1983) by Geoffrey Pogson.

Creon 1. (Stravinsky: *Oedipus Rex*). Bass-bar. Brother of Oedipus' wife, Jocasta. Accused by Oedipus of plotting to seize the throne of Thebes. Created (1927) by Georges Lanskoy (who also created the Messenger—the two roles are usually sung by the same artist).

2. (Creonte) (Haydn: *Orfeo ed Euridice*). Bass. Father of Euridice. Created (1951) by Boris Christoff.

3. (Créon) (Cherubini: *Médée*). King of Corinth and father of Dircé, who is about to marry Jason, the Argonaut who brought the Golden Fleece back to Corinth. Created (1797) by Mons. Dessaules.

Crespel (Offenbach: *Les Contes d'Hoffmann*). Bass or bass-bar. Violinmaker. Father of the sick Antonia. He keeps her hidden in order to protect her. Created (1881) by Hypolite Belhomme.

Cressida (Walton: *Troilus and Cressida*). Sop./mez. Daughter of Calkas, High Priest of Pallas. She is a widow, her husband having been killed in the Trojan Wars, and is about to take her vows as a priestess. Initially she cannot accept Troilus' love, but, tricked by her uncle into spending the night with the Trojan prince, they admit their love for each other and she gives him her crimson scarf. When she is taken to the Greek camp in exchange for a Trojan prisoner, she takes with her the scarf as a token of their eternal love. But she receives no word from Troilus and after ten weeks reluctantly agrees to marry the Greek prince Diomede. When Troilus arrives at the Greek camp it becomes clear that Cressida's maid

CRESSIDA (*Troilus and Cressida*—Walton)

by Susana Walton

William Walton's main difficulty in finding a suitable libretto seems to have been the need for a heroine that appealed to his idealistic view of women. Alice Wimborne, William's muse at the time, wrote to his librettist, Christopher Hassall, that she was encouraging William to accept Christopher's version of Chaucer's *Troylus and Criseide*, because Cressida was more the *Manon* lady whom he obviously preferred to the *Juliet*.

Chaucer's Cressida is a figure caught among the subtle plots of chivalrous love. He defends and idealizes her, he emphasizes her ruling passion, i.e. fear—fear of loneliness, of old age, of death, of love—from which springs the pitiable longing for protection.

William conceived the role to suit the voice of Elisabeth Schwarzkopf, whom he admired and who had recently become the wife of his great friend and supporter in the recording world, Walter Legge. In his view, the chief attraction of her voice was the rich tone and power of her lower register (could this have opened the way for the later mezzo version?), coupled with the excitement of her soaring top notes which gave the listener an added *frisson* at climactic moments as the orchestra surged along with her. But, for some reason, Schwarzkopf rejected the role—it is said because her English was not good enough.

William semi-destroyed a chair or two in Covent Garden while attending rehearsals for the world première in 1954, because of his annoyance at Malcolm Sargent conducting without regard to William's exact tempo markings. Malcolm was very proud of his ability to sight-read scores and obstinately refused to learn the work. So when William remonstrated with him about tempi, Malcolm would complain about the smallness of the musical script (he was too vain to wear his spectacles) or would retaliate by trying to alter the orchestration and frequently instructed the orchestra to ignore 'the old fool'.

In this first production, Cressida was a lovely Hungarian soprano, Magda Laszló. She and the rest of the cast had great difficulty with Sargent's erratic changes of tempi and false leads. Although she did not speak a word of English (and was coached in the language by me, an Argentinian!), her portrayal was brilliantly sung and acted. She looked ethereal yet vulnerable, moving the first-night audience to tears (an experience repeated in Leeds when Judith Howarth sang the role for Opera North's first production in January 1995).

At the 1956 Italian première at La Scala, Milan, the soprano—caught at the wrong time of the month!—sang all the high notes out of tune. William was distraught as he sat in the director's box between Elisabeth Schwarzkopf and Maria Callas—either of whom would have been an ideal Cressida—while the two singers demolished the unhappy soprano, voicing their belief that she would not last the length of the first act before the angry audience whistled her off the stage, and that is exactly what happened.

Cressida remains an exciting vehicle for a superlative singer-actress, with its wide range of emotions: the chaste and frightened oracle of Act 1, the passionate lover of Act 2, and, finally, through adversity, transfigured into the tragic heroine whose final act of immolation clutches at our hearts.

has been burning his letters. As he and Diomede fight, Calkas stabs Troilus in the back.
Rather than be left in the Greek camp as a
whore for the soldiers, Cressida kills herself
with Troilus's sword. Arias: *Slowly it all comes
back; At the haunted end of the day*. This role
was written by Walton with the voice of Elisabeth Schwarzkopf in mind, but she never sang
it on stage, although she did record some of the
arias. (Maria Callas was another soprano Walton would have loved to sing it!) In 1976 the
composer rewrote the music of Cressida for
the mezzo-soprano Janet Baker, who sang it at
Covent Garden that year. Created (1954) by
Magda Laszló. *See also* ARTICLE BY SUSANA
WALTON, p. 62.

Cripps, Mrs (Sullivan: *HMS Pinafore*). *See*
LITTLE BUTTERCUP.

Croissy, Mme de (Poulenc: *Les Dialogues
des Carmélites*). Cont. The old Prioress, who
admits Blanche to the convent and dies soon
afterwards. In her dying moments, she is disturbed by visions of the destruction of their
chapel. Created (1957) by Gianni Pederzini.

Crown (Gershwin: *Porgy and Bess*). Bar. A stevedore, he kills a man during a crap game and
has to flee, leaving his girlfriend, Bess, who
falls in love with Porgy. When Crown tries to
win her back, Porgy kills him. Created (1935)
by Warren Coleman.

Csárdásfürstin, Die (*The Csárdás Princess*)
(Kálmán). Lib. by Leo Stein and Béla Jenbach;
3 acts; f.p. Vienna 1915, cond. Arthur
Guttmann.
    Budapest and Vienna, 18th cent.: Prince
*Edwin Ronald's parents (the Prince and Prin-
cess von und zu *Lippert-Wehlersheim) want
him to marry Countess Anastasia (*Stasi), but
he falls in love with Sylva *Varescu, a cabaret
singer. He coaxes her into signing a marriage
contract committing them to marry within
two months. But she hears that Edwin has become engaged to Stasi and turns up at his party
posing as the wife of Count Boni *Káncsiánu,
an old friend. Boni and Stasi are attracted to
each other. Edwin finds out that his own

mother was originally a singer so his parents
can no longer object to Edwin marrying Sylva.
Boni and Stasi also declare their love.

Cunning Little Vixen, The (*Příhody Lišky
Bystroušky*) (Janáček). Lib. by comp.; 3 acts;
f.p. Brno 1924, cond. František Neumann.
    A forest, summer and autumn: While the
*Forester sleeps, surrounded by birds and in-
sects, a Frog lands on his nose. Attracted by
the frog, the Vixen *Bystrouška is caught by
the Forester who takes her to his house. She
kills the cock and all the hens, bites through
her lead, and runs off into the forest. Playing
cards with the *Schoolmaster and the *Priest,
the Forester taunts the Schoolmaster about
his lack of success in love and is teased in return about the Vixen's escape. They all wander
home through the forest. The Vixen meets and
falls in love with the *Fox. They marry, all the
forest animals taking part in the celebrations.
*Harašta, the poultry-dealer, is accused by the
Forester of poaching. He is lured into the forest by the Vixen, falls over, and she and her
family kill all his chickens. Angry, Harašta
shoots the Vixen. He then marries the gypsy
Terinka, who was fancied by the Schoolmaster. The Forester goes home through the forest
where he has his usual little nap. He dreams of
all the forest creatures, including a little vixen
and a little frog—the grandson of the one
which landed on his nose earlier. Nature is renewing herself.

Cuno (Weber: *Der Freischütz*). Bass. Head forester. Father of Agathe, who wants to marry
Max. Created (1821) by Herr Wauer.

Curio (Handel: *Giulio Cesare*). Bass. Roman
tribune. Wants to marry Cornelia, widow of
Pompey, but she rejects him. Created (1724) by
John Lagarde (or Laguerre).

Curzio, Don (Mozart: *Le nozze di Figaro*).
Ten. Counsellor at law. Created (1786) by
Michael Kelly (who also created Basilio).

Cyril (Sullivan: *Princess Ida*). Ten. Friend who
helps Prince Hilarion break into the Castle
Adamant to search for Ida. He gets drunk, leading to their discovery and capture. Created
(1884) by Durward Lely.

Daland (Wagner: *Der fliegende Holländer*). Bass. A Norwegian sea captain, father of Senta. His ship is anchored in bad weather off the coast of Norway near to where he lives. Out of the mists he sees the Dutchman's ship appear. The Dutchman asks if he can marry Senta in return for great wealth, and Daland agrees, taking him home to meet her. Aria: *Mögst du, mein Kind, den fremden Mann willkommen heissen?* ('Will you, my child, bid this stranger welcome?'). Created (1843) by Karl Risse.

Dalila (Delilah) (Saint-Saëns: *Samson et Dalila*). Mez. Philistine who, rejected by the Hebrew Samson, determines revenge. Woos him and cuts off his hair, the secret of his enormous strength. Aria: *Mon cœur s'ouvre á ta voix* ('My heart opens to your voice'—more often translated as 'Softly awakes my heart'). Among famous singers of this role are Ebe Stignani, Fedora Barbieri, Giulietta Simionato, Shirley Verrett, Agnes Baltsa, and Olga Borodina. Created (1877) by Auguste von Müller.

Dalinda (Handel: *Ariodante*). Sop. A lady-in-waiting to the Princess Ginevra, at the Scottish court. Helps to falsely convince Ariodante of Ginevra's unfaithfulness but ultimately puts the record straight and marries Ariodante's brother Lurcanio. Created (1735) by Cecilia Young.

Daly, Dr (Sullivan: *The Sorcerer*). Bass-bar. Vicar of Ploverleigh. In love with Constance Partlet. Created (1877) by Rutland Barrington.

Danae (Strauss: *Die Liebe der Danae*). Sop. Daughter of Pollux, King of Eos. In order to help her father pay his debts, she must marry a wealthy husband. Her cousins have all been searching for a suitable match for her, and King Midas, the richest man in the world, is coming to see her. First there arrives a man calling himself Chrysopher—it is, in fact, Midas in disguise, and he says he has come to guide her to Midas. She finds him very attractive and the feeling is mutual. When he takes her to meet 'Midas', this turns out to be Jupiter in disguise. He soon senses that Danae is already in love with the real Midas. When Midas turns Danae into a gold statue, Jupiter asks her to choose between them. She chooses Midas, even though he loses his ability to turn everything to gold. They live together in humble circumstances. Jupiter visits them in the hope of persuading Danae to come to him and the wealthy life he can offer her, but she chooses to remain, happily, with Midas. Arias: *O Gold! O süsses Gold!* ('O gold! O sweetest gold!'); *Wie umgibst du mich mit Frieden* ('How you surround me with peace'). Created (1944) by Viorica Ursuleac; (1952) by Annelies Kupper.

Dancaïre (Bizet: *Carmen*). Ten. A smuggler, with whom Carmen associates. Created (1875) by Mons. Potel.

Dancing Master (Strauss: *Ariadne auf Naxos*). (*a*) Spoken in the play of the 1st vers. He was hired to teach Mons. Jourdain, the *bourgeois gentilhomme*, how to dance as part of his learning to be a gentleman. Created (1912) by the actor Paul Biensfeldt; (*b*) Ten. in the opera of the 2nd vers. He teaches the comedians how to perform their dances. Created (1916) by Georg Maikl.

Dandini (Rossini: *La Cenerentola*). Bass. Valet to Prince Ramiro. He and the Prince swap clothes when visiting Cenerentola and her family, and she falls in love with the supposed valet (in reality the prince). Aria: *Come un'ape* ('Like a bee'); duet (with Magnifico): *Un segreto d'importanza* ('A secret of importance'). Created (1817) by Giuseppe de Begnis.

Daniello (Krenek: *Jonny spielt auf*). Bar. A virtuoso violinist. His violin is stolen by the jazz-player Jonny. He is killed by a locomotive carrying all the other characters to a new life in America. Created (1927) by Theodor Horand.

Danilowitsch, Count Danilo (Lehár: *The Merry Widow*). Ten./bar. A cavalry officer, secretary to the legation in Paris. An old flame of Hanna, the 'merry widow'. On principle he will not marry her now that she is so wealthy. He spends his evenings with the girls in the nightclubs. Only when Hanna assures him she will lose her fortune on remarriage, does he relent and admit his love for her—only to learn that, by the terms of her late husband's will, her fortune will pass to her new husband! Aria: *Da geh' ich zu Maxim* ('I go now to Maxim's'). Created (1905) by Louis Treumann.

Dansker (Britten: *Billy Budd*). Bass. An old seaman who warns Billy Budd to beware of the evil master-at-arms, Claggart. When Billy is in irons, awaiting execution, Dansker brings him food, drink, and comfort. Created (1951) by Inia te Wiata.

Danvers, Mrs (Josephs: *Rebecca*). Mez. Housekeeper at Manderley, the stately home where Maxim de Winter and his wife, the late Rebecca, lived and to which he brings his second wife. Mrs Danvers adored Rebecca and remains faithful to her memory, doing her best to make life unpleasant for the new Mrs de Winter (the Girl). She suggests that she should copy an old family portrait as a costume for the Manderley Ball, much to the anger of Maxim—Rebecca had worn the same dress at the previous Ball. When the reason for Rebecca's death is discovered, Mrs Danvers disappears to Rebecca's old room. It is from here that fire breaks out and destroys the house. Created (1983) by Ann Howard.

Daphne (Strauss). Lib. by Joseph Gregor; 1 act; f.p. Dresden 1938, cond. Karl Böhm.

Mount Olympus, mythical times: *Peneios and *Gaea have a daughter *Daphne, a lover of nature, who has no knowledge of human sexual passion. The family and shepherds prepare for a Dionysian feast. *Leukippos admits his love for Daphne, who does not respond. Her maids suggest he should dress as a woman and try to gain her love that way. *Apollo arrives, disguised as a cowherd. He also woos Daphne, but she is shocked by his display of passion. At the feast, Leukippos, attired as a girl, dances with Daphne. Apollo, jealous, exposes him and stops the festivities. Leukippos accuses Apollo of wooing Daphne under false pretences and Apollo kills him. Daphne realizes, too late, that she loved Leukippos and she rejects Apollo. He asks Zeus to grant Daphne her wish to be one with nature and she is transformed into a laurel tree.

Daphne (Strauss: *Daphne*). Sop. Daughter of Gaea and Peneios, an innocent, unaware of human emotions. She identifies with nature, with the flowers and the trees. Worldly pleasure, such as the forthcoming feast of Dionysus, holds no appeal for her. She has known Leukippos since they were both children and regards him rather as a brother. When he declares his love for her, she is shocked and rejects him. Her maids vow to help him win her. When Apollo joins the family, disguised as a shepherd, Daphne's father orders her to take care of him. Apollo, overcome by her beauty, falls in love with her, but when he tells her so, she is frightened. At the feast, she dances with Leukippos, who is dressed as a woman. Apollo reveals Leukippos's true identity and kills him in a fit of jealousy, and Daphne then realizes she loved Leukippos. Apollo, full of remorse, asks Zeus to forgive him and to grant Daphne to him in a non-human form. She gradually turns into a laurel tree, her voice singing a wordless aria. Arias: *O bleib, geliebter Tag!* ('O stay, beloved day!'); *Unheilvolle Daphne!* ('Sorrowstricken Daphne!'); *Ich komme—ich komme—Grünende Brüder* … ('I'm coming—I'm coming—(to join you), green brothers'); *Mondlichtmusik* ('Moonlight music'—the (wordless) Voice of Daphne). The role has been sung by Maria Cebotari, Hilde Gueden, Rose Bampton, Gina Cigna, Annelies Kupper, Ingrid Bjoner, Cheryl Studer, Roberta Alexander, and Helen Field. Created (1938) by Margarete Teschemacher (the first Dresden Countess in *Capriccio* and a well-known Pamina and Jenůfa).

Dappertutto (Offenbach: *Les Contes d'Hoffmann*). Bass/bass-bar. A sorcerer, he bribes Giulietta to obtain for him the soul of Hoffmann. Created (1905) by Maurice Renaud.

Dark Fiddler (Delius: *A Village Romeo and Juliet*). Bar. Owner of a strip of land between the farms owned by the fathers of Vreli and

Sali. He tries to persuade the young lovers to join him and live like vagabonds. Created (1907) by Desider Zador.

Da-ud (Strauss: *Die ägyptische Helena*). Ten. Son of the chieftain Altair. He is killed by Helen's husband Menelaus whilst they are out hunting, as Menelaus thinks he looks like Paris, who had seduced Helen. Created (1928) by Guglielmo Fazzini.

Dauntless, Richard (Sullivan: *Ruddigore*). Ten. Foster-brother of Robin Oakapple, who he reveals to be Sir Ruthven Murgatroyd, true heir to the baronetcy and its accompanying curse. He would love to marry Rose, but cedes her to Robin and settles for one of the bridesmaids. Created (1887) by Durward Lely.

David (Wagner: *Die Meistersinger von Nürnberg*). Ten. Apprentice to Hans Sachs, he has a long-standing relationship with Magdalene, Eva's companion, even though she is older than he is. There is to be a trial for those wishing to become new Masters. Magdalene asks David to ensure that Walther succeeds (so he can enter the song-contest for which the prize is marriage to Eva). David explains to Walther the *Tablatur*, the table of rules by which all songs must be composed. These rules are quite complicated and David soon realizes that Walther's chances of remembering them are remote. David then supervises the other apprentices in setting the scene for the song contest, and explains to Walther how there will be a marker to listen for his mistakes. He knows that Walther will fail, and indeed he does. David knows this means trouble with Magdalene and when they meet she is certainly not pleased with him. He helps Sachs sort out the new shoes ready for the morrow and goes to bed. He is awakened by noise in the street below his window, and looks out to see Magdalene being serenaded by Beckmesser (who thinks he is singing to Eva). He rushes out and starts beating Beckmesser, who is saved by Sachs's dragging David away and sending him into the house. The next day Magdalene tells him the story of her impersonation of Eva and he is reassured, but worried about what Hans Sachs is going to say to him about his behaviour the previous night. He returns to the house, where Sachs is studying a large book. Sachs says nothing and this worries David until he goes up to Sachs and asks his forgiveness. Sachs just asks him to sing his new poem. Suddenly, David remembers—it is Sachs's birthday. He presents him with flowers and ribbons which Magdalene gave him. He also suggests to Sachs that he, too, should take part in the competition for Eva's hand. David is sent to get ready to accompany his master to the song contest. When he emerges, he is amazed to have Sachs announce that he is upgrading him from 'apprentice' to 'journeyman'. He can't wait to tell his fellow apprentices and Magdalene. At the end of the day's events, his pride in being able to serve someone as noble as Sachs is obvious. Arias: *Gleich, Meister! Hier!* ('I'm coming, Master! Here!'); *Der Meister Tön' und Weisen* ('The Masters' tones and melodies'); *'Am Jordans Sankt Johannes stand'* ('On Jordan's banks St John did stand'); quintet (with Sachs, Eva, Walther, and Magdalene), in which his opening lines are: *Wach' oder träum' ich schon so früh?* ('Do I wake or dream so early?'). This is not a 'great' Wagnerian role, but is fun to play and with some good music to sing. Tenors of the calibre of Gerhard Stolz, Gerhard Unger, Anton Dermota, Peter Schreier, and Graham Clark have been happy to make a speciality of it. Created (1868) by Max Schlosser.

Deadeye, Dick (Sullivan: *HMS Pinafore*). Bass. Able Seaman who informs on Josephine and Ralph and thus thwarts their elopement. Created (1878) by Richard Temple.

Death 1. (Holst: *Sāvitri*). Bass. Visits Sāvitri to take her husband. Moved by her inability to continue life without her husband, Death restores him to her. Created (1916) by Harrison Cook.

2. (Ullmann: *Der Kaiser von Atlantis*). Bassbar. He resents the loss of the old ways of dying and the introduction of new mechanized methods and goes on strike. When the Emperor begs him to return to the old ways, he will do so on condition that the Emperor agrees to be the first to die. Created (1944) by Karel Berman (who also sang the Loudspeaker); (1975) by Tom Haenen.

3. (Maxwell Davies: *Taverner*). *See* JESTER.

Death in Venice (Britten). Lib. by Myfanwy Piper; 2 acts; f.p. Snape 1973, cond. Steuart Bedford.

Munich and Venice, 1911: The writer *Aschenbach muses on the drying up of his creativity. In a cemetery he meets the *Traveller, who suggests he goes south, and he decides to go to Venice, meeting an *Elderly Fop on the boat. An *Old Gondolier rows him to his hotel on the Lido. The *Hotel Manager shows him to his room. He watches the guests arriving for dinner, and is attracted by the beauty of the son, *Tadzio, of a Polish family. He sees him again, playing on the beach, and when he later sits on the beach the boy is there. Aschenbach wants to speak to him, but fails to do so. He admits to himself his love for the boy. Aschenbach hears from the *Hotel Barber that there is cholera in the city and everyone is leaving. When the guests have gone, the writer returns to sit on the beach—Tadzio beckons to him, but Aschenbach is dead in his chair.

Death of Klinghoffer, The (Adams). Lib. by Alice Goodman; prol. and 2 acts; f.p. Brussels 1991, cond. Kent Nagano.

In America and on board the *Achille Lauro*, 1985: Based on the hijacking of a cruise ship and the murder of an American Jewish passenger. A wealthy American family plan a cruise. Outside Alexandria, the *Achille Lauro* is hijacked and hostages taken. Waiting to enter a port in Syria, the wheelchair-bound Leon *Klinghoffer is kept apart from the others. The terrorists quarrel among themselves, Klinghoffer is shot and his body thrown overboard. The *Captain and hijackers come to an arrangement—the liner can return to Alexandria if the Palestinians can leave the ship peacefully. After their arrival in port, the Captain has to tell Marilyn *Klinghoffer that her husband is dead. [NOTE: For later performances, the prologue was withdrawn by the composer.]

Demetrius 1. (Britten: *A Midsummer Night's Dream*). Bar. An Athenian in love with Hermia, who in her turn loves Lysander. After much confusion caused by Puck, the lovers are all sorted out, Demetrius with Helena. Quartet (with Helena, Lysander, and Hermia): *Mine own, but not mine own*. Created (1960) by Thomas Hemsley.

2. (Purcell: *The Fairy Queen*). Spoken. Similar to the role in (1) above. Creator (1692) unknown.

Demon, The (Rubinstein). Lib. by Pavel Viskovatov; prol., 3 acts, and an 'apotheosis'; f.p. St Petersburg 1875, cond. Eduard Nápravník.

The *Demon, a fallen angel, sees and falls in love with *Tamara, daughter of Prince *Gudal. He kills Prince *Sinodal who was to have married her. He follows Tamara to a convent where she has retired to recover from her loss. When they meet, the Demon kisses her and she dies as he now possesses her mortal being. But her soul is taken up to heaven. The Demon is once again alone, cursing heaven and earth.

Demon (Rubinstein: *The Demon*). Bar. He is a fallen angel, condemned to a life of suffering. Having arranged for Tamara's future husband to be killed, the Demon appears to her as in a vision. Only her love can end his suffering. Initially she rejects him but he gradually engages her sympathy by describing his own never-ending agony. When he kisses Tamara, she dies. Again he is doomed to loneliness and eternal suffering. Created (1875) by Ivan Mel'nikov.

Desdemona 1. (Verdi: *Otello*). Sop. Wife of Otello. Desdemona is deeply in love with and loyal to her husband, who is jealous and needlessly suspicious of her relationships with other men. Iago, anxious to supplant Cassio as Otello's second-in-command, sets about convincing Otello of Desdemona's affair with Cassio. In her innocence, and at Iago's suggestion, Desdemona intercedes on behalf of the demoted Cassio, further fuelling Otello's suspicions. She forcefully denies her husband's accusations, but he insults her and strikes her. She gives him a handkerchief to wipe his brow, which he throws on the ground. It is retrieved by her maid Emilia, wife of Iago, who takes it from her and uses it as further evidence against Cassio. As Emilia helps her prepare for retirement that night, Desdemona thinks of death. She sings a song she remembers her mother's maid singing (the *Willow Song*) and prays to the Virgin Mary. As she settles to sleep, Otello enters, leans over her and kisses her, but she senses that he is going to kill her. She pleads her innocence and asks him to be merciful—she wants to live. Otello smothers her with a pillow as Emilia comes back into the room and shouts for help. But Desdemona is dying. Otello learns of Iago's treachery and his wife's innocence, stabs himself, and dies next to her. Arias: *Piangea cantando ... Salce! Salce!* ('She wept, singing ... Willow! Willow!'); *Ave Maria* ('Hail, Mary'); duet (with Otello): *Mio*

superbo guerrier!... ('My proud warrior!');
quartet (with Otello, Emilia, and Iago); *Dammi
la dolce e lieta parola del perdono* ('Grant me
the sweet and happy word of pardon'). Fa-
mous interpreters include Emma Albani,
Emma Eames, Nellie Melba, Claudia Muzio,
Dora Labbette, Frances Alda, Eleanor Steber,
Renata Tebaldi, Leonie Rysanek, Sylvia Sass,
Gwyneth Jones, Mirella Freni, Margaret
Price, Renata Scotto, Katia Ricciarelli, Kiri te
Kanawa, and Elena Prokina. Created (1887) by
Romilda Pantaleoni (who was the mistress of
Franco Faccio, conductor of the world première). Verdi himself chose her to sing the role
for the première, but afterwards felt she didn't
really understand the way the part should be
interpreted. She did not have the great career
that her fellow-creators in *Otello* (Tamagno
and Maurel) had.

2. (Rossini: *Otello*). Sop. Daughter of Elmiro.
Loved by Otello but he suspects her of being
unfaithful. He creeps into her room while
she sleeps and stabs her. Created (1816) by
Isabella Colbran (who was married to Rossini
1822–37).

Des Grieux, Chevalier 1. (Massenet:
Manon). Ten. Son of the Comte Des Grieux.
Sees Manon and falls in love with her. He persuades her to abandon the idea of going to a
convent and she agrees to go and live with him
in Paris. She is coaxed away from their home
by de Brétigny, who can give her a life of luxury. Des Grieux decides to enter holy orders.
Manon comes to see him at the church where
he is preaching. He tries to resist her, but in the
end admits his love for her is as strong as ever
and they run away together. They join friends
in a gambling house, where Des Grieux is
accused of cheating and he and Manon are
arrested. Only the intervention of his father
frees him, but Manon is to be deported. Des
Grieux helps to rescue her, but her health has
suffered and she dies in his arms. Aria: *Ah,
fuyez douce image* ('Ah, fly away, sweet image
of love'). Created (1884) by Jean-Alexandre
Talazac.

2. (Puccini: *Manon Lescaut*). Ten. Drinking
with his friends at the local inn, he falls in love
with the young Manon Lescaut, who is being
escorted by her brother to a convent to complete her education. She returns his feeling
and they run away and set up home together.

When he runs out of money, Manon returns to
her older admirer, Geronte. Manon's brother
tells Des Grieux she still loves him and he
determines to find her again. She agrees to
return to him, but insists on stopping to collect
her jewellery. The delay results in her arrest as
a prostitute. She is to be deported and Des
Grieux begs the ship's captain to let him come
on board to be with her. They escape from the
ship and wander in the desert where Manon
becomes weak and ill. Des Grieux refuses to
leave her, but goes to search for water. When
he returns, Manon dies in his arms as he collapses next to her. Arias: *Donna non vidi mai
simile a questa!* ('Never have I seen such a
woman!'); *Ah! non v'avvicinate!* ('Ah! don't
come any nearer!'). Created (1893) by Giuseppe
Cremonini.

Des Grieux, Comte (Massenet: *Manon*).
Bass. Father of the Chevalier des Grieux. Tries
to persuade his son, when deserted by Manon,
not to enter holy orders. Created (1884) by
Mons. Cobalet.

De Sirieux (Giordano: *Fedora*). Bar. A French
diplomat, later Foreign Secretary, to whom
Fedora accuses Count Loris Ipanov of the
murder of her fiancé. Created (1898) by Delf-
ino Menotto.

Despina (Mozart: *Così fan tutte*). Sop. Maid
to Fiordiligi and Dorabella. Is bribed by
Alfonso to help him prove to their fiancés,
Guglielmo and Ferrando, that the sisters can
be unfaithful. When the two 'Albanians'
(Guglielmo and Ferrando in disguise) pretend
to take poison to gain the sisters' pity, the
Dr Mesmer who 'cures' them with a magnet is
the disguised Despina. And when the girls decide to marry these Albanian lovers, Despina,
disguised as the notary Beccavivi, provides
the marriage contract which they all sign.
Arias: *In uomini, in soldati* ('In men, in soldiers'); *Una donna a quindici anni* ('A woman
who's reached the age of 15'). Although designated in the score as a soprano, this role is
often sung by mezzos. Among notable interpreters (sop./mez.) are Elisabeth Schumann,
Roberta Peters, Emmy Loose, Graziella Sciutti,
Hanni Steffek, Lucia Popp, Nan Merriman,
Ileana Cotrubas, Reri Grist, Teresa Stratas,
Marie McLaughlin, Lillian Watson, Ann Murray, and Cecilia Bartoli. Created (1790) by

Dorothea Bussani (whose husband created Don Alfonso).

Desportes, Baron (Zimmermann: *Die Soldaten*). Ten. A young nobleman in the French Army. Seduces Marie, then hands her to his gamekeeper, who rapes her. Created (1965) by Anton de Ridder.

Devereux, Roberto, Earl of Essex
1. (Donizetti: *Roberto Devereux*). Ten. Roberto has returned after a failed military mission in Ireland and has been accused by his enemies of treason. He awaits trial and fears he will be condemned to death and that only the Queen's intervention can save him. Roberto is still loved by Elisabetta (Elizabeth I), but he is in love with Sara who, while he was abroad, has been pushed into marriage with his friend the Duke of Nottingham. He gives Sara the ring once given to him by the Queen, who promised that if he returned it to her she would guarantee his safety. Sara gives him a scarf, which is found next to his heart when he is searched. He waits in the Tower for the Queen's pardon. The Queen waits for him to send the ring to her so that she can reprieve him. But it is brought by Sara, too late—Roberto has been executed. Aria: *Come uno spirito angelico* ('Like an angelic spirit'). Created (1837) by Giovanni Basadonna.

2. (Britten: *Gloriana*). *See* ESSEX, EARL OF.

Dew Fairy (Humperdinck: *Hänsel und Gretel*). Sop. Wakens the sleeping children in the forest when morning comes. Created (1893) probably by Hermine Finck (who created the Witch, the roles often being doubled).

de Winter, Maxim (Josephs: *Rebecca*). Bar. Owner of Manderley, he has recently been widowed by the drowning of his beautiful wife, Rebecca. In Monte Carlo he meets the Girl and marries her, taking her home to Manderley. He loves his new wife, but she believes he is still in love with Rebecca. He is very angry when she wears a costume at the Manderley Ball which is the same one Rebecca wore the previous year. When a ship goes aground, he goes to help in the rescue. Rebecca's boat is found in the bay, her body still in the cabin. For the first time, Maxim confesses to his wife that he hated Rebecca, who was unfaithful to him. One of her old lovers accuses Maxim of killing her. He is able to prove that she knew she was dying of

cancer and drowned herself. Created (1983) by Peter Knapp.

de Winter, Mrs (Josephs: *Rebecca*). *See* GIRL, THE.

de Winter, Rebecca (Josephs: *Rebecca*). Does not appear in the opera which bears her name. She is the dead first wife of Maxim de Winter and her presence is felt throughout the opera.

Dialogues des Carmélites, Les (Dialogues of the Carmelites) (Poulenc). Lib. by composer; 3 acts; f.p. Milan 1957, cond. Nino Sanzogno.

Compiègne and Paris, 1789–92: The Marquis de la *Force worries about his highly strung daughter *Blanche. She announces her intention to join the Carmelite Order, hoping to find peace of mind. She is interviewed by the sick old Prioress, Mme de *Croissy. Sister *Constance has a premonition that she and Blanche will die together. The Prioress entrusts to Mother *Marie the care of Blanche. An outsider, Mme *Lidoine, is chosen as the new Prioress. The Chevalier de la *Force comes to visit his sister and accuses her of staying in the convent for reasons of fear, not devotion. The Father Confessor says his last Mass—he must go into hiding. The Convent is invaded and destroyed. Blanche escapes to her father's house. She hears that the members of the Convent have been arrested, the Father Confessor sentenced to death. The Prioress leads her nuns to the guillotine. Sister Constance is the last to mount the scaffold. She is joined by Blanche—they will die together as she prophesied.

Diana 1. (Cavalli: *La Calisto*). Sop. The chaste goddess, loved by Pan, but in love with Endymion. Creator (1651) unknown.

2. (Diane) (Gluck: *Iphigénie en Tauride*). Sop. The goddess who saves Iphigénie's brother Oreste from being sacrificed at the demand of the King Thoas. Creator (1779) not traced.

3. (Haydn: *La fedeltà premiata*). Sop. Goddess of the Hunt who unites all the pairs of lovers. Created (1781) by Costanza Valdesturla (who sang two roles).

4. (Diane) (Rameau: *Hippolyte et Aricie*). Sop. Goddess who vows to protect the young lovers. Creator (1733) unknown.

Dido 1. (Didon) (Berlioz: *Les Troyens*). Mez. Queen of Carthage, widow of Sychoeus, who was killed by her brother. She gives shelter to the Trojans, who have been shipwrecked near her castle, and falls in love with their leader, Aeneas. When he leaves her in order to fulfil his quest to build a new Troy in Italy, she builds a pyre to destroy all memories of him, stabs herself with his sword and ascends the pyre. Arias: *Chers Tyriens!* ('Dear Tyrians!'); *Adieu, fière cité …* ('Farewell, proud city'); duet (with Aeneas): *Nuit d'ivresse et d'extase infinie!* ('Night of unending ecstasy and rapture!'). Created (1890) by Anne Charton-Demeur.

2. (Purcell: *Dido and Aeneas*). Sop./mez. Queen of Carthage, falls in love with the Trojan Aeneas. A Sorceress plots Dido's downfall. When Aeneas leaves Carthage, Dido dies. Aria: *When I am laid in earth* (Dido's Lament). Created (1683/4) by an unknown schoolgirl.

Dido and Aeneas (Purcell). Lib. by Nahum Tate; 3 acts; f.p. Chelsea, London, probably 1683 or 1684.

Carthage, 13th cent. BC: After Troy's defeat by the Greeks, *Aeneas sails for Italy to found a new Troy (Rome). On the way, his boat comes ashore at Carthage and Queen *Dido falls in love with him. Her confidante, *Belinda, and the whole court are delighted. A *Sorceress plots Dido's downfall. Aeneas hears a spirit telling him to leave Carthage. As he departs, Dido dies.

Dikoj, Savël Prokofjevič (Janáček: *Katya Kabanová*). Bass. A wealthy merchant, uncle of Boris and a friend of the Kabanicha. Somewhat the worse for drink, he makes overtures to the Kabanicha, but is quickly repulsed. He and the young clerk Váňa Kudrjáš argue about the nature of storms. At the end of the opera, it is Dikoj who carries Katya's body from the Volga and places it in front of the Kabanicha. Created (1921) by Rudolf Kaulfus.

Dimitri (Musorgsky: *Boris Godunov*). *See* GRIGORI/DIMITRI.

Diomede (Walton: *Troilus and Cressida*). Bar. The Greek Prince of Argos, in love with the Trojan Cressida. Thinking Troilus has deserted her, Cressida agrees to marry Diomede. When Troilus returns, he and Diomede fight, and Troilus is stabbed in the back by Calkas, Cressida's father. Diomede insists that Cressida remain in the camp for the pleasure of the Greek soldiers. Created (1954) by Otakar Kraus.

Dionysus (Henze: *The Bassarids*). Ten. Leader of the Bacchantes (Greek Dionysus = Roman Bacchus). In disguise, he enables Pentheus to see his own subconscious sexual fantasies and persuades him to dress as a woman and go to Mount Cythaeron, where he is killed. Created (1966) by Loren Driscoll.

Dircé (Glauce) (Cherubini: *Médée*). Sop. Daughter of Créon, the King of Corinth. About to marry Jason, she is poisoned by his vengeful former lover, Médée, the mother of his two sons. Created (1797) by Mlle Rosine.

Diver, Jenny (Weill: *The Threepenny Opera*). Sop. A prostitute bribed by Mrs Peachum to reveal Macheath's hiding-place to the police. Created (1928) by Lotte Lenya (who had married Kurt Weill in 1926).

Doctor (Berg: *Wozzeck*). Bass. Doctor in the army barracks. Uses Wozzeck for dietary experiments. Created (1925) by Martin Abendroth.

Dodon, Tsar (Rimsky-Korsakov: *The Golden Cockerel*). Bass. Is given a Golden Cockerel by the Astrologer to warn him of danger. He leads his army against the enemy and meets the Queen of Shemakha. When he returns with her to his capital, the Astrologer demands her as reward. Dodon kills him and is then killed by the cockerel. Created (1909) by Nikolay Speransky.

Dollarama, Mr (Birtwistle: *The Second Mrs Kong*). Bar. Dead film producer. Created (1994) by Robert Poulton.

Dollarama, Mrs (Birtwistle: *The Second Mrs Kong*). *See* INANNA.

Dolokhov (Prokofiev: *War and Peace*). Bar. An officer, friend of Prince Anatol Kuragin. Creator (1945 vers.) not known; created (1946 vers.) by V. P. Runovsky.

Dominik (Strauss: *Arabella*). Bar. One of three Counts in love with, but rejected by, Arabella. Her mother is quite happy to flirt with the young count, who tells her she is more beautiful than her daughter. Created (1933) by Kurt Böhme.

Domšík of the Bell (Janáček: *The Excursions of Mr Brouček*). Bar. Father of Kunka, he befriends Brouček when he returns to the

Prague of 1420. He is later killed in the Hussite War. His other manifestations are the Sacristan in 1888 Prague and Lunobar on the Moon. Created (1920) by Vilém Zítek.

Donati, Buoso (Puccini: *Gianni Schicchi*). This character, a wealthy old man, is dead at the start of the opera—his relatives are gathered round his bed waiting to find out what his will contains. Rumour has it that he has left all his fortune to a monastery.

Don Carlos (It. vers. *Don Carlo*) (Verdi). Lib. by Joseph Méry and Camille du Locle; rev. by du Locle and trans. into It. by Angelo Zanardini; 5/4 acts; f.p. Paris 1867 (Fr. vers.), cond. Georges Hainl (described below); Milan 1884 (It. vers.), cond. Franco Faccio.

France and Spain, *c.*1560: Don *Carlos has come to France to meet Elisabeth de *Valois, to whom he is engaged. Not recognized by her, Carlos shows her a portrait of the Spanish Infante and she realizes who he is. Her servant *Thibault brings the news that Elisabeth must marry Carlos's father, King *Philip II of Spain. For the sake of her country, she agrees. By the tomb of the Emperor Charles V at San Yuste monastery, Carlos notices that one of the monks strongly resembles his late grandfather. Carlos's great friend Rodrigo, Marquis of *Posa, advises Carlos to go to Flanders to help the oppressed people there. Elisabeth, now Queen, is with her ladies of the court, including Princess *Eboli, when Posa brings her a letter from Carlos asking to see her—he wants her to persuade his father to send him to Flanders. Eboli hopes that Carlos is in love with her. Posa puts the case for the freedom of Flanders to King Philip, who warns him to beware of the *Grand Inquisitor. On the eve of his Coronation, Elisabeth asks Eboli to dress in her clothes and deputize for her. Carlos, thinking she is Elisabeth, declares his love, and is horrified when Eboli removes her veil. She realizes he and the Queen are lovers and vows to expose them. In front of the Cathedral of Valladolid, the people are gathered for an *auto-da-fé* (the burning of the heretics). Carlos begs his father to send him to Flanders, but Philip refuses. Carlos flourishes his sword, is overpowered and taken to prison. In his wife's jewellery casket, Philip finds a miniature portrait of Carlos and accuses her of adultery. Eboli admits her part in the exposure of the Queen and also

confesses that she has been the King's mistress. As Posa visits Carlos in prison, he is shot; Eboli helps Carlos escape. At the San Yuste monastery, Elisabeth says goodbye to Carlos. They are interrupted by the King and the Grand Inquisitor, and as Carlos backs away from them, King Charles's tomb opens and the old Emperor appears, pulling Carlos into the monastery.

Don Giovanni (Mozart). Lib. by Lorenzo da Ponte; 2 acts; f.p. Prague 1787.

Seville, 17th cent.: Don *Giovanni has gone into the *Commendatore's house to seduce his daughter, Donna *Anna. *Leporello waits outside for his master. The Commendatore chases Giovanni, who kills him. Anna, with her betrothed, Don *Ottavio, finds her dead father, and swears she will take revenge on his killer. Donna *Elvira, a past conquest whom he has deserted, is searching for the Don. Leporello tries to send her away by describing Giovanni's terrible character. Giovanni comes upon the party for the forthcoming wedding of *Masetto and *Zerlina and takes a fancy to the girl. She is saved from seduction by Elvira. Anna recognizes Giovanni's voice as that of her father's assassin and plots with Elvira and Ottavio to reveal him. The three conspirators arrive at Giovanni's banquet in masked costumes. They remove their masks and accuse him of murder but again he escapes. Giovanni comes upon the Commendatore's statue in a graveyard, and the statue speaks to him. Giovanni invites him to dinner. When the Don shakes hands with him at their banquet, the Commendatore throws him into the flames of hell.

Donner (Wagner: *Das Rheingold*). Bass-bar. The god of thunder. Brother of Fricka, Freia, and Froh and brother-in-law of Wotan. He has a tendency to think he can solve most things by lashing out with his hammer. He threatens the giants with it when they are about to abduct Freia, and Loge when he can't solve that situation quickly enough. Each time he has to be restrained by Wotan. Once Freia has been taken by the giants, he becomes much more subdued and lethargic, ready to pay them anything to release his sister. It is Donner who orders Froh to point the way to the rainbow bridge so the gods can walk across it to Valhalla. Aria: *Schwäles Gedünst schwebt in der Luft* ('A sultry haze hangs in the air'). Created (1869) by Karl Heinrich.

Don Pasquale (Donizetti). Lib. by Giovanni Ruffini; 3 acts; f.p. Paris 1843.

Rome, early 19th cent.: *Pasquale asks Dr *Malatesta his chances of producing a direct heir—he wants to disinherit his nephew, *Ernesto, who loves *Norina. Malatesta recommends as a bride his 'sister Sofronia' and enlists Norina's help in bringing Pasquale to his senses. 'Sofronia' is led in (Norina, disguised), blindfolded and demure. A wedding contract is prepared by 'a *Notary' (Malatesta's cousin), giving his bride half of Pasquale's worldly goods. Once 'married', 'Sofronia' becomes very dominant, demands many luxuries and causes Pasquale great distress at the money she is spending. She deliberately lets Pasquale know she has a meeting with somebody in the garden. He indeed catches his 'wife' and Ernesto together. Malatesta persuades him to annul his marriage and allow Norina and Ernesto to get married. Relieved to be free again, Pasquale blesses the couple.

Don Quichotte (Massenet). Lib. by Henri Cain; 5 acts; f.p. Monte Carlo 1910, cond. Léon Jéhin.

Spain, the Middle Ages: Don *Quichotte and his servant Sancho *Panza arrive in the square where *Dulcinée is being courted by four men. Quichotte serenades Dulcinée and one of her suitors is jealous and challenges him to a duel. Dulcinée prevents a fight and sends Quichotte off to find her necklace, stolen by a bandit. In the mist Quichotte mistakes windmills for giants and attacks them and is carried up on one of the sails. The bandits are won over by Quichotte's chivalry and give him the necklace they have stolen. He returns it to Dulcinée but still she will not marry him. Don Quichotte dies, imagining Dulcinée in the heavens.

Dorabella (Mozart: *Così fan tutte*). Sop./mez. Sister of Fiordiligi. She is engaged to Ferrando, whose friend Guglielmo is her sister's fiancé. The cynical Alfonso is determined to prove to his friends that all women are fickle and enlists the help of the sisters' maid, Despina. He tricks the sisters into accepting the overtures of two 'Albanians', who are their own fiancés in disguise. At first the sisters reject their overtures, but Dorabella is the first to weaken and decide 'I'll take the dark one'! This is really her sister's fiancé, Guglielmo. After Fiordiligi has also capitulated, a fake double wedding takes place—the notary is the disguised Despina. The marriage contracts are signed and almost immediately the real fiancés return. Who will Dorabella settle for? Arias: *Smanie implacabile* ('May those terrible pangs'); *È amore un ladroncello* ('Love's like a little thief'). Dorabella is the weaker—or flightier—of the two sisters, as witness the fact that she is the first to yield to the overtures of one of the 'Albanians'. In the score Dorabella is a soprano, but it is one of several operatic roles which has been taken over by mezzos. Notable Dorabellas of the past 50 years include Blanche Thebom, Christa Ludwig, Nan Merriman, Tatyana Troyanos, Teresa Berganza, Janet Baker, Brigitte Fassbaender, Frederica von Stade, Maria Ewing, Anne Howells, Marie McLaughlin, Ann Murray, Jennifer Larmore, Susan Graham, Vesselina Kasarova, and Monica Groop (some of whom have also been successful Despinas). Created (1790) by Louise Villeneuve (whose sister created Fiordiligi).

Dörfling, Field Marshal (Henze: *Der Prinz von Homburg*). Bar. His orders on the battlefield are ignored by the Prince, but the Marshal is so impressed by the Prince's honesty that he tears up the death warrant. Created (1960) by Herbert Fliether.

Dorinda (Handel: *Orlando*). Sop. A shepherdess in love with Medoro, and very jealous of his relationship with Angelica. Created (1733) by Celeste Gismondi.

Dorothée (Massenet: *Cendrillon*). Mez. Daughter of Mme de la Haltière, sister of Noémie (they are the 'ugly sisters' of the fairytale), and stepsister of Cendrillon (Cinderella). Created (1899) by Marie de Lisle.

Dosifei (Musorgsky: *Khovanshchina*). Bass. A monk, leader of the Old Believers, who sides with the Khovanskys and dies with them rather than be captured by the Tsar's troops. Creator (1886) unknown; (1911) by Fyodor Chaliapin. It became one of his most famous and inspired roles.

Doubek (Janáček: *Osud*). Boy sop./ten. Illegitimate son of Míla and Živný. Created (radio, 1934) by unknown artist; (stage, 1958) by Milena Jilková/Bohumir Kurfirst.

Douphol, Baron (Verdi: *La traviata*). Bar. Violetta's 'protector'. When Violetta leaves

Alfredo, she writes him a letter telling him she has decided to return to Douphol. Created (1853) by Francesco Dragone.

Dreigroschenoper, Die (Weill). See THREE-PENNY OPERA, THE.

Drum-major (Berg: *Wozzeck*). Ten. He has an affair with Wozzeck's girl, Marie, and the two men fight. Created (1925) by Fritz Soot.

Drummer (Ullmann: *Der Kaiser von Atlantis*). Mez. Announces a state of total war and decrees that everyone shall respect the Emperor. Created (1944) by Hilde Aronson-Lindt; (1975) by Inge Frolich.

Drusilla (Monteverdi: *L'incoronazione di Poppea*). Sop. Lady-in-waiting to Empress Ottavia, wife of Nerone. Wrongly accused of attempting to murder Poppea. Creator (1643) not known.

Dryad (Strauss: *Ariadne auf Naxos*). Cont. One of three nymphs who watch over the sleeping Ariadne on the Island of Naxos. Trio (with Naiad and Echo): *Ein schönes Wunder!* ('A beautiful miracle!'). Created (1912) by Lilly Hoffmann-Onegin; (1916) by Hermine Kittel.

Duke (Massenet: *Chérubin*). Ten. Guardian of Nina, he mistrusts Chérubin's relationship with her, but eventually gives his consent to their marriage. Created (1905) by Mons. Nerval.

Duke Bluebeard's Castle (Bartók). Lib. by Béla Balázs; 1 act; f.p. Budapest 1918, cond. Egisto Tango.

Legendary times: *Judith has married *Bluebeard and returned with him to his castle, which is gloomy and damp. There are seven doors in the big hall. She wants to open a door to let in light and warm air. Bluebeard gives her a key. She opens the first door and finds the walls covered in blood—it is a torture chamber. Behind the second door is Bluebeard's armoury, also bloodstained. The third reveals the treasury of jewels and robes (with blood on them), the fourth the garden (blood-spotted flowers), the fifth Bluebeard's kingdom (the clouds above are blood-red). Despite his reluctance, she opens door No. 6 to reveal a lake of tears. Judith questions Bluebeard and realizes he has killed his former wives. As the seventh door swings open of its own accord, three former wives appear. Bluebeard dresses Judith in the gown, jewels, and crown she has brought from the treasury and she follows the other wives back through the last door, which closes behind them, leaving Bluebeard once again alone.

Dulcamara (Donizetti: *L'elisir d'amore*). Bass. A quack doctor. He sells a love potion to Nemorino to help him win Adina. The potion is in reality wine and Nemorino, under its influence, develops more courage. Adina learns the full story from Dulcamara and confesses her love for Nemorino. Aria: *Uditi, udite, o rustici* ('Listen, listen, O villagers'). A celebrated Dulcamara, Sir Geraint Evans, chose this as his farewell role at the Royal Opera House, Covent Garden, in 1984. Created (1832) by Giuseppe Frezzolini.

Dulcinée (Massenet: *Don Quichotte*). Cont. Adored by many men who all want to marry her. She rejects Don Quichotte's proposal and sends him to look for her necklace, supposedly stolen by a bandit. When he returns it to her, she kisses him, but still refuses to marry him. Aria: *C'est un fou sublime* ('He is a madman of genius'). Created (1910) by Lucy Arbell.

Duncan, King (Verdi: *Macbeth*). Silent role. He is the King of Scotland, father of Malcolm. He declares Macbeth to be thane of Cawdor and is stabbed to death by Macbeth in his ambition to become king. Creator (1847) unknown.

Dunstable, The Duke of (Sullivan: *Patience*). Ten. Dragoon Lieutenant who proposes to Jane. Created (1881) by Durward Lely.

Durham, Lady Harriet (Flotow: *Martha*). See MARTHA (1).

Dutchman (Wagner: *Der fliegende Holländer*). Bar. Long, long ago, the Dutchman tried to sail round the Cape of Good Hope in a furious storm and swore an oath that he would succeed even if it meant sailing for ever. Overhearing this, the Devil condemned him to sail for ever—only if he found a woman who would be faithful to him for life would he be released. Every seven years he is allowed to go on land to search for such a woman. It is the end of seven years and he sails into the Norwegian coast, alongside Daland's ship. The two men meet and he asks permission to meet and marry Daland's daughter, Senta. In return, he offers

Daland great wealth. Daland takes him home to meet Senta, who recognizes him from the portrait which hangs on the wall in their house. The two are immediately attracted to each other, but the Dutchman overhears Erik declaring his love for Senta and assumes she has been unfaithful to him. Thinking himself doomed to sail the seas for the next seven years, he leaves. Senta leaps into the sea in an attempt to follow him. His ship slowly sinks and the two of them are seen rising together above the vessel. Arias: *Die frist ist um* ('The time is up'); *Durch Sturm und bösen Wind verschlagen* ('Driven on through storms and violent winds'); duet (with Senta): *Wie aus der ferne längst vergang'ner Zeiten* ('As from the distance of time long ago'). Created (1843) by Michael Wächter (whose wife created Senta's nurse, Mary).

Dwarf (Zemlinsky: *Der Zwerg*). Ten. Unaware of his own deformity, the Dwarf (*der Zwerg* of the opera's title) has been given as a present to the Infanta, Donna Clara, on her birthday. They become playmates and he falls in love with her. She gives him a white rose, but her love for him is simply childlike. He dislodges a curtain covering a mirror in the palace and sees his own reflection for the first time. Horrified, he begs Clara's assurance that this is not truly his appearance. Cruelly, she tells him she will continue to play with him, but not as a human, only as the animal she considers him to be. Heartbroken, and clutching the white rose, he dies. Created (1922) by Karl Schröder.

Dyer's Wife (Die Färberin) (Strauss: *Die Frau ohne Schatten*). Sop. She has been married to Barak, the Dyer, for over two years but they have not had any children. They have a humble home in which Barak's three brothers also live. She is something of a shrew, but she loves her husband. While he is away selling his cloths, she is visited by the Empress and her Nurse. The Empress is anxious to acquire a shadow—the symbol of fertility—and her Nurse suggests that the Dyer's Wife sells her shadow to the Empress in return for a life of luxury. She is tempted by the thought of an easier life, and at one point tells her husband that she *has* sold it, even though she has not. He is so distressed at the thought of not having a family that he threatens to kill her. She then admits this was not the truth. She and Barak are separated by supernatural forces and each sings of their feelings. When the Empress realizes the distress it will cause if she takes the Wife's shadow, she cancels the Nurse's suggestion. Barak and his Wife are reunited and they hear the voices of their unborn children. Aria: *Barak, ich hab' es nicht getan!* ('Barak, I did not do it!'); duet (with Barak): *Dir angetraut* ('Wedded to you'). Created (1919) by Lotte Lehmann. Since the première this has been a favourite role for Strauss sopranos, among whom have been Eva von der Osten, Viorica Ursuleac, Rosa Pauly, Marianne Schech, Leonie Rysanek, Christel Goltz, Elisabeth Höngen, Birgit Nilsson, Inge Borkh, Christa Ludwig, Gwyneth Jones (*see* EMPRESS), Hildegard Behrens, Pauline Tinsley, Eva Marton, and Christine Brewer.

E

Eboli, Princess (Verdi: *Don Carlos*). Mez. Lady-in-waiting to Elisabeth de Valois (who becomes Queen of Spain). She is in love with the Spanish Infante, Don Carlos, who was betrothed to Elisabeth until his father decided to marry her himself. On the night before the Coronation, Elisabeth sends Eboli to represent her at the festivities—there is a masked ball and Eboli is masked and dressed in the Queen's clothes. Carlos mistakes her for Elisabeth and pours out his love for her. Eboli, realizing that he and the Queen are lovers, determines to expose them to the King (with whom she has had an adulterous relationship). When she admits her role in encouraging the King's jealousy, and begs the Queen's pardon, Elisabeth gives her a choice—exile or a nunnery. Before leaving, she helps Carlos escape from prison where his father has kept him incarcerated. Aria (with chorus): *Au palais des fées* ('In the fairy palace')—known as the Song of the Veil, this is a lovely display-aria for a mez. with a wide range; *O don fatal* ('O fatal gift'). Eboli is traditionally portrayed wearing an eye-patch. There is much controversy about the authenticity of this patch. It is variously said that she needed to wear it because of an injury to her eye in childhood; that she wore it to hide a squint; or that it was worn just to add to the effect of her appearance. Created (Fr. vers. 1867) by Pauline Gueymard-Lauters; (It. vers. 1884) by Giuseppina Pasqua.

Ecclitico, Dr (Haydn: *Il mondo della luna*). Ten. An astrologer in love with Clarice, daughter of Buonafede, who opposes the marriage. Together with his friends, Ecclitico transports Buonafede to 'the moon'—actually Ecclitico's garden changed to look like a lunar landscape. Here Buonafede agrees to his daughter's marriage. Created (1777) probably by Guglielmo

Jermoli (whose wife created Buonafede's maid Lisetta).

Echo (Strauss: *Ariadne auf Naxos*). Sop. One of three nymphs who guard the sleeping Ariadne on the Island of Naxos. Trio (with Dryad and Naiad): *Ein schönes Wunder!* ('A beautiful miracle!'). Created (1912) by Erna Ellmenreich; (1916) by Carola Jovanovič.

Eckbert, Blond (Weir: *Blond Eckbert*). Bar. Husband of Bertha, they live an isolated life. Their only friend is Walther, but Eckbert is suspicious of his friendship with Bertha and kills Walther. When Bertha dies, Eckbert goes off into the wilderness and meets the old woman who brought Bertha up. She reveals that Bertha, his wife, was really his sister who had been abandoned in childhood by their father. The shock drives Eckbert insane and he dies. Created (1994) by Nicholas Folwell.

Edgardo (Donizetti: *Lucia di Lammermoor*). *See* RAVENSWOOD, EDGAR.

Edmondo (Puccini: *Manon Lescaut*). Ten. A student and friend of Des Grieux. Aria (with chorus of students): *Ave, sera gentile* ('Hail, gentle evening'). Created (1893) by Roberto Ramini.

Edrisi (Szymanowski: *King Roger*). Ten. An Arabian sage who warns King Roger about the Shepherd who preaches the new faith of beauty and pleasure. Created (1926) by Maurcy Janowski.

Eduige (Handel: *Rodelinda*). Sop. Sister of King Bertarido of Lombardy. Created (1725) by Anna Vincenza Dotti.

Edwin Ronald, Prince (Kálmán: *Die Csárdásfürstin*). Ten. Son of the Prince and Princess von und zu Lippert-Wehlersheim. His parents want him to marry his cousin Stasi, but he is in love with Sylva, a cabaret singer. When he discovers that his mother in her youth was a singer, his parents' objections to his marriage are overcome. Created (1915) by Karl Bachmann.

Egberto (Verdi: *Aroldo*). Bar. An elderly knight, father of Mina. He kills the man with whom his daughter has an adulterous affair while her husband is fighting in the Crusades. Created (1857) by Ferri Gaetano. *See also* STANKAR, COUNT.

Egisto, L' (Cavalli). Lib. by Giovanni Faustini; prol. and 3 acts; f.p. Venice 1643.

Mythological Greece: *Egisto and *Clori, *Lidio and *Climene, are two pairs of lovers captured by pirates and separated. Egisto and Climene have escaped their captors and set out to find their lovers. But Clori and Lidio have fallen in love with each other. Climene cannot bring herself to kill Lidio and asks that she should die instead. Moved by her request, Lidio falls in love with her again. Clori is sorry for Egisto, who has gone mad, and returns to him.

Egisto (Cavalli: *L'Egisto*). Ten. A descendant of Apollo. Lover of Clori, from whom he is separated by pirates. Goes mad with despair and Clori returns to him. Creator (1643) not known.

Eglantine (Weber: *Euryanthe*). Mez. A guest and supposed friend of Euryanthe, she loves Euryanthe's fiancé, Adolar, and persuades her hostess to betray his trust, thus convincing him of her disloyalty. When Adolar learns the truth, Eglantine is killed by the man she is about to marry. Created (1823) by Thérese Grünbaum.

Eisenstein, Gabriel von (J. Strauss II: *Die Fledermaus*). Ten. Husband of Rosalinde. He has committed a minor offence which carries a short prison sentence and is preparing to serve it. His friend Dr Falke collects him and they pretend to leave for the prison. In reality they go to Prince Orlofsky's ball. There Eisenstein, introduced as 'Marquis Renard' meets 'Chevalier Chagrin' and the two men converse in terrible French. He flirts with a masked Hungarian countess, not knowing it is his wife. Among the guests he recognizes Adele, his wife's maid. At 6 a.m. he leaves for the prison. On arrival he finds that 'Chevalier Chagrin' is

Frank, the prison governor, and that his cell is already occupied—by his wife's singing-teacher, Alfred. Rosalinde and Falke both arrive at the gaol and the confusion is sorted out. Created (1874) by Jani Szika.

Eisenstein, Rosalinde von (J. Strauss II: *Die Fledermaus*). Sop. Wife of Gabriel von Eisenstein. When he leaves to serve a prison sentence, she is serenaded by her singing-teacher, Alfred. She goes to Prince Orlofsky's ball, masked and gowned as a Hungarian countess, and her husband does not recognize her. Also at the ball is her maid, who has 'borrowed' one of her mistress's dresses. Aria: *Klänge der Heimat* ('Strains of my homeland'—the Csárdás). Created (1874) by Marie Geistinger.

Eisslinger, Ulrich (Wagner: *Die Meistersinger von Nürnberg*). Ten. One of the *Meistersinger*, his trade being that of a grocer. Created (1868) by Herr Hoppe.

Elcia (Rossini: *Mosè in Egitto*). *See* ANAÏS.

Elderly Fop (Britten: *Death in Venice*). Bass-bar. A passenger on board the boat taking Aschenbach to Venice. He leads a song about life in Venice. Created (1973) by John Shirley-Quirk.

Elders (Floyd: *Susannah*). The four village Elders (McLean, Gleaton, Hayes, and Ott) who, while trying to find a suitable pool to be used for communal baptism, peer through the trees and see Susannah bathing, naked. Because the sight of her arouses them, they accuse her of shamelessness and encourage the villagers to denounce her and force her to confess her 'sins'. Created (1955) by (respectively) Harrison Fisher, Kenneth Nelson, Dayton Smith, and Lee Liming.

Eléazar (Halévy: *La Juive*). Ten. Jewish goldsmith, father of Rachel. Aria: *Rachel, quand du Seigneur* ('Rachel, when God in his wisdom'). A favourite role of Enrico Caruso. Created (1835) by Adolphe Nourrit (for whom the role was written. It is thought he helped compose parts of the opera, notably the famous aria mentioned above).

Elegy for Young Lovers (Henze). Lib. by W. H. Auden and Chester Kallman; 5 acts; f.p. Schwetzingen 1961, cond. Heinrich Bender.

Austrian Alps, 1910: The poet *Mittenhofer returns every year to write his spring poem. With him are his secretary *Carolina, his doctor, *Reischmann, and his young companion Elisabeth *Zimmer. The doctor's son Toni *Reischmann is also there. At the inn is Hilda *Mack, whose bridegroom was killed on the Hammerhorn on their honeymoon 40 years ago. Crazy, she still waits for his return. The guide Joseph *Maurer tells them a body has been found in a glacier. Elisabeth consoles Hilda. Toni falls in love with Elisabeth, much to the poet's fury. The lovers set off for the mountain slope but are trapped by bad weather and resigned to their death on the mountain. Mittenhofer's poem reflects these events.

Elektra (Strauss). Lib. by Hugo von Hofmannsthal; 1 act; f.p. Dresden 1909, cond. Ernst von Schuch.

Mycenae, ancient times: Queen *Klytämnestra and *Aegisth have murdered her husband Agamemnon. Klytämnestra has two daughters, *Chrysothemis and *Elektra. Elektra awaits the return of her brother Orest (*Orestes) and dreams of avenging her father's death. Klytämnestra consults Elektra about the bad dreams she is having. Elektra tells her they will stop only when someone has been sacrificed, and that sacrifice will be the queen herself. False news of Orest's death reaches them. Elektra realizes that she will have to do the deed single-handed. Orest returns and she urges him to avenge their father. He enters the palace and soon Klytämnestra's screams are heard. Aegisth arrives and meets the same fate as his wife. Elektra's dance of joy becomes her dance of death.

Elektra (Strauss: *Elektra*). Sop. Elektra is one of three children of Klytämnestra and Agamemnon, her sister being Chrysothemis and her brother Orest. When Agamemnon returned from fighting in the Trojan War, he found his wife had taken her lover, Aegisth, to live with her in the palace. Aegisth and Klytämnestra murdered Agamemnon in his bath. Elektra sent Orest away to a safe haven, whilst she and her sister remained at the palace. Elektra is forced to live in the grounds like the animals. Only the youngest of the maids treats her with respect, reminding the others that Elektra is still a princess. She is beaten for her loyalty.

Elektra has buried the axe which was used to murder her father, determined it will be used to avenge his death. Klytämnestra demands to know from Elektra the cure for the nightmares she is having—only the sacrifice of herself will do, her daughter tells her. News (false) arrives of the death of Orest, and Elektra knows she will have to take revenge single-handed, her sister being too frightened to help her. A man enters the courtyard, and slowly Elektra recognizes her brother. She will not let him hold her—she is ashamed of the way she looks after living rough. She impresses on him that it is his duty to avenge their father. While he is in the palace killing Klytämnestra, Aegisth arrives at the gates. Elektra offers to light his way into the palace, and then hears his screams as he meets the same fate as her mother. Elektra's wild dance of triumph ends in her collapse and death. Aria: *Allein! Weh, ganz allein* ('Alone! Alas, all alone'); *Was bluten muss?* ('What blood must flow'); *Orest! Orest!* ('Orestes! Orestes!'—this is the famous Recognition Scene, as Elektra realizes that news of his death was false and he is now here to help her avenge their father).

For all her frenetic rantings and obsession with revenge, the emotion which motivates many of her actions is love—love of her dead father Agamemnon (Michael Kennedy describes her as 'Strauss's Brünnhilde … a classic case of father-fixation'), love for her weaker sister Chrysothemis (even though she curses her when she refuses to help with the murders), and love for her brother Orest, for whose safety she has always been concerned and in whose return she has always had faith. This is one of Strauss's earliest parts for a strong dramatic soprano, and many distinguished artists have appeared in the role, including Marie Gutheil-Schoder, Rosa Pauly, Erna Schlüter, Astrid Varnay, Ingrid Bjoner, Inge Borkh, Christel Goltz, Birgit Nilsson, Anja Silja, Gwyneth Jones, Eva Marton, and Susan Bullock. Created (1909) by Annie Krull. *See also* ELETTRA. *See also* ARTICLE BY SUSAN BULLOCK, p. 78.

Elemer (Strauss: *Arabella*). Ten. One of three Counts in love with Arabella. He is probably the one of whom she is most fond, and she agrees to go for a sleighride with him—but only on condition that her 'brother Zdenko', comes with them. He is eventually rejected by

ELEKTRA (*Elektra*—Strauss)

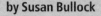

by Susan Bullock

Richard Strauss's Elektra is one of the most strenuous roles in the operatic repertoire. For any soprano undertaking this part, there are a myriad of challenges to overcome, both vocally and dramatically. Elektra is a highly complex woman. She is forced to live in squalor outside the Palace, due to her desire to avenge the murder of her beloved father Agamemnon by her mother Klytämnestra and her mother's lover Aegisth. Elektra's opening monologue sets out her plans for revenge, and is in itself a mammoth piece of singing, encompassing a wide range of vocal colours, from the plangent childlike yearnings to see her father again, to the full-blooded phrases which eventually climb up to a triumphant top C, when she envisages dancing in victory on her father's grave. She dreams of achieving this with the help of her sister Chrysothemis, who lives in the Palace, and her brother Orest who has, since childhood, been exiled by their mother. But Chrysothemis resents Elektra's obsession, feeling it is ruining her chances of having a normal life as a wife and mother. Elektra hopes, deep in her heart, that one day Orest will return and help her.

Strauss employs a vast musical language to express all the twists and turns of Elektra's character. When Chrysothemis talks of freedom and marriage, Elektra uses great sarcasm and violence and at the same time a beautiful lyric sweetness when she tries to persuade her to be an accomplice in the murders. This constant changing of style demands great versatility from an Elektra, and huge attention to Strauss's scrupulous dynamic markings in order to achieve the right sound; the orchestral accompaniment is sometimes so overwhelming that the voice becomes just another part of the overall colour, and at other times (for example when Elektra sings *Von jetzt an will ich deine schwester sein* ('From now on I will be a proper sister') to Chrysothemis), the scoring is almost chamber-music-like in its transparency. In her big confrontation scene with the desperate Klytämnestra, who needs Elektra's help to rid herself of tormented dreams of the murders, Strauss captures perfectly the enigmatic, almost monosyllabic, behaviour of a moody teenage child talking to a parent. He uses a spare, teasing colour in the voice and in the orchestra building up the tension perfectly, before Elektra finally erupts in fury in another vocally challenging passage as she tells her mother that it is indeed Klytämnestra who will be the final sacrifice necessary to assuage her guilt.

When Chrysothemis refuses to help in the murders, following an extraordinary scene between the two sisters which is almost like whispered speech (*Nun muss es hier von uns geschehen*—'Now it is left for us to do'), Elektra decides to act alone, as she has already been told by Chrysothemis (mistakenly) that Orest is dead. However, a strange man arrives, and explains that he needs to see Klytämnestra to confirm that her son Orest is indeed dead. Elektra, now hell bent on destruction, has no time for this man and tells him to leave. He feels that there is something familiar about her and eventually she reveals that she is, despite her ragged appearance, descended from Agamemnon, and is the Princess Elektra. The stranger in turn reveals that he is Orest, her brother, not dead at all, but on a mission to kill Klytämnestra and Aegisth. The famous 'Recognition Scene' when Elektra says that she can now die happy because he has returned, is one of the most beautiful and testing passages in the opera, calling for pure lyrical singing with a true legato line. Orest goes into the Palace to fulfil his mission, and the cries of Klytämnestra's murder fill the air. Aegisth arrives, gloating about the news that Orest is dead, but is shocked and somewhat disarmed to find Elektra being incredibly sweet to him, and using all her feminine wiles to persuade him to go into the Palace, where she knows he too will meet his end. In this scene, Strauss employs the Viennese waltz to emphasize the faux saccharine quality of Elektra's mood. In complete contrast to the preceding highly dramatic and often very violent music, this scene comes as a relief in its lightness of touch, but at the same time, that lightness is laden with danger.

The Aegisth scene offers Elektra a chance to gather her vocal resources before the final part of the opera, which is one of the great Strauss *finales* for female voices. Chrysothemis emerges, bringing news that Orest is within the Palace walls and that the murders have been accomplished. The two sisters sing a final duet, each expressing their own reaction to the news. The two voices weave around each other, whilst the chorus sings offstage, proclaiming Orest, and the orchestra whips up into a frenzy during which Elektra dances herself to death. Her work is done, and despite all the joy around her, she now has nothing else to live for.

The role of Elektra is often misrepresented. It is not just about 'loud' singing. On the contrary it is about enormous stamina, power, subtlety, beautiful line, meticulous attention to dynamic detail and vocal colour, and above all the ability to declaim the text in the same way that an actress in the straight theatre would in order to show the many layers of this fascinating character.

her in favour of Mandryka. Created (1933) by Karl Albrecht-Streib.

Elena (Boito: *Mefistofele*). *See* HELEN OF TROY (4).

Elettra (Mozart: *Idomeneo*). Sop. Greek princess, daughter of Agamemnon. In love with Idamante, son of Idomeneo but realizes she is losing him to the Trojan Princess Ilia. Aria: *Oh smania!* ('O madness'). Created (1781) by Elisabeth Wendling. *See also* ELEKTRA.

Elisabeth 1. (Wagner: *Tannhäuser*). Sop. Niece of the Landgrave. She and Tannhäuser have been in love, but he has been enticed away by Venus and Elisabeth longs for his return. He comes back to take part in the annual song contest and the Landgrave, confident that Tannhäuser will win, offers Elisabeth's hand as the prize. To everyone's horror and disgust, Tannhäuser, influenced by his bacchanalian life with Venus, sings of the sensual aspects of love and the other knights threaten to kill him. Elisabeth throws herself in front of Tannhäuser, prepared to sacrifice herself for him. Tannhäuser is sent to Rome to seek absolution and Elisabeth waits for his return. Feeling there is no hope of his coming back, she dies shortly before he arrives. In answer to Wolfram's prayer, her soul gives Tannhäuser the absolution he craves and he falls across her coffin and dies. Aria: *Dich, teure Halle, grüsse' ich wieder ...* ('Dear Hall of Song, I greet you again'); *Allmächt'ge Jungfrau, hör' mein Flehen!* ('Almighty Virgin, hear my pleading!'). Among notable singers of this role are Meta Seinemeyer, Maria Reining, Maria Müller, Trudi Epperle, Marianne Schech, Leonie Rysanek, Elisabeth Grümmer, Anja Silja, Birgit Nilsson, and Mechthild Gessendorf. Created (1845) by Johanna Wagner.

2. (Verdi: *Don Carlos*). *See* VALOIS, ELISABETH DE.

3. (Henze: *Elegy for Young Lovers*). *See* ZIMMER, ELISABETH.

4. (Maw: *The Rising of the Moon*). *See* ZASTROW, FRAU ELISABETH VON.

5. For Elizabeth I of England, *see* ELISABETTA (1)–(3).

Elisabetta 1. (Donizetti: *Maria Stuarda*). Sop. Queen Elizabeth I of England, daughter of Henry VIII and Anne Boleyn. On her orders, her cousin, Mary Stuart, is held captive in Fotheringay Castle, Mary being her rival for the throne and the love of Leicester. He begs the Queen to see Mary. She does so and there is the famous (but non-historical) confrontation. Elizabeth accuses Mary of treachery and of being involved in the murder of her own husband, Darnley. Mary calls her a vile bastard. Encouraged by Cecil, Elizabeth signs Mary's death warrant. Created (1834, as Irene) by Anna del Serre; (1835) by Maria Malibran.

2. (Donizetti: *Roberto Devereux*). Sop. The Queen is still in love with Devereux, Earl of Essex. She gave him a ring and promised that if he ever returned it to her she would guarantee his safety. He has returned from Ireland and been accused by his enemies of treason. She does not believe this of him, but she does suspect he is unfaithful to her. When she is shown a scarf found near his heart when he was arrested and searched, she recognizes it as belonging to Sara, Duchess of Nottingham, thus confirming her suspicions. As Essex awaits execution, the Queen waits for the ring to arrive so she can reprieve him. It comes too late, brought by Sara as Essex is executed. Aria: *L'amor suo mi fe'beata* ('His love is a blessing to me'); *Vivi ingrato, a lei d'accanto* ('Live, ungrateful man, at her side'). Created (1837) by Giuseppina Ronzi de Begnis.

3. (Britten: *Gloriana*). Sop. Queen Elizabeth I. Cecil warns the Queen to beware of Essex, but she assures him that, though she and Essex do have a close relationship, she is not seeking a husband. The Queen attends the Norwich Masque. At a dance in the Palace of Whitehall, the Queen changes into Lady Essex's dress, and is humiliated by her own ridiculous appearance. She appoints Essex Lord Deputy of Ireland. He returns when his campaign to conquer Tyrone fails and bursts in on the Queen whilst she is dressing and without her wig. Ultimately she is obliged to sign Essex's death warrant. The Queen, in spoken words in the epilogue, addresses the House of Commons. Arias: *Hark, sir! This ring I had at my crowning*; *On rivalries 'tis safe for kings to base their power*. Created (1953) by Joan Cross (and performed memorably by Josephine Barstow in the Opera North production first seen in 1990).

Elisetta (Cimarosa: *Il matrimonio segreto*). Mez. Elder daughter of Geronimo who wants her to marry Count Robinson. Created (1792) by Giuseppina Nettelet.

elisir d'amore, L' (Donizetti). Lib. by Felice Romani; 2 acts; f.p. Milan 1832.

An Italian village, 19th cent.: The wealthy farm-owner *Adina is loved by the poor *Nemorino who is too shy to tell her so. Sergeant *Belcore asks her to marry him and she agrees. Desolate, Nemorino buys from the quack *Dulcamara a love-potion to help him win Adina and he also enlists. At the wedding-feast, Adina delays signing the contract until Nemorino arrives. But Nemorino has inherited money and this makes him very attractive to all the girls. When Adina sees them surrounding him, she realizes where her heart really belongs, buys him out of the army, and confesses that she loves him.

Elizabeth I of England (Donizetti: *Maria Stuarda*; Donizetti: *Roberto Devereux*; Britten: *Gloriana*). *See* ELISABETTA (1)-(3).

'Elle' (Poulenc: *La Voix humaine*). Sop. The sole character in the opera, the Woman, abandoned by her lover and unable to accept the situation, speaks to him on the telephone the day before he is to be married. Created (1959) by Denise Duval.

Elmiro (Rossini: *Otello*). Bass. Desdemona's father. He wants her to marry Rodrigo. Created (1816) by Michele Benedetti.

Elsa von Brabant (Wagner: *Lohengrin*). Sop. Ward of Telramund and sister of Gottfried, the heir to the Brabant throne. Telramund suspects her (wrongly) of murdering her brother. Telramund is in love with her and offended by her refusal to marry him. He accuses her and she stands trial before King Heinrich, refusing to defend herself. She describes a dream in which a knight offered to protect her. In answer to her prayers Lohengrin appears, ready to fight in her defence and declare her innocent. He asks her to marry him and when she agrees tells her that she must never ask him his name or whence he came, a condition to which she consents. Ortrud, now Telramund's wife, preys on Elsa's innocence to make her doubt Lohengrin's integrity, but later attacks her, forcing her to have doubts about her heroic knight. After their wedding, Elsa is unable to contain herself and starts to question Lohengrin about where he comes from and what she should call him. Despite all his warnings to her to trust him, she persists in her questioning. They are interrupted by the arrival of Telramund and his men, ready to fight. Lohengrin kills him. He then accuses Elsa, in front of the king, of betraying his trust and they all condemn her. Lohengrin announces his name and as he does so the boat and swan appear and Elsa realizes that, by her curiosity and insistence, she has lost the man she loves. The swan turns into her brother Gottfried, released by Lohengrin from Ortrud's spell, and as Lohengrin sails away, Elsa collapses in her brother's arms. Aria: *Einsam in trüben Tagen* ('When all my hopes departed'); duet (with Lohengrin): *Fühl ich zu dir so süss mein Herz entbrennen* ('Here in my heart a flame is brightly burning'). Among famous interpreters are Lilian Nordica, Emma Eames, Maria Müller, Eleanor Steber, Maria Reining, Marianne Schech, Helen Traubel, Birgit Nilsson, Elisabeth Grümmer, Heather Harper, Hannelore Bode, Gundula Janowitz, Cheryl Studer, and Karita Mattila. Created (1850) by Rosa Agthe (later Rosa Agthe-Milde).

Elvino (Bellini: *La sonnambula*). Ten. A rich young farmer who is to marry Amina, not knowing she walks in her sleep. When she is seen in the room of Rodolfo, Elvino accuses her of being unfaithful and decides to marry Lisa instead. He then sees Amina sleepwalking across the mill roof, and realizes she is innocent. She wakens to be taken in his arms. Created (1831) by Giovanni Battista Rubini.

Elvira 1. (Mozart: *Don Giovanni*). Sop. Donna Elvira, a lady from Burgos, who has been seduced by Don Giovanni and then deserted by him. She comes to Seville to find him, despite his terrible reputation which is catalogued by his manservant Leporello. She saves the young and newly married Zerlina from his clutches and helps Donna Anna and Ottavio unmask him as a murderer. Aria: *Mi tradì* ('I was betrayed'; this aria did not appear in the f.p., it was added for the Vienna premiére in 1788). This is one of many operatic roles which, described in the score as 'soprano', is equally well sung by a mez. with a good top. In recent years, Agnes Baltsa, Maria Ewing, Della Jones,

Waltraud Meier, and Felicity Palmer are among mezzos who have sung Elvira. Created (1787) by Catarina Micelli.

2. (Bellini: *I Puritani*). *See* WALTON, ELVIRA.

3. (Rossini: *L'italiana in Algeri*). Sop. Wife of Mustafà, the Bey of Algiers. He no longer loves her and orders his slave to marry her, but he has to beg her forgiveness when Isabella leaves him. Created (1813) by Luttgard Annibaldi.

4. (Verdi: *Ernani*). Sop. Ward of the old grandee, Silva, who wants to marry her. She is also loved by Don Carlos, King of Spain, and by Ernani, whom the king outlawed. As her wedding to Silva is planned, Ernani breaks in, hoping to abduct her. Caught by Silva, he refuses a duel, but promises his life in forfeit if Silva ever wants it. Carlo is elected Emperor, forgives Ernani and consents to Ernani and Elvira's wedding. After the ceremony, Silva wreaks his revenge and Elvira throws herself on to Ernani's body. Aria: *Ernani! Ernani! involami* ('Ernani! Ernani! fly away with me'). Created (1844) by Sofia Loewe (Loevve) (who caused havoc by instructing the librettist to write a special aria with which she could close the opera, as she didn't approve of ending with a trio. Verdi stuck to his guns. At the premiére, she apparently sang flat the whole evening). The character on whom Elvira is based, Doña Sol in Victor Hugo's *Hernani*, was one of Sarah Bernhardt's greatest roles.

Elviro (Handel: *Serse*). Bass. Servant of Serse's brother Arsamene. Creator (1738) not known.

Emilia 1. (Verdi: *Otello*). Mez. Wife of Iago and lady-in-waiting to Desdemona. She finally exposes her husband as the instigator of Otello's suspicions, but too late—Otello has killed Desdemona. Created (1887) by Ginevra Petrovich.

2. (Rossini: *Otello*). Sop. Confidante of Desdemona. Created (1816) by Maria Manzi.

Emperor 1. (Strauss: *Die Frau ohne Schatten*). Ten. Emperor of the South Eastern Islands. Out shooting one day, he aimed at a gazelle and the animal resumed its true form, that of the daughter of Keikobad, king of the spirit world. The Emperor married her. They live and love, but have no children. Keikobad sends a messenger: if the Empress does not cast a shadow (i.e. become pregnant), the Emperor will be turned to stone. This does indeed happen, and he is returned to life only after his wife is forgiven by her father because she refused to accept another woman's shadow, thus proving she has learned to show humanity to those worse off than herself. Arias: *Bleib und wache* ('Stay and watch'); *Falke, falke* ('Falcon, falcon'); *Wenn das Herz aus Kristall zerbricht* ('When the heart of crystal is shattered'). Created (1919) by Karl Aagard-Oestvig.

   2. (Ullman: *Der Kaiser von Atlantis*). *See* ÜBERALL, EMPEROR.

Empress (Strauss: *Die Frau ohne Schatten*). Sop. Daughter of Keikobad, king of the spirit world, she is the shadowless lady of the opera's title. Since marrying the Emperor, she has remained part human, part spirit. Despite a loving relationship, she has borne no children. Her father sends his Messenger, to say that unless his daughter casts a shadow—this being the symbol of fertility—within three days, the Emperor will be turned to stone. The Empress and her Nurse journey to earth and visit the humble home of Barak the Dyer and his Wife—they, too, have had no children. But the Wife does have a shadow and the Nurse wants to buy it for the Empress. The Empress at first thinks this a splendid solution, but gradually becomes aware of the distress which it is causing Barak, a simple, dignified, human being, not to have any children. She understands that by taking his Wife's shadow, she will be the cause of disharmony between them. The Empress refuses to be the cause of such anguish, whatever the price. She falters momentarily when she sees her own husband turned to stone, then offers to die with him rather than take another woman's shadow. At this moment of her supreme sacrifice, the Empress is seen to have a shadow of her own. Her husband is restored to life and the voices of their unborn children are heard. Arias: *Ist mein Liebster dahin?* ('Is my loved one there?'); *Wehe, mein Mann* ('Ah, my husband'); *Vater, bist du?* ('Father, is it you?'). Renowned Empresses include Viorica Ursuleac, Elisabeth Rethberg, Ingrid Bjoner, Leonie Rysanek, Gwyneth Jones (who once, while singing the role of the Dyer's Wife, also took over the vocal part of the Empress when the singer of that role lost her voice and could only mime the part!), Julia Varady, Anne Evans, and Cheryl Studer. Created (1919) by Maria Jeritza.

Endymion (Endimione) (Cavalli: *La Calisto*). Cont. *Travesti* role. Shepherd in love with the goddess Diana. Is captured by the jealous Pan and rescued by Diana. Creator (1651) not known.

Enfant et les Sortilèges, L' (Ravel). Lib. by Colette (Sidonie-Gabrielle Colette); 2 acts; f.p. Monte Carlo 1925, cond. Victor de Sabata.

   An old Norman country house: Punished by his *Mother for being rude and naughty, the *Child has a tantrum, throwing things about and hurting the cat. All the ill-treated inanimate objects come to life and taunt him. The cat sings a duet with his mate and in the garden the trees and animals join in the torment, singing of the terrible way they have been treated by the Child. Frightened, the Child calls for his mother. An injured squirrel appears and the Child bandages its paw. Amazed at this act of kindness, the other animals help him call for his mother. As she approaches, he rushes into her arms. Among the objects which come to life are: Louis XV Chair (sop.), Chinese Cup (mezzo alto), Armchair (bass), Teapot (ten.), Grandfather Clock (bar.); various animals join the action.

English Cat, The (Henze). Lib. by Edward Bond; 2 acts; f.p. Schwetzingen 1983, cond. Dennis Russell Davies.

   Lord *Puff, president of the Royal Society for the Protection of Rats, is to marry *Minette and hopes to produce an heir. His nephew *Arnold, worried about losing his inheritance, tries but fails to stop the wedding. Minette, however, is still attracted to a former lover, *Tom. Puff finds them together and starts divorce proceedings. Tom, who turns out to be the long-lost son of a rich lord, learns that Puff's owner is going to drown Minette. He decides to court her sister *Babette instead. About to claim his inheritance from his wealthy father, Tom is murdered.

Enrichetta di Francia (Bellini: *I Puritani*). Sop. Henrietta Maria of France, widowed queen of King Charles I of England. She is helped to escape by Arturo. Created (1835) by Mlle Amigo (probably Maria Amigo, one of two sisters, the elder a mez., the younger a sop.—it cannot be ascertained who created the role).

Enrico 1. (Donizetti: *Lucia di Lammermoor*). *See* ASHTON OF LAMMERMOOR, LORD HENRY.

2. King Henry VIII (Donizetti: *Anna Bolena*). Bass. The King of England is losing interest in his second wife, Anna Bolena (Anne Boleyn), and now favours Giovanna (Jane) Seymour. In his attempts to find Anna guilty of treason, he encourages her old love, Lord Percy, to return. When he finds them innocently together, the King sends Anna to the Tower to await trial. Despite all the protests of Percy, her brother Rochefort, and her page, he sentences her to the scaffold. Created (1830) by Filippo Galli.

3. (Haydn: *L'isola disabitata*). Bass. Friend of Gernando. Accompanies him to rescue his wife from a deserted island and falls in love with her sister. Created (1779) by Benedetto Bianchi.

Ensoleillad, L' (Massenet: *Chérubin*). Sop. A ballet dancer who dances at Chérubin's party and whom the King decides to marry. Created (1905) by Lina Cavalieri.

Entführung aus dem Serail, Die (Mozart). Lib. by Gottlieb Stephanie; 3 acts; f.p. Vienna 1782.

Turkey: *Constanze has been captured by pirates and *Belmonte is looking for her. He comes to Pasha *Selim's house, where he thinks she might be, and meets *Osmin, who is in charge of the Pasha's harem. Osmin loves *Blondchen, Constanze's maid, who is also loved by *Pedrillo, Belmonte's servant. Pedrillo assures Belmonte that Constanze has remained true to him, despite Selim's protestations of love for her. Belmonte and Pedrillo trick Osmin and manage to enter the palace. Pedrillo finds Blondchen and tells her that Belmonte is in the palace. Osmin is drugged and the various lovers are united. As they try to escape down a ladder to catch the boat that will take them home, Osmin recovers and thwarts their escape. The Pasha magnanimously allows them all to depart.

Enzo Grimaldi (Ponchielli: *La gioconda*). *See* GRIMALDI, ENZO.

Erda (Wagner: *Das Rheingold*; *Siegfried*). Cont. Earth goddess. Mother of the three Norns. Also mother, by Wotan, of the nine Valkyries. She rises from the earth only when she sees impending disaster.

Das Rheingold: She first appears at the point where Wotan refuses to surrender the Ring to the giants in payment for their building of Valhalla, and Erda warns him that he will be a victim of the curse which Alberich has put on the Ring and will bring about the earth's—and his own—downfall.

Siegfried: Wotan summons Erda from the depths to ask her how he can overcome all his fears. He also tells her that, now she has borne him the nine Valkyries, he has no further use for her. Aria: *Weiche, Wotan, weiche!* ('Yield, Wotan, yield'); *Stark ruft das Lied* ('Strong is the call of your song'). Created (R. 1869) by Therese Seehofer; (S. 1876) by Luise Jaide.

Ericlea (Monteverdi: *Il ritorno d'Ulisse in patria*). Mez. Nurse to Penelope. Creator (1640) unknown.

Erik (Wagner: *Der fliegende Holländer*). Ten. A hunter. He is in love with Senta, daughter of Daland, and wants to marry her. The Dutchman overhears Erik trying to persuade Senta to agree and assumes her to be no longer faithful to him. Aria: *Willst jenes tag du nicht mehr entsinnen* ('Do you no longer remember the day'). Created (1843) by Herr Reinhold.

Erika (Barber: *Vanessa*). Mez. Vanessa's niece. Is seduced and then deserted by Anatol who marries Vanessa. Erika waits for his return. Created (1958) by Rosalind Elias.

Erisbe (Cavalli: *L'Ormindo*). Sop. Wife of the old King Hariadeno, she falls in love with Ormindo, who turns out to be the king's long-lost son. The king first orders them to be poisoned, but then forgives them. Creator (1644) not known.

Ermione (Rossini). Lib. by Andrea Leone Tottola; 2 acts; f.p. Naples 1819.

Epirus, Greece, about 430 BC: *Orestes leads a Greek delegation to the court of *Pyrrhus. They want the death of Hector's young son *Astynax, to prevent him ever being able to take revenge for the killing of his father. Pyrrhus bribes the boy's mother, *Andromache, to marry him. His rejected wife *Hermione (Ermione), knowing she is loved by Orestes, persuades the latter to kill Pyrrhus, but when he has done so she is furious, having changed her mind because she still loves her husband. Orestes is taken by the Greeks as they flee from the court.

Ernani (Verdi). Lib. by Francesco Maria Piave; 4 'parts'; f.p. Venice 1844, cond. Luigi Carcano (1st violin).

Spain, 1519: *Elvira's guardian, *Silva, wants to marry her. *Ernani the bandit is in love with her and plans to kidnap her. The Spanish king *Carlo tries to persuade her to elope with him, but Ernani's arrival interrupts them. Silva, finding them all together, becomes very aggressive until he realizes who Don Carlo is. Rumours spread of Ernani's death and plans for Elvira's wedding to Silva continue. Ernani arrives in disguise and Silva catches him and Elvira in a passionate embrace. Silva refuses to hand Ernani over to the king—he is a guest and must be protected. Carlo takes Elvira as hostage. Silva challenges Ernani to a duel, which Ernani refuses, agreeing to forfeit his life to Silva once he has taken revenge on Carlo, whom he holds responsible for the death of his father. Ernani gives Silva a horn—when Silva wants him dead, he must sound the horn. Together they plan to rescue Elvira. Carlo overhears Silva and Ernani planning to kill him. He denounces them, but shows mercy at Elvira's pleading and even agrees to Ernani and Elvira's wedding. As everyone celebrates, Silva, thwarted in his own desire to marry Elvira, sounds the horn. Rather than be killed, Ernani stabs himself.

Ernani (Verdi: *Ernani*). Ten. John of Aragon, whose father, the Duke of Segovia, was killed on the orders of the King of Spain, father of the present king, Don Carlo. Ernani has been outlawed by Carlo and has become the leader of a group of bandits. They plan to kidnap Elvira, ward of Silva, with whom Ernani is in love. Silva is planning to marry her himself. When Carlo is declared Emperor, he forgives Ernani for plotting against him and consents to the marriage of Ernani and Elvira. While the nuptials are being celebrated, Silva, jealous and frustrated at not winning Elvira as his own bride, calls for Ernani's death. Rather than be killed, Ernani takes the sword which Silva offers him and stabs himself. Aria: *Come rugiada al cespite* ('Like dew to the drooping bud'); duet (with Elvira): *Ah, morir potessi adesso* ('Ah, to die would be a blessing'). Created (1844) by Carlo Guasco (who, according to a letter Verdi wrote soon after the premiére, was hoarse and sang badly all evening).

Ernesto 1. (Bellini: *Il pirata*). Bar. Duke of Caldora, he has married Imogene after his political opponent, her lover Gualtiero, has

been forced into exile following the battle for the throne of Sicily. The two men meet and fight and Ernesto is killed. Created (1827) by Antonio Tamburini.

2. (Donizetti: *Don Pasquale*). Ten. Nephew of Don Pasquale, he is in love with Norina, of whom his uncle disapproves. He is therefore about to be disinherited. Pasquale is tricked into a totally unsuitable fake marriage and, only too glad to be freed from it, consents to Norina and Ernesto's union. Arias: *Cercherò lontana terra* ('Looking for a distant land'); *Com'è gentil la notte a mezzo april!* ('How gentle is the night in mid-April!'). Created (1843) by Giovanni Matteo Mario (a lifelong companion of Giulia Grisi, the soprano who created Norina).

3. (Haydn: *Il mondo della luna*). Sop. *Travesti* role (originally castrato). A knight, in love with Flaminia, daughter of Buonafede, who opposes the marriage. He helps to trick her father into agreeing to their wedding. Created (1777) by Pietro Gherardi (alto castrato).

Erwartung (Expectation) (Schoenberg). Lib. by Marie Pappenheim; 1 act; f.p. Prague 1924, cond. Alexander von Zemlinsky.

Looking for her lover, the *Woman is scared as she enters the forest—or is it all a nightmare? She hears rustles, birds screeching, someone weeping. She stumbles, falls, cries for help. She feels sure that her lover must be with another woman. Then she sees his bloodstained body.

Escamillo (Bizet: *Carmen*). Bar. A handsome toreador, he is aware of his own good looks and knows how women are attracted to him. He falls in love with Carmen when he meets her in Lillas Pastia's tavern. She was on her way to prison but her escort, the soldier Don José who loves her, allowed her to escape. At this stage, Carmen is still in love with José and does not encourage Escamillo. José deserts from the dragoons and goes with Carmen and her smuggler friends to their mountain camp. There Escamillo visits her and wins her from the jealous Don José. She leaves for Seville with Escamillo to see him fight in the bullring. She proudly joins him in his triumphant arrival, but stays outside the ring when he enters. There she is killed by José. Aria: *Votre toast je peux vous le rendre* ('I can return your toast'); duet (with Carmen): *Si tu m'aimes Carmen* ('If you love me, Carmen'). Created (1875) by Jacques Bouhy.

Eschenbach, Wolfram von (Wagner: *Tannhäuser*). Bar. A knight, one of the Minnesingers left behind by Tannhäuser when he was lured away to the Venusberg. Despite being himself in love with Elisabeth, he tells Tannhäuser that she is pining for him and persuades him to return with them to Wartburg. After Tannhäuser has set off for Rome to plead for absolution, Wolfram waits with Elisabeth for his return and when she gives up hope and dies, Wolfram meets Tannhäuser and prays to the soul of Elisabeth for his forgiveness. Arias: *War's Zauber, war es reine Macht* ('Was it magic, or a divine power'); *Blick' ich umher in diesem edlen Kreiser* ('Looking around at this noble circle'); *Dir, hohe Liebe* ('You, sacred love'); *O du, mein holder Abendstern* ('O star of eve, so pure and fair'). Created (1845) by Anton Mitterwurzer.

Esmeralda (Smetana: *The Bartered Bride*). Sop. Dancer in the circus which comes to the village. Created (1866) by Terezie Ledererová.

Essex, Earl of 1. (Britten: *Gloriana*). Ten. Robert Devereux, husband of Frances and brother of Penelope, Lady Rich. Essex is a favourite courtier of Queen Elizabeth I and entreats her to make him viceroy of Ireland. After the Queen has attempted to humiliate his wife (but only succeeded in making herself look a fool), she appoints Essex to the Irish post he has coveted. He fails in his campaign there and, arriving back in London, bursts in on the Queen when she is only partly dressed and without her wig. Essex tries to incite the Londoners to rebellion and is arrested as a traitor and sentenced to death. Queen Elizabeth signs the death warrant. Aria (2nd lute song): *Happy were he*. Created (1953) by Peter Pears.
   2. (Donizetti: *Roberto Devereux*). See DEVEREUX, ROBERTO.

Essex, Lady (Britten: *Gloriana*). Mez. Frances, Countess of Essex. Her husband is a favourite of the Queen, who is jealous of Frances. At a dance in the Palace of Whitehall, the Queen orders all the ladies to change their clothes. Lady Essex's beautiful gown disappears. It has been taken by the Queen, who appears in it looking ridiculous as it fits very

badly. Lady Essex's humiliation is equally matched by the Queen's. Created (1953) by Monica Sinclair.

Etherea (Janáček: *The Excursions of Mr Brouček*). Sop. A muse, fiancée of the poet Blankytný on the Moon, her other manifestations being Málinka and Kunka. Created (1920) by Emma Miřiovská.

***Étoile, L'* (The Star)** (Chabrier). Lib. by Eugéne Leterrier and Albert Vanloo; 3 acts; f.p. Paris 1877, cond. Leon Rocques.
   On his birthday, King *Ouf wanders round looking for somebody to execute. Accompanied by their secretary *Tapioca, *Hérisson and *Aloés meet Ouf, whom they plan to marry to Princess *Laoula, daughter of their King Mataquin. Everyone is in disguise, the ladies having swopped clothes. The pedlar *Lazuli flirts with both the ladies and when Ouf remonstrates with him, Lazuli insults the King, who now has a victim for execution. His astrologer, *Siroco, warns against this—the stars tell that the King's death will follow shortly after Lazuli's. Lazuli plans to elope with Laoula, but anxious to secure an heir, Ouf allows Laoula to marry Lazuli and appoints them his successors.

Eudoxie, Princess (Halévy: *La Juive*). Sop. Wife of Léopold who, disguised as 'Samuel', has seduced the Jewess Rachel. Created (1835) by Julie Dorus-Gras.

Eugene Onegin (Tchaikovsky). Lib. by comp.: 3 acts; f.p. Moscow 1879 (by students of Moscow Conservatory), cond. Nikolai Rubinstein; f. prof. p. Moscow 1881, cond. Enrico Bevignani.
   The Larin estate and St Petersburg, late 18th cent.: *Tatyana and *Olga sing together, listened to by their mother Mme *Larina and their old nurse *Filipyevna. A neighbour, *Lensky, arrives with his friend *Onegin. Onegin and Tatyana are at once attracted to each other and she writes him a letter, telling him of her feelings. He visits her a few days later and brutally rejects her love, leaving her humiliated. At her name-day party, *Triquet sings to the unhappy Tatyana. Onegin, bored and annoyed with Lensky for bringing him to the party, flirts with Olga, until Lensky angrily challenges him to a duel. They meet at dawn, Onegin accompanied by his valet *Guillot,

Lensky by *Zaretsky. Onegin kills Lensky. He leaves the area and Tatyana marries Prince *Gremin. Years later, at a ball in St Petersburg, Tatyana and Onegin meet and he admits he loves her. She still loves him, but she must remain faithful to her husband and she sends Onegin away.

Eumete (Eumaeus) (Monteverdi: *Il ritorno d'Ulisse in patria*). Ten. Swineherd and former faithful servant of Ulisse, who informs his master of his wife's fidelity all the years they have been apart. Creator (1640) unknown.

Euridice 1. (Gluck: *Orfeo ed Euridice*). Sop. The dead wife of the musician Orfeo, who brings her back from Hades with the help of Amor, the God of Love. Created (It. vers. 1762) by Marianna Bianchi; (Fr. vers. 1774) by Sophie Arnould.

2. (Haydn: *Orfeo ed Euridice*). Sop. Daughter of Creon, who allows her to marry Orfeo. She stands on a snake, is bitten, and dies. When Orfeo finds her, she deliberately steps in front of him, forcing him to look at her and thus bringing about her own death. Haydn's version of this story had to wait 160 years for its première. Created (1951) by Maria Callas.

3. (Monteverdi: *L'Orfeo*). Sop. Created (1607) probably by the castrato Girolamo Bacchini.

4. (Offenbach: *Orpheus in the Underworld*). *See* EURYDICE.

Euridice Hero (Birtwistle: *The Mask of Orpheus*). Mime role. Created (1986) by Zena Dilke.

Euridice Woman (Birtwistle: *The Mask of Orpheus*). Mez. Dies and is looked for in the Underworld by Orpheus. Created (1986) by Jean Rigby.

Euridice Myth/Persephone (Birtwistle: *The Mask of Orpheus*). Mez. Follows Orpheus from the Underworld, he thinking it is the real Euridice. Created (1986) by Ethna Robinson.

Eurimaco (Eurymachus) (Monteverdi: *Il ritorno d'Ulisse in patria*). Ten. Valet to one of Penelope's suitors, lover of her maid Melanto. Creator (1640) unknown.

Europa (Strauss: *Die Liebe der Danae*). Sop. One of the Four Queens who have all been lovers of Jupiter in the past. Created (1944) by Stefania Fratnikova; (1952) by Esther Rethy.

Euryanthe (Weber). Lib. by Helmine von Chézy; 3 acts; f.p. Vienna 1823, cond. Carl Maria von Weber.

France, early 12th cent.: *Lysiart bets his rival nobleman *Adolar that he can prove his bride, *Euryanthe, unfaithful. *Eglantine, in love with Adolar, persuades Euryanthe to tell her the secret of the death of Adolar's sister, who killed herself with poison secreted in her ring. Eglantine removes the ring from the body, but as she emerges from the tomb she meets Lysiart. Lysiart uses the ring to prove to Adolar that Euryanthe has betrayed his trust, because of her love for him, Lysiart. Adolar takes Euryanthe into the mountains, meaning to kill her. When she saves him from being bitten by a snake, he takes pity on her and abandons her in the mountains. She is found by King *Louis VI when he is out hunting. Adolar confronts Lysiart, who is about to marry Eglantine. The King arrives and tells Adolar the truth. Lysiart kills Eglantine. Euryanthe and Adolar are happily reunited.

Euryanthe of Savoy (Weber: *Euryanthe*). Sop. Engaged to Adolar, who is deceived into believing she has been unfaithful. He intends to kill her, but abandons her in the mountains. The truth is revealed to him and they are happily reunited. Created (1823) by Henriette Sontag.

Eurydice 1. (Offenbach: *Orpheus in the Underworld*). Sop. Wife of Orpheus, but they are tired of each other and she is having an affair with Pluto, whom she follows into the underworld. When Orpheus tries, reluctantly, to rescue her, Jupiter arranges for him to look at her, thus ensuring that she remains in the underworld for ever, to the delight of everyone except Public Opinion. Created (1858) by Lise Tautin.

2. (Birtwistle: *The Second Mrs Kong*). Sop. 'Forever lost to Orpheus', who is helped by Kong in his efforts to find her again. Created (1994) by Lisa Pulman. *See also* EURIDICE.

Eva (Wagner: *Die Meistersinger von Nürnberg*). *See* POGNER, EVA.

Evadne (Walton: *Troilus and Cressida*). Mez. Servant of Cressida. On the orders of Cressida's father, Evadne burns all the letters sent by Troilus, leading Cressida to believe he has deserted her. Aria: *Night after night the same.* Created (1954) by Monica Sinclair.

Evangelist (Vaughan Williams: *The Pilgrim's Progress*). Bass. Directs Pilgrim to the Wicket Gate. When Pilgrim is injured in the Valley of Humiliation, the Evangelist gives him the Key of Promise, which he later uses to free himself from prison. Aria: *Be thou faithful unto death.* Created (1951) by Norman Walker.

Excursions of Mr Brouček, The (*Výlety páně Broučkovy*) (Janáček). Lib. by comp., Viktor Dyk, František Procházka, and others; 2 'parts' (4 acts); f.p. Prague 1920, cond. Otakar Ostrčil.

Prague 1888, the Moon, Prague 1420: At the inn, watched by the landlord *Würfl, Mr *Brouček drinks and dreams of life on the moon. In a drunken stupor, he finds himself there. He meets the poet *Blankytný and his fiancée *Etherea (who are just like Brouček's tenant *Mazal and *his* fiancée *Málinka, daughter of the *Sacristan) and Etherea's father *Lunobar (identical to the Sacristan). Etherea and Brouček go together to the Temple of Arts, whose President resembles the innkeeper. Brouček finds life on the moon fairly horrifying and escapes back to earth. Back in Prague, he finds it is 1420, the time of the Hussite Wars. From the chamber of King Wenceslas IV, he is taken home by *Domšik (another Sacristan look-alike). Again, everyone he meets resembles someone from his other life, e.g. Domšik's daughter *Kunka resembles Málinka, the leader *Petřik is Mazal. Domšik is killed in the battle defending the Hussite faith. Brouček has refused to become involved in the fighting. He is charged with cowardice and condemned to be burnt in a barrel. As it is burning, he wakes up—in the barrel he fell into when drunk at the inn.

F

Fabrizio (Rossini: *La gazza ladra*). *See* VIN-GRADITO, FABRIZIO.

Fafner (Wagner: *Das Rheingold; Siegfried*). Bass. A giant. Brother of Fasolt.

Das Rheingold: Fafner and Fasolt have been hired by Wotan to build a castle, Valhalla, as a fortress for the gods. They will receive as payment Freia, Wotan's sister-in-law. When the building is finished, Wotan hesitates about the payment and Fafner becomes impatient. Hearing of the hoard of gold stolen by Alberich from the Rhinemaidens, Fafner decides he will settle for the gold instead of Freia, taking her off to their lair as hostage while Wotan thinks about how he will wrest the hoard from Alberich. Wotan steals the gold and agrees to the giants' bargain. Fafner stands Freia between him and Fasolt and demands that the gold be built up until she is no longer visible. All the gold is used up except the Ring on Wotan's finger, and Fafner insists this be used to close the last gap in the wall of gold. Freia is then freed. Fafner starts to collect the gold, but Fasolt wants the Ring for himself. They fight, and Fafner kills Fasolt—the first manifestation of the curse placed upon the Ring by Alberich. Aria: *Hör', Wotan, der Harrenden Wort!* ('Wotan, hear what we have to say!').

Siegfried: In his cave in the forest, Fafner changes himself into a dragon (could he possibly have known the magic of the Tarnhelm?) to guard the gold. Wotan warns Fafner that a hero will come and fight him for the Ring. Fafner is awakened by the sound of Siegfried's horn. As Fafner rears up to attack Siegfried, the latter plunges his sword through the dragon's heart. Before Fafner dies, he tells Siegfried that he killed Fasolt, the last of the giant race, and warns him that whoever sent him to the cave is also planning to kill him.

Created (*R.* 1869) by Kaspar Bausewein; (*S.* 1876) by Georg Unger.

Fairfax, Col. (Sullivan: *The Yeomen of the Guard*). Ten. Unjustly imprisoned and under sentence of death, he wants to marry to provide himself with a legal heir. He marries the blindfolded Elsie Maynard. He is released by Sergeant Meryll and passed off as Meryll's son Leonard, with whom Elsie falls in love. She is ultimately relieved to find that Leonard and her unknown husband are the same man. Aria: *Is life a boon?; Free from his fetters grim*. Created (1888) by Courtice ('Charlie') Pounds.

Fairy Godmother (La Fée) (Massenet: *Cendrillon*). Sop. Appears to Cendrillon and sends her to the royal ball, giving her a pair of glass slippers to wear. They are charmed, and while she wears them her own family cannot recognize her—but she must leave the ball at midnight. Created (1899) by Georgette Bréjean-Gravière (later Bréjean-Silver, having married the composer Charles Silver).

Fairy Queen, The (Purcell). Lib. anon.; prol. and 5 acts; f.p. London 1692.

This is the same basic plot as in *A Midsummer Night's Dream*, but the characters from the original Shakespeare are played by actors, Purcell's music being performed in self-contained masques which are interwoven with the acts of the play. In the final act Oberon presents to the Duke and his followers a Chinese masque to celebrate the state of marriage. *The Fairy Queen* is thus more accurately described as a 'semi-opera'.

Falke, Dr (J. Strauss II: *Die Fledermaus*). Bar. A friend of the Eisensteins. He collects Eisenstein to escort him to prison, but he has arranged that en route they will go to Prince Orlofsky's party. Here Falke plots his revenge on Eisenstein, who once made a laughing-stock of him in their village by leaving him to walk home alone after a fancy-dress party, wearing the costume of a bat. Aria (with chorus); *Brüderlein und Schwesterlein* ('Brotherhood and sisterhood'). Created (1874) by Ferdinand Lebrecht.

Falstaff (Verdi). Lib. by Arrigo Boito; 3 acts; f.p. Milan 1893, cond. Edoardo Mascheroni.

Windsor, early 15th cent. (the reign of Henry IV): *Falstaff, *Pistol, and *Bardolph are drinking at the Garter Inn, interrupted by Dr *Caius. Falstaff plans to seduce the wives of *Ford and *Page, and thus gain access to their husbands' money. Alice *Ford and Meg *Page decide to teach him a lesson. Ford hears of Falstaff's plans. The Fords' daughter Nannetta *Ford slips away to be alone with *Fenton. The two ladies enlist the help of Mistress *Quickly, who delivers to Ford their replies, making an assignation with Alice. Ford, disguised as Signor Fontana (Master Brook) offers to help Falstaff seduce Alice and they set off to visit her. Falstaff woos her romantically but when Ford is heard outside he hides behind a screen. He is then pushed by the ladies into a laundry hamper, Nannetta and Fenton replacing him behind the screen, where they are 'discovered' during Ford's search for Falstaff and Alice. Meantime, the contents of the laundry-hamper are tipped into the river below. Soaked and shivering, Falstaff arrives at the Garter Inn, where Mistress Quickly hands him a letter suggesting a further meeting with Alice, at midnight in Windsor Park, but he must come disguised as the Black Huntsman who haunts the forest. Masks and costumes are donned by the ladies and husbands and as Falstaff attempts to woo Alice he is terrified by these 'spirits of the forest'. While the others continue to torment him, Nannetta and Fenton slip away. As they gradually remove their masks, Falstaff realizes he has been made to look a fool, but accepts it all in good part. Ford blesses his daughter's union with the man she loves.

Falstaff, Sir John 1. (Verdi: *Falstaff*). Bar. Drinking with his friends Pistol and Bardolph, Falstaff finds he has too little money to pay the bill. However, he has a plan: he has written letters to two wealthy ladies whom he believes to be attracted to him—if he can seduce them, he can get his hands on their husbands' money.

The ladies in question, Alice Ford and Meg Page, compare notes and decide to teach him a lesson. Through their friend Mistress Quickly, they arrange a meeting between Falstaff and Alice at her home. Her husband hears of this and, in disguise, encourages Falstaff and accompanies him to the house in order to see if his wife is being unfaithful. His attempts to catch Alice and Falstaff together fail. Alice shows him Falstaff dragging himself out of the water below—he has been hidden in a laundry-basket and tipped into the river. A further meeting is arranged, in Windsor Park at midnight. Falstaff is told he must come dressed as the legendary Black Huntsman who haunts the forest. The ladies, the Fords' daughter and her sweetheart, and some of the other men all join in tormenting Falstaff. When the disguises are eventually removed, he realizes he has been duped, and takes it all in good part. Arias: *L'Onore! Ladri!* ('Your Honour! Scoundrels!'); *Quand'ero paggio del Duca di Norfolk* ('When I was a page to the Duke of Norfolk'); *Mondo ladro. Mondo rubaldo.* ('Thieving world. Vile world.'); *Tutto nel mondo è burla* ('All in the world's but folly'—this is the astonishing fugue in which everyone joins in the final scene of the opera). Created (1893) by Victor Maurel, the baritone who had six years earlier created Iago in *Otello*. It is hard to think of two more contrasted roles, but they have in common the need for a singer who is also a good actor, and this Maurel was—Verdi admired his acting ability as much as his singing. However, he nearly didn't take part in the première—Maurel behaved as though he had an absolute right to the role, demanding exclusive performing rights in future productions in Italy and abroad (and also an exorbitant fee) and this so angered Verdi that he was ready to withdraw the première from La Scala and even prepared to abandon the work altogether. Maurel eventually backed down and had a triumphant first night. Many baritones have been associated with Verdi's Fat Knight since then—Mariano Stabile first sang it in 1921 under Toscanini at La Scala and between then and 1960 he sang it 1,200 times in an interpretation which many regard as unsurpassed. He had previously sung Ford, and was not the last Ford to graduate to the title role—so did Antonio Pini-Corsi, Leonard Warren and Tito Gobbi (another Iago); a famous German Falstaff in

the late 1930s was the great Wagnerian baritone Hans Hotter; and in Britain the role will
long be associated with Geraint Evans and, in
more recent years, with another Welshman,
Bryn Terfel.

2. (Nicolai: *Die lustige Weiber von Windsor*).
Bass. The same character as above. Created
(1849) by August Zschiesche.

fanciulla del West, La (*The Girl of the Golden West*) (Puccini). Lib. by Guelfo Civin-ini and Carlo Zangarini; 3 acts; f.p. NY 1910, cond. Arturo Toscanini.

California, 1849–50: *Minnie is respected by
the gold miners who drink and play cards in
her pub, served by the bartender *Nick. The
sheriff, Jack *Rance, is keen to marry Minnie
and fights the senior miner, *Sonora, who is
also interested. *Ashby tells them that the
hunted bandit *Ramerrez is in the area. As
Minnie reads to the men, a stranger enters the
pub. He is Dick *Johnson (really Ramerrez)
and Minnie has met him somewhere previously. One of the bandit gang, José *Castro, is
caught and brought to the pub. He manages to
pass a message to Johnson—the bandits aim
to raid the inn and steal the miners' gold. Left
alone with him, Minnie invites Dick Johnson
to her hut later that evening. Minnie's maid
*Wowkle and her lover the red Indian Billy
*Jackrabbit are soon to marry. Johnson arrives
to dine with Minnie. When it is time for him to
leave, a snowstorm is raging outside and Minnie suggests he stay the night. Hearing Rance
and some of the miners arrive, Minnie hides
Johnson. Rance has been in contact with
Johnson's former girlfriend (Nina Michelto-
rina) and now knows that Johnson is the bandit Ramerrez. He even has a picture of him to
prove it to Minnie. They leave and Johnson
confesses to Minnie, explaining how he became a bandit, but she tells him he must go. No
sooner has he left the hut than he is shot by
Rance's men. Minnie hides him in the loft.
Rance comes again to Minnie's hut and finds
nothing. But a drop of blood falls on his hand
from the loft, revealing Johnson's hiding-
place. Minnie offers to play poker with Rance—
she and Johnson will be the prize if Rance wins.
By cheating, she wins and Johnson is free. Near
the miners' camp Rance, unable to understand
Minnie's preference for the bandit, is still trying to catch him. When he is caught the miners

prepare to hang him. Minnie appears, gun in
hand, and reminds them how she has always
been prepared to help them when they
needed her. She asks them to save the man she
loves and they relent and release him, leaving
Johnson and Minnie free to leave the country.

Faninal (Strauss: *Der Rosenkavalier*). Bar. A
nouveau-riche arms dealer, father of Sophie.
In his new-found wealth, he is anxious to
associate with the aristocracy and has promised his daughter Sophie to the coarse Baron
Ochs in marriage. Created (1911) by Karl
Scheidemantel.

Faninal, Sophie von (Strauss: *Der Rosenkavalier*). Sop. The 15-year-old daughter of
the newly rich Faninal. She has been given in
marriage by her father to Baron Ochs. Together with her duenna, she awaits his arrival.
First comes his *Rosenkavalier* (Octavian) to
present to her the traditional silver rose. As
soon as their eyes meet, it is love at first sight.
While they are talking, Faninal's major-domo
announces Ochs's arrival. Sophie is horrified
by the sight of the uncouth, lecherous Baron,
who tries to make her sit on his knee, pointing
out that she now belongs to him. Sophie becomes agitated, Octavian furious, until at last
he draws his sword and the Baron receives a
minor scratch on his arm. Valzacchi and Annina rush in and help him, bringing a message
from 'Mariandel' that she will meet him that
night at the inn. Sophie makes it clear to her
father that she no longer regards Ochs as her
future husband and Faninal threatens to put
her in a convent. After Ochs's adventures with
Mariandel, Sophie and her father come to the
inn, summoned by a servant, and Ochs is seen
as the boor he truly is. Sophie and Octavian are
reunited with her father's blessing. Duet (with
Octavian): *Mir ist die Ehre widerfahren* ('To me
has been given the honour'—the glorious Presentation of the Rose scene); trio (with the
Marschallin and Octavian): *Marie Theres'!…
Hab' mir's gelobt* ('Marie Theres'!…I vowed to
myself'); duet (with Octavian): *Spür' nur
dich…Ist ein Traum* ('I hold only you…It is
a dream'). Singers associated with this role
include Elisabeth Schumann, Hilde Gueden,
Adèle Kern, Rita Streich, Roberta Peters, Helen
Donath, Judith Blegen, Lucia Popp, Ruth
Welting, Rebecca Evans, and Barbara Bonney.
Created (1911) by Minnie Nast.

Farfarello (Prokofiev: *The Love for Three Oranges*). Bass. A devil who uses a large bellows to blow the Prince on his way to look for the three oranges. Created (1921) by James Wolf.

Farlaf (Glinka: *Ruslan and Lyudmila*). Bass. A Prince, former suitor of Lyudmila. Plots with a sorceress to win Lyudmila from Ruslan. Created (1842) by Domenico Tosi.

Farnace (Mozart: *Mitridate, re di Ponto*). Male alto. Elder son of Mitridate and brother of Sifare. In love with his father's fiancée, who in turn loves his younger brother. Finally marries Ismene. Created (1770) by Giuseppe Cicognani (alto castrato) and successfully sung in recent years by the German countertenor (perhaps better described as a male alto) Jochen Kowalski.

Fasolt (Wagner: *Das Rheingold*). Bass-bar. A giant. He and his brother, Fafner, have been commissioned by Wotan to build Valhalla as a fortress for the gods. Their payment will be Freia, Wotan's sister-in-law. When the building is completed, Wotan is reluctant to pay the promised fee. By now Fasolt is feeling amorous towards Freia and becomes angry. Hearing of the hoard of gold from the Rhine, the giants suggest they be given this instead of Freia. After much thought and negotiation, Wotan agrees and hands over the gold, which he steals from Alberich, including the Ring on which Alberich has placed a curse. Fasolt and Fafner fight over the Ring and Fasolt is killed—the Ring has claimed its first victim. Aria: *Halt! Nicht sie berührt!* ('Stop! Do not touch her!'). Created (1869) by Herr Petzer.

Father (Charpentier: *Louise*). Bass. He is less reluctant than her mother to let Louise go to live with her poor poet, Julien. Created (1900) by Lucien Fugère.

Fatima (Weber: *Oberon*). Sop. Maid of Reiza. Sherasmin falls in love with her. Created (1826) by Lucia Elizabeth Vestris.

Fatty (Willy) (Weill: *Aufstieg und Fall der Stadt Mahagonny*). Ten. The 'book-keeper'. On the run from the police for fraud, he helps to found the city of Mahagonny, a place where no one will work and life will be devoted to pleasure. Created (1930) by Hans Fleischer.

Faust (Gounod). Lib. by Jules Barbier and Michel Carré; 5 acts; f.p. Paris 1859, cond. Mons. Deloffre.

Germany, 16th cent.: *Méphistophélès (the Devil) offers to satisfy *Faust's longing for sensual pleasure in return for his help in the underworld. Faust agrees and is transformed into a handsome young nobleman. At a fair, *Valentin asks his friends *Wagner and *Siebel to take care of his sister *Marguerite while he is away at war. Méphistophélès and Faust join the group and both Faust and Siebel are attracted to Marguerite. Siebel leaves her flowers, Méphistophélès adds a jewelbox. Marguerite is delighted with the jewellery. Her guardian, Marthe *Schwerlein, is intrigued by Méphistophélès while Marguerite surrenders to Faust. She bears his child but is disowned by all her friends. Siebel remains faithful. Valentin returns from battle and Faust confesses his role in Marguerite's downfall. They fight a duel and Valentin is killed. On Walpurgis Night, Faust has a vision of Marguerite in prison for infanticide. Méphistophélès helps him get the key to her cell. She refuses to flee with him. As Faust looks on helplessly, her soul rises to heaven.

Faust 1. (Gounod: *Faust*). Ten. The ageing philosopher, Dr Faust, agrees to help Méphistophélès (Satan) in the underworld in return for which Méphistophélès will satisfy Faust's longing for youthful pleasures. Faust meets Marguerite, sister of the soldier Valentin, and falls in love with her. She has his child and is imprisoned for infanticide. Aided by Méphistophélès, Faust enters her cell. She refuses to leave with them, prays for the Lord's help and dies. Faust prays as her soul rises to heaven. Created (1859) by Joseph-Théodore-Désiré Barbot (who learned the role in three weeks, when it became clear that the original choice for the part, Hector Gruyer, was unable to sing it).

2. (Boito: *Mefistofele*). The aged doctor strikes a bargain with the devil (Mefistofele)—his soul for a moment of pure happiness. He falls in love with Margherita, but she is wrongly imprisoned and dies. In classical Greece Faust falls in love with Helen of Troy (Elena). However, as he nears death he realizes how empty is the life the devil has shown him. He appeals to God for forgiveness and redemption, and thus thwarts Mefistofele. Created (1868) by Sig. Spallazzi.

3. (Prokofiev: *The Fiery Angel*). Bar. Met by Ruprecht at the inn where he goes to recover from his injuries after his duel with Heinrich. Creators (1954/5) not traced.

Favell, Jack (Josephs: *Rebecca*). Bar. Former lover of the late Rebecca. He accuses her husband, Maxim de Winter, of causing her death. Created (1983) by Malcolm Rivers.

***Favorite, La* (*The Favourite*)** (Donizetti). Lib. by Alphonse Royer, Gustav Vaez, and Eugène Scribe; 4 acts; f.p. Paris 1840, cond. François-Antoine Habeneck.

Castile, 1340: Abbot *Balthazar's son *Fernand tells his father that he has fallen in love with an unknown woman and must leave the order. Fernand is taken to the island of Léon. There he is greeted by *Inès, Léonor di *Guzman's confidante. Léonor, knowing how he feels, will not tell him that she is King *Alphonse XI's 'favourite'—he wants to divorce his Queen and marry her. Balthazar arrives at court with an excommunication order to be served on the King if he divorces his wife. Fernand, having defeated the Moors, asks for Léonor in marriage. The King consents, finding this a good solution to his difficult position. Léonor sends Inès with a note telling Fernand of her true position. The note fails to reach Fernand and their wedding takes place. Balthazar tells his son the truth. Fernand departs to resume his monastic life. As he is about to be received into holy orders, Léonor arrives—she is ill and wants to see Fernand one last time. They confess their love and she dies at his feet.

Fay, Morgan le (Birtwistle: *Gawain*). *See* MORGAN LE FAY.

***fedeltà premiata, La* (*Fidelity Rewarded*)** (Haydn). Lib. by Haydn and an unknown person; 3 acts; f.p. Eszterháza 1781.

Legendary Cumae, nr. Naples: *Fileno and *Celia decide to part, rather than risk being sacrificed to placate the sea monster. The priest at *Diana's temple, *Melibeo, and the woman he fancies, *Amaranta, try to arrange for Celia to marry Amaranta's brother *Lindoro (whose fickle love is *Nerina). Celia, who thinks Fileno is dead, is saved by satyrs. Melibio, concerned that Amaranta now prefers the Count *Perrucchetto, contrives to make Celia and Perrucchetto the pair to be sacrificed. Fileno, prepared to sacrifice himself to save Celia, attacks the monster, who turns into a grotto from which emerges Diana, who unites Fileno and Celia, Nerina and Lindoro, and Amaranta and Perrucchetto.

Federica (Verdi: *Luisa Miller*). *See* OSTHEIM, FEDERICA, DUCHESS OF.

Fedora (Giordano). Lib. by Arturo Colautti; 3 acts; f.p. Milan 1898, cond. Umberto Giordano.

St Petersburg, Paris, Switzerland, late 19th cent.: Princess Fedora *Romanov goes to visit her fiancé, Count Vladimiro. He has been fatally wounded; his killers, said to be Count Loris *Ipanov and accomplices, have escaped. Fedora swears vengeance. In Paris, she succeeds in making Loris fall in love with her and she denounces him to the police. Loris confesses his act, but says it was an act of honour—he had found out that his wife and Vladimiro were lovers. By now in love with Loris, Fedora goes to live with him in Switzerland. She learns from *De Sirieux, the French Foreign Secretary that, as a result of her instructions, they have discovered that two men conspired to kill her fiancé—one has been arrested, the other has escaped—the latter is, of course, Loris. News reaches Switzerland that Loris's brother has drowned while in prison and their mother has died of grief. Realizing that Fedora has been responsible for implicating his family, Loris curses her. She takes poison, begging his forgiveness as she dies.

Fedora (Giordano: *Fedora*). *See* ROMANOV, PRINCESS FEDORA.

Feldmarschallin, The (Marie Therese, Princess von Werdenberg) (Strauss: *Der Rosenkavalier*). *See* MARSCHALLIN, THE.

Female Chorus (Britten: *The Rape of Lucretia*). Sop. Commentator on the action. She and the Male Chorus recount the historical background to the opera, describe various events taking place on and off-stage and invoke Christianity as the basis for all love and forgiveness. Aria: *She sleeps as a rose upon the night*. Created (1946) by Joan Cross.

Fenena (Verdi: *Nabucco*). Mez. Younger daughter of Nabucco and sister of Abigaille, who is very jealous of Fenena. When held hostage by the High Priest Zaccaria, Fenena (who is a secret sympathiser of the Hebrews) frees the Hebrews held in the Temple. Created (1842) by Giovannina Bellinzaghi.

Fennimore (Delius: *Fennimore and Gerda*). Sop. Leading female character in Delius's opera, f.p. Frankfurt 1919 cond. Gustav Brecher. Married to Erik (created by Eric Wirl), she falls in love with Niels (created by Robert von Scheidt), but when Erik is killed she sends Niels away. He marries the teenage Gerda. Created (1919) by Emma Holt.

Fenton 1. (Verdi: *Falstaff*). Ten. Young man in love with Nannetta, daughter of the Fords (although in the original Shakespeare, he was in love with the Page daughter. See (2)). Aria: *Dal labbro il canto estasia* ('From lover's lips a tender song'); duet (with Nannetta): *Labbra di foco!* ('Lips that are burning!'). Created (1893) by Edoardo Garbin.

2. (Nicolai: *Die lustige Weiber von Windsor*). Ten. In love with Anna Reich (Page). See (1). Created (1849) by Julius Pfister.

Fernand (Donizetti: *La Favorite*). Ten. A young novice in the monastery where his father, Balthazar, is the abbot. He sees and falls in love with a woman, not knowing she is the 'favourite' of the King. He leaves the monastery and goes to the Island of Léon, where he meets Léonor, who will not tell him of her true position. He receives the King's consent to marry her, but after the wedding his father tells him the truth about his new wife. He returns to the monastery. As he is about to take holy orders, Léonor, now very ill, comes to see him for the last time. They confess their love for each other and she dies at his feet. Arias: *Oui, ta voix m'inspire* ('Yes, your voice inspires me'); *Ange si pure* ('Angel so pure'). Created (1840) by Gilbert-Louis Duprez.

Fernandez, Rambaldo (Puccini: *La rondine*). Bar. A rich Parisian banker, in love with Magda de Civry. He showers her with jewellery but Magda makes it clear to him that she is looking for true love such as she once experienced when younger. While he is at Magda's salon, he is visited by the son of an old friend—his name is Ruggero. It soon becomes clear to Rambaldo that Magda has fallen in love with Ruggero. Although he lets it be known that he is willing to take her back, Magda is

not interested. Created (1917) by Gustave Huberdeau.

Fernando 1. (Rossini: *La gazza ladra*). *See* VILLABELLA, FERNANDO.

2. (Beethoven: *Fidelio*). Bass. Don Fernando, the King's Minister. He arrives at the gaol in time to free the prisoners, incl. his old friend Florestan. Aria: *Der besten König's Wink und Wille* ('At the wish and suggestion of the best of kings'). Created (1805) by Herr Weinkopf.

Ferrando 1. (Mozart: *Così fan tutte*). Ten. Fiancé of Dorabella. His friend, Guglielmo, is engaged to her sister Fiordiligi. Don Alfonso bets the two men that all women are unfaithful. Ferrando and Guglielmo pretend to leave for battle, don disguises as Albanians, and are presented to the ladies as old friends of Alfonso. Gradually the women give in to the men's overtures, but each to the 'wrong' man, so Fiordiligi is won over by Ferrando. They agree to a double wedding and a bogus ceremony takes place, the bridegroom being named as Sempronio. Now Ferrando and Guglielmo 'return' from war, each to claim his own original sister! How will the couples finally pair off? Arias: *Un'aura amorosa* ('A breath of love'); *Ah, lo veggio* ('Ah, now I see it'). A popular role for lyric tenors, among whom have been Richard Tucker, Ernst Haefliger, Léopold Simoneau, Anton Dermota, Heddle Nash, Luigi Alva, Richard Lewis, Alfredo Kraus, George Shirley, Peter Schreier, Nicolai Gedda, Alexander Young, David Rendall, Max-René Cosotto, John Aler, Ryland Davies, and Kurt Streit. Created (1790) by Vincenzo Calvesi.

2. (Verdi: *Il trovatore*). Bass. A Capt. in the army of Count di Luna. He recounts the story of the gypsy Azucena and the baby she burnt on the funeral pyre of her mother, setting in motion the confused identities at the heart of this opera. Created (1853) by Arcangelo Balderi.

Fevronia (Rimsky-Korsakov: *The Legend of the Invisible City of Kitezh*). Sop. A maiden who lives in a forest, she falls in love with a huntsman and later discovers he is Prince Vsevolod, joint ruler of the sacred City of Kitezh. During their wedding she is abducted by Tartars, but escapes and is reunited with her Prince in Paradise. Created (1907) by Mariya Kuznetsova.

Fiakermilli (Strauss: *Arabella*). Sop. The mascot at the Cabbies' Ball in Vienna [Fiaker = hansom cab]. Mandryka flirts with her when he believes Arabella to be unfaithful. She sings a florid coloratura aria, embellished with much yodelling, requiring vocal flexibility and control. Aria: *Die Wiener Herrn verstehn sich auf die Astronomie* ('The gentlemen of Vienna understand about astronomy'). This role has been outstandingly sung in recent years by Edita Gruberova, Lillian Watson, Natalie Dessay, Inger Dam Jensen, and Diana Damrau. Created (1933) by Ellice Illiard.

Fidalma (Cimarosa: *Il matrimonio segreto*). Cont. Sister of Geronimo whose household she runs. She is in love with his young clerk Paolino who is secretly married to her niece Carolina. Created (1792) by Dorothea Bussani.

Fidelio (Beethoven). Lib. by Joseph Sonnleither and Georg Friedrich Treitsche; 3 acts (rev. to 2 by Stefan von Breuning); f.p. Vienna 1805, cond. Beethoven.

A fortress near Seville, 18th cent.: *Florestan, secretly imprisoned by his political enemy Don *Pizarro, is in a dungeon guarded by the gaoler *Rocco. Florestan's wife, *Leonore, disguises herself as a man (Fidelio) and comes to work as Rocco's assistant. The young turnkey, *Jaquino, is in love with Rocco's daughter, *Marzelline, who now wants to marry the 'young man' Fidelio. Fidelio overhears Pizarro plotting to kill Florestan before the Minister, Don *Fernando, arrives to inspect the prison. She persuades Rocco to let the prisoners out into the garden for a short while and to let her help him dig the grave for the special prisoner in the dungeon. She realizes it is indeed her husband and resolves to save him. When Pizarro threatens to stab Florestan, she puts herself between them with a pistol. A trumpet sounds—the Minister has arrived. Pizarro flees, Florestan and Leonore are reunited. The prisoners and their families are allowed to join them for the Minister's address. He recognizes his old friend Florestan and assigns Leonore the task of unlocking his chains. Everyone joins in a hymn of praise to the noble Leonore.

Fidelio (Beethoven: *Fidelio*). *See* LEONORE.

Fieramosca (Berlioz: *Benvenuto Cellini*). Bar. Sculptor to the Pope, overlooked in favour of Cellini when the Pope wants a statue to be made. Created (1838) by Jean-Etienne Massol.

Fiery Angel, The (*Ognennyj Angel*) (Prokofiev). Lib. by comp.; 5 acts; f.p. Paris 1954 (concert), cond. Charles Bruck; Venice 1955 (stage), cond. Nino Sanzogno.

Germany, 16th cent.: *Ruprecht falls in love with *Renata who is thought to be a witch. She is searching for Count *Heinrich, who deserted her after a year, believing him to be her protecting angel. Together, Ruprecht and Renata use magic to try to find Heinrich, asking for help from Agrippa *von Nettelsheim. When they meet Heinrich, he and Ruprecht fight a duel. Ruprecht is injured and the guilty Renata promises to love him and nurse him. When he recovers she leaves and enters a convent to atone for her behaviour. Ruprecht meets *Faust and *Mephistopheles. In the convent Renata remains obsessed with her angel, corrupting the nuns with her visions. As Ruprecht and Mephistopheles watch, she is condemned to death.

Fiesco, Jacopo (Verdi: *Simon Boccanegra*). Bass. Father of Maria, who has an affair with the plebeian Boccanegra, of whom the aristocratic Fiesco disapproves. Maria dies and Fiesco can only forgive Boccanegra if he hands over the child Maria had, but the little girl has disappeared. Fiesco is further angered when Boccanegra is elected doge of Genoa. Unknown to everyone involved, Boccanegra's daughter has been adopted and brought up as Amelia Grimaldi. At the Grimaldi palace, 25 years later, she and Boccanegra meet and he recognizes her as his long-lost daughter. Andrea, her guardian, is Fiesco under an assumed name (not knowing who Amelia is). When Boccanegra is poisoned and dying, he tells Fiesco that this is his granddaughter and the two men are finally reconciled before Boccanegra dies. Aria: *Il lacerato spirito* ('The tormented spirit'). Created (1857) by Giuseppe Echeverria; (1881) by Édouard de Reszke.

Figaro 1. (Rossini: *Il barbiere di Siviglia*). Bar. The barber who regularly shaves Dr Bartolo. He assists Count Almaviva in his efforts to meet Bartolo's ward Rosina, whom Bartolo wants to marry. While shaving Bartolo, he manages to secrete the key to the balcony window so the young couple can elope, but their plans are frustrated. However, he finds a notary willing to conduct their wedding ceremony. Aria (one of the most popular of all comic operatic arias): *Largo al factotum* ('Make way for the factotum'); sextet (with Count, Rosina, Bartolo, Basilio, and Berta): *Freddo ed immobile* ('Awestruck and motionless'). This role attracts baritones of a high calibre, and allows them to indulge in a fair degree of comedy. It is interesting to compare the list of singers with that of Mozart's Figaro—some, but by no means all, undertake both roles. Notable singers of the Rossini role have included Giuseppe Taddei, Ettore Bastianini, Tito Gobbi, Sherrill Milnes, Renato Capecchi, Sesto Bruscantini, Hermann Prey, Piero Cappuccilli, John Rawnsley, Samuel Ramey, and Thomas Hampson. Created (1816) by Luigi Zamboni.

2. (Mozart: *Le nozze di Figaro*). Bar. The same barber as above, now valet to Count Almaviva and about to marry Susanna, the Countess's maid, on whom the Count also has designs. Figaro and Susanna will continue to live in the house and serve the Count and Countess, who have given them a room to prepare for themselves close to their master and mistress so that they can be on call as necessary. Figaro helps the ladies to prove to the Count that his wife is totally faithful and, in the end, to reconcile them. Arias: *Non più andrai* ('No more will you go'); *Aprite un po' quegli occhi* ('Open your eyes for a moment'). Although still a comic role, the singers who regularly sing this part do not as a rule undertake the Rossini barber. They have included Willi Domgraf-Fassbänder, Mariano Stabile, Paul Schöffler, Erich Kunz, Rolando Panerai, Titta Ruffo, Cesare Siepi, Sesto Bruscantini, Walter Berry, Giuseppe Taddei, Hermann Prey, Geraint Evans, John Rawnsley, Claudio Desderi, Ruggero Raimondi, and Bryn Terfel (of whom only Bruscantini, Taddei, Prey, and Rawnsley appear in both lists, although there are doubtless others not mentioned here). Created (1786) by Francesco Benucci.

3. (Corigliano: *The Ghosts of Versailles*). Bar. Still Count Almaviva's valet, married for twenty years to Susanna. He is the favourite character of his creator, Beaumarchais, whose ghost enlists his help to change the course of history so that Marie Antoinette, with whom Beaumarchais is in love, will not have to go to the guillotine. Figaro's attempts to rescue her and the entire Almaviva family, who have been captured with her, fail miserably. Created (1991) by Gino Quilico.

Fileno (Haydn: *La fedeltà premiata*). Ten. Beloved of Celia, threatened with being sacrificed to placate the sea monster near Diana's temple. He attacks the monster and Diana blesses his marriage with Celia. Created (1781) by Guglielmo Jermoli.

Filipyevna (Tchaikovsky: *Eugene Onegin*). Mez. Old nursemaid in the Larin family. Tatyana, consumed with love for Onegin, asks her nurse about her own youth and courtship and marriage, and then asks Filipyevna to bring pen and paper so that she can write a letter to Onegin. Created (1879) by Zinaida Konshina.

***Fille du régiment, La* (*The Daughter of the Regiment*)** (Donizetti). Lib. by Jean-François-Alfred Bayard and Jules-Henri Vernoyde Saint-Georges; 2 acts; f.p. Paris 1840.

The Swiss Tyrol, 1815: *Marie, found as a child abandoned on the battlefield, was adopted as a 'daughter' by the 21st Regiment of the French Army. She tells *Sulpice that she has fallen for *Tonio, who saved her life when she almost fell off a precipice. In order to be eligible to marry Marie, he at once enlists as a grenadier. The Marquise de *Birkenfeld announces she is Marie's aunt and removes her from the regiment to her château. Marie objects when the Marquise wants her to marry the son of the Duchesse de *Krakenthorp. The wounded Sulpice comes to the château and then the whole regiment arrives. Tonio begs the Marquise to allow him to marry Marie. The Marquise confesses that Marie is really her illegitimate daughter. She gives her consent to their marriage.

Finn (Glinka: *Ruslan and Lyudmila*). Ten. A good-natured magician. He helps Ruslan find the abducted Lyudmila and provides the ring to break the evil spell put upon her. Aria (one of the longest in all opera): *Lyubyézni sin! Oozh ya zabíl otchízni dálnoï oogryúmi kraï* ('My dear son, I have long forgotten my own gloomy homeland'). Created (1842) by Leon Leonov (the illegitimate son of John Field, the Irish composer and pianist).

finta giardiniera, La (*The Pretend Garden-Girl*) (Mozart). Lib. by ?Giuseppe Petrosellini; 3 acts; f.p. Munich 1775.

Lagonero, mid-18th cent.: Don *Anchise, the Podestà (mayor) has fallen in love with *Sandrina, the gardener's assistant, who is the Marchesa Violante in disguise. She is searching for her lover, the somewhat mad *Belfiore, who stabbed her and went into hiding, thinking she was dead. She is accompanied by *Nardo (her disguised servant Roberto). *Arminda, Don Anchise's niece, is to receive her prospective bridegroom, to the distress of her admirer *Ramiro. The bridegroom turns out to be Belfiore. Anchise wants him to be arrested for the murder of Violante, who has disappeared, so Sandrina has to admit her identity in order to save him. Arminda conspires with the maid *Serpetta, who loves Anchise, to lose Sandrina in a forest, but Nardo overhears them plotting and rescues them. Now Sandrina and Belfiore seem to have lost their minds, but they recover their sanity and fall in love. Arminda settles for Ramiro and Serpetta for Nardo. The Podestà is left alone, hoping another young lady will turn up.

Fiordiligi (Mozart: *Così fan tutte*). Sop. Sister of Dorabella and betrothed to Guglielmo. The sceptical Don Alfonso is determined to prove to his friends that all women are fickle and enlists the help of the sisters' maid, Despina. He tricks the sisters into accepting the overtures of two foreign gentlemen (who are their own fiancés in disguise). Determined to remain faithful to Guglielmo, Fiordiligi admonishes Dorabella for weakening, but gradually she too gives in to her amorous suitor ('I'll take the fair one') who is, in reality, her sister's fiancé, Ferrando. A bogus double wedding takes place but no sooner are the marriage contracts signed than the real fiancés return. How will the men react and who will Fiordiligi settle for? Arias: *Come scoglio* ('Like a rock'); *Per pietà* ('Have pity on me'). The two arias mentioned above are very demanding and wide-ranging, requiring a soprano with a good 'top' to the voice, but also a good downward extension. She is the serious sister, who tries to control the early signs of weakening in her younger sister. Famous interpreters, in all nationalities, include Florence Easton, Ina Souez, Jarmila Novotna, Joan Cross, Eleanor Steber, Susanne

Danco, Lisa Della Casa. Elisabeth Schwarzkopf, Sena Jurinac, Margaret Price, Pilar Lorengar, Elizabeth Harwood, Gundula Janowitz, Irmgard Seefried, Karita Mattila, Carol Vaness, Kiri te Kanawa, Felicity Lott, Amanda Roocroft, Renée Fleming, Barbara Frittoli, and Solveig Kringelborn. Created (1790) by Adriana Ferrarese del Bene (who had a torrid affair with Lorenzo da Ponte. Her sister created Dorabella).

Fiorilla (Rossini: *Il turco in Italia*). Sop. Italian lady, wife of Geronio, but not averse to the attentions of other men. The Turkish Prince Selim finds her attractive, but is unable to decide between her and his old love, Zaida. Narciso also loves Fiorilla. At a masked ball the two ladies dress alike and so do the three men, causing utter confusion. The poet Prosdocimo, anxious to bring the day's events to a happy conclusion, sorts them all out and Geronio forgives Fiorilla for her infidelity. Created (1814) by Francesca Maffei-Festa.

Fisher, King (Tippett: *The Midsummer Marriage*). Bar. A business tycoon, father of Jenifer. A rather aggressive figure, he is opposed to his daughter's wedding to Mark. When she disappears in search of spiritual fulfilment, he assumes she has eloped and tries to follow her. He enlists the help of a clairvoyant, Mme Sosostris, and is warned not to tamper with nature or try to alter its course. He tries to kill Mark, but himself drops dead (presumably from a heart attack). Created (1955) by Otakar Kraus.

Flamand (Strauss: *Capriccio*). Ten. A musician. He is in love with the Countess Madeleine and whilst listening to a sextet in her château, he discovers that the poet Olivier feels the same about her— whom will she choose? The two men represent the two constituents of opera: words and music. Flamand naturally favours the music: *Prima la musica—dopo le parole* ('First the music—then the words'), he replies to Olivier's statement that the words are the most important element. Olivier has written a sonnet for Madeleine and Flamand composes music to it for her birthday, giving rise to great distress and disapproval in the poet and a long discussion—to whom does it now belong, the poet or the composer? The Countess claims it as her present from them both, so it no longer belongs to either of them. Flamand declares his love for her and his desire to marry her and asks her for an answer. She promises to give it to him, in the library tomorrow morning at 11 o'clock. Aria: *Verraten hab' ich meine Gefühle!* ('I have betrayed my feelings!'). Created (1942) by Horst Taubmann.

Flaminia (Haydn: *Il mondo della luna*). Sop. Daughter of Buonafede and sister of Clarice. She is in love with Ernesto, but her father disapproves. She helps to trick him into giving his consent to their marriage. Created (1777) by Maria Anna Puttler.

Flavio (Handel: *Rodelinda*). Silent role. Young son of King Bertarido and Queen Rodelinda of Lombardy. Creator (1725) not known.

Fleance (Verdi: *Macbeth*). Silent. A child, son of Banquo, who manages to escape when his father is assassinated. Creator (1847) unknown. A famous Fleance was the 12-year-old George Christie, who played the role in the Glyndebourne company's production of the opera at the Edinburgh Festival in 1947—his only operatic performance!

Fledermaus, Die (J. Strauss II). Lib. by Carl Haffner and Richard Genée; 3 acts; f.p. Vienna 1874, cond. J. Strauss II.

Vienna, late 19th cent.: Rosalinde *Eisenstein's husband Gabriel von *Eisenstein has to serve a prison sentence for a minor offence, his lawyer, Dr *Blind, being unable to have him released. Rosalinde's singing-teacher, *Alfred, is ready to take advantage of her husband's absence. The maid, *Adele, wants to attend Prince *Orlofsky's party. Eisenstein's friend Dr *Falke helps him fool his wife into thinking he is going to prison that night and the two men go to the Prince's party. The prison governor, *Frank, arrives at the house to collect his prisoner. Seeing Rosalinde with Alfred, he assumes this is her husband and removes him to prison. At the party, Falke explains to Orlofsky that he wants to get his own back on Eisenstein, who once left him to walk back alone through the streets of Vienna dressed as a bat. Wearing a gown she has 'borrowed' from her mistress, Adele arrives at the party with her sister *Ida. Among the guests is a masked Hungarian countess, with whom Eisenstein flirts, not realizing it is his wife. The Prince introduces him to 'Chevalier Chagrin' (Frank in disguise). At 6 a.m. Eisenstein and Frank leave the party to hurry to the gaol, each unaware of the identity of the other. At the prison, the gaoler, *Frosch, is trying to stop Alfred singing. Frank falls asleep at his desk. Adele and Ida arrive, looking for 'Chagrin'. Eisenstein is amazed to see that 'Chagrin' is the governor and to learn that his cell is already occupied! Rosalinde arrives and all is sorted out, Falke admitting that he planned the whole thing.

fliegende Holländer, Der (Wagner). Lib. by comp.; 3 acts; f.p. Dresden 1843, cond. Richard Wagner.

Norway, 18th cent.: *Daland's ship is anchored off the coast in bad weather. The *Steersman is keeping watch. The *Dutchman's ship appears. The Dutchman asks Daland for his daughter in marriage. He will reward Daland with great wealth. Daland agrees. In his house, Daland's daughter *Senta is fascinated by the portrait of a man on their wall. Her old governess *Mary and the other women tease her. *Erik, who would like to marry Senta, announces Daland's return. He enters with the Dutchman whom Senta recognizes from the portrait. The two are drawn together and she is determined to save him. The Dutchman overhears Erik trying to persuade Senta to marry him. Assuming her to be unfaithful and himself to be doomed, he leaves. Senta jumps into the sea to follow him. The Dutchman's ship sinks. She and he are seen together above the shipwreck.

Flint, Mr (Britten: *Billy Budd*). Bass-bar. The Sailing Master on the *Indomitable*. Created (1951) by Geraint Evans.

Flora 1. (Britten: *The Turn of the Screw*). Sop. Child in the charge of the Governess, older sister of Miles. Aria: *Dolly must sleep*. Created (1954) by Olive Dwyer.

2. (Verdi: *La traviata*). See BERVOIX, FLORA.

3. (Menotti: *The Medium*). Cont. Mother of Monica. As Mme Flora (Baba) she holds seances. During one of these, she is terrified by the feel of a cold hand on her throat. She accuses her mute servant, Toby, who is unable to deny it. When he hides behind a curtain she assumes he is a ghost and, frightened, she shoots him. Created (1946) by Claramae Turner.

florentinische Tragödie, Eine (*A Florentine Tragedy*) (Zemlinsky). Lib. trans. by Max Meyerfield from the Oscar Wilde play; 1 act; f.p. Stuttgart 1917, cond. Max von Schillings.

Florence, 16th cent.: The silk-merchant *Simone finds his wife *Bianca with Guido *Bardi, son of the Duke of Florence. The two men start to converse politely, but gradually say what they think and feel and fight a duel. At first Bianca supports Guido, but as Simone kills her lover, she realizes she loves her husband and needed him to demonstrate his strength.

Florestan (Beethoven: *Fidelio*). Ten. A Spanish nobleman, husband of Leonore. Secretly imprisoned by his enemy Pizarro. His wife Leonore dresses as a man (Fidelio) to work at the prison as the gaoler's assistant. She confirms that her husband is the special prisoner being held in a dungeon, whose grave she helps to dig. She manages to give him a little water and bread, but Florestan does not recognize her. She prevents Pizarro stabbing her husband just as the King's Minister arrives to free him and his fellow-prisoners. Aria: *Gott! Welch' Dunkel hier!* ('God! How dark it is here!'); duet (with Leonore): *O namenlose Freude!* ('Oh, nameless joy!'). The role of Florestan demands great vocal stamina from a tenor—the difficult tessitura almost requires a *Heldentenor*. Famous Florestans have included Enrico Tamberlik, Julius Patzak, Torsten Ralf, Jan Peerce, Wolfgang Windgassen, Ernst Haefliger, Jon Vickers, James McCracken, and Anton de Ridder. Created (1805) by Friedrich Christan Demmer.

Florestine (Corigliano: *The Ghosts of Versailles*). Sop./mez. Illegitimate daughter of Count Almaviva and an unknown 'Lady of Rank'. Florestine is loved by Léon, Countess Almaviva's illegitimate son, but promised by her father to Bégearss, a secret Revolutionary. Created (1991) by Tracy Dahl.

Florian (Sullivan: *Princess Ida*). Bar. Friend of Prince Hilarion. He helps the Prince break into the Castle Adamant to search for Ida. Created (1884) by Charles Ryley.

Flosshilde (Wagner: *Das Rheingold*; *Götterdämmerung*). Mez. One of three Rhinemaidens. Created (*R.* 1869) by Fräulein Ritter; (*G.* 1876) by Marie Lammert. *See* RHINE-MAIDENS.

Flower Maidens (Wagner: *Parsifal*). Six sops. These maidens live in Klingsor's magic garden, trying to seduce the Knights of the Grail and interest them in earthly pleasures. When Parsifal meets them, they tease him, but once they realize he is quite happy to play with them, they try to seduce him. They fight among themselves, each claiming to be the most beautiful. When Kundry calls to Parsifal, they metaphorically spring to attention, leaving him and returning to their castle. Created (1882) by Fräulein Horsen, Meta, Pringle, André, Galfy, and Belce (and in the programme for the première they were designated 'Klingsor's Zaubermädchen', i.e. Klingsor's *Magic Maidens*).

Flute 1. (Britten: *A Midsummer Night's Dream*). Ten. A bellows-maker, one of the rustics. Takes the part of the female Thisbe in the play they perform for Theseus and Hippolyta. Aria (as Thisbe): *Asleep, my love?* Created (1960) by Peter Pears.

2. (Purcell: *The Fairy Queen*). Spoken. Similar to the role in (1) above. Creator (1692) unknown.

Fluth, Frau (Nicolai: *Die lustige Weiber von Windsor*). Sop. Character equivalent to Alice Ford. Created (1849) by Leopoldine Tuczek. *See also* FORD, ALICE.

Fluth, Herr (Nicolai: *Die lustige Weiber von Windsor*). Bar. Character equivalent to Ford. Created (1849) by Julius Krauser. *See also* FORD.

Foltz, Hans (Wagner: *Die Meistersinger von Nürnberg*). Bass. By trade a copper-smith, he is one of the *Meistersinger*. Created (1868) by Herr Hayn.

Fontana, Signor (Verdi: *Falstaff*). Name assumed by Ford (in It.; in Eng. 'Master Brook') when, in disguise, he visits Falstaff and offers to help him seduce Alice Ford, his wife. *See* FORD.

Force, Chevalier de la (Poulenc: *Les Dialogues des Carmélites*). Ten. Son of the Marquis, brother of Blanche. Created (1957) by Nicola Filacuridi.

Force, Marquis de la (Poulenc: *Les Dialogues des Carmélites*). Bar. Father of Blanche and the Chevalier. Created (1957) by Scipio Colombo.

Ford (Verdi: *Falstaff*). Bar. Husband of Alice and father of Nannetta. He plans to marry his daughter to old Dr Caius. He learns of Falstaff's plan to seduce his wife and, disguised, offers to help him (in order to spy on his wife and see her reaction). He accompanies Falstaff to the Ford house and is heard coming in to interrupt the meeting. Falstaff is bundled into a laundry-basket and tipped into the river, and Alice is able to point him out to her husband as the fat knight struggles ashore. Ford joins the ladies in teaching Falstaff a further lesson and is himself tricked into consenting to the marriage of his daughter and Fenton, the young man she loves—couples are brought to him, still in disguise, and he blesses their union, only to find he has 'married' Caius to Bardolph and Nannetta to Fenton. He, like Falstaff, accepts the inevitable. Aria: *È sogno? O realtà … Due rami enormi crescon…* ('Am I dreaming? Or is it true …? I feel two enormous horns…'—known as Ford's Jealousy Aria). Created (1893) by Antonio Pini-Corsi, who later became an equally famous Falstaff, as did several other interpreters of Ford, including Mariano Stabile, Leonard Warren, Tito Gobbi, and Bryn Terfel.

Ford, Alice (Verdi: *Falstaff*). Sop. Wife of Ford and mother of Nannetta. She promises to help her daughter, whom Ford wants to marry off to the elderly Dr Caius, while Nannetta wants to marry the man she loves, young Fenton. Falstaff plans to seduce Alice as a way of acquiring some of her husband's money. She enlists the help of Mistress Quickly and Meg Page, and they set about teaching Falstaff a lesson. Ford, told of Falstaff's intentions, is worried his wife might actually be unfaithful. Alice arranges for Falstaff to visit her 'between two and three' when her husband is out. Meg pretends to hear Ford approaching and they hide Falstaff behind a screen. Mistress Quickly announces that Ford really is here. Falstaff is hastily bundled into a laundry-basket, Nannetta and Fenton taking his place. Ford hears the sound of kissing coming from behind the screen, pulls it down and reveals his daughter and her sweetheart. So where is Falstaff? Alice leads him to the window, through which the laundry-basket has been tipped, and there is the Fat Knight, soaking wet, struggling to climb out of the river below. Alice makes a further arrangement with Falstaff—they will meet in Windsor Park at midnight. Everyone dons masks and costumes and Falstaff is teased and tormented by all present, until he finally understands that it was all a joke and takes it in good part. Aria (with the other ladies): *Gaie comari di Windsor! è l'ora!* ('Merry Wives of Windsor! it is the hour!'); *Avrò con me del putti* ('I will have with me little elves'). In recent years, Elisabeth Schwarzkopf, Giulietta Simionato, and Regina Resnik have been famous Alice Fords. Created (1893) by Emma Zilli.

Ford, Nannetta (Verdi: *Falstaff*). Sop. Daughter of Ford and Alice. Her father plans to marry her to old Dr Caius but she is in love with young Fenton. She and Fenton join with her mother in teaching Falstaff—and Ford, for doubting his wife—a lesson. In the final scene in Windsor Park, Nannetta and her friends exchange garments with Fenton and his friends as she cleverly avoids being married to Caius, each of them being disguised. As their union is blessed by her father (under the impression that she has been married to Caius), fairies and goblins dance around the bemused Falstaff. When the truth is revealed, Ford accepts the situation with a good grace. Aria: *Sul fil d'un soffio etesio* ('On the breath of winds'); duet (with Fenton): *Labbra di foco!* ('Lips that are burning!). Created (1893) by Adelina Stehle.

Foreign Princess (Dvořák: *Rusalka*). Sop. Jealous of her rival, she reveals Rusalka's origins to the Prince, thus causing his death when Rusalka breaks her vow and speaks to him. Created (1901) by Marie Kubátová.

Forester (Janáček: *The Cunning Little Vixen*). Bass-bar. Otherwise called the Gamekeeper. He walks through the forest each day, and often stops for a sleep on his way home, happily telling his wife he's been delayed by work. He captures the Vixen and takes her home as a pet, but she escapes back to the forest. He and his friend the Schoolmaster play cards and tease each other—he teases the Schoolmaster about his slowness in courting his girlfriend, the Schoolmaster teases him about the Vixen's escape. It is by following the Forester through the seasons that the story unfolds. The most notable singer of this part in recent years has been Thomas Allen. Created (1924) by Arnold Flögl.

Formoutiers, Countess of (Rossini: *Le Comte Ory*). *See* ADELE (2).

Forth, Sir Riccardo (Bellini: *I Puritani*). Bar. A Puritan colonel, chosen as Elvira's husband but rejected by her in favour of a Cavalier, Arturo. Created (1835) by Antonio Tamburini.

Fortuna (Monteverdi: *L'incoronazione di Poppea*). Sop. One of the goddesses who, in the opera's prologue, debate their own successes and the failure of others. Creator (1643) not traced.

Fortune-Teller 1. (Strauss: *Arabella*). Sop. As the opera opens, Adelaide, Arabella's mother, is consulting the Fortune-Teller, who tells her that her husband will lose more money by gambling. However, she can see in the cards that a stranger is soon coming, from a great distance, and will want to marry Arabella. This is a cameo role which several famous sopranos, well past the prime of their career, have been happy to sing, including Martha Mödl. Created (1933) by Jessyka Koettrik.
  2. (Martin : *Julietta*). Michel meets her during his search for Julietta. She is unable to foretell the future, only the past. Creator (1938) not traced.

***forza del destino, La* (*The Force of Destiny*)** (Verdi). Lib. by Francesco Maria Piave; 4 acts; f. p. St Petersburg 1862, cond. Giuseppe Verdi.
  Spain and Italy, mid-18th cent.: In Spain, Leonora di *Vargas, daughter of the Marchese di *Calatrava, is about to elope with *Alvaro. His gun accidentally goes off, killing the Marchese. Leonora's brother Carlo di *Vargas, swears to avenge his father and pursues Leonora and Alvaro. Leonora, separated from Alvaro, arrives at an inn where the gypsy *Preziosilla tells of wars in Italy. She sees Carlo at the inn and flees, begging for help at a monastery, where Padre *Guardiano allows her to inhabit a sacred cave as a young penitent. Alvaro joins the Spanish army in Italy. He and Carlo meet under false names and swear eternal friendship. Alvaro is injured in battle and nursed by Carlo who, looking through his papers, finds Leonora's portrait and challenges Alvaro to a duel. Their fight is stopped by troops and Alvaro enters a monastery. Five years later, Fra *Melitone and the Father Superior are talking in the monastery when Carlo arrives, demanding to see Padre Raffaele (Alvaro). The two men fight, Carlo is injured and Alvaro seeks help for him from the caves. He and Leonora recognize each other. As he dies, Carlo stabs his sister who dies in Alvaro's arms.

Four Kings (Strauss: *Die Liebe der Danae*). 2 ten., 2 bass. Four nephews of King Pollux, who are trying to find a rich wife for his daughter Danae. Created (1944) by Walter Carnuth, Joszi Trojan-Regar, Theo Reuter, and Georg Wieter; (1952) by August Jaresch, Erich Majkut, Harald Pröglhof, and Franz Bierbach.

Four Queens (Strauss: *Die Liebe der Danae*). Wives of the Four Kings. *See* ALCMENE, EUROPA, LEDA, SEMELE (2).

Fox (Janáček: *The Cunning Little Vixen*). Sop. *Travesti* role. His real name is Zlatohřbítek. He falls in love with the Vixen and, when she becomes pregnant, marries her and they live in the forest with their cubs. To give a greater contrast in vocal timbre between the Vixen and the Fox, the Fox is often sung by a mez. or, in some productions, by a ten. Created (1924) by Božena Snopková.

Francis, Saint (Messiaen: *Saint François d'Assise*). Bar. St Francis of Assisi prays to God to help him reach a state of spiritual grace. At various stages of his journey he is encouraged by an Angel. He finds the strength to embrace a Leper, who is cured. And, in answer to his prayers, he is given the stigmata and experiences the pain and the peace felt by Christ on the cross. Created (1983) by José van Dam.

Frank (J. Strauss II: *Die Fledermaus*). Bar. The Governor of the Prison in which Eisenstein is to serve a sentence. The two men meet at Prince Orlofsky's ball, each unaware of the other's identity—they are introduced to each other as French noblemen (Frank is 'Chevalier Chagrin') and struggle to talk in very poor French. Back at the prison, they are astonished to meet again, now in their natural state. Created (1874) by Herr Friese.

Franz (Strauss: *Intermezzo*). *See* STORCH, FRANZ.

Frasquita (Bizet: *Carmen*). Sop. A gypsy girl, friend of Carmen. Created (1875) by Mme Ducasse.

Frau ohne Schatten, Die (*The Woman without a Shadow*) (Strauss). Lib. by Hugo von Hofmannsthal; 3 acts; f. p. Vienna 1919, cond. Franz Schalk.

Legendary place and time: The South Eastern Islands *Emperor has married the daughter of *Keikobad, master of the spirit world, but she has not cast a shadow, i. e. has not become pregnant. The *Spirit Messenger tells her *Nurse that unless the *Empress casts a shadow the Emperor will be turned to stone. The Empress and the Nurse visit the humble home of *Barak the Dyer, whose Wife (the *Dyer's Wife) has not had children but, being human, she has a shadow. The Nurse offers to buy her shadow in return for a life of luxury—she must refuse Barak's overtures for three days. Barak is banished to a single bed and, seeing his distress, the Empress feels guilty about trying to take the shadow but also about her own husband being turned to stone. The Wife tells Barak she has sold her shadow. He lifts a sword to strike her, but it is snatched from his hand. She realizes she loves him and the Empress cancels the bargain made by the Nurse. The Nurse guides her back to Keikobad's kingdom. Inside the temple she hears the voices of Barak and his Wife searching for each other. The Nurse, now hating them all, sends them in opposite directions. Keikobad's messenger condemns the Nurse to wander for ever amidst those she hates. The Empress is tempted to drink water from the fountain of life—this will give her the Wife's shadow. She refuses to drink and the Emperor is turned to stone. She offers to die with him. Suddenly she casts her own shadow and the Emperor comes back to life—Keikobad has forgiven her because she has learned about humanity. She and the Emperor, also Barak and his Wife, are reunited, their unborn children singing their praises.

Frederic (Sullivan: *The Pirates of Penzance*). Ten. An apprentice pirate who assumes that now he is 21 he can leave their employ, but learns he was born on 29 February and his 21st birthday will be in 1940! To escape the amorous attentions of his old nursemaid, he appeals for a wife and Mabel offers to marry him. Aria: *Oh, is there not one maiden breast?* Created (NY, 1879) by Hugh Talbot.

Frédéric 1. (Delibes: *Lakmé*). Bar. An English officer, who reminds his friend Gérald of his duty as a soldier. Created (1883) by Mons. Barré.

2. (Thomas: *Mignon*). Ten. or cont. A young nobleman who falls in love with Philine, an actress with a troupe of strolling players. Created (1866) by Mons. Vois.

Freia (Wagner: *Das Rheingold*). Sop. Goddess of youth and beauty. Sister of Fricka, Froh, and Donner and sister-in-law of Wotan. Wotan has promised to give Freia to the giants as payment for their building of Valhalla. Her brothers defend her position—Donner by threatening the giants with his hammer. The saving of Freia is crucial to the final outcome of the *Ring*—by being forced to give the giants the gold Ring, on which there is a curse, instead of his sister-in-law, the ultimate downfall of the gods is set in motion. Created (1869) by Henriette Müller.

Freischütz, Der (*The Freeshooter*) (Weber). Lib. by Johann Friedrich Kind; 3 acts; f. p. Berlin 1821, cond. Weber.

Bohemia, mid-17th cent.: *Kilian, a peasant, beats *Max, a forester, in a shooting match. *Cuno, head forester and father of *Agathe, warns Max that if he fails a shooting test before Prince *Ottokar, he will not allow Agathe to marry him. *Caspar gives Max a gun loaded with a magic bullet, forged in the Wolf's Glen. There lives *Samiel, a wild huntsman, to whom Caspar has sold himself, and now plans to sell Max in his place. Agathe and her cousin *Ännchen warn Max not to go to the Glen, but he ignores them. He and Caspar forge seven magic bullets—six will do his bidding, but the seventh will obey Samiel. Max uses six bullets hunting; the seventh is left for the test. He aims at a dove. Agathe, arriving with the Hermit, calls to him not to shoot, but he has already pulled the trigger. Caspar falls, fatally wounded. Samiel, satisfied, frees Max. The Prince, learning about Max's use of magic bullets, banishes him. With the Hermit's intervention, Ottokar forgives Max for using magic bullets in the test, much to Agathe's relief.

Fricka (Wagner: *Das Rheingold; Die Walküre*). Mez. Goddess of marriage, wife of Wotan, and sister of Freia, Donner, and Froh.

Das Rheingold: Fricka is horrified by her husband's contract with the giants—they will build Valhalla and he will give them Freia in payment. She does her best to comfort her sister. Hearing of the Rhine gold from Loge, Fricka is attracted by the prospect of owning the hoard. The giants remove Freia as hostage while Wotan thinks about whether to give them the gold as payment instead of his sister-in-law. After the giants have been paid and Freia has been freed, Fricka joins Wotan in leading the gods across the rainbow bridge to Valhalla. Aria (with Wotan): *Wotan! Gemahl! erwache!* ('Wotan! Husband, awake!').

Die Walküre: Fricka, as goddess of marriage, supports Hunding's right to revenge for the incestuous love between his wife Sieglinde and her brother Siegmund. Fricka's relationship with Wotan has deteriorated and she arrives in her carriage, drawn by rams, to find him on the mountain where his nine daughters by Erda live. Wotan refuses to help in seeking revenge for Hunding or to condemn the twins' relationship and Fricka rails against him and his own unfaithfulness. She makes him promise that he will at least not protect Siegmund in battle and will forbid Brünnhilde to help him, warning him that if he ignores her, the gods will suffer. He gives his promise—Hagen kills Siegmund and Wotan then kills Hagen. Aria: *So ist es denn aus mit den ewigen Göttern?* ('So is it all over, then, with the eternal Gods?').

Created (*R.* 1869) by Sophie Stehle; (*W.* 1870) by Anna Kaufmann.

Friedenstag (*Peace Day*) (Strauss). Lib. by Joseph Gregor; 1 act; f. p. Munich 1938, cond. Clemens Krauss.

A beleaguered town, 1648: It is 24 October, at the end of the Thirty Years War. The people are starving and the army is near to collapse. The Major asks the *Commandant to surrender in order to save them all, but he cannot—he'll fight to the end. He is going to blow up their fortress and offers them all the chance to leave or stay, as they wish. The Commandant's wife, *Maria, chooses to stay with her husband, even though it will mean death. As they are about to light the gunpowder, bells ring to signify that peace has been proclaimed. The Commandant thinks it is all a trick and, seeing the *Holsteiner arrive, draws his sword. Maria intervenes to stop them fighting and they are reconciled. All is rejoicing and peace.

Friedrich Artur, Prince of Homburg (Henze: *Der Prinz von Homburg*). Bar./ten.

General of Cavalry. Sentenced to death for ignoring Marshal Dörfling's orders, he refuses to save himself by acting dishonourably. The Marshal, moved by this attitude, tears up the death warrant, leaving the prince free to marry the Elector's niece, Princess Natalie. Created (1960) by Vladimir Ruzdjak.

Friedrich Wilhelm, Elector of Brandenburg (Henze: *Der Prinz von Homburg*). Ten. Promises his wife's niece, Princess Natalie, to the Prince of Homburg. Sentences the Prince to death for ignoring the Marshal's orders in battle. Created (1960) by Helmut Melchert.

Frith (Josephs: *Rebecca*). Bar. The butler at Manderley, the de Winter family home. Created (1983) by James Thornton.

Fritz (Offenbach: *La Grande-Duchesse de Gérolstein*). Ten. A young recruit in the Gérolstein army, in love with Wanda. The Grand Duchess falls in love with him and promotes him to general. He returns triumphant from battle but still in love with Wanda. Rejected, the Grand Duchess demotes him back to private. Created (1867) by José Dupuis.

Froh (Wagner: *Das Rheingold*). Ten. God of light and joy. Brother of Donner, Fricka, and Freia and brother-in-law of Wotan. He helps Donner rescue Freia from the clutches of the giants. Like his brother, he is devastated by Freia's imminent abduction by the giants, pleads with Wotan to give the giants the gold Ring in payment instead, and is overjoyed to see her return. On Donner's instructions, it is Froh who summons the rainbow bridge across which the gods will walk to Valhalla. Created (1869) by Franz Nachbaur.

From the House of the Dead (*Z mrtvého domu*) (Janáček). Lib. by comp.; 3 acts; f. p. Brno 1930, cond. Břetislav Bakala.

Siberia, 19th cent.: The prisoners, some of whom have been there many years, are nursing their pet eagle with a broken wing. A new prisoner arrives, the aristocratic Alexandr *Gorjančikov who claims to be a political prisoner. He is ordered by the prison commandant to be flogged. Some of the prisoners are sent to work outside, others inside. Luka Kuzmič (whose real name is Filka *Morozov) quarrels with *Skuratov. They each recall their earlier life and Luka tells how he killed a prison officer and was flogged. Working on the river bank, Gorjančikov offers to teach the young boy *Aljeja to read and write. Skuratov tells how he murdered the man his girlfriend was being obliged by her family to marry and was sentenced to prison for life. All the prisoners perform two plays on a makeshift stage. When the second play is over, the prisoners disperse. The short fat prisoner wounds Aljeja, who has to be taken to the prison hospital. The old man, *Šiškov, now tells his story—he was forced into marriage with a girl who everyone thought had been seduced by Filka Morozov, but on their wedding-night he discovered she was still a virgin. Later she admitted she was in love with Filka and having an affair with him. Šiškov, humiliated, killed her. He now realizes that Luka, dying in his bed, is Filka Morotov. The governor, drunk, releases Gorjančikov and Aljeja comes from the hospital to say goodbye to him. As he leaves, the prisoners release the eagle which, like Gorjančikov, soars away to freedom.

Frosch (J. Strauss II: *Die Fledermaus*). Spoken. The gaoler at the prison. He has difficulty trying to stop Alfred singing in his cell. This role provides a great opportunity for a comic actor. Created (1874) by Herr Schreiber.

Frugola (The Rummager) (Puccini: *Il tabarro*). Mez. Wife of the stevedore Talpa. She and her husband dream of owning a country cottage. Her greatest love is her cat. Created (1918) by Alice Gentle.

Furies (Gluck: *Orfeo ed Euridice*). Chorus: SATB. The Furies are the inhabitants of Hades who guard the entrance to the underworld. They threaten Orfeo when he comes to look for Euridice, but the sweetness of his music wins them over and they allow him to enter to search for his loved one.

Fyodor (Musorgsky: *Boris Godunov*). Mez. *Travesti* role. Son of Boris Godunov, sister of Xenia. Is with his father when, demented, Boris dies. Created (1874) by Aleksandra Krutikova.

G

Gaea (Strauss: *Daphne*). Cont. (or mez.). Wife of Peneios and mother of Daphne. She overhears Daphne telling Leukippos, her friend from childhood, that she is not interested in his passionate declarations. Gaea tells her daughter that one day she will recognize real love. Duet (with Daphne): *Daphne! Mutter!* ('Daphne! Mother!'). Some well-known singers have sung this short but rewarding role, including Jean Madeira and Marjana Lipovšek. Created (1938) by Helene Jung (who was also the first Mussel in *Die ägyptische Helena* and created the Housekeeper in *Die schweigsame Frau*).

Galatea (Handel: *Acis and Galatea*). Sop. A part-divine sea-nymph in love with the shepherd Acis. Acis is killed by the giant Polyphemus. Devastated, Galatea transforms Acis into a stream. Created (1718) possibly by Margherita de l'Epine (wife of the composer J. C. Pepusch).

Galitsky, Prince Vladimir (Borodin: *Prince Igor*). Bass. Brother of Yaroslavna, Prince Igor's wife. He is an extravagant and dissolute man. When Igor goes with his son to fight the Polovtsi, he leaves Galitsky to rule the people and take care of Yaroslavna. Created (1890) by Fyodor Stravinsky (father of the composer Igor Stravinsky).

Gama, King (Sullivan: *Princess Ida*). Bar. Father of Princess Ida. Created (1884) by George Grossmith.

Gamekeeper (Janáček: *The Cunning Little Vixen*). See FORESTER.

Gamuret (Wagner: *Parsifal*). Father of Parsifal. He does not appear in the opera. Parsifal does not know who his father is, but Kundry explains to him and Gurnemanz that Gamuret was slain in battle before Parsifal's birth. *See also* HERZELEIDE.

Garibaldo (Handel: *Rodelinda*). Bass. Duke of Turin. Friend of Grimoaldo (who hopes to marry Rodelinda, whose husband Bertarido has been reported killed). Garibaldo feigns love for Eduige, sister of King Bertarido, in the hope that he will inherit the royal money. He tries to kill Grimoaldo, but is himself killed by the returning Bertarido. Created (1725) by Giuseppi Boschi.

Gawain (Birtwistle). Lib. by David Harsent; 2 acts; f.p. London 1991, cond. Elgar Howarth.

*Morgan le Fay manipulates and comments on the action. At New Year in the court of *Arthur and his wife *Guinevere, the *Green Knight challenges someone to hit his neck with an axe, on condition that he return the blow a year later. *Gawain, the knight known for his courtesy, accepts the challenge and decapitates the Green Knight. The Knight retrieves his head, which speaks, telling Gawain to meet him at the Green Chapel. As the seasons change, Gawain sets off. At the castle of Sir Bertilak and Lady de *Hautdesert, he is entertained and the Lady tries to seduce him. Gawain leaves for the Green Chapel, wearing a sash given to him by her Ladyship which will protect him. The Green Knight cuts Gawain lightly with his third blow, and reveals himself as Sir Bertilak. Gawain returns to Arthur's court, ashamed of his cowardice in wearing the protection.

Gawain (Birtwistle: *Gawain*). Bar. Knight at the court of Arthur. After decapitating the Green Knight he has to meet him a year later for a return blow. Saved by a protective girdle given to him by the Lady de Hautdesert, he realizes the Green Knight is Sir Bertilak de Hautdesert. Created (1991) by François le Roux.

gazza ladra, La (*The Thieving Magpie*)
(Rossini). Lib. by Giovanni Gherardini; 2 acts;
f.p. Milan 1817.

Village near Paris, some time in the past:
Giannetto *Vingradito loves Ninetta *Villabella, a servant in the home of his father Fabrizio *Vingradito. She is the daughter of
Fernando *Villabella, a soldier. Fabrizio's wife
Lucia *Vingradito accuses Ninetta of losing a
silver fork. *Isacco comes to sell his wares, but
*Pippo, a young servant, sends him away.
Ninetta's father visits her—he has been condemned to death and has escaped. He gives
her a silver fork and spoon to sell to raise
money to aid him. The pet magpie steals a silver spoon and again Lucia accuses Ninetta, an
accusation apparently substantiated when
Pippo reports seeing Ninetta selling to Isacco
silver with the initials F.V. on it. Ninetta is sent
to prison. Lucia tells Fernando of his daughter's position and when he tries to help her he
is himself arrested. Ninetta prays in front of
the church before her execution. Pippo climbs
up the spire and finds the cutlery in the magpie's nest. Ninetta is saved and her father
pardoned.

Geisterbote (Strauss: *Die Frau ohne Schatten*). *See* SPIRIT MESSENGER.

Gellner, Vincenzo (Catalani: *La Wally*). Bar.
Favoured by her father as a husband for Wally.
Rejected by her, he attempts to kill the man she
loves. Created (1892) by Arturo Pessina.

Geneviève (Debussy: *Pelléas et Mélisande*).
Cont. Daughter of King Arkel and mother of
Golaud and Pelléas by different marriages.
Created (1902) by Jeanne Gerville-Réache.

Gérald (Delibes: *Lakmé*). Ten. English officer
in India, who trespasses into a sacred grove,
sees Lakmé and falls in love with her, thus
earning the wrath of her father, a Brahmin
priest. Despite his love for Lakmé, Gérald, reminded of his duty as a soldier, returns to his
regiment. Lakmé takes poison. Created (1883)
by Jean-Alexandre Talazac.

Gérard, Carlo (Giordano: *Andrea Chénier*).
Bar. Servant of the Contessa di Coigny, he is a
leader of the peasants' revolt and is secretly in
love with the Contessa's daughter, Maddalena,
who is in love with the poet Chénier. When
Chénier is arrested, Maddalena begs Gérard to
have him set free. He is unable to do so, but assists Maddalena to enter the prison so that she
can die with Chénier. Aria: *Nemico della patria*
('An enemy of his country'). Created (1896) by
Mario Sammarco.

Gerda (Delius: *Fennimore and Gerda*). Sop.
Minor character in the opera. Fennimore's
lover Niels, when rejected by Fennimore,
marries the young Gerda. Created (1919) by
Elizabeth Kandt. *See* FENNIMORE.

Gerhilde (Wagner: *Die Walküre*). *See*
VALKYRIES.

Germont, Alfredo (Verdi: *La traviata*). Ten.
Son (*fils*) of Giorgio Germont. Often referred to
as Germont *fils*. At a party at her house, Alfredo
meets the courtesan Violetta Valéry, whom he
has loved from afar for some time—when she
was recently ill, he came daily to ask after her.
He tells her of his feelings and suggests she
give up her way of life and live with him, but
she refuses to consider this. However, we next
meet Alfredo in the country house in which he
and Violetta have been living for three months.
He has been out hunting. Violetta's maid returns from Paris and when questioned by Alfredo admits she has been selling more of her
mistress's possessions to pay the bills and
there are now not many things left to sell. Horrified, Alfredo leaves immediately for Paris to
raise money. By the time he returns, Violetta
has been visited by his father, who has persuaded her to leave Alfredo for the honour of
the family. Alfredo is overcome by Violetta's
passionate appeal to him to declare his love for
her, before she rushes out of the room. A servant brings him a letter from her—she has decided to return to Baron Duphol, her protector
in Paris. His father, who enters at that moment,
is unable to console him. Seeing an invitation
to Flora's party on Violetta's desk, Alfredo departs, sure that he will find her there. At the
party he spends all his time at the gaming-
tables, fully aware of Violetta's entrance, but
giving no sign of having noticed her. The guests
go to supper and Alfredo and Violetta meet
alone, but she will not change her plans. Calling the other guests as witnesses, he throws at
Violetta all the money he has won, putting him
out of her debt. Six months later, Violetta is
dying from consumption. She has received a
letter from Germont *père*—Alfredo went

abroad after the party. His father has told him of the sacrifice Violetta made for their family and he is hurrying back to her. When he arrives, there is a passionate reunion and they declare their love and talk about their plans for the future. However, Alfredo can see that all is not well and, in answer to his questions, Annina confirms that Violetta is dying. As she tells him that her strength is returning, she collapses and dies. Arias: *Libiamo ne' lieti calici* ('Let's drink from the overflowing chalice'—known as the *Brindisi*, i.e. drinking-song); *Un dì felice* ('One happy day'); *Lunge da lei … De miei bollenti spiriti* ('Far from her … My passionate spirit'); duet (with Violetta): *Parigi, o cara* ('We'll leave Paris, my dearest').

The character of Alfredo, like that of his father and of Violetta, develops from act to act. In Act 1 he is the carefree young man-about-town; in Act 2 he changes from the contented partner to the inconsolable rejected lover, to the man set on revenge—hell hath no fury like *this* man scorned, it would seem, as he publicly insults the woman he loves; and in the last act, aware at last of the reason for Violetta's behaviour, he is in turn the ardent suitor, the forgiving son and, ultimately, the bereaved sweetheart. Of all Verdi's tenor roles so far, this is the one with most opportunities for the singer to demonstrate his talent—it contains more solo arias, for one thing—and all great tenors are anxious to sing the part. These have included Jan Peerce, Helge Roswaenge, Tito Schipa, Giuseppe di Stefano, Richard Tucker, Fritz Wunderlich, Carlo Bergonzi, Nicolai Gedda, Franco Bonisolli, Plácido Domingo, Alfredo Kraus, Luciano Pavarotti, Dennis O'Neill, José Carreras, Frank Lopardo, and Roberto Alagna. Created (1853) by Lodovico Graziani.

Germont, Giorgio (Verdi: *La traviata*). Bar. Father (*père*) of Alfredo. Referred to usually as Germont *père*. He visits Violetta to ask her to make the great sacrifice—to give up his son, whose career, his father believes, is jeopardized by her reputation. Also, he has a daughter who has a good marriage prospect, which is going to be ruined if it becomes known that her brother is living with a courtesan, albeit a high-class and popular one—such have the social mores changed in the last 100 years or so. Even while asking her to make the sacrifice, Germont feels

sorry for Violetta, admiring her dignity and believing that she loves Alfredo. But despite learning that she is ill and may not have long to live, he cruelly persists in pointing out to her that, as she ages and looks less glamorous, Alfredo will lose interest in her anyway—so why not do the right thing now and make things better for his family? Violetta gives in, but asks Germont to promise that one day, when she is dead, he will explain her actions to Alfredo. After she leaves for Paris, he does his best to help his son come to terms with the situation, suggesting he would be better coming to the family home, but Alfredo is inconsolable. At Flora's party, Germont observes his son insulting Violetta, admonishes him for his ungentlemanly behaviour, and disowns him. Months later, Germont's conscience troubles him. He writes to Alfredo telling him the whole story and he also writes to Violetta, explaining that this is what he has done. He arrives just in time to embrace her as a daughter before she dies. Aria: *Pura siccome un angelo* ('God gave me a daughter, pure as an angel'); *Di Provenza il mar, il suol* ('The sea and soil of Provence').

At the beginning of the second act, Germont *père* may seem to be something of a prig, but we must remember that he is very much of his time—family honour is everything and he is prepared to ask any sacrifice to marry his daughter to a suitable husband. And he probably truly believes that Alfredo would be better off without the courtesan. Nevertheless, he is honest enough to admire Violetta's spirit and to feel sorry for her even while he asks her to make such a terrible sacrifice, and he accedes to her request that, one day, Alfredo will be told the truth. Indeed, six months later, he does tell his son the whole story. Charles Osborne in his *The Complete Operas of Verdi* (London, 1969) sums up the role beautifully when he tartly comments that *Di Provenza* in its 'stodgy sentimentality is just right for Germont *père*'. Giorgio Germont is not a particularly interesting character, but his two arias in his big scene with Violetta have been enough to make the part attractive for baritones. These have included Mattia Battistini, Robert Merrill, Paolo Silveri, Carlo Tagliabue, Titta Ruffo, Ettore Bastianini, Heinrich Schlusnus, Leonard Warren, Tito Gobbi, Renato Capecchi, Sherrill Milnes, Dietrich Fischer-Dieskau, Rolando Panerai, Sesto Bruscantini, Leo Nucci, Renato Bruson,

Thomas Allen, and Dmitri Hvorostovsky. Created (1853) by Felice Varesi.

Gernando (Haydn: *L'isola disabitata*). Ten. Husband of Costanza whom he rescues from the deserted island on which he left her with her sister thirteen years earlier. Created (1779) by Andrea Totti.

Geronimo (Cimarosa: *Il matrimonio segreto*). Bass. A wealthy deaf merchant. He wants his elder daughter, Elisetta, to marry Count Robinson. His younger daughter, Carolina, is secretly married to his clerk. Created (1792) by Giambattista Serafino Blasi.

Geronio (Rossini: *Il turco in Italia*). Bass. Husband of Fiorilla, he wants to teach his flirtatious wife a lesson and bans all men from the house. The arrival of the Turkish Prince Selim provides the next attraction, but Selim cannot make up his mind between Fiorilla and his old love, Zaida. Geronio comes to a masked ball disguised as Selim, and the two ladies dress identically causing chaos. It is left to the poet Prosdocimo to sort them all out. Geronio forgives his wife and they are reunited. Created (1814) by Luigi Pacini.

Geronte (Puccini: *Manon Lescaut*). *See* RAVOIR, GERONTE DI.

Gertrud (Humperdinck: *Hänsel und Gretel*). Mez. Wife of Peter and mother of Hänsel and Gretel. As there is no food to feed the family, she sends the children to pick strawberries in the Ilsenstein forest, wherein lives the wicked Witch. Created (1893) by Luise Tibelti.

Gertrude 1. (Gounod: *Roméo et Juliette*). Mez. Juliet's nurse. Created (1867) by Mme Duclos.
   2. (Thomas: *Hamlet*). Mez. The Queen, mother of Hamlet, recently widowed and now about to marry Claudius, brother of her late husband the King. She and Claudius have conspired to cause her husband's death and she is terrified that Hamlet will find this out and seek revenge—which indeed he does. Created (1868) by Pauline Guéymard-Lauters.

Geschwitz, Countess (Berg: *Lulu*). Mez. A lesbian who is attracted to Lulu. When she tries to save Lulu from being killed by Jack the Ripper, he murders her also. Created (1937) by Maria Bernhard.

Gessler (Rossini: *Guillaume Tell*). Bass. Tyrannical Austrian Governor of the Swiss cantons of Schwitz and Uri. Brother of Princess Mathilde, with whom the Swiss Arnold is in love. After Tell saves a shepherd fleeing from Austrian troops, Gessler challenges Tell to save his life by shooting at an apple perched on the head of his own son. Created (1829) by Alexandre Prévot (or Prévost), whose son created Leuthold.

Ghita (Zemlinsky: *Der Zwerg*). Sop. Maid to the Infanta, Donna Clara. Ordered to show the Dwarf his reflection in a mirror, she avoids doing so, out of kindness. When he sees himself by accident, she consoles him as, heartbroken, he dies. Created (1922) by Käthe Herwig.

Ghost of Hamlet's Father (Thomas: *Hamlet*). Bass. He appears to his son Hamlet and tells him that Claudius, the King's brother and now married to Gertrude, Hamlet's mother, was responsible for his death. Created (1868) by Mons. David.

Ghost of Hector (Berlioz: *Les Troyens*). *See* HECTOR (2).

Ghosts of Versailles, The (Corigliano). Lib. by William M. Hoffman; 2 acts; f.p. NY 1991, cond. James Levine.
   Palace of Versailles, present time: The ghost of *Beaumarchais hopes to save *Marie Antoinette, the Queen he loves. He summons his favourite character, *Figaro, together with all the others from his earlier works, so they can help him use his art to change the course of history. King *Louis XVI leads the ghosts of the court to watch the play, whose action takes place twenty years after the marriage of Figaro and *Susanna. *Almaviva is now Spanish ambassador to France. *Rosina has given birth to *Cherubino's son, *Léon, and Almaviva has, by an unknown woman, an illegitimate daughter, *Florestine, with whom Léon is in love, although she has been promised by her father to his friend *Bégearss (who is secretly a Revolutionary). One evening at the Turkish Embassy, the Pasha *Suleyman's guests, including the entire Almaviva family, are being entertained by the Egyptian singer *Samira. Revolutionaries break in and capture the aristocrats. When Marie Antoinette's escape is thwarted, she demands that Beaumarchais restage her trial. He

fails to rescue her or the Almaviva family who are imprisoned with her. He says goodbye to Figaro, and also to Marie Antoinette, but she tells him that through his art she has learned to love him. Her execution takes place and she and Beaumarchais are united in Paradise.

Gianetta 1. (Donizetti: *L'elisir d'amore*). Sop. A peasant girl who throws herself at Nemorino when he inherits money from a rich uncle, thus rousing Adina's jealousy. Creator (1832) not traced.

2. (Sullivan: *The Gondoliers*). Sop. Chosen by the gondolier Marco as his wife. Aria: *Kind Sir, you cannot have the heart*; duet (with Tessa): *O my darling … do not forget you married me.* Created (1889) by Geraldine Ulmar.

Giannetto (Rossini: *La gazza ladra*). *See* VINGRADITO, GIANNETTO.

Gianni Schicchi (Puccini: *Il trittico*, part 3). Lib. by Giovacchino Forzano; 1 act; f.p. NY 1918, cond. Roberto Moranzoni.

Florence, late 13th cent.: Buoso *Donati, a rich old man, has just died and his family is gathered round his bed, each hoping to inherit. It is rumoured he has left his fortune to a monastery. *Rinuccio, son of Donati's elderly cousin *Zita, finds the will but does not allow the others to see it until they make him a promise: when they receive their money, they will allow him to marry Lauretta *Schicchi, daughter of the poor Gianni *Schicchi. The old man has indeed left his money to the Church. Rinuccio sends for the wily Schicchi. He agrees to help them for Lauretta's sake. He suggests they suppress the news of Donati's death while he, Schicchi, will disguise himself as the old man and make a new will. They each try to bribe Schicchi to give them the lion's share. The new will is made—and leaves most of the fortune 'to my old friend Gianni Schicchi'. Without revealing their own part in the plot, the relatives are helpless to intervene. Schicchi blesses the union of Lauretta and Rinuccio.

Gianni Schicchi (Puccini: *Gianni Schicchi*). *See* SCHICCHI, GIANNI.

Gil, Count (Wolf-Ferrari: *Il segreto di Susanna*). Bar. Husband of Susanna. He detects the smell of tobacco in the house.

As he does not smoke, he suspects that his wife must have a secret lover. When she keeps slipping out of the house, he assumes she is going to meet her lover. One day he returns unexpectedly and her secret is out—it is she who is the smoker. He is most relieved and decides that he too will smoke. Created (1909) by Herr Brodersen.

Gilda (Verdi: *Rigoletto*). Sop. Daughter of the hunchback court jester, Rigoletto. Since her mother died, her father, who loves her dearly, has kept her secluded in their home, cared for by her nurse Giovanna. The wanton Duke of Mantua has seen her in church and is attracted by her. He slips into the house and introduces himself as a student, Gualtier Maldè. They are interrupted by the sound of somebody arriving and the Duke leaves. It is not her father, however, but the courtiers who are taking revenge on Rigoletto for the gibes they have suffered from his tongue. Knowing nothing of the jester's background, they assume Gilda to be his lover and have come to kidnap her. She is taken to the ducal palace, where the Duke, now revealed in his true colours, seduces her. Learning of this, Rigoletto is bent on revenge and hires an assassin. Gilda overhears the plans to kill the Duke and hand his body over to her father. She vows to sacrifice herself for the Duke and, dressed as a boy, is killed in his stead. When her father opens the sack containing what he believes to be the Duke's body, he finds his dying daughter. Aria: *Caro nome …* ('Dear name that I love'); duet (with Rigoletto): *Piangi, fanciulla, piangi* ('Weep, my child, weep'); quartet (with Rigoletto, the Duke, and Maddalena): *Bella figlia dell'amore* ('Lovely daughter of love'). Apart from the above aria, there are few opportunities for great solo virtuosic singing for the soprano in this role, the entire opera being more dependent on its duets and ensembles, with which it abounds. Gilda and Rigoletto are among the many Verdi daughter–father relationships at the centre of several of his operas. Created (1851) by Teresa Brambilla.

Ginevra (Handel: *Ariodante*). Sop. Daughter of the King of Scotland. In love with Prince Ariodante. Polinesso wants to marry her and convinces Ariodante, falsely, that she has betrayed him. Polinesso, mortally wounded by Ariodante's brother Lurcanio, confesses the truth. Ariodante and Ginevra prepare for their wedding. Created (1735) by Anna Maria Strada (del Pò).

gioconda, La (literally, *The Joyful Girl*) (Ponchielli). Lib. by 'Tobia Gorrio' (Arrigo Boito); 4 acts; f.p. Milan 1876, cond. Franco Faccio.

Venice, 17th cent.: The spy *Barnaba is rejected by *Gioconda. He persuades the mob that her blind mother, La *Cieca, is a witch and they set upon the old lady. She is rescued by the disguised Enzo *Grimaldi, with whom Gioconda is in love, and freed by Alvise *Badoero and his masked wife *Laura, to whom La Cieca gives a rosary in gratitude. Barnaba, aware of Enzo's true identity, and knowing he was Laura's lover, arranges a meeting between him and Laura. They meet on his boat, and passionately embrace. Gioconda arrives on board to confront her rival for Enzo's love. Alvise's boat approaches. Laura prays for help, and Gioconda, recognizing her rosary, helps Laura escape. Alvise, swearing vengeance for his wife's betrayal, gives her poison to drink. Gioconda substitutes a narcotic. Alvise finds Laura, apparently dead. He greets his guests, who are entertained by the famous 'Dance of the Hours' ballet. His guests are told Laura is dead and when Enzo tries to stab Alvise, he is captured by guards. To save Enzo, Gioconda promises herself to Barnaba. Enzo and Laura escape, expressing their gratitude to Gioconda. Rather than fulfil her promise to Barnaba, Gioconda stabs herself. As she dies, Barnaba tells her he has strangled her mother.

Gioconda, La (Ponchielli: *La gioconda*). Sop. Daughter of La Cieca, she is in love with the nobleman Enzo, who is in turn in love with the married Laura. Laura and her husband save La Cieca from the angry mob whipped up by Barnaba. In gratitude, Gioconda helps Enzo and Laura escape, promising herself to Barnaba. Rather than keep her promise, she stabs herself. Aria: *Suicidio!…in questa fieri momenti* ('Suicide…in these awful moments'). Created (1876) by Sig.a Mariani-Masi.

Giorgetta (Puccini: *Il tabarro*). Sop. Wife of Michele, owner of a barge on the River Seine in Paris. She is much younger than her husband. Their only child has died. She is having an affair with Luigi, one of the stevedores who works on the barge. Her husband wonders why she has become so unresponsive to his approaches. She and Luigi discuss with other workers their dreams and hopes and Giorgetta

confesses that her own dream is to return to the bustling life in Paris where she was born. She wishes Michele would sell the barge and return to the city to live. Luigi and Giorgetta have a signal—when it is safe for him to come to her, she will light a match. One evening, after she has gone to their room, her husband stays on deck suspiciously watching her window. He lights his pipe, inadvertently sending the signal to Luigi, whom he catches and kills. Giorgetta returns to the deck, asking to be warmed under her husband's cloak, as they did in the old days. He opens his cloak to reveal the body of her lover. Created (1918) by Claudia Muzio.

Giorgio (Bellini: *I Puritani*). *See* WALTON, GIORGIO.

giorno di regno, Un or finto Stanislao, II (*King for a Day or The False Stanislao*) (Verdi). Lib. by Felice Romani; 2 acts; f.p. Milan 1840, cond. by Giuseppe Verdi.

Brest, France, 1733: It is a time of political unrest in Poland and King *Stanislao is under threat of losing the throne. To keep the attention from his monarch, *Belfiore poses as the king and goes to Baron di *Kelbar's castle in France. Here, the Baron's daughter, Giulietta di *Kelbar, is being forced to marry the old La *Rocca (whose nephew she loves) and the Marchesa del *Poggio (Belfiore's sweetheart) is going to marry the Commander of Brest, whom she does not love but is prepared to wed out of pique as she thinks Belfiore has deserted her. As the 'King', Belfiore is able to forbid both these marriages. News is brought to Brest that the crisis in Poland has been resolved. After his busy day as 'King', Belfiore is able to admit his true identity and claim the Marchesa for himself.

Giovanna 1. (Verdi: *Rigoletto*). Mez. Nurse who cares for Gilda, Rigoletto's daughter. Created (1851) by Laura Saini.

2. *See* SEYMOUR, GIOVANNA (JANE).

Giovanni, Don (Mozart: *Don Giovanni*). Bar. A young nobleman much given to seduction. After he has seduced Donna Anna and is chased from the house by her father, he kills him. His servant Leporello has to help him in his ventures. Elvira, having been seduced and then deserted by Giovanni, comes searching for him. His next attempted seduction is the young about-to-be-married Zerlina, but she is saved by Elvira. Giovanni is unmasked as the killer by Anna and her friends. Escaping them, he comes across her father's statue in the graveyard and, when the statue speaks to him, he invites 'it' to dinner. At their banquet he shakes hands with the Commendatore and is dragged into the flames of hell. Arias: *Finch'han dal vino* ('Now that the wine'—known as the Champagne Aria); *Deh vieni alla finestra* ('Come to the window'); duet (with Zerlina): *'Là ci darem la mano* ('There you will give me your hand'). The Don is really a somewhat cruel man, not caring who gets hurt along the way as long as his own louche desires are satisfied. He thinks nothing of beating his servant, Leporello, to make him help in his ventures and is quite happy to have poor innocent Masetto beaten up in the course of trying to seduce his fiancée, Zerlina. But baritones the world over are happy to portray this unpleasant character. These have included Mattia Battistini, John Brownlee (a very early Glyndebourne Don), Ezio Pinza, Matthieu Ahlersmeyer, Tito Gobbi, Mariano Stabile, Giuseppe Taddei, Cesare Siepi, George London, Dietrich Fischer-Dieskau, Eberhard Wächter, Nicolai Ghiaurov, Kim Borg, Ruggero Raimondi, Bernd Weikl, Benjamin Luxon, Thomas Allen, Samuel Ramey, Ferruccio Furlanetto, and Bryn Terfel. Created (1787) by Luigi Bassi.

Giove (Cavalli: *La Calisto*). *See* JUPITER (5).

Girl, The 1. (Josephs: *Rebecca*). Sop. (the second Mrs de Winter). Companion to Mrs Van Hopper, she meets and falls in love with the recently widowed Maxim de Winter. After their wedding, she returns with him to Manderley, believing that he will never get over the loss of his first wife, Rebecca. Her self-confidence is further undermined by the housekeeper, Mrs Danvers, who emphasizes that she can never take Rebecca's place. At the Manderley Ball, she wears a costume copied from an old family portrait—this was suggested by Mrs Danvers. Maxim is furious—Rebecca had worn the same costume. In a storm, Rebecca's boat is found at the bottom of the bay with her body still in the cabin. Maxim confesses that he hated his first wife, who killed herself when she knew she was dying of cancer. Now he and the Girl can love each other in peace—a peace broken by the

fire which breaks out in Manderley. Created (1983) by Gillian Sullivan.

2. (Ullmann: *Der Kaiser von Atlantis*). Sop. She falls in love with a Soldier from the opposite camp. Created (1944) by Marion Podolier; (1975) by Roberta Alexander.

Giulia (Spontini: *La vestale*). Sop. Forced by her father to become a Vestal virgin, she still loves Licinius. They meet at night when she is guarding the sacred flame. Too late, they realize it has gone out. Giulia is condemned to death—she will not reveal her lover's name. As she descends into her tomb, lightning strikes and the flame is rekindled—Vesta has forgiven her and she and Licinius are reunited. A famous role for Rosa Ponselle and Maria Callas. Aria: *Te che invoco con orrore* ('You, whom I invoke with horror'). Created (1807) by Alexandrine Caroline Branchu.

Giulietta 1. (Bellini: *I Capuleti e i Montecchi*). *See* CAPULET, JULIET (2).

2. (Offenbach: *Les Contes d'Hoffmann*). (This scene was omitted from the première.) Sop. In Venice, Hoffmann falls in love with her. The magician Dappertutto promises her a diamond if she obtains for him Hoffmann's soul. Hoffmann kills a rival, takes the key to Giulietta's room, but sees her floating away in a gondola with someone else. Duet (with Nicklausse): *Belle nuit, ô nuit d'amour* ('Beautiful night, O night of love')—the famous *Barcarolle*. Creator (?1905) not traced.

Giulio Cesare (Handel). Lib. by Nicola Francesco Haym; 3 acts; f.p. London 1724. Egypt, AD 48: *Giulio Cesare (Julius Caesar) has defeated Pompey and returned to Egypt. Pompey's wife (*Cornelia) and son (*Sesto) have agreed a peaceful settlement with Cesare. *Tolomeo has Pompey murdered. *Cleopatra, Tolomeo's sister, comes to Cesare hoping to join him in revenge on Tolomeo. Cesare is attracted by her beauty. Tolomeo orders Sesto's arrest and sends Cornelia to the king's harem, where *Achilla offers her release if she will marry him, an offer she rejects. Cleopatra continues her seduction of Cesare, aided by her confidant, *Nireno, but *Curio interrupts them and Cleopatra reveals her true identity. She urges Cesare to leave as war is being declared on him. When he is believed dead, Cleopatra flees to the Romans. Achilla claims Cornelia as his reward for killing

Cesare, but Tolomeo dismisses him. Achilla leads his troops to join Cleopatra against Tolomeo but she is taken prisoner by Tolomeo's soldiers. However, Cesare is not dead and comes to rescue Cleopatra. Sesto kills Tolomeo and he and his mother are welcomed in peace by Cesare and Cleopatra.

Giulio Cesare (Handel: *Giulio Cesare*). Cont. *Travesti* role (originally castrato). Cesare (Julius Caesar) returns to Egypt after defeating Pompey. When Tolomeo, King of Egypt, has Pompey murdered, Cleopatra joins Cesare in attempting to defeat Tolomeo. Cleopatra is taken prisoner by Tolomeo's troops and Cesare rescues her. Aria: *Va tacito* ('He goes silently') Created (1723) by Senesino (Francesco Bernardi, an alto castrato who created many Handel roles).

Glaša (Janáček: *Katya Kabanová*). Mez. Servant in the Kabanov household. She accompanies Tichon when he tries to find Katya and prevent her drowning herself in the river. Created (1921) by Lidka Šebestlová.

Glauce (Cherubini: *Médée*). *See* Dircé.

Glawari, Hanna (Lehár: *The Merry Widow*). Sop. The merry widow of the opera's title. She has been left a fortune by her late husband but, if she marries a foreigner, her fortune will be lost to her homeland of Pontevedro. She wants to marry an old flame, Count Danilo, but he refuses to be thought to be after her money. When learning that, on remarriage, she loses her fortune, he agrees to marry her. Once she is sure of him, she then admits that her money will pass to her new husband! Aria: *Es lebt' eine Vilja* ('There once lived a Vilja'—about the legendary nymph of the woods). Created (1905) by Mizzi Günther. *See also* ARTICLE BY ADÈLE LEIGH, p. 112.

Gloriana (Britten). Lib. by William Plomer; 3 acts; f.p. London 1953, cond. John Pritchard.
England, towards the end of the reign of Queen Elizabeth I: The Earl of *Essex urges Queen *Elizabeth (Gloriana) to appoint him Viceroy of Ireland. She goes to Norwich, attended by Essex, *Cecil and *Mountjoy, who resent the influence of *Raleigh on the Queen. Essex's sister, Penelope (Lady *Rich) is Mountjoy's lover. They, together with Essex and his wife Frances, Lady *Essex, plot who will succeed the Queen. Essex is appointed to the post in Ireland, but fails in his campaign there. He bursts in on the Queen whilst she is without her wig. Essex tries to persuade the citizens of London to rebel. A *Blind Ballad-Singer reports all this to the people in the street. Essex is condemned to death as a traitor, the Queen signing his death warrant.

Gobineau, Mr and Mrs (Menotti: *The Medium*). Bar. and sop. This couple are regular visitors to Mme Flora's seances. They come to make contact with their daughter, who was drowned in a fountain in their garden in France. Created (1946) by Jacques LaRochelle and Beverley Dame.

Godunov, Boris (Musorgsky: *Boris Godunov*). Bass. Regent to the recently dead young Tsar Fyodor (elder son of Ivan the Terrible). The people persuade Boris to be the new Tsar, not knowing he has murdered the Tsarevich Dimitri, who would have succeeded his brother. Boris has two children: his daughter Xenia was to be married to the Tsar, his son is called Fyodor. When a pretender arrives, claiming to be the resurrected Tsarevich, Boris's guilt overwhelms him and he loses his senses, bidding farewell to his son as he dies.
Russian, American, and English basses have succeeded in this role (Fyodor Chaliapin, Alexander Kipnis, George London, Yevgeny Nesterenko, Nicola Rossi-Lemeni, Robert Lloyd (the first Briton to sing this role at the Kirov Opera, 1990), John Tomlinson, Paata Burchuladze), but there was a period of about twenty years in the 1950s to 1970s when it was almost the exclusive property of Bulgarians, most notably Boris Christoff, Nicolai Ghiaurov, and Nicola Ghiuselev, all of whom had sung smaller roles in the same opera earlier in their career. Created (1874) by Ivan Mel'nikov.

Godvino (Verdi: *Aroldo*). Ten. A young knight who has an affair with Mina while her husband, Aroldo, is fighting in the Crusades. He is killed by her father. Created (1857) by Poggiali Salvatore. *See also* RAFFAELE (1).

Go-Go, Prince (Ligeti: *Le Grand Macabre*). Sop. (*travesti* role) or counterten. Boy prince who rules Breughelland, a land of peasants and monsters (as seen in Bruegel's paintings). While playing childish games with his

HANNA GLAWARI (*The Merry Widow*—Lehár)

by Adèle Leigh

Ever since I first heard Elisabeth Schwarzkopf singing, on an early LP, the role of Hanna Glawari, I wanted to sing the part. I had long felt an affinity with Lehár's music, realizing that the art of singing operetta was very special. You have to 'act' with your voice, and this was what Schwarzkopf was doing. I had never heard anyone else sing 'Vilja' like that.

I had been engaged to sing Musetta and Octavian at the New York City Opera. When offered Hanna Glawari as well, I had to learn it—in English—and be ready in five days. I decided to make my first entrance wearing white rather than the usual black and descended the staircase on to the stage in white satin with masses of glitter on my neck and arms and aigrettes [feathers and sparkles] in my hair. I loved acting the part as well as singing and I knew that this was what I wanted to sing. I sent all the flattering reviews to Joan Ingpen, my agent in London, who was married to the Viennese agent Alfred Dietz. 'Ah, my dear', he said, 'Your Hanna might be OK for the USA or even for London, but Vienna …'

I left Covent Garden after ten years to try my luck on the Continent. Herbert Graf was the Intendant in Zürich and he engaged me for several roles. His assistant was Lotfi Mansouri (later Intendant of San Francisco Opera) and I really enjoyed working with him. Maybe I could persuade Herr Graf to let me try out Hanna in Zürich? 'All right', he agreed, 'but you make your entrance in *black!*'

Lotfi Mansouri taught me that Hanna was not a typical diva. She was a young, vital woman with a mind of her own. So why the *Merry* Widow? Well, although she's newly widowed and in mourning, she didn't really love her rich husband. She married him because Danilo's uncle had told him 'She is beneath you … you must marry someone more "high ranking"'—this has all taken place before the curtain rises. Now she is very, very rich, merry, and enjoying herself in Paris. At the Embassy of Pontevedro, her own country, she again meets Danilo, whom she has not seen since they were sweet-hearts many years ago. My Hanna in Zürich was a success, but still I had the burning desire to sing Glawari in Vienna, where Lehár had his first big triumph with this operetta. One day I had a telephone call from Freddie [Alfred] Dietz: could I come and do a stage audition in Vienna the next day? When I got there, they wanted to hear me sing the Csardas from *Fledermaus* and offered me one performance of Rosalinde, on New Year's Eve. Then I went back to Zürich and waited—six months. The telephone rang and it was Dietz again: 'They're offering you an "informations gastspiel" of *die Witwe* on the last Saturday in June.' This was the last performance of the season, so I had no idea if anyone would be there to report whether they liked me enough to engage me again. They *did* like me, especially the audience and I had to repeat 'Vilja'. To sing Hanna Glawari on the stage of the Vienna Volksoper and to be applauded by such a knowledgeable audience, who know the piece better than you do—I felt that finally I had made it.

ministers, the secret police enter, disguised as birds, and warn him of the people's rebellion. Created (1978) by Gunilla Slättegård.

Golaud (Debussy: *Pelléas et Mélisande*). Bar. Grandson of King Arkel, half-brother of Pelléas and father of Yniold from an earlier marriage. He meets Mélisande when he is out hunting and she is wandering about lost. He brings her home and marries her, and introduces her to Pelléas. Golaud is injured when he falls from his horse, and while Mélisande is nursing him, he notices that a ring he gave her is missing from her finger—she has lost it while out with Pelléas. Golaud suspects her of being unfaithful to him with his brother. He uses his young son to spy on them, but Yniold sees nothing untoward. Golaud later finds them together, saying a passionate goodbye to each other, and he kills Pelléas. Created (1902) by Hector Dufranne.

Golden Cockerel, The (Rimsky-Korsakov). Lib. by Vladimir Bel'sky; prol., 3 acts, and epil.; f.p. Moscow 1909, cond. Emil Cooper.

Legendary Russia: Tsar *Dodon and his sons, *Gvidon and *Afron, are given a *Golden Cockerel by the *Astrologer, which will crow to predict peace or warn of an enemy. Soothed to sleep by *Amelfa, Dodon's dreams are broken by the crowing of the Cockerel. He sends his sons to head the army, then sets off himself with *Polkan. They are defeated and the sons kill each other in battle. The Queen of *Shemakha appears, seduces Dodon, and agrees to marry him. As they process into the capital, the Astrologer demands his reward—the hand of the Queen. Dodon kills him, and is then rejected by Shemakha. The Cockerel pecks Dodon on the head and he dies; the Queen and the Cockerel disappear. It is all an illusion, the Astrologer tells the audience.

Golden Cockerel (Rimsky-Korsakov: *The Golden Cockerel*). Sop. *Travesti* role. Warns the Tsar of enemies. Later pecks him on the head and kills him. Creator (1909) not traced.

Golitsyn, Prince Vassily (Musorgsky: *Khovanshchina*). Ten. The Regent and former lover of the Tsar's daughter. He is condemned to exile. Creator (1886) unknown; (1911) by Ivan Yershov.

Gomez, Don Inigo (Ravel: *L'Heure espagnole*). Bass. A banker who comes to visit Concepción, wife of the clockmaker. To keep him hidden from her other lover she suggests he climb into a clock. Being rather fat, he gets stuck and is unable to climb out to be with her. Created (1911) by Hector Dufranne.

Gondoliers, The, or The King of Barataria (Sullivan). Lib. by W. S. Gilbert; 2 acts; f.p. London 1889, cond. Arthur Sullivan.

Venice and the Island of Barataria, 18th cent.: Marco and Giuseppe *Palmieri, two gondoliers, choose their brides while blindfolded. Giuseppe catches *Tessa and Marco catches *Gianetta. The Duke and Duchess of *Plaza-Toro arrive with their daughter *Casilda and their drummer *Luiz. Casilda was married as a babe to the heir to the throne of Barataria, who is unknown to everyone except Don *Alhambra and the heir's old nurse. She is Luiz's mother and she confirms that the heir is one of the two gondoliers. Casilda and Luiz are secretly in love. Marco and Giuseppe, knowing one of them is the heir, decide to rule jointly and set sail for the island. Their wives are distressed to learn that one of their husbands was married to Casilda as a baby. Then Luiz's mother *Inez admits that she swapped the babies—her own 'son' Luiz is really the prince. All three couples remain happily together.

Gonzalve (Ravel: *L'Heure espagnole*). Ten. A poet in love with Concepción, wife of Torquemada the clockmaker. When he comes to see her while her husband is away, she is being visited by an old banker and a young customer. He hides in a clock and, when her husband returns, pretends he is a customer and buys the clock. Created (1911) by Fernand Francell.

Gorislava (Glinka: *Ruslan and Lyudmila*). Sop. A young maid in love with Prince Ratmir. Created (1842) by Emiliya Lileyeva.

Gorjančikov, Alexandr Petrovich (Janáček: *From the House of the Dead*). Bass. An aristocratic political prisoner, flogged at the commandant's orders as soon as he arrives in the camp. He befriends the young Tartar Aljeja and teaches him to read and write. He is later released by the commandant. Created (1930) by Vlastimil Šíma.

Goro (Puccini: *Madama Butterfly*) Ten. A marriage-broker who has arranged a wedding between the American naval officer Pinkerton and a 15-year-old Japanese girl Cio-Cio-San, known to all her friends as Butterfly. When it seems that Pinkerton has deserted Butterfly and her money is running out, Goro produces the wealthy Japanese Prince Yamadori and tries to persuade Butterfly to marry him. Created (1904) by Gaetano Pini-Corsi (not to be confused with Antonio Pini-Corsi (1858–1918) the baritone who created Schaunard in Puccini's *La bohème* and Ford in Verdi's *Falstaff*).

Gossips (Britten: *Noye's Fludde*). Four girl sops. Friends of Mrs Noye, with whom she spends most of her time drinking and talking. Created (1958) by Penelope Allen, Doreen Metcalfe, Dawn Mendham, Beverley Newman.

Götterdämmerung (Twilight of the Gods) (Wagner). Lib. by Wagner; prol. and 3 acts; f.p. Bayreuth 1876, cond. Hans Richter (excerpts in concert perf., Vienna 1876). The final opera in the cycle *Der Ring des Nibelungen*.

The Valkyries' rock, Gibichungs' court and a forest near the Rhine, mythological times: The *Norns spin the rope which links together the world's knowledge of the past and the future. The rope snaps—the link is broken. *Brünnhilde and *Siegfried descend from their rock. He is about to ride away on her horse, *Grane, and he gives her the gold Ring as a sign of his faithfulness. At the Gibichungs' court, *Hagen plans to steal the Ring which he believes *Alberich possesses. Hagen advises *Gunther and *Gutrune that they must each marry to gain the respect of their subjects, and suggests as their prospective partners Brünnhilde and Siegfried respectively. Gunther will give Siegfried a potion which will make him forget all previous loves and then use Siegfried to gain Brünnhilde. Siegfried arrives and tells them of the Ring and the Tarnhelm. He drinks the potion and immediately falls in love with Gutrune, all memory of Brünnhilde being wiped away. He offers to use the Tarnhelm to disguise himself as Gunther and then woo Brünnhilde. The two men set off for Brünnhilde's rock. Brünnhilde, awaiting Siegfried's return, is visited by her sister *Waltraute, who recounts how their father, *Wotan, is in Valhalla awaiting the end of his world. Will Brünnhilde return the Ring to the Rhinemaidens, thus freeing the gods of its curse? Brünnhilde will not let go of the Ring, a symbol of Siegfried's love. Hearing Siegfried's horn, she rushes to meet him, only to have 'Gunther' drag the Ring from her finger and force her to go with him. They set out for the Gibichung court, where Hagen, asleep, is visited by Alberich to persuade him they must continue with their plan to regain the gold. Siegfried returns, with Gunther leading Brünnhilde and they are greeted by the Vassals summoned by Hagen. Seeing the Ring on Siegfried's finger, Brünnhilde claims him as her husband, which he denies, leaving to arrange his marriage with Gutrune. Rejected and distraught, Brünnhilde reveals to Hagen that Siegfried's back is vulnerable to attack. Brünnhilde and Gunther swear vengeance on Siegfried, calling on Wotan to aid them. Siegfried and Gutrune enter, ready for their marriage and Hagen makes Brünnhilde join Gunther for a double wedding. Later, out hunting, Siegfried meets the Rhinemaidens on a river bank. They warn him that if he keeps the Ring he will die. As he recounts to his hunting companions the story of his life, he looks up to watch Wotan's ravens overhead, and Hagen stabs him in the back. His body is carried back to Gutrune and Hagen and Gunther fight over the Ring, Hagen killing Gunther. As Hagen reaches to take the Ring from his finger, Siegfried raises his hand in the air. Brünnhilde orders Siegfried's body to be placed on a funeral pyre. She puts the Ring on her own finger and rides on her horse into the flames, which spread to destroy the Gibichung court and Valhalla. The Rhine overflows and extinguishes the flames, and Hagen and the Rhinemaidens are seen in the water. The Rhinemaidens triumphantly recover their gold.

Gottfried, Duke of Brabant (Wagner: *Lohengrin*). Silent role. Brother of Elsa and rightful heir to the dukedom of their late father. He has been turned into a swan by the evil Ortrud who hopes her husband will inherit the lands instead. Gottfried appears at the end of the opera, as the swan pulling the boat which is to take Lohengrin away. He is restored to his original image and holds his sister as she collapses. Creator (1850) not known.

Governess (Britten: *The Turn of the Screw*). Sop. Engaged to teach two orphaned children at Bly, she has been ordered never to trouble their guardian. When she realizes that the deceased valet, Quint, and governess, Miss Jessel, have returned as ghosts and are an evil influence on the children, she writes to the guardian. Miles steals the letter. She forces him to admit it was Quint who made him do this, and he dies in her arms. Arias: *Lost in my labyrinth; Sir—dear Sir—my dear Sir; O Miles, I cannot bear to lose you.* This role has attracted eminent singing-actresses, including Elisabeth Söderström, Heather Harper, Catherine Wilson, Helen Donath, Felicity Lott, Valerie Masterson, Joan Rodgers, Susan Chilcott, and Rebecca Evans. Created (1954) by Jennifer Vyvyan.

Grand Duchess of Gérolstein (Offenbach: *La Grande-Duchesse de Gérolstein*). Sop. Reviewing her troops, she takes a fancy to a new recruit, Fritz, and promotes him to general. He leads the troops to battle, much to the chagrin of the army commander, Gen. Boum. When he returns, having won the battle, Fritz rejects her in favour of his girlfriend Wanda. The Grand Duchess joins Boum in plotting his downfall, reduces him to a private and settles for marrying a prince. Aria: *Dîtes-lui* ('Tell him'). Created (1867) by Hortense Schneider.

Grande-Duchesse de Gérolstein, La (Offenbach). Lib. by Henri Meilhac and Ludovic Halévy; 3 acts; f.p. Paris 1867, cond. Jacques Offenbach.
 Mythical Gérolstein, 1720: The *Grand Duchess falls in love with an army private, *Fritz, who is in love with *Wanda. The Duchess upgrades him to general and he is victorious in battle. The army commander, General *Boum, plots his downfall. The Grand Duchess, upset by Fritz's lack of interest in her, joins Boum's plans to degrade Fritz. He is demoted to private again and marries Wanda. The Duchess settles for life with a prince.

Grand Inquisitor (Verdi: *Don Carlos*). Bass. An old man (aged about 90), blind and sometimes needing to be supported, he nevertheless has a strong personality. The King consults him on how to treat his son, who sympathizes with the heretics in Flanders. The Inquisitor points out that God gave his son in order to

save the world, so it would not be wrong for Philip to sacrifice his son for the sake of his country. The Inquisitor tries to denounce the Marquis of Posa, but the King will not listen to this. At his grandfather's tomb, Carlos bids farewell to Elisabeth before leaving for Flanders. Philip demands that the Grand Inquisitor seize his son and punish him. As the Inquisitor reaches out, Carlos is pulled into the safety of the cloisters by his dead grandfather reaching from the tomb. Aria: *Dans ce beau pays* ('In this beautiful country'). Created (1867) by Mons. David; (1884) by Francesco Navarini.

Grand Macabre, Le (*The Grand Macabre*) (Ligeti). Lib. by comp. and Michael Meschke; 2 acts; f.p. Stockholm 1978, cond. Elgar Howarth.
 Breughelland, unspecified time: *Nekrotzar forecasts that the world will end at midnight and forces *Piet the Pot to help him destroy it. *Astradamors pretends to be dead in order to get away from his wife *Mescalina, who has excessive and outlandish sexual urges. She brings him back to life using a spider. Dissatisfied with him as a lover, she begs *Venus to provide her with a man who will respond and Venus sends her Nekrotzar. She dies in ecstasy, to her husband's relief. As *Go-Go, the boy prince who rules Breughelland, plays childish games with his ministers, the secret police break in, disguised as birds, warning him of the people's rebellion. They panic when Nekrotzar announces the end of the world as he collapses in a drunken stupor. Mescalina, on the way to her burial, recognizing him as the cause of her death, leaps out of the hearse and pursues him. *Amanda and *Armando appear from their hiding-place where they have made love throughout all these events, ignorant of everything that has taken place. Has the world ended and have they all been resurrected?

Grane (Wagner: *Die Walküre; Götterdämmerung*). Brünnhilde's horse, on which she carries the pregnant Sieglinde to the Valkyries' rock. In the final act of *Der Ring* (the Immolation), Brünnhilde rides Grane into the fire of Siegfried's funeral pyre.

Green Knight/Sir Bertilak de Hautdesert (Birtwistle: *Gawain*). Bass. Challenges the members of Arthur's court to bestow a blow on his neck with an axe, on condition that he can return the compliment a year later. Is decapitated by Gawain, who later arrives at his castle en route to meet the Green Knight, not knowing that he and his host are one and the same man. Created (1991) by John Tomlinson.

Gregor, Albert (Janáček: *The Makropulos Case*). Ten. Descendant of Ellian MacGregor, a Scottish singer who had an affair with the Czech Baron Prus and had a son, Ferdinand MacGregor. When the Baron died intestate, his estate went to his cousin. The Gregor family contested the will and the case between them and the Prus family has been going on for 100 years, now involving Albert Gregor and Jaroslav Prus. The opera singer Emilia Marty confirms the history of the Gregors and is also able to tell the lawyer where to find the will of Baron Prus which will confirm Gregor's right to the estate. Created (1926) by Emil Olšovský.

Gremin, Prince (Tchaikovsky: *Eugene Onegin*). Bass. An aristocratic retired general, Gremin marries Tatyana after she has been rejected by Onegin. Two years afterwards, at a ball in the Gremin palace in St Petersburg, Onegin meets the Princess, Gremin's wife, and realizes it is Tatyana and that he does love her. Gremin describes to Onegin, whom he has known for some years, what happiness his marriage has brought him, despite the difference in age between himself and Tatyana. Aria: *Lyubvi vse vozrastï pokornï* ('To love all ages are obedient'). Created (1879) by Vasily Makhalov.

Grenvil, Dr (Verdi: *La traviata*). Bass. Friend of and physician to Violetta. He attends her while she is dying of consumption. Created (1853) by Andrea Bellini.

Gretel (Humperdinck: *Hänsel und Gretel*). Sop. Daughter of Gertrud and Peter and sister of Hänsel. As there is no food to eat, she and her brother are sent by their mother to pick strawberries in the forest. They become lost and frightened. They are put to sleep by the Sandman and watched over by angels. When they wake they see a gingerbread house and fence. They taste it and are captured by the Witch, who puts Hänsel in a cage. Gretel rescues him and pushes the Witch into the oven. The oven explodes and the gingerbread fence becomes a row of children who have been

captured and baked by the Witch. Duet (with Hänsel): *Abends wenn ich schlafen gehn* ('In the evening when I go to sleep'). Created (1893) by Marie Kayser (who took over the role at very short notice—*See* HÄNSEL).

Grieux, Chevalier Des 1. (Puccini: *Manon Lescaut*). *See* DES GRIEUX, CHEVALIER (2).

    2. (Massenet: *Manon*). *See* DES GRIEUX, CHEVALIER (1).

Grigori/Dimitri (Musorgsky: *Boris Godunov*). Ten. A novice monk, Grigori hears from his mentor, Pimen, how the young Tsarevich Dimitri was murdered. He realizes he is the same age the Tsarevich would have been and determines to take his identity, defeat the present Tsar, Boris Godunov, and assume the throne of Russia. Created (1874) by Fyodor Komissarzhevsky.

Grigorjevič, Boris (Janáček: *Katya Kabanová*). Ten. Nephew of the rich merchant Dikoj. He is forced to live with him under the terms of his grandmother's will which, following the death of his parents, provided for him and his sister as long as they live with and respect Dikoj. For his sister's sake, he puts up with his uncle's often humiliating attitude to him. Boris tells his friend Váňa Kudrjaš that he has fallen in love with a married woman, Katya Kabanová. They manage to meet one night while her husband is away on business and declare their love. When this is revealed to her husband, Boris's uncle banishes him to Siberia. Boris and Katya meet for the last time and bid each other goodbye. Created (1921) by Karel Zavřel.

Grimaldi, Amelia (Verdi: *Simon Boccanegra*). Sop. Illegitimate daughter of Boccanegra and the late Maria (who was the daughter of Fiesco). After her mother's death she was found wandering and was adopted by Count Grimaldi and brought up as his daughter. She is cared for by her guardian Andrea (who is Fiesco under an assumed name—he does not know Amelia's true identity). Years later she and Boccanegra (now elected Doge) meet. She tells the story of her adoption and shows him the portrait of her real mother in her locket. Boccanegra recognizes his Maria and realizes this is his long-lost daughter. She is to be married to the nobleman Gabriele Adorno. Boccanegra is poisoned by Paolo Albiani, whose hopes of marrying Amelia were thwarted.

Knowing he will die, Boccanegra tells Fiesco the truth and the two men are reconciled. Amelia and Gabriele are married and the dying Boccanegra declares Gabriele his successor. Aria: *Come in quest' ora bruna* … ('In this dark hour … See how the stars and ocean'); duet (with Adorno): *Vieni a mirar la cerual marina tremolante* ('Come and look at the shimmering azure sea'). Created (1857) by Luigia Bendazzi; (1881) by Anna d'Angeri.

Grimaldi, Enzo (Ponchielli: *La gioconda*). Ten. Prince of Genoa, disguised as a sea-captain. Gioconda is in love with him, but he loves Laura, now married to Alvise. The spy Barnaba plots Enzo's downfall, but he and Laura are helped to escape by Gioconda. Created (1876) by Julián Gayarre.

Grimes, Peter (Britten: *Peter Grimes*). Ten. A fisherman. His Apprentice has died—the second one to do so—and the townsfolk are suspicious of his part in this, despite the inquest verdict of 'accidental circumstances'. He insists on having a new Apprentice, even though he has been advised by the court to manage without one in future. Grimes's only real friends are the widowed schoolmistress Ellen Orford, whom he hopes to marry, and the retired Capt. Balstrode. The rest of the Borough mistrust and dislike him—Grimes is something of a loner and does not easily socialize. His only wish is to earn lots of money as a fisherman so that he can afford to marry Ellen. He notices shoals of fish in the sea ('the whole sea's boiling') and is determined to net them, despite bad weather and the risks involved and orders his new apprentice, John, to change and get ready to sail. When John accidentally falls to his death from their cliff-top hut, the townsfolk march to find Grimes. Only Ellen and Balstrode believe him, but they also realize that the townsfolk are baying for his blood and there is no way of saving him. Balstrode advises him to take his boat out to sea and sink it and, watched by Ellen, helps him push it out. Arias: *What harbour shelters peace?*; *Now the Great Bear and Pleiades*; *In dreams I've built myself some kindlier home.* Several excellent British singers have taken up this role, but also tenors from the other side of the Atlantic. These have included Philip Langridge, Anthony Rolfe Johnson, Anthony Roden, Jeffrey Lawton, Jeffrey Lloyd Roberts, the Canadians Jon Vickers

and Ben Heppner, and the American Anthony Dean Griffey, and not forgetting the Australian Ronald Dowd. Created (1945) by Peter Pears. *See also* ARTICLE BY MICHAEL KENNEDY, p. 118.

Grimgerde (Wagner: *Die Walküre*). *See* VALKYRIES.

Grimoaldo (Handel: *Rodelinda*). Ten. Duke of Benevento. When the death of King Bertarido is rumoured, he decides to marry Queen Rodelinda and thus inherit the throne, but she demands that he must first kill her son, the rightful heir. He cannot bring himself to do this. When he is attacked by Garibaldo, his supposed friend, Bertarido comes out of hiding and kills Garibaldo. Grimoaldo cedes all claims to the throne and marries Bertarido's sister. Created (1725) by Francesco Borosini.

Grishka (Rimsky-Korsakov: *The Legend of the Invisible City of Kitezh*). *See* KUTERMA, GRISHKA.

Grose, Mrs (Britten: *The Turn of the Screw*). Sop. Housekeeper at Bly. She has been looking after the children, Miles and Flora, and welcomes the Governess when she arrives. She recognizes that it is the dead valet and governess, Quint and Miss Jessel, who are haunting the house and grounds and tells the Governess their story. At first sceptical of the effect these two are having on the children, she gradually becomes convinced and leaves Bly, taking Flora with her away from their evil influence. Aria: *Dear God is there no end to his dreadful ways?* Created (1954) by Joan Cross.

Grosvenor, Archibald (Sullivan: *Patience*). Bass-bar. An aesthetic poet, who agrees to abandon his high-flown ideals. Patience deems it her duty to love him. Aria: *Prithee pretty maiden.* Created (1881) by Rutland Barrington.

Gualtiero 1. (Bellini: *I Puritani*). *See* WALTON, LORD GUALTIERO.

2. (Bellini: *Il pirata*). Ten. The former Count of Montalto, lover of Imogene and political enemy of Ernesto. After the battle for the Sicilian throne, he has been exiled and lived as a pirate. He is shipwrecked near the castle where Imogene lives with Ernesto, whom she was forced to marry. The two men fight a duel

PETER GRIMES (*Peter Grimes*—Britten)

by Michael Kennedy

Peter Grimes is the hero or anti-hero—there's the rub—of Benjamin Britten's first great opera. It was such an immediate success that bus conductors, as they approached Islington, called out 'Next stop for Sadler's Wells and the sadistic fisherman'. But is Grimes a sadistic fisherman in Britten's presentation of his character? He certainly was in George Crabbe's poem *The Borough* from which Britten and Peter Pears concocted a scenario on which Montagu Slater based his libretto. Crabbe's Grimes hated his father, gambled, drank, turned poacher, and hired three apprentices from the workhouse to help him in his fishing-boat. All three died in suspicious circumstances. Haunted by their ghosts, Grimes went mad and died in an asylum, unmourned.

Britten's Grimes is quite another figure, who underwent several metamorphoses until he became the Grimes we know today, the outsider hounded to his doom by an East Coast fishing community. In a first draft, written in 1942, Britten accepted the apprentices' deaths as murder. But under the influence of Peter Pears, with whom he lived, Britten began to see Grimes in another light. As 'the individual against the crowd', Grimes had 'ironic overtones for our own situation. As conscientious objectors we were out of it … We experienced tremendous tension. I think it was partly this feeling which led us to make Grimes a character of vision and conflict, the tortured idealist he is, rather than the villain he was in Crabbe'.

What Britten did not say was that the 'outsider' Grimes was a symbol of Britten the homosexual. Apart from the fact that in 1943 homosexuality was a criminal offence, Britten would never have publicly confessed to it. He realized that some might detect homo-erotic implications in the subject of Grimes and the apprentices and he set out deliberately to eradicate them. In an early draft, Grimes says to the boy in the hut scene (Act 2, scene 2): 'Work, do not stare. Would you rather I loved you? You are sweet, young. But you must love me, why do you not love me? Love me, darn you.' A later draft of the scene was more sadistic and had Grimes chasing the boy round the hut, slashing at him with his rope and shouting 'By God, I'll beat it out of you. Jump, the dance is on'. Britten the professional composer knew just how much an audience could take in 1945 where sexual overtones were concerned. Through his instinctive dramatic genius, audiences are moved—entirely by the power of the music—by Grimes's fate, in spite of the obvious emotional discrepancies in his character. Britten made him a visionary, but not everyone will agree that he is an idealist. More of a pragmatist—when advised by his friend Captain Balstrode to ask the school mistress Ellen Orford to marry him, Grimes says he will not contemplate marriage until he has made enough money to shut the mouths of the Borough gossips whom he despises.

Grimes, like Britten, is consumed by guilt. Although he has compassion for the first apprentice before his death at sea, giving him the last drinking water, and is rightly acquitted of blame at the inquest, all his actions thereafter are those of a guilty man ('the case goes on in people's minds', he sings). He is perhaps physically cruel to the second apprentice, but the bruises Ellen finds on the boy could have been sustained in what Grimes calls 'the hurly-burly' of manual work. He strikes Ellen in a fit of temper. But he bursts into the Boar Inn during a storm and sings of the Great Bear and Pleiades drawing up the clouds of human grief. ('He's mad or drunk', the customers respond.) Grimes ignores good advice. 'Do not get another apprentice', the coroner tells him, 'get a fisherman to help you', but within hours Grimes is negotiating for a boy from the workhouse. His whole motivation in the opera is to fish the sea dry to make money, and he is shown as a hard worker with a genius for fishing. 'Look, now is our chance', he tells the second apprentice in the hut. 'The whole sea's boiling. Get the nets'. No one else in the Borough notices the shoals of fish, they are too busy hunting the big fish of Grimes himself.

It is guilt which drives Grimes to madness and makes him acquiesce so meekly in Balstrode's instruction to him to commit suicide by sailing out to sea and sinking his boat. But guilt about what? That he was responsible for the second boy's fall to death down the cliff? Yes, and that he, all unknowingly, had some kind of influence on others. In his delirium in the Mad Scene he sings: 'The first one died, just died. The other slipped and died. And the third will ... Accidental circumstances'. Yet Britten's friend Edward Sackville-West, in a 1945 booklet about the opera, wrote that 'it would not do to shirk the fact that Grimes is guilty of manslaughter' and continues about Grimes's 'choleric nature' and 'uncontrollable vein of real ferocity'. Britten must have seen and presumably approved this article. So the real character of Grimes remains an enigma, which is perhaps what Britten the great opera composer intended. 'The case goes on in people's minds.'

and Ernesto is killed. Gualtiero gives himself up and bids Imogene farewell. Created (1827) by Giovanni Battista Rubini.

Guardiano, Padre (Verdi: *La forza del destino*). Bass. A Franciscan monk, the Father Superior at the monastery where Leonora goes for help and peace. He is gentle with her, understanding her distress, and warns her that the solitary life she is proposing for herself will be very lonely. However, thinking that her beloved Alvaro is dead, she is sure that this is what she wants, and the Padre agrees to her request. She will live alone in a sacred cave. He will take her food each day, but otherwise she will see nobody. He warns the monks that they must not attempt to discover her identity. Duet (with Leonora): *Più tranquilla l'alma sento* ('My soul becomes more peaceful'). This duet is in the direct line of father–daughter duets in so many of Verdi's operas. Created (1862) by Gian Francesco Angelini.

Gudal, Prince (Rubinstein: *The Demon*). Bass. A Caucasian Prince, father of Tamara, the Princess who is lusted after by the Demon. Created (1875) by Osip Petrov.

Guglielmo (Mozart: *Così fan tutte*). Bar. Engaged to Fiordiligi, whose sister is engaged to his friend Ferrando. The two men accept a wager from Don Alfonso that he can prove that all women are fickle, including the two sisters. Guglielmo and Ferrando pretend to go to war and return disguised as Albanians. They pursue the sisters, but each is after his friend's fiancée, so Guglielmo wins over Dorabella. She gives him her locket (which contains Ferrando's portrait), as a token of her feelings for him. A bogus double wedding is arranged, the notary being the sisters' maid, Despina, in disguise. After signing the marriage contract (in which Guglielmo is named as Tizio), the men leave the room and return as themselves, back from battle to claim their own fiancées. Confusion ensues—who will now pair off with whom? Arias: *Non siate retrosi* ('Do not be so reluctant'); *Donne mie, la fate a tanti* ('Dear ladies, you treat so many men like this'). As Ferrando appeals to tenors, so this role attracts the deeper vocal ranges, from baritone to bass-baritone. Among the many famous names associated with the part are Roy Henderson, Willi Domgraf-Fassbänder,

Rolando Panerai, Erich Kunz, Sesto Bruscantini, Walter Berry, Hermann Prey, Sherrill Milnes, Geraint Evans, Knut Skram, Håkan Hagegård, Thomas Allen, Thomas Hampson, Anthony Michaels Moore, Simon Keenlyside, and Gerald Finley. Created (1790) by Francesco Bennuci.

Guido Bardi (Zemlinsky: *Eine florentinische Tragödie*). *See* BARDI, GUIDO.

Guillaume Tell (William Tell) (Rossini). Lib. by Étienne de Jouy and Hippolyte Louis-Florent Bis; 4 acts; f.p. Paris 1829, cond. François-Antoine Habeneck.

Switzerland, 13th cent.: *Arnold, son of *Melcthal, loves the Habsburg Princess Mathilde. William *Tell wants to rid their country of Austrian domination. *Leuthold flees from Austrian troops after killing a soldier who assaulted his daughter. He is rowed by Tell across the rapids. No one will reveal Tell's name to the Austrian authorities, who take Melcthal as hostage. Their governor, *Gessler, orders his death and Arnold swears revenge. Tell is recognized as the man who saved Leuthold. Gessler tells him he can save his life by shooting an arrow at an apple placed on the head of his own son, Jemmy *Tell. He shoots the apple, but then drops the arrow with which he was going to kill Gessler. He is imprisoned. As he is being transported by boat, a storm begins and he is freed to control the boat. As they arrive on the shore, Jemmy hands his father a bow which he uses to kill Gessler. Arnold and his soldiers capture the castle and ensure the freedom of their country.

Guillaume Tell (Rossini: *Guillaume Tell*). *See* TELL, GUILLAUME.

Guillot (Tchaikovsky: *Eugene Onegin*). Silent. Onegin's French valet, who accompanies him as his second when he meets Lensky for a duel. Created (1879) by a student at Moscow Conservatory.

Guinevere (Birtwistle: *Gawain*). Sop. Wife of King Arthur at the court of Logres. Created (1991) by Penelope Walmsley-Clark.

Gunther (Wagner: *Götterdämmerung*). Bar. King of the Gibichungs, brother of Gutrune and half-brother of Hagen. Hagen advises Gunther that his standing among his people would be enhanced if he were married and he knows the right bride for him. She is Brünnhilde, who is on a rock surrounded by fire. Gunther is no hero, and cannot see himself breaking through the fire to win his bride, but Hagen assures him that this will be done for him, by none other than Siegfried who, for his pains, will be rewarded with Gutrune's hand in marriage. Siegfried arrives and is welcomed by Gunther as a friend. Gutrune gives Siegfried a drugged drink which makes him forget everything about Brünnhilde and he falls in love with Gutrune. Gunther describes to his visitor his chosen bride and Siegfried happily offers to win her for him. He uses the Tarnhelm to disguise himself as Gunther, sets out, and returns with the reluctant Brünnhilde. The delighted Gunther brings her in to introduce to everyone. She refuses to marry him, considering herself married to Siegfried, despite his apparent betrayal of her. Gunther must hear Siegfried swear on oath that he was not Brünnhilde's husband, before he can either marry her or give his consent to Siegfried's marriage to his sister. Siegfried happily complies, using Hagen's spear on which to swear. Brünnhilde uses the same spear to vow vengeance on Siegfried. Hagen suggests to Gunther that the only way to assuage the embarrassment he has been caused is to ensure Siegfried's death. Gunther is not sure this is the best step, knowing the distress it will cause his sister, but he is too weak to defy both Hagen and Brünnhilde. Out hunting the next day, Hagen kills Siegfried, but not before Gunther has realized that Hagen has used them all to his own ends. Gunther orders his vassals to carry Siegfried's body back to the Gibichung hall. Once there he attempts to prevent Hagen stealing the Ring from the dead Siegfried's finger, but Hagen kills him with his sword. Created (1876) by Eugen Gura.

Gurnemanz (Wagner: *Parsifal*). Bass. A veteran Knight of the Grail. It is from Gurnemanz, at the beginning of the opera, that we learn what has happened before the opening of the drama—how Titurel came to be the King of the Grail and how his son, Amfortas, has a wound that will not heal. It distresses Gurnemanz to see the King of the Grail in such pain—physical and mental. At first he is a defender of Kundry, pointing out to the Knights that it is whenever Kundry is away from them for long periods that misfortune seems to befall them, but one of the Knights wonders if maybe Kundry is responsible for these misfortunes (she is, in fact, responsible for Amfortas's position, for while she seduced him, the evil magician Klingsor inflicted the wound) and eventually Gurnemanz has to admit that Kundry may be under a curse. Gurnemanz describes to the Knights how Amfortas has had a vision of an 'innocent fool' who is the only one who can save him. When Parsifal arrives, having killed a swan, Gurnemanz chastises him, pointing out that all God's creatures are equally important and Parsifal is duly remorseful. Eventually, Gurnemanz begins to wonder if Parsifal will be Amfortas's saviour—his innocence and ignorance are clear, as he does not know his own name or what the Grail is. Many years later, as a very old man living in a hut in the forest, Gurnemanz finds Kundry, almost dead. He rescues her and she insists on being his servant. She draws his attention to someone entering the forest, and Gurnemanz is amazed to see it is Parsifal and even more shocked when he realizes that Parsifal has no idea that it is Good Friday. Parsifal recognizes Gurnemanz, and explains that he is searching for Amfortas so he can return to him the Holy Spear. Gurnemanz tells Parsifal that Titurel has died and Amfortas has promised to unveil the Grail at his funeral, whatever pain this will cause him. He leads Parsifal to meet Amfortas and Parsifal touches his wound with the Spear. Amfortas is healed and Parsifal is acknowledged as the new Guardian of the Grail. Arias: *O wunden-wundervoller heiliger Speer!* ('O wondrous-wounding hallowed spear!'); *Titurel, der fromme Held* ('Titurel, the godly hero'); *O Gnade! Höchstes Heil!* ('O Mercy! Bounteous grace!').

Gurnemanz, as the senior Knight of the Grail, puts the whole story in perspective for the audience, as he describes the events which have taken place before the opera begins (without knowledge of which it would be very difficult to understand what is going on in the opera). His attitude to Kundry is ambivalent— he never seems to know whether she is good or evil and his view of her varies from time to time. He ultimately recognizes that Parsifal is the 'Innocent Fool' that Amfortas has seen in a vision, and he is happy to lead the youth to the ailing Knight. There have been many famous singers of Gurnemanz, including Richard

Mayr, Alexander Kipnis, Josef von Manowarda, Ludwig Weber, Josef Greindl, Jerome Hines, Hans Hotter, Ludwig Weber, Franz Mazura, Hans Sotin, Theo Adam, John Tomlinson, and Manfred Schenk. Created (1882) by Emil Scaria.

Gustavus III (Verdi: *Un ballo in maschera*). (Riccardo, Count of Warwick in Amer. vers.) Ten. King of Sweden (changed to Governor of Boston in the American version). He is in love with Amelia, wife of his loyal secretary and best friend Anckarstroem. He meets her in a wood outside the city and they declare their feelings, but she tells him she will always remain faithful to her husband. They are interrupted by the arrival of Anckarstroem, warning the King of a conspiracy and advising him to return at once to the town by a safe route. Anckarstroem discovers that the lady is his wife and swears vengeance. The King gives a masked ball at his palace, attended by Amelia and Anckarstroem. His page-boy Oscar unwittingly reveals which costume the King is wearing and Anckarstroem shoots him. As he dies, Gustavus swears to his old friend that Amelia has been always faithful and begs everyone present not to avenge his death. Arias: *La rivedrà nell'estasi* ('I shall see her again in ecstasy'); *Ah crudele, e mel rammemori* ('Ah cruel one, to remind me of him'). Created (1859) by Gaetano Fraschini.

Gustl (Lehár: *The Land of Smiles*). See POTTENSTEIN, GUSTAV VON.

Gutrune (Wagner: *Götterdämmerung*). Sop. A Gibichung, sister of Gunther and half-sister of Hagen. It is Hagen who suggests that Gutrune should marry and when she hears about Siegfried she is attracted to him as a suitable husband. When he comes to visit them, she gives him a potion which makes him forget about Brünnhilde and their love, and he falls in love with Gutrune. Brünnhilde, brought to the Gibichungs' hall as a bride for Gunther, swears that she and Siegfried were married. Despite all his denials, Gutrune has doubts. Hagen and the vassals return from their hunting trip carrying Siegfried's body. Gutrune is distraught, but is brushed aside by Brünnhilde as if she were just a silly little girl. She rejects Gunther's sympathy, realizing that between them he and Hagen are responsible for Siegfried's death. Created (1876) by Matilde Weckerlin.

Guzman, Léonor de (Donizetti: *La Favorite*). Mez. She is the King's 'favourite'—he wants to divorce the Queen and marry her. She lives on the Island of Léon with her confidante, Inès. To the island comes Fernand, who has fallen in love with her without knowing who she is. He has left his monastery to follow her. She will not marry him under false pretences, but her efforts to tell him the truth fail. After their wedding his father, the Abbot Balthazar, tells him that his new wife was the King's mistress. Fernand flees to the monastery. Léonor, sick and dying, disguises herself as a novice and goes to see him one last time. They declare their love for each other and she dies at his feet. Aria: *Ô mon Fernand* ('O my Fernand'). Created (1840) by Rosine Stoltz.

Gvidon (Rimsky-Korsakov: *The Golden Cockerel*). Ten. Son of Tsar Didon and brother of Afron. Killed in battle. Creator (1909) not traced.

H

Hagen (Wagner: *Götterdämmerung*). Bass. Half-brother of Gunther and Gutrune, illegitimate son of Alberich. They all share the same mother (Grimhilde, according to Gunther). Hagen is the evil one of the family. He will do anything and use anyone to gain the gold which his father stole from the Rhinemaidens. To this end, he suggests that Gunther should marry Brünnhilde and Gutrune can then marry Siegfried—thus the treasure comes into the family. The fact that Brünnhilde and Siegfried are already married to each other does not present a problem to Hagen. When Siegfried arrives at the Gibichung Hall on his travels, the plan is put into action. First Siegfried is drugged and this makes him forget everything about Brünnhilde and fall in love with Gutrune. Siegfried, now disguised as Gunther by use of the magic Tarnhelm, is dispatched to collect Brünnhilde. While they are away and Hagen is apparently asleep, he is visited by his father, Alberich, who tells his son they will together inherit control of the world from Wotan, providing Hagen remains loyal to him. They must obtain the Ring before Brünnhilde carries out Wotan's wishes and gives it back to the Rhinemaidens. He makes Hagen swear to remain faithful to him. When Siegfried returns, followed by Gunther with the confused and distressed Brünnhilde, a double wedding is planned. Hagen offers his spear on which Siegfried can swear that he was never Brünnhilde's husband, and she uses the same spear to take an oath of vengeance—may this spear bring about Siegfried's death, she says. Thus Hagen is managing to turn those who once loved against each other. On a hunting trip the next day, Hagen kills Siegfried. He and Gunther clash over possession of the Ring and Hagen kills Gunther. Back at their hall Hagen admits—boasts would be a better word—that he killed Siegfried. He reaches out to take the Ring from the dead Siegfried's finger, but to his horror the corpse lifts his arm in the air and Hagen retreats. After Brünnhilde has started the fire in Siegfried's funeral pyre and the Rhine has overflowed to quench the flames, Hagen sees the Rhinemaidens in the river holding aloft the Ring which Brünnhilde has at last thrown to them. He leaps into the water and the Rhinemaidens grab him and pull him down to the bottom of the river. Aria: *Hier sitz ich zur Wacht* ('Here I sit and watch'); trio (with Brünnhilde and Gunther): *So soll es sein* ('So shall it be').

Hagen is the most wicked character in the whole of the *Ring*. Many of the others behave badly at some point of the saga, usually motivated by greed, but only Hagen is truly evil through and through. This is a challenging role for a deep, dark-voiced, bass. Famous Hagens include Édouard De Reszke, Richard Mayr, Walter Soomer, Josef von Manowarda, Alexander Kipnis, Ludwig Hofmann, Ludwig Weber, Josef Greindl, Gottlob Frick, Karl Ridderbusch, Fritz Hübner, Aage Haugland, John Tomlinson, Eric Halfvarson, and Kurt Rydl. Created (1876) by Gustav Siehr.

Hagenbach, Giuseppe (Catalani: *La Wally*). Ten. Loved by Wally, he laughs at her and she orders him to be killed, regrets her decision and rescues him. They die together in an avalanche. Created (1892) by Manuel Suagnes.

Haltière, Mme de la (Massenet: *Cendrillon*). Mez. Second wife of Pandolfe, mother of Noémie and Dorothée and stepmother of Cendrillon. She dominates her husband and treats Cendrillon very badly. Created (1899) by Blanche Deschamps-Jéhin.

Haly (Rossini: *L'italiana in Algeri*). Bass. A servant of Mustafà, the Bey of Algiers, ordered by his master to find him an Italian wife. Aria: *Le femmine d'Italia* ('The women of Italy'). Created (1813) by Giuseppe Spirito.

Ham and Mrs Ham (Britten: *Noye's Fludde*). Treble and girl sop. Son and daughter-in-law of Noye (Noah). They help to build the Ark. Created (1958) by Marcus Norman and Katherine Dyson.

Hamlet (Thomas). Lib. by Michel Carré and Jules Barbier; 5 acts; f.p. Paris 1868, cond. Georges Hainl.

Denmark: Soon after the death of her husband, the King of Denmark, *Gertrude marries his brother, *Claudius. Her son, *Hamlet, loves *Ophélie (Ophelia), sister of *Laërte (Laertes) and daughter of *Polonius. His father's ghost tells Hamlet that he was murdered by Claudius and asks Hamlet to avenge him. Hamlet instructs a band of strolling players to enact a play about the murder of a king. The performance upsets Claudius and Hamlet accuses him of a similar crime and snatches the crown from him. Occupied by the worry about his father's murder, Hamlet refuses to marry Ophélie who, driven mad by his rejection, drowns herself in a lake. Laërte blames Hamlet for his sister's death and they are about to fight when Ophélie's body is carried in. Hamlet is determined to kill himself.

Hamlet (Thomas: *Hamlet*). Bar. Prince of Denmark, son of the late King and of Queen Gertrude. He is distressed by his mother's plan to marry Claudius, his uncle, so soon after his father's death. His father's ghost tells Hamlet that Claudius murdered him, assisted by Gertrude and Polonius, with whose daughter, Ophélie, Hamlet is in love. He must avenge his father's death. He invites a band of strolling players to entertain the wedding guests and instructs them to perform a play about a king who was poisoned—at this point in the performance, Hamlet accuses Claudius of murdering his father and seizes the crown. Preoccupied by all these events, and shocked that Ophélie's father was part of the assassination plot, Hamlet has ignored Ophélie, who is driven to insanity and drowns herself. Her brother Laërte is about to fight with Hamlet, who knows nothing of Ophélie's death, when her body is carried in. Hamlet is determined to kill himself. It is interesting that, whereas in

the Shakespeare play, there is a great deal of inaction and personal meditation, in the opera the librettists have given Hamlet more character and turned the play into a dramatic opera. Created (1868) by Jean-Baptiste Faure.

Hannah, Dame (Sullivan: *Ruddigore*). Cont. Old lover of the late Sir Roderic Murgatroyd. He emerges from his portrait and they recognize each other. Created (1887) by Rosina Brandram.

Hänsel (Humperdinck: *Hänsel und Gretel*). Mez. *Travesti* role. Son of Peter and Gertrud and brother of Gretel. He helps his father make brooms to sell. Is sent with his sister to pick strawberries in the forest. They become lost and are put to sleep by the Sandman and protected by angels. When they wake the next morning, they are captured by the Witch and Hänsel is put in a cage to be fattened up before he is baked. He is rescued by Gretel who pushes the Witch into the oven. Duet (with Gretel): *Abends wenn ich schlafen gehn* ('In the evening when I go to sleep'). Created (1893) by Fräulein Schubert (who was to have created Gretel, but took over the *travesti* role at short notice because of the illness of the intended Hänsel, Pauline de Ahna, the future wife of Richard Strauss).

Hänsel und Gretel (Humperdinck). Lib. by Adelheid Wette (Humperdinck's sister); 3 acts; f.p. Weimar 1893, cond. by Richard Strauss.

Germany, medieval times: Their family is poor and *Hänsel helps his father, *Peter, make brooms and *Gretel knits. Their mother, *Gertrud, sends the children to pick strawberries, as there is no food in the house. Peter is shocked to hear the children are in the Ilsenstein forest—this is where the *Witch lives, and she catches children and bakes them into gingerbread. They set out to find their children. In the forest the children are lost and frightened. A *Sandman throws sand in their eyes. They say their prayers, then fall asleep. Angels guard them. In the morning the *Dew Fairy wakes them. They see a gingerbread house and fence and take a bite. The Witch catches them, putting Hänsel in a cage. Gretel pushes the Witch into the oven. As the oven explodes, the gingerbread fence becomes a row of children who had been baked by the Witch.

Hans Heiling (Marschner). Lib. by Philipp Eduard Devrient; 3 acts; f.p. Berlin 1833.

Hans*Heiling is the mortal son of the *Queen of the Earth Spirits. He leaves the underworld to live near *Anna. She is afraid of him, but he needs her love to make him a true mortal. At a village fête, she dances with *Konrad. When Anna loses her way in a forest, she meets the Queen, who demands that she give up Heiling. Konrad finds her in the forest and they vow their love. Heiling stabs Konrad who survives the attack and he and Anna plan their wedding. Heiling asks the spirits to help him. As he is about to attack Konrad for a second time, the Queen reminds him that he promised to return to her if his heart was broken.

Harašta (Janáček: *The Cunning Little Vixen*). Bass. A pedlar, or poultry-dealer. He wants to marry the gypsy Terinka. The Vixen trips him up in the forest and kills all his chickens. He shoots the Vixen. Created (1924) by Ferdinand Pour.

Hariadeno, King (Cavalli: *L'Ormindo*). Bass. King of Mauritania, husband of Erisbe, who falls in love with Ormindo who turns out to be the king's long-lost son. After first ordering them to be poisoned, Hariadeno later forgives them and cedes his kingdom to them. Creator (1644) not known.

Harlequin 1. **(Arlecchino)** (Leoncavallo: *Pagliacci*). See BEPPE.

  2. (Strauss: *Ariadne auf Naxos*). See COMMEDIA DELL'ARTE TROUPE.

Hata (Smetana: *The Bartered Bride*). Mez. Wife of Micha, mother of Vašek and stepmother of Jeník. Created (1866) by Marie Pisařovicová.

Hate-Good, Lord (Vaughan Williams: *The Pilgrim's Progress*). Bass. Condemns Pilgrim to death in Vanity Fair, for refusing to partake of the pleasures offered to him. Created (1951) by Rhydderch Davies.

Hatred (La Haine) (Gluck: *Armide*). Cont. Warns Armide that Renaud will leave her. Created (1777) by Mlle Durancy.

Haudy, Capt. (Zimmermann: *Die Soldaten*). Bar. Officer in the French Army. Another of Marie's lovers. Created (1965) by Gerd Nienstedt.

Hauk-Šendorf, Count Maximilian (Janáček: *The Makropulos Case*). Ten. An old ex-diplomat, now somewhat confused. In his youth Hauk had an affair with the Spanish gypsy Eugenia Montez, who died some years ago. Fifty years later he attends the opera in Prague and hears the soprano Emilia Marty. He is so struck by her resemblance to his past love that he goes to visit her in her dressing-room. Much to the astonishment of all her other visitors, she seems to know who he is and welcomes him—they even embrace. Hauk is amazed to realize that Emilia and Eugenia are the same person. Created (1926) by Václav Šindler. A gem of a role for a character tenor. *See also* ARTICLE BY NIGEL DOUGLAS, p. 126.

Hautdesert, Lady de (Birtwistle: *Gawain*). Mez. Wife of the disguised Green Knight. Gives Gawain a protective sash to wear which saves him from injury when the Green Knight fulfils his bargain and hits his neck with an axe. Created (1991) by Elizabeth Lawrence.

Hautdesert, Sir Bertilak de (Birtwistle: *Gawain*). See GREEN KNIGHT.

Hawks, Capt. Andy (Kern: *Show Boat*). Spoken. Capt. of the *Cotton Blossom*, a show boat on the Mississippi. Husband of Parthy Ann and father of Magnolia. Created (1927) by Charles Winninger.

Hawks, Magnolia (Kern: *Show Boat*). Sop. Daughter of Parthy and Andy Hawks, captain of the show boat *Cotton Blossom*. She falls in love with the gambler Gaylord Ravenal and marries him despite her parents' reservations. She and her husband take over the roles of entertainers on the boat. They have a daughter, Kim, but Gaylord gambles all their money away and they leave the boat. He leaves them in Chicago and Magnolia finds a job as a singer. Years later, on board the newly fitted show boat, she and Kim become the star turns and Gaylord returns to them. Duets (with Ravenal): *Make believe; You are love; Why do I love you?* Created (1927) by Norma Terris.

Hawks, Parthy Ann (Kern: *Show Boat*). Spoken. Wife of Andy, captain of the show boat *Cotton Blossom*. She disapproves of her daughter Magnolia's relationship with the gambler Gaylord Ravenal. Created (1927) by Edna May Oliver.

MAXIMILIAN HAUK-ŠENDORF (*The Makropulos Case*—Janáček)

by Nigel Douglas

The Slav repertoire is rich in sharply etched cameos for a character tenor, but in my experience there is none to compete with Hauk (*The Makropulos Affair*): in terms of potential impact on the audience per minute spent on stage it is a miniature masterpiece.

It is always amusing, I find, to sketch in for one's self the past history of the characters whom one has to play, and I envisage Hauk's early days as something along these lines. Back in 1870, when he was 20 years old, he visited Andalusia and engaged in a torrid affair with a gypsy girl named Eugenia Montez. His family hauled him home to Prague, married him off to someone dull and plain but socially suitable, and deceived him into believing that his gypsy girl was dead. Since then fifty years have passed and, in his own words, Hauk's existence has been a sort of sleepwalk—until last night, when, on the stage of the Prague Opera, there suddenly appeared before him an apparent reincarnation of his long-lost love.

When you enter for Hauk's first scene, shuffling on some ten minutes after the beginning of Act 2, the public is as baffled as Emilia Marty herself—who can this old lunatic be, sobbing pathetically and having apparently no logical connection with anyone or anything around him? As he attempts, however, somehow to make Marty understand that she is the living image of the woman for whom he sacrificed everything, Janáček gives us a sudden flash of the man Hauk used to be. The orchestra erupts without warning into a fiery flamenco rhythm as the old boy momentarily relives his days of erotic splendour. As he lapses back after only a couple of dozen bars into a lament for his own lost sanity, a state of mind achingly evoked in the strings, the penny drops with Emilia and she calls him by her old pet name of 'Maxi'. Briefly the two of them re-enact the feverish embraces of yesteryear, and although within moments her mood has passed and it is time for him to totter off again, back into his dreamlike existence, what the audience has just witnessed is the only instance during the whole opera of Emilia treating a fellow human being with anything other than contempt.

Naturally, no two directors approach so multifaceted a character from the same angle, and it goes without saying that there are some nowadays who have such charming ideas as decreeing that he should be in the final stages of syphilis. I, however, have been fortunate in that the two directors who have guided my steps in the role, David Pountney and Nikolaus Lehnhoff, both believe in using the score as the source of their ideas. They came up with sharply contrasted readings, Pountney emphasizing the lovable dottiness of the figure, while Lehnhoff saw him as a faded dandy, somewhere between the Elderly Fop in Britten's *Death in Venice* and the Master of Ceremonies in *Cabaret*. But as neither version conflicts with Janáček's inspiration, both are intensely rewarding to perform.

If I were asked to sum up the figure of Hauk in one word it would, I think, be *Chaplinesque*. The audience should be left not quite knowing whether to laugh or cry, and though the old boy's second appearance, in Act 3, is more farcical than the scene I have described, he remains as much a tragic figure as a comic one. The trick of the role—or so I believe—lies in never forgetting, even at your most doddery, that you were once one hell of a fellow.

He-Ancient (Tippett: *The Midsummer Marriage*). Bass. Priest of the Temple, he seems to know Mark from times gone by. Created (1955) by Michael Langdon.

Heavenly Beings, Two (Vaughan Williams: *The Pilgrim's Progress*). Sop. and cont. In the Valley of Humiliation, they revive the injured Pilgrim, giving him a cup of the Water of Life. Created (1951) by Elisabeth Abercrombie and Monica Sinclair.

Hebe (Sullivan: *HMS Pinafore*). Mez. Sir Joseph Porter's first cousin, and in the end the only woman available for him to marry. Created (1878) by Jessie Bond.

Hector 1. (Tippett: *King Priam*). Bar. Eldest son of King Priam and Queen Hecuba, brother of Paris. Fighting in the Trojan War, Hector kills Patroclus, Achilles' friend, and Achilles avenges his friend's death by killing Hector. Created (1962) by Victor Godfrey.
　　2. (Berlioz: *Les Troyens*). Bass. The Ghost of Hector. Son of King Priam, killed in the Trojan War. His ghost urges Aeneas to found a new Troy in Italy. Creator (1890) not traced.

Hecuba (Tippett: *King Priam*). Sop. Wife of King Priam, mother of Hector and Paris. At the time of Paris's birth, Hecuba's dream foretells that Paris will cause the death of Priam. Hecuba is prepared to have her son killed, but Priam allows the baby to be taken by a shepherd. Created (1962) by Marie Collier.

Heerrufer (Wagner: *Lohengrin*). Bar. The King's herald. He summons Lohengrin to come and champion Elsa's cause. This is a small role in which many a baritone destined for fame has made his mark, including Dietrich Fischer-Dieskau (who sang it at Bayreuth in 1954), Eberhard Wächter, Tom Krause, Ingvar Wixell, Bernd Weikl, and Anthony Michaels-Moore. Created (1850) by Herr Pätsch.

Heiling, Hans (Marschner: *Hans Heiling*). Bar. Son of the Queen of the Earth Spirits. He leaves the underworld to live near Anna, but promises his mother to return if ever his heart is broken. Anna meets Konrad and they fall in love. Hans attacks Konrad, who survives. As he is about to attack him again, the Queen reminds Hans of his promise. Created (1833) by Eduard Devrient (the opera's librettist).

Heinrich 1. (Wagner: *Lohengrin*). Bass. König Heinrich der Vogler (Henry the Fowler), King of Saxony. He has gone to Brabant to persuade some of the knights to fight with him to defeat the Hungarian invasion of Germany. In front of the King, Lohengrin reveals his identity. Arias: *Gott grüss' euch, liebe Männer von Brabant!* ('God bless you, worthy people of Brabant!'); *Habt Dank, ihr Lieben von Brabant* ('I thank you, dear people of Brabant'). Notable singers of this role include Josef von Manowarda, Josef Greindl, Gottlob Frick, Ludwig Weber, Theo Adam, Karl Ridderbusch, Kurt Böhme, Hans Sotin, Matti Salminen, and Manfred Schenk. Created (1850) by August Höfer.
　　2. (Prokofiev: *The Fiery Angel*). Silent. Count Heinrich. Renata believes him to be her protecting angel. When they meet, he injures Ruprecht in a duel. Creator (1954) not known.

Helena 1. (Britten: *A Midsummer Night's Dream*). Sop. In love with Demetrius, but he loves her friend Hermia. There is much confusion, caused by Puck, before the lovers are sorted out and reconciled with their partners, Helena with Demetrius. Quartet (with Hermia, Demetrius and Lysander): *Mine own, and not mine own.* Created (1960) by April Cantelo.
　　2. (Purcell: *The Fairy Queen*). Spoken. Similar to the role in (1) above. Creator (1692) unknown. *See also* HELEN OF TROY (3).

Hélène (Elena) (Verdi: *Les Vêpres siciliennes*). Sop. Duchess, sister of the assassinated Duke Frederick of Austria. She is in love with Henri, a young Sicilian. She agrees to help Jean de Procida, a loyal Sicilian, to rout the French and at a masked ball at the Governor's palace they conspire to kill the Governor, Montfort. By now Henri has learned that he is Montfort's illegitimate son, and he foils their attempt. The conspirators are arrested and imprisoned. Henri visits Hélène in prison and tells her the truth of his relationship to Montfort, and she forgives him. Montfort agrees to allow them to marry if Henri acknowledges him as his father. The wedding is planned, but at the last minute Procida tells Hélène that the sound of her wedding bells is the signal for the Sicilians to rise. She tries her best, but it is too late to call a halt to the ceremony. The bells sound and the French are massacred. Aria: *Merci, jeunes amies*

('Thank you, young friends'). This aria, usually known as the *Bolero* (in the score Verdi called it a *Siciliana*), is a wonderful display piece, written in the high register for much of its length. Created (1855) by Sophie Cruvelli (who caused great consternation during the rehearsal period by totally disappearing for several days: she had been on holiday with Baron De Vigier, the man she eventually married). *See also* HELEN OF TROY (1).

Helen of Troy 1. (Hélène) (Offenbach: *La Belle Hélène*). Sop. Queen, wife of Menelaus, who finds her in bed with Paris, who won her in a contest. Instructed by a priest (Paris in disguise) to sail for Cythera. As she obeys, the Trojan War begins. Created (1864) by Hortense Schneider.
   2. (Tippett: *King Priam*). Mez. Wife of the Greek King Menelaus, her abduction to Troy by Paris brings about the start of the Trojan War. Created (1962) by Margreta Elkins.
   3. (Helena) (Strauss: *Die ägyptische Helena*). Sop. Wife of Menelaus and mother of Hermione. At the beginning of the opera Helen and Menelaus are in a ship and Menelaus is approaching his sleeping wife with a dagger, intending to kill her after her unfaithfulness with Paris (whom he has already killed). She is saved by the sorceress Aithra, who causes a storm which shipwrecks them near her palace. Aithra befriends Helen and gives her a special potion—lotus juice—which causes forgetfulness. She gives this to Menelaus, but he then forgets that he did not kill her and assumes she is someone else. Aithra comes to the rescue with a second potion and Helen and Menelaus are reunited. Aria: *Zweite Brautnacht! Zaubernacht* ('Second wedding night! Magic night'). Created (1928) by Elisabeth Rethberg. She was not the soprano Strauss wanted. She had a lovely voice but not the glamour he had in mind for the beautiful Helen of Troy. When Strauss conducted the Vienna première, Helen was sung by Maria Jeritza, on whom he had modelled the role. Other famous exponents have included Viorica Ursuleac, Leonie Rysanek, and Gwyneth Jones. In the British première (1997) by Garsington Opera, Helen was well portrayed by Susan Bullock.
   4. (Elena) (Boito: *Mefistofele*). Sop. Helen of Troy, with whom Faust falls in love when he visits classical Greece under the influence of Mefistofele. Created (1868) by Mlle Reboux.

Helmwige (Wagner: *Die Walküre*). *See* VALKYRIES.

Helson, Hel (Britten: *Paul Bunyan*). Bar. A logger, sent to America by the King of Sweden and appointed as Paul Bunyan's foreman. Tries to usurp Bunyan's position by inciting the men to rebel, but later makes his peace and the two of them help to found the America of the future. Created (1941) by Bliss Woodward.

Henri (Arrigo) (Verdi: *Les Vêpres siciliennes*). Ten. A young Sicilian in love with Hélène, sister of the assassinated Duke Frederick of Austria. Montfort, who is Governor of Palermo since the French occupied Sicily, warns him to keep away from her, a warning he ignores. Questioned by Montfort about his background, Henri soon learns that he is the Governor's illegitimate son. He refuses to acknowledge this. But when Hélène conspires with others to murder Montfort, Henri intervenes. He is denounced by the Sicilians as a traitor and Hélène is imprisoned. Henri visits her and tells her the full story and she forgives him for his actions. He agrees to call Montfort 'father' in return for Hélène's freedom, and the Governor gives his consent to their marriage. Too late, Hélène discovers that the sounding of the bells at her wedding is the sign for the Sicilian uprising and the French are massacred. Aria: *O jour de peine* ('O day of sorrow'). Created (1855) by Louis Gueymard.

Henry (Strauss: *Die schweigsame Frau*). *See* MOROSUS, HENRY.

Henry VIII, King (Donizetti: *Anna Bolena*). *See* ENRICO (2).

Herald (Wagner: *Lohengrin*). *See* HEERRUFER.

Hérisson de Porc Épic (Chabrier: *L'Étoile*). Ten. Husband of Aloès. Ambassador to King Mataquin, whose daughter Laoula is the intended bride of the neighbouring King Ouf. He and his wife escort the Princess to meet Ouf but she falls in love with a pedlar instead. Created (1877) by Alfred Joly.

Hermann (Tchaikovsky: *The Queen of Spades*). Ten. A Russian officer, he has fallen in love, but the lady turns out to be Prince

Yeletsky's fiancée, Lisa. When young, Lisa's grandmother, the old Countess, lived in Paris and gambled heavily, being known as the Queen of Spades. After she lost her husband's fortune, a Count gave her the secret of three winning cards. These she told her husband and a lover, but a ghost warned her not to reveal them to anyone else. Hermann is determined to secure the secret, so he can win and be worthy of Lisa. He hides in the Countess's quarters and when she is alone he demands the secret. Terrified of him, she collapses and dies. Lisa sends him away and drowns herself. The Countess's ghost tells Hermann the three cards—3, 7 and Ace. He gambles on them, winning on the first two, but when he bets everything on the third card and turns it over, it is not the Ace but the Queen of Spades—the Countess has tricked him. He kills himself. Aria: *Ya imeni yeyo ne znayu* ('I don't even know her name'); *Chto nasha zhizn? Ingra!* ('What is our life? A game!'). Created (1890) by Nikolay Figner (whose wife, pregnant, created Lisa).

Hermia 1. (Britten: *A Midsummer Night's Dream*). Mez. In love with Lysander but her father wants her to marry Demetrius. It all works out right and Demetrius loves Helena, leaving Theseus to give permission for Hermia and Lysander to marry. Aria: *Puppet? Why so?*; quartet (with Hermia, Lysander and Demetrius): *Mine own, and not mine own.* Created (1960) by Marjorie Thomas.
   2. (Purcell: *The Fairy Queen*). Spoken. Similar to the role in (1) above. Creator (1692) unknown.

Hermione 1. (Ermione) (Rossini: *Ermione*). Sop. Wife of Pyrrhus. Her husband marries Andromache, widow of the murdered Hector. Hermione asks Orestes, who loves her, to kill her husband. He does so, but she is furious with him, having changed her mind, realizing she still loves her husband. She has Orestes arrested. Created (1819) by Isabella Colbran (wife of Rossini 1822–37).
   2. (Strauss: *Die ägyptische Helena*). Sop. Daughter of Helen and Menelaus. She is at first forbidden by her father to see her mother, who has been unfaithful with Paris (killed by Menelaus), but her parents are reunited with the aid of the enchantress Aithra and Hermione comes to see her beautiful mother. Created (1928) by Anneliese Petrich.

Hermit (Weber: *Der Freischütz*). Bass. Accompanies Agathe to watch Max in a shooting contest. Created (1821) by Herr Gern.

Héro (Berlioz: *Béatrice and Bénédict*). Sop. Daughter of Léonato, Governor of Messina, about to marry Claudio who has just returned from the Moorish wars. Duet with Ursula, her companion: *Nuit paisible et sereine* ('Peaceful and serene night'). Created (1862) by Mlle Montrose.

Herod 1. (Herodes) (Strauss: *Salome*). Ten. Herod Antipas, Tetrarch of Judaea. His second wife is Herodias; and Salome, after whom he lusts, is his 16-year-old stepdaughter. He holds captive the prophet Jochanaan, who has denounced the sinful Herodias, but Herod is still somewhat in awe of Jochanaan, the man of God. Herod is superstitious and not a little mentally disturbed, worried about the way the wind blows and how the moon looks. His desire for Salome is uppermost. 'Dance for me, Salome', he asks, and when she refuses, and all his bribes do not move her, he promises to grant her anything she requests, if she will only dance for him. So she dances and he watches her, fascinated and aroused. Then she claims her reward—the head of Jochanaan on a silver salver. Herod cannot believe his ears. He will give her jewels, his white peacocks, even the Veil of the Temple. But Salome will not be diverted and at last, too weak to argue any longer, Herod sends down into the cistern an executioner to carry out her wishes, at the same time disowning her—she becomes *ein Ungeheuer, deine Tochter* ('a monster, your daughter') he tells Herodias. As Salome's total depravity reaches its climax, Herod can take no more and orders his soldiers to kill her. Arias: *Salome, komm, trink Wein mit mir* ('Salome, come drink wine with me'); *Salome, tanz für mich* ('Salome, dance for me'). Created (1905) by Karl Burrian, who set an example to the rest of the cast during the rehearsal period. Many of them felt the music was too difficult and were ready to return their parts, but Burrian (an uncle of Emil Burrian, the composer) already knew his by heart, thus countering the 'too difficult' accusations. It has become one of the roles relished by tenors, including Julius Patzak, Max Lorenz, Ramon Vinay, Richard Lewis, Helmut Melchert, and,

HEROD (*Salome*—Strauss)

by Robert Tear

'Your father was a camel driver.' King Herod is never allowed to forget his origins. His wife, Herodias, has reminded him every day of their marriage. This inequality is Herod's main problem. Having been born a camel-driver's son, he'd never been privy to the secrets of the princely caste. He was an outsider. Moreover, as he had been placed in position by an invader, he was not trusted by his people. His temperament was that of a peasant. He watched the elements, the stars for portents; superstitious, the moon casting a dubious glance in his direction could drive him to hysteria. Blood on the floor sends him into paroxysms of fear. He is a man with the wrong temperament in the wrong job at the wrong time. A vexatious wife who brought with her a wilful teenage daughter (Salome), didn't make his home life happy, to put it mildly.

The difficulty in acting Herod is that the mood of deranged tension can easily become monochromatic. An imitation of silent film technique is not encouraged. However, it is the most wonderful role to play. I think good advice to future Tetrarchs is, turn down your fidget-acting knob about two notches more than you think is practicable. Herod must be played with intense inward truth. He must lust as if he invented it, hate and fear the same.

The role of Herod is also a joy to sing. It must not be barked. He is given some of Strauss's most lyrical lines: 'Salome, come drink wine with me' is a perfect example of these fluid yet heroic passages. I do not believe that Herod is a *buffo* character. True, it can sometimes seem so, but if this is the case then one part of the tragic quartet has been eliminated. No, he is a real figure, a monster who should evoke some sympathy.

The role is a heavy sing. The orchestra is inevitably too loud. It is musically complicated and should be sung with exactitude. There is a trap for the unwary singer. Having given his all from the end of Salome's dance to the end of the jewel aria, he should find himself all but exhausted. The love-song which Salome sings to John the Baptist's severed head will give Herod twenty minutes rest. This is just the time the voice needs to relax. He must end the opera with a series of high As and a final B flat—cruel in the circumstances. The B flat can sometimes feel like a Z *in alt.*

more recently, Emile Belcourt, Nigel Douglas, Manfred Jung, Robert Tear, Peter Bronder, and Kenneth Riegel. *See also* ARTICLE BY ROBERT TEAR.

2. (Hérode) (Massenet: *Hérodiade*). Bar. Hérode, Tetrarch of Judaea. Husband of Hérodiade and stepfather of Salomé. Orders Salomé and Jean (John the Baptist) to be beheaded. Created (1881) by Mons. Manoury.

Hérodiade (Massenet). Lib. by Paul Milliet and 'Henri Grémont' (Georges Hartmann,

Massenet's publisher); 4 acts; f.p. Brussels 1881 (3 acts), cond. Joseph Dupont; Paris 1884 (final vers., in 4 acts).

Biblical times: Hérode's (*Herod's) wife Hérodiade (*Herodias) hates *Jean (John the Baptist) and his preaching of the coming of the Messiah and his insults about her, but *Salomé admits to *Phanuel that she loves Jean. Hérode is attracted by Salomé. Hérodiade, unaware that Salomé is her long-lost daughter, sees her as a rival for Hérode's love. Salomé does not respond to Hérode's overtures and he orders both her and Jean to be beheaded. Salomé, wanting Hérodiade's head for her part in the plot to behead Jean, kills herself on realizing that she is Hérodiade's daughter.

Herodias 1. (Strauss: *Salome*). Mez. She is the second wife of Herod, Tetrarch of Judaea, and mother of the 16-year-old Salome. She is a cold fish—in order to marry Herod, she killed her first husband who was Herod's brother. Jochanaan has been imprisoned by Herod because of his denunciation of Herodias and she urges her husband to hand him over to the Jews. Herodias is aware that Herod lusts after her daughter, and she treats him with contempt, proud of the way her daughter stands up to him. She supports Salome in her refusal to dance for Herod and in her request to be rewarded with Jochanaan's head on a silver salver—after all, has not the prophet insulted her, Herod's wife? She enjoys the emotional struggle between Salome and Herod until he has to give in to her macabre request. Then Herodias takes the ring from Herod's finger and sends it to the executioner, a sign that it is an order from Herod and must be obeyed. Salome, Herod points out, is truly her mother's child (*Sie ist in Wahrheit ihrer Mutter Kind!*). Created (1905) by Irene von Chavanne.

2. (Hérodiade) (Massenet: *Hérodiade*). Mez. Second wife of Hérode and mother of the long-lost Salomé. Not knowing this is her daughter, she is jealous of her, because Hérode finds her attractive. She encourages Hérode in ordering the beheading of Salomé and John the Baptist. When Salomé realizes that Hérodiade is her mother, she kills herself. Created (1881) by Blanche Deschamps-Jéhin.

Herring, Albert (Britten: *Albert Herring*). Ten. Son of Mrs Herring. He helps his mother to run the greengrocer's and is totally dominated by her. Watching the way Sid and Nancy behave together, he realizes he is missing something, but 'mum' will not allow him to have girlfriends. To his discomfort, he is elected May King, an honour his mother forces him to accept as it carries a prize of 25 sovereigns. At the crowning ceremony, his lemonade is spiked by Sid. Albert discovers he likes the taste, and gradually becomes more and more drunk. Under the influence of the alcohol he goes off the rails and sows his wild oats. He is reported missing, and while everyone is mourning his supposed death he quietly reappears. He remembers little of the previous evening—he admits he has been drinking and with girls and has spent a fair amount of his prize money. He likes his newfound freedom and is not going to allow his mother to dominate him any more. Arias: *He's much too busy; Albert the Good!; Heaven helps those; I can't remember everything.* An outstanding Albert in recent years was John Graham Hall. Created (1947) by Peter Pears.

Herring, Mrs (Britten: *Albert Herring*). Mez. Owner of the local greengrocer's, mother of Albert whom she keeps under her thumb. She insists her son accepts the position of May King as there is a 25 sovereign prize attached to it. When Albert goes missing, Mrs Herring is truly distressed—he is, after all, her only son and, thinking he is dead, she genuinely mourns him. Once he reappears, she rapidly reverts to being the domineering mother, and is totally nonplussed when her son makes it clear that he is no longer prepared to accept this kind of treatment. Aria: *There's one in a frame.* Created (1947) by Betsy de la Porte.

Herrmann (Wagner: *Tannhäuser*). *See* LANDGRAVE, HERRMANN THE.

Herzeleide (Wagner: *Parsifal*). 'Heart's Sorrow'. She is Parsifal's mother. She does not appear in the opera. Parsifal, when questioned, tells Gurnemanz her name, saying that he does not know who his father is. *See also* GAMURET.

Heure espagnole, L' (Spanish Time) (Ravel). Lib. by Franc-Nohain (M. E. Legrand); 1 act; f.p. Paris 1911, cond. Franz Ruhlmann.
    Toledo, 18th cent.: *Torquemada the clockmaker regulates all the clocks once a week. He leaves his wife, *Concepción, to look after *Ramiro, who has brought a watch for repair. Concepción is awaiting her lover, the poet *Gonzalve. To keep Ramiro out of the way, she sends him up and down the stairs carrying clocks. The banker Don *Gomez comes to court her also, hides in one of the clocks and, being fat, becomes stuck. Gonzalve hides in another clock. Ramiro continues carrying clocks up and down the stairs, but her lovers remain inside them. Concepción suggests to Ramiro that he and she go upstairs together—without the clocks. Torquemada returns and

the two occupants of the clocks pretend to be customers, each buying his clock. Ramiro helps to extract Gomez and leaves. As the clocks have now been sold, Ramiro promises to call each morning to tell Concepción the correct time.

Hidraot (Gluck: *Armide*). Bar. King of Damascus, Armide's uncle, a magician. Puts a spell on the crusader knight Renaud so that he falls in love with Armide. Created (1777) by Nicolas Gélin.

High Priest of Dagon (Saint-Saëns: *Samson et Dalila*). Bar. High Priest of the Philistines. Orders Dalila to find out the secret of Samson's enormous strength. Created (1877) by Mons. Milde.

Hilarion, Prince (Sullivan: *Princess Ida*). Ten. Son of King Hildebrand. He was engaged as an infant to Ida. She has gone into hiding and he breaks into the Castle Adamant to reclaim her. Created (1884) by Henry Bracy.

Hilda (Henze: *Elegy for Young Lovers*). *See* MACK, FRAU HILDA.

Hildebrand, King (Sullivan: *Princess Ida*). Bass-bar. His son Hilarion was engaged to Ida in infancy. Created (1884) by Rutland Barrington.

Hippolyta (Britten: *A Midsummer Night's Dream*). Cont. Queen of the Amazons, betrothed to Theseus. Created (1960) by Johanna Peters. Hippolyta does not appear in Purcell's *The Fairy Queen*.

Hippolyte (Rameau: *Hippolyte et Aricie*). Ten. Son of Thésée and stepson of Phèdre. Loved by his stepmother, but in love with Aricie. Exiled by his father, who wrongly thinks he is about to kill Phèdre. The misunderstandings are all unravelled and he and Aricie are united. Created (1733) by Denis-François Tribou.

Hippolyte et Aricie (Rameau). Lib. by Simon-Joseph Pellegrin; prol. and 5 acts; f.p. Paris 1733.

Sparta, Hades and the Forest of Aricia: The goddess *Diana pledges protection of *Hippolyte and *Aricie. Thésée (*Theseus) has made Aricie, descendant of his enemy, take vows of chastity. She and Hippolyte love each other. Hippolyte's stepmother, *Phèdre, loves him too and is furious at Diana's protection of the young lovers. Theseus, in Hades, is warned of the troubles in his home. Phèdre offers Hippolyte the throne and herself, but he rejects her. In her chagrin, she demands he kill her. As he refuses, Theseus arrives and assumes Hippolyte is trying to kill Phèdre. Aricie agrees to share his exile, but Hippolyte is carried off by a monster, apparently dead. His stepmother reveals the truth. Aricie is inconsolable but when Diana brings in her proposed husband she realizes it is Hippolyte, and their union is celebrated.

HMS Pinafore, or The Lass that loved a Sailor (Sullivan). Lib. by W. S. Gilbert; 2 acts; f.p. London 1878, cond. Arthur Sullivan.

On board ship in Portsmouth, mid-19th cent.: Mrs Cripps (known as *Little Buttercup) sells her wares on board. A sailor, Ralph *Rackstraw, loves Josephine *Corcoran, daughter of Capt. *Corcoran who wants her to marry Sir Joseph *Porter, First Lord of the Admiralty. All Ralph's friends (except Dick *Deadeye) help him and Josephine to go ashore to be married that night. Dick tells her father, who tries to prevent their elopement. Mrs Cripps confesses to having mixed up Ralph and Capt. Corcoran as babies, so really Ralph is the captain and Corcoran the simple sailor. Josephine can now marry Ralph and her father settles for Mrs Cripps. Sir Joseph is left to the tender mercies of his cousin *Hebe.

Hobson, Jim (Britten: *Peter Grimes*). Bass. A carrier. He is reluctant to fetch Grimes's new Apprentice, but agrees to do so when Ellen Orford volunteers to accompany him and escort the boy back. Created (1945) by Frank Vaughan.

Hoffmann (Offenbach: *Les Contes d'Hoffmann*). Ten. A poet, based on E. T. A. Hoffmann. In love with the diva Stella who is loved by Lindorf. Hoffmann regales his friend Nicklausse with stories of his past loves, Olympia, Antonia, and Giulietta. All these affairs have been thwarted. Nicklausse points out that all the women Hoffmann has loved have been manifestations of Stella, but adds that the experiences will make him a better poet. Created (1881) by Jean-Alexandre Talazac.

Hohenzollern, Count (Henze: *Der Prinz von Homburg*). Ten. Attached to the Elector, friend of the Prince. Created (1960) by Heinz Hoppe.

Holsteiner, Der (Strauss: *Friedenstag*). Bass. Commander of the army which is besieging the Citadel. When he enters after the bells have rung, the Commandant assumes he has come to fight and draws his sword. However, the Commandant's wife, Maria, intervenes and the two men embrace in peace. Created (1938) by Ludwig Weber.

Horn, Count (Verdi: *Un ballo in maschera*). (Tom in Amer. vers.) Bass. Enemy of King Gustavus, plotting to overthrow him. Created (1859) by Giovanni Bernadoni.

Hotel Barber (Britten: *Death in Venice*). Bass-bar. He trims Aschenbach's hair in the Lido hotel and tells him about the cholera epidemic in Venice. Created (1973) by John Shirley-Quirk.

Hotel Manager (Britten: *Death in Venice*). Bass-bar. Manager at the hotel on the Lido, who keeps Aschenbach's room for him when he tries to leave the city. Created (1973) by John Shirley-Quirk.

Housekeeper (Strauss: *Die schweigsame Frau*). Cont. Housekeeper to Sir Morosus, a retired admiral who cannot bear any noise. She tells his Barber that she would be quite happy to marry him, but the Barber knows Morosus would not contemplate it. Created (1935) by Helene Jung.

Hugh (Vaughan Williams: *Hugh the Drover*). Ten. A drover who falls in love with Mary at first sight and fights her future husband, John, for her hand. John accuses him of being a French spy and he is put in the stocks. When soldiers arrive and recognize him as a loyal English-man, he is released and he and Mary leave town for their new life on the open road. Arias: *Do they call you in the noon-day?*; *Gaily I go to die*. Created (1924) by John Dean.

Hugh the Drover (Vaughan Williams). Lib. by Harold Child; 2 acts; f.p. London 1924, cond. S. P. Waddington.

A small Cotswold town, *c*.1812 (during the Napoleonic wars): *Mary, daughter of the *Constable, is to marry *John the Butcher. *Hugh the Drover, a stranger, falls in love with her and asks her to take to the open road with

him. He fights John, with Mary as the prize. John loses and accuses Hugh of being a French spy. The Constable puts Hugh in the stocks. Mary steals the keys from her father to release him. John goes to visit Mary at home and dis-covers her missing. The Constable and Aunt *Jane find her sitting in the stocks next to Hugh. John urges soldiers to arrest Hugh, but one of them recognizes Hugh as an old and loyal friend. John is press-ganged into the army. Mary and Hugh set off on their life together.

Hugo (Weir: *Blond Eckbert*). Ten. He meets and befriends Eckbert in the forest, but Eckbert sees in him a likeness to Walther, whom Eckbert has killed. *See also* WALTHER (3). Created (1994) by Christopher Ventris.

Huguenots, Les (Meyerbeer). Lib. by Eugène Scribe and Émile Deschamps; 5 acts; f.p. Paris 1836, cond. François-Antoine Habeneck.

France, 1572: The Huguenot Raoul de *Nangis accepts the invitation of the Catholic Comte de *Nevers to a party, much to the hor-ror of his servant, *Marcel. Raoul has fallen in love with Valentine de *Saint-Bris, daughter of the leader of the Catholics, not knowing her identity. She begs Nevers to break off their engagement and sends a note to Raoul via *Urbain, page of Marguerite de *Valois, who encourages Raoul's feelings for Valentine. Raoul agrees to marry Valentine to help pro-mote peace between the Huguenots and Catholics, not knowing she is still engaged to Nevers who intends persisting with the mar-riage. Raoul visits the home of Valentine and Nevers. When *Saint-Bris is heard arriving, Valentine hides Raoul, who overhears a plot to massacre the Huguenots and warns them. Nevers is killed. Saint-Bris orders his men to shoot. Raoul and Valentine are both mortally wounded.

Hunding (Wagner: *Die Walküre*). Bass. A mortal, husband of Sieglinde. They live in a hut with a large ash tree growing up through the roof. He is a big, warrior-like man, of whom Sieglinde is scared. He returns home one evening to find a stranger (Siegmund) in his house, and notes the likeness between this man and Sieglinde. He is suspicious of the man and of the obvious attraction be-tween him and Sieglinde. Hunding questions

Siegmund about his background and reasons for being there. Siegmund tells how, lost in the forest, he defended a girl by killing her brothers and was set upon by their kinsmen. Hunding realizes this is the man he and his huntsmen have been chasing all day.

However, the laws of hospitality prevail and Hunding tells Siegmund he may stay the night, but tomorrow they will fight to the death. Sieglinde, preparing her husband's nightly drink, drugs it. Hunding retires to bed. Next morning he awakens to find the stranger and his wife gone. He sets off in pursuit, invoking the name of Fricka, goddess of marriage, to support him. The two men meet and fight. As Siegmund is about to thrust his sword into Hunding, Wotan appears. With his spear he shatters the sword and Hunding kills Siegmund. Wotan then gestures at Hunding, who himself falls dead. Aria: *Heilig ist mein Herd* ('My hearth is holy'). Although it is not a large part (Hunding appears in about half the first act and only briefly in the second, when he kills Siegmund), the role has

attracted many excellent basses, several of whom have, at other points in their career, essayed Wotan. These include Walter Soomer, Josef von Manowarda, Josef Greindl, Gottlob Frick, Martti Talvela, Karl Ridderbusch, Matti Salminen, Matthias Hölle, Hans Sotin, Manfred Schenk, and John Tomlinson. Created (1870) by Kaspar Bausewein.

Huon, Sir (Weber: *Oberon*). Ten. Knight of Bordeaux. Kills the son of Charlemagne, Emperor of the Franks, and is exiled to Baghdad. There he must kill whoever sits on the Caliph's right hand and then marry the Caliph's daughter. He succeeds, but all except Huon are captured by pirates and he has to rescue the daughter. Oberon uses their evident show of faithfulness to allow himself to be reconciled with his own love, Titania. Created (1826) by John Braham.

Hymen (Purcell: *The Fairy Queen*). Bass. The god of marriage. Creator (1692) unknown.

Iago 1. (Verdi: *Otello*). Bar. Husband of Emilia (who is Desdemona's lady-in-waiting) and Otello's ensign. He hates both Otello and the young lieutenant Cassio, promoted by Otello over his head. He uses Roderigo, a young Venetian hopelessly in love with Desdemona (Otello's wife), to get Cassio demoted. Iago swears an oath of faithfulness to Otello, and then sets about providing false evidence to suggest that Desdemona and Cassio are lovers. He forces Emilia to give him Desdemona's handkerchief which he then shows to Otello, implying that it was found in Cassio's possession. He so convinces the jealous Moor that Otello plans the murder of both Cassio and Desdemona. Iago undertakes to dispose of Cassio—he will force Roderigo into killing him—and Otello will deal with his wife. Otello suffocates Desdemona, but then finds out that Cassio has killed Roderigo and that the stories are all made up by Iago. Aria: *Credo in un Dio crudel* ('I believe in a cruel God'); *Era la notte, Cassio dormì* ('In the night, Cassio slept'); duet (with Otello—the swearing of their oath): *Sì, per ciel marmoreo giuro!* ('Yes, by the marbled heavens, I swear!'). Another superb Verdi baritone role. Created (1887) by Victor Maurel (whose performance, from contemporary accounts, was superb, making him seem like the most important character in the opera—indeed, at one time both Boito and Verdi considered calling the opera *Iago*). Many Italianate baritones have relished this role, including Mariano Stabile, Antonio Scotti, Titta Ruffo, Tito Gobbi, Lawrence Tibbett, Paul Schöffler, Otakar Kraus, Piero Cappuccilli, Peter Glossop, Delme Bryn-Jones, Sergei Leiferkus, Ruggero Raimondi, and Donald Maxwell.

2. (Rossini: *Otello*). Ten. He helps Rodrigo to plot against Otello, knowing Desdemona loves the Moor. He tells Otello that Desdemona is deceiving him. Created (1816) by Giuseppe Ciccimarra.

Ida 1. (J. Strauss II: *Die Fledermaus*). Sop. Sister of Adele (maid of Rosalinde). Ida invites Adele to attend Prince Orlofsky's ball. Creator (1874) not traced.

2. (Sullivan: *Princess Ida*). Sop. Princess Ida, daughter of King Gama, she was engaged when a year old to Prince Hilarion. To escape the consequences, at 21 she enters a women's college, the Castle Adamant. There Hilarion comes to find her. Created (1884) by Leonora Braham.

Idamante (Mozart: *Idomeneo*). Sop./mez. (*travesti* role) (or ten.). Son of Idomeneo. Loved by two women, Elettra and the captured Ilia. When the father he thinks is dead arrives on the shore, Idamante cannot understand why he pushes him away, not knowing that Idomeneo has promised Neptune, in return for saving his life at sea, to sacrifice the first person he sees on arriving in Crete. His father's attempts to save him arouse Neptune's wrath but this is appeased by Ilia's offer to be sacrificed in his place. Neptune agrees to waive his demand if Idomeneo abdicates the throne in favour of Idamante. Aria: *Non temer* ('Do not fear'). This was the only role in which Luciano Pavarotti appeared at Glyndebourne (1964). Created (1781) by the castrato Vincenzo dal (or del) Prato.

Idomeneo (Mozart). Lib. by Giambattista Varesco; 3 acts; f.p. Munich 1781, cond. Christian Cannabich.

Crete, after the Trojan War: *Idomeneo, King of Crete, has sent home the Trojan King Priam's daughter *Ilia, who has fallen in love with Idomeneo's son, *Idamante, whom the Greek princess *Elettra wants to marry. *Arbace announces that Idomeneo's ship has sunk, but Neptune has saved the King in return for Idomeneo's promise to sacrifice the first person he meets on shore. This turns out to be Idamante. When he realizes this is his son, he is distraught. He plans to send Idamante away with Elettra, to the distress of Ilia, who reveals her love for his son. Neptune, furious at Idomeneo's attempts to break his promise in order to save his son, sends a monster in a storm which terrifies the people. Ilia confesses her love for Idamante but he, though he loves her, takes his leave to go and fight the monster. Idamante returns, having learned the reason for his father's rejection of him and offers to be sacrificed to placate Neptune. Ilia offers to take his place. This impresses Neptune, who agrees to release Idomeneo from his promise if he will vacate the throne in favour of Ilia and Idamante. Only Elettra objects.

Idomeneo (Mozart: *Idomeneo*). Ten. King of Crete, father of Idamante. As he returns to Crete after the Trojan War, his ship is saved in a storm by Neptune, who in return asks that the King sacrifice the first person he meets on shore. This turns out to be his own son, Idamante, and he is horrified and tries to send him away to save him. Neptune is angry at this breaking of his promise and sends a monster and storm to terrorize the people. Idamante kills the monster and Neptune accepts Idomeneo's abdication in place of the sacrifice. Aria: *Fuor del mar* ('Saved from the sea'). Interpreters of this role include Franz Klarwein, Richard Lewis, George Shirley, Nicolai Gedda, Wiesław Ochmann, and Anthony Rolfe Johnson, Philip Langridge, and Paul Nilon. Created (1781) by the 66-year-old Anton Raaff.

Ighino (Pfitzner: *Palestrina*). Sop. *Travesti* role. 15-year-old son of the composer Palestrina. Created (1917) by Maria Ivogün.

Igor, Prince of Seversk (Borodin: *Prince Igor*). Bar. Husband of Yaroslavna, father of Vladimir. With his son, he leads his army to fight the Polovtsi, a Tartar tribe, and is captured by their leader, Khan Kontchak. For his entertainment, the *Polovtsian Dances* are performed by Kontchak's slaves. He escapes to save his city and rejoin his wife. Created (1890) by Ivan Alexandrovich Mel'nikov.

Ilia (Mozart: *Idomeneo*). Sop. Daughter of the Trojan King Priam, sent to Crete by Idomeneo. She falls in love with his son, Idamante, and offers herself in his place as a sacrifice demanded by Neptune. Moved by this action, Neptune relents and Idomeneo abdicates in favour of Idamante and Ilia. Aria: *Zeffiretti lusinghieri* ('Gentle breezes'). A delightful role in which sopranos of the calibre of Sylvia McNair, Rebecca Evans, and Melanie Diener have made an impression. Created (1781) by Dorothea Wendling.

Imogene (Bellini: *Il pirata*). Sop. Wife of Ernesto, whom she was forced to marry after her real lover, Gualtiero, was defeated in the battle for the throne of Sicily and exiled. When he is shipwrecked near Ernesto's castle, the two men fight a duel and Ernesto is killed. Gualtiero gives himself up. Created (1827) by Henriette Mérie-Lalande.

Inanna (Birtwistle: *The Second Mrs Kong*). Cont. Mrs Dollarama. Dead former beauty queen. Tries, but fails, to seduce Kong. Created (1994) by Phyllis Cannan.

incoronazione di Poppea, L' (Monteverdi). Lib. by Giovanni Francesco Busenello; prol. and 3 acts; f.p. Venice 1643.

Rome, AD 65: In the prol., *Amor claims superiority over *Fortune and *Virtue as the opera which follows will prove. *Ottone realizes that *Poppea is being unfaithful to him with the Emperor *Nerone (Nero). Poppea's nurse, *Arnalta, warns her that her ambition to be Empress will bring nothing but trouble, but she is sure Cupid is on her side. Nerone's wife, *Ottavia, feels humiliated by his actions. *Seneca, his former tutor, tries to reason with Nerone who becomes very angry. He is calmed down by Poppea, who advises Seneca's death, which the old philosopher welcomes as an act of stoicism. Ottone turns his attentions to *Drusilla, Ottavia's lady-in-waiting, but Ottavia urges him to kill Poppea—it is his duty to do so—and Drusilla cooperates by giving him clothes. Disguised as Drusilla, he attempts to kill Poppea but is prevented by Amor. Drusilla finds herself arrested for the attempt on Poppea's life and sentenced to death by Nerone. Ottone confesses and Nerone banishes them both, leaving the way clear for him to divorce Ottavia and marry Poppea. Ottavia bids farewell to Nerone and to Rome. Nerone proclaims Poppea as Empress—Amor has triumphed.

Incredibile (Giordano: *Andrea Chénier*). Ten. A spy of the Revolution who persuades Gérard to write out the indictment against Chénier. Created (1896) by Enrico Giordano.

Inès (Donizetti: *La Favorite*). Sop. Confidante of Léonor, mistress of the King. Aria (with chorus): *Rayons dorés* ('Bright sunbeams'). Created (1840) by Mlle Elian (or Eliam).

Inez 1. (Sullivan: *The Gondoliers*). Spoken. Foster-mother of the infant prince of Barataria, whom she swapped with her son Luiz to prevent the prince being captured by pirates. Created (1889) by Annie Bernard.

2. (Verdi: *Il trovatore*). Sop. Confidante of Leonora, to whom she confides her love for the troubador Manrico. Created (1853) by Francesca Quadri.

Infanta (Zemlinsky: *Der Zwerg*). Sop. Donna Clara, the Princess. For her birthday she is given, as a playmate, the Dwarf. He is unaware of his own abnormal appearance and falls in love with her. When he sees his own reflection he is terrified. The Infanta cruelly assures him she will continue to play with him, as one would with an animal—she does not regard him as a human. Created (1922) by Erna Schröder.

Inkslinger, Johnny (Britten: *Paul Bunyan*). Ten. An intellectual book-keeper and poet. He is responsible for improving the standard of food in the lumber-camp, but he is restless and realizes life holds more for him than the camp. He leaves and goes to work in Hollywood. Aria: *It was out in the sticks*. Created (1941) by William Hess.

Ino (Handel: *Semele*). Cont. Semele's sister. Created (1744) by Esther Young.

Intermezzo (Strauss). Lib. by composer; 2 acts; f.p. Dresden 1924, cond. Fritz Busch.

Grundlsee and Vienna, 1920s: The composer Robert *Storch, his wife Christine *Storch, and their son *Franz live in a villa beside the Grundlsee. He is leaving for Vienna to conduct and she is packing for him, assisted by their maid *Anna. Christine complains about all her responsibilities. While Robert is away she goes sledging and collides with Baron *Lummer. She helps him rent a room locally and promises Robert's help with his career. A letter arrives for her husband from one Mieze *Maier, couched in affectionate terms and requesting tickets for the opera. Christine at once assumes the worst, orders Anna to pack their bags, and sends a telegram to Robert announcing that she is starting divorce proceedings. Robert, frantic, meets his friend *Stroh, for whom the letter was really intended—Mieze Maier had confused their names. Stroh arrives at Grundlsee to explain the mix-up. Robert arrives home and there is a passionate reunion with his wife.

Iolanthe, or The Peer and the Peri (Sullivan). Lib. by W. S. Gilbert; 2 acts; f.p. London 1882, cond. Arthur Sullivan.

Arcadia and London, imaginary times: *Iolanthe was banished from fairyland 25 years ago for marrying a mortal. The fairies persuade their *Queen to forgive her if she promises to have no contact with her husband. Her 24-year-old son, *Strephon, who is a fairy 'only down to the waist', loves *Phyllis, a ward of chancery, who is also loved by Earls *Tolloller and *Mountararat. The Queen sends Strephon into Parliament to cause chaos among the peers. The fairies start to fall in love with the peers. Their Queen calls them to order, emphasizing that she herself has resisted the charms of the sentry, Private *Willis. The elderly *Lord Chancellor admits he wants to marry Phyllis, his ward, having presumed his wife to be dead. Iolanthe confronts him, thus breaking her promise to the Queen, and he recognizes her as his long-lost wife. The Lord Chancellor persuades the Queen to change the law—any fairy who does *not* marry a mortal shall die! All are now free to pair off accordingly—and Sergeant Willis finds himself with the Queen of the Fairies.

Iolanthe (Sullivan: *Iolanthe*). Mez. Banished from fairyland for marrying a mortal, she has a half-fairy son, Strephon, in love with Phyllis, a ward in chancery. He does not know that his father is the Lord Chancellor, who himself wants to marry Phyllis. Iolanthe reveals herself to her mortal husband to plead for her son. Aria: *He loves! If in bygone years*. Created (1882) by Jessie Bond.

Ipanov, Count Loris (Giordano: *Fedora*). Ten. Thinking him to be the killer of her fiancé, Fedora swears she will make Loris fall in love with her in order to force a confession from him, but she falls in love with him herself.

He admits the deed, but swears it was an act of honour—he had discovered that his wife and Fedora's fiancé were lovers. Fedora has set in motion a chain of investigation which she is not able to halt. Loris's brother is arrested as an accomplice and drowns while in prison and their mother dies of grief. Loris accuses Fedora of being responsible for ruining his family. She takes poison, begging his forgiveness, which he gives her as she dies. Aria: *Amor ti vieta…* ('Love forbids you not to love'). Created (1898) by Enrico Caruso.

Iphigénie 1. (Gluck: *Iphigénie en Aulide*). Sop. Daughter of Agamemnon and Clitemnestre, betrothed to Achille. Her sacrifice is demanded by the goddess Diane (Diana) before the Greeks can proceed to Troy. She is prepared to agree to her father's wish to appease the troops, but is saved by Achille. Created (1774) by Sophie Arnould.

2. (Gluck: *Iphigénie en Tauride*). Sop. Now a priestess of the goddess Diana, Iphigénie is about to sacrifice Oreste (Orestes) as demanded by the king, when she recognizes him as her brother. Created (1779) by Rosalie Levasseur. Maria Callas sang this role at La Scala, Milan, in 1957.

Iphigénie en Aulide (Gluck). Lib. by M. F. L. Lebland du Roullet; 3 acts; f.p. Paris 1774, cond. Christoph Willibald von Gluck.

During the Trojan War, on the island of Aulis: The goddess Diane (*Diana) has decreed that the Greeks can only continue to Troy if they sacrifice *Iphigénie, daughter of *Clitemnestre and *Agamemnon. *Calchas, the High Priest, encourages them to do so. *Achille, who is to marry Iphigénie, tries to defend her, but she agrees to her father's wishes. As the sacrifice is prepared, Achille arrives with his troops to confront Agamemnon and to rescue her. Slaughter is avoided when Calchas announces that the gods are happy and prepared to provide the winds necessary to enable them all to leave for Troy.

Iphigénie en Tauride (Gluck). Lib. by Nicholas-François Guillard; 4 acts; f.p. Paris 1779, cond. Louis-Joseph Francoeur.

After the Trojan War, on the island of Tauris: *Iphigénie, who has become a priestess of the goddess Diane (*Diana), dreams of the deaths of her parents. Oreste (*Orestes) and his friend *Pylade come to Tauris (Scythia) where King *Thoas demands they be sacrificed. In disguise, Oreste tells his sister Iphigénie how her parents died, and that her brother (himself) is also dead. As the decreed sacrifice is about to take place, Iphigénie recognizes Oreste. Pylade kills the savage Thoas and Diana grants Oreste a pardon.

Iras (Barber: *Antony and Cleopatra*). Sop. Attendant on Queen Cleopatra of Egypt. Created (1966) by Belén Amparàn.

Irene (Handel: *Tamerlano*). Cont. Princess of Trebisond, betrothed to Tamerlano. Created (1724) by Anna Vincenza Dotti.

Iro (Irus) (Monteverdi: *Il ritorno d'Ulisse in Patria*). Ten. Jester and glutton. A buffo role, providing comic relief. Killed by Ulisse. Creator (1640) unknown.

Isabella (Rossini: *L'italiana in Algeri*). Cont. An Italian lady shipwrecked near Algiers with her old suitor, Taddeo, whose niece she pretends to be. Mustafà, the Bey, finds her beautiful, but she was on her way to look for her beloved Lindoro. Lindoro is being made to marry the wife the Bey no longer wants. Lindoro and Isabella meet, reaffirm their love and make their escape plans. While Mustafà dines, they depart on an Italian ship. Arias (with chorus): *Cruda sorte!* ('Cruel fate!'); *Pensa alla patria* ('Think of your country'). Created (1813) by Marietta Marcolini.

Isacco (Rossini: *La gazza ladra*). Ten. A wandering pedlar to whom Ninetta sells some silver cutlery to raise money for her father. She is observed by another servant, Pippo, who innocently remarks on this to her mistress. Created (1817) by Francesco Biscottini.

Ismaele (Verdi: *Nabucco*). Ten. Nephew of the King of Jerusalem, he is in love with Fenena (who secretly sympathizes with the Hebrews) daughter of the King of Babylon. Her older sister, Abigaille, is in love with Ismaele and resentful of his love for Fenena. Created (1842) by Corrado Miraglia.

Ismailov, Boris (Shostakovich: *Lady Macbeth of the Mtsensk District*). Bass. A merchant, whose son, Zinovy, is married to Katerina.

Boris wants her for himself and when he discovers she is having an affair with one of the servants, Katerina kills him by putting rat-poison in mushrooms, his favourite food. Created (1934) by Georgy Orlov.

Ismailov, Zinovy (Shostakovich: *Lady Macbeth of the Mtsensk District*). Ten. Son of Boris and husband of Katerina. While he is away, she falls in love with the servant. When he returns and whips her, she and her lover kill him and hide his body in the cellar. Created (1934) by Stepan Balashov.

Ismailova, Katerina (Shostakovich: *Lady Macbeth of the Mtsensk District*). Sop. Wife of Zinovy Ismailov, whose father, Boris, lusts after her. While her husband is working away from home, she falls in love with the new family servant, Sergei. Her father-in-law finds out they are having an affair and she poisons him. When her husband returns and whips her, she and Sergei kill him and put his body in the cellar. During the festivities prior to her marriage to Sergei, the body is discovered and they confess their crime. On the road to Siberia, Sergei is attracted by another convict. Jealous, Katerina pushes the girl off a bridge into the river and jumps in to her own death. Created (1934) by A. I. Sokolova.

Ismene (Mozart: *Mitridate, re di Ponto*). Sop. Daughter of the King of Parthia, chosen by Mitridate as a wife for his elder son, Farnace. Created (1770) by Anna Francesca Varese.

isola disabitata, L' (The Deserted Island) (Haydn). Lib. by Pietro Metastasio; 2 acts ('parts'); f.p. Eszterháza 1779.
    The sisters *Costanza and *Silvia were left on an island by Costanza's husband *Gernando. He and his friend *Enrico, having freed themselves from captivity by pirates after thirteen years, come searching for the sisters. Silvia and Enrico fall in love but Gernando, believing Costanza dead, prepares to die on the island himself. He and his wife find each other and all misunderstandings are happily resolved.

Isolde (Wagner: *Tristan und Isolde*). Sop. An Irish Princess. As the opera opens, she is on board ship, accompanied by her maid and companion Brangäne, travelling from Ireland to Cornwall. She is being escorted by Tristan to meet and marry his uncle, King Mark. Before the opening of the opera, Isolde had been engaged to Morold, who was killed in a fight with Tristan. Tristan was wounded and came to be nursed by Isolde, who was known to have magic healing powers. She did not recognize him as her betrothed's killer until she saw there was a sliver missing from his sword and realized it matched the splinter found in Morold's skull. Isolde wanted to kill Tristan, but when she looked into his eyes she fell in love with him and was unable to carry out her intention. Now she is on her way to marry the King. As the ship approaches the shores of Cornwall, Isolde becomes more agitated, not wanting to meet Mark. She sends Brangäne to fetch Tristan, but he demurs. Isolde decides that, as he is not interested in her, he shall die rather than take her to his aged uncle, and she will gladly die rather than go without the love of Tristan. Brangäne is sent to fetch the box of potions which Isolde's mother gave her, and from these Isolde takes the death-potion and orders Brangäne to mix a drink from it. Tristan comes to tell her to make ready to meet his uncle. Isolde persuades him that, as she spared his life, he must share with her a drink of reconciliation. Together they drink from the potion, but Brangäne has switched the drink and has mixed the love-potion instead. All inhibitions are released and Tristan and Isolde join in a passionate embrace. Tristan's servant and friend, Kurwenal, rushes in to tell them that King Mark is about to come on board. Realizing their predicament, Isolde falls unconscious. In the King's castle Isolde and Tristan plan to meet later that night; they have arranged a signal—the torch outside Isolde's apartment will be extinguished as a sign that it is safe for him to come. Brangäne is reluctant to put out the torch, warning Isolde that she fears a plot to expose them to the King, so Isolde quenches the flame herself, ignoring Brangäne's warning. Tristan enters and he and Isolde, reunited, make passionate love, again ignoring Brangäne warning of trouble ahead. They are brought to their senses by the sudden arrival of Kurwenal—Melot has betrayed his friend Tristan and Mark is on his way to catch the lovers together. Melot challenges Tristan to fight and Tristan deliberately throws himself on to Melot's sword. He is seriously wounded and carried off by Kurwenal. Isolde is sent for to come to Kareol, Tristan's estate in Brittany, where Kurwenal has taken her lover. Isolde was able to heal him once before, now she departs to join him again. She is met by Kurwenal who takes her to Tristan, but as she arrives he dies in her arms. Distraught, she first pleads with him to wake up, then berates him for deserting her, and finally collapses over his body. She recovers consciousness to find Brangäne bending over her, having arrived with Mark who, now aware of the truth about the love-potion, had come to give them his blessing. However, Isolde wants only to be united with Tristan, if not in life, then in death—feelings she pours out in her famous *Liebestod* (love-death). Arias: *Von seinem Lager blickt' er her* ('From his bed he looked up'); *O blinde Augen!* ('Oh, blind eyes!'); *Mild und leise* ('Softly and gently'—this is the *Liebestod*); duets (with Tristan): *Tristan!... Isolde!... Treuloser Holder!* ('Tristan!... Isolde!... Faithless darling!'); *O ew'ge Nacht...* ('O eternal night').

One could argue about the relative difficulties of the roles of Isolde and Brünnhilde, but there can be little doubt that they both represent pinnacles of the soprano canon. Although condensed into one opera, as opposed to the three in which Brünnhilde appears, the role of Isolde demands much from its exponents, in vocal and physical stamina certainly, but especially in emotional terms. Most of her actions are dictated by her feelings rather than by her thoughts—she reacts instinctively to situations and emotions, and Isoldes must be able to run the whole gamut of the acting repertory—anger, distress, passion, despair. At the same time, it is an enormous vocal test for any soprano. There have been famous Isoldes in each generation since its première. These include Emma Albani, Lilli Lehmann, Rosa Sucher, Marie Wittich (the first Salome), Nanny Larsén-Todsen, Florence Austral, Kirsten Flagstad, Frida Leider, Sylvia Fisher, Helen Traubel, Astrid Varnay, Birgit Nilsson, Catarina Ligendza, Johanna Meier, Anne Evans, Waltraud Meier, Christine Brewer, and Nina Stemme (many, of course, equally famous as Brünnhilde). Created (1865) by Malvina Schnorr von Carolsfeld (whose husband created Tristan). *See also* ARTICLE BY CHRISTINE BREWER, p. 141.

Isolier (Rossini: *Le Comte Ory*). Mez. *Travesti* role. Page to Count Ory. He is in love with the Countess Adèle, whom Ory is trying to win. He succeeds where his master fails. Created (1828) by Constance Jawureck.

Isotta (Strauss: *Die schweigsame Frau*). Sop. A member of the troupe run by Morosus's nephew Henry. She poses as a possible wife for Morosus, but her loud chattering and high-flown ideas soon convince him that she would be totally unsuitable. Created (1935) by Erna Sack.

italiana in Algeri, L' (Rossini). Lib. by Angelo Anella; 2 acts; f.p. Venice 1813.

Algiers, time unspecified: *Elvira, wife of *Mustafà, is no longer loved by her husband. The Italian *Lindoro, captured by Mustafà's men, is ordered to marry Elvira. *Zulma says she should accept this, as women do. Mustafà orders *Haly to find him an Italian woman. Among the prisoners of a nearby shipwreck is *Isabella and her old suitor *Taddeo. Isabella has come to seek Lindoro. Mustafà finds her beautiful. Lindoro and Isabella meet and plan their escape together. Lindoro encourages Mustafà to believe that Isabella loves him, but is waiting for him to join the order of *Pappataci*—he must eat, drink, and remain silent. As he dines, the Italians leave on a waiting ship. Mustafà begs Elvira's forgiveness.

Italian Singer 1. (Strauss: *Der Rosenkavalier*). Ten. Present during the Marschallin's levee, he sings to the assembled servants and traders, rudely interrupted by Baron Ochs. Aria: *Di rigori armato il seno* ('With my breast armed with severity'—these words were lifted in their entirety by Strauss from the concluding ballet of *Le Bourgeois Gentilhomme* (Molière, 1670) for which Lully wrote the music). This is a role in which many an aspiring young tenor has first made an impression (and in which Luciano Pavarotti made his Salzburg Festival opera début in 1978). Created (1911) by Fritz Soot (who also created Faninal's Major-Domo and went on to have a long career in roles from Florestan in *Fidelio* to Parsifal).

2. (Strauss: *Capriccio*). Sop. She and the Italian Tenor are artists invited by La Roche to entertain the Countess's house-guests. This scene usually provides an opportunity for very

ISOLDE *(Tristan und Isolde*—Wagner)

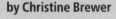

by Christine Brewer

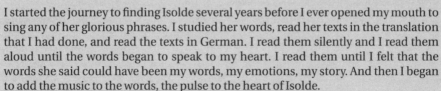

I started the journey to finding Isolde several years before I ever opened my mouth to sing any of her glorious phrases. I studied her words, read her texts in the translation that I had done, and read the texts in German. I read them silently and I read them aloud until the words began to speak to my heart. I read them until I felt that the words she said could have been my words, my emotions, my story. And then I began to add the music to the words, the pulse to the heart of Isolde.

At first glance, Act 1 could be all about Isolde's outrage at being transported to Cornwall by Tristan who killed Morold, the man who was to have been her husband. It could be about her disdain for Kurwenal and the way he speaks to her. (I love the formal language that Wagner gave Isolde to sing when she is talking to Kurwenal. The Irish Princess comes to the fore, and I enjoy singing those phrases with a little biting edge.) However, emotions like anger and disdain are the simpler expressions that lie at the extremes of the spectrum, and the subtle emotions which fuel that anger are more difficult to sustain. I tried to find the deeper emotions that revealed details of her character so that her complexities could be more easily understood. Singing all of Act 1 in a state of fury is not only devastating for the voice, but is boring for the listener. So I looked for indications of Isolde's tender side. One of the most beautiful moments in her narration and curse comes when she is describing how she held the sword over Tristan's head ready to kill him. He looked at her, not at the sword or at her hands, but into her eyes—when she sings *...er sah mir in die Augen...* ('...he looked into my eyes...'), time stands still. This simple phrase illustrates her love for Tristan and she tells how his anguish touched her heart and the sword fell from her hands. But she regains her composure and describes how she healed him so that he could return home and she would never have to see him again. As she continues the narration, she becomes more fired up, and the anger that is directed at Tristan is also anger and guilt directed at herself. How could she fall in love with the man who killed Morold and sent Morold's head to her? How torn with anguish she is! Her bitterness really starts to show as she speaks of the oath he made of thanks and fidelity to her. How could he forget this oath and now hold her captive on his ship as he takes her to marry King Marke? Out of her hurt feelings come the bitterness and the sarcasm and ultimately the fury at the end of this scene. She mocks him several times and I found those moments were most successful when I sang them quietly, almost through my clenched teeth, so that the curse wasn't all shouted.

The sharpness and wit of Isolde appealed to me when I first started singing the role, and I continue to find moments when just one word or phrase can be inflected in a way to show her sarcasm. After the build up to Isolde's meeting with Tristan at the end of Act 1, there are many such opportunities. She always has the upper hand in the final scene of this act. One of the juicier moments is when she mocks Tristan and supposes what he might say to King Marke when he introduces Isolde to him. And this comes after the famous phrase when she tells him that she couldn't possibly kill him now—how would that look when the King sees that she has killed his 'best' knight? It seems that Isolde is keen to make Tristan squirm as much as possible as she convinces him to join her in drinking what she believes is the death potion.

A glorious moment that everyone waits for is what happens after they have tasted this draught—the love potion substituted by her maid Brangäne. All inhibitions are gone—the love potion really isn't necessary to make them fall in love, but to remove those inhibitions. And now the fun begins!

The music at the beginning of Act 2 is full of anticipation and desire. I think of Isolde as a young girl in that first scene with Brangäne. She isn't listening to the hunting horns. She is listening to her heart. She is girlish and some of those glimpses we had of her love for Tristan in Act 1 come out now with no reservations. The tension starts building, and by the time Tristan arrives, the hair on the back of her neck is standing on end.

I enjoy the moments in the love duet when the music is intimate and soft. The more places that the music can be this way, the more exciting the outbursts are. This is one of the things I love about singing this role, the extremes and all the subtleties in between.

At the end of Act 2, I have to really concentrate and not let my emotions get the better of me, because I find King Marke's music and text so moving that I can easily begin to cry (and have done so in several performances). This makes for some difficulties in singing the last few phrases in the act, so I try to hold it together as he pours his heart out.

In the 45 minutes at the beginning of Act 3 before Isolde's entrance, I try to keep in character backstage. After singing two very long acts and not leaving the stage, it is nice to have a break; however, I try not to let down too much. The *angst* that has started building since the first notes of the overture is what sustains me until Isolde's next appearance. There is a real hurt and anger in her voice when she discovers that Tristan has not waited to die with her, but has preceded her in death. Her anguish from waiting for so long to be with him now comes out.

By the time I sing the *Liebestod*, I think Isolde has come to grips with Tristan's death and knows that she will soon be joining him. She is actually 'seeing' his gentle smile and his beautiful eyes open—those same eyes that she spoke of in Act 1. Her senses are heightened as she sees, smells, and feels the starlit night and the pardoning breezes. She smells heaven and the redemption that they will both experience in death. She is able to plunge into the sweet fragrance of death and the sublime music carries her away. It carries me away, too!

funny interplay between the two singers. Duet: *Addio, mia vita, addio* ('Farewell, my life, farewell'). Created (1942) by Franz Klarwein, who later in the run sang Flamand, and by Irma Beilke.

Italian Tenor (Strauss: *Capriccio*). *See* ITALIAN SINGER (2).

Ivan Susanin (Glinka). *See* LIFE FOR THE TSAR, A.

Jack (Tippett: *The Midsummer Marriage*). Ten. Boyfriend of Bella, a mechanic. He is asked to help open the gates through which Jenifer's father wants to go to find his daughter. Created (1955) by John Lanigan.

Jack Point (Sullivan: *The Yeomen of the Guard*). *See* POINT, JACK.

Jackrabbit, Billy (Puccini: *La fanciulla del West*). Bass. A Red Indian, lover of Wowkle, Minnie's maid. Created (1910) by Georges Bourgeois.

Jack the Ripper (Berg: *Lulu*). Bar. Lulu's last client (and a manifestation of Dr Schön), who murders first her, then Countess Geschwitz. Created (1937) by Asger Stig. *See* SCHÖN, DR.

Jaffett and Mrs Jaffett (Britten: *Noye's Fludde*). Treble and girl sop. Son and daughter-in-law of Noye. They help to build the Ark. Created (1958) by Michael Crawford and Marilyn Baker.

Jake (Gershwin: *Porgy and Bess*). Bar. A fisherman, married to Clara. He is lost at sea during a storm. Created (1935) by Edward (Eddie) Matthews.

Jane, Aunt (Vaughan Williams: *Hugh the Drover*). Cont. Sister of the Constable and aunt of Mary, Arias: *Life must be full of care; Stay with us, Mary*—this second aria was added during revisions in 1956. Created (1924) by Mona Benson.

Jane, Lady (Sullivan: *Patience*). Mez. A lady of advancing years, with hopes of ensnaring Bunthorne as a husband. Aria: *Silvered is the raven hair*. Created (1881) by Alice Barnett.

Jano (Janáček: *Jenůfa*). Sop. *Travesti* role. A young cowhand whom Jenůfa has been teaching to read. Created (1904) by Marie Čenská.

Jaquino (Beethoven: *Fidelio*). Ten. A young assistant (turnkey) to the gaoler Rocco and in love with Rocco's daughter, Marzelline. Quartet (with Marzelline, Rocco, and Leonore): *Mir ist so wunderbar* ('What a wondrous feeling'). Created (1805) by Herr Caché.

Jarno (Thomas: *Mignon*). Bass. Leader of a band of gypsies who hold Mignon captive. Creator (1866) not traced.

Jason (Cherubini: *Médée*). Ten. Leader of the Argonauts. He has brought the Golden Fleece from Colchis, aided by Médée, who bore him two sons. He abandoned her and is about to marry Dircé, daughter of the King of Corinth. Determined to avenge herself, Médée first poisons Dircé and then kills her own children. Created (1797) by Pierre Gaveaux.

Javotte (Massenet: *Manon*). Sop./mez. One of three ladies 'of easy virtue' who are found drinking with Morfontaine and de Brétigny. Created (1884) by Mlle Chevalier.

Jean (Massenet: *Hérodiade*) Ten. John the Baptist, whom Salomé loves. He rejects her. He makes insulting remarks about her mother, Hérodiade, who encourages her husband to order Jean's—and Salomé's—execution. Created (1881) by Edmond Verguet. *See also* JOCHANAAN.

Její pastorkyňa (Her Stepdaughter) (Janáček). *See* JENŮFA.

Jemmy (Rossini: *Guillaume Tell*). *See* TELL, JEMMY.

Jenifer (Tippett: *The Midsummer Marriage*). Sop. Daughter of King Fisher. Engaged to Mark, whom she is about to marry. She is something of a feminist before her time, determined not to be submerged by Mark's natural masculinity. 'I want truth, not love', she declares as she postpones her wedding and sets out 'to find herself'. Her father assumes she has eloped with Mark and tries to follow her, but is unable to open the gates through which she has disappeared. She and Mark ultimately find what each is looking for and are reunited. Created (1955) by Joan Sutherland (four years before her famous Covent Garden Lucia precipitated her into the megastar class).

Jeník (Smetana: *The Bartered Bride*). Ten. Son of Micha by his first marriage, stepson of Hata. He is in love with Mařenka, who knows nothing of his past. He agrees to give her up on condition that she marries 'only Micha's son'—he, of course, is the only one who knows the truth. When all is revealed, his father gives them his blessing. Created (1866) by Jindřich Polák.

Jenůfa (Janáček). Lib. by comp.; 3 acts; f.p. Brno 1904, cond. Cyril Metoděj Hrazdira.

A Moravian village, late 19th cent.: Half-brothers Števa *Buryja and Laca *Klemeň, both love Jenůfa *Buryja, stepdaughter of the widowed Petrona Buryjovka, known as the *Kostelnička. Jenůfa is pregnant by Števa. The Kostelnička forbids a wedding—they must wait until Števa stops drinking. Jealous of her love for his brother, Laca slashes Jenůfa's cheek. Having learnt that Jenůfa is pregnant, the Kostelnička keeps her locked away in her cottage where she produces a son. Števa will not agree to marry her and the Kostelnička's hopes rest on Laca. He is so upset about the baby that the Kostelnička tells him it died. Giving Jenůfa a sleeping-draught, she drowns the baby in the icy river and tells Jenůfa the child died. Laca proposes marriage. Wedding preparations take place, but now the Kostelnička is full of guilt and remorse. The Mayor and Mayoress and their daughter *Karolka arrive—she is engaged to Števa. As Grandmother *Buryja blesses the couple, the young farmhand *Jano runs in and announces that a baby's body has been found under the melting ice. The Kostelnička confesses her crime. She is forgiven by Jenůfa and taken away for trial.

Jenůfa (Janáček: *Jenůfa*). *See* BURYJA, JENŮFA.

Jessel, Miss (Britten: *The Turn of the Screw*). Sop. A former governess to the children at Bly. She became pregnant by the master's valet, Quint, and died, as did he. They both come back to haunt the children. Aria: *Here my*

tragedy began; duet (with Quint): *I seek a friend obedient to follow where I lead*. Created (1954) by Arda Mandikian.

Jester (Maxwell Davies: *Taverner*). Bar. Observes the argument between the King and Cardinal over the break with Rome, and points out their selfish reasons for their opinions. He is revealed as Death and corrupts Taverner. Created (1972) by Benjamin Luxon.

Ježibaba (Dvořák: *Rusalka*). Mez. The Witch who grants mortality to Rusalka, but on condition that she remains dumb, otherwise she will die. Created (1901) by Růžena Bradáčová.

Jocasta, Queen (Stravinsky: *Oedipus Rex*). Mez. Sister of Creon, and widow of Laius, the late King of Thebes, and now wife of Oedipus. She has consulted the Oracle who has told her that Laius was killed by his son, but she knows Laius was killed by thieves at a crossroads. Oedipus confesses that, in the past, he killed an old man at a crossroads. It gradually becomes apparent that he killed his own father, and then married his mother. Overcome, Jocasta kills herself. Created (1927) by Hélène Sadoven.

Jochanaan (Strauss: *Salome*). Bar. John the Baptist. He has been imprisoned by Herod in a cistern below the palace terrace, for his insulting comments about Herodias, Herod's second wife. His voice can be heard coming from the cistern, praising God and prophesying the coming of the Messiah. Salome is fascinated by his voice, and wheedles Narraboth into opening the cistern so that the Prophet can emerge and she can see him and touch him. Jochanaan appears, denouncing her mother and stepfather. When she tells him she is Herodias's daughter, he forbids her to come anywhere near him, calling her 'Daughter of Sodom'. All Salome's attempts to attract him fail, and he swears she will never kiss his mouth, cursing her as the daughter of an adulteress and advising her to seek the Lord. He returns to his underground cistern and his voice is heard, causing great arguments among the Jews about the likelihood of the prophet having seen God. No more is seen of Jochanaan until his severed head is brought up to satisfy Salome's gruesome desires. Aria: *Wo ist er?...wo ist sie...?* ('Where is he...where is she...?'). Created (1905) by Carl Perron (who in 1911 became the first Baron Ochs in *Der Rosenkavalier*). *See also* JEAN.

Joe (Kern: *Show Boat*). Bass-bar. Black servant on the *Cotton Blossom*, husband of Queenie. Aria: *Ol' Man River*; duet (with Queenie): *Ah still suits me*. The role was made famous by Paul Robeson, who sang in the London première in 1928. Created (1927) by Jules Bledsoe.

John (Vaughan Williams: *Hugh the Drover*). Bass-bar. The wealthy butcher who is to marry Mary as her father wishes. He fights the drover Hugh for her hand and when he loses accuses Hugh of being a French spy. He is press-ganged into the army. Created (1924) by Gavin Gordon-Brown.

Johnson, Dick (Puccini: *La fanciulla del West*). Ten. A bandit known as Ramerrez. He is being hunted by the sheriff, Jack Rance. An old girlfriend of Johnson has provided Rance with a photograph to prove his identity. Johnson arrives at the inn owned by Minnie and is welcomed by her and when the sheriff tries to question Johnson, Minnie vouches for his identity. She invites him to join her in her cabin for a meal later that evening. They eat and talk about their life and soon declare their love for each other. As it is snowing, Minnie suggests he stays the night. When the sheriff calls to warn her of the dangerous bandit who is in the area, she hides Johnson behind the curtains. Having seen the picture of 'Ramerrez', she orders Johnson to leave. He admits that initially he came to rob her, but now he has fallen in love with her and wants to lead an honest life. He rushes out of her cabin and is immediately shot by the sheriff's men. Minnie pulls him back into her room and helps him up a ladder into her loft. Rance again calls, but finding nothing is about to leave when blood drips from the loft above, revealing Johnson's hiding-place. Minnie coaxes Rance to a game of poker, the winner will decide Johnson's fate. By cheating, she wins and Rance leaves, but the sheriff tells his men where to find the bandit and they capture him. They are about to hang him when again Minnie intervenes and, out of their love and respect for her, they allow Johnson his freedom. He and Minnie leave together to find a new life. Arias: *Oh, non temete...* ('Oh, never fear...'); *Sono un dannato! Io so, Io so!*

('I'm a scoundrel! I know, I know!'); *Ch'ella mi creda libero e lontano* ('Let her think I'm free and far away'). Another of Puccini's great tenor roles, sung by all the greatest Italianate tenors since its creation. Created (1910) by Enrico Caruso.

John the Baptist 1. (Strauss: *Salome*). *See* JOCHANAAN.

  2. (Massenet: *Hérodiade*). *See* JEAN.

Jonny (Krenek: *Jonny spielt auf*). Bar. A Negro jazzband fiddler. He steals Daniello's violin, and leads the other musicians and their friends to a new life in America. Created (1927) by Max Spilcker.

***Jonny spielt auf** (**Jonny strikes up**)* (Krenek). Lib. by comp.; 2 'parts' (11 scenes); f.p. Leipzig 1929, cond. Gustav Brecher.

  Paris and the Alps, mid-1920s: On the top of a glacier, the composer *Max meets the prima donna *Anita. At her house in Europe they start an affair as a result of which Max composes a new opera. In Paris for its première, Anita starts an affair with a violinist, *Daniello. Daniello's violin is stolen by *Jonny, a jazz player at their hotel. The chambermaid, *Yvonne, is blamed for the theft, is sacked and goes to Germany as Anita's maid. Max awaits Anita's return, but learning she has been unfaithful he goes back to the Alps. On a radio, he hears Anita singing an aria from his opera and decides to start again with her. Daniello is crushed by a locomotive on which the others all leave for the USA, led to a new life by Jonny on the violin.

Jorg (Verdi: *Stiffelio*). Bass. An elderly minister who advises Stiffelio which passage to read from the Bible to publicly demonstrate his forgiveness of his wife's adultery. Created (1850) by Francesco Reduzzi. *See also* BRIANO.

José, Don (Bizet: *Carmen*). Ten. A corporal in the dragoons. He sees Carmen when she emerges from the cigarette factory in which she works. She flirts with him and throws him a flower. Micaëla comes to see José, bringing him a letter from his mother suggesting her as a wife for him. As he starts to show interest, Carmen reappears. She has been in a fight and hurt another girl and José is ordered to escort her to gaol. He is unable to resist her when she suggests they could be lovers, and allows her to escape. He is imprisoned for his carelessness, and when released seeks out Carmen in Lillas Pastia's tavern. As they dance, he tells her he must return to barracks and Carmen is angry, wanting him to stay with her. José is jealous when his superior officer shows an interest in Carmen and strikes him. Now he has no option but to desert and go with Carmen and her band of smugglers into the mountains. There Micaëla again finds him, and tells him his old mother is dying. He leaves with her, but not before he has a fight with the toreador Escamillo, who is also in love with Carmen. José later follows them to the bullring. When Carmen tells him she no longer loves him, he kills her. Aria: *La fleur que tu m'avais jetée* ('The flower which you threw me'—known as the *Flower Song*). As with the title-role, French singers have not been to the fore in this role, which is usually sung by an Italianate tenor, such as Beniamino Gigli, Fernando De Lucia, Giuseppe di Stefano, Mario del Monaco, Nicolai Gedda, Franco Corelli, Jon Vickers, James McCracken, Dennis O'Neill, Luis Lima, Plácido Domingo, and José Carreras. Created (1875) by Paul Lhérie.

Josephine (Sullivan: *HMS Pinafore*). *See* Corcoran, Josephine.

Jourdain, Mons. (Strauss: *Ariadne auf Naxos*). Spoken. *The bourgeois gentilhomme*. He appears only in the 1st (1912) vers. In the 2nd vers., he has become one of the richest men in Vienna (and never appears on the stage), at whose house the opera company and the *commedia dell'arte* troupe will entertain his guests. Created (1912) by Victor Arnold.

Jowler, Col. Lord Francis (Maw: *The Rising of the Moon*). Bar. Officer in the 31st Royal Lancers, stationed in Ireland. Created (1970) by Richard Van Allan.

Jowler, Lady Eugenie (Maw: *The Rising of the Moon*). Sop. Wife of Col. Lord Jowler. Selected as one of the conquests for a young cornet wanting a commission in the regiment. Created (1970) by Rae Woodland.

Judith (Bartók: *Duke Bluebeard's Castle*). Mez. Bluebeard's latest wife, she has married against her family's advice. She slowly realizes he has murdered his previous wives and that she will have a similar fate. Created (1918) by Olga Haselbeck.

Judy (Birtwistle: *Punch and Judy*). Mez. Wife of Punch. Killed by him and comes back during his nightmare as the Fortune-Teller, to seek revenge. Created (1968) by Maureen Morelle.

Juive, La (Halévy). Lib. by Eugène Scribe; 5 acts; f.p. Paris 1835, cond. François-Antoine Habeneck.

Constance, Switzerland, 1414: *Rachel, daughter of the Jewish goldsmith *Eléazar, is in love with *Samuel', who works for her father, not knowing he is Prince *Léopold, a young general who has led his army to victory over the Hussites. Léopold swears one of his soldiers, *Albert, to secrecy. The provost *Ruggiero threatens Eléazar with death for working on a Christian holiday, but he is defended by Cardinal de *Brogni, an old friend from Rome. 'Samuel' confesses to being a Christian and adds that he is not free to marry her. He is the husband of Princess *Eudoxie. Rachel denounces him for having seduced a Jewess, and de Brogni condemns them to death for breaking the Lord's laws. To save her husband, Eudoxie persuades Rachel to retract her charge. The Cardinal tells Rachel she too can be saved, by denying her religion, but this she refuses to do. As she is thrown into a boiling cauldron, Eléazar reveals that she is not a Jewess at all, but de Brogni's daughter whom he saved when Rome was sacked many years earlier.

Julia 1. (Spontini: *La vestale*). *See* Giulia.
    2. (Flotow: *Martha*). *See* Nancy (1).

Julian, Kate (Britten: *Owen Wingrave*). Mez. Daughter of Mrs Julian. She is expected to marry Owen Wingrave. She is alarmed when he is disinherited by his grandfather for refusing to become a soldier. She accuses him of cowardice and challenges him to sleep in a haunted room to prove his bravery. When she goes to see him during the night, she finds him dead. Created (1971 TV/1973) by Janet Baker.

Julian, Mrs (Britten: *Owen Wingrave*). Sop. A widow and dependant of the Wingraves, mother of Kate. Many years previously, her brother had been Miss Wingrave's lover. They live at Paramore. Created (1971, TV) by Jennifer Vyvyan; (1973) by Janice Chapman.

Julie (Kern: *Show Boat*). *See* La Verne, Julie.

Julien (Charpentier: *Louise*). Ten. A young penniless poet, who loves Louise. She leaves home to live with him in Montmartre. Created (1900) by Adolphe Maréchal.

Juliet 1. (Gounod: *Roméo et Juliette*). *See* CAPULET, JULIET (1).
2. (Bellini: *I Capuleti e i Montecchi*). *See* CAPULET, JULIET (2).

Julietta (Martinů). Lib. by comp.; 3 acts; f.p. Prague 1938, cond. Václav Talich.
*Michel, a Parisian bookseller, is haunted for years by the voice of a girl whom he heard singing in a town on the coast. He revisits the town to look for her. The town looks the same but the inhabitants have all lost their memory and live only for the present. They are so impressed that he can remember things from his childhood, that they immediately appoint him Commander—but forget they have done so. He does eventually find *Julietta, the girl he seeks. His memories and her fantasies form the basis of the surreal action of this opera.

Julietta (Martinů: *Julietta*). Sop. Her voice has haunted the Parisian bookseller Michel for years. He returns to her seaside town to look for her. Julietta meets Michel in a forest and greets him as if she has always known him. After a scene of passionate love, they argue, she leaves, and he fires a gun at her. Has he killed her? Created (1938) by Ada Horáková.

Juliette (Gounod: *Roméo et Juliette*). *See* CAPULET, JULIET (1).

Julyan, Col. (Josephs: *Rebecca*). Bass-bar. Chief Constable of the county in which Manderley, the de Winter family home, stands. Created (1983) by John Gilbert.

Junius (Britten: *The Rape of Lucretia*). Bar. A Roman general. Learns that his wife has been unfaithful in his absence and is taunted by Tarquinius as a cuckold. Created (1946) by Edmund Donlevy.

Juno 1. (Handel: *Semele*). Cont. Wife of Jupiter, King of the gods. Created (1744) by Esther Young.
2. (Cavalli: *La Calisto*). Sop. Jealous of her husband's desire for Callisto, turns her into a bear. Creator (1651) not known.

Jupiter 1. (Giove) (Monteverdi: *Il ritorno d'Ulisse in patria*). Ten. Approves of Neptune's action when he turns to stone the Phaeacians who have returned Ulisse to Ithaca. Creator (1640) unknown.
2. (Offenbach: *Orpheus in the Underworld*). Bar. King of the gods himself in love with Eurydice. To ensure that she remains near him, he arranges a thunderbolt to make a noise and force Orpheus to look at Eurydice as he leads her from the underworld. Created (1858) by Mons. Désiré.
3. (Handel: *Semele*). Bass. King of the gods, husband of Juno. Created (1744) by John Beard.
4. (Rameau: *Castor et Pollux*). Bass. Father of Pollux, who finally grants him and his twin Castor eternal life. Created (1737) by Mons. Dun.
5. (Giove) (Cavalli: *Calisto*). Bass. Comes to earth to claim Callisto for himself. His jealous wife turns Callisto into a bear. Jupiter places her among the stars as the constellation Ursa Minor. Creator (1651) not known.
6. (Strauss: *Die Liebe der Danae*). Bar. Dressed entirely in gold, he comes to meet Danae, who presumes he is really Midas. She has fallen in love with 'Chrysopher' (Midas in disguise) and Jupiter soon realizes this. No matter what wealth he offers her, she prefers to remain with Midas, who has been stripped of his ability to turn everything to gold. Jupiter has to acknowledge defeat. Arias: *Treulose Danae!* ('Faithless Danae!'); *Auch dich schuf der Gott* ('You also were created by God'). Created (1944) by Hans Hotter; (1952) by Paul Schöffler.

K

Kabanicha (Janáček: *Katya Kabanová*). Cont. Full name is Marfa Ignatěvna Kabanová. She is the widow of a very rich merchant, the mother of Tichon and foster-mother of Varvara. Katya is her daughter-in-law, married to the weak Tichon. Kabanicha is a sour-natured, domineering woman, who resents her son's marriage and disapproves of Katya. On the way home from church, she accuses Tichon of showing her no respect since his marriage and tells him he should treat his wife more firmly. She urges him to travel to a nearby market and sneers at Katya's wish to go with him. Before leaving he must order his wife, in front of his mother, to respect and obey the Kabanicha, and not speak to other men while he is gone. When Katya embraces him, the Kabanicha decries her shamelessness, pointing out that this is her husband, not a lover. After his departure, she nags at Katya for not showing proper distress at her husband's absence. She is visited by a rather drunk Dikoj, who makes overtures to her but is repulsed. While she is occupied with him, Varvara and Katya slip out of the house to meet their lovers. Tichon returns and Katya, overcome with guilt, confesses her unfaithfulness to her husband and her mother-in-law before rushing out into the storm. Tichon goes to search for her, but as a body is seen in the river, the Kabanicha restrains him, saying his wife is not worth his efforts. The body is carried out and placed in front of the Kabanicha, who mockingly bows and thanks the people for their concern and kindness.

The Kabanicha has, superficially, a similar personality to the Kostelnička in *Jenůfa*, but with a difference: the Kostelnička genuinely loves Jenůfa and her actions are all governed by that love, the Kabanicha is a bitter, unloving woman, who feels her position threatened by her daughter-in-law and would thus do anything to humiliate the younger girl. Recent exponents of the role include Ludmila Komancová, Rita Gorr, Leonie Rysanek, Pauline Tinsley, Felicity Palmer, Eva Randová, Sally Burgess, and Josephine Barstow (previously an excellent Jenůfa). Created (1921) by Marie Hladíková.

Kabanová, Katya (Janáček: *Katya Kabanová*). Sop. Wife of Tichon and daughter-in-law of the Kabanicha Her marriage is not the happy state she hoped it would be—her husband is weak and dominated by his mother, who sneers at her love for her husband and denounces Katya—and Tichon—for their lack of respect for her. Katya has noticed Boris, nephew of Dikoj (a friend of her mother-in-law) watching her as she walks home from church. Alone with Varvara, the Kabanicha's foster-daughter, she confesses her unhappiness, her lack of freedom—as a child she liked to be free as a bird—and her dreams, in which she feels as if she is being embraced and wants to give in to her feelings for another man. Tichon is sent away on business by his mother and before he goes is obliged to issue instructions to his wife about her behaviour in his absence, an episode Katya finds humiliating. Varvara encourages her to meet Boris, while she herself meets her own lover, and Katya and Boris give in to their feelings and admit their love for each other. Afterwards Katya is totally guilt-ridden, her mind almost unhinged. When Tichon returns, she confesses her unfaithfulness to him and his mother, naming Boris to them. She then flees from the family home and runs down to the Volga. She hears her husband calling her, but Boris appears and the two lovers console each other, at the same time acknowledging that they must say goodbye. Alone, she cannot face the thought of the future, under the eye of the tyrannical Kabanicha. There is no alternative—she jumps into the river. Aria: *Proč se tak chovají?* ('Why do they behave like this?').

Among famous singers of the role are Rose Pauly, Amy Shuard (the first Katya in England in 1951 and the first in New York in 1961), Libuše Domanínská (an acclaimed Jenůfa), Helena Tattermuchová, Ludmilla Dvořákova, Elisabeth Söderström, Elena Prokina, Eva Jenis, Nancy Gustafson, and Amanda Roocroft. Janáček freely admitted his love and admiration for *Madama Butterfly*, and in the scene where Boris describes to Váňa his love for Katya, the music is clearly influenced by Butterfly's first entrance. Katya and Boris, Varvara and Váňa, during their clandestine meeting, sing a 'double duet' reminiscent of the one between Mimì and Rodolfo, Musetta and Marcello in Act 3 of Puccini's *La bohème*. Created (1921) by Marie Veselá.

Kabanov, Tichon Ivanyč (Janáček: *Katya Kabanová*). Ten. Husband of Katya, son of the Kabanicha. A weak man, totally ruled by his mother. This has gradually undermined his relationship with his wife. Ordered away on business by his mother, he is told what instructions to give to Katya to govern her behaviour during his absence. He weakly demurs but, as always, does as the Kabanicha tells him, humiliating Katya in the process. When he returns, Katya confesses to him and the Kabanicha that she has, in his absence, been unfaithful with Boris. She runs out of the house and despite his mother's efforts to prevent him, Tichon goes with the servant Glaša to find her. He is too late—her body is floating in the river. Even at this point, his mother rules his actions, preventing him rushing to recover her body, telling him she is not worth his efforts. Created (1921) by Pavel Jeral.

Kaiser (Ullmann: *Kaiser von Atlantis, Der*). *See* ÜBERALL, EMPEROR.

***Kaiser von Atlantis, Der, oder Der Tod dankt ab** (The Emperor of Atlantis, or Death Abdicates)* (Ullmann). Lib. by Petr Kien; 4 scenes; dress rehearsal in Theresienstadt concentration camp 1944, cond. Karel Schachter; f.p. Amsterdam 1975, cond. Kerry Woodward.

Present place and time: The Kingdom of Atlantis has overrun all the neighbouring countries. Emperor *Überall rules over them all, even though the people there are dead. The

*Loudspeaker describes how life and death have lost their usual meaning. *Death dislikes this concept and decrees that, from now on, no one shall die. He resents the loss of the old ways of dying and the introduction of new mechanized methods. The *Drummer tries to make everyone obey the Emperor, but Überall realizes that without control of Death, he has no control at all—for instance, a *Girl falls in love with a *Soldier from the opposite camp and the Emperor can do nothing about it. He begs Death to return to the old ways. Death agrees—but only if the Emperor agrees to be the first to die. At first he resists, but then consents, so admitting that he too is human. [NOTE: This opera was written in the concentration camp of Theresienstadt (Terezin). After the dress rehearsal, its proposed 1944 première in the camp was banned when the obvious allusions to Hitler (the Emperor) were noted. A short while later, Ullmann and Kien were sent to Auschwitz, where they both died.]

Káncsiánu, Count Boni (Kálmán: *Die Csárdásfürstin*). Ten./bar. An admirer of the cabaret singer Sylva. He escorts her to a ball at the home of Prince Edwin, with whom she is in love. He is attracted by Edwin's cousin, whom the Prince's parents want him to marry. Created (1915) by Josef König.

Karolka (Janáček: *Jenůfa*). Mez. Daughter of the Mayor and Mayoress of the village. She becomes engaged to Števa after he has rejected Jenůfa. Created (1904) by Růžena Kasparová.

Kaspar, King (Menotti: *Amahl and the Night Visitors*). Ten. One of the Three Kings seeking the Christ Child. Created (1951, TV) by Andrew McKinley.

Kate (Britten: *Owen Wingrave*). *See* JULIAN, KATE.

Katerina Ismailova (Shostakovich). Name under which the rev. vers. of *Lady Macbeth of the Mtsensk District* was staged. In this form, f.p. Moscow 1963. *See* LADY MACBETH OF THE MTSENSK DISTRICT.

Katisha (Sullivan: *The Mikado*). Cont. An elderly lady, keen to marry young Nanki-Poo, the Mikado's son. She is tricked into marrying the comic Ko-Ko. Aria: *Hearts do not break!* Created (1885) by Rosina Brandram.

Katya Kabanová (Janáček). Lib. by comp.; 3 acts; f.p. Brno 1921, cond. František Neumann.

Kalinov, Russia, mid-19th cent.: Katya *Kabanová is married to Tichon *Kabanov, son of Marfa (who is known as *Kabanicha). Boris *Grigorjevič (nephew of *Dikoj) tells his friend Váňa *Kudrjáš (in love with *Varvara, the Kabanovs' foster-daughter), that he is secretly in love with Katya. Katya admits to Varvara her secret passion. While Tichon is away on business, Varvara and Katya slip out and meet their lovers. Varvara and Váňa go for a walk, leaving Katya and Boris together to admit their love. During a storm two weeks later, Váňa and his friend *Kuligin take shelter. They are joined by Varvara and then Boris, to whom Varvara expresses her concern for Katya, who is full of guilt and dreading Tichon's return. When he arrives, she confesses to him and his mother that she has been unfaithful, then runs out. She fails to return and Tichon and the servant *Glaša go in search of her. But Katya has met Boris, whom Dikoj is sending to Siberia. She bids him farewell, then drowns herself in the Volga.

Katya Kabanová (Janáček: *Katya Kabanová*). *See* KABANOVÁ, KATYA.

Kecal (Smetana: *The Bartered Bride*). Bass. A marriage-broker, consulted by her parents about a prospective husband for Mařenka—they want her to marry Vašek, son of Micha and Hata. He talks her lover, Jeník, into giving her up, not realizing that he is also Micha's son. Created (1866) by František Hynek.

Keene, Ned (Britten: *Peter Grimes*). Bar. Apothecary and quack. Supplies Mrs Sedley with her pills. Finds a new Apprentice for Grimes. To cause a distraction and thus avoid an unpleasant scene in the Boar, he leads the crowd in the round *Old Joe has gone fishing*. Created (1945) by Edmund Donlevy.

Keikobad (Strauss: *Die Frau ohne Schatten*). Ruler of the Spirit World and father of the Empress. He does not appear in the opera, but it is Keikobad's edict which sets in motion the whole sequence of events. He is represented by his Spirit Messenger (*der Geisterbote*), who delivers, via the Empress's Nurse, a message from her father: if the Empress does not cast a shadow (i.e. become pregnant) in three days, her husband will be turned to stone.

Kelbar, Baron di (Verdi: *Un giorno di regno*). Bass. Owner of a castle in Brest, father of Giulietta. He acts as host to the man he believes to be the king of Poland, only to find that he is really Cavalier di Belfiore, who wishes to marry Kelbar's niece. Created (1840) by Raffaele Scalese. [NOTE: At the 1981 Wexford Festival this role was sung by Sesto Bruscantini. He also produced the opera, which was shown to be a true *buffo* piece, well worth performance.]

Kelbar, Giulietta di (Verdi: *Un giorno di regno*). Mez. Daughter of the Baron, she is being obliged to marry the old Treasurer, La Rocca. Her wedding is forbidden by the man posing as king of Poland and she is reunited with the man she really loves, La Rocca's nephew. Created (1840) by Luigia Abbadia.

Kennedy, Hannah (Anna) (Donizetti: *Maria Stuarda*). Mez. Lady-in-waiting to Mary Stuart. As her last wish before her execution, Mary asks that Hannah be allowed to accompany her on her walk to the scaffold. Created (1835) by Teresa Moja.

Ketch, Jack (Birtwistle: *Punch and Judy*). *See* CHOREGOS.

Khovanshchina (Musorgsky). Lib. by comp. and Vladimir V. Stasov; 5 acts; f.p. St Petersburg 1886, in a production by the Amateur Musical-Dramatic Club, cond. by Eduard Goldstein; f. professional p. St Petersburg 1911, cond. Albert Coates.

Russia, 1682–9 (the time of accession of Tsar Peter the Great): *Shaklovity, a boyar, warns the Russian rulers that Prince Ivan *Khovansky and his son Andrei *Khovansky are plotting against the state. Khovansky intends crushing the enemies of the throne. The monk *Dosifei, a reactionary Old Believer, warns of trouble ahead. Prince *Golitsyn, regent and former lover of the Tsar's daughter, supports the new Western ideas of Tsar Peter. *Marfa, former lover of Andrei, foretells Golitsyn's ruin. As he meets with Khovansky and Dosifei, Shaklovity interrupts and tells them the Khovanskys have been denounced as traitors and the Tsar's troops are advancing. While Khovansky is being entertained by serving girls, Shaklovity murders him. Golitsyn leaves for exile. The Old Believers, their cause lost, prepare for death, joined by Marfa, Dosifei, and Andrei. The Tsar's soldiers arrive in time to see them all consumed by flames.

Khovansky, Prince Andrei (Musorgsky: *Khovanshchina*). Ten. Son of Ivan Khovansky, leader of the Streltsys. Former lover of Marfa, an Old Believer. He joins her and others in suicide rather than be captured by the Tsar's troops. Creator (1886) unknown; (1911) by Lobinsky.

Khovansky, Prince Ivan (Musorgsky: *Khovanshchina*). Bass. Father of Andrei and leader of the Streltsy Musketeers, a reactionary. He intends crushing the enemies of the throne. He is murdered by Shaklovity. Creator (1886) unknown; (1911) by Sharonoff.

Kilian (Weber: *Der Freischütz*). Ten. A rich peasant who beats the forester Max in a shooting contest. Created (1821) by Herr Wiedemann.

King (Maxwell Davies: *Taverner*). Bass. Not named, but presumably Henry VIII. Wants to break with Rome to rid himself of an unwanted wife. Created (1972) by Noel Mangin.

King Fisher (Tippett: *The Midsummer Marriage*). *See* FISHER, KING.

King of Clubs (Prokofiev: *The Love for Three Oranges*). Bass. Father of the Prince who is unable to laugh and will die if his melancholia is not cured. Created (1921) by Édouard Cotreuil.

King of Egypt (Verdi: *Aida*). Bass. Father of Amneris. He offers his daughter in marriage to Radamès, leader of the triumphant Egyptian army which has invaded his country. Created (1871) by Tommaso Costa.

King of Scotland (Handel: *Ariodante*). Bass. Father of Ginevra, who is loved by Ariodante. Created (1735) by Gustavus Waltz (who once was thought to have been Handel's cook). Handel is supposed to have remarked that 'Gluck knew no more of counterpoint than my cook Waltz'. No proof has been found to support this story.

King Priam (Tippett). Lib. by comp.; 3 acts; f.p. Coventry 1962, cond. John Pritchard.
Troy, about 12th cent. BC: At the time of *Paris's birth, his mother *Hecuba dreams that he will cause the death of his father, *Priam, who orders the child to be killed. Instead he is given to a shepherd, but later reclaimed by Priam and taken to Troy. His elder brother, *Hector, marries *Andromache. The two brothers quarrel, Paris goes to Greece and falls in love with *Helen (wife of the Spartan Menelaus). He takes Helen to Troy, thus starting the Trojan War. In the war, the Greek hero *Achilles has quarrelled with King Agamemnon. Priam wants to attack at once, taking advantage of the split between the two Greeks. He orders both his sons to take part in this fight. Achilles and his friend *Patroclus discuss their chances of returning home after the war. Dressed in Achilles' armour, Patroclus rallies the Greek troops, but Hector kills him (thinking he has slain Achilles). To avenge the killing of Patroclus, Achilles kills Hector. Paris reports Hector's death to his father and Priam secretly begs Achilles to hand over his son's body. Feeling pity, Achilles does so. As Troy burns, Priam retreats into his own world. Paris kills Achilles. Priam is killed by Achilles' son *Neoptolemus.

King Roger (Król Roger) (Szymanowski). Lib. by Jaroslav Iwaszkiewicz and comp.; 3 acts; f.p. Warsaw 1926, cond. Emil Młynarski.
Sicily, 12th cent.: The Arabian sage *Edrisi describes to King *Roger a *Shepherd who preaches the philosophy of beauty and pleasure. The Church sees him as a threat and priests ask the King to put the Shepherd in prison. Roger's wife, *Roxana, asks Roger to hear first what the Shepherd has to say. He is invited to their castle. Roxana and the court are entranced by him and his teachings and follow him when he leaves. Roger searches for them and when he finds them he follows them. The Shepherd appears to Roger as Dionysus, and his followers all dance and sing, before leaving with Roxana. Roger stays behind, he alone having resisted temptation.

Kissinger, Henry (Adams: *Nixon in China*). Bass. American Secretary of State (1973–7) who accompanies Pres. Nixon on his visit to China. Created (1987) by Thomas Hammons.

Klemeň, Laca (Janáček: *Jenůfa*). Ten. Half-brother of Števa Buryja and grandson of Grandmother Buryja. He is in love with Jenůfa (his cousin by virtue of his mother's second marriage, but no blood relation). He is jealous of his brother, whom Jenůfa loves. To make her less attractive to Števa, he impulsively slashes her face with a knife, an act he immediately regrets. He is told by his aunt, the Kostelnička, that Jenůfa has given birth to Števa's baby, which has died. He offers to marry Jenůfa and she agrees, although she does not truly love him. When her baby's body is found and her stepmother confesses to its murder, Laca, with great tenderness and understanding, stands by Jenůfa, wanting to go ahead with the wedding. She realizes that, through all their suffering, she has now found true love with Laca. Created (1904) by Alois Staněk-Doubravský.

Klinghoffer, Leon (Adams: *The Death of Klinghoffer*). Bass. A wealthy American Jewish passenger, paralysed and confined to a wheelchair, is on the cruise-ship *Achille Lauro* when it is hijacked by Palestinian terrorists. He is shot and thrown overboard. Created (1991) by Sanford Sylvan.

Klinghoffer, Marilyn (Adams: *The Death of Klinghoffer*). Cont. Wife of the paralysed Leon Klinghoffer who is shot by terrorists on a cruise-ship. Created (1991) by Sheila Nadler.

Klingsor (Wagner: *Parsifal*). Bass. An evil magician, he has sworn to destroy the Knights of the Grail, who have rejected him. He wanted to join them, but knowing that his sinful and lustful way of life would exclude him, he castrated himself all to no avail. He lives in his castle on the opposite side of the mountain at Monsalvat where the Knights dwell and there he has devised a magic garden peopled by Flower Maidens whom he has trained by his magic powers to seduce the Knights of the Grail. The most important Knight, Amfortas, came to Klingsor's castle intending to destroy him, armed with the Holy Spear which was in Christ's side on the Cross. Amfortas fell for the charms of Kundry, who is totally under the influence of Klingsor, and while she seduced him, Klingsor stole the Spear and used it to inflict a terrible wound on Amfortas which will not heal. Klingsor sees Parsifal arriving and knows that this youth will be the one to heal Amfortas. He summons Kundry and orders her to help him in preventing Parsifal foiling his plans and in bringing him under Klingsor's power for ever. When Kundry is unsuccessful in her efforts to seduce Parsifal, Klingsor advances with the Holy Spear which he throws

at Parsifal. To Klingsor's horror the sword hovers in the air above Parsifal, who grasps it and makes the sign of the Cross at which Klingsor and his castle disappear. Arias: *Die Zeit ist da—Schon lockt mein Zauberschloss den Toren* ('The time has come—My magic castle lures the fool'); *Furchtbare Not!* ('Dire distress!'). In recent years, portrayers of this role have included Hermann Uhde, Gustav Neidlinger (who sang the part at Bayreuth for over ten years in the 1950s and 1960s), Donald McIntyre, and Franz Mazura. Created (1882) by Carl Hill.

Klytämnestra, Queen (Strauss: *Elektra*). Mez. or cont. She was the wife of Agamemnon, and mother of Elektra, Chrysothemis, and Orest. She helped her lover Aegisth murder Agamemnon in his bath and they now live together at the palace. They have banished Elektra to the grounds to live like an animal. The life Klytämnestra has led has left her somewhat raddled, eyelids too heavy to keep open, and she leans for support on her stick and her confidante, jewellery weighing her down. She dreams about the absent Orest coming to take revenge on her. Her nightmares keep her awake—something crawls over her, the marrow melts in her bones, she feels as if her body is rotting away. She asks Elektra what she can do to stop these dreams, and Elektra tells her they will stop when she makes a sacrifice, the sacrifice of a woman—Klytämnestra herself. The queen is terrified: she both hates and fears Elektra. News is given to her that Orest is dead and for the first time she relaxes and laughs—now she is safe. But it is false news, and Orest returns and murders her and Aegisth. Arias: *Ich will nichts hören!* ('I will not listen to you!'); *Ich habe keine guten Nächte* ('I have bad nights'). Of the three female roles in this opera, Klytämnestra provides the greatest opportunity for a singing-actress, but they must resist the ever-present temptation to 'go over the top'. Some mezzos have made it their own, especially Elisabeth Höngen, Jean Madeira, Martha Mödl, Regina Resnik, Maureen Forrester (who sang it in Pittsburgh in 1989 when she was almost 60), Christa Ludwig, Brigitte Fassbaender, and Marjana Lipovšek. Created (1909) by Ernestine Schumann-Heink (who apparently said she would never sing the role again—'it was frightful'. There is a story, maybe apocryphal, that at the dress rehearsal, Strauss called down into the orchestra pit 'Louder! I can still hear Frau Heink!'). *See also* CLITEMNESTRE.

Ko-Ko (Sullivan: *The Mikado*). Bar. Lord High Executioner. Guardian of Yum-Yum, to whom he is engaged. He is tricked into marrying the elderly Katisha, leaving his ward free to marry Nanki-Poo. Arias: *I've got a little list; On a tree by a river... titwillow*. Created (1885) by George Grossmith.

Kolenatý, Dr (Janáček: *The Makropulos Case*). Bass-bar. A barrister, who has been consulted by the present members of the Gregor and Prus families to try to solve the 100-year-old law case aiming to find the rightful heir to the Prus estate. The singer Emilia Marty tells Kolenatý that she can provide proof of Gregor's background and show that his claim is genuine. She tells the lawyer where Prus's will can be found. Created (1926) by Ferdinand Pour.

Kong (Birtwistle: *The Second Mrs Kong*). Ten. 'The idea of him'—the character from the 1933 film, *King Kong*. Falls in love with the girl from Vermeer's painting 'Girl with a Pearl Earring'. They meet, but as they are both 'ideas', and not real people, their love cannot be fulfilled. Created (1994) by Philip Langridge.

Konrad (Marschner: *Hans Heiling*). Ten. A hunter. He meets Anna, bride of Heiling, when she is lost in a forest. They fall in love. Heiling stabs him but he survives and he and Anna plan to be married. He is saved from a second attack by Heiling's mother. Created (1833) by Karl Adam Bader.

Kontchak, Khan (Borodin: *Prince Igor*). Bass. Leader of the Polovtsi, father of Kontchakovna. He captures Prince Igor and his son (who falls in love with the Khan's daughter). Orders his slaves to dance the *Polovtsian Dances* to entertain his prisoners. Has a sneaking admiration for Igor, whom he recognizes as a good leader of his people. Created (1890) by Mikhail Mikhaylovich Koryakin.

Kontchakovna (Borodin: *Prince Igor*). Mez. or cont. Daughter of the Polovtsian leader Khan Kontchak. She falls in love with Vladimir, the captured son of Prince Igor. Created (1890) by Mariya Slavina.

Kostelnička (Petrona Buryjovka) (Janáček: *Jenůfa*). Sop. Widow of Grandmother Buryja's younger son, Tomáš, and stepmother of his daughter, Jenůfa. She is the Sacristan of the village church. Disapproving of Jenůfa's love for Števa, who drinks too much, she bans their wedding until he proves he can remain sober. This apparently unjustified severity towards her stepdaughter is explained when the Kostelnička's Act 1 aria is restored to her. In it she talks of her own unhappy marriage to Jenůfa's father, who drank and squandered her money. She wants to save her step-daughter from a similar fate. Then she finds out that Jenůfa is pregnant and hides her away until after the birth, to avoid the shame which attaches to illegitimacy. Realizing that Števa does not want the responsibility of marriage and fatherhood, the Kostelnička pins her hopes on Laca. He would dearly like to marry Jenůfa, whom he has always loved, but he is reluctant to take on Števa's child. The Kostelnička, prepared to do anything for the sake of Jenůfa's happiness, drowns the baby and tells both Jenůfa and Laca that it died. Now the wedding can go ahead. But the baby's body is found and Jenůfa is accused of its murder, so the Kostelnička confesses. Jenůfa, realizing her stepmother acted out of love for her, forgives her, and she is taken by the Mayor to stand trial. Aria (now restored in most productions): *A tak bychom šli celým životem* ('And that's how we might spend our whole life'). Created (1904) by Leopolda Hanusova-Svobodová. Other exponents of the role include Naděžda Kniplová, Sylvia Fisher, Amy Shuard, Sena Jurinac, Astrid Varnay, Pauline Tinsley, Eva Randova, and Anja Silja. *See also* ARTICLE BY SIR CHARLES MACKERRAS, p. 154.

Kothner, Fritz (Wagner: *Die Meistersinger von Nürnberg*). Bass. A baker. A senior Master, he reads the rules to new members. He calls the roll of the masters who have been invited to attend the song contest and they answer to their names. One of the Masters is found to be absent because of illness and Kothner asks his apprentice to wish him good health. Kothner invites the others to say who will enter the competition to win the prize of Eva's hand in marriage—and adds that they must, of course, be bachelors. He becomes quite cross with Pogner who, as Eva's father, recommends the

KOSTELNIČKA (*Jenůfa*—Janáček)

by Sir Charles Mackerras

Those who have come to know and love Janáček's operas, and particularly *Jenůfa*, will have discovered that the Kostelnička is one of the most interesting and unusual characters in the operatic repertoire. But many facts about her life are not made clear, so that some of her actions might seem difficult to understand. The libretto for the opera was taken from a play by Gabriela Preissová and in 1930, after the opera had become famous, she wrote a novella telling the familiar story once again, but embellishing the events which occurred before and after the period covered by the opera.

The title of the original play and the opera was *Její Pastorkyn'a*, which means 'Her Foster-Daughter'. The opera in English- and German-speaking countries is now known as *Jenůfa*, thus transferring the focus away from the Kostelnička. Many people think her name is 'Kostelnička', but this is her professional title as pew-opener or female sacristan of the local church. Her name is Petrona Buryjovka (*née* Slomková). She was the second daughter of the local magistrate and had married Jenůfa's widowed father, the attractive but dissolute brother of the mill owner.

In the opera, she is portrayed as a grim and disapproving matriarch (Števa calls her a 'sorceress'). We would warm to her more easily if Janáček had retained the aria in which she describes her disastrous marriage [some productions do now restore this aria]: she sees the pattern of her own life about to be repeated by Jenůfa and Števa. What she doesn't know, of course, is that Jenůfa is pregnant and that in forbidding their marriage she is condemning her to bear an illegitimate child. As if to atone for her hasty action, she arranges for the baby to be born in secret.

When Števa admits that he is now engaged to another girl, the Kostelnička decides to pin her hopes of marriage for Jenůfa on his half-brother, Laca, who, although he has disfigured her face with a knife, has been in love with Jenůfa all the time. Laca is nevertheless horrified to hear from the Kostelnička of the birth of Jenůfa's baby and he is about to leave when the Kostelnička hurriedly invents the story that the child has died. There is now nothing left for her to do but make this into fact—to drown the baby and lie about its death to Jenůfa, the only person in the world whom she truly loves. So, this high-minded upholder of the moral values of her small community is trapped by her own impetuous action into being both a liar and a murderess.

In Janáček's opera we do not know what punishment she receives for her crime, though we can observe from the deterioration of her spirit that her conscience is punishment enough in itself. In Preissová's later novel, the Kostelnička returns home after only two years in prison to live out her days with Jenůfa and Laca.

Perhaps the most moving interpretation of the Kostelnička that I have experienced was that of Sena Jurinac, who sang the role towards the end of her career. As a young woman she had sung many performances as Jenůfa, and thus truly seemed to understand the conflicts of the two heroines of this opera.

young knight Walther von Stolzing, and Kothner insists that Walther must undergo the tests like everyone else—he cannot be given preferential treatment to join their guild just because he is a knight. The apprentices hold the tablet on which the rules are written and Kothner reads them to Walther. Walther's singing causes great amusement and mutterings and Kothner loses control of the proceedings. Aria: *Was euch zum Leide Richt, und Schnur, vernehmt nun aus der Tabulatur* ('To make your footsteps safe and sure, these rules come from the Tabulatur'). Created (1868) by Karl Fischer.

Krakenthorp, Duchesse de (Donizetti: *La Fille du régiment*). Sop. A friend of the Marquise de Birkenfeld. The Marquise wants her 'niece' Marie to marry the Duchesse's son. Created (1840) by Mlle Blanchard.

Kristina (Janáček: *The Makropulos Case*). Mez. Daughter of Vítek, clerk to the barrister Dr Kolenatý. She is a singing student and is besotted by the famous opera singer Emilia Marty, whom she watches at rehearsal. Kristina is in love with Janek Prus, son of one of the contenders in the long lawsuit, but tells him they must give up their relationship so that she can concentrate on the higher things of life— her music. Created (1926) by Jožka Mattesová.

Król Roger (Szymanowski). *See* KING ROGER.

Krušina (Smetana: *The Bartered Bride*). Bar. A farmer, husband of Ludmila and father of Mařenka. Owing money to his landlord Micha, he wants his daughter to marry Vašek, Micha's son, to clear the debt. Created (1866) by Josef Paleček.

Kudrjáš, Váňa (Janáček: *Katya Kabanová*). Ten. An engineer and teacher in Dikoj's employ. He is in love with Varvara, the Kabanov foster-daughter. Boris confesses to him his love for Katya. Kudrjáš has a big argument with Dikoj about the nature of storms—Váňa knows they are caused by electricity in the air and wants his employer to install lightning conductors; Dikoj believes they are an act of God when his wrath has been aroused by sinful acts on earth. After Katya confesses her adultery, and Varvara is punished by the Kabanicha for being implicated, Kudrjáš decides they must escape the stifling atmosphere at her home and he and Varvara run away to Moscow. Aria: *Po zahrádce děvucha již ráno* ('Early morning in the garden'). Created (1921) by Valentin Šindler.

Kuligin (Janáček: *Katya Kabanová*). Bar. Friend of Váňa Kudrjáš. Created (1921) by René Milan.

Kundry (Wagner: *Parsifal*). Sop. She has been condemned to roam the world to seek redemption because she laughed at Christ on the Cross. She is under the influence of the evil magician Klingsor and has to help him destroy the Knights of the Grail (who rejected Klingsor). The King of the Knights, Amfortas, came to Klingsor's castle armed with the Holy Spear in order to kill Klingsor. Kundry was forced to seduce Amfortas, and while they were together, Klingsor stole the Spear and used it to attack Amfortas. The wound he inflicted will not heal. Kundry tries to find a herb or ointment that will heal Amfortas, giving it to Gurnemanz to try to assuage her own guilt about the injury. The Knights try to make her tell them how she is implicated in Amfortas's injury, but she stubbornly remains silent. When Parsifal arrives, it is clear that Kundry knows all about him—in fact, she knows far more than he himself knows. Klingsor orders her to seduce Parsifal, and although she does not really want to be involved in Parsifal's destruction, she is so firmly under Klingsor's will that she has no option but to obey him. She tells Parsifal his name and how she remembers him as a baby and she knows that his mother deliberately kept him innocent of worldly affairs. As she kisses him, he rejects her, calling the name of Amfortas. Kundry realizes that Parsifal knows she was the one who seduced Amfortas and is responsible for the wound. She refuses to take him to Amfortas and screams that she will curse the path to the Knight. Klingsor, determined to kill Parsifal, throws the Spear at him, but Parsifal catches it and Klingsor and his castle disappear. Kundry hears Parsifal leaving. Many years later, Kundry, half dead, is found in the forest by Gurnemanz, who revives her. She insists on staying with him as his servant. She indicates to him that a youth has entered the forest and she recognizes Parsifal, who carries the Holy Spear. She washes Parsifal's feet and dries them with her hair. Parsifal, in his turn, baptizes Kundry.

They both go with Gurnemanz to the Knights' castle, arriving in time for Titurel's funeral. With the Spear, Parsifal heals Amfortas's wound. As Parsifal unveils the Grail, Kundry collapses on the ground. Arias: *Nein, Parsifal, du tör'ger Reiner!* ('No, Parsifal, you foolish innocent!'); *Grausamer! Fühlst du im Herzen nur and'rer Schmerzen* ('Cruel one! If you feel in your heart').

Kundry is a most unusual character, different from all the other female roles in Wagner. She is half-good, half-bad—she is riddled with guilt about the agony caused to Amfortas and does her best to find balm to apply to it, but she is under Klingsor's evil control and has no option but to help him in his efforts to destroy the Grail Knights. As can be deduced from the list of singers below, vocally the part has been successfully sung by both sopranos and mezzo-sopranos; dramatically, great histrionics are required from the singer-actress who must nevertheless take care not to be too melodramatic. Interpreters have included Rosa Sucher, Anna von Mildenburg (a mistress of Mahler), Olive Fremstad, Ellen Gulbrandson, Marie Wittich (the first Salome in Strauss's opera, despite her protests that she was too much of a lady to sing that role!), Marie Brema, Eva von der Osten (the first Octavian in *Der Rosenkavalier*), Marta Fuchs, Martha Mödl, Astrid Varnay, Régine Crespin, Christa Ludwig, Amy Shuard, Ludmila Dvořáková, Gwyneth Jones, Janis Martin, Rita Gorr, Eva Randová, Leonie Rysanek, Anne Evans, and Waltraud Meier. Created (1882) by Amelia Materna.

Kunka (Janáček: *The Excursions of Mr Brouček*). Sop. Daughter of the 15th-cent. Hussite Domšík. Her counterparts are Málinka (Prague, 1888) and Etherea (Moon). Created (1920) by Emma Miřiovská.

Kuragin, Prince Anatol (Prokofiev: *War and Peace*). Ten. Although married, he wins the love of Natasha and wants her to go away with him. Creator (1945 vers.) unknown; (1946 vers.) F. A. Andrukovich.

Kurwenal (Wagner: *Tristan und Isolde*). Bar. One of Tristan's retainers and his close friend. He is with his master on board the ship in which Tristan is escorting Isolde to Cornwall where she will marry Tristan's uncle, King Mark. When Brangäne comes to Tristan with a message from her mistress, summoning him to her presence, Kurwenal is angry—how dare anyone speak to his master in this way? Before they land, Isolde and Tristan declare their love, under the influence of the love potion given to them by Brangäne, and arrange to meet that night in the king's castle. Kurwenal arrives to warn them of King Mark's approach. After Tristan has been seriously wounded on the treacherous Melot's sword, Kurwenal carries him back to his estate at Kareol in Brittany and devotedly nurses him. He sends for Isolde to cure Tristan's wound and anxiously awaits her arrival, distressed by his beloved master's rapidly deteriorating condition. At last Kurwenal sees Isolde's ship and describes to Tristan how it is coming nearer. He rushes to meet Isolde. Tristan dies in Isolde's arms. King Mark and Melot also arrive at Kareol, and holding Melot's betrayal responsible for Tristan's death, Kurwenal kills Melot and is fatally wounded in the attack. He dies at Tristan's side—a servant faithful to the end. Aria: *Auf! Auf! Ihr Frauen!* ('Up! Up, you ladies!'); *Mein Herre! Tristan! Schrecklicher Zauber!* ('My Lord! Tristan! Dreadful magic!'); duet (with Tristan): *Wo du bist? In Frieden, sicher und frei!* ('Where are you? In peace, safe and free!'). Among notable portrayers of this role are David Bispham, Jaro Prohaska, Hans Hotter, Gustav Neidlinger, Dietrich Fischer-Dieskau, Walter Berry, Eberhard Wächter, Donald McIntyre, Hermann Becht, and Falk Struckman, many of whom went on to become famous Wotans. Created (1865) by Anton Mitterwurzer.

Kuterma, Grishka (Rimsky-Korsakov: *The Legend of the Invisible City of Kitezh*). Ten. A drunken layabout who curses the wedding of Fevronia and Prince Vsevolod. He is captured with Fevronia and goes mad. Created (1907) by Ivan Yershov.

Kutuzov, Field Marshal Prince Mikhail (Prokofiev: *War and Peace*). Bass. Having lost the Battle of Borodino, he decides to abandon Moscow rather than risk defeat by the French within the city. Napoleon's troops occupy Moscow. Created (1945 vers.) by A. S. Pirogov; (1946 vers.) by N. N. Butyagin.

Kuzmič, Luka (Janáček: *From the House of the Dead*). *See* MOROZOV, FILKA.

Laca (Janáček: *Jenůfa*). *See* KLEMEŇ, LACA.

Lacy, Beatrice (Josephs: *Rebecca*). Mez. Wife of Giles Lacy and sister of Maxim de Winter. She greets the new Mrs de Winter warmly, pleased to see how different she is from Rebecca. Created (1983) by Linda Hibberd.

Lacy, Giles (Josephs: *Rebecca*). Bass-bar. Husband of Beatrice, Maxim de Winter's sister. Created (1983) by Thomas Lawlor.

Lady Macbeth of the Mtsensk District (*Ledi Makbet Mtsenskago Uezda*) (Shostakovich). Lib. by comp. and Aleksandr Preis; 4 acts; f.p. Leningrad (St Petersburg) 1934, cond. Samuil Samosud.

Russia, 1865: Katerina *Ismailova is unhappily married to Zinovy *Ismailov, son of Boris *Ismailov. While her husband is working away, she interrupts *Sergei, the servant, molesting the cook, *Aksinya. Boris himself lusts after Katerina and sends her to her room, but Sergei follows and they make love. Boris catches Sergei leaving Katerina's room and sends for Zinovy. Katerina puts poison into her father-in-law's mushrooms and he dies. Zinovy returns and notices Sergei's belt in Katerina's room and uses it to whip her. She and Sergei kill her husband and hide his body in the cellar. They plan to marry, but at the festivities a drunkard, looking for more drink, finds the body in the cellar. Katerina and Sergei admit their guilt and are arrested. On the road to Siberia they are separated. Sergei is attracted by another young convict, *Sonyetka. Katerina pushes her into the river and jumps in to her own death.

Laërte 1. (Thomas: *Hamlet*). Ten. Brother of Ophélie (Ophelia), son of Polonius (who was, unknown to his children, involved in the plot to kill the King, Hamlet's father). He blames Hamlet's rejection of her when Ophélie loses her reason and drowns herself. Created (1868) by Mons. Collin.

2. (Thomas: *Mignon*). Ten. An actor in a group of strolling players. Created (1866) by Mons. Couderc.

Lakmé (Delibes). Lib. by Edmond Gondinet and Philippe Gille; 3 acts; f.p. Paris 1883, cond. Jules Danbé.

India, mid-19th cent.: *Gérald, an English officer, with his friends and their governess, Mistress *Bentson, has wandered into a sacred grove. There he sees *Lakmé (and her maid *Mallika) and falls in love with her. She is the daughter of *Nilakantha, a Brahmin priest, who determines to punish Gérald for desecrating their holy ground. Nilakantha follows Gérald and his fellow-officer *Frédéric to a crowded market, and orders Lakmé to sing and attract the officer again, so he can identify him. She is able to warn Gérald of her father's plans. When Gérald is slightly injured, Lakmé nurses him in a hut in the forest. Frédéric finds him there and reminds him of his duty as a soldier. Gérald goes with Frédéric. Lakmé takes poison as her father finds her in the hut.

Lakmé (Delibes: *Lakmé*). Sop. Daughter of the fanatical Brahmin priest Nilakantha. In love with a young English officer, Gérald, much disapproved of by her father. When Gérald is persuaded to return to his regiment, Lakmé realizes she has lost him and takes poison. Aria: *Où va la jeune Hindoue?* ('Where is the young Indian girl?'—the famous *Bell Song*). Created (1883) by Marie van Zandt.

Lamoral (Strauss: *Arabella*). Bass. One of three Counts in love with Arabella. Created (1933) by Arno Schellenberg.

Landgrave, Hermann the (Wagner: *Tannhäuser*). Bass. Landgrave of Thuringia, leader of the knights and Minnesingers, whom

Tannhäuser has left in order to live with Venus. Hermann is the uncle of Elisabeth, whom he offers in marriage to the winner of the song contest in the hall of the Wartburg. Created (1845) by Wilhelm Georg Dettmer.

Land of Smiles, The (*Das Land des Lächelns*) (Lehár). Lib. by Ludwig Herzer and Fritz Beda-Löhner; 3 acts; f.p. Berlin 1929.

Vienna and Peking, 1912: Lisa, *Lichtenfels, daughter of Count Ferdinand *Lichtenfels, is admired by Count Gustav (Gustl) *von Pottenstein, but when he declares his love for her she tells him she does not see him as a prospective husband. Prince *Sou-Chong arrives to visit Lisa, but conversation is stilted due to his strict formality. The Prince has to leave in a hurry when informed he has been appointed Prime Minister of his country. He and Lisa declare their love for each other and she goes with him to Peking. His sister, *Mi, is jealous of the freedom she sees in western girls like Lisa. Gustl comes to visit them and he and Mi become fond of each other. Sou-Chong's uncle, *Tschang, insists Sou-Chong must follow Chinese custom and take four wives. Lisa threatens to leave him. Gustl agrees to help her escape and Mi agrees to assist them, distressed though she is to lose them both. Sou-Chong tries to prevent their departure, but sees that it is the only real solution. He and Mi comfort each other in their loss.

Laoula, Princess (Chabrier: *L'Étoile*). Sop. Daughter of King Mataquin, neighbour of King Ouf, whose intended bride she is. However, on her way to meet him she falls in love with a pedlar, Lazuli. Ouf agrees to their wedding and appoints the young couple as his heirs. Created (1877) by Berthe Stuart.

Larina, Mme (Tchaikovsky: *Eugene Onegin*). Mez. A landowner, mother of Tatyana and Olga. The local peasants bring in the harvest and dance for her. Her neighbour, Lensky, calls on her, bringing with him his friend, Eugene Onegin. Once she has greeted them, Mme Larina leaves her guests to be entertained by her daughters. She gives a party for Tatyana on her nameday, to which the two men are invited. To her consternation they quarrel, challenging each other to a duel and she is most upset to think that this can have happened in her house. Created (1879) by Maria Rainer.

La Roche (Strauss: *Capriccio*). Bass. A theatrical impresario, he has been invited by the Count to his sister's château. It is the Countess's birthday and her brother is planning to entertain her with a play which La Roche will produce. It is suggested during the rehearsal that an opera should be written about the events of the day. La Roche sings a long and impressive aria: the guests participating in the entertainment have all been laughing and arguing about the way in which plays are produced and gradually he is losing his patience with their arrogance in thinking that the actors are the ones who really matter in the theatre—after all, what do these young people really know about the art of production? Aria: *Hola, ihr Streiter in Apoll!* ('Enough! You ignorant fools!'). This role is thought to be based on the famous producer Max Reinhardt, who rescued the première of *Der Rosenkavalier* from its incompetent producer and to whom, in gratitude, *Ariadne auf Naxos* was dedicated. Famous singers of La Roche include Paul Schöffler, Hans Hotter (on record only—he never sang it on stage), Karl Ridderbusch, Benno Kusch, Manfred Jungwirth, Ernst Gutstein, Marius Rintzler, Theo Adam, and Stafford Dean. Created (1942) by Georg Hann.

Lastouc, Ruggero (Puccini: *La rondine*). Ten. Son of an old friend of Magda's lover Rambaldo. Ruggero calls at Magda's salon and tells her and her guests that this is his first night in Paris. Her maid Lisette suggests he should go to Bullier's nightclub and they all take their leave of their hostess. After they have gone, Magda sets off for the nightclub in disguise. There she meets and dances with Ruggero and they fall in love, to the distress of Rambaldo. They decide to live together in Nice. Ruggero writes and tells his family of his happiness, but Magda knows that when they learn of her past life they will not welcome her into their family and she tells Ruggero that she can never marry him and must leave him. Duet (with Magda): *Ma come puoi lasciarmi* ('But how can you leave me'). Created (1917) by Tito Schipa.

Laura (Ponchielli: *La gioconda*). Mez. Wife of Alvise, formerly in love with Enzo. Is given a rosary by Gioconda's mother, which Gioconda recognizes when Laura and Enzo are trapped by the spy Barnaba. Gioconda helps the lovers escape. Created (1876) by Maria Biancolini-Rodriguez.

Lauretta (Puccini: *Gianni Schicchi*). *See* Schicchi, Lauretta.

La Verne, Julie (Kern: *Show Boat*). Mez. Married to Steve Baker, she and her husband are the chief entertainers on board the *Cotton Blossom*. A jealous sailor reveals that Julie is partly black and as mixed marriages are illegal, she and Steve have to leave the boat. Years later she is singing in a night-club, but gives up her job to Magnolia Ravenal (*née* Hawks), who has been deserted by her husband and has a little daughter to support. Arias: *Can't help lovin' dat man; Bill*. Created (1927) by Helen Morgan.

Lawrence 1. (Smyth: *The Wreckers*). Bar. Lighthouse keeper, father of Avis, Mark's previous love. Creator (1906) not traced.
    2. (Laurence) (Gounod: *Roméo et Juliette*). Bass. Friar Lawrence. He agrees to secretly marry Romeo and Juliet. When Romeo is exiled and Capulet wants Juliet to marry Paris, Friar Lawrence gives her a potion which, when drunk, will make her simulate death. Thus she avoids the wedding and is taken to the family crypt to await Romeo's arrival. Created (1867) by Mons. Cazaux.

Lazuli (Chabrier: *L'Étoile*). Mez. *Travesti* role. A pedlar who meets and falls in love with Princess Laoula, the intended bride of King Ouf. The King eventually agrees to their marriage and names them as his heirs. Created (1877) by Paola Marié.

Leader of the Players (Britten: *Death in Venice*). Bass-bar. His strolling players entertain the guests at Aschenbach's hotel. Created (1973) by John Shirley-Quirk.

Leandro (Prokofiev: *The Love for Three Oranges*). Bar. Prime Minister (King of Spades), hoping to inherit the throne from the King of Clubs and therefore not anxious to see the Prince cured of his melancholia. Created (1921) by William Beck.

Lechmere (Britten: *Owen Wingrave*). Ten. A young student with Owen at Coyle's cramming establishment. He can't wait to go to war and fight. Created (1971 TV/1973) by Nigel Douglas.

Lecouvreur, Adriana (Cilea: *Adriana Lecouvreur*). Sop. An actress (a real person, she lived 1692–1730, but the plot of the opera is pure fiction). She has fallen in love with Maurizio, not knowing him to be the Count of Saxony, pretender to the Polish throne. She gives him a bunch of violets, which he then passes to his lover, the Princess de Bouillon. The later shows these to Adriana, who gets her own back by talking of the Princess's promiscuity. On Adriana's birthday she receives a box of violets. They are from the Princess and are soaked in poison—their perfume proves fatal. Aria: *Ecco: respiro appena* ('See: I'm hardly breathing'). Created (1902) by Angelica Pandolfini.

Leda (Strauss: *Die Liebe der Danae*). Cont. One of the Four Queens, a previous lover of Jupiter. Created (1944) by Anka Jelacic; (1952) by Sieglinde Wagner.

Legend of the Invisible City of Kitezh and the Maiden Fevronia, The (*Skazaniye o nevidimom grade Kitezke i deve Fevronii*) (Rimsky-Korsakov). Lib. by Vladimir Bel'sky; 4 acts; f.p. St Petersburg 1907, cond. Felix Blumenfeld.
    Legendary Russia: *Fevronia learns that the young man she has promised to marry is Prince *Vsevolod, son of Prince *Yury and joint ruler of the sacred city of Kitezh. Their wedding is cursed by the drunken Grishka *Kuterma. Tartars ransack the city and carry off Fevronia, taking Grishka as their guide. Vsevolod leads his people against their enemy, but in answer to Yury's prayers the city is enveloped in a golden mist and becomes invisible as it disappears into Paradise. Vsevolod is killed, Grishka and Fevronia escape. Grishka goes mad and rushes away from her. The spirit of Vsevalod leads her to him in Paradise.

Leicester, Earl of (Robert Dudley) (Donizetti: *Maria Stuarda*). Ten. Appointed by Queen Elizabeth I as ambassador to France. Mary Stuart, held captive in Fotheringay Castle, appeals to Leicester for help and he begs the Queen to visit her in gaol. He prepares Mary for the visit, counselling her to ask the Queen for forgiveness. The meeting is a disaster and Leicester's pleas for clemency for Mary are ignored as Elizabeth signs the death warrant. Suspecting that Leicester loves Mary, she orders him to witness the execution. Created (1834, as Buondelmonte) by Francesco Pedrazzi; (1835) by Domenico Reina.

Leïla (Bizet: *The Pearl Fishers*). Sop. A young priestess of Brahma. She is loved by the friends Nadir and Zurga, causing enmity between them. Aria: *Comme autrefois dans la nuit sombre* ('As once of yore, in the dark night'). Created (1863) by Léontine de Maësen.

Leitmetzerin, Marianne (Strauss: *Der Rosenkavalier*). Sop. Duenna (chaperone) to Sophie von Faninal. Created (1911) by Riza Eibenschütz (who, interestingly, created the Page in *Salome*, a role designated in the score as 'contralto'; and the Overseer of the Maids in *Elektra*, a soprano part, as well as the Leitmetzerin, which the score describes as 'high soprano').

Lena, Mme (Birtwistle: *The Second Mrs Kong*). Mez. 'The customary sphinx' who guards the barrier between the worlds of the living and the dead. Created (1994) by Nuala Willis.

Lensky, Vladimir (Tchaikovsky: *Eugene Onegin*). Ten. A neighbour of the Larin family, he comes to visit them accompanied by his friend Eugene Onegin. Lensky admits he is in love with the younger Larin daughter, Olga. At Tatyana's birthday party, Onegin flirts with Olga and, angry, Lensky challenges him to a duel. Both men realize that things have gone too far—a duel is out of all proportion to the 'crime', but honour prevents them admitting this. Waiting for Onegin to arrive at the chosen site, Lensky sings his farewell to Olga. To Onegin's horror, Lensky is killed in the duel. Aria: *Kuda, kuda vï udalilis* ('Whither, ah whither are ye fled'). Created (1879) by Mikhail Ivanovich Medvyedev (Bernstein).

Léon 1. (Corigliano: *The Ghosts of Versailles*). Ten. Illegitimate son of Rosina (Countess Almaviva) from her affair with Cherubino. He has fallen in love with Florestine, illegitimate daughter of the Count. Created (1991) by Neil Rosenshein.

    2. (Messiaen: *Saint François d'Assise*). Bar. Friar Léon, a monk to whom St Francis explains his philosophy about suffering leading to perfect joy. Created (1983) by Philippe Duminy.

Léonato (Berlioz: *Béatrice et Bénédict*). Spoken. Governor of Messina, father of Héro. Created (1862) by Mons. Guerrin.

Leone (Handel: *Tamerlano*). Bass. Friend of Tamerlano and Andronico. Created (1724) by Giuseppe Boschi.

Leonora 1. (Verdi: *Il trovatore*). Sop. A duchess, Lady-in-Waiting to the Princess of Aragon. She is loved by Count di Luna and also by the troubador Manrico—she has heard the latter serenading below her window and loves him. The two men fight in battle and she believes Manrico has been killed and vows to enter a convent. She is prevented by the appearance of Manrico, who is about to marry her when he hears that the gypsy Azucena, whom he regards as his mother, has been arrested by the Count's troops. Attempting to rescue her, he is imprisoned with Azucena. To save him, Leonora offers herself to di Luna—but she has taken poison hidden in her ring to avoid the consequences of her offer. As she releases Manrico from prison, she dies at his feet. Aria: *Tacea la notte placida* ('It was a peaceful night'); *D'amor sull'ali rosee* ('Go forth, on rosy wings of love')—this is the aria sung in counterpoint to the famous *Miserere*, which is sung by Manrico (with chorus) from his prison cell. Created (1853) by Rosina Penco.

    2. (Donizetti: *La Favorite*). See GUZMAN, LÉONOR DI.

    3. (Verdi: *La forza del destino*). See VARGAS, DONNA LEONORA DI.

    See also LEONORE.

Leonore (Beethoven: *Fidelio*). Sop. Wife of Florestan. Disguised as a young man, Fidelio, she goes to work as assistant to the gaoler Rocco, determined to save her wrongly imprisoned husband. Rocco's daughter falls in love with Fidelio. In the dungeon, Leonore realizes it is Florestan who is soon to be killed and whose grave she is helping to dig. She gives the weak man bread and water, but he does not recognize her. She throws herself between him and Pizarro when the latter comes to kill Florestan. She is hailed by all as a heroine and is given the privilege of removing Florestan's chains and setting him free. Aria: *Abscheulicher!* ('Abominable man!'); duet (with Florestan); *O namenlose freude!* ('Oh nameless joy!'); ens. (with Florestan, etc.): *O Gott, welch'* *ein Augenblick* ('O God, what a moment'). Leonore is not an easy role to portray, being both vocally and dramatically demanding, but there has been no shortage of sopranos willing to perform the role, some, but not all, of whom fall into the *Heldensopran* class. These include Lotte Lehmann (the regular Salzburg Leonore between 1927 and 1937), Lucie Weidt, Hilde Konetzni, Rose Bampton, Kirsten Flagstad, Martha Mödl, Christel Goltz, Erna Schlüter, Leonie Rysanek, Galina Vishnevskaya, Sena Jurinac, Christa Ludwig, Birgit Nilsson, Gwyneth Jones, Elisabeth Söderström, Anne Evans, and Anje Kampe. Created (1805) by Anna Milder.

Léopold 1. (Halévy: *La Juive*). Ten. Prince of the Empire and married to Eudoxie. Is employed by Eléazar, under the name of 'Samuel', and seduces his daughter Rachel. She saves him from a sentence of death by retracting her accusation. Created (1835) by Mons Lafond.

2. (Strauss: *Der Rosenkavalier*). Silent. Really called Leupold, he is the bastard son of Baron Ochs von Lerchenau, called throughout the opera his Body-Servant (*Leiblakai*). Created (1911) by Theodor Heuser.

Leper, The (Messiaen: *Saint François d'Assise*). Ten. St Francis visits a leper colony. The Leper bitterly rails against his fate, becoming silent only when he hears the voice of the Angel. St Francis embraces him and the Leper is cured. Created (1983) by Kenneth Riegel.

Leporello (Mozart: *Don Giovanni*). Bass. Don Giovanni's manservant. He is obliged to help his master in his amorous adventures, keeping watch for him when he seduces ladies. Tries to convince Donna Elvira of Giovanni's terrible nature by reciting a list of his master's seductions including, in Spain, 1,003 conquests. Forced to change clothes with his master to help assist in yet another seduction, he is mistaken for the Don by Donna Anna and her fellow-conspirators, who are determined to reveal Giovanni as a murderer. He has to run for his life. Terrified when it speaks to them in the graveyard, he fails to prevent Giovanni inviting the Commendatore's statue to dinner. After Giovanni's demise, Leporello departs in search of a new master. Aria: *Madamina, il catalogo è questo* ('My dear lady, here is a

list'—the so-called Catalogue Aria). Created (1787) by Felice Ponziani. *See also* ARTICLE BY BRYN TERFEL, p. 162.

Lescaut 1. (Massenet: *Manon*). Bar. A member of the Royal Guards, cousin of Manon Lescaut whom he is to escort to a convent. However, she falls in love with Des Grieux and leaves with him to live in Paris. When she and her lover are arrested as cheat and prostitute, Lescaut effects their escape, but it is too late: Manon is dying. Created (1884) by Alexandre Taskin.

2. (Puccini: *Manon Lescaut*). Bar. Sergeant in the King's Guards. Brother (in this opera—see above) who is escorting his sister to a convent where she is to complete her education. She runs away with Des Grieux, but when he loses all his money she leaves him and goes to her rich lover. Lescaut knows his sister is unhappy and tells Des Grieux where he can find her. As she is being deported as a prostitute, Lescaut helps Des Grieux to rescue her. Created (1893) by Achille Moro.

Lescaut, Manon 1. (Massenet: *Manon*). Sop. On her way to a convent, she stops off in Amiens where her cousin Lescaut is to meet her and escort her on the rest of her journey. At the inn where her stage-coach calls, she meets and falls in love with the Chevalier Des Grieux. At their home in Paris they are visited by the wealthy de Brétigny, who persuades Manon she will have a much more luxurious life if she departs with him. Living with him a life of wealth, Manon overhears the Comte Des Grieux telling de Brétigny that his son is about to take holy orders. Learning that he is preaching in Saint-Sulpice, she makes her way there. Des Grieux is unable to resist her and they run away together. They join her cousin and his friends in a gambling parlour, where Morfontaine, after losing heavily to Des Grieux, accuses him and Manon of cheating. They are arrested. Des Grieux is freed but Manon is to be deported as a prostitute. Lescaut and Des Grieux help her escape, but she dies in Des Grieux's arms. Aria: *Adieu, notre petite table* ('Farewell, our little table'). Created (1884) by Marie Heilbronn.

2. (Puccini: *Manon Lescaut*). Sop. She is being taken by her brother to complete her education in a convent. Calling at an inn en route, she meets the handsome Des Grieux and the wealthy Geronte, both of whom fall in

LEPORELLO (*Don Giovanni*—Mozart)

by Bryn Terfel

From day one, Leporello fell nicely into my vocal bass-baritone category, which is half the battle. But what an opera! Two men constantly at the centre of the action—tumbling, rolling, throwing each other into skirmishes without any inhibitions. After a night of 'Leporelloing' I feel as if I've played in a rugby international.

One of the most fascinating things about this character is his relationship with his master, Don Giovanni. It is clear that neither one could exist without the other. They feed on one another like parasites, thus creating a strange telepathic understanding. There is no doubt at all who is the master. When the manservant sidekick has time to himself, he grumbles constantly and longs to break free, but he would be unable to do so of his own accord. Leporello's whole being is enhanced by the precarious life his master leads and the unexpected adventures which result from this. On the one hand they reverse, rather badly, the master-servant relationship, and on the other hand, Leporello is thrown by his master into numerous life-threatening situations. Clearly Leporello is a descendant of the *commedia dell'arte* tradition, but he also has a devilishly cynical gusto that has created a lethal weapon to crush the desires of any female admirer of the Don. Donna Elvira, after being subjected by Leporello to the infamous 'Catalogue aria', would testify to this. (I once forgot this essential list on the holy Salzburg stage. I somehow managed to sneak away during Elvira's aria, returning in the nick of time, to the amazement of my Don, to sing a rather harassed *Così ne consolo mille e otto cento*.) In my opinion, being a good servant is important to Leporello: it is evident he takes incredible pride in keeping tally of his master's conquests, and when he serves the Don that final fateful dinner, he does so with the utmost professionalism. But at the same time, his attitude is 'Nothing ventured, nothing gained'. This is highlighted in the final minutes of the opera when, after the soul-searching, conscience-ridden 'Aaaagh' of the Don as he descends into the fires of hell, Leporello, with no regrets, no tears, goes off to the tavern to seek a better master.

I have had a fabulous time with this character, but it is not without its hazards. During a dress rehearsal at the Metropolitan Opera, New York, Leporello was constantly picking up Giovanni's cast-offs: his rings, his sword, cape, hat, boots, mandolin, and the odd conquest—the only thing I didn't have to bend and pick up was the catalyst of the entire drama, the body of the Commendatore after the Don savagely disposes of him in the first five minutes of the work. Unfortunately, the constant tendering and the raked stage played havoc with my back and I slipped a disc, resulting in cancelled performances and keyhole surgery to remove the offending part (from which I am fully recovered and able to throw myself back—no pun intended—into this glorious role). It was a potent reminder of what it is really like to become the overworked manservant. Perhaps when the time comes I should take a leaf out of Leporello's book and go to that same tavern to seek a servant of my own for my future new character.

love with her. She falls for Des Grieux and they run away and set up home together. Des Grieux's money runs out and Manon, hankering after a life of luxury, goes to live with Geronte, who lavishes gifts on her—but she remembers how happy she was with Des Grieux. Her brother visits her and she tells him how she wishes she was back with her true lover. Lescaut informs Des Grieux who comes for her. Keen as she is to leave with him, she is reluctant to leave behind all her jewels. The delay as she collects them is fatal—Geronte reports her to the police as a prostitute and she is arrested and put on a ship to be deported. Des Grieux manages to join her and he and Lescaut rescue her. They become lost in the desert, and Manon, exhausted, begs him to leave her and save himself. He tries to find water, but fails. As he returns to Manon, she is dying. Arias: *Vedete? Io son fedele* ('See, I am faithful to my word'); *In quelle trine morbide* ('In those soft laces'); *Sola, perduta, abbandonata* ('Alone, lost, abandoned'); duet (with Des Grieux): *Cedi, son tua!* ('Give in, I am yours!'). Created (1893) by Cesira Ferrani (who three years later created Mimì in *La bohème*).

Leukippos (Strauss: *Daphne*). Ten. A shepherd, he and Daphne have grown up together, and treat each other as brother and sister. Leukippos tries to tell Daphne that he loves her. She resists his efforts to embrace her, feeling towards him only as a sister. Her maids suggest to him that he should dress as a woman and try to win her affection first as a friend and this he does, dancing with her at the Dionysian feast her father has organized to greet the sun-god Apollo. Apollo also falls in love with Daphne, and reveals to her Leukippos' true identity. The men fight and Leukippos is killed. Only then does Daphne understand that she did truly love him. Duet (with Daphne): *Leukippos, du? Ja, ich selbst* ('Leukippos, is it you? Yes, it is I'). Of the two tenor roles of *Helden* proportions in this opera, Leukippos requires the more lyrical voice, and among those who have been notable in the part are Anton Dermota and Fritz Wunderlich. Created (1938) by Martin Kremer.

Leuthold (Rossini: *Guillaume Tell*). Bass. A shepherd who kills an Austrian soldier who assaulted his daughter. He is saved from capture by Tell, who rows him across the rapids.

Created (1829) by Ferdinand Prévot (or Prévost. His father created Gessler).

Lichtenfels, Count Ferdinand (Lehár: *The Land of Smiles*). Spoken. An army lieutenant, father of Lisa. Creator (1929) not traced.

Lichtenfels, Lisa (Lehár: *The Land of Smiles*). Daughter of Count Ferdinand, she is loved by Gustl, but gently rejects his proposal. She falls in love with Prince Sou-Chong and returns with him to Peking. Their cultural differences prove a difficulty, especially his uncle's insistence that he take four wives. Unable to tolerate the situation and homesick for Vienna, Lisa is relieved when Gustl arrives to visit them. He offers to help her escape from the palace. When the Prince discovers their plan, he acknowledges that this is the only solution and bids her a loving farewell. Created (1929) by Vera Schwarz.

Licinius (Spontini: *La vestale*). Ten. A victorious Roman General, in love with Giulia, now a vestal virgin. He meets her at night when she is guarding the sacred flame. They neglect it and it goes out—a cardinal sin. He is helped to escape, but she is condemned to death. At the last minute, the flame is rekindled by a flash of lightning and the lovers are reunited. Created (1807) by Étienne Laîné.

Lidio (Cavalli: *L'Egisto*). Alto. *Travesti* role. In love with Climene but separated from her when captured. He falls in love with Clori, his friend's betrothed—they too have become separated. But Climene's loyalty moves him and he returns to her. Creator (1643) not known.

Lidoine, Mme (Poulenc: *Les Dialogues des Carmélites*). Sop. The new Prioress, appointed after the death of Mme de Croissy. Created (1957) by Leyla Gencer.

Liebe der Danae, Die (*The Love of Danae*) (Strauss). Lib. by Joseph Gregor; 3 acts; f.p. Salzburg 1944 (dress rehearsal only), cond. Clemens Krauss; Salzburg 1952, cond. Clemens Krauss. [NB In 1944, while rehearsals for the première were taking place, the Nazis ordered the closure of all theatres following the bomb plot against Hitler. Local officials allowed the dress rehearsal to take place in Salzburg before an audience mainly of soldiers—this was the unofficial première. The first official performance was also in Salzburg, in 1952.]

Mythological times: King *Pollux is trying to delay his creditors. He has asked the *Four Kings, his nephews, to find a rich husband for his daughter *Danae, and King *Midas is interested. Danae discusses with her maid *Xanthe how her suitor must be able to offer her as much gold as she has dreamed about. 'Chrysopher' arrives, claiming to be Midas' friend—he has come to prepare her to meet the king—in fact, Chrysopher is Midas in disguise. Danae is attracted to Chrysopher, and he to her. They go together to meet the 'real Midas', who is the disguised *Jupiter about whom Danae has dreamed. Jupiter enters Danae's room, where the *Four Queens are preparing the bridal bed. They all recognize him, for he has been each one's lover in the past. Jupiter warns Midas that if he pursues his relationship with Danae, Jupiter will change him back into the donkey-driver he originally was. To prove to Danae that he is really Midas, he changes everything in the room to gold. As he embraces Danae, she is turned into a golden statue. Jupiter asks her to choose between him and Midas. She picks Midas and is restored to life. Because he loves her, Midas loses his magic touch. In the desert he explains to her that Jupiter usurped his position as soon as he saw Danae's portrait. *Mercury appears to Jupiter and tells him that the gods are all mocking his inability to win Danae. He visits Midas and Danae, but acknowledges his failure—Danae is poor but happy with Midas.

Life for the Tsar, A (*Zhizn' za tsarya*) (Glinka). Lib. by Georgy Fyodorovich Rosen, epil. by Vasily Zhukovsky, rev. by Glinka, monastery scene (added after f.p.) by Nestor Kukolnik; 4 acts and epil.; f.p. St Petersburg 1836, cond. Catterino Cavos.

Russia and Poland, 1613: Ivan *Susanin forbids the wedding of his daughter *Antonida and *Sobinin until the country's future is secure. Sobinin returns from battle to announce that a Romanov has been elected Tsar. At a ball in a Polish fortress, all are confident that the Russians will be defeated. When news of the Tsar's election arrives, soldiers set off to find and capture him. They arrive at Susanin's cottage, demanding to be told the whereabouts of the new Tsar. Susanin sends his ward

*Vanya to warn the Tsar, then misleads the Poles into the forest. At the monastery, Vanya warns of the danger. When Susanin is sure the Tsar is safe, he confesses his deception and is killed. In Moscow, Sobinin, Antonida, and Vanya tell the crowds of Susanin's heroic death.

Lighthouse, The (Maxwell Davies). Lib. by comp.; prol. and 1 act; f.p. Edinburgh 1980, cond. Richard Dufallo.

Edinburgh and a lighthouse, early 20th cent.: Three lighthouse keepers have disappeared and an Edinburgh court is hearing evidence from three officers. These three become the keepers, *Arthur, *Blazes, and *Sandy. They have lived together for many months with tensions developing between them. They imagine ghosts from the past and each believes he is being claimed by 'the Beast'. As the Beast approaches, its eyes are seen to be the lights of the rescue boat. The three men again become the officers, who search for the keepers but find only rats.

Lillas Pastia (Bizet: *Carmen*). *See* PASTIA, LILLAS.

Lillywhite, Atalanta (Maw: *The Rising of the Moon*). Sop. Daughter of the adjutant of the camp in Ireland of the 31st Royal Lancers. Created (1970) by Annon Lee Silver.

Lillywhite, Capt. (Maw: *The Rising of the Moon*). Ten. Adjutant of the camp of the 31st Royal Lancers in Ireland. Father of Atalanta. Created (1970) by John Fryatt.

Lina (Verdi: *Stiffelio*). Sop. Daughter of Count Stankar and wife of the Protestant minister Stiffelio. While he is away preaching, she has an affair with a young nobleman. Ignoring her father's advice, she confesses to Stiffelio, who is devastated by her betrayal and offers her a divorce. He forces her to sign papers annulling their marriage. She then asks him, no longer as her husband, but still as a minister, to hear her confession. He is so moved by her avowal of love for him that, by the passage he reads in church, he publicly forgives her adultery. Created (1850) by Marietta Gazzaniga (Malaspina). *See also* MINA.

Linda di Chamounix (Donizetti). Lib. by Gaetano Rossi; 3 acts; f.p. Vienna 1842, cond. Gaetano Donizetti.

Paris and the French Alps, about 1760: *Antonio, a farmer, and his wife *Maddalena worry they will be evicted. The Marquis de *Boisfleury offers to educate their daughter *Linda at his château. Linda is visited by Carlo di *Sirval, a viscount, whom she knows simply as Carlo, a painter. He is scared to reveal his true identity in case Linda regards his status a barrier to their relationship. Her parents are warned by the *Prefect that it would be better for Linda to stay with his brother in Paris. Linda and her young friend *Pierotto depart for Paris. The Prefect's brother dies and Linda goes to live with Carlo, who knows his mother wants him to marry a wealthy young lady. Antonio comes to see Linda, disgusted with his daughter for apparently being Carlo's mistress. Linda meets Pierotto who tells her that Carlo is going to marry someone else. At this news she becomes mentally disturbed. She and Pierotto return to Chamounix and Carlo comes in search of her, his mother having at last agreed to their marriage. She is happily reunited with Carlo.

Linda di Chamounix (Donizetti: *Linda di Chamounix*). Sop. Daughter of a poor farmer Antonio and his wife Maddalena. She is in love with Carlo, a young painter, not knowing he is the Vicomte di Sirval. He wants to marry her but his mother is against it. When Linda hears that he is to marry someone else she becomes mentally disturbed, but Carlo finds her and tells her that his mother has withdrawn her objections and they can finally marry. Her sanity returns and they are happy together. Linda's great coloratura aria, *O luce di quest'anima* ('O light of this soul') was not heard at the première, but was composed for the first Paris performance later that year. Created (1842) by Eugenia Tadolini (and in Paris by Fanny Tacchinardi-Persiani who in 1835 had been the first Lucia di Lammermoor).

Lindorf (Offenbach: *Les Contes d'Hoffmann*). Bass. A councillor of Nuremberg, he loves Stella, the diva loved by Hoffmann. As Hoffmann tells the stories of his previous unsuccessful loves, it becomes clear that they were all thwarted by manifestations of Lindorf: Coppélius, Dr Miracle, and Dappertutto. Created (1881) by Alexandre Taskin.

Lindoro 1. (Haydn: *La fedeltà premiata*). Ten. An assistant at Diana's temple, brother of Amaranta and recently deserted by Nerina, with whom he is ultimately united. Created (1781) by Leopoldo Dichtler.

2. (Rossini: *L'italiana in Algeri*). Ten. An Italian in love with Isabella. He has been captured by Mustafà's men and serves as his slave. He is ordered to marry Elvira, the wife Mustafà no longer loves. When Isabella arrives at the Bey's house, they reaffirm their love and plan their escape. Arias: *Languir per una bella* ('To languish for a beauty'); *Ah come il cor di giubilo esulte* ('Oh, how my heart exults with joy'). Created (1813) by Serafino Gentile.

3. (Rossini: *Il barbiere di Siviglia*). The name under which Count Almaviva, disguised as a student, woos Rosina.

Linetta, Princess (Prokofiev: *The Love for Three Oranges*). Cont. The princess inside the first orange. She dies of thirst. Created (1921) by Philine Falco.

Lippert-Wehlersheim, Prince Leopold Maria and Princess Anhilte von und zu (Kálmán: *Die Csárdásfürstin*). Spoken roles. The parents of Prince Edwin Ronald. They want him to marry his cousin, the Countess Anastasia (Stasi) and are opposed to his love for a cabaret singer. But it becomes known that Edwin's mother was herself a singer before her marriage, so the parents' objections are overruled. Created (1915) by Max Brod and Gusti Macha.

Lisa 1. (Tchaikovsky: *The Queen of Spades*). Sop. Granddaughter of the old Countess, recently engaged to Prince Yeletsky. (In Pushkin's novel, from which the libretto was adapted, Lisa was a ward of the Countess, not a relative, but she was upgraded in order to put her on a higher social standing than Hermann, who had to be wealthy in order to be worthy of her, hence his desperate need to win money.) Hermann has seen her and fallen in love with her and she is unable to resist him when he declares his feelings. She gives him a key to her room, and on his way there he passes through the Countess's quarters and demands from the old lady the secret of the three cards. The Countess dies of fright and Lisa realizes that, even though he loves her, Hermann has been using her to get to the Countess to satisfy his gambling needs. She drowns herself in the Winter Canal. Aria: *Zachem zhe eti slyozi?* ('Why these tears?'); *Akh, istomilas ya gorem* ('Ah, I am worn out by grief'). Created (1890) by Medea Mei-Figner (she was pregnant at the time; her husband created Hermann).

2. (Bellini: *La sonnambula*). Sop. Hostess of the village inn. In love with Elvino and jealous of Amina, who is to marry him. Does her best to cause trouble between them. Created (1831) by Elisa Taccani.

3. (Lehár: *The Land of Smiles*). *See* LICHTEN-FELS, LISA.

Lisetta (Haydn: *Il mondo della luna*). Mez. Maid to Flaminia and Clarice. She is loved by Cecco, whose master Ernesto is in love with Flaminia. Created (1777) by Maria Jermoli (whose husband created Ecclitico, who is in love with Clarice).

Lisette (Puccini: *La rondine*). Sop. Maid of Magda de Civry. She and the poet Prunier decide to live together. He unsuccessfully attempts to help her make a career on the stage. She returns to her post as Magda's maid. Created (1917) by Ines Maria Ferraris.

Little Buttercup (Sullivan: *HMS Pinafore*). Cont. Nickname of Mrs Cripps, who swapped as babies the ship's captain and a simple sailor. When this is revealed and the captain demoted, she marries him. Aria: *I'm called Little Buttercup*. Created (1878) by Harriet Everard.

Liù (Puccini: *Turandot*). Sop. A slavegirl in the employ of the blind King Timur and his son Calaf (now the Unknown Prince), with whom she is secretly in love. When Timur is overthrown and exiled, she goes with him, caring for him and acting as his escort. They meet Calaf, whom they feared dead. He asks Liù why she is so kind to his father, and she replies that it is because Calaf once smiled at her. She and Timur are arrested by Turandot's guards, who try to make the old man reveal the name of the Unknown Prince. Frightened that Timur will be injured by the guards, Liù tells them that she is the only one who knows the identity of the Unknown Prince. She is tortured but they cannot make her tell them the answer. Turandot calls for the executioner, but Liù snatches a dagger from a soldier and kills herself. Followed by the heartbroken Timur, her body is carried away by the crowd. (The funeral music

for Liù is the last Puccini wrote, and it is here that, at the première, Toscanini laid down his baton.) Arias: *Signore, ascolta!* ('My lord, hear me!'); *Tu, che di gel sei cinta* ('You who are girdled with ice'). The character of the gentle, faithful Liù, is in marked contrast to the ice-maiden Turandot and attracts lyric sopranos as Turandot appeals to dramatic singers. Liù has two beautiful arias, and several German singers, including Lotte Schöne and Elisabeth Schwarzkopf, sang the role both on stage and on record (Schwarzkopf recording it with Maria Callas in the title role). Other exponents include Mafalda Favero (who sang Liù to Eva Turner's Turandot and was also a famous Manon Lescaut), Magda Olivero, Raina Kaba-ivanska, Anna Moffo, Cynthia Haymon, and Yoko Watanabe. Created (1926) by Maria Zamboni.

Lockit, Lucy (Gay: *The Beggar's Opera*). Sop. Daughter of the gaoler at Newgate Prison. Her ex-husband, the highwayman Macheath, is brought to Newgate after his arrest. Lucy and Macheath's new wife, Polly Peachum, meet and quarrel. Created (1728) by Mrs Eagleton. *See also* BROWN, LUCY.

Lockit, Mr (Gay: *The Beggar's Opera*). Bar. The gaoler at Newgate Prison. His daughter Lucy was the first wife of the highwayman Macheath who is now married to Polly Peachum. Created (1728) by Mr Hall. *See also* BROWN, TIGER.

Lodovico (Verdi: *Otello*). Bass. Ambassador of the Venetian Republic. Created (1887) by Francesco Navarrini.

Loge (Wagner: *Das Rheingold*). Ten. He is the God of Fire and most cunning of the gods. It was Loge who urged Wotan to offer Freia as payment to the giants for building Valhalla, promising that when the time came to settle, he would find a way out. Loge brings the news of Alberich stealing the gold from the Rhine-maidens and explains the magic powers of the Ring. Overhearing this (as Loge intended them to), the giants are prepared to accept the gold in lieu of Freia. Loge accompanies Wotan to find Alberich, from whom they will steal the gold. When they return with the hoard, Loge helps to pile up the gold in front of Freia as instructed by the giants. When Freia is free and Wotan is ready to leave, Loge joins the other gods crossing the rainbow bridge into Valhalla, but he alone realizes that, in their greed to rule the world, the gods are hastening their own end. Arias: *Umsonnst such' ich* ('In vain have I searched'); *Wenn doch fasste nicht Wunder* ('Who would not feel wonder'); *Ihrem Ende eilen sie zu* ('They hasten to their end').

Loge does not appear in the rest of *Der Ring*, but in *Die Walküre*, after Wotan has condemned his daughter Brünnhilde to sleep on a rock, he summons up Loge to provide a circle of fire round her to ensure that only a true hero will be able to reach and claim her. The part of Loge is a gift to a character tenor, and many have made a speciality of the role. In recent years these have included Emile Belcourt, Heinz Zednik, Robert Tear, Graham Clark, Kenneth Riegel, Philip Langridge, Nigel Douglas, and Peter Bronder. In addition to these, many an overtly *Heldentenor* has (to use Alan Blyth's phrase) 'slummed it' as Loge later in his career, and no doubt enjoyed the change. These include Wolfgang Windgassen, Jess Thomas, Manfred Jung, and Siegfried Jerusalem (more usually heard as Siegfried or Tristan). Created (1869) by Heinrich Vogl.

Lohengrin (Wagner). Lib. by comp.; 3 acts; f.p. Weimar 1850, cond. Franz Liszt.

Antwerp, first half of 10th cent.: König *Heinrich of Saxony is in Brabant recruiting men to help fight the invading Hungarians. He learns that Friedrich von *Telramund has married *Ortrud because he has been refused by the woman he wanted to marry, his ward *Elsa, who he suspects has murdered her young brother *Gottfried so that she alone can inherit her late father's land. Telramund believes he is now the rightful heir to Brabant instead of Elsa. Elsa has dreamed of a knight (*Lohengrin) who will defend her. The herald (*Heerrufer) summons the knight to appear and he arrives in a boat drawn by a swan. He promises to fight on Elsa's behalf and then marry her, on condition that she must never ask his name or whence he came. Lohengrin wins the fight but spares Telramund's life. The herald announces that Lohengrin will rule Brabant and Telramund will be banished. Lohengrin will marry Elsa and lead the men of Brabant into battle. Telramund accuses his wife of lying about Elsa murdering her brother. He determines to prove to her that Lohengrin won the fight by sorcery.

Ortrud, thwarted in her hopes of ruling Brabant with Telramund, suggests to Elsa that her knight could disappear as easily as he came. As Lohengrin and Elsa approach the church, Ortrud and Telramund try to destroy Elsa's belief in her nameless knight. In their bridal chamber, Elsa's doubts increase and she at last asks her husband his name. Telramund bursts in and Lohengrin kills him. Before Heinrich, Lohengrin announces his name and origin and then declares that he must leave. Ortrud, triumphant, admits it was she who made Gottfried disappear by turning him into a swan. Lohengrin prays and the swan pulling his boat changes into Gottfried, the rightful leader of Brabant. Ortrud collapses, Lohengrin leaves, and Elsa sinks into her brother's arms. [NOTE: At the start of Act 3 the chorus sings the famous Wedding March, *Treulich geführt ziehet dahin* ('Husband and wife, enter within').]

Lohengrin (Wagner: *Lohengrin*). Ten. He arrives on the scene as an unknown knight come to defend Elsa—she has been accused by Telramund of killing her young brother. The knight will then marry Elsa, but she must never ask him his name or want to know from where he has come. He does champion her cause and Telramund is banished from Brabant, but after their wedding Elsa can no longer withhold her questions. Lohengrin announces, in front of the King and his knights, that he will tell them who he is and will then bid them all farewell. He tells them he comes from Montsalvat where his father, Parsifal, is king of the Holy Grail and he is its knight. As he finishes speaking, a swan is seen pulling a boat down the river and as Lohengrin says goodbye to Elsa, Ortrud appears in triumph, telling them that the swan is Elsa's brother whom she, Ortrud, changed by magic into the swan. Lohengrin prays, the swan turns back into Gottfried and a dove descends to guide the boat into which Lohengrin steps to be borne away. Arias: *Nun sei bedankt, mein lieber Schwan!* ('Thank you, my beloved swan!'); *Atmest du nicht mir die süssen Düfte?* ('Will you not share the sweet perfumes with me?'); *In fernen Land* ('In a distant land'). Lohengrin is one of Wagner's most lyrical tenor roles, which does not need a *Heldentenor* to do it justice. (Charles Osborne has written that the most moving Lohengrin he has heard was the Australian tenor Ronald Dowd, also a famous Gerontius!) Exponents of the role include Jean de Reszke, Max Lorenz, Lauritz Melchior, Leo Slezak (who, legend has it, one night did not step on to the boat in time, and as it sailed out of sight into the wings, was heard to ask, as if he'd missed the bus, *Wenn geht der nächste Schwann?* ('When does the next swan go?')), Rudolf Schock, Wolfgang Windgassen, Sándor Kónya, Jess Thomas, James King, René Kollo, Gösta Winbergh, Peter Hofmann, Siegfried Jerusalem, Alberto Remedios, and Paul Frey. Created (1850) by Karl Beck.

Lola (Mascagni: *Cavalleria rusticana*). Mez. Wife of Alfio, she resumes an affair with Turiddu. When Alfio finds out, he kills Turiddu in a duel. Created (1890) by Annetta Guli.

Lord Chancellor (Sullivan: *Iolanthe*). Bar. Guardian of Phyllis, whom he wants to marry. He believes his wife, Iolanthe, to be dead, but she reveals herself to him to plead the cause of her son, who also loves Phyllis. Arias: *The law is the true embodiment; When you're lying awake* (Nightmare Song). Created (1882) by George Grossmith.

Lorenzo (Bellini: *I Capuleti e i Montecchi*). Bar. Capulet's doctor. Sympathizing with Giulietta and her Montague lover Romeo, he helps her avoid the wedding planned for her to Tebaldo by giving her a sleeping potion to simulate death. Created (1830) by Rainieri Pocchini Cavalieri.

Lothario (Thomas: *Mignon*). Bass. A wandering minstrel, slightly confused, who is searching for his long-lost daughter. He helps to rescue Mignon from a band of gypsies. In Italy he hears the story of a marquis whose wife died, and realizes that he himself is the Marquis Cipriano and that Mignon is his daughter. His sanity is restored. Created (1866) by Eugène Battaille.

Loudspeaker (Ullmann: *Der Kaiser von Atlantis*). Bass-bar. Introduces the characters and the action. Created (1944) by Karel Berman (who also created Death); (1975) probably by Tom Haenen.

Louise (Charpentier). Lib. by comp.; 4 acts; f.p. Paris 1900, cond. André Messager.

Contemporary Paris: *Louise loves the penniless poet *Julien and his way of life, but is loyal to her loving, workingclass parents. Eventually she leaves them to live with her poet. At a carnival, Louise's *Mother tells her daughter that her *Father is ill and she should return to see him. He recovers, and her parents try to convince Louise she should stay at home with them, but she has seen another way of life and, after a violent row with her parents, leaves to rejoin Julien.

Louise (Charpentier: *Louise*). Sop. The daughter of working-class parents, Louise falls in love with the poor poet Julien and, despite her parents' objections, she leaves to live with him in Montmartre. She meets her mother at a carnival, and learns that her father is seriously ill. She goes home to see him. He recovers and tries to keep Louise at home, but the life in Paris beckons and she returns to Julien. Aria: *Depuis le jour* ('Since the day'—usually sung in Eng. as 'O day of joy'). Created (1900) by Marthe Rioton.

Louis, King 1. (Weber: *Euryanthe*). Bass. Louis VI. Reveals to Euryanthe's fiancé that she has not been unfaithful, as he has been deceived into believing. Created (1823) by Herr Seipelt.

2. (Corigliano: *The Ghosts of Versailles*). Bar. Louis XVI, executed husband of Queen Marie Antoinette. His ghost leads the other court ghosts to watch Beaumarchais's new play. Created (1991) by James Courtney.

Love for Three Oranges, The (Lyubov k trem Apelsinam) (Prokofiev). Lib. by composer; prol. and 4 acts; f.p. Chicago 1921, cond. Sergei Prokofiev.

'Once upon a time': The *King of Clubs' son, the *Prince, suffers from melancholia and will die if he does not laugh. This suits *Leandro, who wants to succeed to the throne together with *Clarice, the King's niece. The witch, Fata *Morgana, is determined to prevent *Chelio, the King's magician, from helping the situation. The first time the Prince laughs is when Fata Morgana falls over. She puts a spell on him—he will travel the world to find three oranges. Accompanied by *Truffaldino, the Prince sets off, blown on his way by the devil *Farfarello. He finds the oranges in a castle, but Chelio warns that the oranges must be opened only near water. While the Prince sleeps, Truffaldino opens two oranges and out step Princess *Linetta and Princess *Nicoletta. Both die from thirst. The Prince wakes to find Truffaldino gone and two dead princesses nearby. He opens the third orange to reveal Princess *Ninetta and they fall in love. She is saved from death by water provided by observers. *Smeraldina (who wants to marry the Prince), turns Ninetta into a rat and takes her place. They return to the palace. On the throne sits a large rat, but Chelio is able to turn her back into the Princess. Fata Morgana and her conspirators all escape as the rest toast the Prince and his Princess.

Lucette (Massenet: *Cendrillon*). *See* CENDRILLON.

Lucia 1. (Britten: *The Rape of Lucretia*). Sop. A maid and companion of Lucretia. Quartet (with Lucretia, Bianca, and the Female Chorus): *Their spinning wheel unwinds*. Created (1946) by Margaret Ritchie.

2. (Donizetti: *Lucia di Lammermoor*). *See* ASHTON, LUCY.

3. (Rossini: *La gazza ladra*). *See* VINGRADITO, LUCIA.

4. (Mascagni: *Cavalleria rusticana*). Cont. Mamma Lucia, mother of Turiddu, who has rejected the pregnant Santuzza. She is torn between love of her son and pity for the girl. Created (1890) by Frederica Casali.

Lucia di Lammermoor (Donizetti). Lib. by Salvatore Cammarano; 3 acts; f.p. Naples 1835.

Scotland, about 1700: Lucia (Lucy *Ashton) is in love with Edgardo (Edgar *Ravenswood), rival of her brother Enrico (Lord Henry *Ashton of Lammermoor). Her nurse Alisa (*Alice) acts as lookout while she meets her lover. Enrico conspires with Normanno (*Norman) to show her a forged letter supposedly proving Edgardo's infidelity and insists she must marry Arturo (Arthur *Bucklaw) to save the family fortune. As the wedding ceremony ends, Edgardo returns and curses her family and Lucia for betraying him. Raimondo (Raymond *Bidebent) informs the guests that Lucia has murdered her new husband. She appears, mad and covered in blood, collapses and dies. Learning of her death, Edgardo stabs himself.

Lucio Silla (Mozart: *Lucio Silla*). *See* SILLA, LUCIO.

Lucretia 1. (Britten: *The Rape of Lucretia*). Cont. Wife of Collatinus, a Roman general. She is the only Roman wife to remain faithful to her husband, living at home with her old nurse, Bianca, and her servant, Lucia. She is raped by Tarquinius. Despite the forgiveness of her husband, she stabs herself to death. Aria: *How cruel men are to teach us love*; trio (with Bianca, Lucia, and the Female Chorus): *Their spinning wheel unwinds*. Created (1946) by Kathleen Ferrier.

2. (Pfitzner: *Palestrina*). Cont. Dead wife of the composer Palestrina, she appears to him as a vision. Created (1917) by Luise Willer.

Lucy 1. (Menotti: *The Telephone*). Sop. Obsessed by the telephone, Lucy frustrates her boyfriend's attempts to propose to her—every time he tries, the 'phone rings and she answers it. Eventually he realizes there is only one way to keep her attention—he goes out to a public call-box and proposes to her by telephone. She accepts—on condition that he always remembers her number and calls her every day. Created (1947) by Marilyn Cotlow.

2. (Gay: *The Beggar's Opera*). *See* LOCKIT, LUCY.

Ludmila 1. (Glinka: *Ruslan and Lyudmila*). *See* LYUDMILA.

2. (Smetana: *The Bartered Bride*). Mez. Wife of Krušina and mother of Mařenka. They want their daughter to marry their landlord Micha's son, in order to clear their debts. Created (1866) by Marie Procházková.

Luigi (Puccini: *Il tabarro*). Ten. A stevedore in the employ of the barge-owner Michele. Luigi is having an affair with Giorgetta, Michele's wife. He decides to leave the barge and return to work on the shore, but Michele persuades him to stay. The signal for Luigi to come to Giorgetta is a lighted match. When Michele lights his pipe, Luigi mistakes this for the signal and comes to see his lover. Michele catches Luigi, forces a confession out of him then throttles him and hides him under his cloak ready to be shown to Giorgetta. Created (1918) by Giulio Crimi.

Luisa Miller (Verdi). Lib. by Salvatore Cammarano; 3 acts; f.p. Naples 1849, cond. Giuseppe Verdi.

Tyrol, early 17th cent.: Luisa *Miller loves 'Carlo', an unknown peasant. Count *Walter's steward *Wurm loves her. *Miller is told by Wurm the true identity of 'Carlo'—he is Rodolfo *Walter, son of Count Walter, who is Miller's enemy. Rodolfo's father, meantime, has planned his son's wedding to his niece Federica, Duchess of *Ostheim. Rodolfo confesses to Federica his true feelings. Walter's bodyguard captures Miller and Luisa and Rodolfo bribes his father to release them, threatening to reveal the truth of Walter's past and of his title—together with Wurm, he murdered his predecessor and inherited his title. Wurm forces Luisa to put into writing that her love for Rodolfo was prompted by ambition, and that she will marry Wurm. She is then blackmailed into repeating all this to Rodolfo under threat of her father's death. She decides her only way out is to kill herself. She writes her last letter to Rodolfo. Her father is released and when he arrives home she and he agree to go into exile. Rodolfo bursts in and he and Luisa drink poison—at least they will be together in another world. Before they die, Luisa embraces her father and Rodolfo kills Wurm.

Luiz (Sullivan: *The Gondoliers*). Ten. Drummer-boy of the Duke and Duchess of Plaza-Toro and in love with their daughter Casilda. He is later revealed as the heir to the throne of the Island of Barataria. Duet (with Casilda): *There was a time*. Created (1889) by Wallace Brownlow.

Luka (Walton: *The Bear*). Bass. Old servant of Mme Popova. He disapproves of her decision to mourn her husband for the rest of her life, as he is aware that her husband was a philanderer and does not warrant such loyalty. He does his best to protect his mistress from unwelcome visitors and tries unsuccessfully to prevent Smirnov troubling her, reproaching the visitor for his boorish behaviour. Created (1967) by Norman Lumsden.

Lulu (Berg). Lib. by composer; prol. and 3 acts; f.p. (incomplete, 2 acts) Zurich 1937, cond. Robert Denzler; f.p. (completed by Friedrich Cerha) Paris 1979, cond. Pierre Boulez.

Germany, late 19th cent.: *Lulu's lover, *Dr Schön, an editor, and his son *Alwa, a composer, watch Lulu having her portrait painted. They leave and the artist tries to seduce Lulu.

Her husband arrives, has a stroke, and dies. The *Painter marries Lulu, his portraits sell well, and they are rich. Her 'father-figure' *Schigolch visits. Schön wants to end his relationship with Lulu and wed his fiancée. He reveals their past to the Painter, who kills himself. In a theatre, Lulu is dancing to Alwa's music. Schön realizes he cannot live without her and he and Lulu marry, but Alwa still protests his love for Lulu. Schön disapproves of the masculine Countess *Geschwitz, who is attracted to Lulu. Jealous of her various relationships, Schön gives Lulu a gun to kill herself, but she uses it to shoot him. Lulu has cholera and is in the prison hospital. With the help of Schigolch and Geschwitz, Alwa arranges her escape and they leave to live together. The stockmarket collapses, they are poor, and Lulu earns money as a prostitute to keep Alwa and Schigolch, who steal from her clients. Her last client is *Jack the Ripper. He murders her and the Countess who comes to her aid.

Lulu (Berg: *Lulu*). Sop. In turn she marries various men—a Painter, an editor (Dr Schön), his son (Alwa). When they lose all their money, she takes to the streets and is murdered by a client, Jack the Ripper. See above for further details. Created (1937) by Nuri Hadzič.

Lummer, Baron (Strauss: *Intermezzo*). Ten. An impoverished young man of good background whom Christine Storch meets when tobogganing while her husband is away. They go to a dance at a local inn and he tells Christine how his family want him to study law and will not support him in other studies which he prefers. She helps him to find suitable lodgings and writes to her husband about her young escort, but Lummer soon becomes fed up with keeping her company, and meets his girlfriend in his new rooms. He hopes Christine will help him financially but she tells him firmly that he must wait for that until her husband returns. When Storch does return, he feigns jealousy of the Baron, but Christine assures him she is now thoroughly bored with the young man and his constant demands for money. Created (1924) by Theo Strack.

Luna, Count di 1. (Verdi: *Il trovatore*). Bar. A nobleman of Aragon, who inherited the title and estate from his father. His younger brother was snatched as a baby by the gypsy Azucena who is thought to have thrown him into the flames of her mother's funeral pyre, but di Luna doesn't believe his brother to be dead. He has fallen in love with the Duchess Leonora, but she seems to favour the troubador Manrico. The two men fight a duel, and although Manrico wins, he does not kill Luna—something seems to stop him making the final thrust. Later, in battle, Manrico is wounded by Luna and nursed by Azucena in the gypsy encampment. Luna vows to kill Azucena, whose rescue is attempted by Manrico. Now Luna imprisons them both. Leonora offers herself to him in return for Manrico's freedom—an offer he gladly accepts—but she takes poison and dies. He proceeds with Manrico's execution, and as Manrico dies Azucena tells him it was her own son she burned—Luna has just executed his brother. Aria: *Il balen del suo sorriso* ('The flash of her smile'—regarded by many as one of the loveliest baritone solos Verdi ever wrote); *Per me, ora fatale* ('For me, the fatal hour'). Created (1853) by Giovanni Guicciardi.

2. (Pfitzner: *Palestrina*). Bar. Ambassador of the King of Spain. Attends the final meeting of the Council of Trent. Created (1917) by Gustav Schützendorf.

Lunobar (Janáček: *The Excursions of Mr Brouček*). Bar. Father of Etherea, his alter egos in Prague being the Sacristan (1888) and Domšík (1420). Created (1920) by Vilém Zítek.

Lurcanio (Handel: *Ariodante*). Ten. Ariodante's brother, in love with Dalinda, lady-in-waiting to Princess Ginevra. Created (1735) by John Beard.

lustige Weiber von Windsor, Die (The Merry Wives of Windsor) (Nicolai). Lib. by Hermann Salomon Rosenthal; 3 acts; f.p. Berlin 1849, cond. Otto Nicolai.

Sir John *Falstaff writes identical love-letters to Frau *Fluth and Frau *Reich. Frau Fluth arranges to meet him, making sure her possessive husband overhears the arrangements. When she meets Falstaff they are interrupted by Frau Reich, warning of Herr *Fluth's approach. Falstaff is hidden in a laundry basket and thrown into the river. He receives another invitation from Frau Fluth. Reich's daughter Anna *Reich is in love with *Fenton, but her father wants her to marry *Spärlich and her mother wants her to marry Dr *Caius. Anna and Fenton elope and her parents then give their blessing. Falstaff asks everyone to forgive his silly behaviour.

lustige Witwe, Die (Lehár). *See* MERRY WIDOW, THE.

Lyonel (Flotow: *Martha*). Ten. A farmer, foster-brother of Plumkett, but in reality heir to the Earl of Derby. He falls in love with Lady Harriet Durham believing her to be a peasant girl, Martha. Aria: *Ach, so fromm, ach so traut* ('None so rare, none so fair'—known better by the Italian title *M'apparì*). Created (1847) by Aloys Ander.

Lysander 1. (Britten: *A Midsummer Night's Dream*). Ten. An Athenian, in love with Hermia, who is also loved by Demetrius. As a result of the magic juice put on his eyes by Puck, Lysander declares his love for Helena, causing a quarrel between the two girls. It is all sorted out in the end and Theseus gives permission for Lysander to marry Hermia. Quartet (with Hermia, Demetrius, and Helena): *Mine own, and not mine own*. Created (1960) by George Maran.

2. (Purcell: *The Fairy Queen*). Spoken. Similar to the role in (1) above. Creator (1692) unknown.

Lysiart (Weber: *Euryanthe*). Bar. Count of Forêt, rival of Adolar and in love with Euryanthe. Conspires with Eglantine to convince Adolar that Euryanthe has been unfaithful to him. When the truth is told, he kills Eglantine. Created (1823) by Anton Forti.

Lyudmila (Glinka: *Ruslan and Lyudmila*). Sop. Daughter of the Grand Prince of Kiev, Svetozar. About to marry Ruslan, she is abducted by an evil dwarf. Ruslan, with the aid of a benevolent magician, Finn, finds her and breaks the spell put upon her. Created (1842) by Mariya Stepanova.

M

Mabel (Sullivan: *The Pirates of Penzance*). Sop. One of Major-General Stanley's daughters. She offers to marry Frederic to save him from the attentions of his elderly former nursemaid. Aria: *Poor wandering one*. Created (NY, 1879) by Blanche Roosevelt.

Macbeth (Verdi). Lib. by Francesco Maria Piave; 4 acts; f.p. Florence 1847, cond. Giuseppe Verdi.

Scotland, about 1040: The *Witches greet *Macbeth as king of Scotland and *Banquo as the father of future kings. Lady *Macbeth feels Macbeth needs her help to fulfil his ambition and make the Witches' prophecy come true. First, King *Duncan must die. His body is found by *Macduff. Duncan's son, *Malcolm, flees to England and Macbeth is declared King. To confound the Witches' prophecy about Banquo's son, Banquo is assassinated, but his son *Fleance escapes. At a banquet in the castle, Macbeth sees Banquo's ghost. Riddled with guilt about the killings, Macbeth is behaving strangely. He visits the Witches who tell him to beware Macduff, to fear no man 'born of woman', and that he will be safe until Birnam Wood starts to move against him. He resolves to get rid of Macduff and his heirs. Macduff learns of the death of his wife and children and Malcolm urges revenge. Within their castle, Lady Macbeth is sleepwalking, talking of the various murders she and her husband have committed. News of her death is given to Macbeth and he is also told that Birnam Wood is 'moving' (it is the troops within the wood who are advancing). On the battlefield, Macduff recounts to Macbeth the story of his birth—how he was 'untimely ripped' from his mother's womb. So the Witches' omens are being fulfilled as Macbeth is killed by Macduff. Malcolm's troops enter Scotland in triumph.

[NOTE: For the Paris première in 1865, Verdi added the obligatory ballet, but he also took the opportunity to make some revisions—after all, nearly twenty years had passed and he had become a more mature composer. He was better able to recognize weaknesses and better equipped to eliminate them and replace them with stronger elements. He added an aria for Lady Macbeth, rewrote various passages, and altered the finale so that Macbeth is not killed on stage. The work was translated into French. This so-called 'Paris' version (but sung in Italian) is the one most often performed today. The f. prof. p. of this opera in England was given at Glyndebourne in 1938.]

Macbeth (Verdi: *Macbeth*). Bar. An army general, married to Lady Macbeth. He is a weak man, dominated by his wife. At his meeting with the Witches at the beginning of the opera, he is told that he will become king of Scotland, but that Banquo, who will never himself be king, will beget future kings of Scotland. Macbeth and his wife decide to eliminate the opposition. Duncan, the present king, having already declared Macbeth thane of Cawdor, is the first to be killed. Macbeth, at his wife's instigation, kills him in his bed but is too unnerved to take the bloody dagger he used back to the body to make it look as if a servant has done the deed. Next, Banquo and his heirs must die. Banquo is assassinated, but his son escapes. Macbeth sees Banquo's ghost sitting at his table. He again consults the Witches and hears their other prophecies about his immunity from death. After his wife sleepwalks and talks of their terrible deeds, he is given news of her death. Riddled with guilt, his behaviour is becoming more and more erratic. As the English army advances, the troops covered in tree branches, Macbeth sees the whole of Birnam Wood apparently 'moving'. He is killed by

Macduff, and Duncan's son, Malcolm, makes a triumphant return to claim the throne. Duet (with Lady Macbeth): *Tutto è finito! Fatal mia donna!* ('It is done! My fateful lady'—the original Lady Macbeth recorded that there were 151 rehearsals of this duet before Verdi was satisfied that the singers had got it right). Created (1847) by Felice Varesi.

Macbeth, Lady (Verdi: *Macbeth*). Sop. Wife of Macbeth. She is a very strong-minded lady, determined to see her husband become king of Scotland and quite prepared to murder anyone standing in his way. It is at her urging that her husband kills the present monarch, King Duncan. When Macbeth is too unnerved to return to the scene of his crime to replace the dagger he used, Lady Macbeth, undaunted, takes it back for him. But, in her famous sleepwalking scene, her servant and doctor overhear her talking of the dreadful crimes the two of them have committed. This is equivalent to the 'mad scene' of Italian opera of the previous generation (Bellini, Donizetti), so beloved by sopranos, as it gave them the chance to show off both their vocal and histrionic capabilities. Arias: *Vieni, t'affretta* ('Hie thee hither'); *La luce langue* ('The weak light thickens'); duet with Macbeth as above. This is a remarkable role for a singing actress, one of the earliest Verdi roles in which the psychological development of the character is matched by the music's development. Created (1847) by Marianna Barbieri-Nini (who received a tremendous ovation after the sleepwalking scene. Verdi went round to her dressing-room, but the two of them were so overcome they were hardly able to speak).

Macduff (Verdi: *Macbeth*). Ten. A Scottish nobleman. The Witches warn Macbeth to beware of Macduff. It is Macduff who, going to wake King Duncan one morning, finds his body after Macbeth has killed him. Macduff's wife and children are further victims of the Macbeths' ambition to rule Scotland. And it is Macduff who, at the end of the opera, kills Macbeth. Aria: *O figli, O figli miei!* ('O children, my children!'). Created (1847) by Angelo Brunacci.

MacGregor, Ellian (Janáček: *The Makropulos Case*). *See* MARTY, EMILIA.

Macheath, Capt. 1. (Gay: *The Beggar's Opera*). Ten. A highwayman. He has secretly married Polly Peachum. When he is arrested and she visits him in gaol she meets Lucy (daughter of the gaoler at Newgate Prison), who was Macheath's first wife. Macheath is sent for trial to the Old Bailey, but is released and he and Polly renew their life together. Created (1728) by Mr Walker.

2. (Weill: *The Threepenny Opera*). Ten. Known as Mack the Knife. The same as in (1). Created (1928) by Harald Paulsen.

Mack, Frau Hilda (Henze: *Elegy for Young Lovers*). Sop. Widow whose bridegroom met his death on the Hammerhorn Mountain 40 years ago. Demented, she still waits for his return. His body is found encased in ice. This seems to free Hilda from her mad world and she decides to leave the Alps. Created (1961) by Eva-Maria Rogner.

Mack the Knife (Weill: *The Threepenny Opera*). *See* MACHEATH, CAPT. (2).

Madama Butterfly (Puccini). Lib. by Giuseppe Giacosa and Luigi Illica; 3 acts; f.p. Milan 1904, cond. Cleofonte Campanini.

Near Nagasaki, early 20th cent.: The American naval officer *Pinkerton is to marry a 15-year-old Japanese bride, the arrangements being made by the marriage-broker *Goro. The American Consul *Sharpless tries to tell him that the bride, Cio-Cio-San (called *Butterfly), regards this as a binding contract and has even converted to Christianity for the wedding. Her uncle, the *Bonze, curses her for betraying her own religion and the rest of the family join in rejecting her. Her maidservant, *Suzuki, prepares her for her wedding-night and Butterfly and Pinkerton are left alone, she declaring her love for him, he enjoying the flattery of his child-bride. However, Pinkerton soon departs for America. Three years pass. Butterfly, sure he will return, has turned down an offer of marriage from *Yamadori. Sharpless comes to visit Butterfly with a message—Pinkerton's ship will soon dock in Nagasaki. With him will be his American wife Kate *Pinkerton, and Sharpless wants to warn Butterfly. He is horrified to find that she has a son (*Sorrow, or Trouble) and he cannot bring himself to tell her the truth. Butterfly and Suzuki make preparations for Pinkerton's return. He comes to the house with Sharpless, Kate waiting outside. Seeing Suzuki's distress, Pinkerton rushes out, unable to face Butterfly. Suzuki and Sharpless explain to her who Kate is, and tell her that Pinkerton wants to take his son back to America. Butterfly agrees—but Pinkerton must come in person to collect the child. He arrives to find that Butterfly has killed herself with her father's ceremonial dagger.

Maddalena 1. (Verdi: *Rigoletto*). Cont. Sister of the professional assassin Sparafucile. She agrees to help him trap the Duke of Mantua but falls in love with him and begs her brother to spare his life. She takes part in the famous quartet: *Bella figlia dell'amore* ('Lovely daughter of love'). Created (1851) by Annetta Casaloni.

2. (Giordano: *Andrea Chénier*). *See* COIGNY, MADDALENA DI.

3. (Donizetti: *Linda di Chamounix*). Sop. Wife of Antonio, a poor farmer, and mother of Linda. Creator (1842) not traced.

Madeleine, Countess (Strauss: *Capriccio*). *See* COUNTESS (2).

Mad Margaret (Sullivan: *Ruddigore*). Mez. In love with Sir Despard Murgatroyd, the presumed 'bad baron of Ruddigore'. When he discovers he has an elder brother, true heir to the title and the curse which goes with it, the shock brings about her recovery. Any future episode of madness can be cured immediately by someone uttering the word 'Basingstoke'. Created (1887) by Jessie Bond.

Magda (Puccini: *La rondine*). *See* CIVRY, MAGDA DE.

Magdalene (Wagner: *Die Meistersinger von Nürnberg*). Mez. Eva's nurse and companion. She hopes to marry David, Sachs's apprentice. In church, she realizes that Eva's attention is wandering to Walther, the handsome young knight. After the service, Magdalene is sent to retrieve Eva's belongings from their pew in order to leave Eva alone with Walther. Magdalene is anxious that people do not suspect a relationship between these two before the song contest, for the prize is Eva's hand in marriage. Magdalene suggests Walther should learn the way to go about winning her. She asks David to teach Walther the rules of the guild to ensure that he is elected a Master.

She later learns from David that Walther has failed the test. She urges Eva to ask Hans Sachs for help. Eva asks Magdalene to stand at the window, dressed in Eva's cloak, so that Beckmesser, who is coming to serenade Eva, will mistake Magdalene for Eva—Magdalene agrees to this ruse, hoping it will also make David jealous. She is unaware that Eva is planning to elope with Walther, leaving Magdalene behind to confuse her father. David's jealousy is duly aroused and he sets about beating-up Beckmesser. Frightened that he will badly injure the town-clerk, Magdalene screams for help. By now the whole town is awake and only the Night-Watchman's arrival restores sanity. Magdalene explains to David what it was all about. At the contest she is clearly delighted when Walther wins. She hopes that now that Sachs has upgraded David from 'apprentice' to 'journeyman', they too will be able to wed. Magdalene has no solo aria, but sings in many ensembles, including the famous third-act quintet with Eva, Walther, Sachs, and David, where her opening line is *Wach' oder träum' ich schon so fruh?* ('Is this a vision or a dream?'). Created (1868) by Sophie Dietz.

Magistrate (Massenet: *Werther*). *See* BAILLI, LE.

Magnifico, Don (Baron of Mountflagon) (Rossini: *La Cenerentola*). Bass. Father of Tisbe and Clorinda and stepfather of Cenerentola, whom he treats like a servant. He hopes to marry one of his daughters to the Prince and is astonished when the Prince falls in love with Cenerentola. Aria: *Miei rampolli femminini* ('My female offspring'). Created (1817) by Andrea Verni.

Mahoney, Jim (Weill: *Aufstieg und Fall der Stadt Mahagonny*). Ten. One of the emigrants from the industrial life who comes to live in the city of Mahagonny, a town devoted to pleasure. He seduces Jenny. He loses all his money when he bets on a boxing-match and the man he supports is killed. Jenny refuses to help him pay his debts and he is sentenced to the electric chair. He advises all his fellow-dwellers to look at their decadent way of life. As he dies, Mahagonny burns down. Created (1930) by Paul Beinert.

Maier, Mieze (Strauss: *Intermezzo*). Although she does not appear on the stage, this young lady is the cause of all the trouble in this opera. She meets both Robert Storch, husband of Christine, and his fellow-conductor Stroh, and confuses the two names. She writes in affectionate terms to Stroh, asking him for tickets for the opera and suggesting they meet in the bar afterwards. By mistake she sends the letter to Storch and in his absence it is opened by his wife. Assuming that Robert is being unfaithful to her, she starts divorce proceedings. Mieze Maier was based on Mieze Mücke, who did confuse Richard Strauss and Josef Stransky (a conductor who eventually succeeded Mahler in New York), thereby precipitating the crisis in the marriage of Pauline and Richard Strauss which became the basis of the libretto for *Intermezzo*.

Major-Domo (**Haushofmeister**, i.e. head of the household staff**). 1.** (Strauss: *Der Rosenkavalier*). Ten. The Marschallin's majordomo, called Struhan. Created (1911) by Anton Erl; Ten. Herr von Faninal's major-domo. Created (1911) by Fritz Soot (who was also the Italian Singer).
2. (Strauss: *Capriccio*). Bass. He directs the servants to clear up after the guests and brings a message from the poet Olivier to the Countess. Created (1942) by Georg Wieter.
3. (Strauss: *Ariadne auf Naxos*). Spoken. The head of the household of one of the richest men in Vienna. He has to announce to the two assembled companies that his master wishes them to perform their diverse entertainments simultaneously in order to begin the firework display exactly on time. This role, being spoken, is often taken by a famous actor, who enjoys the novelty of taking part in an opera. This is not possible in *Der Rosenkavalier* or in *Capriccio*, for in both these operas the major-domos have to sing. Created (1916) by Anton Stoll.

Makropulos Case, The (*Véc Makropulos*) (Janáček). Lib. by comp.; 3 acts; f.p. Brno 1926, cond. František Neumann.
Prague, *c.*1922: Given the elixir of life by her father, Elina Makropulos trained as an opera singer, becoming one of the best of all time— she has lived for over 300 years. She moved about the world, changing her name (but keeping the same initials) to avoid being exposed. In 1922 she returns to Prague as the opera singer Emilia *Marty. A 100-year-old

lawsuit is nearing its climax: Albert *Gregor claims his ancestor was entitled to the estate of Baron Prus, who died in 1827; Jaroslav *Prus and his family disagree. In Dr *Kolenatý's chambers, his clerk *Vítek is consulted by Gregor. Vítek's daughter *Kristina returns from the theatre where she has watched Marty rehearsing. She and her father leave the office as Dr Kolenatý enters with Marty, who questions him about the Gregor–Prus case. She knows that a will exists somewhere in Prus's house, which would settle the estate with Gregor. She tells Gregor about his ancestor's mother, Ellian MacGregor, and promises to provide any evidence they need. At the theatre, Prus's son Janek *Prus meets Kristina. Marty receives old Count *Hauk-Šendorf, who recognizes her as Eugenia Montez, the gypsy girl he loved, who died years ago. Prus later tells her a sealed envelope was found with the will—he will give it to her in exchange for a night together. After the night in a hotel, Prus hears his son has committed suicide and leaves, meeting Gregor, Kolenatý, and the others coming in. While Marty is dressing, they search through her trunk and find papers in the various names she has used. She admits to being Elina Makropulos, 337 years old, collapses and dies. Kristina burns the formula.

Makropulos, Elina (Janáček: *The Makropulos Case*). *See* MARTY, EMILIA.

Malatesta, Dr (Donizetti: *Don Pasquale*). Bar. Physician and friend of Don Pasquale, who consults him about getting married and producing an heir so he can disinherit his nephew Ernesto, who wants to marry Malatesta's niece Norina, of whom Pasquale disapproves. The doctor and Norina conspire to trick Pasquale, Norina posing as Malatesta's 'sister Sofronia' and 'marrying' Pasquale (in a false ceremony conducted by a 'Notary', Malatesta's nephew). Malatesta then helps Pasquale to catch his 'wife' and her 'lover' (Ernesto) together and the doctor convinces Pasquale he should annul his marriage, return to a life of peace and allow the young couple to wed. Aria: *Bella siccome un' angelo* ('Beautiful as an angel'). Created (1843) by Antonio Tamburini.

Malcolm (Verdi: *Macbeth*). Ten. Son of Duncan, the King of Scotland, and therefore the rightful heir to the throne. After his father's murder by Macbeth, Malcolm flees to England, but leads his troops into battle and enters Scotland with his victorious army to claim his throne. Created (1847) by Francesco Rossi.

Maldè, Gualtier (Verdi: *Rigoletto*). False name used by the Duke of Mantua when he introduces himself to Rigoletto's daughter Gilda. Gualtier Maldè is the 'dear name' (*caro nome*) about which Gilda sings her most famous aria.

Male Chorus (Britten: *The Rape of Lucretia*). Ten. A commentator on the action. He and his female counterpart relate the historical background, comment on off-stage and on-stage events, and finally invoke the Christian ethic—Christ is all. Arias: *Tarquinius does not wait*; *When Tarquinius desires*. Created (1946) by Peter Pears.

Málinka (Janáček: *The Excursions of Mr Brouček*). Sop. Daughter of the local Sacristan and fiancée of Brouček's lodger, Mazal. On the moon her *alter ego* is Etherea and in Prague in 1420 it is Kunka. Created (1920) by Emma Miřiovská.

Mallika (Delibes: *Lakmé*). Mez. Slave of Lakmé (daughter of the Brahmin priest). Created (1883) by Mme Frandin.

Maman (Ravel: *L'Enfant et les sortilèges*). *See* MOTHER.

Mamoud (Adams: *The Death of Klinghoffer*). Bass. A teenage Palestinian who guards the Capt. on the hijacked *Achille Lauro*. Created (1991) by Eugene Perry.

Mandryka (Strauss: *Arabella*). Bar. A wealthy Croatian landowner, a big bear of a man whose uncle, also called Mandryka, was Count Waldner's best friend in his regiment many years ago, and it was to him that Waldner sent his daughter Arabella's photograph in the hope that the elderly man would want to marry her and save Waldner from his impecunious state. When the letter arrived in Croatia, the older man was dead and his nephew fell in love with the beautiful girl in the picture. He has come to ask for her hand in marriage. Mandryka explains all this to Waldner, and also tells him how rich he is. He tactfully suggests that maybe Waldner could use some ready cash at the moment—*Teschek, bedien'*

dich! ('Pray help yourself'), he says, offering high-value notes one after the other. Waldner, of course, cannot resist this generosity, and agrees to introduce Mandryka to Arabella. They meet at the annual Cabbies' Ball and there is an immediate mutual attraction. After they declare their love, Arabella says she will spend the rest of the evening bidding farewell to her girlhood, dancing with her old friends, before settling down with Mandryka. Later in the evening, Mandryka overhears her 'brother' Zdenka arranging for a young officer, Matteo, to have the key for Arabella's room that night. Overcome with distress, he provides champagne for all the guests, drinks rather too much himself, and flirts with the cabbies' mascot (the Fiakermilli). He returns to the hotel with Arabella's parents, and accuses Arabella of being unfaithful to him. Zdenka, now revealed as the girl she really is, confesses that it is she who has been responsible for the mix-up and that it was all done for love. Everyone is forgiven and united with the one they love. The family all retire, either to bed, or to play cards. Mandryka remains in the hotel foyer, thankful that everything has worked out satisfactorily. Suddenly, down the stairs comes Arabella, carrying a glass of water to give to him—an old Croatian tradition to signify the end of her girlhood. He drinks from the glass and then destroys it so that no one else can ever drink from the same glass. Thus their love is sealed. Aria: *Der Onkel ist dahin* ('My uncle is no more'); *Ich habe eine Frau gehabt* ('I had a wife'); duet (with Arabella): *Und du wirst mein Gebieter sein* ('And you will be my lord'); *Die Herren und Damen sind einstweilen meine Gäste!* ('The ladies and gentlemen are meanwhile my guests!'); *Sie gibt mir keinen Blick* ('She doesn't look at me'). Created (1933) by Alfred Jerger. Other famous interpreters include Alexander Kipnis, Hans Hotter, George London, Paul Schöffler, Dietrich Fischer-Dieskau, Bernd Weikl, and Wolfgang Brendel. *See also* ARTICLE BY THE EARL OF HAREWOOD, p. 177.

Manon (Massenet). Lib. by Henri Meilhac and Philippe Gille; 5 acts; f.p. Paris 1884, cond. Jules Danbé.

France, 1720: In an inn in Amiens, Guillot de *Morfontaine and de *Brétigny are dining with three 'actresses', *Pousette, *Javotte, and *Rosette. Manon *Lescaut arrives by coach, to

MANDRYKA (*Arabella*—Strauss)

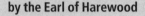

by the Earl of Harewood

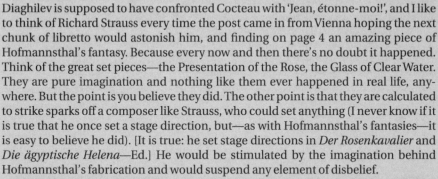

Diaghilev is supposed to have confronted Cocteau with 'Jean, étonne-moi!', and I like to think of Richard Strauss every time the post came in from Vienna hoping the next chunk of libretto would astonish him, and finding on page 4 an amazing piece of Hofmannsthal's fantasy. Because every now and then there's no doubt it happened. Think of the great set pieces—the Presentation of the Rose, the Glass of Clear Water. They are pure imagination and nothing like them ever happened in real life, anywhere. But the point is you believe they did. The other point is that they are calculated to strike sparks off a composer like Strauss, who could set anything (I never know if it is true that he once set a stage direction, but—as with Hofmannsthal's fantasies—it is easy to believe he did). [It is true: he set stage directions in *Der Rosenkavalier* and *Die ägyptische Helena*—Ed.] He would be stimulated by the imagination behind Hofmannsthal's fabrication and would suspend any element of disbelief.

I don't know where the poet 'found' Arabella and her family (originally invented for a projected pre-1914 novel), but that would not have been hard, I imagine, at any time in Vienna. The invention of Mandryka is something quite different. Everyone has an operatic character they believe, had they the voice, they would play with total conviction—Wotan, the Dutchman, Simon Boccanegra, Falstaff. Mandryka would be high on my list.

Waldner's [Arabella's father] trawl of rich comrades from his regimental days is a grubby little device (on his part, not the writer's), but that through it he should catch the *nephew* of his old friend and cause him to fall in love is the kind of notion which deservedly strikes gold. And how Strauss rises to the occasion! He proceeds as soon as he gets into his stride to a musical portrayal of the *coup de foudre*—the overwhelming conviction at the very start of a relationship which insists this is *it!*—described by its protagonist. It's quite unlike anything anywhere else that I know of. The music approaches one climax after another, the orchestra prompts and underlines and acquiesces, and my only worry is whether I should be watching such private revelations at all.

Here is this great backwoodsman (that's what we call them in England if they've inherited wealth and don't come out very often to justify it) falling so totally in love that he is even prepared to pour everything out to someone he's never previously met, simply because he is the father of the unknown beloved! He rushes on, trying to convince with what *he* knows is a completely valid case but is worried another won't recognize. His feelings stream out in an avalanche of excitement as he tries to advance his relatively new circumstances—the vast inheritance from his uncle—and then, in a typical Hofmannsthal twist (accepted with obvious relish by Strauss), twigs that Waldner's cash flow has dried up and would be transformed by a contribution from outside. The moment of comedy passes, as it was always meant to do, and his words before he takes his leave are grave and to the point and touching to listen to. He will wait to hear when it will suit the 'Frau Gräfin' to receive him.

Any listener could be forgiven for thinking this the greatest scene for a male singer in any Strauss opera, greater than anything he had written for Ochs von Lerchenau, its only musical rival to be found, perhaps, in Barak in *Die Frau ohne Schatten*.

The rest of Act 1 is concerned with Arabella and we don't see Mandryka again until the next act, though Arabella makes clear that she has noticed him out of the window. When we do, it is to witness at the Ball the slightly withdrawn greeting Arabella decides is appropriate. Nothing could be simpler, more serious, than his description of the wife who died after only two years of marriage, nothing more ardent than his follow-up, as he starts to understand that Waldner has told Arabella a little more than she was at first prepared to admit. Exuberance gives way to the poetry of the quotation from the *Book of Ruth*, and the engagement is in place, more touchingly and more convincingly perhaps than any other in operatic history.

The essence of Mandryka is contained in the opera's first half. What comes later— bamboozlement by circumstance, jealous fury, whole-hearted repentance—is only a logical follow-up: this is a big-hearted fellow with a countryman's generosity and a countryman's hatred of what he sees as underhand. In his admirable study of Strauss's operas, the townsman William Mann wonders if Arabella could have accepted country life and marriage to what he describes as a farmer (Mandryka would have been pleased: he excuses himself for clumsiness as *ein halber Bauer*—'half a peasant'). He concludes that she would, as she would get compensation for the shallowness of the Viennese life she was giving up.

But what about Mandryka, asks the average even slightly MCP? Somehow, this has always struck me as the prospective operatic marriage to which could be pinned the badge of 'happily ever after' with some confidence—not like the improbable combinations of Turandot and Calaf or Sophie and Octavian, or any of those manipulated, cliché-bound heroes and heroines of baroque operas, beautiful as has been the music which got them into their over-predictable matrimonial situations. Strauss has, I think, provided the answer. If Mandryka's scene with Waldner is unique in opera, his meeting with Arabella, proposal of marriage, and her acceptance constitute something hardly less remarkable: a musically impeccable illustration of the making of an offer which cannot be refused, in this case emotional, on his part a mixture of pent-up excitement and sobriety, on hers of the surrender of a young lady hitherto in control of her feelings. The *coup de foudre* was no *fly-by-night!*

Strauss has something up his sleeve: the use of the Glass of Clear Water as a modern *deus ex machina* (with the staircase music, almost literally), a symbol at the same time of Arabella's forgiveness and her acceptance of the way of life Mandryka has opened for her; this is one of the libretto's finest opportunities. Direction of events has passed from Mandryka to Arabella, and the way he accepts the new turn seems as good an augury for the prospective marriage as anyone, MCP or (reasonably) modern woman, could want.

be met by her cousin *Lescaut. When Chevalier *Des Grieux appears, there is an immediate mutual attraction and Manon agrees to leave with him. They go to Paris, where they are followed by Lescaut and de Brétigny. De Brétigny persuades Manon to go away with him to a life of luxury. Manon overhears Comte *Des Grieux tell de Brétigny that his son is to take holy orders. She slips away and goes to the church where Des Grieux is preaching. Their love is renewed and they run away together. Manon and Des Grieux join Lescaut, Guillot, and their young ladies in a betting parlour. Guillot loses heavily to Des Grieux, then has him and Manon arrested as cheats. Des Grieux is freed, but Manon, declared a prostitute, must be deported. Lescaut and Des Grieux plot her escape. By now she is ill and weak and dies in Des Grieux's arms. *See also* MANON LESCAUT.

Manon (Massenet: *Manon*). *See* LESCAUT, MANON (1).

Manon Lescaut (Puccini). Lib. by Ruggero Leoncavallo, Marco Praga, Domenico Oliva, Giuseppe Giacosa, Luigi Illica (also the comp. and Giulio Ricordi); 4 acts; f.p. Turin 1893, cond. Alessandro Pomé.

France and Amer., 18th cent.: *Des Grieux drinks with *Edmondo and friends. A coach arrives with Geronte di *Ravoir, *Lescaut, and his sister Manon *Lescaut. She is being taken to a convent. Des Grieux and she at once fall in love. Geronte is hoping to take her to Paris, but she and Des Grieux use his carriage to leave together. When Des Grieux has no more money to lavish on her, Manon leaves him and returns to Geronte, although still hankering after the simple life she had with Des Grieux. He searches for and finds her and they plan to leave together, but in her anxiety to collect up her valuable jewels, their departure is delayed and Geronte brings the police to arrest Manon. Lescaut and Des Grieux fail to rescue her from deportation. Des Grieux persuades the captain of the ship to allow him to sail with Manon. They escape into a desert and Manon becomes ill. Des Grieux searches unsuccessfully for water, and Manon dies.

Manon Lescaut (Puccini: *Manon Lescaut*). *See* LESCUAT, MANON (2).

Manrico (Verdi: *Il trovatore*). Ten. The troubador of the title and an officer in the army of the Prince of Biscay. He regards the old gypsy Azucena as his mother. She is reputed to have thrown a baby boy, supposedly the younger son of the old Count di Luna, into her mother's blazing funeral pyre. The old Count is long since dead and his son has inherited his title and estate. Manrico is in love with the Duchess Leonora, lady-in-waiting to the Princess of Aragon, who is also loved by di Luna. Leonora loves the troubador who sings under her window. He and di Luna fight a duel, and although Manrico has the Count at his mercy, he feels unable to make the final thrust—something seems to stop him. Serving in opposing armies, he is later wounded by di Luna, and nursed back to health by Azucena. As Manrico is about to marry Leonora, news reaches him of Azucena's arrest by di Luna. His attempts to rescue her result in his being imprisoned with

her. In return for Manrico's release, Leonora offers herself to di Luna, but to avoid the consequences of his acceptance, she takes poison and dies at Manrico's feet. As di Luna has Manrico executed, Azucena reveals that he was not her real son—that was the baby who was burned in the fire. Di Luna has just killed his own brother. Arias: *Deserto sulla terra* ('Lonely upon the earth'); *Di quella pira l'orrendo foco* ('The hideous fire of that pyre'); duet (with Leonore and chorus): *Miserere—Quel suon, quelle preci solenni* ('The Miserere'—'That sound, those solemn prayers'). There are also lovely duets for Manrico and Azucena and various ensembles in which he sings. *Di quella pira* has become a real showpiece in which tenors who are able to do so hold the famous high C (not in the score as written by Verdi!) until they are red in the face. The role has been sung by most of the great Italianate tenors, from Giovanni Martinelli and Enrico Caruso, through Jussi Björling, Franco Corelli, and Giuseppe de Stefano, to Luciano Pavarotti and Plácido Domingo. Created (1853) by Carlo Baucardé.

Mantua, Duke of (Verdi: *Rigoletto*). Ten. A libertine leaving a trail of discarded young women in his wake. In church he has seen a lovely lady whom he fancies as his next conquest. He does not know she is Gilda, daughter of his court jester, Rigoletto (nobody knows that Rigoletto is a widower with a daughter, and it is generally presumed that the lady is his lover). Disguised as a student, Gualtier Maldè, he manages to slip into Rigoletto's house and make his feelings known to Gilda. When she is abducted by the courtiers and brought to his palace, he seduces her and her father swears revenge. Sparafucile is hired to kill him. Sparafucile's sister Maddalena entices the Duke to a local tavern, where his behaviour is secretly observed by Gilda and her father. Maddalena finds him attractive and her brother agrees not to kill him, on condition that they kill someone else in his place so that their hirer (Rigoletto) can be presented with a body in a sack. This plan is overheard by Gilda, who disguises herself as a man and is mortally wounded when she enters the tavern. As Rigoletto gloats over the sack, his revenge complete, he hears in the distance the Duke's voice singing. Arias: *Questa o quella* ('This one, or that one'); *È il sol* *dell'anima, la vite è amore* ('It is the sun of the soul, life is love'); *La donna è mobile* ('Woman is fickle'); quartet: *Bella figlia dell'amore* ('Fairest daughter of love'). This justly famous quartet is led by the Duke, and he is joined by Maddalena, Rigoletto, and Gilda, each singing of their own thoughts about the scene which is being played out—Maddalena laughing but giving in to the Duke's amorous pleading, the distressed Gilda brought here by her father to observe how the Duke behaves, and Rigoletto bent on vengeance. It has been recorded many times (often coupled with the equally famous sextet from Donizetti's *Lucia di Lammermoor*). The most celebrated disc was made in 1917 with Enrico Caruso, Amelita Galli-Curci, Flora Perini, and Giuseppe de Luca. [NOTE: In the 1832 Victor Hugo play (*Le Roi s'amuse*), on which the libretto is based, the action took place in the French court and the main character was the King but production in this form was forbidden by the censor. In order to have the opera accepted for performance, Verdi and Piave moved the setting and altered the names of the characters, the tenor role becoming the Duke of Mantua.] Created (1851) by Raffaele Mirate.

Mao Tse-tung (Adams: *Nixon in China*). Ten. Chairman Mao of China who, together with his wife (*see* CHING CH'ING), meets Pres. and Mrs Nixon when they visit China. Created (1987) by John Duykers.

Marcel (Meyerbeer: *Les Huguenots*). Bass. A Huguenot soldier, servant of Raoul de Nangis. Created (1836) by Nicolas Levasseur.

Marcellina (Mozart: *Le nozze di Figaro*). Sop. (but more often sung by mez.). Housekeeper to Dr Bartolo. Although twice Figaro's age, she wants to compel him to marry her to repay a loan and in this she is aided by Bartolo who wants to get his own back on Figaro for having helped Almaviva abduct Rosina, Bartolo's ward. She realizes later that Figaro is her long-lost son, of whom Bartolo is the father. Created (1786) by Maria Mandini (whose husband created Count Almaviva).

Marcello 1. (Puccini: *La bohème*). Bar. A painter, who lives with three other bohemians in a garret in the Latin Quarter of Paris. He is working on a painting of the Red Sea. His relationship with Musetta, a grisette, has come to an end after much quarrelling and he knows she is seeing other men. After he and his friends have eaten and drunk their wine to celebrate Christmas Eve, they continue the evening at the popular Café Momus, together with Rodolfo's new-found love Mimì. There Marcello sees Musetta enter with her elderly rich escort. Pointedly trying to ignore each other, it is soon obvious that they are still in love. Musetta sends her escort on a wild goose chase and then joins the bohemians and leaves with them. In February she and Marcello are in a tavern, outside which now hangs his Red Sea painting. Mimì calls him from the inn—she tells him she can no longer stay with Rodolfo, whose jealousy is causing them much anguish. Rodolfo comes from the inn to look for Marcello and sees Mimì. Marcello returns inside and finds Musetta flirting with another man and this starts a furious quarrel. The tender farewells of the one couple merge with the raucous quarrel of the other pair. Back in the attic, Marcello is missing Musetta—once again they have parted and she has taken a wealthy patron. As the four friends cheer themselves up with some horse-play, Musetta arrives: Mimì is downstairs, too ill and weak to climb the stairs. Musetta gives Marcello her earrings to sell to raise money for food and medicine. When they all return, it is too late—Mimì is dead. Quartet (really a double-duet, Marcello and Musetta /Rodolfo and Mimì): *Dunque è proprio finita? / Che facevi?* ('So it's really over?'/'What were you doing?'). There have been many excellent singers of this Italian baritone role, among them Francesco Valentino, Giuseppe Taddei, John Brownlee (who made his Covent Garden début in this role in 1926 on the night of Dame Nellie Melba's farewell, taking over for the last two acts only), Robert Merrill, Rolando Panerai, Ettore Bastianini, Dietrich Fischer-Dieskau (in German), Tito Gobbi, Robert Merrill, Sherrill Milnes, Thomas Allen, and Anthony Michaels-Moore. Created (1896) by Tieste Wilmant (described by Puccini as 'vile' and 'absolutely no good').

2. (Leoncavallo: *La bohème*). Ten. A painter, the leading male role in this version. He is deserted by Musetta, but she later returns to him. Created (1897) by Giovanni Beduschi.

Mařenka (Smetana: *The Bartered Bride*). Sop. Daughter of Krušina and Ludmila. She is in love with Jeník, about whose background she knows nothing. Her parents are anxious for her to marry Vašek, son of their landlord Micha, thus clearing their debts to him. She manages to convince Vašek that this would be unwise. It is later revealed that Jeník is also Micha's son, from his first marriage. Created (1866) by Eleanora Z. Ehrenbergů.

Marfa (Musorgsky: *Khovanshchina*). Mez. An Old Believer, a widow and former lover of Prince Andrei Khovansky. She dies with him as the Tsar's troops approach. Created (1886) by Daria Mikhailovna Leonova; (1911) by Yevgeniya Zbruyeva.

Margherita (Boito: *Mefistofele*). Sop. The girl with whom Faust falls in love. Under the influence of the evil Mefistofele, she is accused of her mother's death and imprisoned. She begs Faust to take her away to some place where they can be happy. When Mefistofele declares this to be impossible, Margherita dies. Created (1868) by Mlle Reboux. *See also* MARGUERITE.

Margret (Berg: *Wozzeck*). Cont. Friend of Wozzeck's mistress Marie. She notices the blood on Wozzeck's hands after he has stabbed Marie to death. Created (1925) by Jessica Koettriss.

Marguerite 1. (Gounod: *Faust*). Sop. Sister of Valentin. She is loved by his friend Siebel. Faust falls in love with her and she bears his child. She is imprisoned for infanticide. Faust, aided by Méphistophélès, gets the key to her cell, but she refuses to leave with them. She prays to the Lord for forgiveness and dies. Aria: *Ah! je ris de me voir* ('Ah! I laugh to see myself')—the *Air de Bijoux* (the Jewel Song). Created (1859) by Marie Caroline Miolan-Carvalho. *See also* MARGHERITA.

2. (Meyerbeer: *Les Huguenots*). *See* VALOIS, MARGUERITE DE.

Maria 1. (Bernstein: *West Side Story*). Sop. Sister of gang-leader Bernado, she falls in love with Tony from a rival gang. Tony mistakenly hears she is dead and allows himself to be killed. Maria intervenes to prevent further bloodshed due to gang rivalry. Arias: *I feel pretty*; *Somewhere*; duets (with Tony): *Tonight*; *One hand, one heart*. Created (1957) by Carol Lawrence.

2. (Gershwin: *Porgy and Bess*). Cont. A shopkeeper on Catfish Row. She discourages Sportin' Life from peddling dope. Created (1935) by Georgette Harvey.

3. (Verdi: *Simon Boccanegra*). *See* GRIMALDI, AMELIA.

4. (Strauss: *Friedenstag*). Wife of the Commandant, whose country is under siege in the Thirty Years War. The people are starving and the army is near to collapse. Her husband is determined to hold out, and is prepared to blow up the Citadel and forfeit their lives rather than surrender. Maria, younger than he and very much in love, tells him how happy he has made her. She refuses to leave him—if he is to die, then so shall she. As bells ring out to signify peace, the enemy army marches to the Citadel, led by the Holsteiner. Her husband presumes they have come to fight and draws his sword, but Maria throws herself between the two men. There has been enough fighting, now is the time for friendship and peace, she tells them, and the two men embrace. Arias: *Wie? Niemand hier?* ('What? No one here?'); *Geliebter, nicht das Schwert!* ('My love, not the sword!'). Created (1938) by Viorica Ursuleac.

'Mariandel' (Strauss: *Der Rosenkavalier*). Name used by Octavian when he disguises himself as a maid, with whom Baron Ochs makes an assignation—which results, as Octavian is a *travesti* role, in a woman playing a man who is now playing a woman, leading to some hilarious situations.

Maria Stuarda (Mary Stuart) (Donizetti). Lib. by Giuseppe Bardari; 2 acts; f.p. Naples 1834 (as *Buondelmonte*, the names and plot changed because the King objected to the opera and f.p. as *Maria Stuarda* in 1835).

England, 1567: *Leicester asks *Elisabetta (Elizabeth I) to grant an interview to her cousin Maria *Stuarda (Mary Stuart), who is imprisoned at Fotheringay. This arouses the Queen's jealousy, as she suspects him of loving Mary. Leicester goes to see Mary and prepare her for the Queen's visit. The confrontation between the two women turns into a slanging match and Elizabeth, encouraged by *Cecil, signs Mary's death warrant. Leicester begs her to be merciful, but she tells him he must witness the execution. *Talbot hears Mary's confession and Leicester watches in despair as Mary, escorted by her companion, Hannah (Anna) *Kennedy, is led to the scaffold.

Maria Stuarda (Donizetti: *Maria Stuarda*). *See* STUARDA, MARIA.

Marie 1. (Donizetti: *La Fille du régiment*). Sop. Abandoned on a battlefield as a child, Marie was adopted as a 'daughter' by the 21st Regiment of Grenadiers. She falls in love with Tonio, who saves her when she nearly falls off a precipice. She is removed from the regiment by the Marquise de Birkenfeld, who claims to be her aunt. In the Marquise's château, Marie finds the ladylike pursuits she is expected to learn boring. Her aunt wants her to marry the Duchesse de Krakenthorp's son. The regiment arrives at the château, and the Marquise sees how much Tonio and Marie love each other. She then admits that Marie is her own illegitimate daughter and gives her consent to their marriage. Arias: *Au bruit de la guerre j'ai reçu le jour* ('I first saw the light in the camp'); *Chacun le sait, chacun le dit* ('Each man knows it, each man says it'). Created (1840) by Juliette Bourgeois.
2. (Berg: *Wozzeck*). Sop. Mother of Wozzeck's son. She is attracted by the Drum-major, making Wozzeck jealous. He kills her, throwing the knife he stabbed her with into a pond. Created (1925) by Sigrid Johanson.
3. (Marie/Marietta) (Korngold: *Die tote Stadt*). Sop. Marie is the dead wife of Paul. She resembles the dancer Marietta, whom he has met and taken home. Marietta is determined to meet the challenge of the dead wife and in a vision helps him exorcise Marie's ghost. Created (1920) by Anny Munchow (Hamburg) and Johanna Klemperer (Cologne, wife of Otto Klemperer, who conducted).
4. (Zimmermann: *Die Soldaten*). See WESENER, MARIE.
5. (Poulenc: *Les Dialogues des Carmélites*). Mez. Mother Marie of the Incarnation. Assistant Prioress, to whom Mme de Croisy entrusts the care of Blanche. Created (1957) by Gigliola Frazzoni.

Marie Antoinette, Queen (Corigliano: *The Ghosts of Versailles*). Sop. The executed wife of King Louis XVI. The ghost of the poet Beaumarchais is in love with her and is determined he can, through art, alter the course of history so that she does not go to the guillotine. Gradually, as she watches his new play, in which all the characters from his previous Figaro plays are recalled, she loses her bitterness about her fate and comes to love the author. Although she finally is retried and again

executed, she can now accept her fate and be happy united with Beaumarchais in Paradise. Created (1991) by Teresa Stratas.

Marietta (Korngold: *Die tote Stadt*). *See* MARIE (3).

Marina (Musorgsky: *Boris Godunov*). Mez./sop. A Polish Princess, who falls in love with the 'false Dimitri'. She appears only in the revised version of the opera, when the 'Polish act' was added. Created (1874) by Yuliya Platonova.

Mark 1. (Wagner: *Tristan und Isolde*). Bass. King Mark (König Marke) of Cornwall, uncle of Tristan who is expected to inherit the throne from Mark. He comes to meet the ship carrying Isolde, escorted by Tristan, from Ireland to marry the King. Mark is unaware that Isolde and Tristan have fallen in love. Melot, supposedly Tristan's friend, in the hope of currying favour, tells the King about Isolde and Tristan's love. Mark is very upset by Tristan's betrayal, for it was Tristan who suggested in the first place that she would be a suitable bride for him. What the King does not know is that Tristan and Isolde were given a love potion by Brangäne, and it is this elixir which is responsible for them declaring their feelings for each other. Mark now becomes compassionate, ready to bless the young lovers, but Tristan, feeling guilty at letting down his uncle, deliberately falls on Melot's sword and is fatally wounded. When Mark arrives to forgive him, Tristan is dead, and Mark's distress is overwhelming. Aria: *Tatest du's wirklich?* ('Have you indeed?'). This is a long aria, lasting almost eight minutes and demands much from the singer. Famous King Marks include Edouard de Reszke, Alexander Kipnis, Josef von Manowarda, Richard Mayr, Ludwig Weber, Josef Greindl, Hans Hotter (although better known as Kurwenal), Paul Plishka, Martti Talvela, Kurt Moll, Matti Salminen, Gwynne Howell, John Tomlinson, and Rene Pape. Created (1865) by Ludwig Zottmayer.
2. (Tippett: *The Midsummer Marriage*). Ten. A young man, an orphan, nothing about his parents being known. He is about to be married to Jenifer when she leaves to search for spiritual awareness and to 'find herself'. He undertakes a similar 'journey', and when they are reunited each is more prepared to accept

the other for what they are. Created (1955) by Richard Lewis.

3. (Smyth: *The Wreckers*). Ten. Lover of Thirza, previously of Avis. Together with Thirza, he warns ships not to come and be wrecked on the coast. As punishment, the lovers are walled up in a cave and left to die in the rising tide. Created (1906) by Jacques Urlus.

Marriage of Figaro, The (Mozart). *See* NOZZE DI FIGARO, LE.

Marschallin, The (Marie Therese, Princess von Werdenberg) (Strauss: *Der Rosenkavalier*). Sop. Wife of the Feldmarschal. She is 32 years old and already regards herself as middle-aged. While her husband is away she is having a passionate affair with 17-year-old Octavian. As they have breakfast, her cousin Baron Ochs arrives. Octavian disguises himself as a maid (Mariandel). The Marschallin recommends Octavian as the bearer of the silver rose to Ochs's new 15-year-old fiancée. It is time for the Marschallin's levee (a morning assembly held regularly by princesses) and her boudoir fills with tradesmen, animal sellers, an Italian Singer who serenades her, her hairdresser, and others. She becomes angry with her hairdresser—he has made her look too old. They all leave and she meditates on the passing years—soon she will be the old princess. When Octavian returns (Quinquin, she calls him) she is in melancholy mood. She knows that one day he will desert her for someone younger—time inexorably passes and sometimes she gets up in the night and stops the clocks. Octavian leaves—without the silver rose, and the Marschallin sends her little black servant Mohammed after him. The Marschallin next appears in Act 3. Summoned by one of Ochs's servants, she arrives at the inn where Ochs is now in trouble, trying to explain to everyone who he is and what his relationship is to 'Mariandel', whom he has tried to seduce. The Marschallin advises him to leave with some semblance of dignity. She acknowledges that she has lost Octavian, Octavian tries to say farewell to her, at the same time having eyes only for Sophie, and Sophie herself is overawed by the whole turn of events. The Marschallin departs, offering a seat in her coach to Faninal, Sophie's father. Arias: *Da geht er hin.* ('There he goes'); *Die Zeit, die ist ein sonderbar' Ding* ('Time is a strange thing'); duet (with Octavian): *Heut' oder Morgen* ('Today or tomorrow'); trio (with Octavian and Sophie): *Marie Theres'!...Hab' mir's gelobt* ('Marie Therese!' ... 'I vowed to myself').

Although the Marschallin appears only in Act 1 and the final part of Act 3, she has remained a favourite role for all great Strauss sopranos, who love the dignity of the character and the soaring vocal lines. Some would regard it as the most celebrated Strauss soprano role in his most celebrated opera. Famous singers of the Marschallin include Lotte Lehmann, Meta Seinemeyer, Viorica Ursuleac, Hilde Konetzni (who took over the role from an indisposed Lotte Lehmann halfway through a performance at Covent Garden in 1938), Frieda Hempel, Anny Konetzni, Maria Reining, Régine Crespin, Christa Ludwig, Lisa Della Casa, Elisabeth Schwarzkopf, Helga Dernesch, Montserrat Caballé, Lucia Popp, Kiri te Kanawa, Felicity Lott, Joan Rodgers, and Renée Fleming. Created (1911) by Margarethe Siems (who a year later created the totally contrasting role of Zerbinetta in *Ariadne auf Naxos*).

Marta 1. (d'Albert: *Tiefland*). Sop. Mistress of landowner Sebastian who, to leave him free to find a rich wife, makes her marry the shepherd Pedro, whom she grows to love. Creator (1903) not traced.

2. (Boito: *Mefistofele*). Cont. A friend of Margherita, with whom Mefistofele flirts. Created (1868) by Mlle Flory.

Martha (Flotow). Lib. by W. Friedrich (Friedrich Wilhelm Riese); 4 acts; f.p. Vienna 1847.

Richmond, about 1710: Bored by the attention of her elderly cousin Lord Tristan *Mickleford, Lady Harriet Durham, maid of honour to Queen Anne, and her maid *Nancy go to Richmond Fair disguised, respectively, as *Martha and Julia. They are given employment by two young farmers, *Plumkett and his foster-brother *Lyonel, but soon find farmhouse work more than they had bargained for. The men fall in love with them but Tristan 'rescues' the ladies during the night. By now 'Martha' acknowledges that she loves Lyonel. The latter sees her out hunting and realizes she is of the aristocracy. Lyonel is in reality of noble birth—he was left with Plumkett's mother as a baby when his father was a fugitive. Lady Harriet, in order to win him back, sets up a mock fair and here the two are reunited, as are Plumkett and Nancy.

Martha 1. (Flotow: *Martha*). Sop. Lady Harriet Durham, Maid of Honour to Queen Anne. To escape the unwelcome attention of her elderly cousin, she and her maid go to Richmond Fair disguised as Martha and Julia. See above for further details. Aria: *Letzte Rose, wie magst du so* ('The last rose of summer'). Created (1847) by Anna Zerr.

2. (Gounod: *Faust*). *See* SCHWERLEIN, MARTHE.

Marty, Emilia (Janáček: *The Makropulos Case*). Sop. An operatic soprano, originally Elina Makropulos, now 337 years old as a result of being given the elixir of life invented by her father, Hieronymous Makropulos, court physician to the Habsburg Emperor Rudolf II, in 1565. If she does not have a further dose, she will soon die. She has travelled the world, changing her name each generation to avoid being exposed. As Ellian MacGregor, a Scottish singer in the early 19th cent., she had an affair in Prague with a Baron Prus and in 1817 had a son, Ferdinand. The late Baron's estate went to his cousin, but then a Ferdinand Gregor appeared and claimed the right to it. The lawsuit has continued for 100 years. As Eugenia Montez, a gypsy girl and her next generation persona, she had a long affair with Count Hauk-Šendorf. Now, in 1922, she is the opera singer Emilia Marty. She is tired of living and world-weary. She is concerned only with memories and her fear of death. She tells the lawyer Kolenatý that she knows of a will hidden in Prus's house which will prove Gregor's claims and tells Gregor of his ancestor's Scottish mother and of the existence of the child who was Prus's illegitimate son. In her theatre dressing-room, she welcomes the batty old Count Hauk-Šendorf, much to everyone else's amazement—she seems to know him. The will is found (exactly where she tells them to look), and with it a second envelope (which she knows to contain the formula for the elixir). She spends the night with Prus in exchange for the envelope and its contents. When she leaves the room to dress, Kolenatý, Gregor, and the rest search through her trunk, and find in it documents in the various names she has used. As she recounts the whole story to them all, she gradually ages until, as an old woman, she

gives the formula to the youngest person present, Kristina (daughter of Kolenatý's clerk), who burns it as Emilia Marty dies.

This role is a great opportunity for a singing actress, covering the whole range of emotions—for most of the opera she seems to be cold and calculating—except in the episode with old Hauk—but as the truth emerges and she feels that death would be a welcome relief, she becomes much softer in her manner. Janáček in his letters repeatedly referred to her as 'the cold one' or 'the icy one' and at times hinted that she resembled Kamila Stösslová, the young married woman who was his muse in the last years of his life. In a famous production by Sadler's Wells first seen in 1964, which put the opera on the map in England, Marie Collier played Emilia Marty and did appear to age before the audience's eyes in the last act. It was a remarkable performance. Other successful exponents of the role include Libuše Prylová, Elisabeth Söderström, Hildegard Behrens, Anja Silja, and Kristine Ciesinski. Created (1926) by Alexandra Čvanová.

Mary 1. (Vaughan Williams: *Hugh the Drover*). Sop. Daughter of the Constable who wants her to marry the wealthy butcher, John. She falls in love with Hugh who fights John for her hand. Hugh is put in the stocks as a spy and Mary joins him there until they are both released to start their life together on the open road. Arias: *In the night-time; Gaily I go to die; Here, queen uncrown'd*. Created (1924) by Muriel Nixon.

2. (Wagner: *Der fliegende Holländer*). Cont. Senta's old nurse. Aria (with chorus): *Du böses Kind* ('You idle girl!'). Created (1843) by Thérèse Wächter-Wittman (the wife of Michael Wächter, creator of the title-role).

3. (Zimmermann: *Die Soldaten*). Bar. Maj. Mary, in the French Army, is one of Marie's numerous seducers. Created (1965) by Camillo Meghor.

Marzelline (Beethoven: *Fidelio*). Sop. Daughter of the gaoler Rocco. She is loved by Jaquino, but becomes attracted by the 'young man' Fidelio (Leonore in disguise), her father's assistant. Aria: *O wär ich schon mit dir vereint* ('Oh, if only I were already joined to you'). Created (1805) by Louise Müller.

Masetto (Mozart: *Don Giovanni*). Bass. Betrothed to Zerlina who, before their wedding day, is tempted by Don Giovanni. Masetto is beaten up by Giovanni and comforted by the contrite Zerlina. Aria: *Ho capito, signor, sì!* ('I understood, yes sir!'). Created (1787) by Giuseppe Lolli (who also created the Commendatore, the two roles frequently being doubled).

Mask of Orpheus, The (Birtwistle). Lib. by Peter Zinovieff; 3 acts; f.p. London 1986, cond. Elgar Howarth and Paul Daniel.

Legendary times: *Apollo (an electronic voice), present at the birth of *Orpheus, gives him gifts of speech, poetry, and music. Orpheus falls in love with *Euridice. She dies, observed by *Aristaeus, and becomes a Myth. Orpheus asks the *Oracle of the Dead how he can search for her in the Underworld. He travels through seventeen arches on his way to the Underworld, each symbolic, and meets *Hades, his wife Persephone, and Hecate, the Goddess of Witches (incarnations of Orpheus, Euridice, and the Oracle). *Charon takes him across the Styx. As he returns from the Underworld, only Persephone/*Euridice Myth follows him. Knowing he will never find her, he hangs himself. (All this takes place as a dream from which Orpheus wakens.) Time flows backwards, thus showing again Orpheus' return from Hades, his descent to it, and Euridice's death. The tide turns and his journey out of the Underworld is followed by Aristaeus' punishment by bees. Orpheus Hero is killed by a thunderbolt from Zeus and his Myth is dismembered by Dionysiac women. Time moves into the future, Orpheus' head floats down the river and *Orpheus Myth is silenced by Apollo, his spiritual father.

Masks, The Three (Puccini: *Turandot*). *See* PING, PANG, and PONG.

Mathilde, Princess (Rossini: *Guillaume Tell*). Sop. Princess of the House of Habsburg, sister of Gessler, the detested governor. She is loved by the Swiss Arnold and remains loyal to him even when he plans to kill her brother. Created (1829) by Laure Cinti-Damoreau.

Mathis (Hindemith: *Mathis der Maler*). Bar. Based on the painter Matthias Grünewald (*c.*1470–1528), whose masterpiece is the Isenheim altarpiece. In a monastery, Mathis is painting a fresco. He asks himself whether he can truly serve God best through his art.

He joins the peasants in their revolt, having helped their leader to escape the Confederate Army. The Cardinal allows him to go free. He soon becomes disillusioned with the cause he has joined and the methods used by the peasants to achieve their goal. In a vision, St Paul, whose features resemble the Cardinal, suggests to him that he would serve God better through his art. Created (1938) by Asger Stig. *See also* ARTICLE BY PETER SELLARS, p. 186.

Mathis der Maler (*Mathis the Painter*) (Hindemith). Lib. by comp.; 7 scenes; f.p. Zurich 1938, cond. Robert Denzler.

Germany, 16th cent.: *Mathis wonders if he is really, through his art, fulfilling God's will. Hans *Schwalb, leader of the peasants, rushes in with his daughter Regina *Schwalb, pursued by von *Schaumberg, leader of the Confederate Army. Mathis gives them his horse to allow them to escape. Cardinal *Brandenburg, Archbishop of Mainz, listens to the arguments of the Catholics and the Protestants. Mathis arrives and sees Ursula (the daughter of *Riedinger) whom he loves. The Cardinal's adviser, *Capito, suggests it would be an advantage to the state if Ursula should marry the Cardinal. She declares openly her love for Mathis, but he has decided to give up love and art and join the peasants in their revolt. The peasants are defeated in battle and Schwalb is killed. The Cardinal, impressed by Ursula's willingness to marry him for the sake of her faith, blesses her but decides to withdraw from the world. He allows the Lutherans to worship openly. Mathis, left alone with the grieving Regina, considers the futility of his life. In a vision St Paul tells him that the best way he can serve God is through his art.

matrimonio segreto, Il (*The Secret Marriage*) (Cimarosa). Lib. by Giovanni Bertati; 2 acts; f.p. Vienna 1792.

Bologna, 18th cent.: *Geronimo, a widowed wealthy merchant whose house is run by his sister *Fidalma, wants to marry off his daughter *Elisetta to the English nobleman Count *Robinson. The Count falls for the other daughter, *Carolina, already secretly married to Geronimo's clerk, *Paolino, who is loved by Fidalma. There is much misunderstanding and Geronimo, very deaf and confused, agrees

MATTHIAS GRÜNEWALD (*Mathis der Maler*—Hindemith)

by Peter Sellars

The 16th-century painter Matthias Grünewald [?1470–1528] is one of the most inspiring and mysterious figures in the history of art. His well-known masterpiece is the Isenheim Altarpiece in Colmar, France, a multi-panelled, layered, visionary creation, evoking the agony of the Crucifixion with terrifying intensity, and the miracles of annunciation, birth, and resurrection with equal tenderness, wonder, and shock. The extreme distended forms of his human subjects in states of ecstasy or suffering, combined with a magical, iridescent use of colour which radiates spiritual force, made him a seminal figure for the German Expressionist painters in the teens and twenties of this century.

Paul Hindemith was one of the leaders of Germany's *avant-garde* in those wild years, collaborating with painters and poets who were bringing a new era of revolutionary struggle into being. This all changed in the thirties. When the Nazis came to power in 1933 Hindemith was one of the few major creative artists who stayed. He somehow felt that his presence and message could help set his country right again, and so, between 1933 and 1935, labouring under virtual house arrest with a ban on public performances of his music and all mention of his name in the press, he wrote *Mathis der Maler* [*Mathis the Painter*]. Like Boris Pasternak writing Dr Zhivago for Stalin, Hindemith's new work was at one level a repudiation of his modernist past, and at another an heroic attempt to communicate with the one man who held the fate of a nation and perhaps the world in his hands. Intended as the next great German opera after *Parsifal* and consciously sourcing the history of German music back to its glory days in the Middle Ages, Hindemith employed a musical palette that would not offend Hitler. Like an alternative *Meistersinger*, the opera concerned the place of an artist in society. Of course it was autobiographical.

Next to nothing is known of the historical Mathis Gothardt Neithardt—even the name Grünewald is a 17th-century fiction. In contrast to his celebrated contemporary Albrecht Dürer [1471–1528], whose every prolific movement was chronicled and debated, very few of Mathis's works exist, and there are very few traces of a professional life. It is almost as if he wanted to vanish. We do know that he served for ten years as court painter to Cardinal Albrecht von Brandenburg in Mainz, and that he left this office in 1526, apparently in solidarity with the Peasant Revolt of 1525. He died two years later.

In what is possibly the richest and most satisfying libretto ever written by a composer, Hindemith plunges this tormented figure into the midst of riots in the streets (Tableau 2), public book burnings (Tableau 3), crying economic and social injustice, and mass extermination (Tableau 4). He rescues the child of a revolutionary leader from the holocaust, and learns to take responsibility for her. Her angelic presence leads him to hear the music of the spheres and to confront his most painful demons. He paints his Isenheim masterpiece and, as the child dies in his arms, he renounces painting. He will learn not to love the world, but a woman, Ursula, who has followed him across his life. And life is more important than art.

In the opera's opening scene, Mathis is finishing a mural on the wall of a shelter for homeless people as the wounded leader of the resistance runs in looking for refuge with the police in hot pursuit. This courageous fighter taunts Mathis: 'You paint what no one wants to look at, what no one wants to see. Have you fulfilled the task God gave you?' What artist does not ask that question day after day? There are days when that question is unbearable; when one asks is anything we're doing enough or adequate? Who wants it? Who needs it? Whom do we serve?

Recent research has suggested that the altarpiece at Colmar was intended to be viewed in a performative context, as a series of successive revelations, as the panels were opened across time to the accompaniment of words and music. The altarpiece was created for a chapel attached to a hospice which specialized in incurable diseases. The real Mathis's work epitomized art that is not a consumer product, a fashion statement, a leisure activity, an apology for the rich, or an obsequious gesture to human authority. It is art that is meant to heal people.

We are trying to touch the divine. Obviously, in this world the politicians have to put a spin on things, even when they themselves know better. Only artists have this margin where they can face up to things, hopefully honestly. You just want to get past the political polarities of Left or Right and say: 'Could we just make space for the human somewhere here?' The idea of an appeal for humanism in the midst of strife is this opera's most beautiful quality and it's Mathis who expresses it.

to the Count's marriage to Carolina, leaving a distraught Paolino turning to Fidalma for help. The young married couple decide to run away together and the Count agrees to marry Elisetta.

Matteo (Strauss: *Arabella*). Ten. A young officer in love with Arabella. She has no time for or patience with him. In an effort to be nearer to her, he befriends her 'brother' Zdenko (in reality her sister, Zdenka) who is herself secretly in love with Matteo. Matteo receives love-letters purporting to come from Arabella and believes that she returns his love (they are in fact written by Zdenka) and this is confirmed when Zdenko gives him a key to Arabella's room so that he can meet her that night. Unknown to Matteo, the lady he meets in the darkened bedroom is Zdenka. As he leaves her room and comes down the stairs in the hotel, whom does he meet just coming into the hotel but Arabella who, of course, denies having just been with him in her bedroom. Total confusion reigns until Zdenka, in her nightdress and every bit a young woman, runs downstairs to confess what she has done. Matteo realizes that this is the young lady he really loves and her parents give them their blessing. The role has been sung by Anton Dermota, Horst Taubmann, Adolf Dallapozza, Georg Paskuda, and René Kollo. Created (1933) by Martin Kremer.

Maurer, Joseph (Henze: *Elegy for Young Lovers*). Spoken role. Mountain guide who announces the discovery of the body of the long-dead Herr Mack. Created (1961) by Hubert Hilten.

Maurizio (Cilea: *Adriana Lecouvreur*). Ten. Duke of Saxony, pretender to the throne of Poland. His lover is the Princesse de Bouillon, but the actress Adriana Lecouvreur is in love with him. He uses Adriana to save the princess being found by her husband in a compromising situation and inadvertently causes the actress's death. Created (1902) by Enrico Caruso.

Maurya (Vaughan Williams: *Riders to the Sea*). Cont. An old woman who has lost her husband and four sons to the sea. Her one remaining son, Bartley, insists on crossing the sea to take horses to Galway Fair. She sees a vision of him and his brother Michael, both riding horses, and realizes this means Bartley, too, will die. When he is drowned, it is almost a relief—now the sea can hurt her no more. Aria: *They are all gone now*. Created (1937) by Olive Hall.

Max 1. (Weber: *Der Freischütz*) Ten. A forester, in love with Agathe. Ashamed of his defeat in a shooting contest, he accepts magic bullets from Caspar to win the next test. Caspar plans to sacrifice him to the wild huntsman, Samiel, but Samiel guides the bullet and it fatally wounds Caspar. Created (1821) by Carl Stümer.

2. (Krenek: *Jonny spielt auf*). Ten. A composer. He writes a new opera for his beloved Anita, who is having an affair with Daniello, a violinist. But she and Max are reunited and set off for a new life in America. Created (1927) by Paul Beinert.

Maximus, The Pontifex (Spontini: *La vestale*). Bass. Condemns Giulia to death for allowing the sacred flame to go out. Created (1807) by Henri-Étienne Dérivis.

Maybud, Rose (Sullivan: *Ruddigore*). Sop. A village maiden, loved by Robin, who is in reality Sir Ruthven Murgatroyd, heir to the baronetcy and its accompanying curse. When he extracts himself from this situation, she agrees to marry him. Aria: *If somebody there chanced to be*; duet (with Robin): *I know a youth*. Created (1887) by Leonora Braham.

Maynard, Elsie (Sullivan: *The Yeomen of the Guard*). Sop. A strolling player, partner of Jack Point. She agrees to marry, while blindfolded, a condemned prisoner, to provide him with an heir, for which she will be well paid. However, he escapes and poses as Sergeant Meryll's son, Leonard, with whom Elsie falls in love! Much to her relief she discovers that Leonard and her unseen husband are one and the same. Aria: '*Tis done! I am a bride*. Created (1888) by Geraldine Ulmar.

Mazal (Janáček: *The Excursions of Mr Brouček*). Ten. A painter. Mr Brouček's tenant in Prague, he is engaged to Málinka. His alter-ego on the Moon is Blankytný and in 15th-cent. Prague it is Petřík. Created (1920) by Miloslav Jeník.

McLean, Little Bat (Floyd: *Susannah*). Ten. Son of one of the village Elders and his sharp-tongued wife, Little Bat hero-worships Susannah. When she is accused of sinful behaviour, he tells her that his parents are forcing him to accuse her of seducing him. Created (1955) by Eb Thomas.

Médée (Cherubini). Lib. by François Benoît Hoffman; 3 acts; f.p. Paris 1797.

Corinth, mythological times: *Dircé (Glauce), daughter of *Créon, is about to marry *Jason. *Médée (Medea), the sorceress, had helped Jason win the Golden Fleece. She had two children by him, and he then abandoned her. She appears at his wedding, swearing vengeance. Ordered by Créon to leave the city, she pleads for one more day to spend with her children (whom she plans to murder). She sends her servant, *Néris, to deliver two presents to Dircé—a cloak and a magic diadem which Apollo gave her. Néris brings the children to see their mother. From the palace come sounds of distress—Dircé has been poisoned by Médée's gifts. As the crowds seek vengeance, Médée kills her children, causes Jason's death, and herself dies in the flames which consume the temple.

Médée (Medea) (Cherubini: *Médée*). Sop. A sorceress. She killed her brother and betrayed her father and the people of Colchis in order to help her lover, Jason, win the Golden Fleece. Having borne him two children, Jason then deserted her and is about to marry Dircé. Médée sends presents to Dircé—they are poisoned and Dircé dies. As the crowds swear to avenge her, Médée, to get her own back on Jason, kills her sons and dies in the flames as the temple burns. Created (1797) by Julie-Angélique Scio (whose husband, Etienne Scio, a composer, played in the second violins at the première).

Medium, The (Menotti). Lib. by comp.; 2 acts; f.p. New York 1946, cond. Otto Leuning.

USA, 'present day' (1940s): Mme *Flora (Baba) is helped by her daughter *Monica and her dumb servant boy *Toby to prepare the room for a séance. Two regulars arrive, Mr and Mrs *Gobineau. The widowed Mrs *Nolan, making her first visit, is convinced she recognizes her daughter during the séance (it is Monica). Suddenly the medium becomes hysterical—someone has clutched at her throat with an ice-cold hand and she is very frightened. She accuses Toby. Being mute, he is unable to deny it and she beats him. She tries to convince all her clients they have been cheated, but they will not believe her. Toby hides behind a curtain. Unable to reply when she calls, she thinks he is a ghost and shoots him.

Medora (Handel: *Orlando*). Alto. An African prince in love with Angelica who had previously been the love of Orlando. Medoro is loved by the shepherdess Dorinda. Created (1733) by Francesca Bertolli.

Mefistofele (Boito). Lib. by comp.; prol., 4 acts and epil.; f.p. Milan 1868, cond. Eugenio Terziani.

Heaven, Germany, and Greece, Middle Ages: *Mefistofele (the Devil) claims he can win the soul of *Faust. Faust and his disciple *Wagner meet Mefistofele who makes a bargain—Faust's soul in exchange for one moment of pure happiness. Faust woos *Margherita and Mefistofele flirts with her friend *Marta. He takes Faust to view the orgies of Walpurgis Night (the Witches' Sabbath). Faust has given Margherita a sleeping-draught to give to her mother, who dies. Margherita is imprisoned and Faust comes to visit her, accompanied by Mefistofele. She begs Faust to take her where they can be happy, but Mefistofele points out that this can never be and Margherita dies. Mefistofele takes Faust to the Greece of classical times where he woos Elena (*Helen of Troy). In the epilogue, Faust awaits death. He begs God's forgiveness and redemption and resists Mefistofele's evil influence.

Mefistofele (Boito: *Mefistofele*). Bass. The devil, he makes a pact with Faust—he will have Faust's soul in exchange for one moment of pure happiness. He takes Faust to see a vision of the Walpurgis Night orgies. He uses his evil influence to bring about the death of Faust's beloved Margherita. But Faust escapes him in the end, begging God's forgiveness and redemption before he dies. Created (1868) by François Marcel Junca. *See also* MEPHISTOPHELES (1).

Meistersinger, Die (The Mastersingers) (Wagner: *Die Meistersinger von Nürnberg*). A guild which existed in Germany and was at its most active in Nuremberg in the 16th cent. Their art of song-writing had very strict rules of structure and presentation.

Meistersinger von Nürnberg, Die (The Mastersingers of Nuremberg) (Wagner). Lib. by Wagner; 3 acts; f.p. Munich 1868, cond. Hans von Bülow (excerpts had been given in concert performances, 1862–8).

Nuremberg, mid-16th cent.: A knight, Walther von *Stolzing, has fallen in love with Eva *Pogner, daughter of Veit *Pogner. A singing competition is to take place and Pogner has promised the winner Eva's hand in marriage. Only Mastersingers can enter and when Eva and her nurse/companion *Magdalene tell Walther this, he determines to join the guild. Magdalene's boyfriend, *David, agrees to teach Walther the rules of the guild. At his initiation ceremony, he has to sing a song which must follow certain rules. As he sings, he is marked by Sixtus *Beckmesser, who is also in love with Eva. Only the cobbler Hans *Sachs is impressed by the young knight and prepared to admit him to the guild, the others insisting that he has failed the test. Learning this, Eva decides to elope with Walther but they are foiled by Sachs. Beckmesser sings to Eva, not knowing that her place at the window has been taken by Magdalene. As he sings, he is 'marked' by Hans Sachs striking with his hammer on the shoes he is making. As his singing gets louder, the neighbours wake up. David finds him apparently serenading Magdalene and starts a fight in which everyone joins. The chaos is brought to an end by the arrival of the *Night-Watchman. Sachs helps Walther shape his song for the competition, writing it down for him. They leave the workroom and Beckmesser enters and, seeing the song, assumes Sachs also to be a rival. Sachs returns and reassures him, even letting him take the copy of the song. The *Meistersinger* gather in the meadow for the contest. Beckmesser sings his own distorted version of Walther's song, causing much laughter and ridicule. In a fury, he tells everyone that it is Sachs's song, which they realize is ridiculous. Sachs announces the real writer, Walther sings his song and is awarded the prize—and Eva's hand.

Meister, Wilhelm (Thomas: *Mignon*). Ten. A student. This is the title-role of the Goethe work on which the libretto is based. Wilhelm helps Lothario search for his long-lost daughter. They rescue Mignon from a band of gypsies who are ill-treating her and Wilhelm falls in love with her. He takes father and daughter to Italy where they learn the truth of their relationship, thus restoring Lothario's sanity. Created (1866) by Léon Achard.

Melanto (Monteverdi: *Il ritorno d'Ulisse in patria*). Sop. Penelope's maid, in love with Eurimaco. Creator (1640) unknown.

Melchior, King (Menotti: *Amahl and the Night Visitors*). Bar. One of the Three Kings

(Magi) seeking the Christ Child. Created (1951, TV) by David Aiken.

Melcthal 1. (Rossini: *Guillaume Tell*). Bass. Patriarch and leader of the Swiss, father of Arnold. He is taken as a hostage and killed by the Austrian troops. His son swears revenge. Created (1829) by Mons. Bonel.

    2. (Melcthal, Arnold) (Rossini: *Guillaume Tell*). *See* ARNOLD (1).

Melibio (Haydn: *La fedeltà premiata*). Bass. High Priest at the temple of Diana, in love with Amaranta. His attempts to find a loving couple to sacrifice to the sea monster are the basis of the plot. Created (1781) by Antonio Pesci.

Mélisande (Debussy: *Pelléas et Mélisande*). Sop. Found lost in a forest by Golaud, who takes her home and she marries him. She finds his castle gloomy and full of foreboding. She is attracted to his younger half-brother Pelléas, with whom she plays innocent games round a fountain. The ring Golaud gave her falls into the water. She returns home to find her husband was injured at the exact time she lost the ring. Pelléas is leaving and comes to say good-bye to Mélisande, who is combing her long hair. It falls over his face, filling him with passion, but they are interrupted by Golaud. She and Pelléas plan one last meeting, and when Golaud finds them together he kills his brother. Mélisande gives birth to a daughter. She is dying but assures Golaud that she has never been unfaithful to him. Aria: *Mes longs cheveux* ('My hair's so long'). Created (1902) by Mary Garden. *See also* ARTICLE BY JOAN RODGERS, p. 191.

Melissa (Sullivan: *Princess Ida*). Mez. Daughter of Lady Blanche. She helps Hilarion and his friends to find Ida. Created (1884) by Jessie Bond.

Melisso (Gluck: *Alcina*). Bass. Guardian of Bradamante, whom he accompanies on her quest to rescue Ruggiero from the clutches of the sorceress Alcina. Created (1735) by Gustavus Waltz.

Melitone, Fra (Verdi: *La forza del destino*). Bass. A Franciscan monk at the monastery where Leonora seeks help. He admits her and ushers her into the presence of Padre Guardiano, the Father Superior. Years later, he and the Father are talking together when her brother Carlo arrives, seeking vengeance. Created (1862) by Achille de Bassini.

Melot (Wagner: *Tristan und Isolde*). Ten. A courtier of King Mark in Cornwall. He poses as a friend of the King's nephew, Tristan, but is jealous of him. It is Melot who informs King Mark that Tristan and Isolde (whom the King is intending to marry) are in love. Tristan is distraught at Melot's betrayal and challenges him to fight. Tristan deliberately falls on Melot's sword and is fatally wounded. Later, Tristan's servant and closest friend, Kurwenal, kills Melot. Created (1865) by Karl Heinrich.

Menelaus (Ménélas) (Offenbach: *La Belle Hélène*). Ten. King of Sparta and husband of Helen. He finds her in bed with Paris. Created (1864) by Herr Kopp.

    2. (Menelas) (Strauss: *Die ägyptische Helena*). Ten. Husband of Helen of Troy and father of Hermione. Having killed her lover, Paris, he is about to kill Helen, who is asleep in their ship. The enchantress Aithra summons a storm which shipwrecks them near her palace, and Menelaus enters her room dragging his wife with him, his dagger in his teeth. Aithra befriends Helen and gives her a potion—lotus-juice—to give to her husband. This will make him forget the unpleasant past. It does, but unfortunately it also makes him forget who she is—he is convinced he has already slain Helen and that the lady he is presented with as his wife is someone else. Aithra eventually provides the antidote and, after many complications, he allows their daughter once again to see her beautiful mother, with whom he is then happily reconciled. Aria: *Im weissen Gewand* ('All dressed in white'); *Totlebendige!* ('Dead yet living!'). Created (1928) by Curt Taucher. This is another of Strauss's 'cruel' tenor roles, requiring lyrical singing from a voice of *Heldentenor* proportions (similar to Bacchus in *Ariadne auf Naxos*). In the 1997 British première by Garsington Opera, Menelaus was well sung by the American tenor John Horton Murray.

Mephistopheles 1. (Méphistophélès) (Gounod: *Faust*). Bass. The Devil, Satan, he offers Faust fulfilment of his desire for youthful pleasure, if Faust will help him in the Underworld. Faust agrees and Méphistophélès leads him to meet Marguerite. She becomes pregnant, kills

MÉLISANDE   (*Pelléas et Mélisande*—Debussy)

by Joan Rodgers

Mélisande is certainly the most complex and elusive character I have ever portrayed on stage. Dramatically satisfying characters often seem to be written for dramatic voices, but Debussy has created this infinitely subtle role for a lighter, *lyric*, voice. It requires a soprano with a warmth in the middle of her voice or a mezzo with a transparency at the top of her range. Mélisande's character requires the singer to draw from a broad palette of vocal colours and to explore the nuances of the text in great detail.

In playing Mélisande, I felt as much (if not more) like an actress than a singer. I was never aware of really 'singing'. In fact, Mélisande does not have a major aria and spends much of her time 'uttering' rather than proclaiming, often holding back while Pelléas and Golaud are pouring out their emotions. This is the essence of her personality—we never really know what she is thinking or feeling. She is actually not a tremendously sympathetic character. The audience often warms more to Golaud—a tormented bear of a man, desperate for Mélisande to give of herself. It is this complete openness of raw emotion that probably allows us to feel for him in a way that we cannot feel for Mélisande.

There are many contradictions in her character—she seems innocent and childlike, but at the same time she is knowing, using her femininity and sexuality to attract first Golaud and then his half-brother Pelléas. The attraction that Golaud feels for her probably lies in this contradictory mixture of child and woman. Yet she frequently manipulates him, sometimes lying to him like a child, sometimes deceiving him like a woman.

One suspects that Mélisande has been abused before meeting Golaud (Maeterlinck begins the drama with her escaping from Bluebeard, who had imprisoned her as one of his wives). As often happens, the abused seek more abuse, as if they expect it. We see this when Golaud drags Mélisande along the ground by her hair—she seems to accept his cruelty as something not to be resisted. The other side of the coin is that the abused, knowing the effects of abuse, go on to abuse others and one could argue that Mélisande abuses Golaud mentally and emotionally by withholding so much of herself from him and by openly transferring her affections to Pelléas. In a sense, Pelléas's personality is a better match for Mélisande's: from their first meeting they develop a relationship based on emotional immaturity and reticence.

She retains this behaviour even on her deathbed where, despite Golaud's piteous outpourings, she continues to withhold all the answers that he is so desperate to discover. 'Tell me the truth', he begs. 'The truth . . .' is her uncommitted reply. Either 'truth' has no relevance for her or it is a concept she cannot understand.

She remains an elusive, impenetrable creature. We are never even sure of the moment of her death—there is no classic half-finished sentence typical of so many dying operatic heroines. Debussy draws his own veil over her. Perhaps he did not want anybody apart from himself to know that moment.

Mélisande has been sung by a succession of illustrious interpreters. It is interesting to think that Debussy wished not for a French singer, but for the Scottish Mary Garden to be his first Mélisande, and Maggie Teyte, another Anglo-Saxon, went on to become a famous exponent of the role. The soprano who has most impressed me on disc as the ideal Mélisande is Suzanne Danco, whose vocal warmth and clarity seem perfectly suited to Debussy's heroine. There has lately been a trend for mezzo-sopranos to sing the role and one can see why. A mezzo voice with its strength in the middle register can cut through some of Debussy's more lush orchestral passages rather more easily than most sopranos. Since the evolution of the traditionally plummy contralto into a more silvery, higher-reaching voice, the role of Mélisande is ideal for the right kind of mezzo-soprano. The one who springs most readily to mind as one of the great modern Mélisandes is, of course, Frederica von Stade. The translucent and silvery timbre of von Stade's voice beautifully conveys the vulnerable, almost ethereal, quality of Mélisande.

the baby, and is imprisoned. Méphistophélès helps Faust enter her cell but, recognizing the evil in Méphistophélès, she refuses to leave with them, and dies. Created (1859) by Emil Balanqué.

2. (Prokofiev: *The Fiery Angel*). Ten. Ruprecht meets him and Faust in an inn. Creators (1954/5) not known.

See also MEFISTOFELE.

Mercédès (Bizet: *Carmen*). Sop. A gypsy and friend of Carmen. Created (1873) by Esther Chevalier.

Mercury 1. (Mercurio) (Cavalli: *La Calisto*). Ten. Persuades Jupiter to come to earth disguised as Diana in order to win Callisto. Creator (1651) not known.

2. (Merkur) (Strauss: *Die Liebe der Danae*). Ten. After Jupiter has failed to win Danae from Midas, Mercury appears to him and tells him that all the gods are mocking him for his failure. Created (1944) by Franz Klarwein; (1952) by Josef Traxel.

Mercutio (Gounod: *Roméo et Juliette*). Bar. A Montague supporter, friend of Romeo. He is killed by Tybalt in a duel. Created (1867) by Auguste Barré.

Merry Widow, The (Léhar). Lib. by Viktor Léon and Leo Stein; 3 acts; f.p. Vienna 1905, cond. Ferencz Lehár.

Paris, 19th cent.: At a party, the Pontevedrin ambassador Baron *Zeta awaits the arrival of the newly widowed Hanna *Glawari. He must

prevent her marrying a foreigner, in order to keep her wealth in Pontevedro. Zeta informs Count Danilo *Danilowitsch, an old flame of Hanna, that he must marry her. Zeta's wife, *Valencienne, is meanwhile having a passionate affair with Camille de *Rosillon. At a party in her house, Hanna sings to her friends of *Vilja, the maid of the woods. Camille takes Valencienne into a garden pavilion, and when Zeta becomes suspicious and spies on them, he sees Camille with Hanna, who has taken Valencienne's place, both to help her friend but also to make Danilo jealous. She confesses this to Danilo and they declare their love for each other, but Danilo will not marry such a wealthy lady. When Hanna explains that, upon remarriage, she will lose all her money, Danilo agrees to marry her. Only then does she tell him her wealth will pass to her new husband.

Meryll, Leonard (Sullivan: *The Yeomen of the Guard*). Son of Sergeant Meryll, a Tower warder, brother of Phoebe. He is impersonated by Col. Fairfax when he escapes from his cell. Created (1888) by W. R. Shirley. *See* FAIRFAX, COL.

Meryll, Phoebe (Sullivan: *The Yeomen of the Guard*). Sop. Daughter of Sergeant Meryll, sister of Leonard. In love with Col. Fairfax, prisoner under sentence of death. She marries the gaoler Shadbolt to buy his silence when Fairfax escapes. Arias: *When maiden loves; Were I thy bride*. Created (1888) by Jessie Bond.

Meryll, Sergeant (Sullivan: *The Yeomen of the Guard*). Bar. Tower warder, father of Phoebe and Leonard. Releases Col. Fairfax, who has been unjustly imprisoned and is to die and passes him off as Leonard. Buys Dame Carruthers's silence by marrying her. Created (1888) by Richard Temple.

Mescalina (Ligeti: *Le Grand Macabre*). Mez. Wife of Astradamors, who does not satisfy her sexual appetite. She begs Venus to send her someone 'well-hung' and Venus chooses Nekrotzar. Mescalina dies in a frenzy of lovemaking, but rises from her hearse when she recognizes her lover and pursues him. Created (1978) by Barbro Ericson.

Messenger (Stravinsky: *Oedipus Rex*). Bassbar. Brings news of the death of King Polybus and of Oedipus' true lineage. Created (1927) by Georges Lanskoy (who also created Creon, the two roles usually being performed by the same singer).

Mi (Lehár: *The Land of Smiles*). Sop. Sister of Prince Sou-Chong. She falls in love with Gustl, but they have to accept that their ways of life are too disparate for a relationship to succeed. Created (1929) by Hella Kürty.

Micaëla (Bizet: *Carmen*). Sop. A peasant girl in love with Don José. She brings messages from his mother, but José is no longer interested in Micaëla, having met Carmen. When he deserts to join Carmen in the smugglers' mountain camp, Micaëla comes to tell him his mother is dying and he leaves with her. Duet (with Don José): *Parle-moi de ma mere* ('Tell me about my mother'); Aria: *Je dis que rien ne m'épouvante* ('I tell myself that nothing daunts me'). Created (1875) by Margherite Chapuy.

Micha (Smetana: *The Bartered Bride*). Bass. Husband of Hata, his second wife, and father of Vašek, proposed husband of Mařenka. Mařenka already has a lover, Jeník, who turns out to be Micha's son by his first wife. Created (1866) by Vojtěch Šebesta.

Michel (Martinů: *Julietta*). Ten. A Parisian bookseller. Whilst on holiday Michel heard, through an open window, the sound of a woman singing. The voice has haunted him for years. He returns to the town to look for her. The villagers have no memory and live only for the present. Because he can remember a toy duck he played with as a child, they appoint him Commander of the town—and immediately forget they have done so. At last he finds the girl, Julietta. They meet in a forest and she seems to know him. There is a passionate reunion, then they argue. As she runs away, Michel shoots at her. There is a scream. Did Michel kill Julietta? He does not know, and goes on searching. At the Central Office of Dreams, where he may pay to have any dream he wishes, people all around him are choosing their dreams. Some of them live there for ever, not wanting to wake up. He hears Julietta calling him and looks for her, but his dream-time is up, he must wake up. He has not found her but will not give up—he will stay in a half-dream world and go on looking.
Created (1938) by Jaroslav Gleich.

Michele (Puccini: *Il tabarro*). Bar. Husband of Giorgetta. Owner of a barge on the river Seine. He is assisted by three stevedores, one of whom, Luigi, unbeknown to Michele, is Giorgetta's lover. Michele cannot understand why Giorgetta rejects his overtures—when he tries to put his arms round her, she offers her cheek to be kissed. Since the death of their only child they have grown apart and Michele is anxious to renew their old relationship. He becomes suspicious, and when she goes below to go to bed he remains on deck. He watches her through a window and wonders why she has remained dressed and for whom she is waiting. He lights his pipe, unwittingly giving Luigi the signal (the lighted match) that all is clear. Hearing someone approach, Michele hides, pouncing on the visitor. It is Luigi, and with his hands on the stevedore's throat Michele forces him to confess his relationship with Giorgetta, then strangles him and hides him under his cloak. When Giorgetta appears and asks to be warmed under her husband's cloak, he throws it back, revealing her dead lover. Aria: *Nulla!... Silenzio!* ('Nothing!...Silence!'). Created (1918) by Luigi Montesanto.

Micheltorena, Nina (Puccini: *La fanciulla del West*). This lady does not appear in the opera. She is an old girlfriend of the bandit Ramerrez (Dick Johnson) and sends the sheriff, Jack Rance, a photograph of her former lover, which he uses to prove Johnson's identity to Minnie.

Michonnet (Cilea: *Adriana Lecouvreur*). Bar. Stage director of the Comédie-Française, Paris, in love with the actress Adriana. Created (1902) by Giuseppe De Luca.

Mickleford, Lord Tristan (Flotow: *Martha*). Bass. Elderly foppish cousin to Lady Harriet Durham ('Martha'). Created (1847) by ?Herr Erl.

Midas (Strauss: *Die Liebe der Danae*). Ten. King of Lydia, he comes in pursuit of Danae. Midas can turn to gold everything he touches, but he does not want Danae to love him for this alone. He presents himself to her as Chrysopher, a friend of Midas, and promises to take her to meet the King. She finds him attractive and he falls in love with her. When he does take her to meet the 'real' Midas, it is Jupiter in disguise. It is too late—she loves Chrysopher/Midas, who embraces her and turns her into a gold statue. Danae chooses to remain with Chrysopher, and Jupiter strips Midas of his ability to turn everything to gold. Midas and Danae go together to live in humble surroundings, and none of Jupiter's pleas or promises will make her leave Midas. Aria: *In Syriens Glut*. ('In Syria's heat'); *Kennst du, Danae* ('Do you know, Danae'). Created (1944) by Horst Taubmann; (1952) by Josef Gostic.

Midsummer Marriage, The (Tippett). Lib. by comp.; 3 acts; f.p. London 1955, cond. John Pritchard.
  A clearing in a wood, 'the present time': *Mark (an orphan) and his bride *Jenifer (daughter of King *Fisher), with their friends, greet the sun on midsummer morning. Dancers emerge, led by *Strephon and followed by the *He- and *She-Ancients, guardians of the Temple. Jenifer postpones their wedding to search for 'truth'. Mark decides he, too, should begin a journey of spiritual discovery. King Fisher, accompanied by his secretary *Bella, assumes his daughter has eloped with Mark, but he cannot open the gates which will allow him to follow her. Bella's boyfriend *Jack attempts to open the gates, but a voice warns him against tampering. Jenifer reappears, dazed by her spiritual experiences. Mark also returns, but sings of earthly passions and again they part to continue their search for fulfilment. The Ritual Dances demonstrate the conflict between male and female, some of it

quite violent. King Fisher brings the clairvoyant Mme *Sosostris to sort out all the mysteries. The Ancients warn him not to meddle with things he does not understand. Mark and Jenifer are seen, together now and transfigured. King Fisher tries to shoot Mark, but dies himself. As Mark and Jenifer symbolize their union, the dancer Strephon collapses and dies at their feet.

Midsummer Night's Dream, A (Britten). Lib. by Benjamin Britten and Peter Pears; 3 acts; f.p. Aldeburgh 1960, cond. Benjamin Britten.
  Set mainly in the wood: *Oberon, King of the Fairies, has quarrelled with his Queen, *Tytania, and plots revenge. He sends *Puck to find a magic herb which, if given to Tytania, will make her fall in love with the next creature she sees. *Hermia loves *Lysander but her father insists she marry *Demetrius, who does love her, and does not love *Helena who is in love with him. Oberon orders Puck to put the herb in Demetrius' eyes and ensure the next person he sees is Helena. The rustics are to perform a play, *Pyramus and Thisbe*, for *Theseus and *Hippolyta. They come to rehearse in the wood. Puck sprinkles the herb juice in the wrong eyes—those of Lysander, who declares his love for Helena, whom he sees when he awakes. Oberon puts the juice on Tytania's eyes. When she awakes, she sees *Bottom wearing an ass's head and declares her love for him. Now all the lovers are falling in love with the wrong person and the two girls quarrel—Puck is ordered to sort it all out. Oberon releases Tytania and Bottom from the spell. The lovers are all reconciled, Lysander with Hermia and Demetrius with Helena. In the Duke's palace, the rustics perform their play and everyone retires to bed. Oberon and Tytania join Puck and the fairies for the last chorus, then depart, leaving Puck alone to end the story.

Mignon (Thomas). Lib. by Michel Carré and Jules Barbier; 3 acts; f.p. Paris 1866.
  Germany and Italy, late 18th cent.: *Lothario searches for his long-lost daughter, assisted by a student, Wilhelm *Meister. They rescue *Mignon from a band of gypsies who are led by *Jarno. They are watched by two strolling players, *Laërte and *Philine. At the theatre in Rothenberg Castle, the players perform. The nobleman *Frédéric is in love with Philine.

Wilhelm is attracted by Mignon, who is injured when the theatre catches fire, and he rescues her. In an Italian *palazzo*, Wilhelm hears the story of how the wife of the owner, Marquis *Cipriano, died. The Marquis, believing his small daughter to be dead also, left Italy. The name seems to have some significance for Lothario, who finds the palace familiar. Mignon recognizes various childhood possessions—Lothario is indeed the Marquis Cipriano and she is his daughter. She and Wilhelm admit their love for each other and her father's sanity is restored.

Mignon (Thomas: *Mignon*). Mez. She is the daughter of Lothario, and she was abducted as a child from her father's Italian castle and is ill-treated by a band of gypsies with whom she travels. She is rescued by Lothario, assisted by Wilhelm Meister, a student, who falls in love with her. In Italy they all learn the truth of their relationships. Aria: *Connais-tu le pays?* ('Do you know the land?'), an aria which became a popular concert item. Created (1866) by Célestine Galli-Marié.

Mikado, The, or The Town of Titipu (Sullivan). Lib. by W. S. Gilbert; 2 acts; f.p. London 1885, cond. Sullivan.

Japan: *Nanki-Poo, a minstrel, comes to Titupu to marry *Yum-Yum, only to learn from the nobleman *Pish-Tush that she is engaged to *Ko-Ko, her guardian, who is Lord High Executioner. *Pooh-Bah, Lord High Everything Else, is ridiculed by Yum-Yum and her friends *Pitti-Sing and *Peep-Bo. Nanki-Poo confesses to Yum-Yum that he is the son of the *Mikado and is trying to escape the attentions of the elderly *Katisha. It is agreed that Nanki-Poo can marry Yum-Yum, but he must be beheaded in a month's time. Katisha is furious. Ko-Ko discovers an ancient law which states that if a man is executed, his bride must be buried alive. Ko-Ko, Peep-Bo, and Pitti-Sing conspire and tell him they have beheaded Nanki-Poo.

They must be punished for killing the Mikado's heir. Nanki-Poo refuses to reappear and confirm that he is alive until he is promised that Ko-Ko will marry Katisha! She agrees to do so, believing Nanki-Poo to be dead. Having sorted them all out, Nanki-Poo can now marry Yum-Yum.

Mikado, The (Sullivan: *The Mikado*). Bass. The supreme potentate, father of Nanki-Poo. Comes to Titipu to seek his missing son, to be told he is dead, although this is not, in fact, true. Aria: *From every kind of man…my object all sublime.* Created (1885) by Richard Temple.

Miles (Britten: *The Turn of the Screw*). Treble. Brother of Flora, he is the younger of the two children in the charge of the Governess at Bly. He is dominated by the ghost of the former valet, Quint, and under his influence steals the Governess's letter to their guardian. The Governess forces him to reveal who made him do it. As he screams Quint's name, he dies in her arms. Aria: *Malo, Malo, Malo I would rather be.* Created (1954) by David Hemmings.

Miller (Verdi: *Luisa Miller*). Bar. An old soldier, father of Luisa. He disapproves of her relationship with Rodolfo, son of his enemy Count Walter. Created (1849) by Achille De Bassini.

Miller, Luisa (Verdi: *Luisa Miller*). Sop. Daughter of Miller, she is in love with the young peasant 'Carlo', not realizing he is Rodolfo, the son of her father's old enemy Count Walter. She is forced by the steward Wurm to write a letter denying her feelings for Rodolfo. When Rodolfo sees it, he accuses her of betrayal and gives her poison to drink—he also drinks it himself. Learning the truth, he manages to kill Wurm before he and Luisa die together. Created (1849) by Marietta Gazzaniga.

Mime (Wagner: *Das Rheingold*; *Siegfried*). Ten. A Nibelung, Alberich's brother. Like the rest of his race, he mines metals in the bowels of the earth where they live.

Das Rheingold: He is dominated and bullied by his brother, but is nevertheless a wily old bird. Mime forges the Tarnhelm from the Rhine gold and, realizing it has magical powers, tries to keep it. Alberich makes himself invisible by use of the Tarnhelm, and then beats up his brother, confiscating the Tarnhelm. Mime explains to Wotan and Loge how Alberich also has a Ring forged from the Rhine gold which gives him absolute power over his fellow creatures.

Siegfried: When the gold was stolen from Alberich, he lost his power over Mime, who ran off into the forest. There he met the dying

Sieglinde, who entrusted to him her newborn son Siegfried, together with the fragments of the sword which belonged to the child's father. He has brought up the boy to manhood, and has made him many swords, but each one Siegfried shatters. Siegfried quizzes Mime about his childhood, wanting to know why he has no mother and why he does not look like Mime. Mime explains how he helped Sieglinde, showing him the pieces of Nothung. Mime is now trying to forge a sword from the fragments, as he is sure the boy would not be able to break it and could use it to kill the dragon Fafner and steal back the gold for Mime. Siegfried goes out and Wotan arrives in his guise as the Wanderer. Wotan and Mime ask each other three riddles—the forfeit for failure is their life. Wotan answers those put to him by Mime and then asks his own. The first two Mime answers. The last question is: 'Who can forge a sword from these fragments?' Mime, frightened, is unable to answer. Wotan tells Mime that the sword can only be forged by a hero who knows no fear. He also warns him that, through this hero, Mime will be killed. Wotan leaves and Siegfried returns. Mime talks to Siegfried of the emotion of fear, which the boy has never experienced. He tells him about the dragon, but this just inspires the boy to want to fight it.

Angry that Mime has not managed to forge the sword, Siegfried snatches up the pieces of metal and himself forges a sword. Mime takes him to Fafner's cave and Siegfried kills the dragon. Licking drops of Fafner's blood off his hand, he finds it has given him the power both to understand the language of the birds and to know what is in Mime's mind. Determined to possess the gold, Mime offers Siegfried a poisoned drink, but realizing what is afoot, Siegfried kills Mime. Arias: *Zwangwolle Plage! Müh ohne Zweck!* ('Forced drudgery! Toil to no end!'); *Einst lag wimmernd ein Weib* ('One day a woman lay whimpering'); *Fühltest du nie im finstren Wald.* ('Have you never felt, in the gloomy forest'); *Wilkommen, Siegfried!* ('Welcome, Siegfried!').

This is one of the *Ring's* rewarding roles for a character tenor, but is nevertheless, especially in *Siegfried*, 'a big sing'. Names that come to mind include Gerhard Stolze, Julius Patzak, Gregory Dempsey, Heinz Zednik, Peter Haage, Paul Crook, Graham Clark, Manfred Jung, John

Dobson, and Peter Bronder. Created (*R.* 1869 and *S.* 1876) by Carl Schlosser.

Mimì 1. (Puccini: *La bohème*). Sop. Mimì is a seamstress, ill with consumption (tuberculosis). After his friends have gone to the Café Momus on Christmas Eve, Mimì knocks on Rodolfo's door. She is on her way to her own room but her candle has blown out and she asks for a light. In a fit of coughing, she has to rest on a chair, dropping her candle which again goes out, and now Rodolfo's candle is also extinguished. She drops her key on the floor and as they search for it their hands meet. They tell each other of their lives and their hopes for the future. Mimì explains that her real name is Lucia and she embroiders silk and satin. They fall in love and hear his friends calling from the street below. They join them at the Café Momus, where Rodolfo buys her a pink bonnet. But, as the weeks go by, they quarrel because of his jealousy and his anxiety about her illness. Mimì explains all this to Marcello and she and Rodolfo say a sad farewell. When Mimì is dying, Musetta brings her to the attic again to Rodolfo. They reminisce about their time together—and the pink bonnet. Their friends all go out on various missions, in order to leave them together to reavow their love—but it is too late. Suddenly, they realize that Mimì is dead. Arias: *Sì. Mi chiamano Mimì* ('Yes. They call me Mimì'); *Donde lieta uscì* ('Back to the place I left'); duets (with Rodolfo); *O soave fanciulla* ('Oh! Lovely girl!'); *Sono andati?* ('Have they gone?'). Created (1896) by Cesira Ferrani (who had earlier created Puccini's Manon and was chosen by Toscanini as the first Italian Mélisande). It has been suggested that Puccini was in love with Ferrani, but as far as can be ascertained, it seems that she was herself in love with Toscanini. Eminent Mimìs over the years have included Alice Esty, Nellie Melba, Geraldine Farrar, Licia Albanese (a famous recording with Beniamino Gigli), Bidú Sayão, Grace Moore, Elsie Morison, Renata Tebaldi, Maria Callas, Victoria de los Angeles, Renato Scotto, Anna Moffo, Mirella Freni, Montserrat Caballé, Katia Ricciarelli, Kiri te Kanawa, Leontina Vaduva, and Angela Gheorghiu, a veritable roll-call of dramatic sopranos.

2. (Leoncavallo: *La bohème*). Sop. A seamstress. She is in love with Rodolfo, but to escape poverty she accepts the proposal of the wealthy Count Paolo. At Christmas she and Rodolfo are reunited, but Mimì, now mortally ill, dies in their attic. Created (1897) by Elisa Frandini.

Mina (Verdi: *Aroldo*). Sop. Daughter of Egberto and wife of the Crusader knight, Aroldo. While her husband is fighting in the wars, she has an affair with a soldier, Godvino. Her father prevents her confessing her adultery to Aroldo and himself kills Godvino. When the whole story comes to light, Aroldo divorces Mina and goes into exile, living in a primitive hut in Scotland. There the outlawed Mina finds him on her wanderings and the two are reconciled. Created (1857) by Marcellina Lotti. *See also* LINA.

Minerva (Monteverdi: *Il ritorno d'Ulisse in Patria*). Sop. Goddess who helps Ulisse to disguise himself as a beggar and return to his wife. Created (1640) probably by Maddalena Manelli.

Minette (Henze: *The English Cat*). Sop. A simple country cat, she becomes the bride of the aristocratic Lord Puff, but she cannot resist her old flame Tom, resulting finally in her divorce. She is drowned by other cats to put her out of her misery. Created (1983) by Inga Nielsen.

Minnie (Puccini: *La fanciulla del West*). Sop. The (golden) girl of the West, she is the owner of 'The Polka', a pub in which the gold-miners gamble and drink. They all respect Minnie, who reads to them and tells them stories from the Bible. She is loved by the sheriff, Jack Rance, who wants to marry her, but she does not return his feelings—she can remember as a child, the love between her parents, and that is the sort of love she wants for herself. A stranger, Dick Johnson, calls at the inn and he and Minnie talk animatedly. Rance suspects this may be the bandit, Ramerrez, but Minnie vouches for him and invites Johnson to her cabin for a meal that evening. In her cabin, she is looked after by her maid, Wowkle, who prepares the meal for them. She tells Johnson how happy she is living here among the miners. The sheriff calls at the cabin to warn Minnie that the bandit is in the area. She hides Johnson behind the curtains. Rance shows her a photograph of the bandit, and she recognizes it as Johnson. After Rance has left, she

turns on him, angry and upset at his deception. He declares his love for her and his intention of leading an honest life in the future, but she insists he leave. No sooner has she closed the door behind him than a shot rings out. The wounded Johnson falls against her door and Minnie drags him in and hides him in her loft. Again Rance arrives and looks round suspiciously. Finding nothing, he is about to leave when blood drips from the loft above, revealing the bandit's whereabouts. Minnie suggests a game of poker. If she wins, Johnson can go free; if she loses, Rance wins her for himself. By cheating, she wins and Rance departs. But he breaks his side of the bargain, telling his men where to find Johnson. They capture him and are about to hang him when Minnie turns on them—do they not owe her anything for the time and love she has given them? Now she is asking them for something—will they not agree to Johnson's freedom? She tells them that Johnson and she will lead an honest life together. The miners accede to her wishes and she and Johnson leave to seek a new life. Arias: *Laggiù nel Soledad, ero piccina* ('Back in Soledad, when I was little'); *Oh, se sapeste* ('Oh, if only you knew'); duet (with Rance): *Una partita a poker!* ('A game of poker!'). Created (1910) by Emmy Destinn.

Miracle, Dr (Offenbach: *Les Contes d'Hoffmann*). Bar. A doctor who forces the sick Antonia to sing, thus causing her collapse and death. Created (1881) by Alexandre Taskin.

Miriam (Rossini: *Mosè in Egitto*). Mez. Sister of Moses and mother of Anaïs. Her daughter is in love with the son of Pharaoh. Created (1818) by Maria Manzi.

Missail (Musorgsky: *Boris Godunov*). Ten. Vagabond, friend of Varlaam, who accompanies the 'false Dimitri' to Poland. Created (1874) by Pavel Dyuzhikov.

Mitridate, King (Mozart: *Mitridate, re di Ponto*). Ten. Father of Farnace and Sifare, and betrothed to Aspasia. While he is absent at war, Farnace declares his love for Aspasia who later confesses her love for Sifare. Mitridate swears revenge, but facing defeat by the Romans, forgives them all. Created (1770) by Guglielmo d'Ettore.

Mitridate, re di Ponto (*Mithridates, King of Pontus*) (Mozart). Lib. by Vittorio Amedeo Cigna-Santi; 3 acts; f.p. Milan 1770.

Crimea, 63 BC: King *Mitridate is at war, leaving his sons, *Farnace and *Sifare, to govern. When they hear that Mitridate is dead, Farnace declares his love for his father's betrothed, *Aspasia, who seeks protection from Sifare. *Arbate brings news that Mitridate is alive. The King arrives home accompanied by *Ismene, whom he presents to Farnace for his future bride. Arbate tells Mitridate of Farnace's actions and Sifare's loyalty, and the King swears vengeance on his elder son. Farnace rejects Ismene and Mitridate suggests she marry Sifare instead. Aspasia has confessed to Sifare that she loves him, but they agree to do the honourable thing and part. Farnace tells Mitridate of Sifare's love for Aspasia. Mitridate swears he will take revenge on his sons and they are arrested. Ismene, still in love with Farnace, frees the men as Mitridate goes to fight the Romans. Facing defeat, he decides to kill himself, forgives everyone and gives Aspasia and Sifare his blessing. Farnace is reunited with Ismene and they all vow to free the world from the tyranny of Rome.

Mittenhofer, Gregor (Henze: *Elegy for Young Lovers*). Bar. A poet, who comes to the Alps every year to write his spring poem. The poem recounts the events in the Alpine inn where he and his companions stay. Created (1961) by Dietrich Fischer-Dieskau.

Mohammed (Strauss: *Der Rosenkavalier*). Silent. The Marschallin's little black page (*der kleine Neger*) (often given incorrectly in programme-books as Mahomet). In the final scene, he runs on to retrieve the handkerchief dropped by Sophie before she left the inn with Octavian. Creator (1911) unknown.

mondo della luna, Il (*The World on the Moon*) (Haydn). Lib. by Carlo Goldoni; 3 acts; f.p. Eszterháza 1777.

Dr *Ecclitico convinces *Buonafede that there is a better life on the moon. Ecclitico and his friend *Ernesto are in love with Buonafede's daughters, *Clarice and *Flaminia respectively, while Ernesto's servant *Cecco loves their maid *Lisetta. Buonafede is against all these unions and to persuade him to give his consent, they give him a potion and tell him it will enable him to go to the moon. They decorate Ecclitico's garden to look like the moon's surface and take Buonafede there. He is tricked into agreeing to the various marriages. When he discovers he has been deceived, he forgives them all and sanctions their weddings.

Monica (Menotti: *The Medium*). Sop. Daughter of the medium Mme Flora. She takes the parts of the various figures her mother 'conjures up' in séances. Created (1946) by Evelyn Keller.

Monostatos (Mozart: *Die Zauberflöte*). Ten. Moor who is in the service of Sarastro. Tries to seduce Pamina but is interrupted by Papageno. His attempts to capture Tamino and Papageno are thwarted when Papageno plays his magic bells and Monostatos and his henchmen break into a good-natured dance. Aria: *Alles fühlt der Liebe Freuden* ('All may feel the joys of love'). Created (1791) by Johann Joseph Nouseul.

Montague, Romeo 1. (Roméo) (Gounod: *Roméo et Juliette*). Ten. Romeo, a Montague, meets and falls in love with the Capulet Juliet and they are secretly married. In a fight he kills Tybalt, Capulet's nephew, and is exiled. When Romeo sees Juliet unconscious he is unaware that, in order to avoid a marriage her father has arranged, she has deliberately taken a potion which makes her simulate death. He believes her to be dead and takes poison. Aria: *Ah! lève-toi soleil* ('Ah! fairest dawn arise'). Created (1867) by Pierre Michot.

2. (Bellini: *I Capuleti e i Montecchi*). Mez. *Travesti* role. Head of the Montagues, in love with Juliet, but forbidden to marry her by her Capulet father. When Romeo sees her in a coma and thinks she is dead, he swallows poison and, as she wakens, he dies in her arms. Arias: *Ecco la tomba* ('Here is the tomb'); *Tu sola, O mia Giulietta* ('You alone, my Juliet'). Created (1830) by Giuditta Grisi.

Montano (Verdi: *Otello*). Bass. The commander in Cyprus, being replaced by Otello. Created (1887) by Napoleone Limonta.

Monterone, Count (Verdi: *Rigoletto*). Bar. An elderly nobleman whose daughter has been seduced by the Duke of Mantua. He denounces the Duke. When Rigoletto, the court jester, mocks him, Monterone puts a father's curse upon him. Created (1851) by Paolo Damini.

Montez, Eugenia (Janáček: *The Makropulos Case*). *See* MARTY, EMILIA.

Montfort, (Monforte) Guy de (Verdi: *Les Vêpres siciliennes*). Bar. French Governor of Sicily since the invasion. Years ago he had an affair and the lady, now dying, has informed him that Henri—his enemy—is his son. Henri refuses to own that Montfort is his father, but he does thwart an assassination attempt by Sicilians, including the lady he loves, Hélène, on the Governor's life. Hélène is imprisoned and in return for her release he agrees to acknowledge Montfort as his father. Montfort now gives his blessing on the young couple, who plan their wedding, but too late they learn that the ringing of the wedding bells is the signal for a Sicilian uprising. The French are massacred. Aria: *Au sein de la puissance* ('In the midst of power'). Created (1855) by Marc Bonnehée.

Moralès (Bizet: *Carmen*). Bar. A sergeant in the dragoons, friend of Don José. Created (1875) by Mons. Duvernoy.

Morfontaine, Guillot de (Massenet: *Manon*). Ten. An old roué, attracted by Manon. Created (1884) by Mons. Grivot.

Morgana (Handel: *Alcina*). Sop. Sister of the sorceress Alcina. Previously the lover of Oronte, with whom she is eventually reunited. Created (1735) by Cecilia Young.

Morgana, Fata (Prokofiev: *The Love for Three Oranges*). Sop. A witch, she protects the evil Leandro. The first time the Prince is able to laugh is at the sight of Fata Morgana when she falls over, legs flying in all directions. To punish him, she makes him fall in love with three oranges and travel the world to find them. Created (1921) by Nina Koshetz.

Morgan le Fay (Birtwistle: *Gawain*). Sop. Aunt of Gawain, who acts as a commentator and manipulator of events. Created (1991) by Marie Angel.

Morold (Wagner: *Tristan und Isolde*). He does not appear in the opera, but is relevant to the action immediately before the start of the opera. He was an Irish knight engaged to Isolde. He went to Cornwall to collect the monies owing to Ireland. He and Tristan fought, Morold was killed and Tristan badly wounded. He was taken to Isolde to be nursed, and initially she did not know who he was. But she saw his sword with a small piece broken off and this matched the piece which had been found in Morold's wound. Determined though she was to avenge Morold's death, she and Tristan fell in love.

Morone, Cardinal Giovanni (Pfitzner: *Palestrina*). Bar. Cardinal Legate of the Pope. He makes a long speech to the final meeting of the Council of Trent, urging all delegates to obey the Pope. Created (1917) by Herr Brodersen.

Morosus, Henry (Strauss: *Die schweigsame Frau*). Ten. Husband of Aminta and nephew and heir of Sir John Morosus. Together with his wife, an opera singer, Henry runs a troupe of travelling theatricals, putting on operas, and known as the Vanuzzi Opera Company. His uncle considers this a disgraceful way to earn a living, making an exhibition of oneself in public, and disowns Henry. Worried that Morosus will take a wife who will then become his heir, Henry sets about deceiving his uncle. Three ladies in Henry's company disguise themselves as prospective brides, and Morosus, totally taken in by this ruse, chooses the most demure and quiet one, called 'Timida' (who is Aminta in disguise). Henry arranges a mock wedding—the lawyer and priest are again disguised members of his troupe. Once married, 'Timida' turns out to be noisy and aggressive, and Morosus cannot wait to be rid of her. Henry offers to find him reason to divorce her, and even poses as her past lover. But eventually he relents and admits to his uncle that it has all been a hoax. Fortunately for him, Morosus can see the joke, admires their acting ability, and reinstates Henry as his heir. Duet (with Aminta): *Dich verlassen? Dich entbehren?* ('Forsake you? Renounce you?') This was the role in which Fritz Wunderlich first came on to the international scene, when he sang it at the Salzburg Festival in 1959. Created (1935) by Martin Kremer.

Morosus, Sir John (Strauss: *Die schweigsame Frau*). Bass. [We would, of course, in England, refer to him as 'Sir John', but neither

Strauss nor Zweig was able to get the hang of the British honours system, and Sir Morosus he became!] A retired Admiral, he lives in London, looked after by his Housekeeper. During his days in the service, a gunpowder magazine exploded near him. Although he was not injured, since then he cannot bear any sort of noise, including loud voices. His heir is his only relative, his nephew Henry, but it is so long since he has heard anything from him that he assumes he must be dead. Morosus is a lonely man and his Barber suggests that maybe he should marry—he would then have company and an heir. However, Morosus would only consider marriage to a silent woman—and where will he find such a creature? Suddenly, a visitor arrives, the long-lost Henry, whom Morosus is delighted to see. Then Henry announces that he has brought his troupe of actors and singers with him, including his wife, Aminta, also a singer. Morosus feels that to perform in public is a disgrace to the family and disinherits Henry. Henry and Aminta hear that Morosus is looking for a wife and set about finding someone suitable. Aminta, Carlotta, and Isotta, all members of the troupe, dress up as prospective brides, and Aminta, disguised as Timida, presents herself as a modest and quiet young lady, whom Morosus at once chooses. No sooner are they married, in a mock-ceremony conducted by more actors, than she throws off all pretence at being the demure miss and becomes a bossy and shrieking virago. Morosus cannot bear it. Henry offers to find him grounds for divorce, but when this ploy fails he and Aminta, feeling guilty at causing Morosus such distress, remove their disguises and he realizes it has all been a pretence. At first angry, he soon sees the funny side, and even admires their acting ability—their troupe must be good, after all. He now 'adopts' Henry and Aminta as son and daughter and thus his rightful heirs. Aria: *Wie schön erst, wenn sie vorbei ist!* ('How beautiful is music, especially when it is over!'). Hans Hotter was long associated with this role. Created (1935) by Friedrich Plaschke.

Morozov, Filka (Janáček: *From the House of the Dead*). Ten. A prisoner who goes by the name of Luka Kuzmič. He tells his story—he is in this Siberian prison because he murdered a

prison officer. When another prisoner, the old man Šiškov, tells his story, it implicates Morozov, who had an affair with Šiškov's wife. As Filka dies and is carried out, Šiškov recognizes him and curses him. Created (1930) by Emil Olšovský.

Mosè in Egitto (Moses in Egypt) (Rossini). Lib. by Andrea Leone Tottola; 3 acts; f.p. Naples 1818.

Egypt, biblical times: *Pharaoh gives permission for *Moses and the Israelites to leave Egypt. Pharaoh's son *Amenophis and Moses's niece *Anaïs, daughter of *Miriam, are in love and he wants her to stay with him when the rest of her people leave. They hide, but are found by her uncle, *Aaron, and Pharaoh's wife *Sinais. As Pharaoh withdraws permission for the Israelites to leave, Moses threatens the death of Amenophis and all other Egyptian first-born sons. Anaïs offers to die in return for Moses and the other Israelites being set free. Amenophis lifts his sword to strike Moses but is himself killed by a bolt of lightning. Moses and the Israelites pray for God's help. The Red Sea parts and they walk across. The pursuing Egyptians are drowned as the waters close over them.

Moser, Augustin (Wagner: *Die Meistersinger von Nürnberg*). Ten. A tailor by trade, he is one of the *Meistersinger*. Created (1868) by Herr Pöppl.

Moses 1. (Schoenberg: *Moses und Aron*). Spoken. He hears God telling him to lead the Israelites from bondage, but he feels unable to convince them to follow him—he is no orator. God tells him to speak to the people through his brother Aaron. Moses explains what he wants to say, but Aaron cannot inspire the Israelites. Moses goes up Mount Sinai to receive the tablets of the law from the Lord. He returns to find that Aaron has built a golden calf for them all to worship. He criticizes Aaron for not being able to accept the idea of God even though he cannot see him in person. Created (1954, radio/1957, stage) by Hans Herbert Fiedler.

2. (Mosè) (Rossini: *Mosè in Egitto*). Bass. Leader of the Israelites. Brother of Miriam and uncle of Anaïs (who, while in captivity in Egypt, has fallen in love with Amenophis, Pharaoh's son). Each time Pharaoh changes his mind about allowing the Israelites to leave their bondage in Egypt, Moses brings down a plague, threatening death to all first-born sons of Egypt, including Pharaoh's son. Amenophis lifts his sword to strike Moses but is killed by a bolt of lightning. Moses urges his tribe to have faith. They pray to God and the Red Sea parts to allow them to walk across, closing again and drowning the Egyptians who try to capture them. Aria and ens.: *Des cieux où tu résides, grand Dieu (Dal tuo stellato soglio)* ('From Thy starry throne, turn to us O Lord'). This, the most famous passage in the opera, was added at its first revival the season after the première. Created (1818) by Michele Benedetti.

3. (Weill: *Aufstieg und Fall der Stadt Mahagonny*). Bar. Trinity Moses. One of three fugitives who found the city of Mahagonny. It is to be their ideal town, where nobody works and pleasure is the main pursuit. In a boxing match he kills one of the inhabitants. Created (1930) by Walther Zimmer.

Moses und Aron (*Moses and Aaron*) (Schoenberg). Lib. by comp.; 3 acts (no music comp. for Act 3, which can be performed in spoken form only); f.p. Hamburg 1954 (radio)/ Zurich 1957 (stage, Acts 1 and 2 only), both cond. Hans Rosbaud.

Biblical times: *Moses hears the voice of God telling him to lead the Israelites to the Promised Land. He is worried—how will he convince the people to follow him? God tells him to speak to them through his brother *Aaron, but Aaron interprets Moses' words only in a literal and simplified form—when he tells them of Moses' idea of 'only one God' visible only to the righteous, the people are sceptical—they need something more concrete. Aaron performs miracles in order to convince them and promises them God will also perform miracles to feed them as they walk through the desert. Moses goes up the Mountain to receive the tablets containing the new laws of God. He is away 40 days and the Israelites grow restless. Aaron builds a golden calf for them to worship and an orgy follows. Moses returns and the people flee. As Aaron follows them, Moses smashes the tablets in frustration. Aaron is next seen in chains. Moses chides him for needing a solid image to

worship, instead of accepting that there is a God. He orders Aaron's release. As soon as he is freed, Aaron dies.

Mother, The 1. (Menotti: *The Consul*). Cont. Mother of Magda Sorel. Created (1950) by Marie Powers.

2. (Menotti: *Amahl and the Night Visitors*). Sop. Mother of the crippled Amahl, she tries to steal from the Three Kings sheltering in her home. Created (1951) by Rosemary Kuhlman.

3. (Charpentier: *Louise*). Cont. Mother of Louise. Tries to prevent her daughter leaving home to live with an impecunious poet. Created (1900) by Blanche Deschamps-Jéhin.

4. (Ravel: *L'Enfant et les sortilèges*). Cont. She punishes the Child for his rudeness and naughtiness. This sets off a chain of events. Created (1925) by ?Mme Orsoni.

5. (Janáček: *Osud*). Mez. Mila's mother, who lives with Mila and Živny. She is mentally unstable and attacks Živny. Mila tries to intervene and she and her mother fall to their death off the balcony. Created (radio, 1934) by Marie Žaludová; (stage, 1958) by Jarmila Palivcová.

Mother Goose (Stravinsky: *The Rake's Progress*). Mez. Keeper of a London brothel who introduces Tom Rakewell to vice and debauchery. Created (1951) by Nell Tangeman.

Mountararat, Earl of (Sullivan: *Iolanthe*). Bass. A peer in the House of Lords, in love with the shepherdess Phyllis. Duet (with Tolloller and chorus); *When Britain really ruled the waves*. Created (1882) by Rutland Barrington.

Mountjoy, Lord (Charles Blount) (Britten: *Gloriana*). Bar. He is one of the Queen's courtiers and his lover is Penelope, Lady Rich, sister of the Earl of Essex. Created (1953) by Geraint Evans.

Murgatroyd, Sir Despard (Sullivan: *Ruddigore*). Bass-bar. The present 'bad baron of Ruddigore', forced by a curse to commit a crime a day. Hating this role, he is delighted to learn that he has an elder brother, Robin (Sir Ruthven) who thus relieves him of the title and curse. He can now marry Mad Margaret. Created (1887) by Rutland Barrington.

Murgatroyd, Sir Roderic (the ghost of) (Sullivan: *Ruddigore*). Bass. Leads the

Murgatroyd ancestors out of their portraits to act as judges on Robin (Sir Ruthven), who does not want to fulfil the family curse which he has inherited—he is required to commit a crime a day. Robin is able to prove that Roderic should never have died, so he is able to remain out of his portrait and marry his old lover, Dame Hannah. Aria: *The ghosts' high noon.* Created (1887) by Richard Temple.

Murgatroyd, Sir Ruthven (Sullivan: *Ruddigore*). Bar. Brother of Sir Despard Murgatroyd. Disguised as Robin Oakapple he woos Rose. He is revealed by his foster-brother as heir to the baronetcy and its curse—he must commit a crime a day. Refusing to lead this life, he will be judged by his ancestors, who emerge from their portraits led by Sir Roderic. Robin is able to prove that Roderic should never have died, so Robin is no longer the bad baron and can marry Rose. Duet (with Rose): *I know a maid.* Created (1887) by George Grossmith.

Musetta 1. (Puccini: *La bohème*). Sop. A grisette who has been Marcello's lover. They have quarrelled and parted and she has found herself a new patron, the elderly but very wealthy Alcindoro. The bohemians come to the Café Momus on Christmas Eve, and there she and Marcello make a great play of not noticing each other, whilst she does her best to make sure he *does* notice her. Pretending that her shoe hurts, she sends Alcindoro to the cobbler to have it adjusted and then joins her old friends for supper. When the bill is presented they are horrified, but Musetta knows just what to do—she places it on Alcindoro's table together with his own account, and they all leave the restaurant before he returns. In a tavern near the Latin Quarter of Paris where they live, Musetta is flirting with another guest and Marcello is furious with her. They quarrel violently and their words ('Viper! Toad! Witch!') are in sharp contrast to the sad farewells which Rodolfo and Mimì are exchanging. So the two couples again part. But Mimì's health is deteriorating and, ill and weak, she is brought by Musetta to the attic to be with Rodolfo. Musetta takes off her earrings and sends Marcello to sell them to raise money for food and medicine, but it is too late. In this final scene, the other, tender, side of the

flamboyant Musetta's nature comes to the fore. She gives Mimì her fur muff to keep her hands warm and then tells her it is from Rodolfo, and she gladly gives up her valuable jewellery to buy the necessary treatment for the sick girl—one might say she is the gold-digger with the heart of gold. Aria: *Quando men vo soletto…* ('As I walk alone'); ens. (with Marcello and with Rodolfo and Mimì): *Dunque è proprio finita? / Che facevi?* ('So it's really over?' / 'What were you doing?'). Created (1896) by Camilla Pasini, considered 'excellent' by the composer. There have been many other excellent Musettas since then, including Hilde Gueden, Margherita Carioso, Anna Moffo, Graziella Sciutti, Ljuba Welitsch (there is a story that a prospective New York Mimì, hearing who was to be the Musetta, took to her heels and ran, unable to face the competition), Adèle Leigh, Dorothy Kirsten, Rita Streich, Elizabeth Harwood, Sona Ghazarian, Hildegard Behrens, Carol Neblett, Ashley Putnam, and Nancy Gustafson.

2. (Leoncavallo: *La bohème*). Mez. A grisette, in love with Marcello, she leaves him to avoid living in constant poverty, but later returns to him and is there when Mimì dies. Created (1897) by Rosina Storchio.

Music Master (Strauss: *Ariadne auf Naxos*). (a) Spoken (1912 vers.). Hired to teach Mons. Jourdain how to be a gentleman. Created (1912) by the actor Jakob Tiedtke; (b) Bar. (1916 vers.). Teacher of the young Composer (who has written an opera to be performed to the guests of one of the richest men in Vienna). He has to sooth the sensitive Composer who is very agitated when told that his opera will have to be curtailed and performed simultaneously with the antics of the comedians. The Music Master tells him that, if he wants to survive in this world, he must make compromises—it is surely better to have his opera performed in this way than not at all. Created (1916) by Hans Duhan.

Mussel, the All-Wise (Strauss: *Die ägyptische Helena*). Mez. An omniscient Seashell who can advise the enchantress Aithra of events taking place anywhere in the world. The Mussel tells of Menelaus' intention to kill Helena on board their ship, thus allowing Aithra to save her by causing the ship to be wrecked in a storm. Created (1928) by Helene Jung.

Mustafà (Rossini: *L'italiana in Algeri*). Bass. The Bey of Algiers. He no longer loves his wife Elvira and orders his captured Italian slave, Lindoro, to marry her. His servant Haly must find him an Italian lady to marry. The lady Haly finds in a shipwreck is Lindoro's lover, Isabella, looking for her beloved. She and Lindoro plot their escape—they fool Mustafà into believing Isabella loves him and slip away while he is busy dining. Realizing she has gone, the Bey returns to Elvira, swearing to have no more to do with Italian women. Aria: *Già d'insolito ardore* ('I already feel excited and afire'). Created (1813) by Filippo Galli.

N

Nabucco (Verdi). Lib. by Temistocle Solera; 4 acts; f.p. Milan 1842, cond. ?Maestro Tutsch (or possibly Giacomo Panizza from the keyboard).

Jerusalem and Babylon, 587 BC: The Assyrian *Nabucco (Nebuchadnezzar) is attempting to overthrow the Hebrew Temple. Nabucco's elder daughter *Abigaille (who is illegitimate) is rejected by the Hebrew *Ismaele in favour of the younger daughter, *Fenena (who is a secret sympathizer with the Hebrews). Fenena, held hostage by the High Priest *Zaccaria, releases the Hebrews held in the Temple. Nabucco orders Jerusalem's destruction. He declares himself god and orders Hebrews and Babylonians to worship him, whereupon he is struck by a thunderbolt and becomes demented. Abigaille attempts to replace him as ruler. Nabucco prays, recovers his sanity, and recognizes Jehovah as the only God. Abigaille takes poison, begs Fenena's forgiveness for trying to destroy her and the Hebrews, and dies. Zaccaria crowns the repentant Nabucco as king. The most famous music in the opera is the Chorus of the Hebrew Slaves, sung by the hostage Hebrews on the banks of the River Euphrates as they dream of home (*Va, pensiero...*—'Go, thoughts...') This chorus was sung spontaneously by the vast public following the cortège at Verdi's funeral in Milan in 1901.

Nabucco (Verdi: *Nabucco*). Bar. King of Assyria, father of the illegitimate Abigaille and of Fenena—a secret sympathizer with the Hebrews whom Nabucco wants to destroy. Declares himself god, becomes demented, but repents and recovers his sanity. He is crowned king by the Hebrew High Priest Zaccaria. Aria: *O prodi miei, seguitemi* ('Follow me, my valiant men'). Created (1842) by Giorgio Ronconi.

Nachtigal, Konrad (Wagner: *Die Meistersinger von Nürnberg*). Bass. One of the Masters, a tinsmith and bucklemaker. Created (1868) by Eduard Sigl.

Nadir (Bizet: *The Pearl Fishers*). Ten. Fisherman, friend of Zurga. Both are in love with the same girl, Leïla. Aria: *Je crois entendre encore* ('Once more I seem to hear'); duet (with Zurga): *Au fond du temple saint* ('From the depths of the holy temple'). Created (1863) by François Morini.

Naiad (Strauss: *Ariadne auf Naxos*). Sop. One of three nymphs who watch over the sleeping Ariadne on the island of Naxos. Trio (with Dryad and Echo): *Ein schönes Wunder!* ('A beautiful miracle!'). Created (1912) by M. Junker-Burchardt; (1916) by Charlotte Dahmen.

Naina (Glinka: *Ruslan and Lyudmila*). Mez. An evil sorceress. Helps Farlaf in his failed attempt to win Lyudmila from Ruslan. Creator (1842) not traced.

Nancy 1. (Flotow: *Martha*). Mez. Maid to Lady Harriet Durham. Disguised as a peasant girl (Julia), she goes with her mistress (who is disguised as Martha), to the fair at Richmond. Created (1847) by Fr. Schwarz.

2. (Britten: *Albert Herring*). Works in her father's bakery. Girlfriend of Sid. She and Sid encourage Albert to 'go off the rails' and support him when, by getting drunk and spending the night with girls, he earns the wrath of the village and his mother. Aria: *What would Mrs Herring say?* Created (1947) by Nancy Evans (who was then the wife of Walter Legge, who later married Elisabeth Schwarzkopf. Nancy Evans became the wife of the opera's librettist).

Nangis, Raoul de (Meyerbeer: *Les Huguenots*). Ten. A Huguenot nobleman. He has fallen in love with a woman he has seen but whose identity he does not know. She is the Catholic Valentine de Saint-Bris, betrothed to the Comte de Nevers. She returns Raoul's love but her fiancé will not release her. During her father's attempted massacre of the Huguenots, she joins Raoul and they are both killed by her father's soldiers. Duet (with Valentine): *O ciel, où courez-vous?* ('O heavens, where are you rushing off to?'). Created (1836) by Adolphe Nourrit.

Nanki-Poo (Sullivan: *The Mikado*). Ten. Son of the Mikado. A minstrel, he has come to Titipu to marry Yum-Yum, only to be told that she is to marry her guardian, Ko-Ko. The elderly Katisha has set her heart on the Mikado's son. He is given permission to marry Yum-Yum, on condition that he is beheaded after a month. His friends conspire to save him and at the same time trick Ko-Ko into marrying Katisha. Aria: *A wandering minstrel I*; duet (with Yum-Yum): *Were you not to Ko-Ko plighted*. Created (1885) by Durward Lely.

Nannetta (Verdi: *Falstaff*). *See* FORD, NANNETTA.

Narciso (Rossini: *Il turco in Italia*). Ten. Young man in love with Geronio's wife Fiorilla. Created (1814) by Giovanni David.

Nardo (Mozart: *La finta giardiniera*). Bar. Really Roberto, servant of the Marchese Violante (who is disguised as Sandrina, the gardener's girl). Created (1775) probably by Giovanni Rossi.

Narraboth (Strauss: *Salome*). Ten. A young Syrian captain of the Guard. He is so fascinated by the Princess Salome that he allows himself to be persuaded to let the imprisoned Jochanaan come out of his underground cistern because Salome wants to see him. When he sees the way Salome drools over the prophet, Narraboth is so distressed that he kills himself. Aria: *Wie schön ist die Prinzessin Salome heute nacht!* ('How beautiful is the Princess Salome tonight!'). Created (1905) by Rudolf Jäger.

Narrator 1. (Britten: *Paul Bunyan*). Bar./ten. Sings the Ballad Interludes—these inform the audience of the events which are not happening on the stage but which it is necessary to know in order to follow the opera. Created (1941) by Mordecai Bauman.

2. (Britten: *Owen Wingrave*). Ten. The ballad-singer who tells of an earlier young Wingrave who hated fighting, even in childhood, and was killed by his father as a coward. Created (1971, TV/1973) by Peter Pears (who also created Sir Philip Wingrave, the two roles to be taken by the same singer).

Natalie of Orien, Princess (Henze: *Der Prinz von Homburg*). Sop. Niece of the Electress and col.-in-chief of a dragoon regiment. Promised in marriage to the Prince and pleads with the Elector for her fiancé's death warrant to be rescinded. Created (1960) by Liselotte Fölser.

Nedda (Leoncavallo: *Pagliacci*). Sop. Wife of Canio, the leader of a troupe of strolling players. She is having an affair with a villager, Silvio, but refuses to reveal his name. As Columbine in the play, she is stabbed by the clown Pagliaccio (Canio). Dying, she whispers her lover's name. Canio kills him also. Created (1892) by Adelina Stehle.

Nefertiti (Glass: *Akhnaten*). Cont. Wife of Akhnaten. Withdraws into isolation with him, away from their people. Created (1984) by Milagro Vargas.

Nekrotzar (Ligeti: *Le Grand Macabre*). Bar. The Grand Macabre of the title. He announces the coming of the end of the world. When Venus is trying to find a suitably virile and 'well-hung' lover for Mescalina, Nekrotzar offers himself and is accepted. Mescalina dies in a violent embrace by him. Nekrotzar collapses in a drunken stupor. Has he brought about the end of the world? Or was he a charlatan? Created (1978) by Erik Saedén.

Nemorino (Donizetti: *L'elisir d'amore*). Ten. A poor young peasant in love with the wealthy Adina, who seems to prefer Belcore. To help him woo her, he buys a love-potion (really wine) from the quack Dulcamara and becomes very drunk, which gives him false courage. When he inherits money from a rich uncle, all the girls throw themselves at him, making Adina admit her love for him. Aria: *Una furtiva lagrima* ('One furtive tear'). Created (1832) by Giambattista Genero.

Neoptolemus (Tippett: *King Priam*). Son of Achilles, who kills Priam to avenge his father's murder by Priam's son Paris.

Neptune (Nettuno) (Monteverdi: *Il ritorno d'Ulisse in patria*). Bass. Angry with the Phaeacians for returning Ulisse to Ithaca, he turns them and their ship to stone. Creator (1640) unknown.

Nerina (Haydn: *La fedeltà premiata*). Sop. A nymph, fickle in love, who has recently deserted Lindoro. Created (1781) by Costanza Valdesturla.

Néris (Cherubini: *Médée*). Mez. Servant of Médée. It is Néris who is instructed by her mistress to deliver gifts to Dircé which cause her death by poisoning. Created (1797) by Mme Verteuil.

Nero (Nerone) 1. (Monteverdi: *L'incoronazione di Poppea*). Sop. *Travesti* role (but has been sung by a ten.) (originally castrato). Emperor of Rome. Married to Ottavia but in love with Poppea, wife of Ottone. He banishes Ottone who has attempted to kill Poppea and leaves Ottavia in order to marry Poppea and declare her empress. Created (1643) possibly by the castrato Stefano Costa.

2. (Handel: *Agrippina*). Sop. *Travesti* role (originally castrato). Son of Agrippina by her first marriage. She is ambitious that he should succeed her present husband, Claudio, as Emperor of Rome. Created (1709) by Valeriano Pellegrini (castrato).

Nettelsheim, Agrippa von (Prokofiev: *The Fiery Angel*). Ten. A philosopher who is asked for help by Ruprecht and Renata in their search for her angel. Created (1954) by Jean Giraudeau; (1955) not traced.

Nevers, Comte de (Meyerbeer: *Les Huguenots*). Bar. Catholic nobleman, engaged to Valentine de Saint-Bris. Anxious to help the king in his wish to create peace between Catholics and Huguenots, he invites the Huguenot Raoul to his party, not knowing Raoul is in love with Valentine. Insists on marrying Valentine. Is killed during Saint-Bris's attempts to massacre the Huguenots. Created (1836) by Prosper Dérivis.

Nibelungen, Die (Wagner: *Der Ring des Nibelungen*). The Nibelungs are dwarfs who live in the depths of the earth. They mine precious metals, and are forced by Alberich, who becomes all-powerful by possessing the Tarnhelm and Ring made from the Rhine gold, to dig for gold to increase Alberich's hoard. The two main characters in this class are the brothers Mime and Alberich.

Nick (Puccini: *La fanciulla del West*). Ten. Bartender at 'The Polka', an inn owned by Minnie (the girl of the title). Created (1910) by Albert Reiss.

Nicklausse (Offenbach: *Les Contes d'Hoffmann*). Mez. *Travesti* role. Friend to whom the poet Hoffmann tells the stories of his previous unhappy love affairs. Nicklausse points out to the poet that all those he has loved have been manifestations of the same woman. He assures Hoffmann that his work will be all the more inspired for his sad experiences in love. Created (1881) by Marguerite Ugalde.

Nicoletta, Princess (Prokofiev: *The Love for Three Oranges*). Mez. The princess hidden in the second orange. She dies of thirst. Created (1921) by Frances Paperte.

Nieces I and II (Britten: *Peter Grimes*). 2 Sop. 'Nieces' of 'Auntie', the landlady of 'The Boar', and its main attraction. Quartet (with Auntie and Ellen Orford): *From the gutter*. Created (1945) by Blanche Turner and Minnie Bower.

Night-Watchman (Nachtwächter) (Wagner: *Die Meistersinger von Nürnberg*). Bass. He first appears after Eva and Walther have decided to elope, and his horn is heard as he leaves the scene. He reappears at the end of the second act to quell the riot that is taking place among the crowds after Beckmesser's attempts to serenade Eva. Aria: *Hort ihr Leut', und lasst euch sagen* ('Hark, good people, to what I say'). Created (1868) by Ferdinand Lang.

Nilakantha (Delibes: *Lakmé*). Bass-bar. A Brahmin priest, father of Lakmé. Disapproves of her relationship with an English officer. Created (1883) by Mons. Cobalet.

Nina (Massenet: *Chérubin*). Sop. Ward of the Duke, she is in love with Chérubin. When he realizes that Chérubin loves her too, the Duke gives his blessing. Created (1905) by Marguerite Carré.

Ninetta 1. (Rossini: *La gazza ladra*). See VILLABELLA, NINETTA.

2. (Prokofiev: *The Love for Three Oranges*). Sop. The princess inside the third orange, with whom the Prince falls in love. She is turned into a rat by Smeraldina, but turned back again by the King's magician, Chelio. Created (1921) by Jeanne Dusseau.

Nino, Ghost of (Rossini: *Semiramide*). Bass. King of Babylon, murdered by his wife Semiramide and her lover. His ghost appears to Arsace and tells him he is the king's son and must avenge his death.

Nireno (Handel: *Giulio Cesare*). Cont. *Travesti* role (originally castrato). Confidant of Cleopatra and Tolomeo. Created (1724) by Giuseppe Bigonzi (alto castrato).

Nixon in China (Adams). Lib. by Alice Goodman; 3 acts; f. p. Houston 1987, cond. John DeMain.

Based on the visit by the American President to China in 1972: Richard *Nixon flies to China, accompanied by his wife Pat *Nixon and the American Sec. of State, Henry *Kissinger. They meet *Mao Tse-tung and his wife (*Chiang Ch'ing) and have political discussions with *Chou En-lai. They are guests at a banquet in the Great Hall of the People, are shown round cultural centres, and are taken to see a revolutionary ballet devised by Mao's wife.

Nixon, Pat (Adams: *Nixon in China*). Sop. Wife of American President. She accompanies her husband on his visit to China. Aria: *I don't daydream and don't look back*. Created (1987) by Carolann Page.

Nixon, President Richard (Adams: *Nixon in China*). Bass. American President. He goes in 1972 to China to meet Chairman Mao in an attempt to improve relationships between their countries. Aria: *Achieving a great human dream*. Created (1987) by James Maddalena.

Noémie (Massenet: *Cendrillon*). Sop. Daughter of Mme de la Haltière, sister of Dorothée, and stepsister of Cendrillon. One of Cindarella's 'ugly sisters'. Created (1899) by Jeanne Tiphaine.

Nolan, Mrs (Menotti: *The Medium*). Mez. A newcomer to the séance held by Mme Flora. She wants to contact her late daughter. Created (1946) by Virginia Beeler.

Nora (Vaughan Williams: *Riders to the Sea*). Sop. Younger daughter of Maurya and sister of Cathleen. Her father and brothers have drowned at sea. Created (1937) by Marjorie Stevenson.

Norina (Donizetti: *Don Pasquale*). Sop. A young widow, the niece of Dr Malatesta. She is in love with Ernesto, Pasquale's nephew, but Pasquale disapproves of their relationship. She plots with Malatesta to trick Pasquale. She poses as Malatesta's demure sister Sofronia and 'marries' Pasquale in a fake ceremony. After the wedding she becomes a harridan, spending all his money and dominating him— he can't wait to return to peaceful bachelorhood. She deliberately drops a note where Pasquale will find it, and he learns that she is meeting her 'lover' (Ernesto). He catches them together in the garden. He agrees to annul their marriage and offers his blessing on the young couple. Arias: *So anch'io la virtù magica* ('I also know the magic virtue'). Created (1843) by Giulia Grisi (lifelong companion of G. M. Mario, the tenor who created Ernesto).

Norma (Bellini). Lib. by Felice Romani; 2 acts; f.p. Milan 1831, cond. Vincenzo Bellini.

Rome, *c.*50 BC: *Norma, the High Priestess, is the daughter of the High Priest *Oroveso, who wants war against the Romans. She is in love with the Roman *Pollione and has borne him two children. He has forsaken her for an unknown woman. This is *Adalgisa, an acolyte in the temple. Adalgisa comes to confess her love to Norma and is horrified to discover that Pollione has been Norma's lover. She determines to send him back to Norma, but fails. As Norma nobly decides to sacrifice herself to the gods to enable the Gauls to defeat the Romans, Pollione's love for her is renewed and he joins her in the flames.

Norma (Bellini: *Norma*). Sop. High Priestess, daughter of the druid Oroveso. Has borne two children to the Roman Pollione, who has now fallen in love with the acolyte Adalgisa. Norma sacrifices herself in the cause of winning a battle and Pollione mounts the pyre and joins her in the flames. Aria: *Casta Diva* ('Chaste goddess'); duet (with Adalgisa): *Mira, o Norma!* ('See, Norma'). Created (1831) by Giuditta Pasta. *See also* ARTICLE BY ANDREW PORTER, p. 208.

NORMA (*Norma*—Bellini)

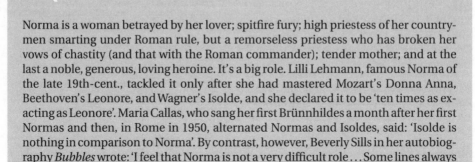

by Andrew Porter

Norma is a woman betrayed by her lover; spitfire fury; high priestess of her country-men smarting under Roman rule, but a remorseless priestess who has broken her vows of chastity (and that with the Roman commander); tender mother; and at the last a noble, generous, loving heroine. It's a big role. Lilli Lehmann, famous Norma of the late 19th-cent., tackled it only after she had mastered Mozart's Donna Anna, Beethoven's Leonore, and Wagner's Isolde, and she declared it to be 'ten times as exacting as Leonore'. Maria Callas, who sang her first Brünnhildes a month after her first Normas and then, in Rome in 1950, alternated Normas and Isoldes, said: 'Isolde is nothing in comparison to Norma'. By contrast, however, Beverly Sills in her autobiography *Bubbles* wrote: 'I feel that Norma is not a very difficult role . . . Some lines always want to make me giggle.'

Norma the play was written in 1831 for the great tragedienne Mme Georges; the author, Alexandre Soumet, described her traversal of 'the entire circle of passions that can be contained in the female heart'—the Greek Niobe, Shakespeare's Lady Macbeth, Chateaubriand's Velléda—rising in the final mad scene 'to heights of inspiration which will perhaps never again be scaled'. *Norma* the opera was composed later that year for the La Scala [Milan] début of the great soprano tragedienne Giuditta Pasta. Bellini and his librettist, Felice Romani, omitted Soumet's mad scene (in which a Medea-recalling Norma, having killed one of her children, flings herself together with the other over a precipice); instead, in a noble finale, their heroine entrusts the children to her father's care and resolutely mounts the pyre in expiation of her transgression. Bellini composed the piece with exceptional care. His autograph score reveals many changes, large and small. Indications such as *con devota fierezza* [with devout pride], *con voce cupa e terrible* [with a 'covered' and dreadful voice], *con tutta la tenerezza* [with all tenderness], *canto vibrato* [with a quiver in the voice] abound.

Many sopranos hesitated to essay it. In the first 80 years of Metropolitan Opera [New York] history only five sang it: Lehmann, Rosa Ponselle (35 years after Lehmann, and only in her tenth Met season), Gina Cigna, Zinka Milanov, and Callas. Kirsten Flagstad learned the role but decided against it; Dusolina Giannini took it to dress rehearsal and then withdrew. But when the Met mounted a new production of Norma in 1970 for Joan Sutherland, six different sopranos soon appeared in it. Esther Mazzoleni, a celebrated Italian Norma early this century, spoke out in her retirement: 'I simply cannot understand what is happening nowadays. They all sing Norma—the coloraturas, the lyrics, the spintos [and she named names]. How can they do justice to this terrifying score? It's a travesty of what Bellini wrote, and the audience takes a lot of punishment.'

Nearly a century of *Norma* performances can now be heard on record. Adelina Patti never sang the role, but she recorded 'Casta Diva' in 1906, when she was 63. Her breaths are short, her tone and style pure and beautiful. Lehmann's *Norma* recordings were made in 1908; at 59 she still had strong, sure tone, astounding flexibility, shapely trills. Hanslick [Eduard Hanslick (1825–1904), a celebrated Austrian music critic] had written of her in 1885, 'her Norma was characterized in slow cantilena by the most beautiful portamento and the securest, finest intonation, in the florid passages by a pure and fluent coloratura, never a coquettish intrusion but noble, serious.' Yet—as Bonynge [Richard Bonynge (b1930), Australian conductor and husband of Dame Joan Sutherland] suggested—a 'complete' Norma has perhaps not existed. For Hanslick also said (and listening to Lehmann's records we may well agree) that 'one may conceive of a thunder of passion more imposing, of lightning flashes of jealousy and anger more incendiary'.

For those, we turn to Callas. Norma was the role she sang most often: ninety times, in eight countries. She recorded it officially twice, and several live performances also survive. I heard Callas's Covent Garden Normas of 1952 and 1953, when she was 'large', and the Paris Normas of 1964, when she was slender and elegant. In all of them she was noble, powerful, delicate, intent. And since then? I won't be as harsh as Mme Mazzoleni, for I've heard other Normas with merits, some considerable. But none who so memorably brought the great role to life with Gluckian grandeur and Romantic variety of passion, tenderness, and force.

Norman (Normanno) (Donizetti: *Lucia di Lammermoor*). Ten. A supporter of Lucia's brother Enrico. He helps Enrico to deceive Lucia into believing that her lover, Edgardo, has been unfaithful. Created (1835) by Teofilo Rossi.

Norns (Wagner: *Götterdämmerung*). 1st cont., 2nd mez., 3rd sop. Probably daughters of Erda. They spin a rope and recount the events which have led to the beginning of this final opera of the cycle. They foretell the end of the gods—and, as if to emphasize this, the rope they are spinning breaks. Trio: *Welch Licht leuchtet dort?* ('What light shines there?'). Created (1876) by (1) Johanna Wagner, (2) Josephine Scheffzsky, and (3) Friederike Grün.

Notary (Donizetti: *Don Pasquale*). Bar. Carlino, a cousin of Dr Malatesta, who acts as notary for the false wedding of Pasquale and 'Sofronia' (Norina). Created (1843) by Federico Lablache (son of Luigi Lablache, who created Pasquale). *See also* DESPINA.

Nottingham, Duke of (Donizetti: *Roberto Devereux*). Bar. Husband of Sara, with whom Devereux (Earl of Essex) is in love. He realizes that Sara also loves Devereux. When Devereux is sentenced to death, he prevents his wife taking to Queen Elizabeth the ring which would be the sign for the Queen to reprieve Devereux, allowing her to go only when it is too late to save her lover. Aria: *Forse in quel cor sensibile*

('Perhaps in that sensitive heart'). Created (1837) by Paolo Barroilhet.

Nottingham, Sara, Countess of (Donizetti: *Roberto Devereux*). Mez. Is loved by and loves Devereux, but while he was in Ireland she was forced into marriage with the Duke of Nottingham. Devereux gives her a ring given to him by the Queen and which will guarantee his safety. Sara gives him a scarf, which is found near his heart when he is arrested and searched. It is recognized by the Queen and by Nottingham, who both realize the significance of it. When Devereux is sentenced to death, her husband delays her taking the ring to the Queen until it is too late to reprieve Devereux. Aria: *All'afflitto è dolce il pianto* ('Weeping is sweet to one who sorrows'). Created (1837) by Almerinda Granchi.

Nourabad (Bizet: *The Pearl Fishers*). Bass. High Priest of Brahma. He finds the virgin priestess Leïla and fisherman Nadir together and Nadir is arrested. Later, when he realizes Leïla has previously saved his life, he frees the two lovers. Created (1863) by Mons. Guyot.

Novice (Britten: *Billy Budd*). Ten. A new young sailor on HMS *Indomitable*. Created (1951) by William McAlpine.

Noye (Britten: *Noye's Fludde*). Bass-bar. Noah, father of Sem, Ham, and Jaffett. He is warned by God of the forthcoming flood. He builds an ark in which all his family and animals ride out the storm. After the storm, Noye sends a raven, then a dove, to see if the land is dry before he leads everyone out of the ark. Created (1958) by Owen Brannigan.

Noye, Mrs (Britten: *Noye's Fludde*). Cont. Wife of Noah and mother of Sem, Ham, and Jaffett. She spends most of her time drinking and chatting with the Gossips and has to be carried into the ark by her sons to save her from being drowned in the flood. Created (1958) by Gladys Parr.

Noye's Fludde (Britten). Lib. from Alfred W. Pollard's edn. of *English Miracle Plays, Moralities and Interludes*; 1 act; f.p. Orford 1958, cond. Charles Mackerras.

*Noye (Noah) is told by God that the earth is to be flooded. Everyone except Noye and his family will be destroyed. Noye must build a ship to save them. He is helped by his sons, *Sem, *Ham, and *Jaffett and their wives. Mrs *Noye drinks and chats with her friends (the *Gossips). As the rain starts, the *Voice of God tells Noye to go into the Ark with his family and all their animals. Mrs Noye has to be forcibly carried in by her sons. After the storm, Noye is the last to leave the ark, the Voice of God giving him his blessing. Incorporates hymns sung by the Congregation (the audience).

nozze di Figaro, Le (*The Marriage of Figaro*) (Mozart). Lib. by Lorenzo da Ponte; 4 acts; f.p. Vienna 1786, cond. Wolfgang Amadeus Mozart.

The Almavivas' château, near Seville, 18th cent.: The Count *Almaviva's valet, *Figaro, and the *Countess's maid, *Susanna, are about to be married. The Count is delaying the wedding as long as possible to give him time to seduce Susanna himself. The page *Cherubino is besotted with the Countess and gives the Count cause for suspicion. The music-master, *Basilio, enjoys causing trouble between them all. *Bartolo, the Countess's former guardian, assists his elderly housekeeper *Marcellina in her efforts to force Figaro to marry her to repay a loan. The Count sends Cherubino off to war. Marcellina and Bartolo are revealed as Figaro's long-lost parents. The Countess and Susanna hatch a plot to catch out the Count in an illicit assignation in the garden (they send him a note via *Barbarina, daughter of the gardener, *Antonio, and Cherubino's latest love). They will exchange clothes and so fool him. After many complications, all is sorted out and the Count asks forgiveness for doubting his wife's fidelity.

Nurse (die Amme) (Strauss: *Die Frau ohne Schatten*). Mez. To her has been entrusted the care of the Empress, and to the Nurse comes Keikobad's Messenger: if the Empress does not cast a shadow (i.e. become pregnant) in three days, the Emperor will be turned to stone. The Empress begs her Nurse to help her find a shadow, and together they travel to earth, where, dressed as peasants, they visit the poor Dyer Barak and his Wife, a couple also childless. But the Wife has a shadow and the Nurse offers to buy it in return for untold riches. The Wife is tempted, but the Empress is moved by the obvious distress which it is causing Barak to have no children and she refuses to take the shadow at the cost of another's happiness. The Nurse is furious and continues to tempt her, pointing out again the fate that awaits the Emperor. The Nurse returns with the Empress to Keikobad's kingdom, but fears his wrath and tries to prevent the Empress entering his temple. The Empress parts from the Nurse, who is cast into a boat by the Spirit Messenger, doomed to wander for ever amongst those she hates. Arias: *Abzutun Mutterschaft* ('To renounce motherhood'); *Fort von hier!* ('Right away from here!'). Of the three leading female roles in this opera, the Nurse (*Amme*) is the most disturbing. She despises mankind's unscrupulous way of life, yet is unable fully to understand the elevated world of the Emperor. The one thing that fills her with trepidation is the power of Keikobad. Rudolf Hartmann aptly described the Nurse as 'a dangerous female Mephistopheles who exudes evil to the point of self-destruction'. It is a superb character-part and among those who have made an impression in the role are Eva von der Osten (the first Octavian in *Der Rosenkavalier*), Elisabeth Höngen, Martha Mödl, Brigitte Fassbaender, and Jane Henschel. Created (1919) by Lucie Weidt.

Oakapple, Robin (Sullivan: *Ruddigore*). *See* MURGATROYD, SIR RUTHVEN.

Oberon, or The Elf King's Oath (Weber). Lib. by James Robinson Planché; 3 acts; f.p. London 1826, cond. Carl Maria von Weber.

*Oberon has quarrelled with *Titania and vowed not to be reconciled until they find two lovers who are faithful despite all temptations. *Puck has unsuccessfully searched for such a couple. He has heard that *Huon, a young knight, has killed Emperor Charlemagne's son and been condemned to go to Baghdad, where he must kill whoever sits on the Caliph's right hand and marry the Caliph's daughter, *Reiza. Oberon gives Huon a fairy horn and magic goblet, and Huon leaves accompanied by *Sherasmin, his squire. They manage to escape with Reiza and her maid, *Fatima, with whom Sherasmin has fallen in love. Pirates capture all but Huon who, with the help of Puck and of the magic horn, rescues them all. He and Reiza have thus remained faithful, freeing Oberon to be reconciled with Titania.

Oberon 1. (Britten: *A Midsummer Night's Dream*). Counter-ten. (or cont.). King of the Fairies. Uses Puck to help wreak revenge on his queen, Tytania. Magic juice is used on her eyes and she falls in love with Bottom wearing an ass's head. Aria: *I know a bank*. In recent times this role has been well sung by James Bowman and Michael Chance. Created (1960) by Alfred Deller.

2. (Weber: *Oberon*). Ten. Has quarrelled with Titania and will only be reconciled if they have proof that lovers can be constant and true to each other through all trials and tribulations. He uses the rescue of Reiza by the knight Huon (with the aid of Puck) as proof that this is possible. Created (1826) by Charles Bland.

3. (Purcell: *The Fairy Queen*). Spoken. As for (1), but in the final scene he presents to the Duke a Chinese masque to celebrate the state of marriage. Creator (1692) unknown.

Obigny, Marchese d' (Verdi: *La traviata*). Bass. 'Protector' of Flora and a friend of Violetta. Created (1853) by Arnaldo Silvestri.

Ochs auf Lerchenau, Baron Anton (Strauss: *Der Rosenkavalier*). Bass. Cousin of the Marschallin. He arrives to visit her while she is having breakfast with her young lover Octavian, who quickly dresses as a chambermaid. Ochs alternates between asking the Marschallin to recommend to him a nobleman who can take the traditional silver rose to his new fiancée, the young Sophie von Faninal, and flirting with the maid, whose name is given as 'Mariandel'. The Marschallin knows just the right person—Octavian, of course. Teased by the Marschallin for flirting with the maid when he has just got engaged, he explains that men do not mate by the calendar—there is no time of month or day when he is not ready for a woman. He suggests that 'Mariandel' would be an ideal maid for his new bride. He uses his own bastard son, Leupold, as his 'body-servant'. During the Marschallin's morning levee, Ochs negotiates with her lawyer to draw up his marriage settlement and Valzacchi, an Italian intriguer, and his partner Annina, offer their services to the Baron. Leupold brings the silver rose to the Marschallin. At the Faninal mansion, Ochs arrives to meet his bride shortly after she and Octavian have met and fallen in love over the presentation of the rose. His disreputable servants cause chaos by chasing the Faninal maids around the house. When he sets eyes on Sophie, he ogles her and attempts to pull her on to his knee, pointing out that she is now his. She is revolted by him, and Octavian promises her he will prevent this marriage. He draws his sword and he and Ochs parry, Ochs receiving a superficial wound and making a great fuss about his injury. While he is being attended to, Valzacchi and Annina (now in Octavian's employment) bring Ochs a message from 'Mariandel', who has agreed to meet him at an inn. Ochs waltzes with glee. At the inn that night, Ochs supervises the setting up of the room where he will dine with 'Mariandel', making sure there is a bed in an alcove. Before his arrival, Octavian, Valzacchi, and Annina have hidden accomplices behind windows and trapdoors, ready to frighten Ochs. 'Mariandel' arrives, and Ochs dismisses the waiters—Leupold will serve dinner. He does his best to seduce her, encouraging her to drink wine, and is interrupted by comings and goings through the trapdoors, which 'Mariandel' denies seeing. A veiled lady claims him as her husband, her children all screaming 'Papa'. Ochs loses his wig and becomes more and more confused. The Police Commissar arrives amidst the chaos, and Ochs claims 'Mariandel' as his fiancée, which she rigorously denies. First Faninal, summoned by Valzacchi, and then the Marschallin, brought by the worried Leupold, arrive and gradually the truth comes out. The Marschallin advises Ochs to leave with a little dignity intact. Arias: *Das lieg' ich!* ... ('Here I lie'); *'Ohne mich, ohne mich'* ('Without me, without me').

This famous bass role—at one time Strauss considered calling the opera *Ochs auf Lerchenau*—is ever-popular. Strauss did not, however, see him entirely as a *buffo* role—he pointed out that he is only 35 years old, a nobleman (albeit a boorish one), who knows how to behave in the presence of his cousin the Princess, although he is inwardly a bounder: 'Viennese comedy, not Berlin farce', said Strauss. Vocally it demands a true bass—the end of the *Ohne mich* waltz drops very low and has to be held for several bars (many basses cannot resist the temptation to sink even lower and hold it even longer!). Richard Mayr was the first Vienna Ochs, and other famous exponents of the part include Fritz Krenn, Paul Knüpfer, Kurt Böhme, Ludwig Weber, Otto Edelmann, Oskar Czerwenka, Theo Adam, Donald Gramm, Jules Bastin, Kurt Moll, Walter Berry, Michael Langdon (who sang it over 100 times worldwide), Kurt Rydl, Manfred Jungwirth, John Tomlinson, and Franz Hawlata. Created (1911) by Carl Perron (who had, six years earlier, created Jochanaan in *Salome*).

Octavia 1. (Monteverdi: *L'incoronazione di Poppea*). *See* OTTAVIA.

2. (Barber: *Antony and Cleopatra*). Mez. Sister of the Roman Emperor, she marries Antony, who leaves her to return to Cleopatra in Egypt. Created (1966) by Mary Ellen Pracht.

Octavian (Strauss: *Der Rosenkavalier*). Sop. (often sung by mez.). *Travesti* role. The 17-year-old Count Rofrano, latest lover of Marie Therese, a 32-year-old Princess (wife of the field marshal—Feldmarschal—thus she is called the (Feld)Marschallin) who calls him by his pet-name, Quinquin. When the opera opens, they have clearly been making love. Their breakfast is interrupted by the arrival of her cousin, Baron Ochs, who consults her about whom he should use to present the traditional silver rose to his new fiancée, Sophie von Faninal. Octavian, unable to leave, disguises himself as a chambermaid, 'Mariandel', with whom Ochs is soon flirting (as Octavian is a *travesti* role, this gives rise to a situation in which a female singer impersonates a man who then impersonates a woman). The Marschallin recommends Octavian as the Knight of the Rose (the *Rosenkavalier* of the title). After the Baron leaves, Octavian finds his lover in melancholy mood—she knows that, sooner or later, he will leave her for a younger woman. This comes about sooner than she has anticipated, for as Octavian presents the silver rose to Sophie, they fall in love at once and he becomes embroiled in a fight with Ochs, whose marriage to Sophie Octavian is now determined to prevent. In his disguise as 'Mariandel', Octavian has an assignation with Ochs at a rather seedy local inn, where 'she' has to resist the Baron's overtures and his efforts to get her drunk—'she' has already noted the conveniently placed bed in an alcove. Octavian has hired Valzacchi and Annina, intriguers, who arrange for people to be hidden around the inn to frighten Ochs throughout their meeting, until he becomes very confused about the situation and even the police become involved. It finally needs both Sophie and the Marschallin to arrive at the inn to sort things out, and for Ochs to realize that he has been fooled by them all. Octavian is left in the room with Sophie, whom he loves, and the Marschallin, his so recent lover, and stands between the two of them, not sure which way to move next. The Marschallin acknowledges that she has lost him to the younger girl, and he tries to explain to her how he feels about her, despite his love for Sophie. With great dignity, she releases him from their relationship and leaves. He and Sophie vow their love for each other. Aria: *Nein, nein, nein, nein! I trink' kein Wein* ('No, no, no, no! Oi'll not drink no wine'); duet (with the Marschallin): *Heut' oder Morgen...* ('Today or tomorrow'); duet (with Sophie): *Mir ist die Ehre widerfahren...* ('To me has been given the honour'— the Presentation of the Rose); trio (with Sophie and the Marschallin): *Marie Theres'!... Hab' mir's gelobt* ('Marie Therese!'... 'I vowed to myself'); duet (with Sophie): *Spür' nur dich... Ist ein Traum* ('I hold only you'... 'It is a dream'). Created (1911) by Eva von der Osten. Like the Marschallin and Sophie, this has been a favourite role for Strauss sopranos from the first performance to the present day. Many an Octavian has gone on to become a famous Marschallin, including Lotte Lehmann, Germaine Lubin, Tiana Lemnitz, Sena Jurinac, Christa Ludwig, and Felicity Lott. Other notable singers of the role include Lucrezia Bori, Vera Schwarz, Conchita Supervia, Margit Angerer, Eva Hadrabova, Jarmila Navotna, Janet Baker, Brigitte Fassbaender, Ann Murray, Susan Graham, and Angelika Kirchschlager.

Octavius Caesar (Barber: *Antony and Cleopatra*). Ten. Roman Emperor. His sister, Octavia, marries Antony. Antony deserts her to return to Cleopatra and the Emperor, angry at his betrayal, declares war on him. Created (1966) by Jess Thomas.

Odoardo (Handel: *Ariodante*). Ten. A courtier with the King of Scotland. Created (1735) by Michael Stoppelaer.

Oedipus (Stravinsky: *Oedipus Rex*). Ten. Son of King Laius and Queen Jocasta, and now husband of Jocasta. Considered to be the son of and heir to King Polybus' throne. Oedipus promises to find the murderer of King Laius, and thus rescue Thebes from the plague. His wife tells him that Laius was killed by thieves at a crossroads. Frightened, Oedipus confesses to her that years ago he killed an old man at a crossroads. A messenger announces the death of King Polybus and tells Oedipus he was not really the king's son. He was found on a

mountain and raised by Polybus, but was the son of Laius and Jocasta. Realizing he has killed his own father and married his mother, Oedipus blinds himself with Jocasta's brooch and is sent into exile by his people. Created (1927) by Stéphane Belina-Skupievsky.

Oedipus Rex (*King Oedipus*) (Stravinsky). Lib. by Jean Cocteau; 2 acts; f.p. (concert) Paris 1927, cond. Igor Stravinsky; (stage) Vienna 1928, cond. Franz Schalk.

Mythological Thebes: A *Speaker introduces the events. *Creon, having consulted the Oracle, informs the people that the plague will not cease until the murderer of King Laius has been found. *Oedipus promises to find him. The blind *Tiresias refuses to give any helpful information. Oedipus accuses him and Creon of plotting to seize the throne of Thebes. Oedipus' wife, *Jocasta, tells that the Oracle has lied—it said that Laius would be killed by his son, but he was, in fact, killed by thieves at a crossroads. Oedipus confesses that he killed an old man at a crossroads. The death of King *Polybus of Corinth is announced by a *Messenger, who reveals that Oedipus was not really Polybus' son, but the son of Laius and Jocasta. Oedipus realizes it was he who killed his father and married his mother. He blinds himself with Jocasta's brooch and is expelled from Thebes.

Oktavian (Strauss: *Der Rosenkavalier*). *See* OCTAVIAN.

Old Gondolier (Britten: *Death in Venice*). Bass-bar. He rows Aschenbach from Venice to the Lido. Created (1973) by John Shirley-Quirk.

Olga (Tchaikovsky: *Eugene Onegin*). Mez./cont. Daughter of Mme Larina and younger sister of Tatyana. She makes Lensky jealous by flirting with his friend Eugene Onegin at her sister's birthday party, thus being partly responsible for the tragedy that ensues. Aria: *Ya ne sposobna k grusti tomnoy* ('I am no good at languid melancholy'). Created (1879) by Alexandra Devitskaya.

Olivier (Strauss: *Capriccio*). Bar. Poet in love with Countess Madeleine. He writes a sonnet for her birthday and is very upset when his rival, the composer Flamand, sets it to music. As they are both in love with the Countess, he was hoping that his words would impress her more than Flamand's music: *Prima le parole—dopo la musica!*, he says ('First the words—then the music!'). This gives rise to an argument—to whom does the work now belong, the poet or the composer? Madeleine settles the argument—it is her present from them both and it now belongs to her. After Olivier leaves the château, he sends a message to the Countess via her Major-domo—he will meet her at 11 o'clock the next morning in her library (exactly the same arrangement she has made with Flamand) in order to learn how the opera will end—in other words, does she choose the poet or the composer? Aria (the sonnet he has written): *Kein andres, das mir so im Herzen loht* ('Your image in my ardent bosom glows'). Created (1942) by Hans Hotter.

Olympia (Offenbach: *Les Contes d'Hoffmann*). Sop. A mechanical doll created by the inventor Spalanzani, her eyes provided by Coppélius. Believing her to be Spalanzani's daughter, Hoffmann falls in love with her. She is destroyed by Coppélius. Aria: *Les oiseaux dans la charmille* ('Birds in the hedgerows'). Created (1881) by Adèle Isaac.

Onegin, Eugene (Tchaikovsky: *Eugene Onegin*). Bar. A friend of Lensky, he is brought to the Larin house and there meets the two daughters, Lensky's fiancée Olga and her elder sister Tatyana, who quickly falls in love with him. She writes a letter to him, confessing her feelings. When they next meet, he rejects her love, pointing out that he can regard her only in a brotherly way. Bored at her birthday party, he flirts with her sister Olga, thus making Lensky jealous and Lensky challenges him to a duel. They meet at dawn, each realizing that the joke has gone too far, neither wanting to proceed, but both, for the sake of honour, feeling the duel must take place. To his horror, Onegin kills Lensky and rapidly leaves the area. Some two years later he is invited to a party at Prince Gremin's palace and recognizes Gremin's wife as Tatyana. He realizes he is in love with her. He contrives to see her alone and she sends for him the next day. He declares his love, but she points out that she is now married and must remain loyal to her husband, while admitting that she still loves Onegin. She bids him farewell and he collapses in despair.

Aria: *Uvï, somnen'ya net* ('Alas, there is no doubt'). Created (1879) by Sergey Vasilyevich Gilev.

Ophélie (Thomas: *Hamlet*). Sop. Daughter of the chief minister, Polonius. She is in love with Hamlet, son of the late king, and is unaware that her father has been involved in the plot to kill the King. When Hamlet, upset at learning the truth, rejects her, she loses her sanity and drowns herself in a lake. Aria: A *vos jeux, mes amis* ('To your games, my friends')—in this famous mad scene, she imagines that she is married to Hamlet and sings about the beautiful girl who draws her faithless lovers to a watery grave. Created (1868) by Christine Nilsson.

Oracle of the Dead/Hecate (Birtwistle: *The Mask of Orpheus*). Sop. Orpheus consults the Oracle in his efforts to bring Euridice back from the Underworld. Created (1986) by Marie Angel.

Orestes 1. (Orest) (Strauss: *Elektra*). Bar. Son of Klytämnestra and Agamemnon, brother of Chrysothemis and Elektra, who sent him away to safety after their mother and her lover Aegisth murdered his father. Elektra waits for his return—she is sure he will come and avenge their father, but news (false) reaches the palace of his death, much to Klytämnestra's relief and Elektra's distress. He arrives in the grounds and sees Elektra, but does not recognize this unkempt wild woman as his sister. It is some time, also, before she realizes who he is—only after the servants throw themselves at his feet and Orest comments that even the dogs recognized him, does Elektra believe it is her brother. Created (1909) by Carl Perron (who, four years earlier, had been the first Jochanaan in *Salome* and was to become, in 1911, the first Baron Ochs in *Der Rosenkavalier*—a remarkable record).

2. (Oreste) (Gluck: *Iphigénie en Tauride*). Bar. Brother of Iphigénie and son of Agamemnon and Clitemnestre (see above). Comes to Tauride and is about to be sacrificed at the decree of King Thoas, when his sister recognizes him and he is pardoned by the goddess Diana. Created (1779) by Henri Larrivée.

3. (Oreste) (Offenbach: *La Belle Hélène*). Sop. Travesti role. Son of Agamemnon (see above) and nephew of Helen. Created (1864) by Léa Silly.

4.(Oreste) (Rossini: *Ermione*). Ten. He leads a Greek delegation to the court of Pyrrhus, demanding the death of Hector's young son, to avoid him ever being able to take revenge for his father's death. He loves Hermione, and at her request he kills her unfaithful husband. But she changes her mind, regrets the act, and has him arrested. Created (1819) by Giovanni David.

Orfeo 1. (Gluck: *Orfeo ed Euridice*). Cont. (*travesti* role)/ten. (originally castrato). A musician, who goes to Hades to search for his dead wife. He is forbidden to look at her, but cannot resist turning round as he leads her out of the underworld. Again she dies. The God of Love takes pity on him, moved by the intensity of the lament he sings, and brings her back to life again. The famous lament is *Che farò senza Euridice* ('What shall I do without Eurydice', but always sung in English as 'What is life for me without you?'). The role is a favourite with many great mez. and cont., and has been sung most famously by Pauline Viardot, Clara Butt, Kathleen Ferrier, and Janet Baker, and by the counterten. Jochen Kowalski. Created (It. vers. 1762, Vienna) by Gaetano Guadagni (alto castrato); (Fr. vers. 1762, Paris) by Joseph Legros (ten.).

2. (Haydn: *Orfeo ed Euridice*). Ten. After being forced by Euridice to look at her, thus causing her death, Orfeo takes poison. Created (1951) by Tygge Tyggeson.

3. (Monteverdi: *L'Orfeo*). Ten./sop. Orfeo is taken to Heaven by his father Apollo to see his beloved Euridice in the stars. Created (1607) by Francesco Rasi (the ten. and composer).

See also ORPHEUS.

Orfeo L' (Monteverdi). Lib. by Alessandro Striggio jnr.; prol. and 5 acts; f.p. Mantua 1607.

Mythological Greece: For the main outline of the story, see *Orfeo ed Euridice* (Gluck) below: the main differences being that Euridice is alive at the beginning of the opera, and when *Orfeo attempts to cross the Styx, the boatman *Charon refuses to let him pass. Orfeo's impassioned plea has no effect, and he has to wait for Charon to fall asleep, lulled by the music, to take over the boat himself. After *Euridice's death (for the second time), Orfeo is consoled by his father, *Apollo, and they both return to Heaven where Orfeo will see Euridice in the stars. This can probably claim to be the first great opera, representing an immense advance in style compared with Monteverdi's predecessors.

Orfeo ed Euridice (Gluck). Lib. by Ranieri da Calzabigi; 3 acts; f.p. Vienna 1762 (first version, in Italian); Paris 1774 (second version, in French, as *Orphée et Eurydice*).

Mythological Greece: *Euridice is dead, mourned by her distraught husband *Orfeo. *Amor (Cupid), the God of Love, tells Orfeo he may go into Hades, but that if he rescues Euridice he must not look at her until they have crossed the Styx—if he disobeys, or tries to explain, she will die. At the entrance to Hades, Orfeo wins the sympathy of the *Furies with his music and is allowed to search for his beloved. When he finds her, he takes her by the hand to lead her from Hades. She, of course, cannot understand why he will not look at her; he capitulates to her pleading and embraces her. She immediately dies. Touched by the depth of his grief and the beauty of the lament he sings, Amor restores Euridice to life.

Orfeo ed Euridice (Haydn). Full title is *L'anima del filosofo, ossia Orfeo ed Euridice* (*The Spirit of Philosophy, or Orpheus and Euridice*). Lib. by Carlo Francesco Badini; 4 acts; f.p. Florence 1951, cond. Erich Kleiber.

This mythological story is the same as that for Gluck's opera described above, but ends differently: *Euridice (daughter of Creonte) deliberately walks in front of *Orfeo to compel him to look at her. She dies and he, distraught, takes poison. Comp. 1791, the première was given at the Florence Maggio Musicale, the cast incl. Maria Callas as Euridice and Boris Christoff as her father.

Orford, Ellen (Britten: *Peter Grimes*). Sop. A widow and the Borough school mistress. She hopes to marry Grimes and tries to defend him against the Borough. When he decides to go against advice and take another apprentice, and the carrier, Hobson, is reluctant to fetch the boy for him, Ellen offers to go with Hobson, thus calming everyone down. Outside the church, she sits embroidering and talking to the apprentice John, and she notices his coat is torn and then finds a bruise on his neck. As she questions him about it, Grimes comes to take the boy to sea, despite poor weather, as he can see there are many fish to be caught ('the whole sea's boiling', he tells the boy). Her attempts to prevent him taking the boy to sea in a storm fail. After the boy's death, she accompanies Balstrode when he tells Grimes to take his boat out to sea and sink it as the only way out of the dilemma. Arias: *Embroidery in childhood; Glitter of waves and glitter of sunlight*. Some outstanding sopranos have sung this role, among them Heather Harper, Josephine Barstow, Nancy Gustafson, Susan Chilcott, Amanda Roocroft, and Christine Brewer. Created (1945) by Joan Cross.

Orlando (Handel). Lib. anon. after Carlo Sigismondo Capeci's *L'Orlando*; 3 acts; f.p. London 1733.

No specific time or place: *Orlando, a knight, loves *Angelica, Queen of Cathay, but she now prefers the African prince, *Medoro, who in turn is loved by the shepherdess *Dorinda. Racked with jealousy, Orlando loses his reason. He throws Angelica into a cave. The magician *Zoroastro restores Orlando to sanity and Dorinda tells him he has murdered Angelica and Medoro. He is filled with remorse and determined to kill himself, but the lovers appear, saved by the magician, and Orlando blesses their union.

Orlando (Handel: *Orlando*). Countertenor (originally castrato). A knight. He is in love with Angelica and, demented when she prefers Medoro, loses his reason. When he recovers he gives the lovers his blessing. Created (1733) by Senesino (the alto castrato Francesco Bernardi).

Orlofsky, Prince (J. Strauss II: *Die Fledermaus*). Mez. *Travesti* role (but has been sung by a tenor, e.g. Robert Tear at Covent Garden in 1978). A young, rich, bored Russian prince. Nothing amuses him, until he hears the story of how Eisenstein left Falke alone to walk through the village after a fancy-dress party dressed as a bat. At the party which Orlofsky gives, Falke plots to get his own back on Eisenstein. Orlofsky's guests are entertained lavishly—everyone must drink champagne with him. Many productions use this scene as an opportunity to interpolate well-known singers and dancers to add to the entertainment. Aria: *Ich lade gern mir Gäste ein* ('I like inviting guests'—usually referred to as

Chacun à son goût—'Each one to his own taste'). Created (1874) by Irma Nittinger.

Ormindo, L' (Cavalli). Lib. by Giovanni Faustini; prol. and 3 acts; f.p. Venice 1644.

*Ormindo is in love with *Erisbe, wife of the old King *Hariadeno. Ormindo's friend *Amida is also in love with Erisbe, to the distress of his former lover, *Sicle. Disguised as a gypsy, Sicle reads Amida's palm and reveals his past to Erisbe, who leaves by boat with Ormindo. Hariadeno orders their arrest and tells his captain, *Osman, to poison them. As they are dying, Hariadeno relents. Osman has anyway substituted a sleeping draught for the poison. The old king realizes that Ormindo is his long-lost son and gives him both his wife and his kingdom.

Ormindo, Prince (Cavalli: *L'Ormindo*). Ten. Long-lost son of King Hariadeno. Falls in love with the king's wife Erisbe. Leaves with her in a boat. Hariadeno orders them to be poisoned, but later relents. On discovering Ormindo's true identity, the King cedes both his kingdom and his wife to his son. Creator (1644) not known.

Oronte (Handel: *Alcina*). Ten. Commander of Alcina's troops, in love with Morgana. Created (1735) by John Beard.

Oroveso (Bellini: *Norma*). Bass. High Priest of the temple and father of Norma. Wants to wage war against the Romans, not knowing that his daughter is in love with a Roman. Created (1831) by Vincenzo Negrini (not, as often stated, Carlo Negrini, only born in 1826 and a tenor).

Orpheus 1. (Orphée) (Offenbach: *Orpheus in the Underworld*). Ten. Married to Eurydice, whom he loathes. She dies and goes to the underworld, but Public Opinion insists he rescue her. He is relieved to find that Jupiter, in love with Eurydice, arranges for her to remain there for ever. Created (1858) by Mons. Tayau.

2. (Birtwistle: *The Second Mrs Kong*). Counterten. 'Forever singing his loss', he loses his head, which is rescued by Kong, who helps him in his search for Eurydice. Created (1994) by Michael Chance. *See also* ORFEO.

Orpheus Hero (Birtwistle: *The Mask of Orpheus*). Mime role. Created (1986) by Graham Walters.

Orpheus in the Underworld (*Orphée aux enfers*) (Offenbach). Lib. by Hector Crémieux and Ludovic Halévy; 4 acts; f.p. Paris 1858, cond. ?Offenbach.

Mythical times: *Eurydice and *Orpheus loathe each other! She is having an affair with *Pluto. When she is bitten by a snake and dies, Orpheus is relieved, but *Public Opinion insists he see *Jupiter to demand her return. However, Jupiter falls for Eurydice and only reluctantly does he agree to Orpheus rescuing his wife—he must not look at her on the way out of the underworld, or she will again die. The bang of a thunderbolt, arranged of course by Jupiter, makes Orpheus jump and turn round. Eurydice is condemned to remain in the underworld, to the delight of everyone concerned—except Public Opinion.

Orpheus Man (Birtwistle: *The Mask of Orpheus*). Ten. Given the gifts of speech, poetry, and music by his spiritual father, Apollo. Falls in love with Euridice and searches for her in the Underworld after she dies. Is killed by a thunderbolt from Zeus. Created (1986) by Philip Langridge.

Orpheus Myth/Hades (Birtwistle: *The Mask of Orpheus*) Ten. Is dismembered by Dionysiac women. Created (1986) by Nigel Robson.

Orsini, Paolo (Wagner: *Rienzi*). Bass. A nobleman of Rome who is unsuccessful in his attempt to assassinate Rienzi. A long-standing feud exists between the Orsini and the Colonna families. Created (1842) by Michael Wächter.

Ortel, Hermann (Wagner: *Die Meistersinger von Nürnberg*). Bass. One of the *Meistersinger*, by trade a soap-boiler. Created (1868) by Herr Thoms.

Ortlinde (Wagner: *Die Walküre*). *See* VALKYRIES.

Ortrud (Wagner: *Lohengrin*). Mez. Wife of Telramund, who married her only after Elsa refused him. It is their ambition to gain the throne of Brabant from Elsa's brother Gottfried. She worships pagan gods and practises sorcery. She has turned Gottfried into a swan, which pulls the boat which carries Lohengrin. Ortrud is a strong character, who dominates Telramund. She plots to undermine Elsa's faith in Lohengrin. She convinces Elsa that she has her welfare at heart, but at the wedding of Elsa and Lohengrin, Ortrud shows her true vicious nature, demanding the throne. When Elsa refuses, she declares that Lohengrin also uses sorcery, placing further doubts in Elsa's mind. However, she is finally defeated when Lohengrin's prayers are answered and Gottfried is released from Ortrud's power and returns to claim his throne. Ens. (with Elsa and chorus): *Zurück, Elsa!* ('Go back, Elsa!'). A good Ortrud should exude evil from every pore. In the first act she is on stage almost throughout without singing until the last few minutes but, if the role is well characterized, we should always be aware of her presence and her glowering glances. Well-known interpreters have included Ernestine Schumann-Heink, Marie Brema, Margarete Klose, Astrid Varnay, Rita Gorr, Christa Ludwig, Ludmilla Dvořáková, Ursula Schröder-Feinen, Gwyneth Jones, Elizabeth Connell, Eva Randová, and Gabriele Schnaut. Created (1850) by Josephine Fastlinger.

Ory, Count (Rossini: *Le Comte Ory*). Ten. Amorous young Count who disguises himself in futile attempts to win the hand of the beautiful Adèle, sister of Count of Formoutiers. He loses her to his own page, Isolier. Duet (with Isolier): *Une dame de haut parage* ('A high-born lady'); trio (with Adèle and Isolier): *A la faveur de cette nuit obscure* ('Under cover of this dark night'). Created (1828) by Adolphe Nourrit.

Oscar (Verdi: *Un ballo in maschera*). (Also Oscar in Amer. vers.) Sop. Page, attendant on the King. Begs for mercy for Mme Arvidson, about to be exiled for sorcery. In all innocence, reveals which costume the King is wearing at the masked ball, thus enabling his secretary, Anckarstroem, to shoot him. Dying, the King falls into the faithful Oscar's arms. Arias: *Volta la terra* ('The earth turns'); *Saper vorreste di che si veste* ('You want to know how he is dressed'). Created (1859) by Pamela Scotti.

Osiride (Rossini: *Mosè in Egitto*). *See* AMENOPHIS.

Osman (Cavalli: *L'Ormindo*). Ten. Captain of King Hariadeno's boats. Ordered to kill the king's wife Erisbe who has run away with Ormindo. Substitutes a sleeping-draught for the poison, thus saving her life. Creator (1644) not known.

Osmin (Mozart: *Die Entführung aus dem Serail*). Bass. Keeper of Pasha Selim's harem, he is a bloodthirsty character. He has fallen in love with Blondchen, who has been captured together with her mistress and is being held in the harem. When her true lover Pedrillo, and his master Belmonte, attempt to enter the harem, they have to drug Osmin to enable them to rescue their ladies. Before they manage to leave, Osmin recovers and again prevents their escape. Created (1782) by Ludwig Fischer.

Ostheim, Federica, Duchess of (Verdi: *Luisa Miller*). Mez. A young widow, niece of Count Walter. She has known the count's son Rodolfo since childhood. Her husband, the Duke, has died and she expects to marry Rodolfo, but he tells her honestly that his heart is with another, he loves Luisa. Created (1849) by Teresa della Salandri.

Osud (Fate) (Janáček). Lib. by comp. and Fedora Bartošová; 3 'scenes'; f.p. Brno Radio 1934, cond. Břetislav Bakala; f. stage p. Brno 1958, cond. František Jílek.

A spa town, *c*.1900: The composer *Živný* meets his ex-mistress, Míla *Valková*, and learns that she gave birth to his son a year previously. They decide to live together, with their son *Doubek*. Míla's *Mother*, who is mentally unstable, lives with them. Živný writes an opera telling the story of their affair and how they are now married. He is attacked by Míla's mother. When Míla tries to intervene, both she and her mother fall off a balcony to their death. Twelve years later, students rehearse Živný's opera and he tells them of its background. He hears the voice of his dead wife, collapses and dies.

Otello 1. (Verdi). Lib. by Arrigo Boito; 4 acts; f.p. Milan 1887, cond. Franco Faccio (among the orchestral cellos was the then unknown Arturo Toscanini, and in the violins were father and son, Antonio and Lorenzo Barbirolli, grandfather and father of John Barbirolli).

Cyprus, late 15th cent.: The Venetians celebrate victory over the Turks. The new governor, *Otello*, accompanied by his wife *Desdemona, arrives to replace *Montano. His ensign, *Iago, is jealous of Otello and *Cassio. He plots with *Roderigo to turn Otello against Cassio and Otello appoints Iago to replace him. Iago suggests to Cassio that he ask Desdemona to intercede with Otello on his behalf. He then plants in Otello's mind suspicions about Cassio and Desdemona. This increases when Desdemona pleads on Cassio's behalf. Otello becomes angry, throwing down the handkerchief she offers him to wipe his face. It is retrieved by her maid *Emilia (Iago's wife) and Iago snatches it from her. Iago arranges for Otello to overhear Cassio talking about his latest mistress, and Otello assumes this means Desdemona. He and Iago plan to kill both Cassio and Desdemona. Desdemona retires to bed. Otello comes in and kisses her and she senses that he is going to kill her. He smothers her as Emilia enters the room and announces that Cassio has killed Roderigo. She calls for help and Iago, Cassio, *Lodovico, and Montano come running. Emilia exposes Iago, who escapes. Otello stabs himself, dying next to Desdemona.

2. (Rossini). Lib. by Francesco Maria Berio di Salsa; 3 acts; f.p. Naples 1816.

Venice, 16th cent.: The plot has a similar ending to the Verdi opera, but varies in the earlier acts: *Iago and *Rodrigo (note the different spelling) plot *Otello's downfall. *Desdemona's letter to Otello is intercepted by her father, *Elmiro, who thinks it was sent to Rodrigo, whom he wants her to marry. Iago gives Desdemona's letter to Otello, who suspects it was meant for Rodrigo and the two men fight. *Emilia comforts her mistress. Otello is exiled by the Senate. He returns and stabs Desdemona. Iago, before he kills himself with remorse, tells the truth. Grief-stricken, Otello stabs himself.

Otello 1. (Verdi: *Otello*). Ten. Moor of Venice and general in the Venetian army. Married to Desdemona. He is appointed to succeed Montano as the new governor in Cyprus. His ensign, Iago, is jealous of him and the young lieutenant Cassio, and makes Otello suspicious of a relationship, totally innocent, between Desdemona and Cassio. Racked with jealousy, Otello smothers Desdemona. Finding that his suspicions were unfounded and that Iago was plotting against him, Otello stabs himself, and dies next to his beloved Desdemona. Arias: *Esultate!* ('Rejoice!'); *Ora e per sempre, addio* ('Now and forever, farewell'); *Dio, mi potevi scagliar* ('God, it has pleased you to heap on me'); duet (with Desdemona): *Già nella notte* ('Now in the silent night'); duet (with Iago—the 'oath'): *Sì, per ciel* ('Heaven see me swear'). Many Verdi scholars regard this as his greatest opera. Certainly the title role is one of the peaks of Italian opera, and wise tenors do not attempt it until they are at the height of their powers. Others, equally wisely, do not attempt it on stage at all (among them Enrico Caruso and Luciano Pavarotti). It demands a heroic voice with a baritonal quality and considerable physical and emotional stamina. But from its creator onwards, the greatest of Italianate tenors have aspired to the part, among them Giovanni Zenatello, Giovanni Martinelli, Leo Slezak (said to rival Tamagno's interpretation), Lauritz Melchior, Frank Mullings, Helge Roswaenge, Ramon Vinay, Ludwig Suthaus, Charles Craig, Jon Vickers, Mario del Monaco (who sang this role over 400 times), James McCracken, Carlo Cossutta, Giuseppe Giacomini, Plácido Domingo, Jose Cura, and Ben Heppner. Created (1887) by Francesco Tamagno. *See also* ARTICLE BY PLÁCIDO DOMINGO, p. 220.

2. (Rossini: *Otello*): Ten. The Moor of Venice. In love with Desdemona but suspects her of being unfaithful with Rodrigo whom her father wants her to marry. Rodrigo and Iago are plotting against Otello. Otello interrupts the proposed wedding and claims Desdemona for himself. He and Rodrigo fight and Otello is exiled by the Senate, but returns and enters Desdemona's room while she is asleep. Despite her protestations of innocence, he stabs her, but on learning the truth he stabs himself. Created (1816) by Andrea Nozzari.

Otho (Monteverdi: *L'incoronazione di Poppea*). *See* OTTONE.

Ottavia (Monteverdi: *L'incoronazione di Poppea*). Sop./mez. Wife of the Emperor Nerone, who is now in love with Poppea. She plots Poppea's death by the hand of her (Poppea's) husband Ottone, but this fails and Nerone deserts Ottavia to marry Poppea. Arias: *Disprezzata regina* ('Spurned Queen'); *Addio Roma* ('Farewell Rome'). Created (1642) by Anna Renzi.

Ottavio, Don (Mozart: *Don Giovanni*). Ten. Fiancé of Donna Anna. A rather weak character, he nevertheless loves Anna and helps her to uncover the murderer of her father, the libertine Don Giovanni. Arias: *Dalla sua pace…* ('Upon her peace of mind')—this aria, added for the Vienna première, is often omitted; *Il mio tesoro, intanto* ('Meanwhile, my treasure'). Created (1787) by Antonio Baglioni.

Ottokar, Prince (Weber: *Der Freischütz*). Bar. Banishes Max from his kingdom for cheating by using magic bullets in a shooting contest, but is persuaded to forgive him. Created (1821) by Herr Rebenstein.

Ottone 1. (Handel: *Agrippina*). Alto. Lieutenant to Claudio, Roman Emperor, and named by him as his successor after Ottone has saved his life. However, Ottone loves Poppea and renounces the throne to marry her. Created (1709) by Francesca Vanini.

2. (Monteverdi: *L'incoronazione di Poppea*). Mez. Husband of Poppea, cuckolded by the Emperor Nerone. Plots to kill his wife, fails and is banished from Rome by Nerone. Creator (1643) not known.

Ouf I, King (Chabrier: *L'Étoile*). Ten. On his birthday, King Ouf is in disguise, trying to provoke one of his subjects into criticizing him so that he can have them executed. He hopes his proposed marriage to Princess Laoula, daughter of his neighbour King Mataquin, will bring peace between their countries. However, Laoula falls in love with a pedlar, Lazuli, who offends Ouf. Ouf decides he must be executed but is warned against this by his astrologer. He eventually yields to the need to provide a successor, blesses the marriage of Laoula and Lazuli, and appoints them as his heirs. Created (1877) by Michel-René Daubray (Thibaut).

Owen Wingrave (Britten). Lib. by Myfanwy Piper; 2 acts; f.p. BBC TV 1971, cond. Benjamin Britten; London 1973, cond. Steuart Bedford.

London and Paramore, late 19th cent.: Owen *Wingrave comes from a family of soldiers, but he hates fighting, unlike his friend *Lechmere who can't wait to be in the thick of battle. They are both at *Coyle's military establishment. Owen tells Coyle he cannot become a soldier. His aunt, Miss *Wingrave, is determined he

OTELLO *(Otello*—Verdi)

by Plácido Domingo

The year was 1975 and the place was Hamburg, when I first performed in *Otello* at the age of 34. Every well-meaning person and vocal expert had warned me that undertaking this part at such an early age would bring about undoing to my voice. Of course, I had doubts myself. After all, it is not only considered the most dramatic part in the accepted Italian repertoire, but the second act alone is as demanding as any full-length Italian opera—and the three other acts are not exactly sinecures. What convinced me was an analytical knowledge of my voice and the assurance that the circumstances for my first Otello were right—namely, the musical guidance of the conductor James Levine (making his European début), the histrionic supervision of the director August Everding, and the support of Katia Ricciarelli as Desdemona and Sherrill Milnes as Iago. Since that September day I have sung the role a total of 110 times so far. Not only hasn't it hurt my voice, but it has actually made the rest of my repertoire easier for me.

I spoke above of 'analytical knowledge of my voice'. Indirectly I have to thank nature for this. I started out as a baritone and in order to fulfil what musical experts saw as my future—a career as a tenor—I had to build my voice upwards like a stonemason, brick by brick, always being cognisant of technique. Thus when Otello entered not only into my vocal cords but into my entire body and most definitely into my psyche, it crystallized in many ways what I had striven for so hard. In a sense, it became a vocal revelation.

Of course, when I accepted the challenge of the role I was not certain of the outcome. To assure myself that I had not forced the voice, I scheduled a *Tosca* between the second and third performances of *Otello*. The *Tosca* did convince me that I had not lost the ability to sing lyrically, but it also gave me a bloody nose. In singing the cry 'Vittoria, Vittoria!' I made the usual dramatic fall to the floor—and landed on my nose!

People have asked whether there is a connection between singing Otello and singing Wagner's Parsifal or Siegmund. All three are dramatic parts and all three can—and should—be sung with *bel canto* technique.

There are directors who see in *Otello* a racial issue. I do not believe that Shakespeare, Boito, or Verdi had this in mind. To me it is above all a drama of emotions between three people: Desdemona is motivated by sexual curiosity and subsequent love; Iago is motivated by ambition and frustration; and Otello is the exotic stranger who is suspicious of everyone. Had Shakespeare chosen to set the plot in England instead of in Venice, the exotic foreigner might have been a Viking or a Tartar instead of a Moor. However, what *Otello* is, in my mind, is a play of outsized emotions and for this reason a production should provide spaciousness for the action. Unfortunately, I have been in more than one production which could best be described as cramped. Those productions, with their 'concepts' are, in my opinion, anti-musical. Yes, *Otello* could be performed on an almost bare stage, but not in little cubicles. Both music and action are too grandiose for that.

will follow the family tradition. Mrs *Julian and her daughter Kate *Julian believe Owen will change his mind and are hostile towards him when he arrives at Paramore, the family country house. All are present at a dinner party, but only Mrs *Coyle pleads for Owen's principles. Sir Philip *Wingrave, his grandfather, is furious with him, calls him a traitor, and disinherits him. Kate accuses him of cowardice and dares him to sleep in a haunted room to prove his bravery. During the night she goes to the room and finds Owen dead.

Page (Strauss: *Salome*). Mez. *Travesti* role. Page to Herodias, he is aware that Salome is in some way abnormal. He tries to warn the young Syrian captain Narraboth not to worship her, as no good will come of it. Created (1905) by Riza Eibenschütz. *See* Leitmetzerin, Marianne.

Page, Meg (Verdi: *Falstaff*). Mez. One of the 'Merry Wives of Windsor' whom Falstaff proposes to seduce with the intention of getting his hands on their husbands' money. She and Alice Ford are good friends and compare the letters they have received from the Fat Knight. Together with Mistress Quickly they hatch a plan to teach him a lesson. Her husband does not appear in the opera. Created (1893) by Virginia Guerrini.

Pagliacci (Clowns) (Leoncavallo). Lib. by comp.; prol. and 1 act; f.p. Milan 1892, cond. Arturo Toscanini.

Montalto, Calabria, about 1870: The disabled clown *Tonio tells the audience they will see a real-life drama. *Canio is head of a troupe of strolling players. His wife *Nedda is having an affair with one of the villagers, *Silvio, and rejects Tonio's overtures. He, in revenge, tells Canio of his wife's planned meeting with her lover. *Beppe, another trouper, prevents Canio beating Nedda when she refuses to name her lover. Canio puts on his clown make-up as the villagers gather for the performance: Columbine (Nedda) is serenaded by Harlequin (Beppe), then by Taddeo (Tonio). Pagliaccio (Canio) overhears Harlequin and Columbine arrange to meet later and assumes he is her lover. Canio stabs her. Silvio rushes to the stage to try to save Nedda and Canio kills him also.

Pagliaccio (Leoncavallo: *Pagliacci*). *See* Canio.

Painter (Berg: *Lulu*). Ten. Marries Lulu but kills himself when he learns of her promiscuous past. Created (1937) by Paul Feher.

Palestrina (Pfitzner). Lib. by comp.; 3 acts; f.p. Munich 1917, cond. Bruno Walter.

Rome and Trent, 1563 (at the end of the Council of Trent): *Palestrina's son *Ighino and his pupil *Silla discuss the composer's unwillingness to write music since the death of his wife *Lucretia. Cardinal *Borromeo warns Palestrina that the Council of Trent may ban the new polyphonic music and urges him to compose a Mass that will convince Pope *Pius IV that the new music can be as devout as plainchant, otherwise he will be imprisoned. As he reluctantly starts to compose his *Missa Papae Marcelli*, the spirit of his wife encourages him; by morning it is finished. The Council holds its final meeting and is addressed by Cardinal *Morone, Legate of the Pope, one of his listeners being the Spanish King's ambassador, Count *Luna. Music is among the subjects discussed. Two weeks later Palestrina learns that his secret Mass is being sung in St Peter's—to save him from prison, his choristers have given it to the papal authorities. The Pope comes to demand his services as composer and Palestrina accepts his destiny.

Palestrina, Giovanni Pierluigi da (Pfitzner: *Palestrina*). Ten. The composer (*c.*1525–*c.*1594) who took his name from his birthplace. Choirmaster to Pope Julius III and wrote many masses, but when Pius IV became pope he was dismissed because he was married. In the opera he stopped writing music when his wife died, but was persuaded to write a papal mass to prove the suitability of the new polyphonic music for use in churches. When Pius IV heard his *Missa Papae Marcelli*, he appointed him his official composer. Created (1917) by Karl Erb.

Palmieri (Verdi: *Tosca*). This character does not appear in the opera but is referred to by Scarpia. Having promised Tosca that Cavaradossi's execution will be staged for the benefit of onlookers, and he will then be free to leave with Tosca, he pointedly instructs Spoletta to execute Cavaradossi 'as in the case of Palmieri' (nod, nod, wink, wink, as we would say today): Palmieri, a previous prisoner, had clearly been killed in the same way Cavaradossi will now be executed. This should have aroused Tosca's suspicions.

Palmieri, Giuseppe (Sullivan: *The Gondoliers*). Bar. A gondolier, brother of Marco. Blindfolded, he picks Tessa as his wife. Reigns jointly with his brother on the Island of Barataria until it is proved that neither gondolier is the true heir to the throne. Duet (with Marco): *We're called Gondolieri*. Created (1889) by Rutland Barrington.

Palmieri, Marco (Sullivan: *The Gondoliers*). Ten. A gondolier, brother of Giuseppe. He picks Gianetta as his wife. In the belief that one of them is the heir to the throne of Barataria, he reigns jointly with his brother, but the real heir is Luiz, the drummer. Aria: *Take a pair of sparkling eyes*. Created (1889) by Courtice ('Charlie') Pounds.

Pamina (Mozart: *Die Zauberflöte*). Sop. Daughter of the Queen of Night, she has been captured by Sarastro. Tamino falls in love with her portrait and sets out to rescue her. She accompanies him through various trials after which Sarastro allows them to be together. Aria: *Ach, ich fühl's, es ist verschwunden* ('Ah, I feel 'tis gone for ever'); duet (with Papageno): *Bei Männern, welche Liebe fühlen* ('All men who can feel love'). Created (1791) by Anna Gottlieb (who, at the age of 12 in 1786, had created Barbarina in *Le nozze di Figaro*).

Pandarus (Walton: *Troilus and Cressida*). Ten. Brother of Calkas, uncle of Cressida. He encourages Cressida to accept Troilus' love, because he sees the connection with the Trojan royal family as a means of rescuing his family from the disgrace brought about by Calkas's desertion to the enemy. He is a well-intentioned dilettante figure, an entrepreneur who sets in motion events with which he is ill-equipped to cope, a fact he acknowledges in

Act 3 when he says 'To ease the world's despair was never worth the trying'. So when Cressida is taken to the Greek camp and he goes with Troilus to rescue her, he is helpless to halt the events which lead to the deaths of both the young lovers. Trio (with Cressida and Troilus): *On jealousy's hot grid he roasts alive*. Created (1956) by Peter Pears.

Pandolfe (Massenet: *Cendrillon*). Bass-bar. Father of Lucette (Cendrillon), he is dominated by his second wife, Mme de la Haltière. However, he loves his daughter and when he sees how unhappy she is after the royal ball, where she and Prince Charming have fallen in love but been parted, he promises to take her away to his country house. Aria: *Viens, nous quitterons cette ville* ('Come, we will leave this town'). Created (1899) by Lucien Fugère.

Pang (Puccini: *Turandot*). Ten. One of the three Ministers of the Emperor Altoum (the Three Masks), he is Supreme Lord of Provisions. Created (1926) by Emilio Venturini.

Panza, Sancho (Massenet: *Don Quichotte*). Bar. Servant of Don Quichotte. He accompanies his master on various quests and takes care of him at all times. Created (1910) by André Gresse.

Paolino (Cimarosa: *Il matrimonio segreto*). Ten. Geronimo's young clerk. He is loved by Geronimo's sister Fidalma but is secretly married to Geronimo's younger daughter, Carolina. Created (1792) by Santi Nencini.

Paolo 1. (Verdi: *Simon Boccanegra*). *See* ALBIANI, PAOLO.

2. (Leoncavallo: *La bohème*). Bar. Wealthy Count, for whom Mimì deserts Rodolfo. Created (1897) by Lucio Aristi (who also created Colline).

Papagena (Mozart: *Die Zauberflöte*). Sop. First appears as an old crone and tells Papageno that she is his prospective bride. Only when he agrees to save her life by marrying her does she turn into the young and beautiful girl of his dreams, but she then disappears, leaving Papageno suicidal. The Three Boys remind him of his magic bells. He plays them and she returns to him. Duet (with Papageno): *Pa-Pa-Pa-Pa-Pa-Pa-Papageno!* Created (1791) by Barbara Gerl (whose husband created Sarastro).

Papageno (Mozart: *Die Zauberflöte*). Bar. A bird-catcher. He meets Tamino and goes with him to rescue Pamina, having been given magic bells to protect him. Though frightened, he rescues Pamina and takes her to meet Tamino. He also wards off the evil moor Monostatos and his followers by playing the bells and luring them away. He accompanies Tamino to his trials, but is unable to remain silent as ordered. Determined to find love for himself, he meets an old crone who, to his horror, declares herself to be his future bride. When he agrees to save her from incarceration by marrying her, she miraculously turns into the young and beautiful Papagena. Arias: *Der Vogelfänger bin ich ja* ('I am the bird-catcher'); *Ein Mädchen oder Weibchen* ('A maiden or a little wife'); duet (with Pamina): *Bei männern* ('All men'). Created (1791) by Johann Emanuel Schikaneder (the opera's librettist. When the opera had its British première, this role was taken by Michael Balfe, the composer of *The Bohemian Girl*.

Paris 1. (Pâris) (Offenbach: *La Belle Hélène*). Ten. Son of King Priam. Disguised as a shepherd, he wins Helen in a contest. Her husband finds them in bed together and Paris makes a quick getaway. Disguised as a priest, he instructs Helen to atone for her sins by sailing with him to Cythera. He throws off his disguise when they are on the ship. The Trojan War is about to begin. Created (1864) by José Dupuis.

2. (Tippett: *King Priam*). Boy sop. & ten. Second son of King Priam and Queen Hecuba, younger brother of Hector. At his birth, his mother dreams he will one day cause the death of his father. His abduction of Helen, wife of the Greek King Menelaus, causes the Trojan War and brings about Priam's death. Created (1962) by Philip Doghan (boy)/John Dobson (adult).

3. (Gounod: *Roméo and Juliette*). Count Paris. Bar. This is the man selected by her father as Juliet's husband, but she has already secretly married Romeo. Created (1873) by Mons. Laveissière.

Parpignol (Puccini: *La bohème*). Ten. A travelling toy-seller, followed by the children in the Café Momus. Created (1896) by Dante Zucchi.

Parrowe, Rose (Maxwell Davies: *Taverner*). Mez. Wife of the composer, she gives evidence against him when he is tried for heresy. Created (1972) by Gillian Knight.

Parsifal (Wagner). Lib. by Wagner; 3 acts; f.p. Bayreuth 1882, cond. Hermann Levi (but excerpts had been given in concert performance in 1878 and 1880). *Parsifal* was described by Wagner as a *Bühnenweihfestspiel*—a stage dedication play.

Spain, Middle Ages: *Amfortas is the King in charge of the Grail (the chalice in which the blood of Christ on the Cross was caught) and the Spear which pierced Christ's side. These are kept in Monsalvat, the Castle of the Knights of the Grail which was built by Amfortas's father *Titurel. Amfortas was seduced by *Kundry, who is controlled by the magician *Klingsor and lives in the grounds of his castle on the other side of the mountain. Klingsor stole the Spear and wounded Amfortas in the side. He was brought back to Monsalvat by *Gurnemanz, but his wound will not heal and he is becoming increasingly weak and unable to carry out the ritual unveiling of the Grail. In a dream, Amfortas is told that only an 'innocent fool, wise through compassion', will be able to help him. A young man arrives at the castle—he does not even know his own name. Suspecting he may be the long-awaited saviour of Amfortas, Gurnemanz takes him into their castle where he watches Amfortas's agony as he unveils the Grail. In his magic castle, Klingsor orders Kundry to seduce the youth. He resists Klingsor's *Flower Maidens but is unable to resist Kundry—she calls him *Parsifal, the name he heard in a dream about his mother and Kundry then kisses him. Suddenly, he knows how sinful longing can have terrible effects, and he can feel the pain of Amfortas's wound. Unable to make him submit to her, Kundry calls Klingsor. Parsifal takes the Spear and Klingsor's castle collapses. Years later, the suffering Amfortas refuses to unveil the Grail. Gurnemanz, now a very old man, finds Kundry half-dead in the forest. When Parsifal enters with the Spear, Gurnemanz anoints him as their new king and Parsifal gives Kundry absolution. He places the tip of the Spear on Amfortas's wound, which at once heals—the sin (present since Amfortas's seduction by Kundry) has now been removed from the

Spear. Parsifal orders the Grail to be unveiled. Kundry dies.

Parsifal (Wagner: *Parsifal*). Ten. He appears on the scene for the first time after a dead swan falls to the ground in Monsalvat, where the Knights of the Grail live (but those who know the earlier opera *Lohengrin* will have heard his name, for Lohengrin announces that he is the son of Parsifal). He does not know he has done any wrong by killing the bird and is surprised to be severely reprimanded by the elderly knight Gurnemanz, who impresses on him the sanctity of all life. Mortified, Parsifal breaks his bow and arrows. Questioned by Gurnemanz, it quickly becomes clear that he is unaware of his origins and does not even know his own name. The only person who seems to know anything about him is Kundry, who describes how his mother kept him innocent of worldly affairs. He left his mother to follow a band of knights that passed by and has been wandering ever since, not knowing until now that his mother has died. He has no perception of the significance of the Grail and on arrival at the castle is distressed to see the agony suffered by Amfortas when he attempts to uncover the chalice. However, Parsifal instinctively understands that he, in some way, will be involved in the release of Amfortas from his suffering. When he leaves the Knights' castle and wanders further, he comes to the magic garden of the sorcerer Klingsor, inhabited by the beautiful Flower Maidens. He is happy to play innocently with them, but they scatter at the sound of Kundry's voice. It is now that she tells him his name and then attempts to seduce him, kissing him passionately. He repels her advances, calling to an unknown lord for redemption and asking Kundry to lead him to Amfortas. Kundry shouts for Klingsor to help her and the magician throws the Holy Spear at Parsifal and is astonished to see the Spear suspended in mid-air above the youth. Parsifal grasps it and instinctively crosses himself whereupon Klingsor and his garden disappear. Parsifal sets off on his wanderings once again, this time in pursuit of Amfortas. Many years later, he meets Gurnemanz in the forest. Parsifal describes to the now very old knight how he has travelled far in his efforts to find the suffering Amfortas and return the Holy Spear to its rightful place. Gurnemanz promises to lead him to Amfortas, and then Kundry appears. Parsifal recognizes her, but her demeanour has changed. She washes his feet and dries them with her hair. Gurnemanz anoints him with balsam given to him by Kundry and appoints him King of the Grail. Parsifal baptizes Kundry, thus redeeming her from Klingsor's evil spell. Gurnemanz leads them to the castle of the Grail. There, the funeral of Titurel, Amfortas's father, is taking place. Amfortas, unable to bear his suffering any longer, tears off his bandages and asks his fellow-knights to kill him. Parsifal steps forward and touches Amfortas's wound with the Holy Spear and the wound is at once healed. As Parsifal uncovers the Grail and sinks to his knees in prayer, Kundry falls lifeless at his feet. Arias: *Zu ihm, des tiefe Klagen* ('To him whose deep lamenting'); *Nur eine Waffe taugt* ('Only one weapon serves').

Parsifal is usually called an 'innocent fool', but he is better described as naïve rather than foolish. His first experience of fear is when he sees the agony suffered by Amfortas, and by instinct rather than intelligence or logic he acknowledges his own potential to remove that suffering. By the end of the opera, the 'innocent fool' has become the 'compassionate saint' whose first act is to redeem Kundry from the evil influence which has made her responsible for the pain which Parsifal observed in Amfortas, felt within himself, and finally cured. Although the opera lasts about 4½ hours, Parsifal himself sings for only about twenty minutes throughout and that often in short exchanges with other characters—Gurnemanz, Kundry, Amfortas—rather than long arias. And dramatically it is the least demanding of Wagnerian tenor roles. Nevertheless, it has attracted many notable singers, among whom should be mentioned Ernest van Dyck, Erik Schmedes, Lauritz Melchior, Max Lorenz, Helge Roswaenge, Wolfgang Windgassen, Ramon Vinay, Jon Vickers, James King, René Kollo, Peter Hofmann, Manfred Jung, Siegfried Jerusalem, Warren Elsworth, and Plácido Domingo—by no means all of them acknowledged Wagnerian tenors. Created (1882) by Hermann Winkelmann.

Parson (Janáček: *The Cunning Little Vixen*). *See* PRIEST.

Partlet, Constance (Sullivan: *The Sorcerer*). Sop. Daughter of Mrs Partlet, a pew opener. In love with the vicar, Dr Daly. Created (1877) by Giulia Warwick.

Pascoe (Smyth: *The Wreckers*). Bass. Local headman and preacher, husband of Thirza (who is now in love with Mark). Created (1906) by Walter Soomer (who shortly after this became a Bayreuth regular from 1906 to 1925 in such roles as Amfortas, Hagen, Hunding, Sachs, and Wotan).

Pasha Selim (Mozart: *Die Entführung aus dem Serail*). *See* SELIM, PASHA (1).

Pasquale, Don (Donizetti: *Don Pasquale*). Bass. An elderly bachelor, he disapproves of his heir, his nephew Ernesto, having a relationship with Norina, a poor young widow. He decides to marry, produce a direct heir, and disinherit Ernesto. But Norina is Malatesta's niece and he sets out to trick Pasquale into giving his consent to the young couple's marriage. Malatesta produces the ideal bride for Pasquale, his demure 'sister Sofronia' (Norina) and a Notary (his cousin) to marry them. Pasquale soon wishes he'd remained a bachelor, as 'Sofronia's' nature changes totally after their marriage. When he catches his 'wife' and her lover (Ernesto) together in the garden he is only too anxious to agree to annul his marriage and give his blessing to the union of Norina and Ernesto. Aria: *Un foco insolito mi sento addosso* ('I'm in the grip of an unaccustomed fever'); duet (with Malatesta): *Cheti, cheti, immantinente* ('Ever so quickly, we'll do down'). Created (1843) by Luigi Lablache (whose son Federico, created the Notary).

Pastia, Lillas (Bizet: *Carmen*). Spoken. Landlord of the inn where Carmen meets Escamillo while she awaits the arrival of Don José. Created (1875) by Mons. Nathan.

Patience, or Bunthorne's Bride (Sullivan). Lib. by W. S. Gilbert; 2 acts; f.p. London 1881, cond. Arthur Sullivan.
England, 19th cent.: The poet Reginald *Bunthorne loves the dairymaid *Patience, the only young lady of his acquaintance who is not in love with him. Patience rejects her other admirer, the poet Archibald *Grosvenor, because she doesn't know what love is. Lady *Jane, worried about her own advancing years, encourages Bunthorne to challenge Grosvenor to abandon his highflown poetic ideas and become an ordinary person, then he can marry Patience. The Dragoon Lieut., the Duke of *Dunstable, proposes to Jane, leaving Bunthorne the only man with no bride.

Patience (Sullivan: *Patience*). Sop. A dairymaid who has not yet experienced love. She rejects Bunthorne's attentions and decides it is her duty to love and marry another poet, Archibald Grosvenor. Aria: *Long years ago*. Created (1881) by Leonora Braham.

Patroclus (Tippett: *King Priam*). Bar. Close friend of Achilles. Upset because his friend will not fight in the Trojan War, he dresses in Achilles' armour and joins the battle, being killed by Hector. Created (1962) by Joseph Ward.

Paul (Korngold: *Die tote Stadt*). Ten. A young widower obsessed with the memory of his dead wife, Marie. He is attracted to the dancer Marietta, who reminds him of his wife. He takes her to his home, where he has carefully preserved all Marie's belongings. After she leaves, he has a vision in which he kills Marietta. When he wakes, the ghost of Marie has been exorcized. Created (1920) by Richard Schubert (Hamburg) and Karl Schröder (Cologne).

Paul Bunyan (Britten). Lib. by W. H. Auden; prol. and 2 acts; f.p. Columbia Univ., NY, 1941, cond. Hugh Ross.
United States, in 'early times': Paul *Bunyan is a giant logger who, in American folklore, 'grew as tall as the Empire State Building'. Throughout the opera there are ballad commentaries sung by a *Narrator. In the prol. we hear Paul Bunyan will be born when the moon turns blue—which it then does. His foreman at the lumberjack's camp is the Swede Hel *Helson, and a book-keeper, Johnny *Inkslinger, becomes Bunyan's second-in-command. Bunyan's daughter, *Tiny, falls in love with the new cook, *Slim. Some of the men want to become farmers. As the lumberjacks get various other jobs and move away, the camp gradually breaks up and they all appreciate Paul's teaching that 'America is what you make it'.

Pauline (Tchaikovsky: *The Queen of Spades*). Cont. Friend and confidante of Lisa. Created (1890) by Maria Dolina.

Peachum, Mr 1. (Gay: *The Beggar's Opera*). Bass. A 'fence', father of Polly. He is head of his gang of pick-pockets. He plots against the highwayman Macheath, not realizing Polly has married him. He helps to have Macheath arrested and sent to gaol. Created (1728) by Mr Hippisley.

   2. (Weill: *The Threepenny Opera*). Jonathan Jeremiah Peachum. Bar. As in (1). Created (1928) by Erich Ponto.

Peachum, Mrs 1. (Gay: *The Beggar's Opera*). Mez. Wife of Peachum and mother of Polly. She is angry to find that her daughter has secretly married the highwayman Macheath and helps to have him arrested. Created (1728) by Mrs Martin.

   2. (Weill: *The Threepenny Opera*). Mez. As in (1). Created (1928) by Rosa Valetti.

Peachum, Polly 1. (Gay: *The Beggar's Opera*). Sop. Daughter of Mr and Mrs Peachum. She has fallen in love with the highwayman Macheath and, knowing her parents will disapprove, has married him secretly. When her father finds out, she urges her husband to hide. He is arrested and sent to gaol. Visiting him there, she meets his former wife and the two women quarrel. She and Macheath are united when he is released. Created (1728) by Lavinia Fenton (who later became the Duchess of Bolton).

   2. (Weill: *The Threepenny Opera*). Sop. As in (1). Created (1928) by Roma Bahn.

Pearl (Birtwistle: *The Second Mrs Kong*). Sop. Vermeer's 'Girl with a Pearl Earring'. Whilst being painted, she learns from a mirror that she will meet Kong. She finds him by computer, but their love is doomed to failure, as they are both 'ideas', not real people. Created (1994) by Helen Field.

Pearl Fishers, The (Les Pêcheurs des perles) (Bizet). Lib. by Eugène Cormon and Michel Carré; 3 acts; f.p. Paris 1863, cond. Mons. Deloffre.

   Ceylon, antiquity: The fishermen have elected *Zurga their king. *Nadir, after a long absence, has a fond reunion with Zurga. They had both fallen in love with the young priestess *Leïla but sworn to give her up rather than threaten their friendship. *Nourabad, the High Priest, brings in the veiled virgin to pray for the safety of the pearl fishers. It is Leïla, and she

and Nadir recognize each other. They are discovered together by Nourabad and the guards and Nadir is caught as he tries to flee. Zurga, as king, is prepared to forgive the couple, until he realises that it is Leïla. He swears revenge on Nadir. Leïla pleads with him and gives him a necklace given to her by a fugitive whose life she once saved. He recognizes it as his necklace and Leïla as his rescuer. He allows the couple to escape.

Pedrillo (Mozart: *Die Entführung aus dem Serail*). Ten. Servant of Belmonte. In love with Blondchen, whom he attempts to rescue from captivity while his master tries to rescue Blondchen's mistress, Constanze. Created (1782) by Johann Ernst Dauer.

Pedro, Don 1. (Berlioz: *Béatrice et Bénédict*). Bass. An army general. Plots with others to trick Béatrice and Bénédict into admitting their love for each other. Created (1862) by Mons. Balanqué.

   2. (d'Albert: *Tiefland*). A farmer, who marries Marta and fights with and strangles her ex-lover, Sebastian. Creator (1903) not traced.

Peep-Bo (Sullivan: *The Mikado*). Mez. Sister of Yum-Yum and Pitti-Sing, wards of Ko-Ko. Trio (with her sisters): *Three little maids from school*. Created (1885) by Sybil Grey.

Pelléas (Debussy: *Pelléas et Mélisande*). Ten./ high bar. Son of Geneviève, grandson of Arkel, and half-brother of Golaud. Golaud meets and marries Mélisande; she and Pelléas are attracted to each other. Golaud spies on them but can find nothing untoward in their relationship. Pelléas decides to leave the family castle. While he and Mélisande are saying a passionate goodbye, Golaud enters and in a fit of jealousy he kills Pelléas. Aria: *Ah! Je respire enfin!* ('Ah! I can breathe at last!'). Created (1902) by Jean Périer.

Pelléas et Mélisande (Debussy). Lib. by composer from Maeterlinck's text; 5 acts; f.p. Paris 1902, cond. André Messager.

   Kingdom of Allemonde, time unspecified: The King of Allemonde is *Arkel, his daughter is *Geneviève, who has two sons by different marriages, *Pelléas and *Golaud. Golaud has a son, *Yniold, from an earlier marriage. Out hunting, Golaud finds the lost *Mélisande and persuades her to follow him home. He marries her and takes her to meet his family in their castle. Mélisande and Pelléas enjoy each other's company. Playing with the ring Golaud has given her, she loses it in the fountain. Golaud, injured in a fall from his horse, notices the ring is missing. Pelléas is leaving and goes to say farewell to the now pregnant Mélisande. Golaud worries about their relationship and uses Yniold to spy on them in Mélisande's room. The child has nothing improper to report. Pelléas and Mélisande say a passionate farewell, declaring their love. But Golaud has been watching. He rushes forward and kills Pelléas. Mélisande dies after giving birth to a daughter. Despite her denials, Golaud remains unsure of her fidelity.

Peneios (Strauss: *Daphne*). Bass. A fisherman, husband of Gaea and father of Daphne. Ens. (with Gaea and the Shepherds): *Seid ihr um mich* ('Are you with me?'). Although Peneios does not have a big solo number, singing mainly in ensembles, the role has nevertheless attracted some notable artists, including Paul Schöffler and Kurt Moll. Created (1938) by Sven Nilsson.

Penelope 1. (Monteverdi: *Il ritorno d'Ulisse in patria*). Mez/cont. The wife of Ulisse, mother of Telemaco. She awaits her husband's return from the Trojan Wars but does not recognize him when he arrives, dressed as a beggar. Then he describes the quilt on their bed, which only he can know, and she is overwhelmed to realize this is her Ulisse. Aria: *Di misera regina* ('Wretched queen'). Created (1640) probably by Giulia Paolelli.

   2. (Britten: *Gloriana*). *See* RICH, LADY (1).

Pentheus (Henze: *The Bassarids*). Bar. Grandson of Cadmus, he succeeds his grandfather, King Cadmus, to the throne of Thebes. His mother Agave is a worshipper of Dionysus who, in disguise, shows Pentheus his own subconscious sexual fantasies. Horrified, Pentheus dresses as a woman and goes to Mount Cythaeron to see the Dionysian life for himself. There he is killed by the Bacchantes, who tear him limb from limb, led by his mother, who does not recognize him. Created (1966) by Kostas Paskalis.

Percy, Riccardo (Lord Richard Percy) (Donizetti: *Anna Bolena*). Ten. A former lover of the Queen and still in love with her. The King accuses them of adultery and Anna is sent to the Tower. Percy's protests of her innocence are ignored and he is committed to die with her on the scaffold. Created (1830) by Giovanni Battista Rubini.

Pereda (Verdi: *La forza del destino*). Name used by the disguised Carlo. *See* VARGAS, DON CARLO DI.

Perrucchetto, Count (Haydn: *La fedeltà premiata*). Bar. Falls in love with Amaranta, with whom his union is finally blessed by the goddess Diana. Created (1781) by Benedetto Bianchi.

Peter (Humperdinck: *Hänsel und Gretel*). Bar. Husband of Gertrud and father of Hänsel and Gretel. He is a broom-maker. Created (1893) by Ferdinand Wiedey.

Peter Grimes (Britten). Lib. by Montagu Slater; prol. and 3 acts; f.p. London 1945, cond. Reginald Goodall.

   The Borough, a small fishing town on the East Coast, about 1830: At the inquest on the death of *Grimes's Apprentice, *Swallow, the Coroner, decides that he died 'in accidental circumstances', but the people of the Borough suspect Grimes of causing the death. His only friends are Ellen *Orford who goes with the carrier, *Hobson, to bring the new *Apprentice found for him by Ned *Keene, and Capt. *Balstrode. In the Boar (run by *Auntie and her two *Nieces), Mrs *Sedley, the town gossip, is meeting Keene to collect her tablets. *Boles, who is drunk, is prevented by Balstrode from attacking Grimes. Ellen finds a bruise on the young apprentice's neck and the townsfolk assume Peter is beating him. In his hut, Grimes hears the men, led by Rev. Horace *Adams, marching toward his hut. He rushes to get out to sea and the boy falls from the hut and is killed. When the boy fails to return, Ellen realizes the Borough will again accuse Grimes of being responsible for his death. Balstrode advises Grimes to take his boat out to sea and scuttle it.

Peter Grimes (Britten: *Peter Grimes*). *See* GRIMES, PETER.

Petřík (Janáček: *The Excursions of Mr Brouček*). Ten. A leader in the Hussite War in 15th-cent. Prague. His other manifestations are Mazal (Prague 1880) and Blankytný (Moon). Created (1920) by Miloslav Jeník.

Phanuel (Massenet: *Hérodiade*). Bass. Chaldean astrologer. It is to Phanuel that Salomé admits her love for John the Baptist. Phanuel knows that Salomé is Hérodiade's daughter. Created (1881) by André Grene.

Pharaoh (Faraone) (Rossini: *Mosè in Egitto*). Bar. King of Egypt. Husband of Sinais, father of Amenophis. He gives permission for Moses and the Israelites to leave bondage in Egypt, but changes his mind—in return, Moses brings down a plague on the Egyptians. Created (1818) by Raniero Remorini.

Phébé (Phoebe) (Rameau: *Castor et Pollux*). Sop. A Spartan princess in love with Pollux. Created (1737) by Marie Antier.

Phèdre (Phaedra) (Rameau: *Hippolyte et Aricie*). Mez. Wife of Thésée and step-mother of Hippolyte whom she loves. She tries to prevent the union of Hippolyte and Aricie, is rejected by her stepson, and later confesses the truth. Created (1733) by Marie Antier.

Phénice (Gluck: *Armide*). Sop. Confidante of Armide. Created (1777) by Mlle Lebourgeois.

Philine (Thomas: *Mignon*). Sop. An actress with a band of strolling players. The nobleman Frédéric falls in love with her. She is jealous of Mignon, who is loved by Wilhelm Meister, to whom Philine is attracted. Created (1866) by Marie Cabel.

Philip II, King (Verdi: *Don Carlos*). Bass. King of Spain, father of the Infante Don Carlos, who has been betrothed to Elisabeth de Valois in an attempt to bring peace between their countries. Philip decides to marry Elisabeth himself, and for the sake of her country she agrees, although she is in love with Carlos. Philip is suspicious of the relationship between his wife and his son. Despite her denials of unfaithfulness, he has Carlos arrested and imprisoned, assured by the Grand Inquisitor that he can even have him killed for the sake of the faith of the country. At the tomb of his father, the Emperor Carlos V, Philip hides and watches Elisabeth bid farewell to Carlos. Philip orders him to be arrested, but is thwarted as the tomb of the Emperor opens and Carlos is dragged inside to the safety of the cloister. Arias: *Elle ne m'aime pas!* ('She does not love me!'); duet (with Posa): *Votre regard hardi s'est levé sur mon trône* ('Your daring glance has been raised to my throne'). This is one of three male roles in the lower register in this opera (the others being Posa and the Grand Inquisitor), and Verdi's skill in differentiating between them vocally can be heard in the various duets and ensembles. Created (Fr. vers. 1867) by Louis-Henri Obin; (It. vers. 1884) by Alessandro Silvestri.

Philosopher (Massenet: *Chérubin*). Bar./bass. Guardian of Chérubin. He encourages Chérubin's love for Nina and discourages him from becoming involved with the dancer L'Ensoleillad. Created (1905) by Maurice Renaud.

Phyllis (Sullivan: *Iolanthe*). Sop. An Arcadian shepherdess and ward in Chancery. She is loved by many—most of the peers in the House of Lords, her guardian the Lord Chancellor, and Strephon, son of Iolanthe, who is the one she loves. Duet (with Strephon): *None shall part us from each other*. Created (1882) by Leonora Braham.

Pierotto (Donizetti: *Linda di Chamounix*). Cont. *Travesti* role. An orphaned musician from Savoy and young friend of Linda, with whom she goes to find work in Paris. It is Pierotto who tells Linda he has heard that Carlo, with whom she is in love, is going to marry someone else and this results in Linda losing her reason. Created (1842) by Marietta Brambilla.

Piet the Pot (Ligeti: *Le Grand Macabre*). Ten. He represents the common man and is drunk most of the time. He is forced to help Nekrotzar announce the news of the end of the world. Created (1978) by Sven-Erik Vikström.

Pike, Florence (Britten: *Albert Herring*). Cont. Housekeeper and companion to Lady Billows. She vetoes every girl suggested as May Queen, as she knows something about each of them which makes them unsuitable as they are no longer virgins. Created (1947) by Gladys Parr.

Pilgrim (Vaughan Williams: *The Pilgrim's Progress*). Bar. The name given by the composer to the character called Christian in Bunyan's book. He goes through various hardships and temptations on his journey to the Celestial City without being corrupted. He passes through the River of Death to ascend to the Gates of the City where he is welcomed by the angels. Created (1951) by Arnold Matters. *See also* ARTICLE BY URSULA VAUGHAN WILLIAMS, p. 230.

PILGRIM (*The Pilgrim's Progress*—Vaughan Williams)

by Ursula Vaughan Williams

Bunyan's *The Pilgrim's Progress* was written some time between 1667 and 1675 and when Ralph Vaughan Williams was a child in the 1870s it was read by almost everyone in England. Some read it for the religious allegory—the author's intention—but others found it, with all its adventures, as exciting as the story of Robinson Crusoe. Like R. M. Ballantyne (*The Coral Island*), Bunyan's story is a fairy tale with dragons and lions and strange beasts, as well as virtuous people helping the pilgrim (Bunyan called him Christian) on his way to the Celestial City.

RVW's mother read *The Pilgrim's Progress* to him and his older brother and sister, together with Shakespeare's plays, Greek legends, poetry, and fairy stories. The richness of the English language and the noble prose of the King James Bible were part of their inheritance, a reader's world given to children.

In 1906 RVW was asked by some young people to write music for a dramatic adaptation of parts of Bunyan's book. He then began to think about it as the subject of an opera, but it wasn't until the early 1920s that he again wrote music for it. The episode he chose was that of Pilgrim (the name he preferred) seeking the Delectable Mountains, seeing in the distance the Heavenly City, and the dark and dangerous water he would have to cross before he found peace. He listened to the Shepherds, and he met the Celestial Being who touched his heart with an arrow to lead him to the Celestial City.

For the next 25 years Ralph worked on and off on a full operatic version. He began it with the great hymn-tune York (harmonized by John Milton, the poet's father). Then Bunyan himself is seen writing the book in Bedford Gaol. After the war, as I sat in RVW's study, I became very involved with the opera. He asked me to write words for a song for Lord Lechery—rather fun, as he wrote another set. We sent typed copies to the tenor Steuart Wilson to choose between them and mine won. I knew about Bunyan's people and did some research from the Bible. I said to Ralph that I found his speech-rhythms so much in character as well as so good. 'So good', he replied, 'that none of the critics noticed'.

When the opera was produced at Covent Garden in 1951, RVW disliked a lot of the staging. Some critics said it belonged to a cathedral, but RVW insisted it was a stage piece. He had supportive letters from his publisher Hubert Foss, the composer Rutland Boughton and the critic Frank Howes, but far more important were several from Professor E. J. Dent, an expert on opera, who said: 'It is an opera, and its only place is the theatre. *The Pilgrim's Progress* is undoubtedly the greatest and the most moving contribution of modern times to the national repertory of musical drama'.

It was dropped after a few performances in London and the provinces and Ralph said 'The Pilgrim is dead and that's that'. But in 1954 it was produced at Cambridge by Dennis Arundell, an actor, writer, musician, and a splendid producer. Cambridge University made amends to RVW for the deficiencies of Covent Garden, and probably no other service to his music gave him more satisfaction.

Eric Blom wrote: 'He is not just exquisite, or gracious, or mellifluous; there is an unworldly nobility about many of those strains which are neither archaic nor modern, though they often sound both at once, but belong to all time or none. I am a keen Handelian, but when it comes to the Alleluias at the end of this work of Vaughan Williams's, they seem to me authentically celestial and those in *Messiah* only full of a fine courtly Georgian swagger.'

This was the best that was said about this work until 1992, when Joseph Ward produced it at the Royal Northern College of Music in Manchester. He was an actor as well as a producer, and we discussed the opera from the viewpoint of Bunyan's lines 'So I awoke, and behold it was a dream'. As a dream the opera took in all the people who had saved Pilgrim and frightened him. The menace of Apollyon and the dangers of Vanity Fair were vividly exciting—and the Alleluias were sung as marvellously as they could be.

Ward had given the opera a vision more like the one RVW would have hoped for, and fulfilled his dream. RVW had used words by Plato (translated by F. J. Church) about his oratorio *Sancta Civitas* and these are equally applicable to the opera, since both were visions of the Celestial City. 'A man of sense will not insist things are exactly as I have described them. But I think he will believe that something of the kind is true of the soul and her habitations, seeing that she is shown to be immortal and that it is worthwhile to stake everything on this belief. The venture is a fair one, and he must charm his doubts with spells like these.'

Pilgrim's Progress, The (Vaughan Williams). Lib. by comp.; prol., 4 acts, epil.; f.p. London 1951, cond. Leonard Hancock.

A Morality (the composer's description of the work): *Bunyan is seen in Bedford gaol writing the end of his book. As he finishes, *Pilgrim appears, a burden on his back, setting out for the Celestial City. An *Evangelist directs him to the Wicket Gate. He kneels before the cross and is armed for his journey. In the Valley of Humiliation he is wounded in a fight. Two *Heavenly Beings revive him and the Evangelist gives him the Key of Promise. In Vanity Fair, Pilgrim rejects the pleasures on offer and Lord *Hate-Good condemns him to death. In prison he remembers the key he was given and walks free. A *Woodcutter's boy directs him to the Delectable Mountains where the Three *Shepherds invite him to rest a while. When he leaves them he passes through the River of Death and ascends to the Celestial City. Bunyan offers his book to the audience.

Pimen (Musorgsky: *Boris Godunov*). Bass. An old monk and chronicler who has given up a life of power, preferring the peace of the monastery. In answer to questions from his novice, Grigori, Pimen recalls the murder of the Tsarevich Dimitri, son of Ivan the Terrible

and brother of the dead Tsar Fyodor, and tells how, had he still been alive, Dimitri would have been the same age as Grigori. Created (1874) by Vladimir Vasiliyev

Ping (Puccini: *Turandot*). Bar. One of the three Masks, Emperor Altoum's ministers. He is Grand Chancellor of China. Created (1926) by Giacomo Rimini.

Pinkerton, Benjamin Franklin (Puccini: *Madama Butterfly*). Ten. Lieutenant in the US Navy. His ship has docked at Nagasaki and he has arranged through a marriage broker to marry a 15-year-old Geisha, Cio-Cio-San, known to everyone as Butterfly. His friend Sharpless, the US Consul in Nagasaki, strongly disapproves of this marriage. Although he has bought a house for his bride, Pinkerton regards her as a temporary amusement whereas Sharpless knows how Butterfly has fallen in love with her prospective husband. Butterfly and her family arrive for the wedding and she tells Pinkerton how she has forsaken her own religion so that they can have a real Christian wedding. This has alienated her relatives who are making a great fuss. Pinkerton orders them to leave and he and Butterfly are united in a passionate love duet as they retire for the night.

Three years later, Butterfly awaits Pinkerton's return—he has gone to America, promising her he will return 'when the robins nest'. He does not know that Butterfly has borne his son. He writes her a letter to say that he now has an American wife and he sends this to Sharpless, asking him to explain the situation to Butterfly before Pinkerton arrives in Nagasaki in his ship, the Abraham Lincoln. Pinkerton arrives at the house with Sharpless and is greeted by Butterfly's maid, Suzuki, who soon learns the truth and sees Kate, Pinkerton's wife, waiting in the garden. At last Pinkerton, seeing how the house has been made ready to welcome him, realizes the distress he has caused. Unable to face Butterfly, he runs from the house, once again leaving Sharpless to do the explaining—Pinkerton wants to take his son back to America to be raised there by him and Kate. He receives, through Sharpless, a message from Butterfly—he can have his son, but he must come in person to collect him. He arrives at the house just after Butterfly has stabbed herself with her father's ceremonial sword and she dies as he enters to claim his child. Aria: *Addio, fiorito asil* ('Farewell, flowery refuge'); duet (with Butterfly): *Bimba dagli occhi pieni di malía* ('Dear child, your eyes full of witchery').

Pinkerton is not the most likeable of men—he is quite happy to marry the young Cio-Cio-San, with no intention of taking his wedding vows seriously, boasting to Sharpless even before the wedding has taken place that he will probably marry an American wife when he returns to the USA. He gives no thought to the damage this might do to Butterfly, and it is only when he returns three years later and learns that Butterfly gave birth to their son after he left her, that the tragedy of the situation dawns on him. Even then his primary concern is to take his son back to America, regardless of the cost to Butterfly—and indeed it costs her her life. Pinkerton sings in duet with Butterfly and with Sharpless and in many ensembles, but has no major solo aria. The short aria he sings in the second act was added by Puccini after the première to pacify the tenor who resented having no big solo. Nevertheless, the role has attracted many great Italianate tenors, including Enrico Caruso, Beniamino Gigli, Richard Tucker, Ferruccio Tagliavini, Carlo Bergonzi, Giuseppe di Stefano, Nicolai Gedda, Jussi Björling, Luciano Pavarotti, Plácido Domingo, and Jerry Hadley. Created (1904) by Giovanni Zenatello.

Pinkerton, Kate (Puccini: *Madama Butterfly*). Mez. American wife of Lieut. B. F. Pinkerton, the American Navy officer who married Butterfly. She goes with her husband to ask Butterfly to allow them to take his son back to America. (The role is larger in the first version of the opera than in the revision.) Creator (1904) not traced.

Pippo (Rossini: *La gazza ladra*). Cont. *Travesti* role. A young peasant of the village who works for the Vingradito family. He informs his master that he saw Ninetta selling silver to a pedlar—her mistress is accusing her of stealing it from the family. As Ninetta is being led to execution, Pippo climbs up the church spire and finds the missing silver in the nest of the family's pet magpie. Created (1817) by Teresa Gallianis.

pirata, Il (Bellini). Lib. by Felice Romani; 2 acts; f.p. Milan 1827, cond. Vincenzo Bellini.

Sicily, 13th cent.: *Imogene has been forced to marry *Ernesto. Her real lover, *Gualtiero, has been exiled since the battle for the Sicilian throne and has led a piratical life. His fleet is shipwrecked and washed up on the coast near Ernesto's castle. Imogene offers shelter to the sailors and then recognizes Gualtiero. She cannot leave her husband and their child to be with him. Ernesto and Gualtiero fight a duel and Ernesto is killed. To Imogene's distress, Gualtiero gives himself up to the Council of Knights and bids her farewell.

Pirate King (Sullivan: *The Pirates of Penzance*). Bass. Head of the pirates to whom Frederic is apprenticed. Created (NY, 1879) by Giovanni Chiari Broccolini (originally called John Clark, born in Cork, Ireland).

Pirates of Penzance, The, or The Slave of Duty (Sullivan). Lib. by W. S. Gilbert; 2 acts; f.p. New York 1879, cond. Sullivan; simultaneously in Paignton, Devon, cond. Ralph Horner (with a second-rate cast, for the sole purpose of securing the English copyright).

Cornwall, about 1875: *Frederic becomes a full member of the pirate band on his 21st birthday. He has decided that, as he disagrees with the actions of the *Pirate King and his followers, he will leave their employ. *Ruth, his former nursemaid, wants to marry him. He appeals to Major-General *Stanley's numerous daughters to help him and *Mabel offers to marry him. Frederic now commands the Sergeant of Police and his men to arrest the pirates. Ruth explains that Frederic was born on 29th February, so his 21st birthday will not be for another 60 years! Therefore he is still committed to the pirates. The pirates are revealed as 'noblemen gone wrong', are forgiven their evil deeds and allowed to marry the Major-General's daughters. So Frederic can marry Mabel.

Pish-Tush (Sullivan: *The Mikado*). Bar. A noble lord who breaks the news to Nanki-Poo that Ko-Ko has been promoted to Lord High Executioner. Created (1885) by Frederick Bovill.

Pistol (Verdi: *Falstaff*). Bass. A follower and drinking companion of Falstaff. Created (1893) by Vittorio Arimondi.

Pittichinaccio (Offenbach: *Les Contes d'Hoffmann*). Ten. Servant and admirer of Giulietta. She floats away in a gondola with him just as Hoffmann comes to claim her. Created (?1905) by Pierre Grivot.

Pitti-Sing (Sullivan: *The Mikado*). Mez. Sister of Yum-Yum and Peep-Bo, wards of Ko-Ko. Trio (with her sisters): *Three little maids from school*. Created (1885) by Jessie Bond.

Pius IV, Pope (Pfitzner: *Palestrina*). Bass. Pope at the time of the conclusion of the Council of Trent. He makes decisions about the use of polyphonic music in church services. After hearing Palestrina's latest Mass, he appoints him his composer. Created (1917) by Paul Bender.

Pizarro, Don (Beethoven: *Fidelio*). Bar. Governor of the prison. He has secretly imprisoned his political enemy Florestan and is determined to kill him before the King's Minister arrives to inspect the gaol. He is foiled by Florestan's wife Leonore who, disguised as a young man, Fidelio, has come to work at the gaol. Aria (with chorus): *Ha! Welch ein Augenblick!* ('Ha, what a moment!'). Created (1805) by (Friedrich) Sebastian Mayer.

Plaza-Toro, Duchess of (Sullivan: *The Gondoliers*). Cont. Mother of Casilda. Created (1889) by Rosina Brandram.

Plaza-Toro, Duke of (Sullivan: *The Gondoliers*). Bar. Father of Casilda, who was married as a babe to the heir to the throne of Barataria. Aria: *In enterprise of martial kind*. Created (1889) by Frank Wyatt.

Plumkett (Flotow: *Martha*). Bass. Young farmer who falls in love with Lady Harriet's maid Nancy, believing her to be a peasant girl called Julia. Created (1847) by Karl Johann Formes.

Pluto (Pluton) (Offenbach: *Orpheus in the Underworld*). Ten. God of the underworld, in love with Eurydice. He arranges for her to live with him in the underworld. Jupiter, who is in love with her, insists she must be returned and Pluto has to foil an attempt by Jupiter to carry her off. Created (1858) by Mons. Léonce.

Podestà (Mozart: *La finta giardiniera*). *See* ANCHISE, DON.

Poggio, Marchesa del (Verdi: *Un giorno di regno*). Sop. Niece of Baron di Kelbar, she is a young widow. She is in love with the Cavalier di Belfiore but, angry because she thinks he has deserted her, she is going to marry old La Rocca. The 'King of Poland', a guest in the Baron's castle, uses his royal prerogative to forbid the wedding. He is, of course, Belfiore in disguise. Created (1840) by Antonietta Marini.

Pogner, Eva (Wagner: *Die Meistersinger von Nürnberg*). Sop. Daughter of Veit Pogner. Her long-standing nurse and companion is Magdalene. Her father has promised her in marriage to the winner of the next Masters' song contest. Unknown to him, she has fallen in love with the young knight Walther von Stolzing. Although she is to be allowed to veto the choice of husband, her father insists she can only marry a member of the Masters' guild, which Walther is not. Walther asks Eva's father to back his request to join the guild, which Pogner gladly does, but adds that he will be subject to the tests that all applicants have to face. Walther sings his song to the gathered assembly, marked by the town-clerk Beckmesser, who himself has ambitions to marry Eva. The knight is failed by the marker.

Eva learns of this later from Hans Sachs, whom she knows is very fond of her, but he does not seem willing to help Walther. Later, Walther and Eva meet and arrange to elope that night. Eva asks Magdalene to dress in her cloak and stand at her window so that her father will think she is at home and she can then slip out to meet Walther. The plan works, but Sachs watches them, blocks their escape, and takes her back to her home. Understanding what the problem is, Sachs sets about coaching Walther. The next morning Eva visits the cobbler to collect her new shoes and while she is there, Walther arrives. She expresses her gratitude to Sachs for helping them so selflessly—she knows that, in his own way, he also loves her. At the meadow on the bank of the River Pegnitz, Eva is led into the arena by her father and seated on her throne to listen to the competitors. Walther sings and is clearly the winner. Eva places the victor's myrtle wreath on his head. She is very upset when he refuses it. Sachs explains to him why he should accept it and, as he capitulates, Eva places the wreath on Sachs's head. The young couple join Sachs in praising 'holy German art'. Aria: *O Sachs! Mein Freund! Du teurer Mann!* ('O Sachs! My friend! You dear man!'); quintet (with Sachs, Walther, Magdalene, and David—Eva opens the ensemble): *Selig, wie die Sonne* ('As blissfully as the sun').

Eva is not a *Heldensopran* role like Brünnhilde, or even Sieglinde or Senta and, as well as many acknowledged Wagnerians, an equal number of non-Wagnerian sopranos have enjoyed fame in the role. These have included Tiana Lemnitz, Maria Müller, Elisabeth Schwarzkopf, Lisa Della Casa, Gré Brouwenstijn (who also sang Elisabeth at Bayreuth for two seasons), Hilde Gueden, Trude Eipperle, Hannelore Bode, Sena Jurinac, Felicity Lott, Nancy Gustafson, and Renée Fleming. Created (1868) by Mathilde Mallinger.

Pogner, Veit (Wagner: *Die Meistersinger von Nürnberg*). Bass. One of the Masters, a goldsmith, and father of Eva. He has decided that the prize for the winner of the forthcoming song contest will be his daughter's hand in marriage. He knows the town-clerk, Beckmesser, hopes to marry Eva, though the idea does not appeal to him. Walther von Stolzing, a young knight, asks Pogner to help

him join the guild of Masters. Pogner is happy to do this (for then Walther can enter the contest and, if he wins, Eva would marry into the aristocracy) but warns him he will have to have an audition and pass the tests like everyone else. When Walther sings at the audition, it soon becomes clear that he does not know any of the Masters' rules of composition. Beckmesser, acting as marker, fails him, but Pogner points out that the town-clerk has a vested interest. He wonders how he can work things out so that Walther is admitted to their guild and whether to enlist the help of the one person he really respects, the cobbler Hans Sachs. Talking to his daughter, she fails to tell him that, member of the guild or not, she is planning to elope with the young knight that very evening. Sachs prevents their departure and returns her to her home, without Pogner realizing what has been happening. At the start of the contest, taking place in a meadow on the banks of the River Pegnitz, Pogner leads his daughter to her throne and takes his own seat with his colleagues, worrying about the result. He is fond of Eva and concerned for her happiness. Sachs whispers to him to have courage. When Walther sings his song, it is obvious that he will be the winner, much to Pogner's (and no doubt Eva's) relief. Pogner takes the chain of office and prepares to place it round Walther's neck to admit him to the guild. He realizes he owes his and his daughter's happiness to Sachs, to whom he pays homage. Aria: *Das schöne fest, Johannestag* ('The lovely festival, St John's Day'). Created (1868) by Kaspar Bausewein.

Poindextre, Alexis (Sullivan: *The Sorcerer*). Ten. Grenadier Guardsman, son of Sir Marmaduke. In love with Aline. He sets the whole plot in motion by requesting a love-potion from the sorcerer John Wellington Wells. Created (1877) by George Bentham.

Poindextre, Sir Marmaduke (Sullivan: *The Sorcerer*). Bass-bar. An elderly baronet, father of Alexis. He is in love with Lady Sagazure. Created (1877) by Richard Temple.

Point, Jack (Sullivan: *The Yeomen of the Guard*). Bar. A strolling player who comes to the Tower of London with his partner Elsie Maynard, whom he loves. She marries a condemned prisoner who is then released. She is clearly in love with her husband and Jack Point, heartbroken, collapses at their feet. Aria: *I have a song to sing, O!* Created (1888) by George Grossmith.

Polinesso (Handel: *Ariodante*). Cont. *Travesti* role. Duke of Albany who wants to marry Ginevra, daughter of the King of Scotland. Conspires to convince Ariodante that Ginevra has been unfaithful to him. Is killed by Ariodante's brother Lurcanio. Created (1735) by Maria Negri.

Polish Mother, The (Britten: *Death in Venice*). Silent dancer. Mother of Tadzio, staying at the same hotel as Aschenbach. Created (1973) by Deanne Bergsma.

Polkan (Rimsky-Korsakov: *The Golden Cockerel*). Bass. General in Tsar Didon's army. Creator (1909) not traced.

Polk, Sam (Floyd: *Susannah*). Ten. Elder brother of Susannah, they have lived together since the death of their parents. They are very poor and he is regarded by the village community as an unscrupulous drunkard, to be feared. While he is out hunting, Susannah is raped by the visiting preacher. When Sam learns of this, he takes his gun, finds the preacher carrying out baptisms, and shoots him. Sam then has to flee the village. Created (1955) by Walter James.

Polk, Susannah (Floyd: *Susannah*). Sop. An attractive girl of 19 years, she has lived with her brother on their farm since their parents died. The village Elders find her attractive, much to the disgust of their wives. The Elders peer through some trees, trying to find a pool to use for baptisms, and see Susannah, naked, bathing. They denounce her as shameless and sinful and the village decides she must confess or be banished from the church. Susannah has no idea what she's done to be treated as an outcast, until informed by Little Bat McLean, who is being forced by his parents to falsely accuse her of seducing him. Sam and the preacher, Olin Blitch, persuade her to go to church, where she sits alone at the back. Hearing Blitch call for sinners to confess, she starts to walk towards him, but realizes what she is doing and rushes out of the church. The preacher follows her home to console her. She breaks down and sobs and as he puts his arms round her his

own passions are aroused and he takes her, too shattered to protest, to bed, where he discovers she is a virgin. When her brother returns from hunting and hears about Blitch's behaviour, he shoots him. The villagers advance on the farm, threatening Susannah, who scares them off with her brother's gun. She is left alone. Created (1955) by Phyllis Curtin.

Pollione (Bellini: *Norma*). Ten. Roman proconsul in Gaul, former lover of Norma and father of her two children. Has deserted her for Adalgisa, an acolyte in the temple. When Norma decides to sacrifice herself in the cause of the Gauls defeating the Romans, Pollione realizes he still loves her and joins her in the flames. Created (1831) by Domenico Donzelli.

Pollux 1. (Rameau: *Castor et Pollux*). Bass. Son of Jupiter and Leda and twin of Castor. Agrees to take Castor's place in Hades to allow him to return to life and Télaïre. Jupiter relents and grants them both immortality. Created (1737) by Claude Chassé de Chinais.
 2. (Strauss: *Die Liebe der Danae*). Ten. King of Eos and father of Danae. He is being hounded by his creditors, demanding the money he owes them. He manages to pacify them by telling them that his four nephews, all Kings, and their wives are trying to find a rich husband for his daughter, and the richest man in the world, King Midas, is coming to see her and wants to marry her. Created (1944) by Karl Ostertag; (1952) by Lázló Szemere.

Polonius (Thomas: *Hamlet*). Bass. Father of Ophélie and chief minister. He was involved in the murder of Hamlet's father, the King. Created (1868) by Mons. Ponsard.

Polybus, King of Corinth (Stravinsky: *Oedipus Rex*). Does not appear in the opera. A messenger announces his death and then throws the fat in the fire: Polybus had been presumed to be the father of Oedipus, and Oedipus thus considered his rightful heir, but on his deathbed he admits that Oedipus, abandoned on a mountainside, although found and raised as Polybus' son, was in fact the son of Laius and Jocasta. *See* OEDIPUS.

Polyphemus (Handel: *Acis and Galatea*). Bass. Giant in love with Galatea. Kills Acis. Aria: *O ruddier than the cherry.* Creator (1718) not traced.

Pompeo 1. (Berlioz: *Benvenuto Cellini*). Bar. Friend of Fieramosca. Killed by Cellini. Creator (1838) not known.

2. (Pompeo Sesto) (Handel: *Giulio Cesare*). *See* SESTO, POMPEO.

Pong (Puccini: *Turandot*). One of Emperor Altoum's Ministers (the Three Masks). He is Supreme Lord of the Imperial Kitchen. Created (1926) by Giuseppe Nessi.

Pooh-Bah (Sullivan: *The Mikado*). Bass-bar. Lord High Everything Else of the town of Titipu. He informs Nanki-Poo that Yum-Yum's wedding to her guardian will take place that very day. Aria: *Young man, despair*. Created (1885) by Rutland Barrington.

Popova, Yeliena Ivanovna (Walton: *The Bear*). Mez. A young widow, she has sworn to be faithful to the memory of her husband for the rest of her life, even though she is well aware that he was unfaithful on more than one occasion. She lives alone, cared for by her protective old servant Luka, takes care of Toby, the family horse and refuses all visitors. Smirnov pushes past Luka and insists on seeing her, as her late husband owed him money for Toby's oats. She promises that her bailiff, when he returns next week, will pay him, but the caller insists the debt must be paid today and refuses to leave until it is—his creditors are all pursuing him. As they argue, he is gradually becoming attracted to her and proposes a duel to settle the argument. She agrees—but she has never before handled a gun so he will have to show her. As he demonstrates how to hold the pistol, he declares his love and they finish up embracing. Aria: *I was a constant, faithful wife*; duet (with Smirnov): *You don't seem to know how to behave in the presence of a lady*. The above arias are delightful parodies of many in opera and provide audiences with a wonderful guessing-game. Created (1967) by Monica Sinclair.

Poppea 1. (Handel: *Agrippina*). Sop. Loved by Ottone, whom Claudio wants to succeed him as Roman emperor. Ottone renounces the throne to marry her. Created (1709) by Diamante Maria Scarabelli.

2. (Monteverdi: *L'incoronazione di Poppea*). Sop. Wife of Ottone, she is loved by the Emperor Nero. Is watched over by the god Cupid (Amor) who prevents her husband murdering her. Marries Nero and is declared Empress of Rome. Aria: *Signor, deh, non partire* ('Sir, do not go away'); duet (with Nero): *Pur ti miro, pur ti godo* ('I gaze on you, I delight in you'). Created (1643) possibly by Anna di Valerio. *See also* ARTICLE BY SYLVIA MCNAIR, p. 237.

Porgy (Gershwin: *Porgy and Bess*). Bass-bar. A crippled resident of Catfish Row. He gives a home to Bess when she is deserted by Crown and falls in love with her. When Crown tries to reclaim her, Porgy kills him. All the other residents refuse to give evidence against him and the police release him. By this time Bess has left for New York. He determines to find her. Arias: *I got plenty o' nuttin'*; *Bess, you is my woman now*; *Oh Lord, I'm on my way*. Created (1935) by Todd Duncan.

Porgy and Bess (Gershwin). Lib. by du Bose Heyward and Ira Gershwin; 3 acts; f.p. Boston 1935, cond. Alexander Smallens.

Charlestown, S. Carolina, in the recent past: In Catfish Row, a Negro tenement, *Crown kills a man and flees, leaving behind his girlfriend *Bess, who is given shelter by the crippled *Porgy. The widow, *Serena, is joined in mourning by other residents of Catfish Row, including *Clara and *Jake. Bess grows to love Porgy. *Sportin' Life tries to sell dope. Bess is persuaded by Porgy and *Maria to go to the annual island picnic. She finds that Crown has been hiding there and wants her to stay with him, but she returns to Porgy. Crown comes back to claim Bess and in a fight Porgy kills him. While Porgy is being questioned by police, Bess leaves for New York. Porgy is released by the police as no one will give evidence against him. He decides to follow Bess and find her.

Porter, Rt. Hon. Sir Joseph (Sullivan: *HMS Pinafore*). Bar. First Lord of the Admiralty. The ship's captain wants him as a husband for his daughter, Josephine, who loves a simple sailor. He has many lady cousins who visit him on board—and he marries one of them. Aria: *I am the monarch of the sea*. Created (1878) by George Grossmith.

Posa, Rodrigo, Marquis de (Verdi: *Don Carlos*). Bar. A loyal supporter of King Philip II of Spain and close friend of the Infante,

POPPEA (*L'incoronazione di Poppea*—Monteverdi)

by Sylvia McNair

Poppea is not what we'd call 'a nice girl'. She is Ambition Gone Wrong. Her ambition to become Nero's [Nerone's] wife and Empress of Rome burns out of control and she uses her extremely potent sexual powers to manipulate Nero into doing everything she wants. To ascend to the throne she must make sure anyone who might resist her is removed.

Her husband, Ottone, the General of Nero's army, is the first to be thrown aside. Next is Seneca, Nero's Secretary-of-State and life-long counsellor. At Poppea's urging, Nero fires him. When told he has been relieved of his duties, Seneca does the only thing he knows to be honourable: he takes his own life. Last, but hardly least, is Nero's wife, Ottavia. Nero puts her out to sea in a boat with no sail: it is a death sentence. With all the 'obstacles' removed, Poppea becomes Nero's wife and ascends to the throne—she has achieved her ambition.

It would be hard in this modern age to find anyone who is perfectly type-cast to play the role of somebody as wicked as Poppea. Ironically, the music that Claudio Monteverdi created for Nero and Poppea to sing is some of the most exquisitely beautiful in all of opera. I dare say the music of *L'incoronazione di Poppea* has almost made this story about two deeply disturbed people and what they did in order to get what they wanted, into something noble.

Poppea is the antithesis of every role I've ever played. I usually play the young, desirable goodie-goodies, sweet and pure and smart—parts I like to think I'm most suited for! But Poppea, one of the most wicked of all female operatic characters, is a *real* acting challenge. Maybe that's why I like it so much—I can let my imagination as an actress run wild because nothing seems too outrageous when interpreting this horror. And playing a sex goddess on stage is actually great fun.

If one looks carefully at the text for the love duets Nero and Poppea sing, one can easily imagine the staging of a private orgy. Poppea speaks specifically about the softness and sweetness of her breasts, and the music, even without the words, describes graphically their pleasures in bed—Poppea knows what Nero likes. But a wise stage producer knows that *less* is *more*, that people who are fully clothed are much sexier, much more attractive and potent than people who are not, and he or she will accomplish far more *real* sensuality by avoiding the staging of an orgy.

One of the highlights of my professional life was working on this opera with that most amazing musician, Nikolaus Harnoncourt, for the Salzburg Festival of 1993. His knowledge and his skill in this repertoire are unequalled and the inspiration he provides is as rich and colourful as any singing actress could ever hope for. I loved every minute of it.

Don Carlos. Carlos tells Posa of his love for Elisabeth, now married to his father. The Marquis advises him to try to forget his frustration by going to Flanders and helping the people there who have been oppressed by the Catholic rule imposed on them by Spain. Posa asks the King to allow Carlos to go to Flanders, begging him to treat the people there less severely. The King, whilst admiring Posa's liberal ideals, nevertheless warns him to beware of the Grand Inquisitor. He also asks Posa to watch Carlos and Elisabeth, about whose relationship he is suspicious. At the *auto-da-fé*, the King rejects Carlos's pleas on behalf of the heretics, and Carlos draws his sword. To avoid bloodshed, Posa steps in and takes the sword from him. Knowing his friend is now in danger, Posa visits Carlos in prison and deliberately stands where he can be seen by his enemies. Posa is shot. As he dies, he tells Carlos that Elisabeth will be waiting for him the next day at the monastery of San Yuste to say goodbye to him. Aria: *Carlos écoute…Ah! Je meurs l'âme joyeuse* ('Carlos, listen…Ah! I die with a happy soul'). In the Schiller play from which this opera libretto was fashioned, Posa is a more dominant role, being the main character in the attempt to save Flanders from Philip's tyrannical rule. In the opera, he is less important for this purpose than Don Carlos, but his death aria is one of the most beautiful in the opera. Created (Fr. vers. 1867) by Jean-Baptiste Faure; (It.vers. 1884) by Paul Lhérie. *See also* ARTICLE BY THOMAS HAMPSON, p. 239.

Pottenstein, Gustav von ('Gustl') (Lehár: *The Land of Smiles*). Ten. A lieutenant in the dragoons. In love with Lisa, but gently rejected by her. After she goes to Peking with Prince Sou-Chong, Gustl is posted there as a military attaché and visits them. He is attracted to the Prince's sister. But it becomes clear that the two cultures will not be compatible and he and Lisa leave China together, each saying farewell to the one they loved. Created (1929) by Willi Stettner.

Poussette (Massenet: *Manon*). Sop./mez. One of three ladies 'of easy virtue', drinking companions of Morfontaine and de Brétigny. Created (1884) by Mlle Molé-Truffier.

Prefect, The (Donizetti: *Linda di Chamounix*). Bass. He suggests to Antonio and Maddalena that their daughter Linda should go and live in Paris with his brother. When the brother dies, Linda goes to live with Carlo. Created (1842) by Prosper Dérivis.

Pretty Polly (Birtwistle: *Punch and Judy*). High sop. Searched for by Punch after he has killed Judy and their baby. She rejects him and appears as the Witch in his nightmare. Returns his love when he redeems himself by killing the hangman. Created (1968) by Jenny Hill.

Preziosilla (Verdi: *La forza del destino*). Mez. A young gypsy-girl. At the inn in the village of Hornachuelos, near Seville, she tells fortunes and advises the men to join the army and fight in Italy against the Germans. Arias (with ens.): *Al suon del tamburo* ('To the sound of the drum'); (with soldiers) *Rataplan* ('Ratatat'). Created (1862) by Constance Nantier-Didiée (who apparently tried to prevent the engagement of Caroline Barbot as Leonora; Verdi protested and Barbot was engaged).

Priam 1. (Berlioz: *Les Troyens*). Bass. King of Troy. Father of Cassandra and Hector, who orders the wooden horse of the defeated Greeks to be placed before Athene's Temple. Creator (1890) not known.

   2. (Tippett: *King Priam*). Bass-bar. King of Troy. Husband of Hecuba, father of Hector and Paris. He begs Achilles to return the body of his murdered elder son. During the destruction of Troy he is killed by Achilles' son. Created (1962) by Forbes Robinson.

Priest (or Parson) (Janáček: *The Cunning Little Vixen*). Bass. A friend of the Forester and the Schoolmaster. The bass usually also sings the part of the Badger. Created (1924) by Jaroslav Tyl.

Prima Donna (Strauss: *Ariadne auf Naxos*). Sop. The soprano in the Prologue who is to sing the role of Ariadne in the *opera seria*. See ARIADNE/PRIMA DONNA.

Prince 1. (Dvořák: *Rusalka*). Ten. Marries the water-sprite, Rusalka, but they both break the conditions under which they were allowed to marry. He dies and she returns to the lake. Created (1901) by Bohumil Pták.

   2. (Prokofiev: *The Love for Three Oranges*). Ten. Son of the King, he suffers from melancholia and will die unless he is made to laugh. He laughs at Fata Morgana, the evil witch, who in revenge makes him fall in love with three oranges and travel the world to find them. Created (1921) by José Mojica.

   3. (Prince Charming) (Prince Charmant) (Massenet: *Cendrillon*). Sop. *Travesti* role. The Prince is melancholy, and is ordered by his father to marry. At the royal ball, princesses parade before him, but he is not interested until an unidentified beautiful young lady appears. They fall in love at once. At midnight she disappears, leaving behind her glass slipper. The

RODRIGO, MARQUIS DE POSA (*Don Carlos*—Verdi)

by Thomas Hampson

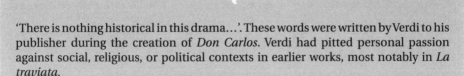

'There is nothing historical in this drama…'. These words were written by Verdi to his publisher during the creation of *Don Carlos*. Verdi had pitted personal passion against social, religious, or political contexts in earlier works, most notably in *La traviata*.

Already historically compromised by the great German dramatist Friedrich Schiller [1759–1805], the story of Don Carlos presents a complex backdrop of political-religious—i.e. public—conflict by which the very personal dilemmas of love, jealousy, family, and faith are brought into sharp relief. But with *Don Carlos* the essentially metaphoric use of historical context accomplishes the recreation of the ambiguity of successive moments found in reality. There is no scene in the opera that ends in the same political or personal context in which it starts. One is caught in the ebb and flow of events in King Philip II's life as mercurially manipulated by his son, set against the backdrop of absolutist religious fervour.

The Marquis de Posa is the most metaphorical figure in the opera, not least because the very essence of his existence and behaviour would have been impossible in Philip II's court. Posa's mission (but not the man himself) is historically founded: to free Flanders of oppression. Even more to the point is his unwavering determination to realize for himself and 'his kind' *self-determination*.

Verdi's concern that Posa would be perceived only as a martyred hero, not only demonstrates the composer's understanding of the theatre public's hunger for cliché, but also illuminates his 'use' of Posa in this work. Posa is a constant and consistent force throughout the opera. His unwavering mission which, in fact, borders on the zealous, finds him in the role of confidant to the very source (Philip) of the massacre he protests, just as it prepares him to become a murderer in the name of protection of his only ally (and therefore hope), Carlos. He compromises one apparent allegiance to fortify the appearance of another (*auto-da-fé*) in order to attain the greater goal of his 'beliefs' and he is even treasonous in the simple act of serving as messenger-boy for his love-sick friend, Carlos.

Each event, however, is greater than Posa's participation in it. If anything, Posa's metaphoric existence as the emerging cry for self-determination and greater democratic ideals, though it is very sympathetic, is suffocated in a larger social, personal, political, religious conundrum that requires a dramatic martyrdom to achieve any permanence to his character's existence.

The challenge artistically to a role like Posa is, in fact, to avoid the heroic. If one sings exactly as the master wrote, constant in his use of pianissimi, trills, phrase markings, rests, there emerges a character who is more intent on finding his way in each new circumstance rather than an operatic figure bent on delivering his message. Posa is intentionally given a separate musical tone for each of his 'partners'—Elisabeth, Carlos and, most importantly, Philip—regardless of what it is he has to say. His lyricism is not impotence, but a rather pliant, even manipulating, dialogue. His outbursts are always born of passion that surprises even himself and thus require immediate further dialogue. Throughout all Verdi's revisions and translations from the original French libretto, the role of Posa remained intact, the only character not to be altered in form, tessitura, presence, and, therefore, intent.

Complex personalities in tumultuous times breed contradictions, but as fascinating as these ambiguities and contexts are, *Don Carlos* remains a great dramatic plea for the supremacy of the personal experience. Human behaviour and its often obscure manifestations dictate that the world will always have its Posas, but the fragile, flickering light of reason harboured in the passions and love born from the individual experience is our greatest warning—and therefore our worthier contemplation.

Prince searches the land until he finds the one person on whose foot the slipper will fit—Cendrillon. Duet (with Cendrillon): *Toi, qui m'es apparue* ('You who have appeared before me'). Created (1899) by Mlle Gmelen.

  4. (Rossini: *La Cenerentola*). See RAMIRO.

Prince Igor (Borodin). Lib. by comp. (scenario by V. V. Stasov); prol. and 4 acts; f.p. St Petersburg 1890, cond. Karl Kuchera.

  Poutivl, 1185: *Yaroslavna begs her husband Prince *Igor and his son *Vladimir not to go to war with their army against a Tartar tribe, the Polovtsi, but they will not listen. She is left in the care of her profligate brother Prince Vladimir *Galitsky. Igor is defeated and captured and the Polovtsi army attacks Poutivl. In captivity in Khan *Kontchak's camp, Vladimir falls in love with his captor's daughter *Kontchakovna. Kontchak's slaves are ordered to entertain his captives by singing and dancing (the *Polovtsian Dances*). Igor decides to escape and save Poutivl, but Vladimir is undecided—he does not want to leave Kontchakovna. She settles the matter by rousing the camp and having him held, while his father succeeds in escaping. Impressed by Igor's determination to save his home town, and moved by the young lovers' plight, Kontchak allows his daughter and Vladimir to remain together in the camp. In Poutivl, Yaroslavna is relieved and delighted to see her husband return.

Prince Igor (Borodin: *Prince Igor*). See IGOR, PRINCE.

Princess Ida, or The Castle Adamant (Sullivan). Lib. by W. S. Gilbert; 3 acts; f.p. London 1884, cond. Arthur Sullivan.

  King Hildebrand's Palace and the Castle Adamant: King *Gama's daughter *Ida was engaged at the age of 1 year to King *Hildebrand's

son *Hilarion. To escape from this situation, when she is 21 she enters the Castle Adamant, a women's college from which men are barred and where Lady *Blanche is in charge. Hilarion, with his friends *Cyril and *Florian, goes to find her. The men climb over the walls and enter the castle, stealing and donning women's clothes. Florian is recognized by his sister *Psyche, and she and her friend *Melissa agree to help them in their quest. Cyril gets drunk and they are all discovered and captured. Ida acknowledges her love for Hilarion.

Princess Ida (Sullivan: *Princess Ida*). See IDA (2).

Prinz von Homburg, Der (Henze). Lib. by Ingeborg Bachmann; 3 acts; f.p. Hamburg 1960, cond. Leopold Ludwig.

  Fehrbellin, Germany, 1675: *Friedrich Wilhelm, Elector of Brandenburg, promises in marriage to *Friedrich Artur, Prince of Homburg, his niece Princess *Natalie. The Prince is so absorbed by thoughts of their future together that, on the battlefield, he commands his troops to attack without heeding the orders of Field Marshal *Dörfling or advice of his friend *Hohenzollern. He is court-martialled and sentenced to death. Natalie begs for his release. The Elector will grant this only if the Prince can argue honestly that the sentence is unjustified. This he will not do, preferring death to dishonour. Natalie plans to free him using her own troops. The Prince is led to his execution, but as his blindfold is removed he sees that the Elector, moved by the Prince's refusal to act dishonestly, has torn up the death warrant leaving him free to marry Natalie.

Prioress (Poulenc: *Les Dialogues des Carmélites*). See CROISSY, MME DE AND LIDOINE, MME.

Procida, Jean de (Verdi: *Les Vêpres siciliennes*). Bass. Ex-leader of the Sicilian patriots against their French aggressors, he has returned from exile and is taking every opportunity to incite the people to rise up against their invaders. He is part of a plot to assassinate the French Governor, thwarted by the interception of the young Sicilian, Henri (who has discovered that he is the Governor's illegitimate son). Aria: *Ô toi, Palermo* ('O, Palermo)'). [This character is based on the real Procida, a distinguished doctor born in Salerno and physician to Emperor Frederick II. Through his involvement in politics he became a conspirator of international repute and appears in history books.] Created (1855) by Louis-Henri Obin.

Prosdocimo (Rossini: *Il turco in Italia*). Bar. A poet who is writing a play based on the events which he observes around him. In order to be able to end his play happily, it is left to him to sort out the various couples who become involved with each other. Created (1814) by Pietro Vasoli.

Prunier (Puccini: *La rondine*). Ten. (originally bar.). A poet, friend of Magda de Civry. He reads Magda's hand and tells her that she may, like the swallow (*la rondine*) find a bright future, but there is also tragedy in store. Prunier is secretly in love with Magda's maid Lisette. He promises to help her make a career as a singer and she leaves to live with him, but the stage episode ends in disaster and he persuades Magda to take her back. Duet (with Magda): *Chi il bel sogno di Doretta poté indovinar?* ('Who can interpret Doretta's beautiful dream?'). Created (1917) by Francesco Dominici.

Prus, Janek (Janáček: *The Makropulos Case*). Ten. Son of Jaroslav Prus, contender in a long lawsuit. Janek falls in love with Kristina, daughter of the law clerk Vítek, but she gives him up for her art (she is training to be a singer). His hopeless love for the diva Emilia Marty leads him to commit suicide. Created (1926) by Antonín Pelz (who later changed his surname to the Czech spelling of Pelc).

Prus, Jaroslav (Janáček: *The Makropulos Case*). Bar. A Hungarian nobleman, descendant of Baron Prus (with whom Emila Marty, in her days as Elina Makropulos, had an affair

and to whom she had borne a son). He is one of the present contestants in a lawsuit which has gone on for 100 years. The old Baron was believed to have died intestate and with no known children and his cousin had inherited his estate. The Gregor family are claiming it belongs to them, as their ancestor was the Baron's illegitimate son. Emilia Marty is able to locate the old Baron's will, hidden in Prus's house, together with an envelope containing the formula for the elixir of life. She needs another dose in order to survive. Prus gives it to her in exchange for a night with her in a hotel—not a very successful night, we gather, as her coldness has been something of a barrier between them. As he leaves her, he is brought the news that his son has committed suicide for love of Emilia. Created (1926) by Zdeněk Otava.

Psyche, Lady (Sullivan: *Princess Ida*). Sop. Professor of Humanities at the Castle Adamant. Sister of Florian, whom she recognizes when he breaks in with Hilarion to find Ida. Created (1884) by Kate Chard.

Public Opinion (Opinion Publique) (Offenbach: *Orpheus in the Underworld*). Mez. Introduces the opera and insists that Orpheus descends to the underworld to rescue Eurydice. Is not happy with the outcome whereby Eurydice goes off with Jupiter. Created (1858) by Marguerite Macé.

Publio (Mozart: *La clemenza di Tito*). Bass. Captain of the Praetorian Guard, who arrests Sesto for plotting against Tito. Aria: *Tardi s'avvede d'un tradimento* ('He is late to notice betrayal'). Created (1791) by Gaetano Campi.

Puck 1. (Britten: *A Midsummer Night's Dream*). Spoken. Boy acrobat, serving Oberon. He is sent to find magic herb juice which, when squeezed on the eyes, will make the recipient fall in love with the first live creature seen on waking. He causes great confusion by putting the juice on the eyes of all the wrong people. Created (1960) by Leonide Massine II (son of the ballet dancer).

2. (Weber: *Oberon*). Mez. *Travesti* role. Is used by Oberon to find a couple true to each other despite all trials and temptations, as Oberon has sworn not to be reconciled with Titania until such a couple is found. Puck aids Huon in his rescue of Reiza, thus fulfilling his

master's request. Created (1826) by Harriet Cawse.

3. (Purcell: *The Fairy Queen*). Spoken. Called Robin Goodfellow and similar to the role in (1) above. Creator (1692) unknown.

Puff, Lord (Henze: *The English Cat*). Ten. Pedigree cat, President of the Royal Society for the Protection of Rats. Uncle of Arnold, who hopes to inherit from him. He learns that his new bride, Minette, has been flirting with her old flame Tom. Society demands a divorce. Created (1983) by Martin Finke.

Punch (Birtwistle: *Punch and Judy*). High bar. Each of his murders is preceded by a war-cry—he kills his wife, Judy, their baby, the Doctor, and the Lawyer. His love for Pretty Polly is rejected until he earns redemption by killing the hangman (the booth-operator who is responsible for him). Created (1968) by John Cameron.

Punch and Judy (Birtwistle). Lib. by Stephen Pruslin; 1 act (in 9 sections with prol. and epil.); f.p. Aldeburgh 1968, cond. David Atherton.

Legendary times: *Choregos opens his Punch-and-Judy booth; he comments on the action. *Punch sings a lullaby to his baby, whom he then throws in the fire. *Judy discovers the body and he stabs her, later killing the Doctor and the Lawyer. Three times Punch searches for *Pretty Polly, but each time she rejects him. When he kills Choregos, a nightmare begins in which his disguised victims come back to seek revenge. Condemned to death, Punch is in prison. The hangman is Jack Ketch (the disguised Choregos) and Punch tricks him into putting the noose round his own neck and hangs him. By killing the Hangman, Punch earns redemption and Pretty Polly returns his love. Choregos sings the epilogue.

Puritani, I (Bellini). Lib. by Carlo Pepoli; 3 acts; f.p. Paris 1835, cond. Vincenzo Bellini.

Near Plymouth, England, the time of the English Civil War (mid-17th cent.): Elvira *Walton, daughter of Lord Gualtiero *Walton, the Puritan governor general, is to marry Riccardo *Forth, a Puritan colonel. Her uncle Giorgio *Walton convinces her father that she should marry the man she loves, a Cavalier, Arturo *Talbot. *Enrichetta, the French widowed queen of Charles I, is to be tried as a spy and Arturo is determined to save her. Riccardo allows her and Arturo to escape. Elvira's wedding is thus postponed and in a famous mad scene, she imagines being married to Arturo, but he has been sentenced to death for his part in the plot. Giorgio pleads with Riccardo to save Arturo as the only way of ensuring Elvira's sanity. He agrees, on condition that if Arturo is fighting on the side of the Royalists, he must die. Three months later Arturo returns, explains why he disappeared and begs Elvira's forgiveness. Despite her joy at seeing him, her unbalanced mind thinks he is leaving her again. When Riccardo announces the death sentence on Arturo, Elvira is so shocked that she recovers her mind. She and Arturo are united as a messenger announces the end of the war.

Pylade (Gluck: *Iphigénie en Tauride*). Ten. Compatriot of Oreste, with whom he is to be sacrificed on the orders of King Thoas. Is saved by Iphigénie sending him away with a message to her sister Electra. Created (1779) by Joseph Legros.

Pyrrhus (Pirro) (Rossini: *Ermione*). Ten. Husband of Hermione. When he leaves her and marries Andromache, she has him killed, but then regrets her action. Created (1819) by Andrea Nozzari.

Queen Elizabeth I 1. (Donizetti: *Maria Stuarda*). *See* ELISABETTA (1).

2. (Britten: *Gloriana*). *See* ELISABETTA (3).

Queenie (Kern: *Show Boat*). Cont. Black servant on the *Cotton Blossom*, married to Joe. Aria: *Hey fella!*; duet (with Joe): *Ah still suits me*. Created (1927) by Aunt Jemima Tess Gardella.

Queen of Night (Königin der Nacht) (Mozart: *Die Zauberflöte*). Sop. Mother of Pamina. She is greatly concerned for her daughter's safety and promises her in marriage to Tamino if he rescues her from the 'evil' Sarastro. Arias: *O zitter nicht, mein lieber Sohn!* ('O do not tremble, my dear son!'); *Der Hölle Rache kocht in meinem Herz* ('The revenge of hell boils in my heart'). Created (1791) by Josepha Hofer (*née* Weber, sister of Mozart's wife Constanza).

Queen of Spades, The (Pikovaya dama) (Tchaikovsky). Lib. by Modest Tchaikovsky and comp.; 3 acts; f.p. St Petersburg 1890, cond. Eduard Nápravník.

St Petersburg, late 18th cent.: *Hermann's fellow-soldiers, *Surin and *Chekalinsky, gamble. He tells his fellow-officer *Tomsky that he is in love but does not know the lady's name. Prince *Yeletsky announces his engagement to *Lisa, who arrives with her grandmother the *Countess. Hermann realises that it is Lisa he loves. Tomsky tells him the story of the old Countess: in her youth she lost heavily at cards and a Count gave her the secret of three cards which would always win. After she revealed the secret to her husband and a lover, a ghost told her she would die if she told a third man the secret. Alone in her room after her friend *Pauline and other girls have left, Lisa is confronted by Hermann and gives in to his avowal of love. At a ball, Lisa slips Hermann the key to her room which he must reach through her grandmother's quarters. He hides in the Countess's room. Her maids prepare her for bed and leave. Hermann emerges and tries to make her tell him the three cards' secret. He threatens her with a gun and she dies of shock. Hermann is visited by the Countess's ghost, who tells him '3, 7, ace'. Lisa and Hermann again declare their love, but he leaves her to go and gamble. Distressed, she drowns herself. Gambling for very high stakes, Hermann wins with the 3, then with the 7. For the third game Hermann bets on the Ace, but when he turns over the card it is the Queen of Spades—the Countess has fooled him. Hermann stabs himself.

Queen of the Earth Spirits (Marschner: *Hans Heiling*). Sop. Mother of Hans Heiling. When he leaves the underworld to live near the girl he loves, the Queen makes him promise to return if ever his heart is broken. Created (1833) by Maria Theresia Lehmann-Löw.

Queen of the Fairies (Sullivan: *Iolanthe*). Cont. Banished Iolanthe from Fairyland for marrying a mortal, but forgives her and sends her son, Strephon, into Parliament to cause chaos among the peers. She herself cannot resist the charms of the sentry, Sergeant Willis. Aria: *Oh, foolish fay*. Created (1882) by Alice Barnett.

Queen of the Gypsies (Balfe: *The Bohemian Girl*). Cont. Jealous of the kidnapped Bohemian girl, Arline, has her arrested on a false charge. Created (1843) by Miss Betts.

Quichotte, Don (Massenet: *Don Quichotte*). Bass. The knight errant, prepared to fight anyone to defend the woman he loves, the beautiful Dulcinée. He mistakes windmills for giants and is carried up on their sails. Despite his chivalry, Dulcinée will not marry him. He dies, dreaming of meeting her in heaven. Arias: *Je suis le chevalier errant* ('I am a knight errant'); *Marchez dans mon chemin* ('Walk with me on my way'). Created (1910) by Fyodor Chaliapin.

Quickly, Mistress (Verdi: *Falstaff*). Mez. One of the Merry Wives of Windsor, friend of Alice Ford and Meg Page. She agrees to help Alice and Meg, both of whom Falstaff is trying to seduce to get at their husbands' money. She acts as the carrier of notes from the two ladies to Falstaff, arranging a meeting for him with Alice at the Ford home, telling him to be there *dalle due alle tre* ('from two to three') when Ford will not be at home. During that meeting, it is Mistress Quickly who warns Alice that her husband, jealous and suspicious, has returned and is about to enter the room to try and catch her with Falstaff. Aria: *Reverenza!* ('Your worship'). In the right hands this is a delightful role, and can be very amusing as long as the humour is not overdone—it's all there in the music and just needs to be sung 'straight'. Created (1893) by Giuseppina Pasqua (wife of the conductor Leopoldo Mugnone; she was Eboli in the 1884 revision of *Don Carlo*).

Quince 1. (Britten: *A Midsummer Night's Dream*). Bass. A carpenter, one of the rustics. He 'produces' the play they are to perform for the wedding of Duke Theseus and Hippolyta. Aria: *Gentles, perchance you wonder at this show*. Created (1960) by Norman Lumsden.

2. (Purcell: *The Fairy Queen*). Spoken. Similar to the role in (1) above. Creator (1692) unknown.

Quint, Peter (Britten: *The Turn of the Screw*). Ten. A former manservant at Bly. He was responsible for the death of the then governess, Miss Jessel, who had become pregnant by him and died in childbirth. He died when he slipped on an icy road. He comes to haunt the children, especially Miles, on whom he has an evil influence. He makes Miles steal a letter written by his present Governess, telling his guardian what is happening at Bly and asking for help. Ultimately Miles admits, to his Governess, who is ruling his actions. Aria: *So! She has written*; duets (with Miss Jessel): *On the paths, in the wood; I seek a friend obedient to follow where I lead*. Many leading Brit. tenors have relished this role: Graham Clark, Arthur Davies, Robert Tear, Philip Langridge, Paul Nilon, and Ian Bostridge. Created (1954) by Peter Pears.

R

Rachel (Halévy: *La Juive*). Sop. Daughter of Eléazar, a Jewish goldsmith, she is the Jewess of the opera's title. She falls in love with 'Samuel', who confesses to being the Christian Prince Léopold and married to Eudoxie. Sentenced to death by Cardinal de Brogni for breaking the Lord's laws, she refuses to save herself by denouncing her Judaism. As she dies in a boiling cauldron, Eléazar reveals that she is not a Jewess, but the daughter of Brogni, whom he saved years earlier when Rome was sacked. Created (1835) by Marie Cornélie Falcon.

Rackstraw, Ralph (Sullivan: *HMS Pinafore*). Ten. A sailor in love with the captain's daughter Josephine, he tries to elope with her as her father disapproves and wants her to marry someone of higher rank. Little Buttercup reveals that she swapped the two men as babies, so Ralph is really the captain and the captain a simple sailor. Aria: *A maiden fair to see*. Created (1878) by George Power.

Radamès (Verdi: *Aida*). Ten. Captain in the Egyptian army. He is in love with Aida, daughter of the Ethiopian Amonasro, who has become slave-girl to the Egyptian Princess Amneris. His ambition is to lead the Egyptian troops so that he can again see Aida. To celebrate his victory, the King of Egypt offers his daughter as Radamès's bride. He dare not refuse without causing offence and being accused of treason. The night before his wedding, he arranges to meet Aida for the last time on the banks of the river. As he says his last farewell to her, he does not realize that she, reluctantly and forced by her father, is trying to extract from him the troops' invasion plans so that the Ethiopians can be a step ahead. When Radamès's bride-to-be, Amneris, emerges from the temple, Amonasro thrusts himself forward with the intention of killing her. He is prevented by Radamès and allowed to escape with his daughter, while Radamès offers himself as a prisoner of the King of Egypt. He is incarcerated in a tomb below the temple altar. There he finds Aida hiding and waiting for him, so they can die together. Aria: *Celeste Aida* ('Heavenly Aida'); duet (with Aida): *Pur ti riveggo, mia dolce Aida* ('At last I see you again, my sweet Aida'). *Celeste Aida*, one of the most famous of all Italian tenor arias, is also one of the most difficult. The tenor singing the part of Radamès has been on stage a very short while before he reaches the aria, with no time to 'warm up'—he just has to sing it 'cold'. Also, the aria ends on a very high note (a top B flat), which the score indicates as 'very quiet and dying away'. The temptation for the tenor is usually too great, and the last note rings out loudly and (one hopes) triumphantly. Famous interpreters include Aureliano Pertile, Giovanni Martinelli, Richard Tucker, Mario Filippeschi (who began his musical career as a clarinettist), Hans Hopf, Mario del Monaco, Jussi Björling, Franco Corelli, Carlo Bergonzi, Jon Vickers, Plácido Domingo, and Luciano Pavarotti. Created (1871) by Pietro Mongini.

Raffaele 1. (Verdi: *Stiffelio*). Ten. A young nobleman who has an affair with Lina, wife of the Protestant minister Stiffelio. He is killed by Lina's father Count Stankar. Created (1850) by Raineri Dei. *See also* GODVINO.

2. (Verdi: *La forza del destino*). Name assumed by Leonora's sweetheart when he enters a monastery. *See* ALVARO, DON.

Ragonde (Rossini: *Le Comte Ory*). Cont. Stewardess of the Castle of Formoutiers, and companion to Countess Adèle. Created (1828) by Mlle Mori.

Raimbaud (Rossini: *Le Comte Ory*). Bass. Friend of Count Ory. Created (1828) by Henri-Bernard Dabadie.

Raimondo 1. (Donizetti: *Lucia di Lammermoor*). *See* BIDEBENT, RAYMOND.

2. (Wagner: *Rienzi*). Cardinal, the Papal Legate who excommunicates Rienzi. Created (1842) by Gioachino Vestri. (In his *Life of Richard Wagner*, i, Ernest Newman describes how, during a break in rehearsals, the cast went out for lunch, leaving Wagner sitting on the stage. He was unable to join them, as he had no money, but did not want anyone to realize this. Vestri, however, must have had an idea of the position, for he came back and brought Wagner a piece of bread and a glass of wine.)

Rake's Progress, The (Stravinsky). Lib. by W(ystan) H(ugh) Auden and Chester Kallman; 3 acts; f.p. Venice 1951, cond. Igor Stravinsky.

England, 18th cent.: Anne *Trulove and Tom *Rakewell are to marry, her father *Trulove being apprehensive. Nick *Shadow tells Tom he has inherited a fortune. Tom leaves with him for London to sort out his finances. In her brothel, *Mother Goose tries to teach Tom about vice and takes him to bed. Anne knows she must go and rescue Tom, who is becoming bored with the rich life in London. Shadow suggests he marry *Baba the Turk and when Anne arrives he begs her to leave him—Baba is his wife. He later rejects Baba and dreams of abolishing the world's misery. His life degenerates until he is bankrupt and his possessions have to be sold by the auctioneer *Sellem. Baba advises Anne to go to Tom. Shadow, now seen to be the devil, claims Tom's soul as payment for his services. He suggests a game of cards to decide Tom's fate. Urged by the voice of Anne, Tom wins. Shadow, angry, leaves, condemning Tom to a life of insanity. Anne visits him in Bedlam and sings him to sleep before leaving with her father. Awaking and finding Anne gone, Tom dies.

Rakewell, Tom (Stravinsky: *The Rake's Progress*). Ten. In love with Anne Trulove, he wishes he was rich. A strange character, Nick Shadow, tells him he has inherited a fortune. Shadow offers his services free for a year and a day and they leave for London. Tom undergoes various adventures: in a brothel he is initiated into a life of vice; he marries Baba the Turk; he loses all his money and becomes bankrupt. Shadow claims his soul in payment

for his services and Tom asks to gamble for it. Tom wins, and angrily Shadow condemns him to a life of madness. In Bedlam, Anne visits him—Tom imagines he is Adonis and she is Venus. He sleeps, and when he wakes she is gone. Tom dies. Arias: *Since it is not by merit*; *With roses crowned, I sit on ground*, *Adonis is my name*. Created (1951) by Robert Rounseville.

Raleigh, Sir Walter 1. (Britten: *Gloriana*). Bass. Capt. of the Guard. The Queen relies on him for sensible advice. This is resented by Essex and Mountjoy. Aria: *Both lords are younglings*. Created (1953) by Frederick Dalberg.

2. (Donizetti: *Roberto Devereux*). Bass. It is Raleigh who, together with Lord Cecil, informs the Queen that when Essex was searched a silk scarf was found next to his heart. She recognizes it as belonging to Sara, Duchess of Nottingham. Creator (1837) not traced.

Ramerrez (Puccini: *La fanciulla del West*). Name by which the bandit being hunted by the sheriff is known. *See* JOHNSON, DICK.

Ramfis (Verdi: *Aida*). Bass. The High Priest, who blesses Radamès as he leads the Egyptian army and accompanies the Egyptian Princess Amneris to the temple the night before her marriage to Radamès, so that she can spend the night in prayer. Created (1871) by Paolo Medini.

Ramiro 1. (Rossini: *La Cenerentola*). Prince of Salerno. Looking for a suitable wife, he swaps clothes with his valet—he wants to be loved for himself, not his position and wealth. Cenerentola falls in love with what she believes to be the valet but her stepfather wants one of his own daughters to marry the prince and excludes her from the royal ball, to which she is taken by Ramiro's tutor. She gives the 'valet' a bracelet, keeping its identical partner for herself. She leaves the ball and the Prince goes from house to house searching for her. He recognizes the servant Cenerentola (Cinderella) as the girl he loves, confirmed when their bracelets match. He and Cenerentola are married. Aria: *Sì, ritrovarla io giuro* ('Yes, I swear to find her again'); duet (with Cenerentola): *Un soave non so che* ('A sweet something'). Created (1817) by Giacomo Guglielmi.

2. (Mozart: *La finta giardiniera*). Sop. *Travesti* role. A knight, in love with the Podestà's niece, Arminda. Created (1775) by Tommaso Consoli (sop. castrato).

3. (Ravel: *L'Heure espagnole*). Bar. A muleteer. Comes to the shop of the clockmaker Torquemada and interrupts assignations between Torquemada's wife Concepción and her lovers. She keeps him occupied carrying clocks up and down the stairs, and is impressed with his strength. Created (1911) by Jean Périer.

Rance, Jack (Puccini: *La fanciulla del West*). Bar. Sheriff who is trying to track down the notorious bandit Ramerrez. Rance is keen to marry Minnie, owner of the saloon where the miners gamble and drink. He keeps declaring his love for her, but she does not return his feelings. He learns from Ashby, a Wells Fargo agent, that the bandit is somewhere in their area and Ashby gives him a photograph of Ramerrez. A stranger, Dick Johnson, arrives at the inn and is welcomed by Minnie; Rance is both jealous and suspicious. He calls that evening at Minnie's cabin to warn her that Dick Johnson is the bandit Ramerrez and shows her the photograph to prove it. Minnie laughs and sends them away. As Dick Johnson leaves Minnie's house, he is shot by Rance's men. Minnie hides him in her loft and again Rance visits her. He wants to make love to her but she again rejects him. As he is about to leave, blood drips down from the attic above and Johnson is discovered. Rance agrees to Minnie's bargain—they will play poker and if she wins, Johnson will be let free; if she loses, Rance will win her love. By cheating, Minnie wins, and Rance departs. Determined to catch his quarry, Rance rejoins his men in the forest and indicates to them Johnson's hiding-place. They capture him, but as they are about to hang him, Minnie intervenes. The miners support her pleas and she and Johnson leave together. Aria: *Minnie, dalla mia casa son partito* ('Minnie, I left my home'). Created (1910) by Pasquale Amato.

Rangoni (Musorgsky: *Boris Godunov*). Bass. A Jesuit, confessor to Princess Marina of Poland. He reminds her of her duty to convert Russia to Catholicism if she mounts the throne as consort to the Tsar. Created (1874) by Ossip Palechek.

Raoul (Meyerbeer: *Les Huguenots*). *See* NANGIS, RAOUL DE.

Rape of Lucretia, The (Britten). Lib. by Ronald Duncan; 2 acts, f.p. Glyndebourne 1946, cond. Ernest Ansermet.

In or near Rome, 500 BC: The *Male and *Female Choruses sketch in the historical background. Throughout the opera they comment on the Christian aspects of the relationships. They recount how *Tarquinius has seized power in Rome. He and his fellow officers, *Collatinus and *Junius, have had their wives spied on in their absence and only *Lucretia, wife of Collatinus, has remained faithful. Tarquinius rides to Rome to prove Lucretia can also be tempted. Lucretia and her companions, *Bianca and *Lucia, are at home. Tarquinius arrives, claiming his horse is lame, and is given a bed for the night. He goes to Lucretia's room and when she refuses him, he rapes her. She confesses to Collatinus, but despite his forgiveness she kills herself. The Choruses invoke the Christian ethic—Christ is all.

Ratcliffe, Lieut. (Britten: *Billy Budd*). Bass. Second Lieutenant aboard *HMS Indomitable*. Created (1951) by Michael Langdon.

Ratmir (Glinka: *Ruslan and Lyudmila*). Cont. *Travesti* role. A Khazar prince, previous suitor of Lyudmila. Is loved by Gorislava. Helps Ruslan to find the abducted Lyudmila. Created (1842) by Anfisa Petrova.

Ravenal, Gaylord (Kern: *Show Boat*). Bar. A gambler, he comes on board the *Cotton Blossom* and falls in love with the captain's daughter, Magnolia. They marry and take over the leading roles as entertainers on the show boat. They have a daughter, Kim, but Gaylord leaves them when he has gambled away their money and can no longer support them. Years later, a gentler, reformed character, he returns to the boat and rejoins his wife and daughter. Duets (with Magnolia); *Make believe; You are love*. Created (1927) by Howard Marsh.

Ravenal, Kim (Kern: *Show Boat*). Sop. Daughter of Gaylord and Magnolia. She and her mother become the star turns on the refitted show boat. Created (1927) as child by Eleanor Shaw, as adult by Norma Terris (who also created Magnolia).

Ravenal, Magnolia (Kern: *Show Boat*). *See* HAWKS, MAGNOLIA.

Ravenswood, Edgar (Edgardo) (Donizetti: *Lucia di Lammermoor*). Ten. There is long-standing rivalry between his family and the Ashtons of Lammermoor. Lucia's brother Enrico, on learning that Edgardo and Lucia love each other, conspires to break up the relationship so his sister can marry Arturo Ashton and save the family fortune and reputation. While Edgardo is in France fighting the Stuart cause, Lucia reluctantly marries Arturo. Edgardo returns as the wedding ceremony finishes and accuses Lucia of betraying him. He curses her and the House of Lammermoor. Enrico challenges him to a duel, but after hearing that Lucia has gone mad and died, Edgardo kills himself with his sword. Aria: *Tombe degl'avi miei...* ('Tombs of my fathers'); duet (with Lucia): *Sulla tomba* ('Over the tomb'); the famous sextet (with Enrico, Lucia, Raimondo, Arturo, and Alisa, which he opens in duet with Enrico): *Chi mi frena in tal momento?* ('Who curbs me at such a moment?'). Created (1835) by Gilbert-Luis Duprez.

Ravoir, Geronte di (Puccini: *Manon Lescaut*). Bass. Treasurer-General in Amiens, a wealthy man. He is at once attracted by Manon when she stops at the inn on her way to a convent. He orders a carriage to take her to Paris, but she and Des Grieux have fallen in love and they use the carriage to elope. When Des Grieux's money runs out, Manon returns to Geronte, who lavishes money on her—a luxurious home in Paris and an abundance of jewels—but she is not happy and again leaves him to go with Des Grieux. Catching them together, Geronte summons the police and asks them to arrest Manon as a prostitute. Created (1893) by Alessandro Polonini.

Rebecca (Josephs). Lib. by Edward Marsh; 3 acts; f.p. Leeds 1983, cond. David Lloyd-Jones.
    Monte Carlo and Manderley, 1930s: In Monte Carlo, Mrs *Van Hopper informs her companion that they are to return to England. The *Girl is upset to be leaving Maxim *de Winter. He is a widower, his wife, Rebecca *de Winter, having drowned in her boat. He offers to take her back to England as his wife. At Manderley they are greeted by Maxim's sister Beatrice *Lacy and her husband Giles and the estate manager, Frank *Crawley. Mrs de Winter

meets *Frith, the butler, and the housekeeper, Mrs *Danvers, who had adored Rebecca. During the Manderley Ball, rockets announce that a ship has gone ashore. The salvage-men find Rebecca's boat at the bottom of the bay, her body in the cabin. In front of Col. *Julyan, Jack *Favell, a lover of Rebecca, accuses Maxim of causing her death, but it emerges that Rebecca, knowing she was dying of cancer, drowned herself. As husband and wife embrace, fire breaks out. Manderley is destroyed, and with it all trace of the first Mrs de Winter.

Rebecca (Josephs: *Rebecca*). *See* DE WINTER, REBECCA.

Redburn, Mr (Britten: *Billy Budd*). Bar. First Lieutenant aboard *HMS Indomitable*. Created (1951) by Hervey Alan.

Red Whiskers (Britten: *Billy Budd*). Ten. A press-ganged man who is brought to *HMS Indomitable* at the same time as Billy Budd. Created (1951) by Anthony Marlowe.

Reich, Anna (Nicolai: *Die lustige Weiber von Windsor*). Sop. Anne Page. *See* FORD, NANNETTA. Created (1849) by Louise Köster.

Reich, Frau (Nicolai: *Die lustige Weiber von Windsor*). Mez. *See* PAGE, MEG. Created (1849) by Pauline Marx.

Reich, Herr (Nicolai: *Die lustige Weiber von Windsor*). Bass. The character equivalent to Meg Page's husband (who does not actually appear in Verdi's *Falstaff*). Creator (1849) not traced.

Reischmann, Dr Wilhelm (Henze: *Elegy for Young Lovers*). Bass. Father of Toni. Physician of the poet Mittenhofer, he accompanies him to the Alps. Created (1961) by Karl Christian Kohn.

Reischmann, Toni (Henze: *Elegy for Young Lovers*). Ten. Son of the poet Mittenhofer's physician. He falls in love with the poet's companion and dies with her on the mountain. Created (1961) by Friedrich Lenz.

Reiza (Weber: *Oberon*). Sop. Daughter of Haroun al Raschid, the Caliph of Baghdad. Is carried away by Huon, then captured by pirates. Huon rescues her. Created (1826) by Mary Anne Paton.

Rémendado (Bizet: *Carmen*). Ten. A smuggler, friend of Dancaïre, and associate of Carmen. Created (1875) by Mons. Barnolt.

'Renard, Marquis' (J. Strauss II: *Die Fledermaus*). *See* EISENSTEIN, GABRIEL VON.

Renata (Prokofiev: *The Fiery Angel*). Sop. Since she was a child, she has been visited by a protecting angel. It disappeared when she grew up, but she thought her lover, Heinrich, was the embodiment of the angel. He deserted her after a year and she is searching for him. She enlists Ruprecht's help. When they meet Heinrich, the men fight a duel and Ruprecht is injured. After nursing him back to health, Renata enters a convent to atone for her sinful behaviour. She corrupts the nuns with her story of the angel and is sentenced to death. Created (1954) by Lucienne Marée; (1955) by Dorothy Dow.

Renato (Verdi: *Un ballo in maschera*). *See* ANCKARSTROEM, CAPT.

Renaud (Rinaldo) (Gluck: *Armide*). Ten. A knight in the First Crusade. Falls in love with Armide under a spell put on him by her magician uncle. Is rescued by two fellow knights and leaves her. Created (1777) by Joseph Legros.

Rheingold, Das (*The Rhine Gold*) (Wagner). Lib. by Wagner; 1 act; f.p. Munich 1869, cond. Franz Wüllner (although Wagner had conducted excerpts in concert performance in Vienna in 1862). Prol. (in 4 scenes) to the trilogy *Der* *Ring des Nibelungen*.
  The Rhine and mountains, mythological times: *Alberich is trying to catch the *Rhinemaidens *Wellgunde, *Woglinde, and *Flosshilde, at the bottom of the Rhine. They evade him and Wellgunde tells him that whoever can make a ring from the Rhine gold, which they guard, will inherit the world. Woglinde adds that if he wants to achieve this, he will have to renounce love. He curses love and grabs the gold. High in the mountains, *Wotan is awakened by his wife, *Fricka. He has had a castle (Valhalla) built by the giants *Fasolt and *Fafner. In payment, he has promised them Fricka's sister *Freia, who is being protected by her brothers *Froh and *Donner, but the giants want their pound of flesh and take Freia

off with them. *Loge announces the theft of the gold by Alberich and the giants agree to let Freia go in return for the gold. Wotan and Loge set off for Nibelheim (where the dwarfs dwell deep in the earth, mining precious metals) to find the gold. They come to a cave where Alberich's brother *Mime has made a Tarnhelm (a magic helmet) from some of the gold. Its wearer can turn himself into any form he wishes. Alberich is wearing the gold Ring. At Loge's suggestion, Alberich uses the Tarnhelm to turn himself into a toad, and Wotan and Loge capture him. Back in the mountains, they force Alberich to give up the hoard of gold and as they pull the Ring from his finger, Alberich curses it—whoever owns it will die. Fasolt and Fafner bring in Freia. She will be saved only if totally hidden from view by the hoard of gold. The gold is built up around her, but a final gap remains and the giants demand the Ring to close this gap. Wotan is advised by *Erda to give up the Ring and Freia is freed. As Fasolt and Fafner struggle to possess the Ring, Fafner kills Fasolt—the Ring has brought about its first curse. The gods cross the rainbow bridge to enter Valhalla—only Loge realizes that, in their efforts to rule the world, they are bringing about their own downfall.

Rhinemaidens (Wagner: *Das Rheingold*; *Götterdämmerung*). 2 sops., 1 mez. They live at the bottom of the Rhine and possess a hoard of gold. They are chased by the dwarf Alberich, who first wants to be friendly, but then sees the gold and decides to steal it. They tell him that whoever makes a Ring from the gold will inherit the world, but in order to do this he would have to renounce love for ever. He steals the gold. The Rhinemaidens finally regain the hoard, but only after it has reaped its curse many times. Trios: *Heiajaheia!... Rheingold!...*; *Frau Sonne sendet licht Strahlen* ('The sun goddess sends down beams of light'). *See also* FLOSSHILDE, WELLGUNDE, WOGLINDE.

Ribbing, Count (Verdi: *Un ballo in maschera*). (Samuel in Amer. vers.) Bass. An enemy of the King, plotting to overthrow him. Created (1859) by Cesare Bossì.

Riccardo 1. (Verdi: *Un ballo in maschera*). *See* GUSTAVUS III, KING.
  2. (Bellini: *I Puritani*). *See* FORTH, SIR RICCARDO.

Rich, Lady (Britten: *Gloriana*). Sop. Penelope, sister of the Earl of Essex. She is the lover of Lord Mountjoy. She plots with him, and with the Earl and Countess of Essex, how the four of them will choose who is to succeed the Queen when she dies. After Essex has been sentenced to death for supposed treason, Lady Rich pleads with the Queen not to sign the warrant for his execution. The Queen, regarding Penelope's attitude as rather haughty, refuses her pleas and seals her brother's fate. Created (1953) by Jennifer Vyvyan.

Riders to the Sea (Vaughan Williams). Text by J. M. Synge; 1 act; f.p. London 1937, cond. Malcolm Sargent.

An island off the west coast of Ireland, early 20th cent.: *Nora believes clothes taken from a drowned man belong to her brother Michael. Her sister *Cathleen agrees and they hide them from their mother, *Maurya, who has already lost her husband and four sons at sea. Her last surviving son, *Bartley, is to cross the sea to take horses to Galway Fair. The women try to dissuade him and, when he insists, the sisters coax Maurya into taking him food for the journey. When Maurya returns, she tells of having seen Bartley riding with Michael and the sisters tell her Michael is dead. She realises she has had a vision and that Bartley will also drown. His body is carried in.

Riedinger (Hindemith: *Mathis der Maler*). Bass. A wealthy Lutheran citizen of Mainz, father of Ursula, who is loved by Mathis. Created (1938) by Albert Emmerich.

Riedinger, Ursula (Hindemith: *Mathis der Maler*). Sop. Daughter of Riedinger, she is loved by the artist Mathis. The Cardinal's adviser tells her it would be an advantage to the state if she marries the Cardinal. Impressed by Ursula's willingness to marry him for the sake of her faith, the Cardinal blesses her but decides to withdraw from the world. Ursula admits her love for Mathis, but announces that she has decided to give up love and art and join the peasants in their revolt. Created (1938) by Judith Hellwig.

Rienzi, Cola (Wagner: *Rienzi*). Ten. Brother of Irene, he is the Tribune of the people, supporting them against the nobles who try to crush them. (Historically Rienzi lived from 1313 to 1354. In 1347 he defeated the Patricians and was elected Tribune. He was assassinated.) One of his followers is Adriano Colonna, who is in love with Rienzi's sister Irene. Adriano's father Stefano is plotting with the nobles to murder Rienzi. When Stefano is killed in the fight, Adriano's loyalty is tested and he swears to avenge his father's death. As Rienzi attempts to enter the church to address the people, the Cardinal proclaims his excommunication. The Capitol is set on fire and Rienzi and his loyal sister perish in the fire. Arias: *Erstehe, hohe Roma, neu!* ('Arise, great Rome, anew!'); *Allmächt'ger Vater* ('Almighty Father'—known as Rienzi's Prayer). Created (1842) by Joseph Tichatschek.

Rienzi, der Letzte der Tribunen (*Rienzi, the last of the Tribunes*) (Wagner). Lib. by comp.; 5 acts; f.p. Dresden 1842, cond. Karl Reissinger.

Rome, mid-14th cent.: Adriano *Colonna is in love with Irene *Rienzi and agrees to support her brother Cola *Rienzi who is trying to seize power from the noblemen in Rome. He is supported by *Baroncelli and Cecco del *Vecchio and proclaims the freedom of Rome, being declared Tribune. Led by Stefano *Colonna, the nobles of Rome secretly plan Rienzi's murder. Adriano warns Rienzi. Attempts to stab him fail and Paolo *Orsini and his co-plotters are sentenced to death. Rienzi agrees to pardon them if they will swear allegiance to the new laws of Rome. They agree, but break their word and plan to march against Rienzi. Adriano's loyalty is divided between his father and Rienzi. Rienzi leads his men against the conspirators and Stefano Colonna is killed. Adriano swears vengeance and plots with Baroncelli and Cecco to kill Rienzi. As they prevent him entering the church, Cardinal *Raimondo announces Rienzi's excommunication. Only Irene remains loyal to her brother. The crowds set fire to the Capitol. Rienzi and Irene stand on the burning balcony. Adriano tries to rescue them but the town collapses, killing them all. Once more the nobles are free to overrule the people.

Rienzi, Irene (Wagner: *Rienzi*). Sop. Sister of Cola Rienzi. She is loved by Adriano, son of Stefano Colonna, Rienzi's greatest opponent. Created (1842) by Henriette Wüst (who later married a Dresden actor, Hans Kriete, from whom Wagner borrowed money for the printing of the scores of *Rienzi, Der fliegende Holländer*, and *Tannhäuser*).

Riff (Bernstein: *West Side Story*). Bar. Leader of the Jet gang, he is killed during gang rivalry. His death sets off the chain of events which lead to the final tragedy. Created (1957) by Mickey Calin (later Callan).

Rigoletto (Verdi). Lib. by Francesco Maria Piave; 3 acts; f.p. Venice 1851, cond. Giuseppe Verdi.

Mantua, 16th cent.: The Duke of *Mantua is giving a ball. He flirts with the Countess *Ceprano, watched by her husband, Count *Ceprano, and the court jester *Rigoletto who, since his wife died, has kept his daughter *Gilda hidden away, looked after by her nurse *Giovanna. He does not know that the Duke fancies her. Old *Monterone, whose daughter has been one of the Duke's conquests, curses both the Duke and his jester. The curse frightens Rigoletto. The Duke enters the house and tells Gilda of his feelings. As revenge for the jester's jibes, Ceprano decides to kidnap Gilda. Finding Gilda is a prisoner in his palace, the Duke 'visits' her. She rushes to her father—she has been seduced. The jester determines to murder his master and enlists the help of a professional assassin, *Sparafucile, whose sister *Maddalena will assist him. Rigoletto takes his daughter to a tavern where she can see for herself the Duke drinking and consorting with whores—one of whom is the helpful Maddalena, who falls in love with him. Sparafucile agrees to spare his life on condition that they kill whoever next arrives at the tavern and substitute the body for the Duke's. Gilda overhears this plan, dresses as a young man, enters the inn and is killed. Rigoletto is handed a sack containing a body. Then he hears the Duke's voice in the distance. In the sack he discovers his dying daughter. Monterone's curse is complete.

Rigoletto (Verdi: *Rigoletto*). Bar. A widower, father of Gilda and court jester to the Duke of Mantua. He is a hunchback and spends his professional time making snide comments about the Duke's guests. Despite all his sourness, Rigoletto mourns the loss of his wife and truly loves his daughter, whom he keeps well hidden from undesirable suitors. To get his own back on Rigoletto for his jibes, Count

Ceprano arranges to abduct Gilda. He even enlists the jester's help, pretending it is all an innocent prank, and Rigoletto allows himself to be blindfolded and then holds the ladder down which his daughter is removed from the house. When the Duke seduces Gilda, Rigoletto vows revenge and hires the assassin Sparafucile and his sister Maddalena to kill the Duke. Maddalena falls in love with the Duke, and she and her brother decide to substitute another body in his place. Unknown to them all, Gilda dresses as a man and comes to the tavern. She is killed and put into the sack which is handed over to Rigoletto, who believes it contains the Duke's body. As he gloats over his revenge, he suddenly hears, in the distance, the Duke's voice, singing… Inside the sack he finds his dying daughter. This is one of the most spine-chilling moments in the opera—or, indeed, in any opera—as it dawns on the devoted father who is in the sack. Aria: *Pari siamo!* ('How we are alike!'); *Cortigiani, vil razza dannata* ('Vile, damned race of courtiers'); duets (with Gilda), including: *Ah! Deh non parlare al misero* ('Do not speak to me of my lost love'); quartet (with Gilda, the Duke of Mantua, and Maddalena): *Bella figlia dell'amore* ('Fair daughter of love'). Created (1851) by Felice Varesi.

Rigoletto is the first of the three 'middle-period' Verdi operas (the other two being *Il trovatore* and *La traviata*) and in it are found some of the great Verdi 'hallmarks' to which his earlier operas have been leading—the forceful, even vicious, baritone, the tender father–daughter duet, and the superb quartet (which, together with the sextet from *Lucia di Lammermoor*, is justly regarded as one of the greatest ensembles of 19th-cent. Italian opera). Since its creation this role has been sung by many great baritones, including Tito Ruffo, Mario Sammarco, Giuseppe de Luca, Tito Gobbi, Heinrich Schlusnus, Giuseppe Taddei, Leonard Warren, Ettore Bastianini, Sherrill Milnes, Paolo Gavanelli, and Alan Opie. *See also* ARTICLE BY FRANK JOHNSON, p. 252.

Rinaldo (Gluck: *Armide*). *See* RENAUD.

Ring des Nibelungen, Der (*The Ring of the Nibelung*) (Wagner). Described by the composer as *Ein Bühnenfestspiel für drei tage und einen Vorabend* ('A stage festival play for three days and a preliminary

RIGOLETTO (*Rigoletto*—Verdi)

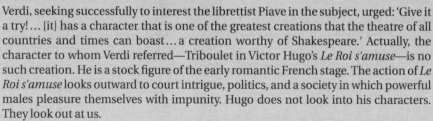

by Frank Johnson

Verdi, seeking successfully to interest the librettist Piave in the subject, urged: 'Give it a try!… [it] has a character that is one of the greatest creations that the theatre of all countries and times can boast… a creation worthy of Shakespeare.' Actually, the character to whom Verdi referred—Triboulet in Victor Hugo's *Le Roi s'amuse*—is no such creation. He is a stock figure of the early romantic French stage. The action of *Le Roi s'amuse* looks outward to court intrigue, politics, and a society in which powerful males pleasure themselves with impunity. Hugo does not look into his characters. They look out at us.

But Triboulet, when turned into Rigoletto by Verdi and Piave, really is the great creation which Verdi over-generously saw in Hugo's play. The action of *Rigoletto* looks inward. Court intrigue, politics, and powerful men engaged in what we would now call blokiness, are simply the setting for a look inward to the soul of the central figure caught up in it all and wishing, like so many of us, that the world was not as it was.

Verdi's Rigoletto is often called Shakespearean, *Pari siamo* ('We are alike') being compared to a Shakespearean soliloquy. In any previous 19th-cent. Italian opera, including Verdi's, it would have been an aria with a swelling melody used twice. The 1851 Verdi chose instead an interior monologue. It is true then that Rigoletto as a character is Shakespearean, but he is something more. The character looks forward far more than back. Rigoletto is the precursor of the ambiguous figures in the plays of the 20th cent., including our own time. He is both good and evil. The duets with his daughter Gilda tell us that he is the first; the humiliating of Count Monterone that he is also the second. As with most people, there is more good in him than evil, as the music for his fatherly love shows. But, as with many people, circumstances caught him up in evil early on and he cannot escape it.

Also, like most of the great characters in 20th-cent. drama, he is not what he seems. There are elements in him of Arthur Miller's Willy Loman and of John Osborne's Archie Rice. Like them, his work necessitates his wearing a mask which hides what he feels. The Duke of Mantua does not know that he hates him. The courtiers do not know that he has a daughter. It is not until she sees him in his working clothes in the Duke's palace that Gilda knows what her father does for a living.

Verdi foreshadows another Italian dramatist, Luigi Pirandello (1867–1936) whose works are about role-playing and the difference between appearance and reality. It is now accepted that *Rigoletto* changed opera musically. *Rigoletto*'s score is so much more advanced than what went before. But, just as importantly, with the character of Rigoletto, Verdi advanced 19th-cent. Italian opera as drama. Because of this ambiguity, the character is more real than any since those of Monteverdi's *The Coronation of Poppea*. He looks forward to Berg's Wozzeck and Britten's Grimes. And to 20th-cent. Man. Freud would have recognized Rigoletto as a standard patient. He is a divided soul; like most of us.

evening'). The Nibelungs are a race of dwarfs who live in the bowels of the earth and mine for precious metals. Wagner wrote the librettos as well as the music, the composition spreading over 28 years. F.p. as a complete cycle: Bayreuth 1876, cond. Hans Richter. *See* RHEINGOLD, DAS; WALKÜRE, DIE; SIEGFRIED; GÖTTERDÄMMERUNG.

Rinuccio (Puccini: *Gianni Schicchi*). Ten. Nephew of Zita (cousin of the recently deceased Buoso Donati). He is in love with Lauretta, daughter of the poor peasant Gianni Schicchi, but his relatives (gathered for the reading of Buoso's will) are against the marriage. They search for Buoso's will, worried by rumours that he has left his fortune to a monastery. When the will is found, they discover that he has indeed left everything to the church. Rinuccio suggests prevailing upon Gianni Schicchi to help them by forging a new will, on condition that they will then withdraw their objection to his marriage with Lauretta. Schicchi agrees to help, but when the new will is read out they discover that Schicchi will inherit the money himself. There can be no further barrier to the marriage of Lauretta and Rinuccio and Schicchi gives them his blessing. Aria: *Firenze è come un albero fiorito* ('Florence is like a flowering tree'). Created (1918) by Giulio Crimi.

Rise and Fall of the City of Mahagonny, The (Weill). *See* AUFSTIEG UND FALL DER STADT MAHAGONNY.

Rising of the Moon, The (Maw). Lib. by Beverley Cross; 3 acts; f.p. Glyndebourne 1970, cond. Raymond Leppard.

County Mayo, Ireland, 1875: When the 31st Royal Lancers arrive in Ballinvourny, among them are Capt. *Lillywhite and his daughter Atalanta *Lillywhite, Col. *Jowler and his wife Eugenia, and Major von *Zastrow and his wife Elisabeth. The only remaining monk in the requisitioned monastery is Brother *Timothy. Young Cornet *Beaumont wants to join the Lancers, and as part of his initiation test he has to conquer all three women in one night. He manages the two married ladies without much trouble. When he attempts to enter Atalanta's room, he is interrupted by Zastrow's arrival with the Irish Cathleen *Sweeney. Beaumont tricks Zastrow into Atalanta's room and is himself left with Cathleen. Next day, to save the honour of those involved, Beaumont resigns his commission and the regiment leaves the village.

ritorno d'Ulisse in patria, Il (*The Return of Ulysses to his Homeland*) (Monteverdi). Lib. by Giacomo Badoaro; prol. and 3 acts; f.p. Venice 1640.

Legendary Ithaca: The allegorical figures Time, Fortune, and Love discuss their domination of Human Frailty, as revealed in the opera proper. *Ulisse (Odysseus) went off to the Trojan War, leaving his wife *Penelope and their son *Telemaco. Twenty years later Penelope is inconsolable, despite the efforts of her nurse *Ericlea. She is uninterested in suitors trying to win her hand, although her maid *Melanto is having a romance with one of their valets, *Eurimaco. Ulisse has been rescued by Phaeacians and brought back to Ithaca. *Minerva disguises Ulisse as an old man and sends him to find his faithful servant *Eumete, who tells him of his wife's fidelity. Penelope agrees to marry whoever wins a contest using Ulisse's bow, but the suitors do not have the strength to string the bow. Disguised as a beggar, Ulisse fights his old enemy, the glutton *Iro. The beggar is made welcome by Penelope and asks to join the archery contest. He strings the bow and kills the suitors. Penelope still does not believe he is her husband. She is convinced when he describes accurately the quilt on their bed, which only he can know.

Roberto Devereux (Donizetti). Lib. by Salvatore Cammerano; 3 acts; f.p. Naples 1837.

England, 1598: *Elisabetta (Queen Elizabeth I of England) loves Roberto *Devereux (Earl of Essex) and wants to save him from a charge of treason after he returns from Ireland. But he loves Sara, Duchess of *Nottingham, who has been forced to marry the Duke of *Nottingham. He gives Sara a ring, given to him by the Queen (with the promise that she would always grant his wish if he returned the ring to her). Sara gives him a scarf. When the Queen is shown this sign of his infidelity, Roberto is sent to the Tower. As he is executed, Sara brings the ring to the Queen—her husband had deliberately prevented her bringing it sooner, in order to ensure Essex's death. Elisabetta has the husband and wife arrested. She then announces her abdication.

Robinson, Count (Cimarosa: *Il matrimonio segreto*). Bass. An English lord whom Geronimo wants to marry his elder daughter Elisetta. He falls for the younger Carolina, already secretly married. Created (1792) by Francesco Benucci.

Rocca, La (Verdi: *Un giorno di regno*). Bass. Treasurer to the estates of Britanny and uncle of Edoardo di Sanval, with whom the Baron's daughter is in love, although she is being forced to marry La Rocca. Created (1840) by Agostino Rovere.

Rocco (Beethoven: *Fidelio*). Bass. Father of Marzelline. He is the chief gaoler at the prison where Pizarro has secretly confined Florestan in the dungeon. Marzelline falls in love with her father's new assistant, Fidelio (Florestan's wife Leonore in disguise). Aria: *Hat man nicht auch Gold beineben* ('Unless you have money to hand as well'). Created (1805) by Herr Rothe.

Roche, Comtesse de la (Zimmermann: *Die Soldaten*). Mez. Her son falls in love with Marie. To protect him from her, she takes Marie as a companion. Created (1965) by Liane Synek.

Rochefort, Lord (George Boleyn) (Donizetti: *Anna Bolena*). Bass. Brother of Anna, the wife of Enrico (Henry VIII). He tries to save his sister from the scaffold when she is accused by her husband of adultery and treason. He is sentenced to die with her. Created (1830) by Lorenzo Biondi.

Roche, La (Strauss: *Capriccio*). *See* LA ROCHE.

Rodelinda (Handel). Lib. by Nicola Francesco Haym; 3 acts; f.p. London 1725.
   Milan, 7th cent.: King *Bertarido, *Rodelinda's husband and father of *Flavio, is reported to have died in battle. *Grimoaldo, her husband's enemy, wants to marry Rodelinda, but she rejects him. His friend *Garibaldo declares his love for *Eduige, Bertarido's sister, because he wants to inherit her money—she really loves Grimoaldo. Bertarido, in disguise, observes his wife agreeing to Grimoaldo's proposal, not knowing it is under threat of Flavio's death. However, Rodelinda declares that it is not possible for her to be the wife of Grimoaldo and, at the same time, mother of the true future king, so she requests Grimoaldo to murder Flavio in

her presence. He cannot bring himself to do this. An old friend, *Unulfo, brings about the reunion of Bertarido and Rodelinda, whereupon Grimoaldo arrests Bertarido and sentences him to death. Eduige and Unulfo plot his escape and Unulfo manages to lead him to freedom. Garibaldo tries to kill Grimoaldo, but Bertarido kills Garibaldo. Grimoaldo gives up all claim to Bertarido's inheritance and marries Eduige.

Rodelinda, Queen of Lombardy (Handel: *Rodelinda*). Sop. Wife of King Bertarido, mother of Flavio. When it is rumoured that her husband has been killed in battle, she is forced to accept the proposal of Grimoaldo, or her son will be killed. Bertarido overhears this, and cannot understand what is happening. Rodelinda asks Grimoaldo to kill Flavio in front of her, for, she declares, she cannot be the wife of a usurper of her husband's crown and, at the same time, be mother of the rightful heir. Grimoaldo is unable to bring himself to do this. Bertarido escapes and is reunited with his wife and son. Created (1725) by Francesca Cuzzoni.

Roderigo 1. (Verdi: *Otello*). Ten. A gentleman of Venice, whose hopeless passion for Desdemona is encouraged by Iago in his plot to arouse Otello's suspicions. This is a smaller role than in the Rossini opera. *See* RODRIGO (1). Created (1887) by Vincenzo Fornari.
   2. (Rossini: *Otello*). *See* RODRIGO (2).

Rodolfo 1. (Puccini: *La bohème*). Ten. A poet who lives in poverty with his three bohemian friends, Marcello, Colline, and Schaunard, in a garret in the Latin Quarter of Paris. He decides to remain behind when his colleagues leave to spend Christmas Eve at the local Café Momus. As he finishes an article, there is a knock at the door. Mimì, pale and fragile, is on her way to her own room and her candle has blown out—please will he relight it for her? Invited in, she has a fit of coughing and collapses in a chair, her candle and door-key falling to the floor. Rodolfo revives her with some wine and they both search for the key on the floor. He finds it and surreptitiously slips it in his pocket. Their hands touch—hers are very cold—and their eyes meet. They tell each other who they are and what they do and then declare their love. They depart for the Café Momus where they join the others and Rodolfo buys Mimì a pink bonnet. Marcello's old love Musetta soon joins them. However, Rodolfo's jealousy and worry about Mimì's health cause many problems, and they decide they will be better apart. Months pass and Rodolfo misses his love. Then there is a knock at the door and Musetta arrives—she has brought the very sick Mimì to be with Rodolfo. The young couple reminisce about their past times together and declare their continued love. The others tactfully leave them together, but when they all return they realise, before Rodolfo does, that Mimì has died. Seeing their faces, it gradually sinks in and, sobbing, he throws himself on Mimì's lifeless body. Aria: *Che gelida manina!* ('What an icy little hand!'—the famous 'Your tiny hand is frozen'); duets (with Mimì): *O soave fanciulla* ('Oh! lovely girl … in the moonlight!'); *Sono andati? … Ah Mimì, mia bella Mimì* ('Have they gone? … Ah Mimì, my beautiful Mimì'). Created (1896) by Evan Gorga. He was ill for most of the rehearsal period and was, in fact, not good enough for the role, although chosen by Puccini. The music had to be transposed down for him and his career was short—he later did well as an antique dealer. Unusual is the Italianate tenor who does not want to sing this role. Among those who have shone in it are Alessandro Bonci, Fernando De Lucia, Aureliano Pertile, Dino Borgioli, Enrico Caruso (who sprang to international fame after singing the role opposite Nellie Melba at Monte Carlo in 1902), Giovanni Martinelli, Beniamino Gigli, Jan Peerce and Richard Tucker (brothers-in-law), Joseph Hislop, Ferruccio Tagliavini (who made his début in this role in Florence in 1939), Fritz Wunderlich (in German), Jussi Björling, Giuseppe Di Stefano (who recorded it opposite Maria Callas), Carlo Bergonzi, Nicolai Gedda, Luciano Pavarotti, Plácido Domingo, José Carreras, Jerry Hadley, and Roberto Alagna—to mention only the most famous.

2. (Leoncavallo: *La bohème*). Bar. A poet, in love with the seamstress Mimì. She leaves him to marry a wealthy count, but returns a year later, very ill, and dies in his arms. Created (1897) by Rodolfo Angelini-Fornari.

3. (Bellini: *La sonnambula*). Bass. A Count, who returns to the village after his father's death to claim his lands. He stays at the local inn and flirts with the hostess, Lisa. Into his room sleepwalks Amina. Lisa assumes she has an assignation with Rodolfo and reports this to Amina's prospective husband, Elvino, who calls off the wedding. Created (1831) by Luciano Mariani.

4. (Verdi: *Luisa Miller*). See WALTER, RODOLFO.

Rodrigo 1. (Verdi: *Don Carlos*). See POSA, RODRIGO, MARQUIS OF.

2. (Rossini: *Otello*). Ten. Desdemona has been promised to him in marriage by her father, but he realizes she loves Otello. He and Iago plot against the Moor, who interrupts the wedding ceremony and claims Desdemona for himself. Rodrigo and Otello fight and Otello is exiled. Created (1816) by Giovanni David.

Rofrano, Count Octavian (Strauss: *Der Rosenkavalier*). See OCTAVIAN.

Roger II, King (Szymanowski: *King Roger*). Bar. King of Sicily, husband of Roxana. Is asked by the church to imprison the Shepherd who is preaching a life of beauty and pleasure. Dissuaded from doing so by his wife, who is fascinated by the Shepherd and follows him to a Dionysian existence. The King manages to resist the temptation to join them. Created (1926) by Eugeniusz Mossakowski.

Romanov, Princess Fedora (Giordano: *Fedora*). Sop. A Russian princess, engaged to Count Vladimiro. She arrives in St Petersburg to find him dying from wounds inflicted by assassins thought to be Count Loris Ipanov and accomplices. She swears to avenge her fiancé. In Paris, she manages to make Loris fall in love with her, then accuses him of the crime. He confesses, but adds that it was an act of honour—he had discovered that his wife and Vladimiro were lovers. Now herself in love with Loris, Fedora goes to live with him in Switzerland. But the chain of investigation she has set in motion continues. Loris's brother is arrested and drowns while in prison and their mother dies of grief. Realizing that Fedora is responsible for hounding his family, Loris curses her. She swallows poison, begging his forgiveness as she dies. Aria: *Dio di giustizia* ('O God of justice'). Created (1898) by Gemma Bellincioni.

Romeo 1. (Gounod: *Roméo et Juliette*). See MONTAGUE, ROMEO (1).

2. (Bellini: *I Capuleti e i Montecchi*). *See* MONTAGUE, ROMEO (2).

Roméo et Juliette (Gounod). Lib. by Jules Barbier and Michel Carré; 5 acts; f.p. Paris 1867, cond. M. Deloffre.

Verona, 13th cent.: Having arrived, uninvited, at a ball in the Capulet palace, Romeo *Montague and his friends *Mercutio and *Benvolio, all masked, see Juliet *Capulet and her nurse *Gertrude. Juliet's father, Count *Capulet, calms down Tybalt (*Tebaldo), who is angry with the Montagues for daring to be present. Romeo and Juliet meet, declare their love and agree to marry. Friar *Lawrence performs their marriage ceremony. The Montagues' page, *Stéphano, taunts the Capulets and in the duels which ensue, Romeo kills Tybalt and is exiled by the Duke of Verona. Juliet's father tells her she must marry Count *Paris. Neither she nor Gertrude dare tell him she is already married. Friar Lawrence gives her a potion to take, which will make her unconscious and apparently dead. She drinks it, collapses, and is taken to the Capulet crypt. Romeo appears, but seeing Juliet he believes she really is dead, and he drinks poison. Juliet wakens to find Romeo dying. She stabs herself with his sword.

Romilda (Handel: *Serse*). Sop. Daughter of Ariodate and sister of Atalanta, in love with Arsamene. She rejects the overtures of Serse and remains faithful to Arsamene. Created (1738) by Elisabeth Du Parc ('La Francesina').

rondine, La *(The Swallow)* (Puccini). Lib. by Giuseppe Adami; 3 acts; f.p. Monte Carlo 1917, cond. Gino Marinuzzi.

Paris and Nice, *c.*1820: It is Ruggero *Lastouc's first night in Paris. He joins Magda de *Civry in her salon together with her maid *Lisette and the poet *Prunier, and they decide to go to a popular nightclub, Bullier's. When the others set off, Magda also departs for Bullier's, but in disguise. At the club she dances with Ruggero and they fall in love, to the annoyance of Magda's lover, Rambaldo *Fernandez. Magda and Ruggero live together in Nice, but she knows his family will never approve of her once they know of her past life with Rambaldo. Prunier and Lisette are also living together. Realizing she can never marry Ruggero, Magda decides to leave. [NOTE: In the first version of the opera, it was Ruggero who accepted the situation and left Magda.]

Rosalinde (J. Strauss II: *Die Fledermaus*). *See* EISENSTEIN, ROSALINDE VON.

Rosenkavalier, Der *(The Knight of the Rose)* (Strauss). Lib. by Hugo von Hofmannsthal; 3 acts; f.p. Dresden 1911, cond. Ernst von Schuch.

Vienna, mid-18th cent.: The *Marschallin is having breakfast with her lover *Octavian when her cousin Baron *Ochs arrives. Octavian disguises himself as a maid, 'Mariandel', with whom Ochs flirts. He asks the Marschallin to recommend a nobleman to take to his fiancée, Sophie von *Faninal, the traditional silver rose. The Marschallin recommends Octavian. At her levee, her room is soon filled with hairdressers, tradesmen, an *Italian tenor, and *Valzacchi and *Annina (Italian intriguers). Ochs's son *Leupold (Leopold) gives her the silver rose and she reflects on the passing years. Octavian leaves and her page *Mohammed runs after him with the silver rose. In the grand hall at *Faninal's home, Octavian presents it to Sophie and there is an immediate attraction. Ochs arrives and Sophie is horrified by him. Chaperoned by Marianne *Leitmetzerin, Octavian promises Sophie he will prevent her marriage to Ochs. Ochs and he spar, the Baron receiving a minor scratch. Annina tells Ochs that 'Mariandel' will meet him that evening. In a private room at the inn, Octavian, Valzacchi and Annina rehearse the opening of trapdoors and windows, which they plan to use to frighten Ochs. 'Mariandel' arrives and as Ochs makes advances, 'apparitions' appear. Ochs calls the police, but Valzacchi has sent for Sophie and Faninal who refute his story. As Octavian discards his female clothing, the Marschallin enters and advises Ochs to leave. She then invites Faninal, Sophie, and Octavian to ride with her in her carriage.

Rosette (Massenet: *Manon*). Sop./mez. One of three 'ladies of easy virtue' found drinking with Mortfontaine and de Brétigny. Created (1884) by Mlle Rémy.

Rosillon, Camille de (Lehár: *The Merry Widow*). Ten. A French aristocrat in love with Valencienne, wife of the Pontevedrin ambassador. Duet (with Valencienne): *Sieh' dort den* *kleinen Pavillon* ('See there the little pavilion'). Created (1905) by Karl Meister.

Rosina 1. (Rossini: *Il barbiere di Siviglia*). Mez. Ward of the elderly Dr Bartolo, who wants to marry her. She is wooed by the student Lindoro, whom she does not know is Count Almaviva in disguise. He enters the house and they confess their love for each other, but her guardian is suspicious. Almaviva returns, this time disguised as a pupil of her music teacher, Basilio (supposedly ill). During their singing lesson, Bartolo falls asleep and the young couple move closer to each other. With the help of the barber Figaro, they plan their elopement, but are thwarted in their attempts when a ladder placed under the balcony window is removed. However, Figaro coaxes the notary hired by Bartolo to marry Almaviva and Rosina. Aria: (the 'letter scene'): *Una voce poco fa* ('The voice I heard a while ago'); sextet (with Figaro, Bartolo, Basilio, Berta, and Almaviva): *Fredda ed immobile* ('Awestruck and motionless'). Created (1816) by Geltrude Righetti-Giorgi.

2. (Corigliano: *The Ghosts of Versailles*). Sop. Wife of Count Almaviva. In the 20 years since her maid, Susanna, married Figaro, Rosina has had a son, Léon, the result of an affair with Cherubino, and Almaviva refuses to acknowledge him. They have all been recalled to take part in a further Beaumarchais play, in which the poet attempts to alter the course of history in order to save the woman he loves, Queen Marie Antoinette. Created (1991) by Renée Fleming. *See also* COUNTESS (1).

Rossweisse (Wagner: *Die Walküre*). *See* VALKYRIES.

Rostova, Natasha (Prokofiev: *War and Peace*). Sop. She is loved by the widowed Prince Andrei, but she falls for the charms of Prince Anatol (who is already married). Andrei volunteers for the Russian army. He is injured and Natasha's family flee occupied Moscow, taking him with them. She begs his forgiveness for leaving him, but too late—he is dying. Created (1945 vers.) by M. A. Nadion; (1946 vers.) by T. N. Lavrova.

Roucher (Giordano: *Andrea Chénier*). Bass. A friend of the poet Chénier. He obtains a forged passport for him and tries to persuade him to leave Paris before he is arrested as

a counter-revolutionary. Created (1896) by Gaetano Roveri.

Roxana, Queen (Szymanowski: *King Roger*). Sop. Queen of Sicily, wife of King Roger II. Fascinated by the preachings of the Shepherd, she follows him and joins his life of Dionysian pleasure. Created (1926) by Stanislawa Korwin-Szymanowska (sister of the opera's composer).

Ruddigore, or The Witch's Curse (Sullivan). Lib. by W. S. Gilbert; 2 acts; f.p. London 1887, cond. Arthur Sullivan.

Cornwall, 18th cent.: Rose *Maybud is desired by Robin Oakapple (Sir Ruthven *Murgatroyd in disguise), who is too shy to tell her of his feelings. His foster-brother, Richard *Dauntless, offers to help, but proposes to her himself. Rose chooses Robin in preference. The present 'bad baronet of Ruddigore' is Sir Despard *Murgatroyd, loved by *Mad Margaret. He is forced by an old curse to commit a crime a day. He hates this life and is relieved to learn that Robin is, in fact, his elder brother and thus the real heir to the title and the curse. Robin must be judged by his ancestors for not committing a daily crime. The ancestors emerge from their portraits, led by Sir Roderic *Murgatroyd. They compel Robin to carry off a lady. He dispatches his servant to find one and he returns with Dame *Hannah. She and Roderic recognize each other as old lovers. Robin is able to prove that Roderic should never have died in the first place, so he can now be united with Hannah; Robin, no longer subject to the curse, can embrace Rose.

Ruggero (Puccini: *La rondine*). *See* LASTOUC, RUGGERO.

Ruggiero 1. (Halévy: *La Juive*). Bar. Provost of Constance. Threatens death to the Jews who work on a Christian holiday. Created (1835) by Henri-Bernard Dabadie.

2. (Handel: *Alcina*). Mez. *Travesti* role (originally castrato). Bradamante's future husband, loved by Alcina who has taken him to her magic island. Bradamante comes to rescue him. Created (1735) by Giovanni Carestini.

Ruprecht (Prokofiev: *The Fiery Angel*). Bar. A knight who helps the distressed Renata to try and find her ex-lover, Heinrich, whom she believes to be her protecting angel. When the two men meet, Ruprecht is wounded in a duel. Renata nurses him, then enters a convent. As he recovers in an inn, he meets Faust and Mephistopheles. Created (1954) by Xavier Depraz; (1955) by Rolando Panerai.

Rusalka (Dvořák). Lib. by Jaroslav Kvapil; 3 acts; f.p. Prague 1901, cond. Karel Kovařović.

*Rusalka, a water sprite, wants to be human in order to be loved by the *Prince. The witch *Ježibaba agrees to her request, but on two conditions: Rusalka will be struck dumb and the Prince must remain true to her—if either breaks these conditions, they will die. The *Water Goblin warns against this path, but Rusalka will not heed his warning. She and the Prince are married, but the evil *Foreign Princess reveals Rusalka's true origin and the Prince rejects her. Regretting his action, he returns to her, but when she speaks to him and kisses him he dies. Rusalka returns to the lake.

Rusalka (Dvořák: *Rusalka*). Sop. A water sprite, daughter of the Spirit of the Lake. Becomes human in order to marry a Prince. When they break the conditions imposed on them by the Witch Ježibaba, the Prince dies and Rusalka returns to the lake. Aria: *Měsíčku na nebi hlubokém* ('O moon in the velvet heavens', often sung in English as 'O silver moon'). Created (1901) by Růžena Maturová.

Ruslan (Glinka: *Ruslan and Lyudmila*). Bar. A Knight of Kiev, in love with Lyudmila. She is abducted by an evil dwarf, and he rescues her and breaks the spell put upon her. Created (1842) by Osip Petrov.

Ruslan and Lyudmila (Glinka). Scenario by Konstantin Bakhturin from lib. by Valerian Shirkov and others; 5 acts; f.p. St Petersburg 1842, cond. C. Albrecht.

Kiev, legendary times: *Lyudmila, daughter of *Svetozar, is to marry *Ruslan. A minstrel, the *Bayan, forecasts that despite the trials ahead, true love will win through. Lyudmila consoles her previous suitors, Prince *Ratmir (loved by *Gorislava) and Prince *Farlaf. Suddenly it goes dark and Lyudmila disappears. Her father promises her in marriage to whosoever finds her. The magician *Finn tells Ruslan that the abductor is the dwarf *Chernomor, whose strength lies in his long beard. Ruslan finds a magic sword which can defeat the dwarf. Ruslan and the others set out to find Lyudmila, but as they approach her Chernomor puts a spell on her. Ruslan cuts off the dwarf's beard and finds his love, but she is still under the spell and is now abducted by Farlaf, helped by the evil enchantress *Naina. Ratmir declares his love for Gorislava. Finn gives him the magic ring which will waken Lyudmila, and he and Ruslan set off for Kiev to break the spell. Their wedding can now take place.

Rustics 1. (Britten: *A Midsummer Night's Dream*). They perform a play for Duke Theseus on his marriage to Hippolyta. *See* Bottom, Quince, Flute, Snug, Snout, Starveling.

2. (Purcell: *The Fairy Queen*). Similar to the roles in (1) above.

Ruth (Sullivan: *The Pirates of Penzance*). Cont. A pirate maid, old nursemaid of Frederic, whom she fancies as a husband. Created (NY, 1879) by Alice Barnett.

Sachs, Hans (Wagner: *Die Meistersinger von Nürnberg*). Bass. One of the senior Masters, a cobbler. His apprentice is David. Living opposite the Pogner family, he has watched Eva grow up and is very fond of her. At the assembly of the Masters at which Pogner offers Eva as the prize at the next song contest, Sachs suggests that the people of Nuremberg have the casting vote, but he has to abandon the idea when it becomes clear that all the other Masters are against him. He accepts that Eva herself shall have the final say in whom she is to marry. He backs up Pogner in his suggestion that Walther von Stolzing shall enter the contest, even though he is not a Master, emphasizing that the only true concern in this contest is art. He is attracted by the young knight's singing, recognizing his talent but ignorance of the rules. He criticizes Beckmesser for being so against Walther, pointing out that he has a vested interest—he would like to marry Eva. Sending David to bed, Sachs settles in the shade of the elder tree outside his door and considers how best to help Walther. As he sits and works at his last, Eva visits him. She is concerned that Beckmesser might win her hand in marriage, and makes it clear that she would consider Sachs a more suitable husband. Sachs lightly tells her he is too old, and she starts to question him about those who have taken part in the auditions that day. As their discussion proceeds, it is obvious that her interest is in Walther. And whilst he approves of the knight as her future husband, Sachs nevertheless feels some jealousy, acknowledging to himself his own feelings for Eva. Realizing that she is planning to elope with Walther, Sachs determines to stop them, knowing this to be a foolish solution. He watches Beckmesser arrive to serenade Eva and agrees to listen to him singing, but he will act as 'marker' and he marks the mistakes by hammer-blows on his last. This causes great aggravation as Beckmesser struggles to be heard above the hammering. All the time, Sachs is keeping a watchful eye on Walther and Eva, and as they try to escape under cover of a riot which begins in the street, he pushes Eva into her father's house and drags Walther into his shop. The next morning, David interrupts Sachs's reveries, reminding him that today is his name-day. Sachs sends David off to dress for the contest and lapses into his famous *Wahn* ('madness') monologue, ruminating on man's inhumanity to man. He resolves to help Walther, explaining to him the rules of the contest, how the song must be written and sung. Walther sings his song and Sachs gives him hints on its performance. While the two men are inside changing, Beckmesser comes in, sees Walther's song, assumes it to be by Sachs and takes it. Sachs returns and offers to allow Beckmesser to keep the song, assuring him that he, Sachs, will not compete for Eva's hand. Beckmesser departs, Eva arrives, dressed ready for the contest and asks Sachs to adjust her shoes. As he does so, Walther returns and the young couple are clearly seen to be in love. Walther sings part of his song and Eva knows he is going to win the contest, thanks to Sachs's help and self-sacrifice. Sachs upgrades David from Apprentice to Journey-man and they all depart for the meadow where the song-contest will take place. As Sachs rises to speak to the Masters, the crowd break into a great paean of praise for him, *Wach auf* ('Awake'). Beckmesser sings, making a terrible mess of the song he has acquired from Sachs, and then Sachs urges them all to allow Walther to have his turn. The easy winner, Walther at first refuses to accept admission to the Masters' Guild, but Sachs points out to him that he must respect the Holy German Art which has ensured his victory, and Sachs places the Master's chain round

Walther's neck. The crowd hail Sachs's wisdom. Arias: *Was duftet doch der Flieder, so mild ...* ('How mild is the scent of the elder'—known as the *Fliedermonolog*); *Wahn! Wahn! Überall Wahn!* ('Madness! Madness! Everywhere madness!'—the *Wahnmonolog*); *Verachtet mir die Meister nicht* ('Do not scorn the Masters').

This long role has been a favourite with Wagnerian bass-baritones since its first performance. Sachs is the character round whom the whole opera revolves and he manipulates the situation to bring about the outcome he considers best. Among famous interpreters of Sachs are Anton van Rooy, Walter Soomer, Jaro Prohaska, Rudolf Bockelmann, Paul Schöffler, Otto Edelmann, Hans Hotter, Gustav Neidlinger, Otto Wiener, Josef Greindl, Theo Adam, Hans Sotin, Norman Bailey, Bernd Weikl, Dietrich Fischer-Dieskau, and John Tomlinson. Created (1868) by Franz Betz. *See also* ARTICLE BY SIR JOHN TOMLINSON, p. 261.

Sacristan 1. (Puccini: *Tosca*). Bass. He potters about the church, and cleans the brushes which the artist Cavaradossi is using for his painting of the Madonna. He announces the defeat of Bonaparte and tells Cavaradossi that, in celebration, Tosca will sing that night at the Farnese Palace, residence of Baron Scarpia. Created (1900) by Ettore Borelli.

2. (Janáček: *The Excursions of Mr Brouček*). Bar. Sacristan of St Vit's Cathedral, Prague, and father of Málinka. On the Moon he is represented by Lunobar and in Prague in 1420 he is Domšík. Created (1920) by Vilém Zítek.

Saint-Bris, Comte de (Meyerbeer: *Les Huguenots*). Bar. Catholic nobleman, governor of Louvre, father of Valentine. He plots the capture of Raoul as part of his plan to massacre the Huguenots. In the course of the fighting, he orders his men to shoot, not knowing his daughter is in love with Raoul and has joined him. They are both killed by his soldiers' bullets. Aria: *Pour cette cause sainte, obéisses sans crainte* ('For this sacred cause, obey without fear'). Created (1836) by Mons. Serda.

Saint-Bris, Valentine de (Meyerbeer: *Les Huguenots*). Sop. Daughter of the Comte de Saint-Bris, leader of the Catholics. She is engaged to the Catholic Comte de Nevers, but falls in love with the Huguenot Raoul de Nangis. She is killed, together with Raoul, by

her father's soldiers, not having been recognized as his daughter. Aria: *Parmi les pleurs* ('Amid my tears'); duet (with Raoul): *Ô ciel, où courez-vous?* ('O heavens, where are you rushing off to?'). Created (1836) by (Marie) Cornélie Falcon.

Saint François (Messiaen: *Saint François d'Assise*). *See* FRANCIS, SAINT.

Saint François d'Assise (St Francis of Assisi) (Messiaen). Lib. by comp.; 3 acts (8 tableaux); f.p. Paris 1983, cond. Seiji Ozawa.

St *Francis explains to Friar *Léon that only through suffering can man reach perfect joy. St Francis prays to God that he will be able to overcome his natural revulsion at the sight of ugliness. He is enabled to embrace a *Leper, thus curing him. The *Angel comes to the monastery in search of St Francis, who recognizes him as a messenger from God. St Francis prays to experience the pain Christ experienced on the cross and to feel the love in his heart which made it possible for Christ to die in peace. This is granted to him and he bears the stigmata. As he nears death, the Angel and the Leper come to visit him.

Sali (Delius: *A Village Romeo and Juliet*). Ten. (as a boy, sop.). Son of a farmer, Manz, he falls in love with Vreli, the daughter of his father's rival. When her father tries to separate them, Sali hits him and the injury results in the farmer losing his mind. The villagers are critical of the young lovers. To escape, they walk to an inn, the Paradise Garden, and take a barge on to the river. They scuttle the barge and sink in each other's arms. Created (as an adult) (1907) by Willi Merkel.

Salome (Strauss). Lib. by comp.; 1 act; f.p. Dresden 1905, cond. Ernst von Schuch.

Tiberias, Galilee, about AD 30: The Syrian captain *Narraboth is enchanted by *Salome, daughter of *Herodias, second wife of *Herod. He is warned by the *Page not to keep looking at Salome. In a cistern below the terrace *Jochanaan (John the Baptist) is imprisoned—he has insulted Herodias. Salome is captivated by Jochanaan's voice and orders the guards to allow him out. When she tells Jochanaan she is Herodias's daughter, he rants against her and her mother. She wants to touch him and kiss him; he curses her and returns to his cistern. Narraboth, distressed by her behaviour, kills

HANS SACHS 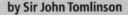 (*Die Meistersinger von Nürnberg—Wagner*)

by Sir John Tomlinson

The Mastersingers' Guild in 16th-cent. Nuremberg represents for Wagner the traditional skills and values lovingly, carefully, proudly applied, but crucially lacking adventure, individuality, and forward thinking.

On the day before Midsummer day in 1542, at a meeting of the Guild, Eva, the young and beautiful daughter of the rich goldsmith Veit Pogner, is offered in marriage by her father as the prize to the winner of the annual singing contest. There are three contenders: Sixtus Beckmesser, the rigid, rulebound, soulless perfectionist, the 'Marker' of the Guild, who tries every trick in the book to win Eva (and, thereby, her fortune); Walther von Stolzing, a young visiting knight who has fallen madly in love with Eva (and she with him), who hopes to be accepted as a Master but who, at the audition, sings with such passionate, swirling romanticism that he is disdainfully rejected by the reactionary Guild; and Hans Sachs, a workmanlike shoemaker who, when not at his last, retires to the shade of the elder tree by his front door where he finds solace with the muse in his other life as poet and composer.

Since the tragic death of his wife and children, Sachs, now perhaps 50 years old (somewhat older than Beckmesser, incidentally), has watched Eva growing up and has for her a generous paternal love. Sometimes her beauty tempts him to think he could be a suitable partner for her, but deep down he knows he is too old. Eva's father would certainly approve of such a marriage and Eva herself, a week ago, would happily have accepted. But since Walther's arrival on the scene … Sachs quickly senses that the pair love each other and he decides to do everything he can to bring them together. Hence the story of *The Mastersingers*, the events of the ensuing 24 hours in the life of the Nuremberg community, at once funny and lively but also philosophical, sobering, and perhaps even tragic.

Hans Sachs is the only character in the opera to be based on fact, and the poem by the real, historical Sachs is sung on stage in the final scene of the opera. By any yardstick, this is the longest of all operatic roles: he is on stage for four hours, singing for much of that time, and stamina is a fundamental necessity. However, Wagner was not a composer to make impossible demands on a singer (although he deliberately comes close to the limit), and he does not ask of a Sachs the dramatic power and continuous intensity of, say, a Wotan. The part of Sachs is written by Wagner on a human scale, sometimes almost *parlando*, with warm natural recitatives, thoughtful probing monologues and soaring public orations. Bass, bass-baritone, or baritone voices are all potentially suitable; and indispensable alongside the stamina, is a voice of great expressiveness together with acting ability and a stage personality capable of portraying this charismatic and multifaceted character.

To return to Nuremberg: Sachs cleverly weaves his plans to outwit Beckmesser, persuade the Masters of the validity of Walther's new music and, finally, despite his own love for Eva, bring the young pair together and ensure a 'happy ending' to Wagner's 'comedy' (his own description).

Sachs, then, is a 'bringer-together': from the beginning, as a democrat, he seeks to bring the people's voice into the élitist Mastersingers' circle; he works tirelessly in trying to understand Walther's inspired singing and to enhance it by structuring it with the old musical forms he himself has perfected; the rift between the aristocracy and the people is bridged by his own efforts; he unites, against all the odds, Eva and Walther; and, in his own humble and devoted way, he even unites shoemaking and art.

Only in one strand of the story does he divide rather than unite: his own maltreatment of Beckmesser. Sachs's skill in mischief-making gets the better of him when he comically destroys Beckmesser's attempt to serenade Eva and the resulting noise provokes a riot in the streets. Sachs allows him to make a complete fool of himself by attempting the performance of Walther's new song—Sachs would say a necessary evil, because only in this way can Walther be summoned to show how the song *can* be sung and so win the day. Sachs, however, in his *Wahn* [delusion, or madness] monologue, amidst his agonizing for the world in general, regrets his own particular form of cruelty and loss of control towards a fellow Master and later admits to himself the discomfort of the hypocrisy and dishonesty involved in sacrificing the pedantic marker for the success of his own, albeit altruistic, plan: the sordid means to a worthy end.

There is a ruthless single-mindedness about Sachs. Such is the destruction of Beckmesser's public image that one could easily imagine him putting an end to his own life and no amount of caring explanation on Sachs's part could prevent it. Audiences like to bathe in the wisdom, humility, intelligence, and humanity of Hans Sachs. But Wagner always painted with all colours of the spectrum, and the darker shades of mischief, anger, and self-pity are all there—and Sachs knows it. That's what makes him human.

himself. Herod leers at Salome—he asks her to dance for him, offering her generous bribes. She agrees only when offered anything she wants to choose. She dances, then claims her reward: the head of Jochanaan on a silver salver. Herod is revolted, Herodias proud of her daughter. All appeals to Salome fail and Herod sends down an executioner who returns from the cistern with Jochanaan's head. Salome drools over the head and kisses the mouth. Herod, horrified, orders his soldiers to kill her.

Salome 1. (Strauss: *Salome*). Sop. The daughter of Herodias and therefore Herod's stepdaughter—her father was his brother, her mother's first husband, murdered to allow Herodias to marry Herod. Hearing the voice of the imprisoned Jochanaan coming from the cistern below the palace terrace, she demands that the soldiers bring him out so she can see him, until Narraboth, the young captain who is besotted with her, agrees to what she asks. Now she wants to talk with Jochanaan and touch his white body, but he rejects her. Then

she wants to kiss his mouth, his scarlet mouth. Again he rejects her, this daughter of an adulteress and, in the manner of a child refused what she wants, she tells him how she hates his body, his hair, his mouth, and doesn't want him at all. He returns to his cistern and Herod and Herodias join Salome on the terrace. Salome knows that Herod lusts after her, and finds his glances disturbing. She resists his pleas to drink wine with him ('I am not thirsty, Tetrarch') and to eat fruit with him ('I am not hungry, Tetrarch'). He asks her to dance for him, and she acquiesces only when he agrees to reward her with anything she desires. She dances the Dance of the Seven Veils (and in most productions these days the soprano does the dance herself) and claims her prize—the head of Jochanaan on a silver platter. Nothing, no offer of jewels, money, even the Veil of the Temple, will satisfy her. This is the only prize she wants, and Herod has to agree. As an executioner descends, Salome hovers over the cistern, disappointed not to hear the prophet scream. The severed head is brought up and handed to her, and thus begin the last twenty minutes of this opera, a perverted *Liebestod* for Salome. Totally depraved, she drools over the head and speaks to it—why will Jochanaan not open his eyes and look at her? Now he can no longer resist her—at last she can kiss his mouth—it tastes bitter—is it the taste of blood or the taste of love? As her mother watches and approves, Herod can take no more and orders his soldiers to kill her. She is crushed by their shields. Arias: *Du wirst das für mich tun, Narraboth* ('You will do this for me, Narraboth'); *Jochanaan! Ich bin verliebt in deinen Leib* ('I am in love with your body'); *Ah! Du wolltest mich nicht deinen Mund küssen lassen, Jochanaan!* ('Ah! you didn't want me to kiss your mouth, Jochanaan'); *Ah! Ich habe deinen Mund geküsst* ('Ah! I have kissed your mouth').

Salome is described by Strauss as a 16-year-old princess with the voice of an Isolde, and this gives some clue to the difficulties the composer put in the way of the singer—she must sound young and innocent, the depravity gradually overtaking her as the work proceeds, until the final long embodiment of evil. Among famous Salomes, e.g. Emmy Destinn, Maria Jeritza, Maria Cebotari, Christel Goltz, Birgit Nilsson, Josephine Barstow, Hildegard Behrens, and Catherine Malfitano, probably the most famous was the Bulgarian soprano Ljuba Welitsch (1913–96), who sang it in the presence of the composer at a performance given to mark his 80th birthday in Vienna in 1944. Created (1905) by Marie Wittich (who regarded the role as indecent, especially the Dance of the Seven Veils, famously declaring at an early rehearsal 'I won't do it, I'm a respectable woman').

2. (Salomé) (Massenet: *Hérodiade*). Sop. Unknown to Salomé, she is the daughter of Hérodiade, second wife of the Tetrarch Hérode. She is in love with Jean (John the Baptist) who rejects her. Hérode finds her attractive and Hérodiade sees her as a rival. She despises Hérodiade who is reviled by Jean. When she discovers that she is Hérodiade's daughter, Salomé kills herself. Created (1881) by Marthe Duvivier.

Samiel (Weber: *Der Freischütz*). Spoken. The Wild Huntsman in the Wolf's Glen—a manifestation of the devil—to whom Caspar has sold himself. He guides the bullet which fatally wounds Caspar, thus sparing Max's life. Created (1821) by Herr Hillebrand.

Samira (Corigliano: *The Ghosts of Versailles*). Mez. An Egyptian singer who entertains Pasha Suleyman's guests, including all the Almaviva household, at a party at the Turkish Embassy. Created (1991) by Marilyn Horne.

Samson (Saint-Saëns: *Samson et Dalila*). Tenor. Leader of the Hebrews against the Philistines. The Philistine Dalila, mortified by Samson's earlier rejection of her, uses her charm to make Samson admit that he really does love her. She then cuts off his hair, the secret of his enormous strength, and betrays him to her own people, who capture and blind him. God restores his strength, and Samson destroys the Philistine temple, killing his aggressors and himself. Among notable singers of this role in the past 50 years are Mario del Monaco, Jon Vickers, James King, Plácido Domingo, and José Carreras. Created (1877) by Franz Ferenczy.

Samson et Dalila (*Samson and Delilah*) (Saint-Saëns). Lib. by Ferdinand Lemaire; 3 acts; f.p. Weimar 1877, cond. Eduard Lassen.

Gaza, 1150 BC: *Samson rouses the Hebrews to revolt against their Philistine oppressors. Their prayers attract the attention of the satrap of Gaza, *Abimélech, who rebukes them and attacks Samson, who slays him. The Philistine *Dalila begs Samson, who has previously rejected her, to visit her again. The *High Priest of Dagon enlists her help to overthrow Samson—she must obtain from him the secret of his enormous strength. Samson arrives and surrenders totally to Dalila, admitting his strength lies in his hair. Dalila cuts it off and summons the Philistines, who are now able to overcome him. The Hebrews feel he has betrayed them. Dalila and the High Priest mock Samson, who prays to God that he might, just once, have back his strength. This granted, he pulls down the pillars supporting the temple, killing his enemies and himself.

Samuel (Halévy: *La Juive*). Name used by Léopold to obtain work with Rachel's father, the goldsmith Eléazar. *See* LÉOPOLD (1).

Sandman (Humperdinck: *Hänsel und Gretel*). Sop. *Travesti* role. He throws sand in the eyes of the two children when they are lost in the forest, thus making them go to sleep. Creator (1893) not traced.

Sandrina (Mozart: *La finta giardiniera*). Sop. The Marchese Violante Onesti, disguised as a gardener's assistant at the house of the mayor. She is searching for her beloved, Belfiore, who has gone into hiding after he stabbed her and believed her to be dead. He arrives as the prospective husband of the mayor's niece, but she admits her identity and they are reunited. Created (1775) by Rosa Manservisi.

Sandy/Officer 3 (Maxwell Davies: *The Lighthouse*). Ten. A lighthouse-keeper, who tries to keep the peace between his colleagues. Created (1982) by Neil Mackie.

Sangazure, Aline (Sullivan: *The Sorcerer*). Sop. Daughter of Lady Sangazure, betrothed to Alexis Poindextre. Created (1877) by Alice May.

Sangazure, Lady (Sullivan: *The Sorcerer*). Cont. A 'Lady of Ancient Lineage', mother of Aline. She is in love with Sir Marmaduke Poindextre, whose son is engaged to her daughter. Created (1877) by Mrs Howard Paul.

Sante (Wolf-Ferrari: *Il segreto di Susanna*). Silent role. The servant of Count Gil and Countess Susanna. Created (1909) by Herr Geiss.

Santuzza (Mascagni: *Cavalleria rusticana*). Sop. A village girl in love with a young soldier, Turiddu. He returns from the army and she becomes pregnant, but he rejects her and returns to a former love, Lola, now married. In revenge she informs Lola's husband of his wife's unfaithfulness, leading to a duel in which Turiddu is killed. Arias: *Voi lo sapete, o mamma* ('You know well, mamma'); *Inneggiamo, il Signor non è morto* ('Let us sing of the Lord now victorious'—known as the Easter Hymn). Although relatively short, this role continues to attract outstanding sopranos and mezzo-sopranos, among whom may be mentioned Giulietta Simionato, Zinka Milanov, Eileen Farrell, Maria Callas, Renata Tebaldi, Fiorenza Cossotto, Victoria de los Angeles, Elena Souliotis, Elena Obraztsova, Rita Hunter, and Julia Varady. Created (1890) by Gemma Bellincioni (whose husband created Turiddu).

Sanval, Edoardo di (Verdi: *Un giorno di regno*). Ten. A young official, nephew of La Rocca. He is in love with Giulietta, who is being forced to marry his uncle. The situation is saved by the false 'King of Poland'. Created (1840) by Lorenzo Salvi.

Sarastro (Mozart: *Die Zauberflöte*). Bass. High Priest of Isis and Osiris. Considered to be evil by the Queen of Night, he is actually very sympathetic and protective towards Pamina, the Queen's daughter, and protects her from the brutish moor Monostatos. Sarastro loves Pamina but accepts that she will be the wife of Tamino, whom she loves. He and his priests order Tamino to undergo various ordeals to prove his suitability to marry her. Arias: *O Isis und Osiris* ('O Isis and Osiris'); *In diesen heil'gen Hallen* ('Within these holy bounds'). Created (1791) by Franz Xaver Gerl (whose wife created Papagena).

Satyavān (Holst: *Sāvitri*). Ten. A woodcutter, husband of Sāvitri. He returns from the forest and dies in his wife's arms. When she makes it clear to Death that her own life is worthless without her husband, Satyavān is restored to life. Created (1916) by George Pawlo.

Sāvitri (Holst). Lib. by comp.; 1 act; f.p. London 1916 (amateur), cond. Herman Grunebaum.

A forest in India, time unspecified: *Death tells *Sāvitri that he has come for her husband *Satyavān. Sāvitri at first tries to protect her husband, then invites Death to stay. Satyavān dies. Death offers to grant Sāvitri a wish, and she asks for life. He agrees to this—she has it already, he says. But, she points out, life for her must mean life for her husband also. Death departs and Satyavān returns to life.

Sāvitri (Holst: *Sāvitri*). Sop. Wife of Satyavān. She dreams of impending doom. Death appears to take her husband. Seeing her distress as he dies, Death offers her a wish and she wishes for life, but this must mean the return of her husband. Death grants this to her. Created (1916) by Mabel Corran.

Scaramuccio (Strauss: *Ariadne auf Naxos*). *See* COMMEDIA DELL'ARTE TROUPE.

Scarpia, Baron (Puccini: *Tosca*). Bar. Chief of Police who lusts after the opera singer Tosca, lover of the painter Cavaradossi. After the defeat of Napoleon, he attends the celebratory *Te Deum* in the church where Cavaradossi is painting the Madonna. Kneeling to participate in the prayers, Scarpia mutters about how he hopes to persuade Tosca to be his. Back at his residence, Tosca can be heard singing off-stage at the party given by Queen Caroline of Naples. Scarpia sends Sciarrone to deliver a note to Tosca to ensure that she comes to his apartment. Spoletta tells him they have arrested Cavaradossi for hiding a political fugitive. He is to be tortured and Scarpia hopes that by forcing Tosca to witness this, she will then succumb to him to save her lover. Tosca does indeed agree to be his, but first he must give her a written guarantee of safe passage for herself and Cavaradossi. He writes and signs this, then lustfully approaches her. With a knife she has taken from his table, Tosca kills him—no one need ever again be afraid of the evil Scarpia. But Scarpia has tricked her—Cavaradossi is executed by a firing squad as soldiers discover Scarpia's body. Arias: *Tarda è la notte* ('Night is late'); *Già, mi dicon venal* ('Yes, they say that I am venal'). Created (1900) by Eugenio Giraldoni. It is interesting that Scarpia appears for only a short while in Act 1 and not at all in Act 3. He has no major solo aria, most of his role consisting of exchanges with Tosca and his policemen during Act 2. Nevertheless it is a role aspired to by all great Italianate baritones, of whom Tito Gobbi, especially in his performances with Maria Callas as Tosca, was outstanding. Other names worth noting in this part include Dino Borgioli, Marcel Journet, Mariano Stabile, Lawrence Tibbett, Marko Rothmüller, George London, Leonard Warren, Giuseppe Taddei, Gabriel Bacquier, Kim Borg, Raimund Herincx, Dietrich Fischer-Dieskau, Sherrill Milnes, Sergei Leiferkus, Bryn Terfel, and Otakar Kraus. *See also* ARTICLE BY SIR JONATHAN MILLER, p. 266.

Schaumberg, Sylvester von (Hindemith: *Mathis der Maler*). Ten. An officer in the Confederate Army. Created (1938) by Max Theo Zehntnera.

Schaunard 1. (Puccini: *La bohème*). Bar. A musician, one of four bohemians. He arrives back at their garret on Christmas Eve with a supply of food—a herring and some bread—and a bottle of wine. In vain he tries to tell his friends how he earned the money from an eccentric Englishman: he was hired to play until the owner's parrot died! After three days

he bribed a servant girl to give the bird a piece of poisoned parsley and the parrot obliged by dying, so he was able to stop playing but he had earned enough money to feed them all for Christmas. His efforts to explain all this are constantly interrupted by his colleagues, interested not so much in how he earned the money, but in the food and fuel it provides. In the last act, it is Schaunard who realizes that Mimì is dying, and who, at the end, whispers to Marcello that she is dead. Created (1896) by Antonio Pini-Corsi (who had, in 1893, created Ford in Verdi's *Falstaff* and was to sing the first Happy in Puccini's *La fanciulla del West* at the New York Met in 1911).

2. (Leoncavallo: *La bohème*). Bar. A similar role to that in (1). Created (1897) by Gianni Isnardon.

Schicchi, Gianni (Puccini: *Gianni Schicchi*). Bar. A 50-year-old peasant, father of Lauretta. She is in love with Rinuccio, whose elderly rich cousin, Buoso Donati, has just died and left all his money to the Church. Rinuccio's family is against his marriage to the daughter of a poor peasant. Rinuccio calls on Schicchi to help the family regain their inheritance. The cunning Schicchi suggests that they keep the death of Buoso quiet while he (Schicchi) poses as the old man and writes a will which he will hand to the lawyer as Buoso's last testament. The family agree, each trying to bribe him to leave them the most money. Schicchi writes the will and hands it to the lawyer. He reads it out—it states that Buoso has left the bulk of his estate to 'my dear old friend Gianni Schicchi'! Without revealing their own part in the deception, the family is unable to protest. Schicchi can now give his blessing to the marriage of his daughter to Rinuccio. Created (1918) by Giuseppe De Luca.

Schicchi, Lauretta (Puccini: *Gianni Schicchi*). Sop. Daughter of Gianni Schicchi. She is in love with Rinuccio, but her father is very poor and Rinuccio's family are against their marriage. When Rinuccio's wealthy elderly cousin Buoso Donati dies, leaving his money to the local church, Rinuccio arranges for Gianni Schicchi to rewrite the will in favour of all Buoso's relatives on condition that they then agree to his marriage. Schicchi cleverly wills the fortune to himself, thus ensuring Lauretta's future, so she and Rinuccio can

SCARPIA (*Tosca*—Puccini)

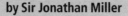

by Sir Jonathan Miller

Who is Scarpia and how should he be played? One answer might be that he's the voluptuary sadist who appears in *Tosca* and that he should be played as Puccini self-evidently meant him to be portrayed, as he was 'done' until meddlesome modern directors started to *un*do him. And the fact is that 'traditional' productions have perpetuated a more-or-less standardized version of the character, in the belief that the longevity of such a characterization guaranteed that it must have been what Puccini intended, so that messing around with alternatives is as blameworthy as putting a moustache on the Mona Lisa. But *that* argument just won't wash. In contrast to pictures and sculptures, which continue to exist without subsequent efforts on the part of other artists, the continued existence of an operatic character depends on periodic reconstruction. Unless the producer makes the questionable assumption that precedent is the best guide to such a process, the character in question inexorably 'develops' from one production to the next and not necessarily along the lines hypothetically intended by the composer and his librettist. Through no fault of his own, Puccini was unable to allow for the fact that posterity is a foreign country where they do and feel things differently. So the character of Scarpia is therefore less determined than some critics fondly imagine. Since Puccini composed his opera, the world has undergone social and political changes which he could not possibly have foreseen. As a result, the reasons for reviving the opera in the 1990s are not quite the same as they would have been in the 1950s, let alone in 1910. When a late 20th-cent. producer confronts the task of realizing *Tosca*, he does so in the knowledge that political tyranny has been perpetrated by people conspicuously *un*like the somewhat cliched villain of traditional productions. What is more, the modern director is familiar with what one can loosely call 'psychology' so that his approach to someone such as Scarpia will inevitably take an 'interpretative turn' which prevents him from taking the character at his face value. A literate producer is bound to take account of the notion of the 'banality of evil', which means that the 'monstrosity' of Scarpia cannot be represented in conventional terms. On the contrary, the suavely lecherous connoisseur of wine and pain seems almost comic by comparison with the bureaucratic mediocrities of the Gestapo, the OVRA [the Italian Fascist Secret police, 1942–3], or the KGB. In fact, the pen-pushing clerkiness of such real characters is much more alarming than the Grytpipe-Thynne [of the Goons] silkiness of traditional opera. And the succession of three tourist locations is just another distraction, as there's nothing more irritating for the cast than the sound of an audience applauding their own recognition of Sant' Andrea, the Palazzo Farnese, and the Castello Sant' Angelo.

As someone who grew up during the Second World War, the *notionally* Napoleonic setting of *Tosca* seems to me thin and unconvincing by comparison with the one which Rossellini projected in his painfully unwatchable film *Rome Open City*. The narrative parallels are sufficiently close to allow an almost frictionless transposition and the character of Scarpia undergoes an intriguing metamorphosis, without dishonouring or deforming the words and music which were written for him. He emerges as someone disconcertingly 'ordinary', sorting and signing papers, absent-mindedly sipping cold coffee, apparently indifferent to or even mildly irritated by the screams of the tortured Cavaradossi in the next room, outside which a drab typist imperturbably takes down the interrogation.

And in the seductive assault upon the distraught Tosca, following her ironic question as to the 'price' of the deal, it is interesting to turn the traditional scene on its head and to find that it is still consistent with the music. Instead of having the desirable diva on her knees, something insufferably painful happens if it is *Scarpia* who abases himself, slithering disgustingly at her feet, begging for an unattainable satisfaction of his self-loathing, masochistic lust.

Just *one* way of 'doing' him, but quite interesting, I think!

marry. Aria: *O! Mio babbino caro* ('Oh! My dear little daddy', more often translated as 'O my beloved father'). Created (1918) by Florence Easton.

Schigolch (Berg: *Lulu*). Bass. An old man, father-figure of Lulu, and possibly an ex-lover. Created (1937) by Herr Honisch.

Schlemil, Peter (Offenbach: *Les Contes d'Hoffmann*). Bass. Lover of Giulietta, killed by Hoffmann. Creator (?1905) not known.

Schön, Dr (Berg: *Lulu*). Bar. A newspaper editor. Father of Alwa. Marries Lulu, but disapproves of her various relationships and gives her a gun to shoot herself, but she uses it to kill him. His *alter ego*, Jack the Ripper, later kills her. Created (1937) by Asger Stig.

Schoolmaster (Janáček: *The Cunning Little Vixen*). Ten. Friend of the Forester, with whom he plays cards. The tenor usually sings also the part of the Mosquito. Created (1924) by Antonin Pelz (who later changed his surname from the German spelling as given here to the phonetic Czech spelling, Pelc).

Schwalb, Hans (Hindemith: *Mathis der Maler*). Ten. Father of Regina. Leader of the rebelling peasants, he is helped to escape by Mathis. Created (1938) by Ernst Mosbacher.

Schwalb, Regina (Hindemith: *Mathis der Maler*). Sop. Daughter of Hans Schwalb, leader of the peasants' rebellion. Created (1938) by Leni Funk.

Schwarz, Hans (Wagner: *Die Meistersinger von Nürnberg*). Bass. One of the *Meistersinger*. He is a stocking-weaver. Created (1868) by Herr Grasser.

schweigsame Frau, Die (*The Silent Woman*) (Strauss). Lib. by Stefan Zweig; 3 acts; f.p. Dresden 1935, cond. Karl Böhm.

London, about 1760: Sir *Morosus*'s *Housekeeper* thinks he needs a wife. His *Barber* says it will have to be a quiet woman, as Morosus cannot abide noise, but Morosus doubts the existence of such a one. He is visited by his longlost nephew and heir, Henry *Morosus*, who is married to *Aminta*. They run a travelling opera company. Disapproving of both his wife and their way of life, Morosus disinherits Henry and starts to search for a silent wife. The Barber presents three possibilities (all played by members of Henry's troupe, *Isotta*, *Carlotta*, and Aminta). Morosus settles for the only quiet one—'Timida' (who is Aminta in disguise). A 'wedding ceremony' is arranged, with actors as the lawyer and priest. No sooner are they 'married' than 'Timida' turns into a veritable virago. Morosus is only too glad to be rescued by his nephew, who offers to arrange grounds for a divorce. Isotta and Carlotta swear that 'Timida' has had other men before she married Morosus and Henry, now in disguise, admits that he was one of her lovers, but the 'judge' is not prepared to accept this evidence as grounds for divorce and Morosus is desperate. At this point Henry and Aminta decide things have gone far enough and tell the old man the truth. They remove their disguises—it has all been a hoax. Morosus sees the joke and accepts their opera company; he will even see their operas if they make him laugh as much as this. Henry is reinstated as his heir, Aminta is accepted, and Morosus thanks his lucky stars he is still a bachelor.

Schwerlein, Marthe (Gounod: *Faust*). Mez. Friend and neighbour of Marguerite, to whom Méphistophélès is attracted. Created (1859) by Mlle Duclos.

Schwertleite (Wagner: *Die Walküre*). *See* VALKYRIES.

Sciarrone (Puccini: *Tosca*). Bass. A member of Baron Scarpia's police who helps in the arrest and torture of Cavaradossi. Created (1900) by Giuseppe Girone.

Seashell, Omniscient (Strauss: *Die ägyptische Helena*). *See* MUSSEL, THE ALL-WISE.

Sebastiano (d'Albert: *Tiefland*). Bar. Wanting to marry a wealthy girl, he has chosen a husband for his long-standing mistress, Marta, but he expects her to remain as his mistress. He takes Marta up the mountain to meet the man in question, the poor shepherd Pedro. On her wedding night, Sebastiano hides in her bedroom, but Marta avoids him. Gradually Sebastiano realises that Marta has grown to love her husband and the rich girl Sebastiano wants to marry has learned of his reputation and is no longer interested. Trying to reclaim Marta, he and Pedro fight and Sebastiano is killed. Creator (1903) not traced.

Second Mrs Kong, The (Birtwistle). Lib. by Russell Hoban; 2 acts; f.p. Glyndebourne 1994, cond. Elgar Howarth.

Fact and fiction, the past, the present, and the future: *Anubis rows the souls of the dead to the World of Shadows. They relive memories: Mr *Dollarama finds his wife *Inanna in bed with her guru and shoots them. *Orpheus looks at *Eurydice and so loses her. *Vermeer sees *Pearl and falls in love with her, but she knows she will meet *Kong—'the idea of him'. Pearl, now a picture on a wall, sees the film of *King Kong* on television. She searches for him by computer and they fall in love. Kong is determined to find Pearl. The sphinx Madame *Lena tries unsuccessfully to seduce Kong. Kong meets a sinister figure, the Death of Kong, fights him and wins, so knows he will not ever die. He and Pearl meet, but their love cannot be fulfilled, for they are both just 'ideas', not real people.

Secretary, The (Menotti: *The Consul*). Mez. Secretary at the consulate who obstructs all Magda's efforts to obtain a visa so that she can join her husband, John. In the end she takes pity on Magda, but it is too late—John has returned and been arrested by the secret police. Created (1950) by Gloria Lane.

Secret Marriage, The (Cimarosa). *See* MATRIMONIO SEGRETO, IL.

Sedley, Mrs (Britten: *Peter Grimes*). Sop. (but often sung by cont.). A widow and the village gossip. Gets her pills from the quack Ned Keene. Aria: *Murder most foul it is*. Created (1945) by Valetta Iacopi.

***segreto di Susanna, Il* (Susanna's Secret)** (Wolf-Ferrari). Lib. by Enrico Golisciani; 1 act; f.p. Munich 1909, cond. by Felix Mottl.

Count *Gil smells tobacco in the house and suspects his wife, *Susanna, of having a secret lover. As soon as he leaves the house, their servant *Sante brings her the cigarettes so she can relax. Almost immediately her husband returns. She hides the cigarette behind her back and as he tries to grab it he burns himself. Her secret is out and he lights a cigarette also.

Selim, Pasha 1. (Mozart: *Die Entführung aus dem Serail*). Spoken role. Owner of the palace in which Constanze and Blondchen are held captive. An apparently severe man, he shows his softer side by allowing both ladies to depart with their lovers, much to the annoyance of Osmin, keeper of the Pasha's harem, who would like Blondchen for himself. Created (1782) by Dominik Jautz.

2. (Rossini: *Il Turco in Italia*). Bass. A Turk who was engaged to his slave, Zaida. He is attracted by Fiorilla, wife of Geronio, but as he is about to sail away with her he sees Zaida and now has to choose between the two women. After much confusion and hilarity caused by everyone dressing up in each other's clothes, he settles for the faithful Zaida. Created (1814) by Filippo Galli.

Sellem (Stravinsky: *The Rake's Progress*). Ten. An auctioneer, he is to sell Tom Rakewell's possessions after Tom has become bankrupt. Aria: *An unknown object draws us ... fifty—fifty-five, sixty*. Created (1951) by Hugues Cuenod.

Sem and Mrs Sem (Britten: *Noye's Fludde*). Treble and girl sop. Son and daughter-in-law of Noye. They help to build the Ark. Created (1958) by Thomas Bevan and Janette Miller.

Semele (Handel). Lib. by William Congreve; 3 acts; f.p. London 1744 (concert perf.).

Temple of *Juno in Thebes: *Semele, daughter of *Cadmus, King of Thebes, is about to marry Prince *Athamas, who is loved by *Ino, Semele's sister. The wedding is abandoned when *Jupiter intervenes because Semele calls on the gods to save her from a loveless marriage and Jupiter is then attracted to her. He takes her off with him. His wife Juno is not pleased. She calls for help from *Somnus, disguises herself as Ino, and persuades Semele to ask Jupiter to appear to her in his full glory as a god. When he reluctantly does so, Semele dies—Juno knew that since Semele is a mortal, she would be unable to withstand his divine power. Ino is now able to marry Athamas.

Semele 1. (Handel: *Semele*). Sop. Daughter of Cadmus, King of Thebes. She asks the gods to save her from a loveless marriage with Athamas. Jupiter, King of the Gods, intervenes and falls in love with her. When, at the bidding of Juno, Jupiter appears to Semele in his divine form, she is consumed by flames and dies. Created (1744) by Elisabeth Duparc ('Francesina').

    2. (Strauss: *Die Liebe der Danae*). Sop. One of the Four Queens who have been lovers of Jupiter. Created (1944) by Maud Cunitz; (1952) by Dorothea Siebert.

Semiramide (Rossini). Lib. by Gaetano Rossi; 2 acts; f.p. Venice 1823.

Ancient Babylon: Queen *Semiramide is the widow of King Nino. Her daughter, the Princess *Azema, loves the young commander *Arsace, the man her mother hopes to marry. Semiramide names Arsace as the new ruler. The Ghost of *Nino tells Arsace that he is his son and that his mother was an accomplice to his murder by her ex-lover *Assur. Arsace must avenge his father. Arsace attempts to strike Assur, but Semiramide steps between them and is killed. Arsace is accepted as the new king.

Semiramide (Rossini: *Semiramide*). Sop. Queen of Babylon, widow of Nino, who has been murdered by her lover Assur, who hopes to marry her and thus ascend the throne of Babylon. She loves the young commander Arsace, not realizing he is her own son. When he attempts to kill Assur, she steps between

them and is herself killed. Aria: *Bel raggio lusinghier* ('Bright ray of hope'). Created (1823) by Isabella Colbran (who was Rossini's wife from 1822 to 1837; this was the last of many roles he created for her).

Sempronio (Mozart: *Così fan tutte*). Name used by Ferrando in his disguise as an Albanian. *See* FERRANDO (1).

Seneca (Monteverdi: *L'incoronazione di Poppea*). Bass. A philosopher and previously tutor to Nero. Stoically accepts his own death by suicide when so ordered by an angry Nero. Creator (1643) not known.

Senta (Wagner: *Der fliegende Holländer*). Sop. Daughter of the Norwegian sea-captain Daland. She is teased by her old nurse and the other women for her obsession with the portrait of a man which hangs on the wall. She recounts the story of the Dutchman who is doomed to sail the seas for ever unless he finds a faithful wife. Her father returns, bringing with him a stranger, whom she recognizes from the portrait to be the Dutchman. He wants to marry her and, determined to save him, she readily agrees. The hunter Erik, who is in love with her, tries to persuade her to marry him instead. Overhearing this conversation, the Dutchman presumes Senta to be unfaithful and himself to be doomed. He leaves. Senta follows him, jumping into the sea. As his ship sinks, Senta and the Dutchman are seen together rising above the waves. Aria: *Johohoe! … Traft ich das Schiff im Meere an* ('Yoho! … Have you seen the ship upon the ocean'—Senta's Ballad). Created (1843) by Wilhelmina Schröder-Devrient.

Serena (Gershwin: *Porgy and Bess*). Sop. Wife of Robbins who is killed by Crown. Aria: *My man's gone now*. Created (1935) by Ruby Elzy.

Sergeant of Police (Sullivan: *The Pirates of Penzance*). Bass-bar. Head of the police who are to arrest the pirates. Aria: *When a felon's not engaged in 'is employment*. Created (NY, 1879) by Fred Clifton.

Sergei (Shostakovich: *Lady Macbeth of the Mtsensk District*). Ten. A young servant in the employ of the Ismailov household. He and Katerina fall in love. Her jealous father-in-law finds out and she poisons him. Her husband returns and whips her. When her father-in-law's body is found, Katerina and Sergei confess their guilt and are arrested. On the road to Siberia, Sergei is attracted by a young girl convict. Jealous, Katerina pushes her off a bridge into the river, before drowning herself. Created (1934) by Pyotr Zasetsky.

Serpetta (Mozart: *La finta giardiniera*). Sop. Maid at the house of the Podestà (mayor) and secretly in love with him. Created (1775) probably by Teresina Manservisi (who created either this role or that of the mayor's niece Arminda).

Serse (*Xerxes*) (Handel). Lib. by Nicola Minato and Silvio Stampiglia; 3 acts; f.p. London 1738.

King Serse's Court, Persia: *Serse, engaged to *Amastre, falls in love with *Romilda (daughter of Serse's army commander *Ariodate), fiancée of his brother *Arsamene, and instructs Arsamene to convey his feelings. Arsamene does so, overheard by Romilda's sister *Atalanta, who is in turn in love with Arsamene. *Elviro, Arsamene's servant, tells Amastre of these intrigues. Even though Romilda rejects Serse, he tries to force his brother to marry Atalanta, telling Romilda that her betrothed is unfaithful. Dressed as a man, Amastre is aware of the various machinations. Arsamene and Romilda are married by Ariodate, and when Serse discovers this he commands his brother to kill his new wife. Amastre reveals her true identity and Serse repents his behaviour and is reconciled with Amastre.

Serse (Handel: *Serse*). Mez. *Travesti* role (originally castrato). Xerxes, King of Persia, is engaged to Amastre but falls in love with Romilda, his brother's fiancée. His attempts to win Romilda from Arsamene cause many misunderstandings but are unsuccessful and he is ultimately reconciled with Amastre. In his most famous aria, *Ombra mai fu* ('Never was nature's own shade'), he praises the tree which gives him shade. This is popularly known as Handel's *Largo* (despite being marked *larghetto* in the score). Created (1738) by Caffarelli (the castrato Gaetano Maiorano).

Servilia (Mozart: *La clemenza di Tito*). Sop. Sister of Sesto, loved by his friend Annio. Aria: *S'altro che lacrime per lui non tenti* ('If you do nothing for him but shed tears'); duet (with Annio): *Ah, perdonna al primo affetto* ('Ah,

forgive my former love'). Created (1791) by Sig.a Antonini.

Sesto 1. (Mozart: *La clemenza di Tito*). Sop./mez. *Travesti* role (originally castrato). Young Roman nobleman, friend of Annio. Helps Vitellia plot to assassinate Tito. Arrested and sentenced to death, but forgiven by Tito. Arias: *Parto, parto* ('I am going'); *Deh, per questo istante solo* ('Ah, for this single moment'). Created (1791) by Domenico Bedini (sop. castrato).

2. (Handel: *Giulio Cesare*). Sop. *Travesti* role (or ten.). Sesto Pompeo, son of Cornelia and Pompey. Arrested by Tolomeo who murdered Sesto's father. Sesto avenges his father by killing Tolomeo. Sesto and his mother are finally united in peace with Cesare and Cleopatra. Created (1724) by Margherita Durastanti.

Seymour, Giovanna (Jane) (Donizetti: *Anna Bolena*). Mez. Lady-in-Waiting to the Queen (Anna Bolena) and now the King's mistress. Her conscience troubles her, torn between her loyalty to the Queen and the thought of being her successor. She first begs the King to release her, then pleads with Anna to confess to adultery (which she has not committed) and beg the King's forgiveness. Created (1830) by Elisa Orlandi.

Shadbolt, Wilfred (Sullivan: *The Yeomen of the Guard*). Bar. Gaoler at the Tower of London. He loves Phoebe, Sergeant Meryll's daughter, and eventually wins 'Phoebe's hand, not Phoebe's heart'. Created (1888) by W. H. Denny.

Shadow, Nick (Stravinsky: *The Rake's Progress*). Bar. He is the devil in disguise. By telling Tom Rakewell he has won a fortune and offering his services free for a year and a day, Shadow tempts Tom away from Anne, his bride-to-be, to a life of debauchery. When all Tom's money is gone, they play cards, the stake being Tom's soul. Tom wins and in anger Shadow condemns him to a life of insanity. Aria: *I burn! I freeze!* Created (1951) by Otakar Kraus.

Shaklovity (Musorgsky: *Khovanshchina*). Bar. A boyar who warns the Russian rulers against the Khovanskys. He murders Prince Ivan Khovansky. Creator (1886) unknown; (1911) by Tartakoff.

Sharkey, Sam (Britten: *Paul Bunyan*). Ten. One of two Bad Cooks. He leaves the camp when the loggers complain about the poor food they serve. Duet (with Benny): *Sam for soups, Ben for beans*. Created (1941) by Clifford Jackson.

Sharpless (Puccini: *Madama Butterfly*). Bar. The US Consul in Nagasaki and friend of Lieut. Pinkerton. The two men meet at Butterfly's house and Sharpless makes it clear to Pinkerton that he considers his happy-go-lucky attitude to his forthcoming marriage to the young Butterfly to be irresponsible and unfair. Sharpless points out that the girl clearly loves him and can therefore easily be hurt, but Pinkerton treats the situation lightly. Shortly after their wedding night, he sails for America. Three years later, Butterfly is still confident that he will come back to her as he promised. Sharpless visits her—he has had a letter from Pinkerton in which he explains that he now has an American wife and he has asked the Consul to break this news to Butterfly. As soon as she sees the letter, Butterfly assumes her husband is returning to her and keeps interrupting all attempts to read the letter to her. Sharpless, aware of the upset it will cause, suggests she should marry the wealthy Yamadori. Butterfly now produces the son who was born after his father left for America. The Consul, unable to proceed with his news, promises Butterfly he will write and tell Pinkerton about the child, although he knows it is too late and that Pinkerton is already on his way to Japan. As Butterfly rests in an adjoining room, Sharpless accompanies Pinkerton to the house and they are admitted by her maid, Suzuki. It is Sharpless who explains to Suzuki that they have come to discuss the future care of the child. Butterfly enters the room and Sharpless explains to her that Pinkerton has an American wife, Kate. He asks Butterfly to let the child return with them to America and she agrees on condition that Pinkerton comes himself to collect his son. Sharpless leaves with Kate to pass on this condition to Pinkerton. When the two men return, Butterfly is dying.

Sharpless is a sympathetic person, who has forced upon him all the cruel acts which Pinkerton, in his cowardly way, avoids. Sharpless has to break the bad news to Butterfly, for whom he clearly feels sorry, and he no doubt could see the eventual outcome from the beginning, hence his attempts to dissuade Pinkerton from marrying Butterfly in the first place. Sharpless does not have any great aria to sing, usually appearing in conversational duets or ensembles. However, his Act 2 scene with Butterfly, when he tries to read her her husband's letter, is most moving and there has never been a shortage of baritones willing to undertake this role—in fact, one rarely sees a poor Sharpless on the stage. Well-known artists in this role have included John Brownlee, Giuseppe Taddei, Tito Gobbi, Rolando Panerai, Hermann Prey, Delme Bryn-Jones, Ingvar Wixell, and Juan Pons. Created (1904) by Giuseppe De Luca.

She-Ancient (Tippett: *The Midsummer Marriage*). Priestess of the temple. Together with the He-Ancient, she warns King Fisher not to interfere with the course of Nature—not to meddle with powers he cannot control. Created (1955) by Edith Coates.

Shemakha, Queen of (Rimsky-Korsakov: *The Golden Cockerel*). Sop. She seduces Tsar Didon after a battle and returns with him to his capital, where the Astrologer demands her for himself. She repulses Didon. Created (1909) by Aureliya Dobrovol'skaya.

Shepherd 1. (Wagner: *Tristan und Isolde*). Ten. Appears in Act 3, piping a beautiful refrain. He keeps watch for signs of the ship bringing Isolde back to Tristan. Created (1865) by Herr Simons.

2. (Szymanowski: *King Roger*). Ten. Preaches the philosophy of beauty and pleasure as a way of life. The Queen is entranced by him and follows him to a Dionysian existence. Only the King is able to resist him. Created (1926) by Adam Dobosz.

3. (Puccini: *Tosca*). Treble/mez. On the roof of Castel Sant' Angelo, just before dawn, Cavaradossi awaits execution. The bells of the local sheep can be heard, and a song sung by a shepherd boy (sung usually by a boy soprano or a mez.). Aria: *Io de' sospiri* ('I give you sighs'). Cecilia Bartoli, at the age of nine, made her début in this role.

4. (Wagner: *Tannhäuser*). Sop. *Travesti* role. He sings of the coming of spring. As the pilgrims pass on their way to Rome, he falls to his knees in prayer. Aria: *Frau Holda kam aus* *dem Berg hervor* ('Dame Holda came near from the hill'—Holda was the goddess of spring). Creator (1845) unknown.

Shepherds of the Delectable Mountains (Vaughan Williams: *The Pilgrim's Progress*). Bar., ten., bass. Three Shepherds welcome Pilgrim and invite him to rest in the Delectable Mountains before resuming his journey to the Celestial City. Created (1951) by (respectively) John Cameron, William McAlpine, and Norman Walker. [NOTE: This episode was written as a separate work and as such received its f.p. in 1922 cond. Arthur Bliss. The three shepherds were created by Archibald Winter (bar.), Leonard A. Willmore (ten.), and Keith Falkner (bar.). It was later incorporated (shortened) into *The Pilgrim's Progress* as Act IV, scene 2 as described above.]

Sherasmin (Weber: *Oberon*). Ten. Squire of Sir Huon of Bordeaux, who accompanies Huon when he goes to find and marry Reiza. Sherasmin falls in love with her maid. Created (1826) by John Fawcett.

Show Boat (Kern). Lib. by Oscar Hammerstein II; 2 acts; f.p. Washington DC 1927 (prior to the opening in New York six weeks later), cond. Victor Baravelle.

On the banks of the Mississippi, at the World Fair (1893), and on the *Cotton Blossom*, 1890–1927: Capt. Andy *Hawks and his wife Parthy Ann *Hawks run a show boat, the *Cotton Blossom*. Their daughter Magnolia *Hawks falls in love with Gaylord *Ravenal, a gambler, and they marry despite her parents' objections. On the boat, the chief stars are Julie *La Verne and her husband Steve *Baker. The black servants are *Queenie and her man *Joe. It emerges that Julie is partly black and therefore she and Steve are no longer wanted on the boat. Magnolia and Ravenal take over their roles. Years pass— Gaylord loses his money gambling and cannot support his wife and their daughter Kim. They leave the boat, separate, and Magnolia finds a job as a singer. In 1927, on the modernized show boat *Cotton Blossom*, Magnolia and Kim become the stars and Gaylord, a somewhat reformed character, returns to them. Things on the river just keep rolling along.

Shuisky, Prince (Musorgsky: *Boris Godunov*). Ten. He is a boyar, but is in league with the Polish people. He brings Boris the news that a pretender to the Russian throne has arisen in Poland, claiming to be the resurrected Dimitri, murdered by Boris. Created (1874) by P. Vasiliyev.

Sicilian Vespers, The (Verdi). *See* VÊPRES SICILIENNES, LES.

Sicle (Cavalli: *L'Ormindo*). Sop. Former lover of Amida, who forgets her when he falls in love with the king's wife. Creator (1644) not known.

Sid (Britten: *Albert Herring*). Bar. Assistant in the butcher's shop. Boyfriend of Nancy. He tries to encourage Albert to break loose from his mother's apron-strings, telling him what he is missing in life. At the May King ceremony, he spikes Albert's drink. When Albert eventually returns to the shop, having spent the night on the tiles, Sid and Nancy support him in his rebellion. Aria: *Tickling a trout, poaching a hare*. Created (1947) by Frederick Sharp.

Sidonie (Gluck: *Armide*). Sop. Confidante of Armide. Created (1777) by Mlle Châteauneuf.

Siebel (Gounod: *Faust*). Mez. *Travesti* role. A youth in the village, in love with Marguerite, to whom he brings flowers, but she falls in love with Faust. Created (1859) by Amélie Faivre.

Siegfried (Wagner). Lib. by Wagner; 3 acts; f.p. Bayreuth 1876, cond. Hans Richter (Wagner had conducted excerpts in concert performance in Vienna, 1863). Third opera in the cycle *Der Ring des Nibelungen*.

Mime's cave, the forest and a rocky mountain, mythological times: *Mime is unsuccessfully trying to forge a new sword from the shattered Nothung—he was given the fragments by a dying woman (*Sieglinde) who asked him to care for her son, *Siegfried, and he has raised the child to young manhood. The *Wanderer (*Wotan) enters and insists they ask each other riddles, their lives being the stake. The Wanderer answers Mime's three questions, then puts his own. The third one— who will repair Nothung?—Mime is unable to answer. Only someone who has never known fear, explains the Wanderer. Mime determines to take Siegfried to see the dragon *Fafner (previously a giant) to teach him fear, planning to kill him once he has slain the dragon, who guards the gold. To Mime's chagrin, Siegfried forges the sword. The Wanderer meets

*Alberich outside Fafner's cave, and tells him of Mime's plans to steal the gold. When Mime and Siegfried appear, Siegfried carves a reed-pipe from a piece of wood. He then kills Fafner who warns him, before he dies, that Mime wants to kill him. Licking some of Fafner's blood off his hand, Siegfried acquires the ability to understand birdsong. From Fafner's cave he takes the Tarnhelm and the Ring. Mime offers Siegfried a drink, but the dragon's blood has also made it possible for him to know Mime's real thoughts, and he realizes the drink is poisoned. He kills Mime with his sword. The Woodbird (*Waldwogel) leads Siegfried to *Brünnhilde's rock, where the Wanderer is waiting. He has asked *Erda what he can do to prevent the inevitable destiny of the world and the fall of the gods from power. Siegfried uses Nothung to break the Wanderer's spear. Fearlessly, he climbs through the fire to awaken Brünnhilde. They proclaim their love and laugh at the thought of the end of the world and the gods.

Siegfried (Wagner: *Siegfried; Götterdämmerung*). Ten. Mortal son of Sieglinde and Siegmund. Wotan has ordained that he will be a hero. His mother died when he was born and had asked Mime to look after her son. She gave him for safekeeping the fragments of Siegmund's sword, to be kept for her son.

Siegfried: In his cave, Mime is trying to forge a sword which young Siegfried will not break. Mime is a good smith, but every sword he has made, Siegfried has broken. As he works, Siegfried enters, leading a large bear on the end of a rope. Highly amused by Mime's terror at the sight of the animal, he explains how he found the bear when he was looking for a companion whose company he would find more congenial than Mime's, emphasizing how he dislikes the dwarf and can't tolerate being with him. He picks up the latest sword and smashes it against the anvil. He starts to ask about his mother and Mime tells him that he has been both father and mother to him. Siegfried is not fooled—he knows he does not look like Mime, as animals look like their parents. Siegfried persists with his questions and Mime recounts the story of his birth, showing him the sword fragments in evidence. Siegfried insists Mime must forge a sword from the pieces. With it, Siegfried tells him, he will leave the cave and hopes never to see Mime again. All in all, he is very cruel in the things he says to Mime who has, after all, brought him up since he found him as a baby. He storms out, leaving Mime still worrying about forging the sword. By the time he returns, Wotan (disguised as the Wanderer) has visited Mime and told him that the only one who will be able to forge the sword from the fragments is one who has known no fear. Mime questions Siegfried about various situations in which the average person would be scared, but each time Siegfried makes it clear he felt no fear and Mime realizes that Siegfried does not know the meaning of fear. He will take him to the dragon's cave to learn what fear is. Siegfried is willing, but wants his sword first and, dismissing Mime's efforts, sets about attempting the forging himself. Despite Mime's derisory comments, Siegfried succeeds where Mime failed, and in triumph smashes the finished weapon down and splits the anvil in half. Off they go to the forest and the dragon Fafner's cave, where Mime hopes also to use Siegfried to gain the gold for himself. Siegfried sits outside Fafner's cave, watching a bird overhead while Mime goes to prepare food (the beautiful music for this episode being known as the Forest Murmurs). Fafner rears up and Siegfried, fearless, plunges his sword into its heart. Getting some of the dragon's blood on his hand, he licks it off and discovers, to his amazement, that he can now understand what the birds are singing. The Woodbird tells him that the treasure in the cave (the Ring and the Tarnhelm) is now his and that he must not trust Mime—he has been given the ability to know what is in Mime's mind. He gathers the gold from the cave. Mime brings him a drink, but he knows it is poisoned—Mime wants to kill him and take the treasure for himself. Siegfried kills Mime with his sword. Again the Woodbird comes to him and promises to lead him to where he will find the friend he is seeking. At the mountain on which Brünnhilde sleeps, Wotan watches as Siegfried climbs up to and through the ring of fire. When he first sees Brünnhilde, covered with her shield and helmet, he presumes it to be a man, but after he has removed the armour he realizes it is a woman. He leans over and kisses her. Slowly, Brünnhilde awakes and they greet one another with declarations of love. Arias: *Nothung! Nothung! Neidliches Schwert!*

('Nothung! Nothung! Trusty sword!'); *Du holdest Vöglein!* ('You pretty bird!'); *Selige Öde auf sonniger Höh'! … Dass ist kein Mann!* ('Blessedly bare on the sunny summit! … That is no man!').

Götterdämmerung: As dawn breaks, Brünnhilde and Siegfried emerge from a cave where they have, the music tells us, made passionate love. She lends him her horse and he rides off to seek further adventures, first giving her the Ring to keep as a token of his love. He arrives at the Hall of the Gibichungs, where live Gunther and his sister Gutrune and their half-brother Hagen (son of Alberich). In his plans to recover the gold for himself, Hagen has suggested the other two should marry—Gutrune with Siegfried, Gunther with Brünnhilde. He will give Siegfried a potion which will make him forget Brünnhilde and fall in love with Gutrune. When Siegfried arrives, this is exactly what happens. Gunther will consent to their marriage if Siegfried will help *him* gain Brünnhilde, as Gunther will be unable to penetrate the ring of fire. With no memory of Brünnhilde and their love, Siegfried agrees to bring Brünnhilde to him—he will use the Tarnhelm to disguise himself as Gunther. Brünnhilde hears his horn as he approaches and rushes to greet him, only to be met by a total stranger—it is Siegfried-as-Gunther. He seizes the Ring from her finger and takes her with him back to Gibichung Hall. There she is forced to watch as he gets ready to marry Gutrune, while she is prepared for her wedding with Gunther. By now Siegfried has resumed his own form, and she looks on in disbelief as he shows no sign of recognition. On his finger, she sees the Ring. Now she is totally confused. The only thing of which she is sure is that Siegfried has betrayed her and their love. Siegfried, of course, has no idea what she is so distressed about, having no conception of what he has done. He is prepared to swear on oath that he never was married to Brünnhilde and Hagen offers his own spear for Siegfried to swear on. In her jealousy, anger, and despair, Brünnhilde also takes an oath—she prays that the spear will kill Siegfried. Siegfried cannot understand all these ravings and asks Gunther to calm his bride and they can all partake of the wedding feast. Hagen suggests that the only answer to everything is Siegfried's death. Next day, when the men are out hunting, Siegfried drinks from a horn into which Hagen has put

an antidote to the previous potion and then remembers the past and knows he betrayed Brünnhilde. He turns to look at two ravens (Wotan's birds) flying overhead and as he turns his back, Hagen stabs him. As Siegfried dies, he speaks Brünnhilde's name, vowing to wake her again with his kiss. His body is carried home through the forest to the waiting women. Hagen makes to take the Ring from Siegfried's finger, but is terrified as the dead Siegfried's hand rises into the air. Brünnhilde, by now aware of the truth, orders the building of a funeral pyre. On this is laid Siegfried's body. As the flames surround it, Brünnhilde mounts her horse and rides into the flames. Arias: *Vergass ich alles was du mir gabst* ('If I forget everything that you gave me'); *Gunther, wehr deinem Weibe* ('Gunther, watch your wife'); *Brünnhilde, heilige Braut!* ('Brünnhilde, holy bride!').

Siegfried, like Wotan and Brünnhilde, vocally needs a singer of *Helden* quality. Although he only appears in the last two operas of the tetralogy, the role tries the most experienced tenor, especially at the present time, when good heroic tenors are somewhat thin on the ground. Nevertheless, over the years there have been some memorable singers of this part, and these include Max Alvary, Ernst Krauss, Lauritz Melchior, Max Lorenz (who, with the exception of two years, sang it in every cycle at Bayreuth from 1933 to 1952), Wolfgang Windgassen, Hans Hopf, Jean Cox, Alberto Remedios, Manfred Jung, Reiner Goldberg, René Kollo, and Siegfried Jerusalem. Created (*S.* and *G.* 1876) by Georg Unger.

Sieglinde (Wagner: *Die Walküre*). Sop. Twin sister of Siegmund and daughter of Wotan by a Wälsung. She is locked in a loveless marriage with Hunding and they live in a hut with a large ash tree growing up through the roof. Lodged in the trunk is a shining sword. While Hunding is out, she finds a stranger (Siegmund) collapsed on her hearth and insists he rest until her husband returns. She and the stranger are attracted to each other. When her husband returns, she is clearly frightened of him and feels threatened. She takes his armour and is sent off to prepare a meal. At the table, she sits opposite Siegmund. Their glances are intercepted by Hunding. As the two men talk and it becomes clear that there will be a fight the next day, Sieglinde does her best surreptitiously to draw the stranger's attention to the sword in the tree. She drugs her husband's drink and when he is asleep, she returns to where Siegmund is resting. She tells him of her unhappy marriage and how, on her wedding day, a stranger thrust the sword into the tree. Many have unsuccessfully tried to withdraw it and she realizes that the man who put it there was her father, Wotan, and that only her twin brother, from whom she was separated as a baby, will be able to do so. The two are soon locked in a passionate embrace, declaring their love. She questions him—was he the son of Wolfe? Yes, he was, and he triumphantly pulls the sword (Nothung) out of the tree. She admits her own true identity and together they flee from Hunding's house. Sieglinde, feeling guilty about their incestuous love, collapses in his arms. Brünnhilde arrives and Siegmund leaves the scene with her. Sieglinde recovers to find herself alone with, in the distance, the sound of Hunding's horn as he chases them through the forest. A flash of lightning reveals to her Hunding and Siegmund fighting. As Hunding kills Siegmund, Brünnhilde arrives, sweeps Sieglinde on to her horse and gallops off to the Valkyries' mountain. Sieglinde, without Siegmund, wants only to die, but Brünnhilde insists she must live for the sake of her unborn child. Wotan is heard approaching, and Brünnhilde insists Sieglinde escapes his wrath by fleeing into the forest to have her child. She gives Sieglinde the fragments of Siegmund's shattered sword, assuring her that one day the son she bears will be a hero who will forge a new sword from the pieces. Sieglinde escapes—we learn from Mime (in *Siegfried*) that he finds her in the forest, dying, and that she gives her baby and the shattered sword into his keeping. Arias: *Eine Waffe lass mich dir weisen* ('Let me show you a sword'); *Du bist der Lenz* ('You are the spring'); *Hinweg! Hinweg! Flieh die Entweihte* ('Be off! Be off! Flee the curse upon me!'). Many singers of Sieglinde, who has some of the most lyrical music in the *Ring*, have later become eminent Brünnhildes. Among the most notable of these are Helen Traubel, Kirsten Flagstad, Astrid Varnay, Birgit Nilsson, Ava June, Gwyneth Jones, Jeannine Altmeyer, Anne Evans, Cheryl Studer, and Waltraud Meier.

Created (1870) by Therese Vogl (whose husband sang Siegmund).

Siegmund (Wagner: *Die Walküre*). Ten. Twin brother of Sieglinde, son of Wotan by a Wälsung. Siegmund stumbles into the hut of Sieglinde and Hunding and collapses on the floor, where Sieglinde finds him and gives him a drink of water. There is an immediate attraction between them, although they have no idea of their relationship. They share a cup of wine and Sieglinde insists he rest until her husband returns. He tells her that he calls himself Woeful. Hunding returns and is suspicious of the stranger. He tries to persuade Siegmund to reveal his name, which the young man is reluctant to do. As they all sit eating, Sieglinde wordlessly draws Siegmund's attention to a sword buried high up in the trunk of the ash tree. In answer to further questioning by Hunding, Siegmund explains that he is one of twins. One day he came home to find his mother dead and his sister gone. He and his father became separated and since then he has wandered around the earth. He met a young girl being bullied into marriage by her brothers, and he killed the brothers. Now he is being hunted by their friends. To Siegmund's horror, Hunding admits that he is one of them. In the name of hospitality, Siegmund may stay the night. Tomorrow, they fight. After Sieglinde and Hunding have retired to bed, he drugged by his wife, Siegmund remembers his father telling him that 'in adversity' he would show him his sword. In the light from the burning fire he sees something shining in the tree to which Sieglinde was earlier trying to draw his attention. Sieglinde returns and explains how the sword comes to be there, thrust there by a stranger during her wedding feast. All attempts to remove it have failed. She has realized that the man must have been her father and only the man for whom the sword was intended will have the strength to withdraw it. Siegmund and Sieglinde declare their love, and gradually they learn that they are brother and sister and that Siegmund is indeed the one for whom the sword was intended. He pulls out the sword, waving it in triumph. Together, they flee from the hut and Hunding. Sieglinde develops a guilty conscience about their incestuous passion, but Siegmund repeats his vows of love. They hear the sound of Hunding's hunting horn approaching and Sieglinde collapses. Brünnhilde appears. She has come to guard Siegmund in his fight with Hunding and to take him to Valhalla. When she confirms that Sieglinde cannot go with them, he refuses to go. She warns him that if he remains where he is, his life is in danger, but he is adamant— he will not leave without his sister. Hunding approaches and the two men fight. Siegmund is about to thrust his sword into Hunding, when Wotan appears and stretches out his spear. Siegmund's sword shatters on the spear and Hunding kills him. Arias: *Friedmund darf ich nicht heissen* ('I cannot call myself "Peaceful" '); *Ein Schwert verhiess mire der Vater* ('My father promised me a sword'); *Winterstürme wichen dem Wonnenmond* ('Winter storms have vanished before Maytime'). Exponents of this role have included Lauritz Melchior, Karl Elmendorff, Max Lorenz, Franz Völker, Ramon Vinay, Wolfgang Windgassen, James King, Charles Craig, Peter Hofmann, Siegfried Jerusalem, Warren Ellsworth, René Kollo, Poul Elming, and Plácido Domingo. Created (1870) by Heinrich Vogl (whose wife sang Sieglinde).

Siegrune (Wagner: *Die Walküre*). *See* VALKYRIES.

Sifare (Mozart: *Mitridate, re di Ponto*). Mez. *Travesti* role (originally castrato). Son of Mitridate, brother of Farnace. He falls in love with his father's fiancée, Aspasia. Created by Pietro Benedetti (sop. castrato).

Silent Woman, The (Strauss). *See* SCHWEIGSAME FRAU, DIE.

Silla (Pfitzner: *Palestrina*). Mez. *Travesti* role. 17-year-old pupil of Palestrina. Created (1917) by Fraulein Strüger.

Silla, Lucio (Mozart: *Lucio Silla*). Ten. A Roman dictator. He tries to persuade the daughter of his old enemy to marry him as a means of ending civil war. She, however, is now the betrothed of one of his senators. The young couple plan to kill him, but Silla relents, forgives them all and abdicates. Created (1772) by Bassano Morgnoni.

Silva, Don Ruy Gomez de (Verdi: *Ernani*). Bass. A grandee of Spain, guardian of Elvira, whom he wants to marry, even though she loves the outlawed Ernani and is also loved by the King. Finding her embracing Ernani, he challenges him to a duel, which Ernani refuses, promising Silva his life as forfeit, after he has avenged his father's death by killing the King. Silva receives a horn from Ernani—if he sounds it, it will signal his desire for Ernani's death. Don Carlos is declared Emperor and consents to Ernani and Elvira's marriage. At the celebrations, Silva wreaks revenge for his thwarted ambition to marry Elvira himself. He sounds the horn call (possibly an early use by Verdi of *Leitmotif* which was soon to become Wagner's trademark). Created (1844) by Antonio Selva.

Silvia (Haydn: *L'isola disabitata*). Sop. Sister of Costanza. They have been left on a desert island and await rescue. Created (1779) by Luigia Polzelli (with whom Haydn had a relationship which lasted for many years).

Silvio (Leoncavallo: *Pagliacci*). Bar. A villager in love with Nedda, wife of Canio. He tries to save Nedda when Canio stabs her during a performance of their play, but Canio kills him also. Created (1892) by Mario Ancona.

Simon Boccanegra (Verdi). Lib. by Francesco Maria Piave/Arrigo Boito; prol. and 3 acts; f.p. Venice 1857, cond. Giuseppe Verdi/ Milan 1881, cond. Franco Faccio. [NOTE: There are two versions of this opera. It had its première in 1857 and was totally revised nearly 25 years later. The later version is the one usually performed today and is therefore described here.]

In and around Genoa, 14th cent.: The city is ruled by two warring factions, the plebeians and the patricians. The patrician Jacopo *Fiesco disapproves of his daughter Maria's love for the plebeian Simon *Boccanegra. She dies, and her father will only forgive Boccanegra if he hands over the illegitimate daughter Maria bore him. But the young Maria has vanished. To Fiesco's fury, Boccanegra is elected doge by the manipulations of the plebeians, led by Paolo *Albiani. It is 25 years later. In the palace of her guardian Andrea (who is Fiesco living under another name), Amelia *Grimaldi waits for her sweetheart, the patrician Gabriele *Adorno, whose father was killed by Boccanegra. She fears the Doge wants her to marry Paolo. She and Gabriele persuade Andrea (Fiesco) to give their union his blessing. Boccanegra arrives and realizes that Amelia is his long-lost daughter. In the council chamber, the Doge is told that Amelia has been kidnapped by Paolo, but she escapes. Boccanegra curses whoever tried to harm Amelia. Paolo plans to kill the Doge, and puts poison in his water jug. He tells Gabriele that Boccanegra lusts after Amelia. Amelia is unable to explain to her lover the truth. Boccanegra drinks the poisoned water and falls asleep. Gabriele, about to kill the sleeping Doge, is interrupted by Amelia. The Doge wakes up and Gabriele learns the truth—they are father and daughter. Boccanegra promises Gabriele that he can marry Amelia if he can bring about a peaceful settlement between the plebeians and the patricians. As the poison starts to take effect, Boccanegra tells Fiesco that Maria is his granddaughter. Boccanegra and Fiesco are reconciled and Amelia and Gabriele married. The dying Doge names Gabriele Adorno as his successor.

Simon Boccanegra See BOCCANEGRA, SIMON.

Simone (Zemlinsky: *Eine florentinische Tragödie*). Bass. A silk-merchant married to Bianca. He discovers she is having an affair. The two men fight a duel and her lover is killed. His wife declares her love for her husband—now she realizes what a strong and dominant man he is. Created (1917) by Felix Fleischer.

Sinais, Queen (Amaltea) (Rossini: *Mosè in Egitto*). Sop. Wife of Pharaoh. She realizes that Pharaoh's son Amenophis is in love with Moses' niece. Created (1818) by Friderike Funk.

Sinodal, Prince (Rubinstein: *The Demon*). Ten. About to marry Princess Tamara, his death is engineered by the Demon. Created (1875) by Fyodor Komissarzhevsky.

Siroco (Chabrier: *L'Étoile*). Bass. Court Astrologer to King Ouf. Created (1877) by Mons. Scipion.

Sirval, Vicomte Carlo di (Donizetti: *Linda di Chamounix*). Ten. In love with Linda, he is frightened to tell her his true identity in case it acts as a barrier to their relationship, and she knows him only as Carlo, a painter. They go to Paris and she lives with him in all innocence. There her father visits her and assumes she is Carlo's mistress. However, his mother is against their marriage and tries to persuade Carlo to marry a wealthy young aristocratic lady. When Linda hears of this she goes mad

and returns to her parents' home. Carlo follows her, his mother having at last agreed to their marriage, and he restores Linda's sanity by singing to her his old love-song. Created (1842) by Napoleone Moriani.

Šiškov (Janáček: *From the House of the Dead*). Bar. A prisoner who tells his story: he was forced to marry a girl who had reputedly been seduced by one Filka Morozov. On their wedding night he discovered she was a virgin and he was full of remorse. She later told him she did love Morozov and had an affair with him *after* they were married. In his humiliation, he killed her. Now, in the prison, he recognizes the dying Luka as Filka Morozov and curses his body as it is carried out. Created (1930) by Géza Fischer.

Skuratov (Janáček: *From the House of the Dead*). Ten. He tells how he comes to be in the Siberian prison camp. He murdered the man his girlfriend was forced by her family to marry. Created (1930) by Antonín Pelc (originally Pelz, under which name he created roles in other Janáček operas).

Slim, Hot Biscuit (Britten: *Paul Bunyan*). Ten. Arrives at the lumber-camp, admitting he is lonely and trying to 'find himself'. Takes over as the camp cook. Falls in love with Tiny, the daughter of Paul Bunyan. When the camp breaks up, they go off to run a hotel in Manhattan. Arias: *I come from open spaces; In fair days and in foul*. Created (1941) by Charles Cammock.

Smeraldina (Prokofiev: *The Love for Three Oranges*). Mez. Servant of Fata Morgana. She wants to marry the Prince and turns his princess into a rat. Created (1921) by Jeanne Schneider.

Smeton (Donizetti: *Anna Bolena*). Cont. *Travesti* role. The Queen's page and a court musician, in love with his mistress. In an attempt to save her from the scaffold, he admits (falsely) to adultery with the Queen. Created (1830) by Henrietta Laroche.

Smirnov, Grigory Stepanovitch (Walton: *The Bear*). Bar. A landowner who supplied oats for the late Popov's horse, for which he is owed 1,300 roubles. He forces his way past the servant into Mme Popova's drawing-room, demanding to be paid. He cannot accept her promise that her bailiff will pay him next week—the debt must be paid today, as his creditors are chasing him and the bank is demanding interest. If he does not receive his money today he will become a bankrupt and will hang himself! He becomes more and more aggressive until she regally sweeps out of the room. Her servant, Luka, tries to persuade him to leave, but he stays his ground, demanding vodka to sustain him. Reproached by Luka for his behaviour, he realizes he does look untidy and has behaved badly towards a lady. By now he is captivated by the spirited Popova. When she returns, he suggests they settle their quarrel by a duel and she sends for her late husband's pistols. But she has never before handled a gun. By the time Smirnov has shown her how to hold it, Luka returns to find them in a passionate embrace. Arias: *Grodzitov is not at home; Madame je vous prie*; duet (with Popova): *Yes, I do know how to behave.* The first aria is a description of all his debtors, the second a parody on the Russian tendency to use French phrases as a sign of aristocratic breeding. Created (1967) by John Shaw.

Smith, Jenny (Weill: *Aufstieg und Fall der Stadt Mahagonny*). Sop. She leads a group of young ladies to live in the city of Mahagonny, a place devoted to pleasure. She is seduced by Jim Mahoney, but when he is unable to pay his drinking debts, she refuses to help him and he is sentenced to death. Created (1930) by Mali Trummer.

Snout 1. (Britten: *A Midsummer Night's Dream*). Ten. A tinker, one of the rustics who perform a play for Duke Theseus and Hippolyta. He plays the part of the Wall. Aria: *In this same interlude it doth befall.* Created (1960) by Edward Byles.
2. (Purcell: *The Fairy Queen*). Spoken. Similar to the role in (1) above. Creator (1692) unknown.

Snug 1. (Britten: *A Midsummer Night's Dream*). Bass. A joiner, one of the rustics who perform a play for Duke Theseus and Hippolyta. He takes the part of the Lion. Aria: *You ladies, you whose gentle hearts do fear.* Created (1960) by David Kelly.
2. (Purcell: *The Fairy Queen*). Spoken. Similar to the role in (1) above. Creator (1692) unknown.

Sobinin, Bogdan (Glinka: *A Life for the Tsar*). Ten. A soldier fighting for the Tsar. Engaged to Antonida, daughter of the peasant Ivan Susanin. Created (1836) by Leon Leonov (the illegitimate son of John Field, the Irish composer and pianist).

Sofronia (Donizetti: *Don Pasquale*). The name used by Norina when she poses as a bride for Don Pasquale. *See* NORINA.

Soldaten, Die (*The Soldiers*) (Zimmermann). Lib. by composer; 4 acts; f.p. Cologne 1965, cond. Michael Gielen.
Flanders, 'present day': *Wesener's daughter *Charlotte sits with her sister *Marie as she writes to the mother of her fiancé *Stolzius. The French officer *Desportes wants to take Marie to the theatre, but her father forbids it, lecturing her on the dubious morals of soldiers. The chaplain disapproves of theatre and its debauchery, which is defended by Capt. *Haudy. Desportes seduces Marie, whose grandmother foretells her downfall. Stolzius becomes batman to Maj. *Mary, with whom Marie has yet another relationship. The Comtesse de la *Roche, to discourage her son's involvement with Marie, engages her as a companion. Marie runs away to join Desportes who, to be rid of her, offers her to his gamekeeper, who rapes her. Stolzius poisons Desportes, then kills himself. Marie is reduced to begging as a prostitute.

Soldier (Ullmann: *Der Kaiser von Atlantis*). Ten. In the midst of war, he falls in love with a Girl from the opposite camp. Realizing he is powerless to stop them, the Emperor also realizes that he cannot have power over Death. Created (1944) by David Grunfeld; (1975) by Rudolf Ruivenkamp.

Somarone (Berlioz: *Béatrice et Bénédict*). Bass. A musician who composes the bridal march for Hero and Claudio and conducts the orchestra and chorus. Created (1862) by Victor Prilleux.

Somnus (Handel: *Semele*). Bass. God of sleep. He puts Ino, Semele's sister, to sleep, so that Juno can impersonate her and influence Semele's behaviour with Jupiter. Created (1744) by Henry Reinhold.

sonnambula, La (The Sleepwalker) (Bellini). Lib. by Felice Romani; 2 acts; f.p. Milan 1831, cond. Vincenzo Bellini.

A Swiss village, early 19th cent.: The orphan *Amina is to marry the wealthy farmer *Elvino. She is grateful to the mill-owner, *Teresa, who has been like a mother to her. The inn hostess, *Lisa, in love with Elvino, is jealous. During the civil wedding, Count *Rodolfo returns to claim his lands. He flirts with Lisa. Through the window comes Amina. Lisa, not realizing that Amina is sleepwalking, assumes she has come to meet Rodolfo and reports this to Elvino. Rodolfo leaves the sleeping Amina to rest on the sofa, where Elvino and Lisa find her. Waking, she swears she is innocent, but Elvino cancels the wedding ceremony. The villagers seek Rodolfo to ask him to explain the truth, as also do Amina and Teresa. Elvino announces he will marry Lisa instead. Amina is seen sleepwalking across the roof of the mill. Now convinced, Elvino puts his ring back on her finger and she awakes to find him with her. The villagers escort them to their wedding.

Sonora (Puccini: *La fanciulla del West*). Bar. The leader of the gold miners. He fights with the sheriff, Jack Rance, because both men are interested in Minnie. She intervenes and separates them. Created (1910) by Dinh Gilly.

Sonyetka (Shostakovich: *Lady Macbeth of the Mtsensk District*). Cont. A young convict killed by Katerina Ismailova, jealous when her lover showed interest in the girl. Created (1934) by Nadezhda Welter.

Sophie 1. (Massenet: *Werther*). Sop. Fifteen-year-old sister of Charlotte. Created (1892) by Fr. Mayerhofer.

2. (Strauss: *Der Rosenkavalier*). *See* FANINAL, SOPHIE VON.

Sorcerer, The (Sullivan). Lib. by W. S. Gilbert; 2 acts; f.p. London 1877, cond. Arthur Sullivan.

Ploverleigh, an English village, 19th cent.: Sir Marmaduke *Poindextre's son Alexis *Poindextre is engaged to Lady *Sangazure's daughter Aline *Sangazure. Constance *Partlet loves Dr *Daly, the vicar of the village. Sir Marmaduke and Lady Sangazure are also in love. Alexis asks the sorcerer, John Wellington *Wells, to find a potion which will make everyone fall in love with the first person he

sees—married people to be excluded. Wells puts his potion in the drinks at the village tea-party and everyone gets mixed up with the wrong partner. They are saved only when Wells agrees to die in order to negate the effect of the potion. He disappears in a flash of fire and the various lovers are then correctly paired.

Sorceress (Purcell: *Dido and Aeneas*). Mez. Determined to bring about Dido's downfall, she sends her disguised 'trusty elf' to tell Aeneas he must leave at once for Italy—she knows this will result in Dido's death. Created (1683/4) by an unknown schoolgirl.

Sorel, John (Menotti: *The Consul*). Bar. Husband of Magda, he is hunted by the secret police for taking part in a clandestine meeting. He flees the country, leaving behind his wife and baby. When the baby dies, he returns to be with Magda, but is arrested almost at once. Created (1950) by Cornell MacNeill.

Sorel, Magda (Menotti: *The Consul*). Sop. Wife of John Sorel and mother of their baby. When her husband flees the country to escape arrest by the secret police, Magda tries to obtain a visa to join him. Her attempts to see the Consul are frustrated by the bureaucratic Secretary. The baby dies and John returns to be with his wife. Magda, hoping to forestall the police, kills herself so her husband will have no reason to stay. But it is too late—he has been arrested. Created (1950) by Patricia Newey.

Sorrow (or Trouble) (Dolore) (Puccini: *Madama Butterfly*). Silent. The young son of Butterfly and Pinkerton, born after his father has returned to America. Creator (1904) unknown.

Sosostris, Mme (Tippett: *The Midsummer Marriage*). Cont. A clairvoyant, summoned by King Fisher to untangle the mysteries surrounding his daughter and her fiancé and their rather strange friends who dance before the temple on midsummer day. Sosostris is a vague figure, not really human, more like an oracle of ancient times. 'I am what has been, is and shall be'. Created (1955) by Oralia Dominguez.

Sou-Chong, Prince (Lehár: *The Land of Smiles*). Ten. A Chinese prince, he falls in love with Lisa in Vienna and she returns with him to Peking, where he has been declared Prime

Minister. Their cultural differences cause problems, especially his uncle's insistence that he follow Chinese custom and take four wives. Lisa cannot tolerate this and leaves Peking. Despite his love for her, he accepts that this is the only real solution and lovingly bids her farewell. Arias: *Von Apfelblüten einen Kranz* ('A crown of apple blossoms'); *Dein ist mein ganzes Herz* ('Yours is my heart alone'). Created (1929) by Richard Tauber. This latter aria became Tauber's signature tune (widely known as 'You are my heart's delight') and he sang the role and the song round the world.

Spalanzani (Offenbach: *Les Contes d'Hoffmann*). Ten. An inventor who made the mechanical doll Olympia, with whom Hoffmann falls in love. Created (1881) by Mons. Gourdon.

Sparafucile (lit. **Shotgun**) (Verdi: *Rigoletto*). Bass. A professional assassin hired by Rigoletto to kill the Duke of Mantua, who has seduced Rigoletto's daughter Gilda. Sparafucile's sister Maddalena agrees to help him by posing as a whore in a tavern and attracting the Duke to her. Maddalena urges her brother to let the Duke go free, and he agrees to do so on condition that whoever enters the inn next will be killed in his place. The next person to enter is killed—it is Gilda in disguise. Created (1851) by Feliciano Ponz.

Spärlich (**Slender**) (Nicolai: *Die lustigen Weiber von Windsor*). Ten. Chosen as a husband for Anna Reich by her father. Created (1849) by Eduard Mantius.

Speaker (Stravinsky: *Oedipus Rex*). Spoken. Announces that a story will unfold which will reveal the truth about Oedipus. Created (1927) by Pierre Brasseur.

Spermando (Ligeti: *Le Grand Macabre*). *See* ARMANDO.

Spirit Messenger (**Der Geisterbote**) (Strauss: *Die Frau ohne Schatten*). Bar. Messenger of Keikobad, ruler of the spirit world. He visits the Nurse to inform her that Keikobad has decreed that unless his daughter, the Empress, casts a shadow (i.e. becomes pregnant) within three days, the Emperor will be turned to stone. When the Nurse shows a total lack of feeling for humanity, the Spirit Messenger prevents her entering Keikobad's temple,

throws her into a boat and condemns her to spend the rest of her days wandering amongst those she hates. Created (1919) by Josef von Manowarda.

Spoletta (Puccini: *Tosca*). Ten. A police agent who assists Scarpia in the arrest and torture of Cavaradossi. After Tosca agrees to Scarpia's condition for Cavaradossi's release—that she must give herself to the Baron—Scarpia tells her there must be a mock execution and he gives his orders for this to take place to Spoletta: '...as in the case of Palmieri', says the Baron, and Spoletta repeats his orders: '*Just* like Palmieri'. Created (1900) by Enrico Giordani.

Sportin' Life (Gershwin: *Porgy and Bess*). Ten. A pedlar of dope ('happy dust'). Gives some to Bess and, under its influence, she leaves for New York while Porgy is being questioned by the police. Created (1935) by John W. Bubbles.

Squeak (Britten: *Billy Budd*). Ten. A ship's corporal. Claggart uses him to spy on Billy. Created (1951) by David Tree.

Stanislao, King (Verdi: *Un giorno di regno*). King of Poland (who does not appear in the opera) at the time of the wars of the Polish succession. His right to the throne has been challenged. To keep attention away from him, his friend Belfiore poses as King. *See* BELFIORE (2).

Stankar, Count (Verdi: *Stiffelio*). Bar. A retired colonel, father of Lina and father-in-law of the priest Stiffelio. He suspects his daughter of having had an affair in her husband's absence. He forbids her to confess to her husband, and himself kills her lover. Created (1850) by Filipo Colini. *See also* EGBERTO.

Stanley, Major-General (Sullivan: *The Pirates of Penzance*). Bar. Father of Mabel and other daughters. Aria: *I am the very model of a modern major-general*. Created (NY, 1879) by J. H. Ryley.

Starveling 1. (Britten: *A Midsummer Night's Dream*). Bar. A tailor, one of the rustics who perform a play for Duke Theseus and Hippolyta. Takes the part of Moonshine. Aria: *This lanthorn doth the horned moon present*. Created (1960) by Joseph Ward.

2. (Purcell: *The Fairy Queen*). Spoken. Similar to the role in (1) above. Creator (1692) unknown.

Stasi, Countess (Anastasia, Countess) (Kálmán: *Die Csárdásfürstin*). Sop. A cousin of Prince Edwin, whose parents want him to marry her and announce his engagement. His true love, Sylva, turns up at their party and Stasi falls in love with Sylva's escort, Count Boni. Created (1915) by Susanne Bachrich.

Steersman (Wagner: *Der fliegende Holländer*). Ten. Daland's steersman. Aria: *Mit Gewitter und Sturm aus fernem Meer* ('Through thunder and storm, from distant seas'). Created (1843) by Wenzel Bielezizky.

Stella (Offenbach: *Les Contes d'Hoffmann*). Sop. An opera singer with whom Hoffmann is in love. She is the model for all the other women loved by him—Olympia, Antonia, and Giulietta—but she deserts him and leaves with Lindorf. Created (1881) by Adèle Isaac.

Stéphano (Gounod: *Roméo et Juliette*). Sop. *Travesti* role. Page to Romeo. Created (1867) by Mlle Daram.

Števa (Janáček: *Jenůfa*). See BURYJA, ŠTEVA.

Stiffelio (Verdi). Lib. by Francesco Maria Piave; 3 acts; f.p. Trieste 1850, cond. Giuseppe Verdi.

Germany, early 19th cent.: The minister *Stiffelio is away preaching. His wife *Lina has an affair with *Raffaele. Her father, *Stankar, forbids her to confess to her husband and he challenges Raffaele to a duel. During the fight, Stiffelio returns. On hearing the truth about Raffaele and Lina, he wants to fight Raffaele himself. The old minister, *Jorg, reminds Stiffelio of his standing as a minister of the faith. Stiffelio offers to divorce Lina, who protests her love for him. She appeals to him as a minister to hear her confession and tells him that, in her heart, she still loves him. Deciding to punish Raffaele, Stiffelio sees Stankar emerge from the next room, in which he finds Raffaele's body—Stankar has killed him. In the church, Stiffelio is about to preach and Stankar and Lina are in the congregation. He opens the Bible at the story of the woman taken in adultery. By reading this to the congregation, Stiffelio publicly forgives his wife. See also AROLDO.

Stiffelio (Verdi: *Stiffelio*). Ten. A Protestant minister, once the leader of a persecuted sect. He lived in the house of his supporter, Stankar, whose daughter Lina he married. The older minister, Jorg, worries that Stiffelio's love for his wife detracts from his devotion to the church. Stiffelio returns from a preaching mission and is told of a man seen escaping from a lady's bedroom window, dropping his notebook as he ran. The notebook is handed to Stiffelio, who burns it, not wishing to read of what is clearly an adulterous relationship, and all are impressed by his morality. However, Lina and Raffaele are agitated—they are the couple involved and her father is clearly suspicious. When the truth comes out, Stiffelio is devastated. He tells Lina their marriage can be annulled and, despite her protests, encourages her to sign the necessary forms. She asks that he, now not as her husband but as a minister, hear her confession. Moved by her protestations of love, Stiffelio returns to the church to preach. He opens the Bible at the story of the woman taken in adultery. Created (1850) by Gaetano Fraschini. See also AROLDO.

Stolzing, Walther von (Wagner: *Die Meistersinger von Nürnberg*). Ten. A young Franconian knight who is visiting Nuremberg. He has fallen in love with Pogner's daughter Eva. Walther's first appearance is in church, as he attracts Eva's attention and she gives her nurse, Magdalene, the slip and meets Walther after the service. Magdalene returns in time to hear him asking Eva if she is already engaged to be married, and tells him that Eva has been offered by her father as the prize to the winner of the forthcoming song-contest. Only members of the Mastersingers' Guild are allowed to enter the competition, as Pogner is determined his daughter must marry a Master. Magdalene's sweetheart, David, instructs Walther in the art of singing required for the competition. Walther is staggered to hear of all the rules which apply, and cannot imagine how he is going to become a Master and win the contest. As Pogner appears, Walther asks him to allow him to take part in the contest. Pogner agrees (after all, a noble knight as son-in-law appeals to him) but insists that Walther must abide by the rules and this involves an audition. To the gathered Masters, Pogner proposes Walther as a possible candidate. Walther explains that he learned how to sing from reading the works of Walther von der Vogelweide, a 12th-cent. Minnesinger. He sings his song and is laughed at by them all, especially Beckmesser, who acts as 'marker' and fills his slate with adverse marks. However, Hans Sachs has realized that for all his lack of experience and ignorance of the rules, Walther's singing has an artistic quality which deserves consideration. That night Walther meets Eva and tells her he has no chance of winning the contest and asks if she is prepared to elope with him, to which plan she agrees. But Sachs has overheard their conversation and knows this would lead to disaster. He keeps an eye on them that evening as Beckmesser comes to serenade Eva and the whole town, disturbed by his noise, starts a riot. Hoping to escape under cover of this noise, Eva and Walther are foiled by Sachs, who pushes her into her father's house and drags Walther into his shop. The next morning, Walther tells Sachs he had a dream and Sachs encourages him to use his dream as the basis for the song he will sing in the contest. Sachs also explains to him how the Masters' rules are there to uphold tradition and are not to be scoffed at. As Walther sings his song, Sachs gives him hints on the way it should be performed, the key relationships, harmonies, number of verses, etc. Sachs now sends Walther to dress appropriately for the competition and when he emerges Eva has arrived, also adorned for the day in white. She has come to ask the cobbler to adjust her shoes, but she and Walther stare at each other in such a way that it is quite obvious to Sachs that they are deeply in love. Walther demonstrates his song to Eva who is totally overwhelmed by it and grateful to Sachs for helping him. At the song contest, Beckmesser sings first—he has stolen Walther's song but he has no idea how to render it and makes a laughing-stock of himself. Sachs then invites the Masters to hear Walther sing the same song, and as he does so it is clear that he will be the winner. He is taken to the throne where Eva sits and he kneels before her as she places the victor's wreath on his head. Her father steps forward to put the Masters' chain of office round Walther's neck, but at this point the young knight rebels and announces that he does not wish to belong to this Guild whose members made things so difficult for him at his audition. Sachs points out to him that he is

the winner not because he is of noble birth, but because of his artistic ability—he should not repulse membership of the Guild or mock German Art. Contrite, Walther agrees to accept their honour. Eva takes the victor's wreath from him and places it on Sachs's head. Sachs, in his turn, takes the chain from Pogner and puts it round Walther's neck. Arias: *Am stillen Herd in Winterzeit* ('At the quiet hearth in wintertime'); *'Fanget an!'* (' "Begin!" '); *'Morgenlich leuchtend in rosingen Schein'* (' "Shining in the morning's rosy light" '); quintet (with Eva, Sachs, David, and Magdalene): *Selig, wie die Sonne* ('As blissfully as the sun').

Walther von Stolzing is the typical impetuous youth, madly in love, ready to discard all the old traditions by which the Masters have lived, but susceptible to the gentle but persuasive handling meted out by Hans Sachs, whom he learns to respect. It is not a *Heldentenor* role in the same way as are those of Siegfried or Tristan, and can be—and has been—successfully sung by Mozartian tenors. Among famous Walthers one can single out Max Lorenz, Ludwig Suthaus, Hans Hopf, Wolfgang Windgassen, Rudolf Schock, Peter Anders, Jess Thomas, René Kollo, Alberto Remedios, Siegfried Jerusalem, Plácido Domingo, Gösta Winbergh, and Ben Heppner. Created (1868) by Franz Nachbaur.

Stolzius (Zimmermann: *Die Soldaten*). Bar. A draper in Armentières, in love with Marie and distressed by the affairs she has with several soldiers in the town. He poisons one of her lovers, Desportes, then kills himself. Created (1965) by Claudio Nicolai.

Storch, Christine (Strauss: *Intermezzo*). Sop. Wife of the conductor Robert Storch and mother of young Franz. She has an apparently shrewish nature, in contrast to her rather placid husband. In fact, she complains to her maid Anna, she would prefer it if Robert would sometimes be more masterful and less gentle with her, and she would then respect him more. Now he is about to leave for a concert engagement in Vienna and she and Anna are doing his packing. All the time she grumbles—either he is at home too much instead of having a normal job to go to every day, so he gets under her feet, or, as now, he leaves her by herself at home to look after their son and handle all the household bills and responsibilities. No sooner has he left than the telephone rings and a friend invites her to go skating. On the toboggan run she bumps into the young Baron Lummer. Blaming him at first for the accident, she changes her attitude when she realizes who he is and she goes dancing with him at a nearby inn. She helps him find suitable and cheap lodgings but he soon asks her for money to help him with his studies. He must wait for that kind of help, she says, until her husband returns. A letter arrives for Robert, which Christine opens. It is couched in affectionate terms, asks for tickets for the opera, and suggests they meet afterwards, and is signed Mieze Maier. She at once assumes the worst, sends Robert a telegram accusing him of being unfaithful and announcing that she will divorce him. She talks to their son, telling him how much better a person she is than his father. She visits her solicitor and starts divorce proceedings. At home she starts to pack all her things, having sent Baron Lummer to Vienna to try to discover the identity of the unknown Mieze Maier. Then Stroh arrives, ready to explain the whole misunderstanding. Delighted that it is all sorted out and eagerly awaiting her husband's return, Christine nevertheless greets him coldly, implying that the mistake was all his in the first place. To her astonishment—and secret delight—he rounds on her and tells her exactly what he thinks of her behaviour, before storming out of the room. The Baron arrives and Storch comes in, pretending he is jealous of Christine's relationship with Lummer. But she soothes him with the news that she is bored with the younger man and his demands for money. Christine and Robert are now free for a great reconciliation. Duet (with Robert): *Es ist sicher kein Gaune* ('I'm sure he's no crook'). Created (1924) by Lotte Lehmann.

Legend has it that Pauline Strauss did not know the subject of her husband's latest opera until she attended the première. Lotte Lehmann had spent time at the Strauss house, studying Pauline's way of talking and moving and it was clear that the opera was based on reality. There had indeed been an episode in 1902 when Pauline had threatened divorce. Her husband had received a letter from a lady which was meant for another conductor. It was hardly a loveletter, being couched in quite formal terms and asking for some opera tickets, but Pauline assumed her husband was having an affair and went to see her solicitor.

In recent years the more famous exponents of the role have been Hanni Steffek, Elisabeth Söderström, Lucia Popp, and Felicity Lott. *See also* ARTICLE BY DAME FELICITY LOTT, p. 284.

Storch, Franz (Strauss: *Intermezzo*). Spoken. The 8-year-old son of Christine and Robert Storch. Known to his family as *der kleine Franzl* ('little Franz'). When his mother believes her husband is having an affair, she sits next to the child's bed and tells him how terrible his father is. The child, who worships his father, does not want to listen and defends his father. Created (1924) by Fritz Sonntag.

Storch, Robert (Strauss: *Intermezzo*). Bar. Hofkapellmeister, husband of Christine and father of young Franz. He is a famous conductor and much in demand. He is about to leave for Vienna and his wife is packing his suitcases and trunks and grumbling about him all the time. But he has heard it all before and smiles knowingly. Whilst in Vienna, Storch and his colleagues, including another conductor, Kapellmeister Stroh, play his favourite card game of Skat. The men are discussing Storch's affable nature as opposed to his shrewish wife, but he defends her, saying how he finds her stimulating—and anyway, he knows what she is truly like deep down. At this point a telegram arrives for him from Christine telling him that she is going to divorce him—she has opened a letter to him from one Mieze Maier and has assumed the worst. His distress is obvious as he hurriedly leaves the room. He wanders round the Prater in Vienna, quite distraught—he cannot explain who the writer of the letter is, as he does not know her, and he cannot return to his home because of his engagements in Vienna. Stroh finds him and explains that the letter was meant for *him*, and that Mieze Maier has mixed up their names. Furious, Storch insists that Stroh return at once to prove this to Christine. When Storch returns home, Christine is quite cold with him, but for once he does not take her nagging lying down—he gives her a long overdue piece of his mind and storms out of the room. When he returns, he displays jealousy over Christine's relationship with Baron Lummer, but she quickly assures him she is bored with the young man and there is a final scene of passionate reconciliation. Duet (with Christine): *Es ist sicher kein Gaune*

CHRISTINE STORCH (*Intermezzo*—Strauss)

by Dame Felicity Lott

I have sung Christine in two productions of *Intermezzo*: first at Glyndebourne in 1983, in English, and in Munich, from 1988 onwards, in German. The Glyndebourne production, by John Cox, was very glamorous, with a parade of gorgeous 1920s clothes designed by Martin Battersby. Learning it first in English was a tremendous bonus for me (and presumably for the audience, too). *Intermezzo* is really a play that just incidentally happens to be sung, and Christine never stops talking—mostly in song, but occasionally she breaks into speech, and sliding in and out of the two idioms is surprisingly difficult! The music almost never stops, so one has to time the speech quite carefully. One passage I could never learn, in either language, was when she struggles with her accounts, adding up columns of figures aloud, with Baron Lummer supplying most of the answers. I always had to have the numbers written down—they are pretty elementary ($7 + 4 = 11$, $+ 3 = 14$, etc.), but somehow the combination of song, speech, and mathematics was more than my brain could handle!

Christine is, of course, Strauss's beloved wife Pauline, who must have been a prickly character. That Strauss loved her is not in doubt, and his stage persona, Robert Storch, tells his friends that he much prefers a wife who is outwardly difficult but who has a good heart—though some of the stories about her make one wince. I was very flattered when a grandson of Richard Strauss, whom I met after a performance of *Intermezzo* in Munich, said he wished his grandmother had been like me! Strauss portrays Christine as a many-faceted character, quite unpredictable and certainly not dull. She's a dreadful nag to her husband in the first scene (when he's about to leave for some months in Vienna); she's very short with the servants; and she's rather girlish with Baron Lummer when she thinks (mistakenly) that someone is interested in *her* for a change. To the Baron she launches into a long hymn of praise of her husband, reveals her loneliness when he has to leave her, and totally loses her temper when she thinks Robert is being unfaithful with Mieze Maier (based, of course, on a real incident in the Strauss marriage). Christine is a huge challenge to play, and just about the most wonderful role I've ever done, although I thought I would never be able to learn it. Musically it is very difficult and it's also extremely long, comparable with Isolde in terms of singing-time on stage.

Clothes are quite a feature, with about ten quick changes of costume in the wings— the music doesn't stop, so you have to stand like a dummy while dressers peel clothes off, slide new ones on, tidy hair, fix hats, powder nose, offer water, and then rush back on! I will never forget my first costume fitting in Munich. At that time, I hadn't ever done a new production in Germany, so I hadn't been involved in long rehearsals to get to grips with the language: my German was rudimentary—'*Butter, bitte*'—that sort of thing. The costume designers and fitters all spoke with thick Bavarian accents and I couldn't understand a word. I could *feel* them thinking: 'How is this pathetic woman going to cope with this huge role in our theatre in Strauss's home town?' But scripted is always easier than unscripted and with time I even managed to work in a bit of Bavarian here and there [her German is now fluent—Ed.]. The producer was Kurt Wilhelm and we got on famously from the start. I kept putting in bits of John

Cox's 'business' from Glyndebourne, e.g. trying to pack the lampshades in the suitcase, and he loved all of them—John should have had a credit in the programme! Gustav Kuhn conducted in both productions: I shall always be grateful to him for recommending me to Wolfgang Sawallisch, then music director in Munich.

After you have ranted and raged, laughed and cried, tobogganed, danced, harangued lawyers, landladies, servants, gold-digging suitors, and changed clothes in between each outburst, husband comes home and Strauss pulls out all the stops and, for the reconciliation scene, produces the most demanding music of the evening. I still think it's my favourite role!

('I'm sure he's no crook'). Created (1924) by Josef Correck, who for the première was made up to look like Strauss. The stage set was deliberately designed to resemble the room in the Strausses' home and the story was based on a true episode in their marriage, which Strauss had found extremely painful. After Correck other well-known singers of Storch have included Alfred Jerger, Dietrich Fischer-Dieskau, and Hermann Prey.

Street Singer (Weill: *The Threepenny Opera*). Bar. (doubles the role of Tiger Brown). Early in the action, sings the famous aria *Mack the Knife*. Created (1928) by Kurt Gerron.

Strephon 1. (Sullivan: *Iolanthe*). Bar. Son of the fairy Iolanthe and the mortal Lord Chancellor, a fairy 'down to the waist'. An Arcadian shepherd, he is in love with Phyllis, ward of the Lord Chancellor who also wants to marry her. Iolanthe reveals herself to her husband in order to plead for her son. Aria: *Good morrow, good mother*; duet (with Phyllis): *None shall part us from each other*. Created (1882) by Richard Temple.

2. (Tippett: *The Midsummer Marriage*). Dancer. Leader of the dancers who perform the Ritual Dances in front of the temple on midsummer day. At the end, as Mark and Jenifer are united, he dies at their feet—the ultimate sacrifice. Created (1955) by Permin Trecu.

Stroh (Strauss: *Intermezzo*). A conductor. A friend of Robert Storch, the two men often playing cards together. While they are both working in Vienna, a young lady, having confused the two conductors, writes to Stroh in affectionate terms but sends the letter by mistake to Storch's house. It is opened by Storch's wife Christine, who immediately decides to divorce her husband. Stroh is sent to see her with proof of her husband's innocence. Created (1924) by Hanns Lange.

Stromminger (Catalani: *La Wally*). Father of Wally. Created (1892) by Ettore Brancaleoni.

Struhan (Strauss: *Der Rosenkavalier*). *See* MAJOR-DOMO (1).

Stuarda, Maria (Mary Stuart) (Donizetti: *Maria Stuarda*). Sop. (but sometimes sung by mez.). Mary, Queen of Scots, daughter of James V and mother of James VI of Scotland (James I of England), whose father was Lord Darnley, her second husband. Imprisoned in Fotheringay Castle by Queen Elizabeth I, her cousin and rival for the throne and the love of the Earl of Leicester. She is visited in gaol by the Queen, with disastrous results. Elizabeth accuses her of treason and of being involved in Darnley's murder. She in turn calls Elizabeth a 'vile bastard'. Now nothing can save her. Leicester's pleas for mercy go unheeded as Elizabeth signs Mary's death warrant and orders Leicester to witness her execution. Talbot hears her confession and her last wish is that she be escorted to the scaffold by her companion Hannah (Anna) Kennedy. She maintains her innocence and her dignity to the end. Arias: *Guarda: su' prati appare...* ('Look: in these fields appear...'); *Deh! Non piangete!* ('Alas! Do not weep!'). Created (1834, as Bianca) by Giuseppina Ronzi de Begnis; (1835) by Giacinta Puzzi-Tosi. *See also* ARTICLE BY DAME JANET BAKER, p. 286.

Suleyman, Pasha (Corigliano: *The Ghosts of Versailles*). Spoken. He hosts a party at the Turkish Embassy and entertains Beaumarchais, Queen Marie Antoinette, and all the

MARY STUART   (*Maria Stuarda*—Donizetti)

by Dame Janet Baker

'Why on earth do you want to play Mary Stuart, she's such a silly woman.' This reaction from a friend of mine has justification, regarded from the viewpoint of English history. From Donizetti's, which was shared by almost all Europe and certainly by Mary herself, the Catholic position was quite clear: Elizabeth was a usurper and Mary the rightful sovereign of England. Such an attitude puts a different light on all Mary's behaviour, misguided and ill-advised as she may have been, and was the one I tried to cultivate in my study of the opera. I deliberately refrained from reading any material about her and concentrated only on the woman who emerged from the composer's score.

She is an absolute gift for the singer: each scene paints a different side of her character, musically and dramatically. Her first appearance, as a vulnerable young woman let out into the air from her prison, leads on to a passionate expression of womanhood in her scene with Leicester and then the final extraordinary confrontation with Elizabeth, which demands the utmost in physical and emotional energy.

Maria Stuarda is written in such a way that all the singing takes place in consecutive scenes and asks a great deal of the performer, since there is no chance to rest the voice between appearances. The only chances for recovery are the intervals between acts, of course, and one gap for Elizabeth's part in Act II, but it is preferable for a singer to have shorter scenes which allow her to leave the stage more often. Donizetti doesn't do this here and the tremendous vocal concentration necessary to sustain the role entails careful pacing if one is to survive with enough in reserve for the final scenes.

Pacing a role is not back-pedalling in any way—the singing goes on just the same but the energy-drain is carefully controlled so that enough emotional resources are available at all times. It takes great experience to judge exactly what is needed so that one phrase is not favoured at the expense of another. But it is vital for the individual to learn what those needs are and how much personal energy is there to be drawn upon.

In Act 1, Mary goes from playful young woman to imperious queen. In Act 2 she is older, lacking in vitality and hope. She has to summon up more and more charisma as the opera moves to its close and the great confession scene strips her of all pretence, all illusion. Cleansed of her guilt and of the past, she is prepared for the final 'goodbye' to her faithful courtiers. Her make-up, wig, and costume change and she is transformed into the younger, attractive Mary, ready to face death with a courage which she will inspire in the chorus who surround her in the final scenes. For me, this was always a very important point in the opera. When one is on stage with many people, all acting their parts with integrity, an enormous feeling of strength and goodwill flows between the performers. They helped me to give everything I had for the rest of the opera, especially when I was aware that my own energy levels were low. The atmosphere stemming from the chorus replenished me and gave me tremendous support.

Whatever one may believe about the historical Mary, one thing emerges: her undeniable effect on the people who surrounded her. Her small group of faithful friends who suffered incarceration with her, and even her gaolers, were suffused with human compassion for this woman. To inspire that kind of devotion for so many years without hope of reward (she had nothing to give) suggests a person of quite remarkable character. This was the Mary I thought about, tried to imagine, and grew to know during the months of study and the weeks of rehearsal, and I loved her.

One point about singing the *bel canto* repertoire. For singers, composers like Donizetti are heaven, because they wrote at a time when the voice was paramount. They had to let the vocal sound come through the orchestral writing or the audience would soon have let them know about it. Well, times have changed; the glories of Verdi, Wagner, Puccini, and Strauss are without question, but it seems to me that the unique art of accompanying the voice takes second or even third place to the needs of orchestral sound and the demands of modern producers. Until such time as the voice, particularly the *young* voice, is protected with vigilance from the pit, we will continue to have stars with short careers.

Mary Stuart was a joy to sing and a joy to play. She remains for me a cherished memory.

Almaviva household. Created (1991) by Ara Berberian.

Sulpice (Donizetti: *La Fille du régiment*). Bass. A sergeant in the French Grenadiers, to whom Marie confesses her love for Tonio. Created (1840) by Mons. Henri (or Henry).

Suor Angelica (Sister Angelica) (Puccini: the second part of *Il trittico*). Lib. by Giovacchino Forzano; 1 act; f.p. NY 1918, cond. Roberto Moranzoni.

Italy, late 17th cent.: Sister *Angelica has been in a convent for seven years and is upset at having no news of her family during this time. The Principessa La *Zia (her aunt, the Princess), comes to visit her and tells her that the illegitimate child which Angelica had years ago has died. Now all Angelica wants is to join her child in heaven. She takes poison, then remembers that suicide is a mortal sin and she will be damned. She prays to the Madonna to forgive her. She sees a vision of the Madonna bringing her son to lead her into heaven.

Surin (Tchaikovsky: *The Queen of Spades*). Bass. Russian officer, friend of Hermann. Created (1890) by Hjalmar Frey.

Susanin, Ivan (Glinka: *A Life for the Tsar*). Bass. A peasant, loyal to the Tsar, father of Antonida. Concerned for the future of Russia and its safety from Polish invasion. When Polish soldiers come in search of the Tsar, he leads them into the forest, giving the Tsar chance to escape. When his deception is discovered, he is shot and hailed by his countrymen as a hero. Created (1836) by Osip Petrov.

Susanna 1. (Mozart: *Le nozze di Figaro*). Sop. Countess Almaviva's maid, about to marry Figaro, the Count's valet. They will live in rooms near their master and mistress, but Susanna knows the Count wants to seduce her. She plots with the Countess to catch him out in his amorous adventures. Aria: *Deh vieni, non tardar* ('Come now, do not delay'); duet (with Countess): *Che soave zeffiretto* ('What a gentle little breeze'). Created (1786) by Nancy Storace. Arguments continue as to whether this or Baron Ochs (*Der Rosenkavalier*) is the longest role in all opera. Certainly there is very little time during the opera when Susanna is not on the stage and it is a long and tiring role. It should not be regarded as a typical soubrette part, as it demands far more from its singer than the average 'cunning servant-girl' to which that term is applied. There have been many delightful Susannas over the years. In the 20th century alone, the list is formidable, including Audrey Mildmay (wife of John Christie of Glyndebourne), Maria Cebotari, Adele Kern, Irmgard Seefried, Alda Noni, Hilde Gueden, Jeanette Sinclair, Rita Streich, Anna Moffo, Graziella Sciutti, Anneliese Rothenberger, Edith Mathis, Mirella Freni, Reri Grist, Ileana Cotrubas, Marie McLaughlin, Sylvia

McNair, Alison Hagley, Rebecca Evans, Dorothea Röschmann, and Nuccia Focile.

2. (Wolf-Ferrari: *Il segreto di Susanna*). Sop. Countess, wife of Count Gil. He suspects her of having a lover, as he can smell tobacco on her and in their home. She keeps slipping out of the house by herself, he presumes to meet her admirer. Her secret is that she smokes, and she goes out to buy cigarettes. Gil returns unexpectedly one day while she is relaxing with a cigarette and catches her. Her secret is out. Created (1909) by Frau Tordel.

3. (Corigliano: *The Ghosts of Versailles*). Sop. Wife for the last twenty years of Figaro, Count Almaviva's valet. She is one of the characters summoned back by their creator, Beaumarchais, to help him rescue Marie Antoinette from her historical fate. Created (1991) by Judith Christin.

Susannah (Carlisle Floyd). Lib. by comp.; 2 acts; f.p. Tallahassee (Florida State Univ.) 1955, cond. Karl Kuersteiner. [NOTE: The story is updated from the Book of Susannah in the *Apocrypha*.]

Tennessee, present day: In the village, Susannah *Polk is taking part in a square dance, watched by the village *Elders and a visiting preacher, Olin *Blitch. Susannah lives with her brother Sam *Polk. She is escorted home by Little Bat *McLean, son of one of the village Elders, who hero-worships her. The Elders, looking for a pool for the communal baptisms, peer through trees and see the naked Susannah bathing. They denounce her as shameless and decree she must publicly confess her sinful behaviour or be excommunicated. She is ignored by everyone, though she has no idea what she's done to cause offence until Little Bat tells her. His parents are making him accuse her of seducing him. The preacher visits her at home to comfort her, but is overcome by his own feelings and takes her to bed, Susannah being too shattered to even protest. He discovers she is a virgin and tries to convince the Elders of her innocence, but they treat him with disdain. When Sam comes home and hears what has happened, he hunts down Blitch and shoots him. The villagers advance on Susannah's farm and threaten her, but she drives them away with a gun. Even the faithful Little Bat is rejected, leaving Susannah alone.

Susanna's Secret (Wolf-Ferrari). *See* SEGRETO DI SUSANNA, IL.

Suzuki (Puccini: *Madama Butterfly*). Mez. Butterfly's loyal and devoted servant. She does not believe that Pinkerton will come back to Butterfly and is not surprised when she learns the true reason for his return. She is fiercely protective towards her mistress, though cross with her for being so loyal to a man she feels is unworthy of such devotion. Duet (with Butterfly): *Scuoti quella fronda di ciliegio* ('Shake that branch of the cherry tree'). Created (1904) by Giuseppina Giaconia.

Svetozar (Glinka: *Ruslan and Lyudmila*). Bass. Grand Prince of Kiev, father of Lyudmila. Creator (1842) not traced.

Swallow (Britten: *Peter Grimes*). Bass. Lawyer and Magistrate. He is the Coroner at the inquest on Grimes's dead Apprentice, and decides the death was due to 'accidental circumstances'. Aria: *Peter Grimes, I here advise you;* quartet (with Nieces and Keene): *Assign your prettiness to me.* Created (1945) by Owen Brannigan.

Sweeney, Cathleen (Maw: *The Rising of the Moon*). Sop. Daughter of the local innkeeper in the Irish village where the 31st Royal Lancers are stationed. She is in love with young Cornet Beaumont. Created (1970) by Anne Howells.

Sylva (Kálmán: *Die Csárdásfürstin*). *See* VARESCU, SYLVA.

tabarro, Il (The Cloak) (Puccini: the first part of *Il trittico*). Lib. by Giuseppe Adami; 1 act; f.p. NY 1918, cond. Roberto Moranzoni.

Paris, about 1915: On *Michele's barge on the river Seine, he is aided by three stevedores, *Talpa, *Tinca, and *Luigi and Talpa's wife *Frugola. Michele's wife *Giorgetta goes to meet Luigi, her lover. Michele, suspicious, asks Giorgetta to remember their past happiness, but she avoids him and he is sure she has been unfaithful. He lights his pipe and Luigi mistakes the light as a signal from Giorgetta. Michele drags a confession out of him and then chokes him to death, hiding his body under his cloak and gleefully revealing it to Giorgetta.

Taddeo 1. (Rossini: *L'italiana in Algeri*). Bar. An old Italian who is shipwrecked with Isabella whom he loves and poses as her uncle when she makes plans to avoid the attentions of Mustafà, Bey of Algiers. Created (1813) by Paolo Rosich.

2. (Leoncavallo: *Pagliacci*). *See* Tonio (2).

Tadzio (Britten: *Death in Venice*). Silent dancer. A young, beautiful, Polish boy. Aschenbach is attracted to him and watches him playing beach games with his friends, but never plucks up the courage to speak to him. Created (1973) by Robert Huguenin.

Talbot 1. (Donizetti: *Maria Stuarda*). Bar./bass. Earl of Shrewsbury. He urges Elizabeth I to be merciful to her cousin Mary. When the Queen signs Mary's death warrant, Talbot hears Mary's confession before she walks to the scaffold. Created (1834, as Lamberto) by Federico Crespi; (1835) by Ignazio Marini.

2. (Bellini: *I Puritani*). Ten. Lord Arturo Talbot, a Cavalier in love with Elvira, daughter of a prominent Puritan. When he helps the French widowed Queen escape, Elvira thinks he is deserting her and goes mad. As he returns, the shock of hearing he is sentenced to death jolts her back to normality. They are united as the end of the Civil War is announced. Aria: *A te o cara* ('To you, beloved'). Created (1835) by Giovanni Battista Rubini.

Talpa (The Mole) (Puccini: *Il tabarro*). Bass. Husband of Frugola. He is a stevedore on Michele's boat. Created (1918) by Adamo Didur.

Tamara, Princess (Rubinstein: *The Demon*). Sop. Daughter of Prince Gudal, she is engaged to marry Prince Sinodal. The Demon has him killed and himself attempts to gain Tamara's love. When he kisses her for the first time, she dies. Created (1875) by Wilhelmina Raab.

Tamerlano (Handel). Lib. by Nicola Francesco Haym; 3 acts; f.p. London 1724.

Prusa, capital of Bothinia, *c.*1402: *Tamerlano (Tamburlaine), engaged to Princess *Irene, has defeated and captured *Bajazet, Emperor of the Turks. However, both Tamerlano and his ally *Andronico, unbeknown to each other, have fallen in love with Bajazet's daughter *Asteria. Bajazet refuses permission for Tamerlano to marry his daughter, even though Andronico has supported his plea, having been promised the throne and the Princess Irene in return for his loyalty should Tamerlano's suit prove successful. Andronico declares his own love for Asteria and she reciprocates. Tamerlano orders the death of Bajazet and Asteria but his plans are thwarted by Irene. Bajazet commits suicide. Tamerlano agrees to marry Irene, yielding Asteria to Andronico.

Tamerlano (Handel: *Tamerlano*). Cont. *Travesti* role (originally castrato). Emperor of the Tartars. Engaged to Irene, Princess of Trebisond. He defeats the Turkish Emperor Bajazet and falls in love with his daughter Asteria, but agrees to marry Irene, leaving Asteria free to marry his friend and ally Andronico. Created (1724) by Andrea Pacini (castrato).

Tamino (Mozart: *Die Zauberflöte*). Ten. An Egyptian Prince. Rescued from a snake by the Three Ladies, they show him a picture of Pamina, daughter of the Queen of Night, and he falls in love with her image. The Queen promises he can marry her if he rescues her from the 'evil' Sarastro. Aided (and at times hindered!) by the bird-catcher Papageno, he sets out to find her. Sarastro realizes they are in love but insists Tamino undergo severe trials to prove his worthiness. This he does and Sarastro gives them his blessing. Aria: *Dies Bildnis its bezaubernd schön* ('This picture is enchantingly beautiful'). Created (1791) by Benedikt Schack (whose wife created the Third Lady).

Tannhäuser (Wagner). Lib. by comp; 3 acts; f.p. Dresden 1845, cond. Richard Wagner.

Thuringia (near Eisenach), early 13th cent.: *Tannhäuser wants to be freed from the bacchantine orgy which goes on in the grotto of the Venusberg. With all its drawbacks, he prefers a human existence and begs *Venus to release him. She curses him and those who tempt him away. At the foot of the Venusberg he hears a *Shepherd singing of spring and watches pilgrims passing. The *Landgrave appears with his knights. They recognize Tannhäuser, who left their company years ago. Wolfram von *Eschenbach tells him *Elisabeth is missing him and he agrees to rejoin them. In the hall of the Wartburg castle, Wolfram (himself in love with her) leads Tannhäuser to meet Elisabeth. Wolfram announces a song contest in which the entrants, in their song, must clearly state the essence of love. The winner can marry Elisabeth. Walter von der *Vogelweide, *Biterolf, and Wolfram each sing, defining love in moral terms. Tannhäuser, when it is his turn, sees love as a sensual experience and advises them to visit the Venusberg to learn about it. The knights, disgusted, attempt to kill him, but Elisabeth intervenes. The Landgrave orders him to make a pilgrimage to Rome to beg forgiveness. In the Wartburg valley, Elisabeth vainly awaits his return. Dying, she is ready to sacrifice herself in his place. Tannhäuser returns—the Pope has refused forgiveness and he must accept eternal damnation. Wolfram prays to Elisabeth in heaven and Tannhäuser dies as her coffin is carried in. The pilgrims hail his forgiveness.

Tannhäuser (Wagner: *Tannhäuser*). Ten. A knight who has been lured away from the Wartburg by the beautiful Venus. He is now tired of the eternal debauchery in the Venusberg and would like to return to normal life, forgiven for his sin of giving in to temptation. The Landgrave and other Minnesingers whom he left, pass by and recognize him. They tell him that the Landgrave's niece, Elisabeth, has been unhappy since his departure and he agrees to return with them and take part in a singing contest, for which the prize will be Elisabeth's hand in marriage. The other contestants sing of the moral aspects of love, but Tannhäuser, remembering life at the Venusberg, sings of the sensual pleasures he experienced with Venus. The other knights threaten him with their swords, but Elisabeth steps between them. The Landgrave advises him to follow the pilgrims to Rome and beg forgiveness from the Pope. Elisabeth awaits his return, but he does not come with the other returning pilgrims and, exhausted, she prepares to die, while Wolfram waits outside to greet Tannhäuser. He arrives, tired and unhappy—the Pope has refused him absolution and he sees no alternative but to return to Venus. Wolfram tells him how Elisabeth prayed for him. Her funeral procession passes, and Tannhäuser falls down on her coffin and dies. Arias: *Ha, jetzt erkenne ich sie wieder die schöne Welt* ('Ha, now again I see the beautiful world'); duet (with Elisabeth): *Gepriesen sei die Stunde* ('Blessed hour of meeting'); *Inbrunst im Herzen* ('The heat within my heart'—Tannhäuser's Narration). Created (1845) by Joseph Tichatschek (who had created Rienzi in Dresden three years earlier).

Tantris (Wagner: *Tristan und Isolde*). This is the name under which Tristan first presents himself to Isolde, when he comes to seek her healing powers for a wound inflicted when he killed Morold, Isolde's betrothed. 'Tantris' is, of course, a simple anagram of 'Tristan'.

Tapioca (Chabrier: *L'Étoile*). Bar. Secretary to Hérisson, Ambassador to King Mataquin. Created (1877) by Mons. Jannin.

Tarquinius (Britten: *The Rape of Lucretia*). Bar. An Etruscan Prince who, having succeeded his father, has assumed power in Rome. He is determined to prove that no women are chaste, and rides to Rome to Lucretia's house. When she repels him, he rapes her. Aria: *Can you deny your love's dumb pleading?* Created (1946) by Otakar Kraus.

Tatyana (Tchaikovsky: *Eugene Onegin*). Sop. Daughter of Mme Larina and sister of Olga. She falls in love with Eugene Onegin when he is brought to their house by his friend Lensky, who loves Olga. Unable to sleep that night, Tatyana asks her old nurse about her own young days and how she knew when she was in love. She confesses her thoughts about Onegin to Filipyevna and then writes him a letter admitting her feelings for him. When next they meet, Onegin humiliates her by rejecting her love. At her birthday party she finds it difficult to respond when Mons. Triquet sings to her, and she morosely watches Onegin flirting with her sister. He is challenged to a duel by the jealous Lensky and Lensky is killed. Onegin leaves town. Tatyana marries the wealthy Prince Gremin. Two years later, at a ball in St Petersburg, she and Onegin meet again. He realizes he is in love with her and she admits that she still loves him. However, she is determined to remain loyal to Gremin and sends the now despairing Onegin away. Aria: *Puskay pogibnu ya* ('Even if it means I die'). This is the famous letter-song, a long 12-minute showpiece for the soprano. It is around this letter-song that Tchaikovsky developed much of the music for the opera. Tatyana was the character who attracted him to Pushkin's verse, rather than the Onegin of Pushkin's title. The role requires a dramatic soprano with great vocal flexibility. One of the most famous interpreters in recent years was Galina Vishnevskaya (wife of the cellist/conductor Mstislav Rostropovich), a fine dramatic singer. She chose this as her operatic retirement performance, in Paris in 1982. Created (1879) by Maria Klimentova, a 21-year-old student at Moscow Conservatory; she had a successful professional career, singing with the Bolshoy for ten years, and she continued to sing the role of Tatyana throughout her career.

Taupe, Monsieur (Strauss: *Capriccio*). Ten. The old man who acts as the prompter for the play being organised by the Count for his sister Madeleine's birthday. M. Taupe hides in a corner and falls fast asleep at the beginning of the rehearsal, waking up only after everyone has left. His name is a witty play on words by Strauss, Taupe being the French for 'mole'. Created (1942) by Carl Seydel.

Taverner (Maxwell Davies). Lib. by comp.; 2 acts; f.p. London 1972, cond. Edward Downes.
England, 16th cent.: In court, the composer John *Taverner is being tried by the *White Abbot for heresy. His wife Rose *Parrowe and his father Richard *Taverner give evidence against him. He is pardoned by the *Cardinal, who wants to retain him as musician. The *King wants to split from Rome, the Cardinal demurs, and the *Jester (later revealed as Death) tells of the selfish motives for their views. Death summons Taverner and preaches to him until the composer renounces music in favour of a patently false Jesus. After the Reformation, Taverner becomes the prosecutor and sentences the White Abbot to be burned at the stake. The people gather to watch. But it is Taverner who, by turning his back on music, has destroyed his own life.

Taverner, John (Maxwell Davies: *Taverner*). Ten. The composer, son of Richard, husband of Rose Parrowe. In pre-Reformation England, he is tried for heresy, but after the Reformation he sentences the White Abbot to death, while destroying his own creativity. Created (1972) by Ragnar Ulfung.

Taverner, Richard (Maxwell Davies: *Taverner*). Bar. Father of the composer, gives evidence against him in his trial as a heretic. Created (1972) by Gwynne Howell.

Tebaldo 1. (Bellini: *I Capuleti e i Montecchi*). Ten. A Capulet partisan and the husband chosen for Giulietta by her father. Created (1830) by Lorenzo Bonfigli.
   2. (Tybalt) (Gounod: *Roméo et Juliette*). Ten. Nephew of Capulet's wife. He is killed by Romeo in a duel, resulting in Romeo's exile from Verona. Created (1867) by Mons. Puget.
   3. (Verdi: *Don Carlos*). *See* THIBAULT.

Télaïre (Rameau: *Castor et Pollux*). Sop. Daughter of the Sun, beloved of the dead Castor, also loved by his twin Pollux. Created (1737) by Marie Pélissier.

Telemaco (Telemachus) (Monteverdi: *Il ritorno d'Ulisse in patria*). Ten. Son of Penelope and Ulisse. Created (1640) possibly by

Costantino Paolelli (whose mother and father are thought to have created his parents.)

Telephone, The (Menotti). Lib. by comp.; 1 act; f.p. New York 1947, cond. Leon Barzin.

*Lucy is obsessed by the telephone. *Ben tries to propose to her, but every time he reaches the crucial point in the conversation, the telephone rings and she has a long conversation with friends. In desperation he goes out and telephones her from a public telephone.

Tell, Guillaume (William Tell) (Rossini: *Guillaume Tell*). Bass. He is determined to free his country of Austrian domination. He saves a shepherd who has killed an Austrian soldier, and is caught by the tyrannical governor Gessler. To free himself, he has to shoot at an apple placed on his son's head. This he does successfully, but then he admits his plan to shoot Gessler. He is arrested. His son helps him to escape and defeat the Austrians. Created (1829) by Henri-Bernard Dabadie (whose wife created Tell's son, Jemmy).

Tell, Jemmy (Rossini: *Guillaume Tell*). Sop. *Travesti* role. Son of Guillaume (William) Tell. His father has to shoot at an apple perched on Jemmy's head. After Guillaume has been captured by Austrian troops, Jemmy helps him to fight and free Switzerland from Austrian domination. Created (1829) by Louise-Zulme Dabadie (whose husband created Guillaume Tell).

Telramund, Friedrich von (Wagner: *Lohengrin*). Bar. Count of Brabant. He was appointed by the dying Duke of Brabant to be guardian of the Duke's children, Elsa and Gottfried, the heir to the throne. Telramund is anxious to marry Elsa and share her inheritance. But she refuses him and he marries Ortrud instead and the two of them set about trying to gain the throne themselves. Gottfried has disappeared and Telramund accuses Elsa of murdering him, not knowing that Ortrud, who practises sorcery, has turned Gottfried into a swan. Telramund fights Elsa's champion, Lohengrin, and is defeated. Despondent, he is only too glad to let Ortrud plan the next step in their campaign and agrees with her suggestions for undermining Elsa's faith in Lohengrin. He is prepared, as part of this scheme, to accuse Lohengrin of sorcery. At the cathedral where Elsa and Lohengrin are to be married,

he tells Elsa that he will visit them that night and wound Lohengrin, who will then reveal his identity. But when he comes into their bridal chamber Elsa warns Lohengrin, who kills Telramund. Aria: *Dank, König, dir* ('Thank you, my lord'); *Durch dich musst' ich verlieren* ('It's you who have destroyed me'). Interpreters have included Jaro Prohaska, Hermann Uhde, Gustav Neidlinger, Ramon Vinay, Dietrich Fischer-Dieskau, Donald McIntyre, Leif Roar, Guillermo Sarabia, and Ekkehard Wlaschiha. Created (1850) by Feodor von Milde.

Tenor (Strauss: *Ariadne auf Naxos*). Ten. The tenor in the Prologue who will sing the role of Bacchus in the *opera seria. See* Bacchus.

Teresa 1. (Berlioz: *Benvenuto Cellini*). Sop. Daughter of Balducci, the papal treasurer. In love with the Florentine goldsmith Cellini. Created (1838) by Julie Dorus-Gras.

2. (Bellini: *La sonnambula*). Mez. Foster-mother of the orphaned Amina. Created (1831) by Felicità Baillou-Hilaret.

Terinka (Janáček: *The Cunning Little Vixen*). She is a gypsy girl. She does not appear in the opera, but is spoken of by the poacher Harašta, who marries her, and the Schoolmaster who also is in love with her.

Tessa (Sullivan: *The Gondoliers*). Mez. Chosen by the gondolier Giuseppe as his wife. Aria: *When a merry maiden marries*; quartet (with Gianetta, Marco, and Giuseppe): *O my darling ... do not forget you married me.* Created (1889) by Jessie Bond.

Thaddeus (Balfe: *The Bohemian Girl*). Ten. A polish nobleman and soldier, who takes refuge in a gypsy camp and falls in love with Arline, the eponymous heroine. Created (1843) by Mr W. Harrison.

Thaïs (Massenet: *Thaïs*). Sop. A 4th-cent. courtesan. Attempts to persuade her to give up her immoral life eventually succeed, but at the expense of her health. She dies, dreaming of divine forgiveness. Created (1894) by Sibyl Sanderson (the work being written for her, Massenet's favourite soprano at that time).

Thésée (Rameau: *Hippolyte et Aricie*). *See* Theseus (3).

Theseus 1. (Britten: *A Midsummer Night's Dream*). Bass. Duke of Athens, about to be married to Hippolyta. In their honour, the rustics perform their play, *Pyramus and Thisbe*. Aria: *The iron tongue of midnight hath told twelve (Lovers to bed)*. Created (1960) by Forbes Robinson.

2. (Purcell: *The Fairy Queen*). The Duke. Spoken. Similar to the role in (1) above. Creator (1692) unknown.

3. (Thésée) (Rameau: *Hippolyte et Aricie*). Bass. King of Athens, husband of Phèdre and father of Hippolyte by a previous marriage. Created (1733) by Chassé de Chinais.

Thibault (Verdi: *Don Carlos*). Sop. (Tebaldo in It. vers.) *Travesti* role. A page to Elisabeth de Valois, who brings the news that she is to marry King Philip of Spain, not his son to whom she is engaged. Created (Fr. vers. 1867) by Leonia Leviely; (It. vers. 1884) by Amelia Garten.

Thirza (Smyth: *The Wreckers*). Mez. Wife of the preacher Pascoe, in love with Mark. She disapproves of the villagers' luring of ships to be wrecked, and together with Mark she sabotages their efforts. As punishment, the lovers are walled up in a cave and left to drown as the tide rises. Created (1906) by Paula Doenges.

Thoas (Gluck: *Iphigénie en Tauride*). Bass. King of Tauris, who demands the sacrifice of Oreste and Pylade but is outwitted by Iphigénie. Created (1779) by Mons. Moreau.

Three Boys (or **Genii) (Drei Knaben)** (Mozart: *Die Zauberflöte*). Sop., sop., mez. (sometimes sung by boy trebles). They guide Tamino in his search for Pamina. Probably created (1791) by Anna (Nanny) Schikaneder (niece of the librettist) (1st), Pater Anselm Handelgruber (treble) (2nd), Franz Anton Maurer (treble) (3rd).

Three Ladies (Drei Damen) (Mozart: *Die Zauberflöte*). Sop., sop., mez. Attendants of the Queen of Night. They rescue Tamino from a serpent and show him a picture of the Queen's daughter Pamina, with whom he falls in love. Created (1791) by Mlle Klöpfer (1st), Mlle Hofman (2nd), and Elisabeth Schack (3rd) (whose husband created Tamino).

Threepenny Opera, The (Die Dreigroschenoper) (Weill). Lib. by Bertolt Brecht; 3 acts; f.p. Berlin 1928, cond. (from the piano) Theo Mackeben.

London, 1900: A *Street Singer tells of Mack the Knife (*Macheath) who has eloped with Mr and Mrs *Peachum's daughter Polly *Peachum. Her parents are determined to hand him over to the police. Macheath goes into hiding but he is given away by Jenny *Diver, a prostitute bribed by Mrs Peachum. He is arrested by Commissioner Tiger *Brown whose daughter Lucy was supposed to marry Macheath. With Lucy *Brown's help, Macheath escapes but is again betrayed and again arrested. Polly goes to say goodbye before he is hanged. At the last minute he is pardoned and released. He is given a castle, made a peer, and he and Polly are reunited. *See also* BEGGAR'S OPERA, THE.

Tichon (Janáček: *Katya Kabanová*). *See* KABANOV, TICHON IVANYČ.

Tiefland (The Lowlands) (d'Albert). Lib. by Rudolf Lothar [Rudolf Spitzer]; prol. & 2 acts; f.p. Prague 1903.

The Pyrenees and the Lowlands of Catalonia, early 20th cent.: On the mountains, the shepherd *Pedro dreams of marriage. Wealthy *Sebastiano and his mistress *Marta arrive. Deciding he wants to marry a *rich* girl, Sebastiano orders Marta to marry Pedro and go to live in the village below—but she must continue as his mistress. Marta insists that she and Pedro sleep in separate rooms, but realizing that Sebastiano is already in her room, she stays the night with Pedro. *Tommaso, the wise old man of the village, suggests to Marta that she tell her husband the truth. Pedro decides to return to the mountains, and Marta, now in love with him, begs to accompany him. When Sebastiano comes to look for Marta, he is confronted by Pedro, they fight and Pedro strangles him.

'Timida' (Strauss: *Die schweigsame Frau*). Name used by Aminta when she poses as a prospective wife for Sir Morosus, uncle of her husband Henry.

Timothy, Brother (Maw: *The Rising of the Moon*). The only monk remaining in the monastery now used as the officers' mess for the 31st Royal Lancers stationed in Ireland. Created (1970) by Alexander Oliver.

Timur (Puccini: *Turandot*). Bass. The blind exiled King of Tartary, father of Calaf (the Unknown Prince, who is to attempt to answer Turandot's three riddles). He has fled, aided only by the slave-girl Liù, and thought his son to be dead until he saw him in the crowd. Fearful that Calaf will be killed if his identity is known, Timur is determined to keep it a secret. He begs Calaf not to take part in Turandot's dangerous competition. Timur is arrested by Turandot's guards, who try to make him reveal the Unknown Prince's name. Created (1926) by Carlo Walter.

Tinca (The Tench) (Puccini: *Il tabarro*). Ten. A stevedore who helps on Michele's barge. He drinks heavily in order to forget the misery of his existence. Created (1918) by Angelo Bada.

Tiny (Britten: *Paul Bunyan*). Sop. Daughter of Paul Bunyan. She falls in love with Slim, the new cook and when the camp breaks up she goes to help him run a hotel in Manhattan. Aria: *Whether the sun shines (Mother, O Mother)*. Created (1941) by Helen Marshall.

Tiresias 1. (Stravinsky: *Oedipus Rex*). Bass. The blind Seer who refuses to help Oedipus discover the truth about the death of King Laius. He is accused by Oedipus of plotting to seize the throne of Thebes. Created (1927) by Kapiton Zaporojetz.
2. (Henze: *The Bassarids*). Ten. A blind old prophet. Created (1966) by Helmut Melchert.

Tisbe (Rossini: *La Cenerentola*). Mez. Daughter of Don Magnifico, sister of Clorinda and stepsister of Cenerentola. She is one of the 'ugly sisters' of the fairy-tale. Created (1817) by Teresa Mariani.

Titania 1. (Weber: *Oberon*). Spoken. Wife of Oberon, with whom she has quarrelled over the faithfulness of lovers. Created (1826) by Miss Smith.
2. (Purcell: *The Fairy Queen*). Spoken. Similar to the role in (1) above. Creator (1692) unknown. *See also* TYTANIA.

Tito Vespasiano, Emperor (Mozart: *La clemenza di Tito*). Ten. Roman emperor, anxious that his people see him not as a dictator but as a clement ruler. Loved by Vitellia who, jealous of his plan to marry someone else, plots his death. She fails and he forgives her and Sesto, her accomplice. Arias: *Del più sublime soglio...* ('From the most sublime throne...'); *Se all'impero, amici Dei* ('If from the empire, benevolent gods'). Created (1791) by Antonio Baglioni. *See also* ARTICLE BY MARTIN ISEPP, p. 295.

Titurel (Wagner: *Parsifal*). Bass. Father of Amfortas. He is a former ruler (the first) of the Kingdom of the Grail, and has now handed over to his son. Gurnemanz describes how Titurel was given the care of the Grail (the chalice from which Christ drank at the Last Supper) and the Spear (which was in Christ's side on the Cross). When he became too old to continue caring for these relics, Amfortas took over the responsibility. Titurel's voice is heard as he pleads with his son, now seriously injured, to perform the tasks of his office. Amfortas, weak and in pain, asks his father to do it himself, but Titurel says he is too old. Titurel dies, his funeral being the final scene in the opera. Created (1882) by August Kindermann. Although this is not a large role, and Titurel never appears on stage, only his voice being heard, many famous basses have happily sung the part. In this century these have included Richard Mayr, Josef von Manowarda, Josef Greindl, Hermann Uhde, Hans Hotter, Theo Adam, David Ward, Ludwig Weber, Martti Talvela, Karl Böhme, Karl Ridderbusch, Hans Sotin, and Matti Salminen.

Titus, Emperor (Mozart: *La clemenza di Tito*). *See* TITO VESPASIANO, EMPEROR.

Tizio (Mozart: *Così fan tutte*). Name used by Guglielmo in his Albanian disguise. *See* GUGLIELMO.

Toby 1. (Menotti: *The Medium*). Dancer. A mute servant boy to Mme Flora, the medium. She accuses him of clutching at her throat during a séance. Unable to deny it, he hides behind a curtain and she is convinced he is a ghost and shoots him. Created (1946) by Leo Coleman.
2. (Walton: *The Bear*). The horse (never seen) which belonged to Madame Popova's late husband. It is the price of Toby's oats which is the cause of the debt she must now settle.

Tolloller, Earl (Sullivan: *Iolanthe*). Ten. Member of the House of Lords. One of the many men in love with Phyllis. Aria: *Of all the*

TITO   (*La Clemenza di Tito*—Mozart)

by Martin Isepp

As befits a character created to celebrate the coronation of an emperor of the Enlightenment, Mozart makes Tito a noble figure whose music is invariably beautiful and melodic; however, *clemenza* is a very undramatic virtue and, moreover, Tito's main function in the plot is to be the catalyst for the treachery of others (Sesto, Vitellia, even Servilia, by her decision not to marry him). So the singer's greatest challenge is to make Tito interesting, charismatic, and believable. Throughout the opera his position and his goodness set him apart. In the only ensemble in which he appears (Trio, No. 18) he sings to Sesto *Avvicinata* (Approach) twice; apart from that, for all three characters, every line is an aside and so there is no real ensemble dramatically. In the Act 2 finale, all the others sing his praise in ensemble, but he sings alone, his isolation as complete as ever. His one dramatic aria (No. 20), 'If you need a hard heart to rule, either take away my empire or give me another heart' (*Se all'impero* ...) reaffirms, in its middle section, his noble credo: 'If I cannot get loyalty by love, I care nothing for loyalty born of fear', sentiments which explain why the magnificent choruses proclaim his people's love for him.

Tito perhaps suffers more than the other characters from the fact that Mozart was so pressed to complete the opera that he reportedly gave the composition of the secco recitatives to Süssmayr [Franz Xaver Süssmayr (1766–1803), the Austrian composer and conductor who assisted in the completion of Mozart's Requiem (K626)]. If he had written them himself, he would no doubt have put a lot of the 'character' into them, as was his wont. One can imagine a wonderfully dramatic scene between Tito and Sesto, his greatest friend, after he has been brought in to explain himself at the end of Act 2; but as it is, the exchanges which follow go for very little. However, Tito's two *orchestral* recitatives are enormously dramatic and go to the heart of the character. Act 2 sc. 7 sees him agonizing over whether to sign Sesto's death warrant, or to give him an opportunity to justify himself. Recitativo No. 25 contains the moment when, just as he is about to pardon Sesto, Vitellia confesses to being the real villain. Tito's anguished outburst, 'When, you just Gods, will I find one faithful soul?', can sound almost petulant, but I remember in Nicholas Hytner's production at Glyndebourne (1991), the eloquent fury with which Philip Langridge invested this passage, making it the emotional climax of his performance and causing the citizens of Rome to recoil before him.

Being *an opera seria*, harking back to an earlier style, there is a good case for extensive ornamentation, which can help all the principal characters to gain more flexibility in the vocal line. However, interpreters of the title role should respect the essential lyricism of his arias and sing the phrases with great simplicity, being careful not to let the ornamentation distort the vocal line. In that way, Tito's character comes over in all its noble integrity.

young ladies I know, duet (with Mountararat and chorus): *When Britain really ruled the waves*. Created (1882) by Durward Lely.

Tolomeo (Ptolemy) (Handel: *Giulio Cesare*). Cont. *Travesti* role (originally castrato). King of Egypt, brother of Cleopatra. Has Pompey beheaded and his widow (Cornelia) and son (Sesto) arrested. Is killed by Sesto in revenge for his father's murder. Created (1724) by Gaetano Berenstadt (alto castrato).

Tom (Henze: *The English Cat*). Bar. He chases and kisses his old girlfriend, Minette, now the bride of Lord Puff. Society demands that such behaviour results in divorce and Minette is then drowned. Tom is imprisoned, but released when found to be the long-lost son of a wealthy nobleman. He claims his inheritance and sets his cap at Babette, Minette's sister. He is killed before he can sign his will, so his money goes to society. Minette's ghost joins him in a duet as he dies. Created (1983) by Wolfgang Schöne.

Tommaso (d'Albert: *Tiefland*). Bass. The wise village elder, said to be 90 years old. Having heard how Marta came to be Sebastiano's mistress, he advises her to tell her husband, Pedro, the truth of her situation and feelings, and thus escape Sebastiano's influence for ever. Creator (1903) not traced.

Tomsky, Count (Tchaikovsky: *The Queen of Spades*). Bar. A friend to whom Hermann confesses his love of Lisa. Tomsky tells his fellow-officers of the Countess's youth in Paris, of how she was a gambler known as the Queen of Spades, and of how she came to possess the secret of the three cards which will always win. It is this secret which Hermann is determined to learn. Created (1890) by Ivan Mel'nikov.

Toni (Henze: *Elegy for Young Lovers*). *See* REISCHMANN, TONI.

Tonio 1. (Donizetti: *La Fille du régiment*). A Tyrolean peasant who saves Marie when she nearly falls off a precipice. They fall in love and he hangs around the camp to see her again and is arrested as a spy. He joins the Grenadiers to be eligible to marry her. She is removed from the regiment by the Marquise de Birkenfeld to a château, so he and the rest of the Grenadiers follow her. When the Marquise sees how much they are in love, she gives her consent to their

marriage. Duet (with Marie): *De cet aveu si tendre* ('Of that vow so tender'). Created (1840) by Mécène Marié de l'Isle.

2. (Leoncavallo: *Pagliacci*). Bar. Disabled member of a troupe of strolling players, led by Canio, whose wife, Nedda, Tonio covets. Nedda rejects him and in revenge he tells Canio that she has a lover, with tragic results. In the prologue, he informs the audience of the drama to follow: *Si può? Signore, Signori* ('By your leave, ladies and gentlemen'). Created (1892) by Victor Maurel.

Tony (Bernstein: *West Side Story*). Ten. A member of the Jet gang, he falls in love with Maria, sister of Bernardo, leader of a rival gang. Tony kills Bernardo. Maria forgives him, but he is informed mistakenly that she is dead and allows himself to be killed. Duets (with Maria): *Tonight; One hand, one heart*. Created (1957) by Larry Kert.

Torquemada (Ravel: *L'Heure espagnole*). Ten. A clockmaker, married to Concepción. While he is out each week setting the town's clocks, she is visited by her lovers. He pretends not to know what is going on and sells the clocks to the various men he finds hiding within them (they are hiding from him). Created (1911) by Mons. Cazeneuve.

Tosca (Puccini). Lib. by Giuseppe Giacosa and Luigi Illica; 3 acts; f.p. Rome 1900, cond. Leopoldo Mugnone.

Rome, 1800: In the church of S. Andrea della Valle, the *Sacristan potters about. When he leaves, the republican fugitive *Angelotti emerges from his hiding place. The painter *Cavaradossi helps him to hide from Baron *Scarpia's secret police. Scarpia lusts after Cavaradossi's lover, *Tosca, a prima donna. When Angelotti's escape is discovered, Cavaradossi is arrested by Scarpia's henchmen, the agent *Spoletta and the policeman *Sciarrone, and is tortured. Tosca promises herself to the hated Scarpia on condition that he allows Cavaradossi and herself to leave the country. He apparently agrees to this, but will have to stage a mock execution 'as in the case of *Palmieri'. As he approaches her, Tosca kills him. She is allowed to see Cavaradossi and tells him he will face a firing squad but Scarpia has promised her it will be a mock execution—when the soldiers leave him for dead, the two of them can then leave Rome. But Scarpia has tricked her and Cavaradossi is executed. Tosca throws herself from the battlements.

Tosca, Floria (Puccini: *Tosca*). Sop. A prima donna in love with the painter Cavaradossi, and desired by Baron Scarpia. She visits Cavaradossi in the church where he is painting a portrait of the Madonna. She accuses him of painting the face of the Madonna with the features of the beautiful Marchese Attavanti. What she does not know is that Cavaradossi has given shelter to the Marchese's brother Angelotti, an escaped political prisoner. Tosca departs and the Sacristan brings news of Bonaparte's defeat. To celebrate, Tosca will sing that evening at a concert in the Farnese Palace, residence of Scarpia. After the concert she is summoned to the Baron's room. Cavaradossi has been arrested and is being tortured to make him reveal Angelotti's hiding-place. He is guarded by Spoletta and Sciarrone. Before he is dragged away to be tortured further, he orders her to say nothing, but unable to bear the sound of his suffering, she blurts out Angelotti's hiding-place. She begs for Cavaradossi's freedom and Scarpia is prepared to grant it—at a price: Tosca must be his. Overcome with disgust and shame, she agrees, and Scarpia orders his thugs to carry out a mock execution. Tosca insists he write out a safe conduct pass for herself and Cavaradossi. While he is doing this, she notices, on his dinner-table, a sharp knife and she makes a decision—she picks up the knife and hides it behind her back. Scarpia finishes writing and approaches Tosca, ready to extract the promised bargain. Tosca stabs him. Before she leaves the room she must find the letter allowing her and Cavaradossi to leave Rome. The note is still in Scarpia's hand and she has to prise it from his fingers. Now her innate religious devotion comes to the fore. She takes two candles from the table and places them next to the body and puts a crucifix on his chest. She grabs her cloak and leaves. Allowed to see Cavaradossi before his 'execution', she explains what she has done and how he must fake death until all the soldiers have left—he must give a convincing performance. But Scarpia has tricked her and after the firing-squad has left she discovers that Cavaradossi really has been shot. Scarpia's body has been found, and to evade the pursuing soldiers, Tosca jumps from the battlements. Aria: *Vissi d'arte* ('I have lived for art'—this aria is almost always a show-stopper, so much so that Maria Callas is said to have considered excluding it in order to avoid a break in the continuity of the action); duets (with Cavaradossi): *Quale occhio al mondo può star di paro* ('What eyes in the world can compare'); *O dolci mani...* ('O sweet hands.'). Created (1900) by Hariclea Darclée.

Tosca is a great opportunity for a singing actress, covering the whole gamut of emotions. In the first act she displays her religious fervour, her love for Cavaradossi, and her jealousy at the thought that he might show interest in another woman. In the second act she has to be first the diva (singing offstage), then the broken woman who witnesses her lover being tortured. Self-disgust and shame are displayed at the thought of having to give herself to Scarpia. Then—and surely it is a spur-of-the-moment decision, as she sees the knife on the table—she has the strength, physical and psychological, to kill the Baron, and the presence of mind to remember to tear the necessary note from his hand. After she has stabbed Scarpia, she screams at him to die: *Muori dannato! Muori!* ('Die accursed! Die!') and when he has stopped moving she looks down on his body in amazement: *È avanti a lui tremava tutta Roma!* ('And before him all Rome trembled!'). But she should have smelled a rat—when Scarpia ordered the mock execution of Cavaradossi to be 'as with Palmieri' she really should have asked what happened to Palmieri! No doubt the greatest Tosca of our lifetime—or may be any lifetime—has been Maria Callas, but others who have shone in the role include Emmy Destinn, Claudia Muzio, Maria Jeritza, Gina Cigna, Maria Caniglia, Ljuba Welitsch, Milka Ternina, Zinka Milanov, Régine Crespin, Renata Tebaldi, Birgit Nilsson, Leontyne Price, Grace Bumbry, Galina Vishnevskaya, Montserrat Caballé, Mirella Freni, Galina Gorchakova, Raina Kabaivanska, and Catherine Malfitano.

Tote Stadt, Die (*The Dead City*) (Erich Korngold). Lib. by 'Paul Schott' (Julius and Erich Korngold); 3 'scenes'; f.p. Hamburg and Cologne (simultaneously) 1920, cond. Egon Pollak and Otto Klemperer respectively.

Bruges, late 19th cent.: *Marie is dead, and her husband *Paul is obsessed with her memory. He meets the dancer Marietta and invites her home, but when she sees a picture of Marie and realizes how alike they are, she leaves. In a vision, Paul sees friends who have either deserted him or died, and Marietta rises from a tomb to exorcize the ghost of his dead wife. She destroys all Marie's carefully preserved possessions. Incensed, Paul uses a plait of Marie's hair to strangle Marietta. He wakes, the plait is untouched—the memories remain, but he can now live in the present instead of the past.

Traveller, The (Britten: *Death in Venice*). Bass-bar. (who also sings Elderly Fop, Old Gondolier, Hotel Manager, Hotel Barber, Leader of the Players, Voice of Dionysus). Aschenbach meets him in the cemetery and it is his suggestion that the novelist should 'go south', as a result of which Aschenbach travels to Venice. Created (1973) by John Shirley-Quirk.

Traviata, La (The Fallen Woman) (Verdi). Lib. by Francesco Maria Piave; 3 acts; f.p. Venice 1853, cond. Gaetano Mares.

Paris and nearby, 1850: Among the guests at Violetta *Valéry's party in August, are her physician Dr *Grenvil, her friend Flora *Bervoix (escorted by the Marchese d'*Obigny), Violetta's escort Baron *Douphol, Alfredo *Germont, and other friends. Alfredo tries to persuade her to give up her life as a courtesan and go away with him. They go to live in a country house near Paris. After three months, Alfredo hears from her maid, *Annina, that Violetta has sold most of her possessions to support them. He leaves for Paris to sort out his affairs. In his absence, Violetta is visited by Alfredo's father, Giorgio *Germont. He tells her of his daughter, whose prospects of a good marriage are threatened because of her brother's association with a courtesan. He begs Violetta to give up Alfredo for ever. Alfredo returns from Paris and Violetta tells him she is going out for a while. Annina brings him a letter from her, in which she writes that she is returning to her old admirer, Baron Duphol. Germont *père* tries to comfort his son, but Alfredo sets his heart on revenge. At a party given by Flora, Violetta attends with Duphol. Alfredo is present and wins at the gaming tables. In front of all the guests,

he throws his winnings at Violetta in return for her services. His father disowns him. The following February Violetta is dying from consumption, nursed by Annina. She has received a letter from Alfredo's father. Giorgio has told his son of Violetta's sacrifice for their family and Alfredo is on his way to her. There is a passionate reunion as they express their love for each other and their dreams of the future. But it is too late—Violetta dies.

Triquet,   Mons. (Tchaikovsky: *Eugene Onegin*). Ten. An old French tutor who sings, in French, a tribute to Tatyana at a party given in her honour on her birthday. Aria: *A cette fête conviée* ('What a cordial celebration'). Created (1881) by D. V. Tarkhov.

Tristan 1. (Wagner: *Tristan und Isolde*). Ten. (*Heldentenor*). A Cornish knight, nephew of King Mark of Cornwall. Before the opera opens, he killed Morold, who was to marry the Irish Princess Isolde. She swore revenge. Tristan was injured in the fight with Morold and his boat landed in Ireland, where Isolde nursed him back to health. He was presented to her as 'Tantris', and at first she did not know who he was, but she saw his sword with a small piece missing from the blade and realized that this matched exactly the piece of metal which had been lodged in Morold's skull. She vowed to kill Tristan, but could not bring herself to do so, for when she looked into his eyes they fell in love. She allowed him to return to Cornwall where, as King Mark's favourite nephew, he was due to inherit the throne. The King's courtiers suggested he should marry the princess of whom Tristan spoke, and Tristan, despite his own feelings for Isolde, offered to escort her from Ireland to meet her elderly bridegroom. This is where the opera begins, as they sail towards Cornwall. Isolde is accompanied by her maid Brangäne and Tristan by his loyal servant and friend Kurwenal. Brangäne enters his quarters to summon him to speak to her mistress, but he refuses to go. However, as they approach the coast, Isolde sends a message that she will not disembark unless he comes to her first. When he enters her apartment, she is clearly upset that he has avoided her throughout the journey, but he explains that this was the best plan for both of them. Isolde reminds him that, as the slayer of Morold, he is still in her debt and must drink with her a draught of reconciliation—Brangäne will prepare the drink. Unknown to Tristan, Isolde has chosen a death-potion for them both, but Brangäne surreptitiously exchanges it for a love-potion. As soon as Tristan and Isolde drink the fluid, they fall into each other's arms and declare their love. Kurwenal interrupts their passionate embrace to warn them King Mark is about to come on board. After their first few days at Mark's castle, Tristan and Isolde arrange a meeting in her apartment. Once together, they have eyes and ears for no one else and ignore Brangäne's warning of treachery ahead—she is sure that Tristan's friend Melot will betray them to the King. Kurwenal bursts in to the room to try to save them, but is closely followed by Mark and Melot. Mark laments the betrayal by his favourite nephew and Tristan is genuinely upset at having caused his uncle such distress. He is unable to explain his actions (for he is unaware of having taken the love-potion). He asks Isolde if she will follow him even unto death and she at once concurs. Melot approaches with his sword drawn and Tristan deliberately falls on to Melot's sword. Seriously wounded, he collapses into Kurwenal's arms as Isolde throws herself at his inert body. Kurwenal carries the unconscious Tristan to the boat and takes him to his estate in Kareol, Brittany, to nurse him. It is clear that his condition is deteriorating, and Kurwenal sends for Isolde—her magic healing powers cured him once, and hopefully will do so again. Slowly Tristan recovers consciousness, but makes it clear he would rather stay oblivious to the world—oblivion is the only state which appeals to him now that he has lost Isolde. When Kurwenal explains to him that he has sent for her, Tristan rallies a little to express his thanks to Kurwenal for his loyalty all the years they have known each other. Kurwenal describes to his master the slow approach of the ship carrying Isolde and Tristan sends him to bring her to his room. He tears off his bandages, rouses himself from his couch, and lurches towards Isolde. In her arms, he sinks to the ground, dead. The last word he speaks is 'Isolde'. The arrival of Mark to forgive him and give the couple his blessing has come too late. Arias: *O König, das kann ich dir nicht sagen* ('O King, I cannot tell you that'); *Welches Sehnen! Welches Bangen!* ('What longing! What fearing!'); *Muss ich dich so verstehn*

('Must I understand you thus'); *O diese Sonne!* ('Oh, this sun!'); duets (with Isolde): *Isolde!... Seligste Frau!* ('Isolde!...Blessed lady!'); *Isolde! Geliebte!* ('Isolde! Beloved!'); *Lausch, Geliebte!...O ew'ge Nacht, süsse Nacht!* ('Listen, beloved!...O eternal night, sweet night!').

Although this is one of the world's great love stories, in a way Tristan brings about his own problems, albeit for the best of reasons. Having fallen in love with Isolde after killing Morold, whom she was going to marry, his sense of honour—and guilt—makes him reject his feelings in order to bring her to his uncle as a bride. Because he doesn't trust himself to stay in control, he avoids her on the journey and this causes her to insist on seeing him and hence she makes the decision to give them both a death-potion rather than lose him in life. At this point Brangäne intervenes, with ultimately tragic results. The role is one of the pinnacles of the *Heldentenor* repertory, requiring physical, mental, and vocal stamina—there are episodes in which Tristan sings, almost without interruption, for up to 10 minutes at a time. It comes as a great relief to him to be able to lie 'dead' throughout the seven minutes of Isolde's *Liebestod* although, if the Isolde does her stuff properly, even listening can be draining, and more than one Tristan has shed silent tears during this climax of four hours' emotional outpouring. There have been famous singers of Tristan in every generation. These include Heinrich Vogl, Jean De Reszke, Max Alvary, Lauritz Melchior, Max Lorenz, Ramon Vinay, Ludwig Suthaus, Set Svanholm, Wolfgang Windgassen (who sang it in every Bayreuth production between 1957 and 1970), Spas Wenkoff, Jon Vickers, Peter Hofmann, Siegfried Jerusalem, Jeffrey Lawton, Ben Heppner, and Robert Gambill. Created (1865) by Ludwig Schnorr von Carolsfeld (whose wife, Malvina, created Isolde).

2. (Flotow: *Martha*). *See* MICKLEFORD, LORD TRISTAN.

Tristan und Isolde (Wagner). Lib. by Wagner; 3 acts; f.p. Munich 1865, cond. Hans von Bülow.

In a ship, Cornwall and Brittany, legendary times: *Isolde, with her maid *Brangäne, is being escorted from Ireland to Cornwall to marry, unwillingly, King *Mark. Also on the ship are *Tristan and his friend *Kurwenal.

Kurwenal tells the story of how they all come to be here: *Morold, engaged to Isolde, was killed by Tristan. Before he was killed, he injured Tristan. Not realizing this was the man who had killed her fiancé, Isolde nursed Tristan back to health. When she recognized him, she had to resist her inclination to kill him, as she was falling in love with him. Now he is taking her to marry his uncle, the King. Believing that her love for Tristan is unrequited, Isolde decides to drink a deathly potion. Tristan, who does love her but knows she is to marry the King, agrees to share the poison with her. However, Brangäne has substituted a love-potion, which they both drink and fall passionately in love. Once they arrive at King Mark's castle, Isolde arranges a signal to tell Tristan it is clear for him to come to her—she will extinguish a blazing torch near the door. Brangäne suspects that *Melot, supposedly Tristan's friend, is plotting against the lovers and is reluctant to put out the torch. Isolde does the job herself. Tristan arrives and the lovers embrace, ignoring Brangäne's warning that it is almost daybreak. Kurwenal comes to tell them of King Mark's impending arrival. The King enters, with the treacherous Melot, and accuses Tristan of betraying him. As Tristan kisses Isolde, Melot draws his sword and Tristan deliberately falls on it. In his castle in Brittany, Tristan is nursed by Kurwenal. A tune played by a *Shepherd rouses him from his coma and he and Kurwenal await the arrival of Isolde's ship. As she arrives, the sick Tristan rushes to meet her, collapses, and dies. King Mark and Melot arrive. Melot and Kurwenal fight, Melot is killed and Kurwenal mortally wounded. Brangäne tells Isolde how King Mark, having heard about the elixir, had come to forgive Tristan. Isolde collapses over Tristan's body.

trittico, Il (*The Tripytch*) (Puccini). Three one-act operas designed to be given on the same evening and f.p. New York 1918, cond. Roberto Moranzoni. *See* TABARRO, IL; SUOR ANGELICA; GIANNI SCHICCHI.

Troilus (Walton: *Troilus and Cressida*). Ten. Prince of Troy, son of King Priam. He loves Cressida, daughter of Calkas, the High Priest of Pallas. Troilus suspects that Calkas is a traitor. When Calkas deserts to the enemy, his brother Pandarus sees his chance to save the family from this disaster by encouraging Cressida to accept Troilus' love and Troilus and Cressida spend the night together in her uncle's house. Troilus vows to rescue the Trojan captain Antenor, who has been taken prisoner by the Greeks. The Greek prince Diomede takes Cressida to join her father in exchange for the Trojan prisoner Antenor; Troilus swears he will rescue her. On his arrival at the Greek camp, he finds that, thinking he has deserted her, she has married Diomede and in the ensuing fight Troilus is killed by Calkas. Aria: *Child of the wine-dark wave*. The librettist made it clear that he based the plot of the opera on Chaucer's poem, not on Shakespeare's play. His intention was to set the private tragedy of the lovers against the larger tragedy of the Trojan War. Created (1954) by Richard Lewis.

Troilus and Cressida (Walton). Lib. by Christopher Hassall; 3 acts; f.p. London 1954, cond. Malcolm Sargent.

Troy, 12th cent. BC: *Cressida knows her father *Calkas plans to surrender to the Greeks, against the wishes of the Trojan captain *Antenor (who is later captured by the enemy). Her uncle *Pandarus encourages her to respond to the love of *Troilus. They spend the night together and, as a token of her love, she gives Troilus her crimson scarf. The Greek *Diomede arrives and demands that Cressida return with him in exchange for the release of Antenor. Troilus gives her the scarf to keep as a token of their love. After ten weeks in Greece with no word from Troilus, Cressida agrees to marry Diomede, unaware that her maid *Evadne has, on Calkas' orders, been burning Troilus' letters. Troilus and Pandarus arrive at the Greek camp, and seeing the scarf on Diomede's helmet, there is a fight, Troilus being stabbed in the back by Calkas. Diomede demands that Cressida remain in the camp as a soldier's whore. She grabs Troilus's sword and kills herself.

trovatore, Il (*The Troubadour*) (Verdi). Lib. by Salvatore Cammarano; 4 acts; f.p. Rome 1853, cond. Emilio Angelini.

Biscay and Aragon, 15th cent.: *Ferrando recounts the events which took place before the opera begins: Old Count di *Luna had two baby sons. An old gypsy put the 'evil eye' on the younger baby and was burnt as a witch. Her daughter *Azucena, who had a baby of her own, swore to avenge her. She snatched the other di Luna baby to throw into the flames of her mother's funeral pyre. Demented, she threw a baby—but was it the Luna baby or her own? Always bent on revenge, she brought the remaining baby up as her son, the troubador *Manrico. He is now an adult and Azucena an old lady. Old Count di Luna is dead, his elder son has inherited the title, but has never believed that his brother died. Both di Luna and Manrico are in love with *Leonora. The two men fight a duel. Manrico wins, but does not kill di Luna, who later injures Manrico in battle. He is nursed by the old gypsy Azucena (his apparent mother), who tells him the story of throwing a baby into the fire. Azucena is arrested and insists that Manrico is her son; di Luna plans to burn her to avenge his baby brother's death. Manrico goes to Azucena's rescue, but is captured and imprisoned with her. Leonora offers herself to di Luna in exchange for Manrico's release, but to avoid belonging to di Luna, she has already taken poison and dies at Manrico's feet. Now di Luna sentences Manrico to death, and brings Azucena to watch the execution. As Manrico dies, Azucena tells di Luna that it *was* her own baby she threw in the fire all those years ago. Now di Luna has killed his own brother.

Troyens, Les (The Trojans) (Berlioz). Lib. by comp.; 5 acts; f.p. Acts 3–5 (Part II) (*Les Troyens à Carthage*), Paris 1863, cond. Mons. Deloffre; f.p. Acts 1 & 2 (Part I) (*La Prise de Troie*), Karlsruhe 1890, cond. Felix Mottl (Part II also being given, so it was the first complete performance).

Troy and Carthage, 12/13 cent. BC. Part 1: After ten years, the Trojans have driven out the Greeks, who have left behind a large wooden horse as an offering to Pallas Athene. King *Priam's daughter *Cassandra foretells the destruction of Troy and urges her fiancé, the Asian Prince *Coroebus, to save himself by leaving, but he ignores her advice. As the people attempt to destroy the wooden horse, their leader is devoured by serpents. *Aeneas regards this as a sign of Athene's anger at their sacrilege. King Priam, whose son Hector was killed in the war, orders the horse to be placed before Athene's Temple. The Ghost of *Hector tells Aeneas to escape and found a new Troy in Italy. Coroebus is killed and Cassandra resolves to die, rather than fall into the hands of the

Greeks. She invites the other Trojan women to join her. Those not prepared to do so, leave. Cassandra stabs herself and she and the remaining women die.

Part II: In Queen *Dido's house in Carthage, the people celebrate and promise to defend her. Dido is unhappy. Her husband was killed by her brother. Her sister *Anna urges her to marry again. Driven ashore by a storm, Trojans are given shelter and explain Aeneas' plan to build a new Troy in Italy. When the Numidians attack Carthage, Aeneas leads the Trojans and Canthaginians together into battle. Dido and Aeneas shelter from a storm and acknowledge their love for each other. Reluctantly Aeneas and the Trojans set sail for Italy. Deserted, Dido stabs herself with Aeneas' sword and ascends the pyre which she has built to burn all memories of her lover.

Truffaldino 1. (Prokofiev: *The Love for Three Oranges*). Ten. Court jester and friend of the Prince, but unable to make him laugh. He accompanies him on his search for the three oranges. Truffaldino opens the first two oranges and the princesses who step out die of thirst. Created (1921) by Octave Dua.

2. (Strauss: *Ariadne auf Naxos*). *See* COMMEDIA DELL'ARTE TROUPE.

Trulove (Stravinsky: *The Rake's Progress*). Bass. Father of Anne, he is worried about her forthcoming marriage to Tom Rakewell. Created (1951) by Raphael Arié.

Trulove, Anne (Stravinsky: *The Rake's Progress*). Sop. Daughter of Trulove, she is to marry Tom Rakewell. He is tricked into going to London with Nick Shadow (the devil in disguise), and marries Baba the Turk. Worried at not hearing from Tom, Anne sets out to find him, but when she does he tells her he is married to Baba. Still in love with him, she tries to save him from the degenerate path along which he is going. By the time Anne catches up with Tom, he is insane in Bedlam. He thinks she is Venus come to rescue him and she tenderly sings him to sleep before leaving with her father. Arias: *Quietly, night, find him and caress*; *I go to him*; *Gently, little boat*. Created (1951) by Elisabeth Schwarzkopf.

Tschang (Lehár: *The Land of Smiles*). Bar. Uncle of Prince Sou-Chong. He insists the Prince must follow Chinese custom and take four wives. Created (1929) by Adolf Edgar Licho.

Turandot (Puccini). Lib. by Giuseppe Adami; 3 acts; f.p. Milan 1926, cond. Arturo Toscanini. [NOTE: When Puccini died in November 1924, the opera was completed except for the final scene and the closing duet. Franco Alfano completed the score, using Puccini's sketches. Toscanini did not include this part of the score at the première, laying down his baton when he reached the point at which Puccini had finished.]

Peking, ancient times: The Princess *Turandot will marry any prince who can find the answers to three riddles. Those who fail must die. Among the crowds in the streets is old *Timur. He has lost his throne and is penniless and blind. *Ping, *Pang, and *Pong (the Three Masks), ministers of the Emperor *Altoum, join Timur and his guide *Liù in trying to prevent an Unknown Prince (Timur's son *Calaf) attempting to answer the riddles, but they all fail. Turandot announces her riddles and Calaf answers them correctly. He offers her one chance of freedom—if she can discover his name by daybreak he will release her and die; if not, she must marry him. She agrees, and decrees that all the ministers will die if the Prince's name is not discovered. The guards bring in Timur and Liù. Turandot tries to force Timur into revealing the name, but Liù announces that she alone knows the answer. She resists all attempts to make her speak his name and kills herself with a dagger. Calaf and Turandot are left alone. She responds to his kiss. He tells her his name—now his life is in her hands. Turandot summons the people and tells them: the Prince's name is Love. All celebrate with her.

Turandot, Princess (Puccini: *Turandot*). Sop. The cold and cruel Princess, daughter of the Emperor Altoum, who has declared that she will marry whichever prince can give the answer to the three riddles she asks. If they fail, the penalty is death and several have already been executed. The latest victim is the Prince of Persia and she is about to supervise his execution. An Unknown Prince declares his intention of taking part in the contest, despite the pleas by his blind father Timur, the exiled King of Tartary, to desist. Even Turandot's father asks him to reconsider, feeling that enough

lives have been lost already. Nothing will deter the Unknown Prince. Turandot herself explains why she has devised this trial: many thousands of years earlier her ancestress was betrayed when the city was overrun by a foreign conqueror. She died in exile of a broken heart. Turandot's intention is to avenge her unknown predecessor. She puts the first question: 'What is the phantom that is born every night and dies every day?' The Prince answers correctly: 'It is that which inspires me—it is Hope'. She puts the second riddle: 'What is it that is sometimes like a fever, yet grows cold when you die?' Again he gives the correct answer: 'It is Blood'. Turandot is starting to be worried—no one has got this close before to answering all the riddles correctly. She puts the third question: 'What is the ice that sets you on fire?' The Prince hesitates, but then answers her: 'You are the ice which sets me on fire—Turandot'. Turandot begs her father to release her from the pact she has made, but Altoum points out that her oath is sacred. The Prince gives her one last chance—she must guess his name before morning. If she succeeds, he is willing to die, but if she fails, she is his. Turandot orders the whole population to stay awake all night—no one must sleep until the Unknown Prince's identity is discovered. She has his old father, Timur, arrested and tortured to make him tell the name, but Liù declares that she alone knows the answer and she then kills herself. The Prince accuses Turandot of cruelty. He then kisses her and tells her his name—now his life is in her hands. She summons her people and addresses them: The Unknown Prince's name is—LOVE. She submits to him, all resistance gone. Aria: *In questa reggia* ('In this palace'). Turandot is the most vocally 'heroic' of the Puccini heroines, demanding great stamina and vocal control from its exponents, who have included Claudia Muzio, Maria Jeritza, Eva Turner, Gina Cigna, Amy Shuard, Birgit Nilsson, Maria Callas, Ghena Dimitrova, Eva Marton, and Gwyneth Jones. Created (1926) by Rosa Raisa.

turco in Italia, Il (*The Turk in Italy*) (Rossini). Lib. by Felice Romani; 2 acts; f.p. Milan 1814.

Naples, 18th cent.: *Prosdocimo is writing a play, observing the action around him. *Zaida was engaged to the Turk *Selim, but rivals persuaded him to condemn her to death. She was saved by *Albazar. *Geronio wants to cure his wife, *Fiorilla, of her obsession with men. Selim arrives by boat and is attracted by Fiorilla (who is also loved by *Narciso). Geronio bans all men, Turk or Italian, from his house. Selim, about to sail off with Fiorilla, sees Zaida and they are reunited, to Fiorilla's chagrin. The two ladies tell Selim to choose between them, but he cannot make up his mind. Prosdocimo warns Geronio and Narciso that Selim will kidnap Fiorilla that night at a masked ball. Zaida comes to the ball dressed identically to Fiorilla, with Geronio and Narciso disguised as Selim. There is total confusion, and only Prosdocimo can work out how the correct couples can be brought together. He can now complete his play with a happy ending.

Turiddu (Mascagni: *Cavalleria rusticana*). Ten. A young soldier, son of Mama Lucia. He leaves his lover, Lola, and joins the army, and when he returns she has married Alfio. He seduces Santuzza who becomes pregnant, and he then rejects her. When Santuzza tells Alfio of his wife's affair, Alfio kills Turiddu in a duel. Created (1890) by Roberto Stagno (whose wife created Santuzza).

Turn of the Screw, The (Britten). Lib. by Myfanwy Piper; 2 acts; f.p. Venice 1954, cond. Benjamin Britten.

Bly, a country house, middle of 19th cent.: After a short prologue setting the scene, the *Governess arrives at Bly where she is to teach the orphaned *Flora and *Miles, who are being looked after by the housekeeper, Mrs *Grose. She has been engaged by their guardian and instructed never to trouble him. In the garden one evening, the Governess sees a man on the tower, and later sees him looking in through a window of the house. She describes him to Mrs Grose who recognises him as Peter *Quint, the master's former valet. He had been responsible for their then governess, Miss *Jessel, becoming pregnant, and she had died. Quint slipped on an icy road and also died. The Governess realizes the children can also see and hear the ghosts. She is sure they are an evil influence and, despite her promise, she writes to the guardian and tells him what is happening. Quint forces Miles to steal the letter. Mrs Grose decides to take Flora away from the house. The Governess stays behind with Miles, determined to defeat Quint's influence. She forces Miles to admit who told him to take the letter. As he screams Quint's name, he falls dead in the Governess's arms.

Tutor (Rossini: *Le Comte Ory*). Bass. He searches for and exposes Ory in the Castle of Formoutiers. Created (1828) by Nicholas-Prosper Levasseur.

Tybalt (Gounod: *Roméo et Juliette*). *See* TEBALDO.

Tye, Queen (Glass: *Akhnaten*). Sop. Widow of the Pharaoh Amenhotep III, and mother of Akhnaten. Created (1984) by Marie Angel.

Tytania (Britten: *A Midsummer Night's Dream*). Sop. King Oberon's Queen of the Fairies. Her Indian page causes trouble between them and Oberon uses a magic juice sprinkled on her eyes to make her fall in love with the first live creature she sees. This turns out to be Bottom, wearing his ass's head. Aria: *Be kind and courteous to this gentleman*; duet (with Oberon): *Ill met by moonlight*; ensemble (with Puck, Oberon, and the Fairies): *Now the hungry lion roars*. Created (1960) by Jennifer Vyvyan. *See also* TITANIA.

Überall, Emperor (Ullmann: *Der Kaiser von Atlantis*). Bar. He becomes angry when Death, fed up with the new mechanized ways of dying, goes on strike. When he begs Death to let people start dying again, Death agrees on condition that the Emperor is the first. He initially resists, but finally agrees and leaves through a mirror with Death. (This role was a clear allusion to Hitler.) Created (1944) by Walter Windholz; (1975) by Meinard Kraak.

Ulisse (Ulysses) (Monteverdi: *Il ritorno d'Ulisse in patria*). Ten. (though more usually sung by a bar.). Husband of Penelope and father of Telemaco. He has been away fighting in the Trojan Wars. His wife has been faithful throughout the twenty years of his absence, but she does not recognize him on his return. She is convinced only when he describes accurately something which only her husband can know—the quilt which is on their bed. Created (1640) possibly by Francesco Paolelli (whose wife and son are thought to have created Penelope and Telemaco).

Ulrica (Verdi: *Un ballo in maschera*). See ARVIDSON, MME.

Unknown Prince, The (Puccini: *Turandot*). See CALAF.

Unulfo (Handel: *Rodelinda*). Alto. *Travesti* role (originally castrato). Nobleman, counsellor to Grimoaldo. A secret friend of Bertarido, the deposed king, whom he helps to escape and regain his throne. Created (1725) by the castrato Andrea Pacini.

Urbain (Meyerbeer: *Les Huguenots*). Mez. (originally, sop., but rewritten by comp.). *Travesti* role. Page to the Princess Marguerite de Valois (sister of the king). Carries a message from Valentine to Raoul. Aria: *Une dame noble et sage* ('A wise and noble lady'). Created (1836) by Mlle Flécheur.

Ursula (Berlioz: *Béatrice et Bénédict*). Cont. Companion of Héro, the daughter of the Governor of Messina. Duet with Héro: *Nuit paisible et sereine* ('Peaceful and serene night'). Created (1862) by Mme Geoffroy.

Valencienne (Lehár: *The Merry Widow*). Sop. Wife of Baron Zeta, the Pontevedrin ambassador in Paris. She is passionately loved by Camille. Duet (with Camille): *Sieh' dort den kleinen Pavillon* ('See there the little pavilion'). Created (1905) by Annie Wünsch.

Valentin (Gounod: *Faust*). Bar. A soldier, brother of Marguerite. Created (1859) by Mons. Reynald.

Valentine (Meyerbeer: *Les Huguenots*). *See* SAINT-BRIS, VALENTINE DE.

Valéry, Violetta (Verdi: *La traviata*). Sop. A courtesan, the 'fallen woman' of the opera's title. At a large party in her house, Alfredo Germont, who has admired her for some time, declares his love, not knowing that her days are numbered (tuberculosis being incurable then). Although she resists his efforts to coax her to give up her life as a courtesan, nevertheless we next see them in her country house, where they have lived together for three months. Annina, her maid, has returned from selling more of her mistress's possessions in order to pay the bills. When Alfredo learns this, he rushes off to Paris to raise funds. Violetta opens an invitation to a party at the home of her friend Flora, but has no interest in rejoining her old companions. She is visited by Alfredo's father. He clearly believes she is bleeding his son dry. Violetta shows him the bills she herself has paid. Germont tells her he has come to ask her to give up Alfredo, for two reasons: first, his career would stand a better chance if he wasn't with her, and second, Alfredo's sister is engaged to a most suitable husband, whose family will break off the engagement if news of Alfredo's relationship with Violetta becomes known. At first she resists, but gradually she is worn down and agrees to his request, asking him to promise that, when she is dead, Alfredo will be told the truth. She also asks him to stay nearby to console his son after she has left. Germont agrees, respecting her dignified bearing and even sympathizing with her position. Violetta accepts Flora's invitation. Just before she leaves, Alfredo returns, and she begs him passionately to say how much he loves her. He is devastated a few moments later to be handed a letter by a servant in which Violetta explains that she is returning to her former 'protector', Baron Douphol. Alfredo's father vainly attempts to console him. At Flora's, Violetta arrives with the Baron, and is shocked to see Alfredo, who is winning at the gaming tables. She begs him to go, insisting that she loves the Baron. Humiliated when he throws his winnings at her feet, and weak from her illness, she faints. Some months later, Violetta is dying, looked after by Annina and her old friend Dr Grenvil. She takes out a letter which she has read many times. It is from Giorgio Germont. He has told his son the truth, and Alfredo is on his way to Violetta. She wonders if he will arrive in time. He does, and takes Violetta in his arms, talking of their life in the future. It is too late. Violetta dies. Arias: *È strano!…Ah, fors'è lui…* ('It's strange…Was this the man…?'); *Sempre libera* ('Always free'); *Dite alla giovine, si bella e pura* ('Tell your daughter, so beautiful and pure'); *Di lagrime avea d'uopo…Amami, Alfredo* ('I felt like crying… Love me, Alfredo'); *È tardi!…Addio, del passato* ('Too late!…Farewell, happy dreams'); duet (with Alfredo): *Parigi, o cara* ('We'll leave Paris, my dearest'). Created (1853) by Fanny Salvini-Donatelli (whose large build made the suspension of disbelief in her consumption and death scene extremely difficult and was one of the contributory factors to what Verdi described as 'a fiasco' of a première).

La traviata is the third of Verdi's central trilogy, coming after *Rigoletto* and *Il trovatore*. It had its première in the same year as *Trovatore*, and for much of the time Verdi was completing the score, he was supervising the *Trovatore* première in Rome. Like the other principals (the Germonts, father and son), Violetta is a more developed and developing character than any of Verdi's previous heroines. The whole opera is on a more intimate and personal plane—no great marches, no battles, and no great choral set-pieces. Violetta requires a singer with a flexible coloratura, but the *Helden* quality of the *Trovatore* Leonora is not necessary. It is an advance on the *Rigoletto* Gilda, in that Violetta is on the stage for much longer and has more to sing and the range of emotions she shows is much wider than in the previous two works. It has been the favourite role of many famous sopranos, from Nellie Melba and Amelia Galli-Curci to Maria Callas, who recorded it six times and was, for me, the nonpareil of modern Violettas. In his *The Callas Legacy* (London, 1977), John Ardoin described the role as 'tailor-made for her [Callas's] awareness as an artist and her sensibilities as a woman ...' *See also* ARTICLE BY MARIE McLAUGHLIN, p. 307.

Valková, Míla (Janáček: *Osud*). Sop. She had an affair with the composer Živný, but they parted because her mother did not consider him good enough for her. Míla was pregnant and gave birth to their son. She and the composer meet again and renew their love. They marry and set up home together with their son and Míla's mother, who is mentally unstable. She attacks Živný and, when Míla intervenes, mother and daughter fall from a balcony and are both killed. This character is thought to be based on Kamila Urválková, who did have an affair with a composer, who then wrote an opera about it—but this was not Janáček. The composer was called Čelanský and he wrote an opera called *Kamila*. Created (1934, radio) by Marie Bakalová; (1958, stage) by Jindra Pokorná.

Valkyries (Wagner: *Der Ring des Nibelungen*). The nine warrior daughters of Wotan and Erda. In addition to Brünnhilde, they are as follows: 3 sop. (Gerhilde, Helmwige, Ortlinde), 4 mez. (Waltraute, Rossweisse, Siegrune, Grimgerde), 1 cont. (Schwertleite). Apart from Brünnhilde and Waltraute, they sing for the most part as an ensemble. The famous Ride of the Valkyries in *Die Walküre* occurs as they assemble with their dead heroes at the beginning of the third act. Created (1870, in the order listed above) by: Fräulein Leonoff, Possart, Müller, Heinauer, Tyroler, Eichheim, Ritter, Therese Seehofer (who had created Erda in the première of *Das Rheingold* in Munich in 1869).

Valois, Elisabeth de (Verdi: *Don Carlos*). Sop. Daughter of Henri II of France, betrothed unseen to the Infante of Spain, in the hope of ending the wars between their two countries. She is attracted to a young Spaniard she meets and is delighted when she realizes this is Carlos, her future husband. However, his father, King Philip, decides to marry Elisabeth himself, and for the sake of her country she has to agree. Carlos, now her step-son, asks her to persuade his father to send him to Flanders. On the eve of Philip's Coronation, Elisabeth sends her lady-in-waiting, Eboli, to deputize for her at the festivities, masked and dressed in the queen's clothes. Mistaking her identity, Carlos declares his love, thus giving away their secret and Eboli vows to expose them. The King accuses Elisabeth of adultery after finding Carlos's portrait in her jewel-box, his attention having been drawn to it by Eboli, who admits her involvement and also her adultery with Philip. Elisabeth is unable to pardon her adultery—she can go into exile or into a nunnery. At the monastery at San Yuste, Elisabeth kneels in prayer near the tomb of Carlos's grandfather. She says farewell to Carlos who is about to leave for Flanders. They are interrupted by the arrival of the King and the Grand Inquisitor, come to arrest Carlos, but the tomb opens and Carlos is dragged inside. Aria: *Toi qui sus le néant des grandeurs de ce monde* ('You who knew the emptiness of the pomp of this world'); duet (with Carlos): *De quels transports* ('What rapture'). Created (Fr. vers. 1867) by Marie-Constance Sasse; (It. vers. 1884) by Abigaille Bruschi-Chiatti.

Valois, Marguerite de (Meyerbeer: *Les Huguenots*). Sop. Sister of the French king, betrothed to the Huguenot Henri IV de Navarre. In support of her brother's wish to bring to an end the conflict between the Catholics and the Huguenots, she encourages the love between

VIOLETTA (*La traviata*—Verdi)

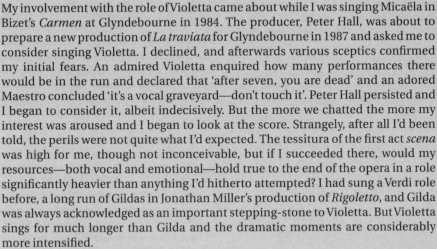

by Marie McLaughlin

My involvement with the role of Violetta came about while I was singing Micaëla in Bizet's *Carmen* at Glyndebourne in 1984. The producer, Peter Hall, was about to prepare a new production of *La traviata* for Glyndebourne in 1987 and asked me to consider singing Violetta. I declined, and afterwards various sceptics confirmed my initial fears. An admired Violetta enquired how many performances there would be in the run and declared that 'after seven, you are dead' and an adored Maestro concluded 'it's a vocal graveyard—don't touch it'. Peter Hall persisted and I began to consider it, albeit indecisively. But the more we chatted the more my interest was aroused and I began to look at the score. Strangely, after all I'd been told, the perils were not quite what I'd expected. The tessitura of the first act *scena* was high for me, though not inconceivable, but if I succeeded there, would my resources—both vocal and emotional—hold true to the end of the opera in a role significantly heavier than anything I'd hitherto attempted? I had sung a Verdi role before, a long run of Gildas in Jonathan Miller's production of *Rigoletto*, and Gilda was always acknowledged as an important stepping-stone to Violetta. But Violetta sings for much longer than Gilda and the dramatic moments are considerably more intensified.

Dramatically, Violetta held no terrors for me. I had enjoyed the Dumas novel and read the play [*La Dame aux camélias*], and the moving story of Marguerite Gautier (whose role-model was undoubtedly the courtesan Marie Duplessis, one of whose lovers Dumas *fils* was reputed to have been) had always enthralled me. To portray her in the opera was a dream which I never expected to come to fruition. The journey from pleasure-seeker to a figure of tragic stature, shadowed by a quest for absolution, had provided a superb vehicle for romantic actresses since the first performance of the play, and for singing actresses since the opera was written, and therein lay my initial fears: I would have to contend with following in the footsteps of Muzio, Ponselle, Callas, and Scotto, in a role in which I would, for the first time, be singing the prima donna of the title.

The more I studied the score, initial worries that one is expected to sound like Joan Sutherland in the first act, Mirella Freni in the second, and Montserrat Caballé in the rest (or, indeed, like Maria Callas all the way through) fell away as it became apparent to me that Verdi's dynamics call for a lyric soprano with some coloratura ability. If the vocal sound is too meaty, or *spinto*, the role loses the important elements of fragility and vulnerability essential if Violetta is to be convincing. By this stage I knew I wanted to sing it: the role has to offer one of the most rewarding challenges in the repertoire. She is one of Verdi's most fully rounded characters, with an underlying dramatic truth to every phrase and not a superfluous note, not even in the hysterical desperation of the first act coloratura, where Violetta is trapped in a vain and superficial world from which she sees no escape. Verdi's understanding of her situation may well derive from his own life with the soprano Giuseppina Strepponi, who as his mistress rather than his wife suffered many closed doors in a society which must have regarded her position as similar to that of Violetta. He also paints a picture of a person dying, alone and abandoned, which is more realistic and dramatically rewarding than, say, Puccini's Mimì in *La bohème*, who dies a little too beautifully.

I look back on the Glyndebourne *Traviata* as a wonderful and challenging experience, clouded for me only by one real—but major—problem: the emotional output the role required. I could not leave her at the stage door. Violetta became a part of me and my long-suffering family had to contend with her all that summer. At the end of the run I traded her for the more familiar territory of the *Figaro* Susanna at Salzburg and have not—yet—returned.

the Catholic Valentine and the Huguenot Raoul, allowing her page to deliver messages for them. Aria: *A ce mot s'anime et renaît la nature* ('At this word Nature revives and renews itself'); duet (with Raoul): *Beauté divine, enchantresse* ('Beauty divine, enchantress'). Created (1836) by Julie Dorus-Gras.

Valzacchi (Strauss: *Der Rosenkavalier*). An Italian intriguer, partnered by Annina. They are hired by Baron Ochs to investigate Sophie, his future wife. They watch Sophie and Octavian together and, suspicious of their obvious attraction for each other, they call Ochs's attention to them. Octavian manages to bribe the intriguers into working for him instead of the Baron and they take part in the plans to dupe the Baron and catch him in a compromising position. Created (1911) by Hans Rüdiger.

Vanessa (Barber). Lib. by Gian Carlo Menotti; 4 acts; f.p. New York 1958, cond. Dmitri Mitropoulos.

Vanessa's country house, about 1905: *Vanessa's lover *Anatol left twenty years ago and she waits for his return, living with her mother, the old *Baroness, and her niece *Erika. Anatol arrives, but it is her lover's son: his father is dead. Anatol seduces Erika, but then becomes attached to Vanessa. Erika, now pregnant, attempts to kill herself, but recovers. Vanessa and Anatol marry and leave for Paris. Erika will wait for him to return.

Vanessa (Barber: *Vanessa*). Sop. Deserted by her lover Anatol, she has waited twenty years for his return. He has died, and his son, also called Anatol, now arrives. He seduces her niece, who becomes pregnant. He then marries Vanessa and takes her to Paris, leaving

Erika to wait for him as Vanessa waited for his father. The part was refused by Maria Callas, who found it lacking in melody. Created (1958) by Eleanor Steber.

Van Hopper, Mrs (Josephs: *Rebecca*). Mez. An American, on holiday in Monte Carlo, with her companion, the Girl, who is destined to become the second Mrs de Winter. She cruelly tells the Girl that Maxim de Winter cannot possibly love her, as he will never get over the death of his first wife, the beautiful Rebecca. Created (1983) by Nuala Willis.

Vanuzzi (Strauss: *Die schweigsame Frau*). Bass. A member of Henry Morosus's troupe of travelling players, after whom the company was named. Created (1935) by Kurt Böhme.

Vanya 1. (Glinka: *A Life for the Tsar*). Cont. *Travesti* role. An orphan, ward of Ivan Susanin. Is sent to warn the Tsar of approaching Polish troops. Created (1836) by Anna Vorobyova (later Anna Petrova, wife of Osip Petrov, the creator of Ivan Susanin).

2. (Janáček: *Katya Kabanová*). *See* KUDRJÁŠ, VÁŇA.

Varescu, Sylva (Kálmán: *Die Csárdásfürstin*). Sop. Cabaret singer with whom Prince Edwin falls in love. After their engagement, she becomes known as the 'Csárdás Princess' of the opera's title. His parents disapprove of the relationship. But he discovers that his mother used to be a singer, thus overcoming their objections. Created (1915) by Mizzi Günther.

Vargas, Don Carlo di (Verdi: *La forza del destino*). Bar. Son of the Marchese di Calatrava and brother of Leonora. When his father is killed, albeit accidentally, by Alvaro, Leonora's lover, Carlo vows vengeance. He follows them when they escape but Leonora and Alvaro become separated and each believes the other dead. At an inn, disguised as a student, Pereda, Carlo is encouraged to join the army fighting the Germans in Italy. In the army camp he meets Alvaro. Not knowing each other's identity, they become firm friends. When Alvaro is injured, Carlo finds his sister's portrait among Alvaro's papers and realizes the truth. He and Alvaro begin to fight a duel but are separated by the troops and Alvaro enters a monastery. Years later, Carlo arrives at the monastery demanding to see 'Padre Raffaele', who is Alvaro. Again they fight, and Carlo is fatally wounded. Summoning help from a nearby cave, Alvaro recognizes Leonora. As she gives her brother the last rites, Carlo stabs her. He has avenged his father. Aria: *Urna fatale del mio destino* ('Fatal urn of my destiny'); duet (with Alvaro): *Da un lustro ne vo in traccia* ('For five years I've been searching for you'). It was just after opening the *urna fatale* on the stage of the Metropolitan Opera, New York, in 1960 that the baritone Leonard Warren 'pitched forward like an oak felled' (Rudolf Bing: 5000 *Nights at the Opera*) and was pronounced dead by the company doctor. Created (1862) by Francesco Graziani.

Vargas, Donna Leonora di (Verdi: *La forza del destino*). Sop. Daughter of the Marchese di Calatrava, brother of Carlo di Vargas. She is in love with the half caste Alvaro but her father has forbidden their marriage. As they try to elope, the Marchese intercepts them. Alvaro's gun accidentally goes off, killing her father. She and Alvaro flee, but become separated and each believes the other to have died. Leonora knows her brother is pursuing them both, determined to avenge their father's death. She seeks refuge in a monastery, requesting permission to spend the rest of her life in solitary confinement in a sacred cave. Years later, Alvaro comes to the monastery and becomes a monk. There Carlo seeks him out and the two men fight a duel. Carlo is fatally wounded and Alvaro calls to the cave for someone to give him absolution. He and Leonora recognize each other, but as she gives her brother the last rites, Carlo stabs her. In Alvaro's arms at last, Leonora dies. Arias: *Me pellegrina ed orfana* ('As wanderer and orphan'); *Madre, pietosa Vergine* ('Holy Mother, compassionate Virgin'); *Pace, pace, mio Dio* ('Peace, give me peace, O Lord'). Created (1862) by Caroline Barbot.

Varlaam (Musorgsky: *Boris Godunov*). Bass. A vagabond who accompanies Grigori to Poland. There Grigori pretends to be the dead Dimitri, pretender to the Russian throne. Created (1874) by Osip Petrov.

Varvara (Janáček: *Katya Kabanová*). Mez. Foster-daughter in the Kabanov house. She is younger than Katya, but the two become firm friends and it is to Varvara that Katya confesses her love for another man, Boris. Varvara steals the key of the garden gate from the Kabanicha, giving it to Katya so she can go and meet Boris one night. At the same time, Varvara meets her own lover, Váňa Kudrjáš. During these meetings, a 'double-duet' takes place, Varvara and Váňa in the foreground, Katya and Boris in the distance. After Katya's breakdown and confession, Varvara is punished by the Kabanicha for her part in the conspiracy. She and Váňa decide to leave together and go to Moscow. Duet (with Kudrjáš): *Chod'si divka do času* ('You may stay out till it's dark'). Created (1921) by Jarmila Pustinská.

Vašek (Smetana: *The Bartered Bride*). Ten. Son of Micha and Hata, he has a marked stammer. He is proposed as a husband for Mařenka, in order to clear her parents' debts to his father, their landlord. He meets Mařenka without realizing she is his prospective bride. She tells him he should not marry 'Mařenka', who will arrange his death if they are forced to marry, as she loves somebody else. When the circus comes to town, he is persuaded to take over for one of the troupe who is drunk— the part is that of a bear who dances with the beautiful Esmeralda. Created (1866) by Josef Kysela.

Vecchio, Cecco del (Wagner: *Rienzi*). Bass. Roman citizen who supports Rienzi in his attempts to serve the people and defeat the nobles, but turns against him and encourages the people to call for his death. Created (1842) by Karl Risse.

Venus 1. (Wagner: *Tannhäuser*). Sop. (mez. in later Paris vers.). The goddess who lures Tannhäuser to the grotto in her mountain (the Venusberg), where he enjoys the perpetual orgy—for a short while. When he has had enough and wants to return to his normal human life, whatever its drawbacks, Venus is furious and warns him that one day he will return and beg to be taken back. Created (1845) by Wilhelmine Schröder-Devrient.

2. (Vénus) (Ligeti: *Le Grand Macabre*). Sop. Asked by Mescalina to send her a satisfactory lover, she chooses Nekrotzar. Created (1978) by Monika Lavén.

Vêpres siciliennes, Les (The Sicilian Vespers) (Verdi). Lib. by Eugène Scribe and Charles Duveyrier; 5 acts; f.p. Paris 1855.

In and near Palermo, 1282: The French have invaded Sicily and Palermo is ruled over by the Governor Guy de *Montfort. He warns *Henri, still loyal to the late Duke Frederick of Austria, who was executed on the Governor's orders, to resist his attraction to the Duke's sister *Hélène. Jean de *Procida, ex-leader of the Sicilian patriots, encourages anti-French feeling among the crowds. Henri refuses to attend the governor's reception and is arrested. Montfort recalls his own relationship with a young lady many years ago. She is dying and has just told him that Henri—his enemy—is his illegitimate son. Henri repulses his overtures. However, he does intervene to prevent Montfort being murdered by Hélène and Procida. They are imprisoned and Henri is cursed by the Sicilians as a traitor. When Hélène learns the full story, she forgives Henri. Montfort declares that, providing Henri will acknowledge him as his father, he will pardon them all and allow the young couple to marry, thus sealing a French-Sicilian entente. The wedding is planned. At the last minute, Hélène hears from Procida that her wedding bells will be the signal for a Sicilian uprising. Her attempts to call a halt to the ceremony fail and the French are massacred.

Vere, Capt. Edward Fairfax (Britten: *Billy Budd*). Ten. Capt. of HMS *Indomitable*. First seen as an old man, remembering the action on his '74' in the war against the French. He is loved by his men, who call him 'Starry Vere' and Billy is thrilled to be part of the crew. Vere chairs a court-martial after Billy strikes Claggart dead in front of him. The captain knows it was an accident but, despite Billy's entreaties, he refuses to intervene to save his life. In an epilogue, Vere recalls the trial and how he was the only one who could have saved Billy Budd from the gallows. Arias: *I am an old man*; *Claggart, John Claggart, beware!* Among successful singers of this role are Jean Cox, Graham Clark, Nigel Douglas, Philip Langridge, and Anthony Rolfe Johnson. Created (1951) by Peter Pears.

Vermeer (Birtwistle: *The Second Mrs Kong*). Bass. 'Left behind by Pearl', the artist who created 'Girl with a Pearl Earring', he falls in love with her but loses her to Kong. Created (1994) by Omar Ebrahim.

vestale, La (The Vestal Virgin) (Spontini). Lib. by Étienne de Jouy; 3 acts; f.p. Paris 1807, cond. Gaspare Spontini.

Ancient Rome: *Giulia has been forced by her father to become a priestess in the Temple of Vesta. She still loves *Licinius, the Roman leader who, with his friend *Cinna, plots her abduction. Giulia has to crown the triumphant leader, and during the ceremony he learns that she is to guard the sacred flame that night—it must never be extinguished. He meets her there, but they neglect the flame, which goes out. Cinna helps Licinius to escape, but Guilia is condemned to death for refusing to name the man she was with. Licinius admits his guilt to Pontifex *Maximus, pleading for him to show mercy to Guilia, but he refuses. As Giulia is about to be entombed, lightning strikes the altar and the flame is rekindled, showing the forgiveness of Vesta. Giulia and Licinius are reunited.

Vilja (Lehár: *The Merry Widow*). Not a character in the opera, but the legendary Maid of the Woods, who does not return the love of a huntsman. Her story is told, in a famous aria, by Hanna Glawari, the Merry Widow.

Villabella, Fernando (Rossini: *La gazza ladra*). Bass. A soldier. Father of Ninetta. After a fight with his commander, he is sentenced to death. He escapes and, disguised as tramp, visits his daughter. He asks her to sell a silver fork and spoon to raise money for him—they belong to him and have his initials on them. His daughter is accused of stealing the cutlery and sent for trial. Fernando risks his life to help her but is himself arrested. When the true 'thief' is discovered, his daughter is freed and Fernando receives a royal pardon. Created (1817) by Filippo Galli.

Villabella, Ninetta (Rossini: *La gazza ladra*). Sop. Daughter of Fernando. She is a servant in the house of the Vingradito family, whose son, Giannetto, has fallen in love with her. When some silver cutlery is missing, her mistress accuses Ninetta of stealing it. Ninetta is observed by one of the other servants selling cutlery to a pedlar to raise money for her father (who gave her his own silver to sell). Ninetta is imprisoned and sentenced to death. On the way to her execution, she stops outside the church to pray and one of her friends climbs up the church spire and finds the missing cutlery in the pet magpie's nest. Ninetta is set free. Arias: *Di piacer mi balza il cor…Tutto sorridere* ('My heart is bounding with joy…I see everything smiling'); *Deh tu reggi in tal momento il mio cor…* ('Merciful God, support my heart at this moment'). Created (1817) by Teresa Giorgi-Belloc.

Village Romeo and Juliet, A (Delius). Lib. by comp.; 6 'tableaux'; f.p. Berlin 1907, cond. Fritz Cassirer.

Switzerland, mid-19th cent.: Two rival farmers plough their land, each anxious to gain the strip of land between their fields, owned by the *Dark Fiddler. The farmers' children *Sali and *Vreli are forbidden to play together, but resume their friendship when they are older and fall in love. They meet the Dark Fiddler, but refuse to join him on the road. When Vreli's father tries to separate them, Sali hits him and the blow results in his losing his mind and being confined to an asylum. The villagers are critical of their behaviour. At an old inn, the Paradise Garden, they take a barge out on to the river, float away, and pull the plug, sinking together.

Vingradito, Fabrizio (Rossini: *La gazza ladra*). Bass. A wealthy farmer, husband of Lucia and father of Giannetto. He is happy that his son has fallen in love with the family maid, Ninetta, daughter of an honourable soldier. Created (1817) by Vincenzo Botticelli.

Vingradito, Giannetto (Rossini: *La gazza ladra*). Ten. Son of Lucia and Fabrizio, a rich farmer. He has been away fighting in the wars. On his return he falls in love with Ninetta, the family maid, daughter of a soldier. His father is delighted but his mother disapproves and accuses Ninetta of stealing the missing family

silver. She is arrested, tried, and found guilty. Another of the servants finds the missing items in the nest of the pet magpie. Created (1817) by Savino Monelli.

Vingradito, Lucia (Rossini: *La gazza ladra*). Mez. Wife of Fabrizio and mother of Giannetto. She does not approve of her son falling in love with the family maid, Ninetta. She accuses the girl of stealing the family silver. Created (1817) by Marietta Castiglioni.

Violante, Marchesa (Mozart: *La finta giardiniera*). *See* Sandrina.

Violetta (Verdi: *La traviata*). *See* Valéry, Violetta.

Virtù (Monteverdi: *L'incoronazione di Poppea*). Sop. The goddess of virtue, who debates with the goddesses of Fortune and Love, their own virtues and the shortcomings of others. Creator (1643) not traced.

Vítek (Janáček: *The Makropulos Case*). Ten. Father of Kristina, he is a solicitor's clerk in the chambers of Dr Kolenatý. Created (1926) by Valentin Šindler.

Vitellia (Mozart: *La clemenza di Tito*). Sop. Daughter of the deposed Emperor Vitellius. Rejected by the Emperor Tito in favour of another bride, she plots his assassination. He escapes death and displays his clemency by forgiving her. Arias: *Deh, se piacer mi vuoi* ('Ah, if you wish to please me'); *Non più di fiori* ('No more flowers'). Created (1791) by Maria Marchetti-Fantozzi.

Vixen Bystrouška (Janáček: *The Cunning Little Vixen*). *See* Bystrouška, Vixen.

Vladimir (Borodin: *Prince Igor*). Ten. Son of Prince Igor. Goes with his father to fight the Polovtsi and falls in love with Kontchakovna, the daughter of their leader. Created (1890) by Grigorii Ugrinovich.

Vladimiro, Count (Giordano: *Fedora*). Fedora's fiancé. He does not appear in the opera. Fedora goes to visit him, and on arrival finds he has been fatally wounded. His killers, said to be Count Loris Ipanov and accomplices, have escaped. Fedora swears vengeance.

Vogelgesang, Kunz (Wagner: *Die Meistersinger von Nürnberg*). Ten. One of the Masters, a furrier. Created (1868) by Karl Heinrich.

Vogel, Niklaus (Wagner: *Die Meistersinger von Nürnberg*). He does not appear in the opera. He is one of the *Meister* but is absent at roll-call and his apprentice informs the others that Vogel is ill. Good wishes are sent to him by Kothner. (Maybe Wagner was superstitious—there are already twelve Mastersingers in the opera!).

Vogelweide, Walther von der 1. (Wagner: *Tannhäuser*). Ten. A Thuringian knight who takes part in the song contest. Created (1845) by Herr Schloss.

2. (Wagner: *Die Meistersinger von Nürnberg*). Vogelweide does not appear in this opera, but is named by the young knight Walther von Stolzing as his 'Master', from whom he learned to love poetry.

Voice of Apollo (Britten: *Death in Venice*). Counter-ten. (off-stage). Aschenbach hears his voice whilst watching Tadzio playing on the beach. Aria: *He who loves beauty worships me*. Created (1973) by James Bowman.

Voice of God (Britten: *Noye's Fludde*). Spoken. Warns Noye of the forthcoming flood and tells him to build a ship (the Ark) to save his family and animals. Created (1958) by Trevor Anthony.

Voix humaine, La (*The Human Voice*) (Poulenc). Lib. by Jean Cocteau; 1 act; f.p. Paris 1959, cond. Georges Prêtre.

Present time: The Woman ('*Elle*'), abandoned by her lover, who is to be married the next day, tries to commit suicide. She speaks to him on the telephone for the last time. She veers between the past, the unpalatable present, and hysteria, unable to accept the reality of the situation. Finally he hangs up, and the telephone falls from her hand.

Vreli (Delius: *A Village Romeo and Juliet*). Sop. Daughter of Marti, a farmer in conflict with his neighbour, with whose son Vreli falls in love. In a fight, her father is injured and confined to an asylum. To escape the criticism of the villagers, she and her lover take a barge on the river and scuttle it, death together being preferable to life apart. Created (1907) by Lola Artôt de Padilla (daughter of the Belgian mez. Désirée Artôt and the Spanish bar. Mariano Padilla y Ramos).

Vsevolod, Prince (Rimsky-Korsakov: *The Legend of the Invisible City of Kitezh*). Ten. Son of Prince Yury and joint ruler of Kitezh, a sacred city. When lost in a forest while hunting, he meets and falls in love with Fevronia. Tartars abduct her during their wedding, and threaten to destroy the city. His father's prayers are answered when the city is enveloped in mist and transported to Paradise, from where his spirit rescues Fevronia and brings her and the Prince together again. Created (1907) by Andrey Labinsky.

Wagner 1. (Gounod: *Faust*). Bar. Friend of Valentin. Created (1859) by M. Cibot.

2. (Boito: *Mefistofele*). Ten. A pupil of Dr Faust. Creator (1868) not traced.

Waldner, Graf (Count) Theodor (Strauss: *Arabella*). Bar. Father of Arabella and Zdenka and husband of Adelaide. He gambles heavily, leaving his family impoverished. He sends Arabella's photograph to a wealthy old army fellow-officer in the hope that he would want to marry her. However, he has died and it is his nephew, Mandryka, who turns up to see the young lady in the photograph. Waldner lets it be known that he has a cash shortage, and is delighted when Mandryka produces a large wad of notes and suggests that Waldner help himself. Created (1933) by Friedrich Plaschke.

Waldner, Gräfin (Countess) Adelaide (Strauss: *Arabella*). Mez. Wife of Count Waldner and mother of Arabella and Zdenka. She is still young at heart and not above a little flirtation herself. At the ball she is quite happy to point out to one of Arabella's rejected suitors, Count Dominik, that, with her elder daughter married, she herself will often be alone in the future. Created (1933) by Camilla Kallab.

Waldvogel (Woodbird) (Wagner: *Siegfried*). Sop. Hearing the Woodbird in the forest, Siegfried tries to imitate its song. After he has killed the dragon Fafner and sucked some of the dragon's blood off his hand, he is able to understand the bird's song. The bird tells him that now that he has killed Fafner, he can claim the Nibelungs' gold and warns him that Mime is planning his death. In answer to Siegfried's questions about a future wife, the bird describes Brünnhilde, asleep on her rock surrounded by fire. The Woodbird leads Siegfried to the rock. Aria: *Hei! Siegfried gehört nun der Nibelungen Hort!* ('Hey! The Nibelungs'

treasure now belongs to Siegfried!'). Created (1876) by Marie Haupt.

Walküre, Die (Wagner). Lib. by Wagner; 3 acts; f.p. Munich 1870, cond. Franz Wüllner (excerpts had been cond. by Wagner in concert perf. in Vienna in 1862). The second opera in the cycle *Der Ring des Nibelungen*.

A house in the forest and on the rocky mountain, mythological times: While *Hunding is out hunting, a stranger (*Siegmund) arrives at the house exhausted. Hunding's wife, *Sieglinde, allows him to rest. Hunding returns and is suspicious of the visitor. Siegmund reveals that he has killed a man and was being pursued by the dead man's friends. Hunding admits to being one of the pursuers. The laws of hospitality force him to offer a stranger shelter for the night—but tomorrow, they fight. Preparing Hunding's bedtime drink, Sieglinde puts a sleeping-draught in it and she rejoins Siegmund. She shows him a sword high in a tree in the middle of the house. No one has had the strength to pull the sword out of the tree. Siegmund is able to do so, calling the sword Nothung. As they talk together and fall in love, they realize they are twins, separated years earlier when their mother was murdered. Their father was Wälse (Siegmund calls him Wolfe). Next morning Siegmund and Sieglinde flee, with Hunding in pursuit. *Wotan orders his favourite daughter *Brünnhilde to make sure Siegmund wins the fight with Hunding. However, Wotan's wife *Fricka, the goddess of marriage, supports Hunding's right to revenge—Wotan agrees to withdraw Brünnhilde's protection from Siegmund. When he arrives on the mountain, Brünnhilde's warns Siegmund that he will be killed, but he refuses to escape to Valhalla without Sieglinde, who is pregnant with their child. Defying her father, Brünnhilde protects him with her shield.

Furious, Wotan shatters Siegmund's sword with his spear and Hunding kills Siegmund. Wotan then causes Hunding's death. Brünnhilde gathers up the pieces of Siegmund's shattered sword, sweeps Sieglinde on to her horse and gallops off. She joins her sisters, the *Valkyries, but they are scared of their father and will not help her protect Sieglinde, who is sent into the forest to await the birth of her child. This child will be the noblest hero of them all, called *Siegfried, and one day he will make the fragments of the sword into a new weapon. Angry with his daughter, Wotan sentences Brünnhilde to sleep on the mountain, where she will be taken by the first man to find her. He grants her one wish—he will surround her with fire, so only a hero who knows no fear will be able to reach her.

Wally (Catalani: *La Wally*). Sop. Daughter of Stromminger. In love with Hagenbach, but her father wants her to marry Gellner. When Hagenbach rejects her, she orders his death, later regretting her decision and saving him. Declaring their love for each other, they are caught in an avalanche and killed. (Although he did not conduct the première of the opera, Toscanini named his daughter after this character.) Created (1892) by Hariclea Darclée.

Wally, La (Catalani). Lib. by Luigi Illica; 4 acts; f.p. Milan 1892, cond. Edoardo Mascheroni.

Tyrol, 1800: *Wally, daughter of *Stromminger is in love with Giuseppe *Hagenbach, but her father wants her to marry Vincenzo *Gellner. At her father's 70th birthday party she rejects Gellner and retreats to the mountains with her friend *Walter. After her father's death, Wally is wealthy and Gellner tries to persuade her to marry him, but she still wants Hagenbach, who laughs at her when she declares her love for him. She orders Gellner to kill him, but later regrets her hastiness. When Hagenbach comes to apologize to Wally, Gellner catches him and pushes him down a ravine. Wally climbs down to save him. They admit their love for each other but, united at last, they die in an avalanche.

Walter 1. (Catalani: *La Wally*). Sop. *Travesti* role. Friend of Wally. Created (1892) by Adelina Stehle.

2. (Verdi: *Luisa Miller*). Bass. Count Walter. An old enemy of Luisa Miller's father. He wants his son Rodolfo to marry Federica, a young widow who is his niece. Created (1849) by Antonio Selva.

3. (Verdi: *Luisa Miller*). Ten. Rodolfo, son of Count Walter. He is in love with Luisa Miller, but their fathers are sworn enemies. He lives in the village disguised as a peasant called 'Carlo'. His father wants him to marry the young widow Federica, but he tells her the truth—that his heart is given to another. When he thinks Luisa has betrayed him, he resolves to poison both her and himself. Succeeding, he learns before he dies that she has been loyal to him and he kills his father's steward, Wurm, who has caused all the trouble between them. Aria: *Quando le sere al placido…* ('When at eventide in the peace…'). Created (1849) by Settimio Malvezzi.

Walther 1. (Wagner: *Die Meistersinger von Nürnberg*). *See* STOLZING, WALTHER VON.

2. (Wagner: *Tannhäuser*). *See* VOGELWEIDE, WALTHER VON DER.

3. (Weir: *Blond Eckbert*). Ten. Only friend of Eckbert and his wife Bertha, to whom Bertha tells the story of her early years—he seems to have known this story already. Eckbert, suspicious of Walther's relationship with Bertha, kills him. He, Hugo, and the old woman who raised Bertha are the same person. *See also* HUGO. Created (1994) by Christopher Ventris.

Walton, Elvira (Bellini: *I Puritani*). Sop. Daughter of Gualtiero. She loves the Cavalier Arturo, but is being forced to marry the Puritan Riccardo. Arturo in his efforts to save the French widowed Queen, escapes with her. Elvira, thinking he has deserted her, becomes unbalanced. In a famous mad scene she imagines being married to Arturo. When he returns he is sentenced to death. This shocks Elvira into recovery and she and Arturo are united. Aria (Mad Scene): *Qui la voce sua soave* ('It was here his sweet voice'). Created (1835) by Giulia Grisi.

Walton, Giorgio (Bellini: *I Puritani*). Bass. Brother of Gualtiero and uncle of Elvira. He is a retired Puritan colonel. He persuades his brother to allow Elvira to marry the man she loves, the Cavalier Arturo. Created (1835) by Luigi Lablache.

Walton, Lord Gualtiero (Bellini: *I Puritani*). Bass. A Puritan, father of Elvira. He wants her to marry a Puritan, but she loves the Cavalier Arturo. Created (1835) by Luigi Profeti.

Waltraute (Wagner: *Die Walküre; Götterdämmerung*). Mez. One of the nine Valkyries, daughters of Wotan and Erda.

Die Walküre: Waltraute appears only as one of the group, though it is she who has the most to say. She tells her sisters that Wotan would be angry if they deliver their dead heroes to him before Brünnhilde has rejoined them.

Götterdämmerung: Waltraute is the only one of the Valkyries who appears in this opera. Without telling her father, who has forbidden his other daughters to have any contact with Brünnhilde, she has gone to visit her. She warns of the inevitable downfall of the gods and tells Brünnhilde that in her absence Wotan has set off to wander the world. Waltraute pleads with her sister to return the Ring to the Rhine whence it came. But Brünnhilde is deaf to her pleas—for her the Ring is a symbol of Siegfried's love and she will not give it up. Aria (known as Waltraute's Narration): *Höre mit Sinn, was ich dir sage!* ('Listen sensibly to what I have to say to you!'). Created (*W.* 1870) by Fräulein Müller; (*G.* 1876) by Luise Jaide.

Wanda (Offenbach: *La Grande-Duchesse de Gérolstein*). Sop. Girlfriend of Fritz, whom the Grand Duchess wants to marry. Created (1867) by Élise Garait.

Wanderer (Wagner: *Siegfried*). The guise under which Wotan appears in the third episode of *The Ring. See* WOTAN.

War and Peace (*Voina y Mir*) (Prokofiev). Lib. by comp. and Mira Mendelson; 5 acts (2 parts); f.p. Moscow 1945 (concert), cond. Samuil Samosud; Leningrad (St Petersburg) 1946 (stage), cond. Samuil Samosud.

Russia, 1812: Prince Andrei *Bolkonsky falls in love with Natasha *Rostova. She has also attracted the attention of Prince Anatol *Kuragin. Andrei's father insists they spend a year apart. At a party, Natasha falls for Anatol's charms. His friend *Dolokhov tries to dissuade him from eloping with Natasha, but they do not listen to him. As they attempt to leave a party, Natasha is waylaid by her aunt, Maria Dmitrievna *Akhrosimova and friend Count Pierre *Bezukhov, who tell her Anatol is

married. Pierre admits his own love for her. He tells Anatol he must give up Natasha and leave Moscow. News arrives—Napoleon has crossed the Russian border. Andrei volunteers for the Russian army. Field Marshal *Kutuzov, having lost the Battle of Borodino, decides to abandon Moscow rather than risk defeat. In French occupied Moscow, Pierre learns that Natasha's family have left, taking with them the wounded Andrei. Natasha begs Andrei to forgive her, but it is too late—he dies. Pierre, freed by partisans, dreams that he now may win Natasha's love.

Water Goblin (also called the **Spirit of the Lake**) (Vodník) (Dvořák: *Rusalka*). Bass. He warns Rusalka not to agree to the conditions imposed on her by the witch in return for allowing her to become human and marry the prince. The Water Goblin is sure it will lead to disaster—and he is proved right. Created (1901) by Václav Kliment.

Wellgunde (Wagner: *Das Rheingold; Götterdämmerung*). Sop. One of three Rhinemaidens. Created (R. 1869) by Therese Vogl; (G. 1876) by Marie Lehmann.

Wells, John Wellington (Sullivan: *The Sorcerer*). Bar. Sorcerer from J. W. Wells and Co., Family Sorcerers. He puts a love potion into the drinks at the village tea-party, causing everyone to fall in love with the wrong person. He agrees to die to negate the spell and disappears in a flash of smoke. Aria: *My name is John Wellington Wells.* Created (1877) by George Grossmith.

Werdenberg, Princess Marie Therese von (Strauss: *Der Rosenkavalier*). Wife of the field marshal, hence the Feldmarschallin (or Marschallin). *See* MARSCHALLIN.

Werther (Massenet). Lib. by Édouard Blau, Paul Milliet, and Georges Hartmann; 4 acts; f.p. Vienna 1892, cond. Hans Richter.

Near Frankfurt, 1780: The widowed Magistrate (Le *Bailli) and his younger children are looked after by the two eldest daughters, *Charlotte and *Sophie. Charlotte is engaged to *Albert but has fallen for the young poet *Werther. However, she promised her dying mother she would marry Albert. After their marriage, Albert suggests to Werther that Sophie would be a suitable bride for him.

Charlotte pleads with Werther to stay away from her. Werther asks Albert to lend him his pistols and Albert instructs Charlotte to fetch them for him. In his study, Charlotte finds Werther dying from gunshot wounds. They confess their love for each other and Werther dies in her arms.

Werther (Massenet: *Werther*). Ten./bar. A dreamy, melancholy young poet who falls in love with Charlotte who is engaged to somebody else. He visits her in her new married home and she begs him to leave her alone. He asks her husband to lend him his pistols. Charlotte, worried what he might do, rushes to his study where she finds him dying from gunshot wounds. He declares his love for her and she for him. He dies in Charlotte's arms. Arias: *J'aurais sur ma poitrine* ('I should have on my breast'); *Pourquoi me réveiller?* ('Why wake me up?'). [In 1902 Massenet transposed this role for the baritone Mattia Battistini, who, as far as can be ascertained, sang it only in Italian. Battistini's own copy of the vocal score, containing all the alterations to the vocal line, came to light recently and its first performance was given by Seattle Opera. The British première of this version was given by the Royal Northern College of Music in Manchester in March 1997.] Created (1892) by Ernst van Dyck.

Wesener (Zimmermann: *Die Soldaten*). Bass. A merchant in Lille, father of Charlotte and Marie. Created (1965) by Zoltan Kelemen.

Wesener, Charlotte (Zimmermann: *Die Soldaten*). Mez. Sister of Marie and daughter of Wesener. Created (1965) by Helga Jenckel.

Wesener, Marie (Zimmermann: *Die Soldaten*). Sop. Daughter of the merchant Wesener, sister of Charlotte. She falls in love with Stolzius, but has many affairs with various soldiers, including Baron Desportes and Capt. Mary. After being raped, she turns to prostitution. Created (1965) by Edith Gabry.

Western Union Boy (Britten: *Paul Bunyan*). Ten. He delivers the 'telegram from overseas' which informs Bunyan that the King of Sweden is sending his best logger to be his foreman. In the last scene he brings telegrams which decide the future of all the main characters. Created (1941) by Henry Bauman.

West Side Story (Bernstein). Lib. by Arthur Laurents and Stephen Sondheim; 2 acts; f.p. Washington DC 1957, cond. Leonard Bernstein.

New York, 1950s: *Riff's Jets and *Bernardo's Sharks are rival gangs. *Tony, a Jet, falls in love with *Maria, Bernardo's sister. As Tony tries to break up the gang rivalry, Riff is killed. In his fury, Tony kills Bernardo. Maria forgives him and they decide to leave the town together. He hides for the night with the Jets, but a confused message tells him, wrongly, that Maria is dead. Distressed, he allows himself to be killed by the Sharks. Maria intervenes to prevent further bloodshed.

White Abbot (Maxwell Davies: *Taverner*). Bar. Tries Taverner for heresy. After the Reformation, he is himself sentenced to be burned at the stake. Created (1972) by Raimund Herincx.

Wilhelm Meister (Thomas: *Mignon*). *See* MEISTER, WILHELM.

Willis, Private (Sullivan: *Iolanthe*). Bass. Sentry at the Palace of Westminster. The Queen of the Fairies settles on him as a husband. Aria: *When all night long*. Created (1882) by Charles Manners.

Wingrave, Gen. Sir Philip (Britten: *Owen Wingrave*). Ten. Owen's grandfather. He comes from a family of soldiers, many of whom have died in battle. He is horrified when Owen declares he will not follow the family tradition, and disinherits him. Created (TV 1971/stage 1973) by Peter Pears.

Wingrave, Miss (Britten: *Owen Wingrave*). Sop. Owen's aunt. She cannot accept Owen's decision not to become a soldier. She ushers him in to see his grandfather, confident that the old man will make him change his mind. Created (TV 1971/stage 1973) by Sylvia Fisher.

Wingrave, Owen (Britten: *Owen Wingrave*). Bar. The last of the Wingraves, a family of soldiers. He refuses to follow this tradition, as he hates fighting. He is disinherited by his grandfather, thus threatening the future of Kate Julian, who is expecting to marry Owen. She taunts him and suggests that to prove he is not a coward, he should spend the night alone in a haunted room in the house. When she goes to see him during the night, she finds him dead.

Created (TV 1971/stage 1973) by Benjamin Luxon.

Winter, Maxim de (Josephs: *Rebecca*). *See* DE WINTER, MAXIM.

Winter, Mrs de (Josephs: *Rebecca*). *See* GIRL, THE.

Winter, Rebecca de (Josephs: *Rebecca*). *See* DE WINTER, REBECCA.

Witch 1. (Humperdinck: *Hänsel und Gretel*). Mez. Lives in the Ilsenstein forest to which she tempts young children with gingerbread. She catches them and bakes them alive in her oven and turns them into gingerbread. She is pushed into her own oven by Gretel and herself turned into gingerbread. Created by Hermine Finck (a future wife of the composer Eugen d'Albert).

2. (Verdi: *Macbeth*). Spoken. Three witches who hail Macbeth as Thane of Cawdor and King of Scotland: he and his wife set about making sure their prophecy comes true. They also warn him to beware of Macduff (who eventually kills him), that Banquo's descendants will become kings (thus sealing his and their fate—they must be killed), that he need fear nothing from man 'born of woman' (on the battlefield Macduff tells Macbeth how he was 'ripped untimely' from his mother's womb, i.e. not born naturally), and that he will be safe until Birnam Wood moves to Dunsinane (which it appears to do when the troops in the forest, advancing against him, are camouflaged by branches from the trees). Creators (1847) not known.

Woglinde (Wagner: *Das Rheingold*; *Götterdämmerung*). Sop. One of three Rhinemaidens. Created (*R*. 1869) by Anna Kaufmann; (*G*. 1876) by Lilli Lehmann.

Wolfram (Wagner: *Tannhäuser*). *See* ESCHENBACH, WOLFRAM VON.

Woman, The 1. (Schoenberg: *Erwartung*). Sop. The only character in the opera, she is looking for her lover, convinced he must be with another woman. She enters the forest. In the darkness of the trees she hears rustles, birds screeching, someone weeping. She is even frightened by her own shadow; she stumbles, falls, cries for help. By the time she reaches the road again she is exhausted, scratched and dishevelled. Then she sees his bloodstained body, shot dead by his other lover. All her attempts to revive him fail. Created (1924) by Marie Gutheil-Schoder.

2. (Poulenc: *La Voix humaine*). *See* 'ELLE'.

Woodbird (Wagner: *Siegfried*). *See* WALDVOGEL.

Woodcutter's Boy (Vaughan Williams: *The Pilgrim's Progress*). Sop./treble. He directs Pilgrim to the Delectable Mountains, where he meets the Shepherds. Created (1951) by Iris Kells.

Wordsworth, Miss (Britten: *Albert Herring*). Sop. Headmistress of the school. She rehearses the village children to sing at Albert's crowning and joins them in: *Glory to our new May King*. Created (1947) by Margaret Ritchie.

Wotan (Wagner: *Das Rheingold*; *Die Walküre*; *Siegfried*). Bass-bar. Ruler of the gods. Husband of Fricka and father of the Valkyries by the earth-goddess Erda. He has also fathered mortal children. Before the start of the opera, he gouged out one of his eyes in his quest to acquire wisdom. His ambition to rule the world leads to the downfall of the gods.

Das Rheingold: Wotan has asked the giants, Fasolt and Fafner, to build a castle for him (Valhalla) from within which he will reign supreme. He has committed himself to giving the giants his sister-in-law, Freia, in payment and ignores all his wife's pleadings and rantings. He is relying on the wily Loge to come up with a bright idea to avoid paying the giants as promised. When Loge does come, it is with the news that Alberich has stolen the gold from the Rhine and has made a Ring which gives him power over the whole world. If they could obtain it, they could pay the giants with the gold in lieu of Freia. Wotan and Loge descend to Nibelheim. They watch Alberich forcing his fellow dwarfs to work for him—they must all do his bidding because he has the Ring. Wotan is determined to steal the gold, including the Ring from Alberich's finger. He and Loge capture Alberich and take the gold and the Ring. As Wotan puts the Ring on his own finger, Alberich utters a terrible curse on it—it will bring no one happiness and death to all who wear it. They return to the mountain and give the gold to the giants, but Wotan wants to keep the Ring. When all the hoard of gold is stacked in front of Freia, there is a small chink through which her eyes are visible. This must be blocked, and the only gold remaining is the Ring on Wotan's finger, with which he is understandably reluctant to part. Erda rises from the earth and warns Wotan of his folly if he keeps the Ring—it will end in his own destruction. Reluctantly he adds it to the rest of the gold and Freia is freed. The giants fight over the Ring and Fafner kills Fasolt—already the curse is working. Wotan and Fricka lead the gods across the rainbow bridge into Valhalla. Aria: *Abendlich strahlt der Sonne Auge* ('The sun's eye sheds its evening beams').

Die Walküre: Wotan has nine daughters (the Valkyries) by Erda, his favourite being Brünnhilde whom he asks to make sure his son Siegmund wins his fight with Hunding. Fricka, Wotan's wife, arrives and, as the goddess of marriage, supports Hunding against his wife Sieglinde, who has eloped with her brother Siegmund. Fricka makes Wotan swear not to help Siegmund. After she has gone, he explains to Brünnhilde what has happened. He also tells her the story of her own background, the warning he had from Erda, and his own wrongdoings which have left him in fear of Alberich regaining the gold. He was hoping that Siegmund would help him, but now Fricka has extracted this promise from him. To his amazement and anger, Brünnhilde, who has always obeyed his every wish, refuses to listen to Fricka's command—she will not protect Hunding. Wotan knows he will have to take matters into his own hands, or risk Fricka's wrath. When Siegmund and Hunding fight, he holds his own spear in front of Hunding and Siegmund, striking out, shatters his sword on the spear. In retaliation, Wotan causes Hunding to die. Wotan storms off to find and punish his disobedient daughter. On their mountain, he finds her surrounded by her sisters. They beg him to forgive her but he is adamant—she must be punished. Brünnhilde reveals herself and tells her father she is ready for whatever punishment he wishes to bestow. Wotan declares her no longer to be his daughter, although it is clear that it costs him dearly so to treat his favourite child. She will be put to sleep on a rock and will belong to the first man who finds her and wakes her. The other Valkyries plead in vain and are dismissed. Brünnhilde asks Wotan to explain to her what

her terrible sin has been, as she knows she only did what, deep in his heart, he wanted to do himself. But he is determined to carry out his threat. She begs her father at least to ensure that the man who reaches the rock on which she will sleep is a hero—will he not surround the rock with fire to make it difficult for anyone but a hero to find her? Loving her dearly as he does, Wotan agrees to her request. He embraces her lovingly and bids her farewell. He lays her on the rock, covered by her helmet and shield, and summons Loge to start the fire, which makes a circle round the sleeping Brünnhilde. He, as well as she, now knows that only a brave hero will be able to reach his beloved daughter. Arias: *Als junger Liebe Lust mir verblich* ('When young love's pleasures faded in me'); *Ein andres ist's: achte es wohl* ('It is something else: listen carefully'); *Lebwohl, du Kühnes, herrliches Kind!* ('Farewell, you bold, wonderful child!'—Wotan's Farewell).

Siegfried: While Mime is unsuccessfully trying to forge a sword from its fragments, Wotan enters, disguised as the Wanderer. He has been travelling round the world awaiting the end he knows is inevitable. In his efforts to get rid of the stranger who is interrupting his efforts, Mime suggests they ask each other three riddles—whichever one is unable to answer forfeits his life. Wotan answers Mime's questions without difficulty, then puts his own. The first two pose no problem, but the last question—who will be able to make the sword Nothung?—causes Mime great distress as he is unable to answer. The only person who will be able to forge the sword is one who knows no fear, says Wotan. Mime's life is now in his hands and, before he leaves, he warns the dwarf to watch his head. Outside the dragon Fafner's cave, Wotan meets Alberich and tells him that Mime will bring a hero who will kill the dragon and take the gold. Later he summons Erda, and tells her how he has had to punish their daughter Brünnhilde. He asks her, as the world's wisest woman, to tell him how he can overcome his worries. Erda is unable to help him. Telling her that he no longer fears the downfall she forecast but, tired of battling, accepts it as inevitable, he dismisses her back to her sleep in the bowels of the earth. No sooner has she left than Siegfried appears. In answer to Wotan's questions, Siegfried describes how he has forged the sword, killed the dragon, gained the gold, and is now seeking the rock on which Brünnhilde sleeps. Siegfried becomes impatient with this stranger and his questions and Wotan in his turn becomes angry and aggressive, telling Siegfried he will not find the rock he is seeking. The conversation becomes heated and Wotan reveals that his spear once shattered the sword which Siegfried holds. At this point, Siegfried realizes that this must be the man responsible for his father's death. With one stroke of his sword, Siegfried smashes Wotan's spear. Wotan gathers up the pieces of his spear and tells Siegfried he will hinder him no more—he must continue in his quest to find Brünnhilde's rock. Arias: *Heil dir, weiser Schmied!* ('Greeting to you, wise smith!'); *Wache, Wala! Wala! Erwach!* ('Waken, Wala! Wala!, awake!'); *Die Unweisen, ruf' ich ins Ohr* ('To you, unwise one, I address these words'); *Kenntest du mich, kühner Spross* ('If you only knew me, insolent youth').

Götterdämmerung: Wotan does not appear in this opera, but we gather from Waltraute that he returned to Valhalla and there awaits his end. There he will ultimately die with the rest of the gods as Valhalla burns in the fire started by Siegfried's funeral pyre.

Created (*R.* 1869 and *W.* 1870) by August Kindermann (who later created Titurel in the première of *Parsifal* in 1882); (*S.* 1876) by Franz Betz (who originally had been engaged to sing Wotan in the Munich première, but withdrew from the production. Wagner was not too pleased with Betz's performance, especially when he forgot the Ring at a vital point and had to go off into the wings to retrieve it). Great Wotans do not grow on trees. Each generation produces only two or three bass-baritones of true *Helden* quality, able to meet this most demanding of operatic roles. These have included Anton van Rooy, Carl Perron, Walter Soomer, Friedrich Schorr, Rudolf Bockelmann, Hermann Uhde, Hans Hotter, Thomas Stewart, David Ward, Theo Adam, Donald McIntyre, Hans Sotin, Norman Bailey, Siegmund Nimsgern, John Tomlinson, James Morris, and Bryn Terfel.

Wowkle (Puccini: *La Fanciulla del West*). Mez. Squaw to Billy Jackrabbit and maid of Minnie (the girl of the golden west). Created (1910) by Marie Mattfeld.

Wozzeck (Berg). Lib. by comp.; 3 acts; f.p. Berlin 1925, cond. Erich Kleiber.

Germany, *c.* 1830: *Wozzeck shaves his *Captain who moralizes about him having a child by *Marie without being married to her. When Wozzeck and his friend *Andres are in a field, Wozzeck becomes agitated, feeling the place is haunted. Marie is teased by her friend *Margret for showing too much interest in the soldiers, especially the *Drum-major. The *Doctor in the soldiers's camp uses Wozzeck for dietary experiments in return for a small fee. Wozzeck takes the money to Marie, who has been given earrings by the Drum-major. The Doctor and Captain taunt Wozzeck about Marie's affair. Wozzeck sees her dancing with the Drum-major and knows the rumours are true. He and the Drum-major fight. Marie and Wozzeck walk near a lake in the woods. Wozzeck cuts her throat. Later he returns to the scene to find the knife he used and throws this in the lake. Slowly he walks into the water and drowns. Their child is told his mother is dead.

Wozzeck, Franz (Berg: *Wozzeck*). A soldier, servant to the Captain. He has a son by Marie and the Captain taunts him about this. Wozzeck tells him that you have to be rich to have such high morals. Marie has an affair with the Drum-major and the next time Wozzeck meets him, the two men fight. In his jealousy, Wozzeck takes Marie for a walk by a lake in the woods. He kisses her then cuts her throat. Frightened when Marie's friend Margret notices blood on his hands, he searches for the knife he used, throws it into the pond, then walks into the water and drowns himself. Wozzeck is a very simple fellow, not subtle or scheming. He has been aptly described by Stephen Walsh as a 'representative of the downtrodden proletariat'. He does not find it easy to express himself or even to understand his own feelings (he was based on a true character, a soldier who was executed in 1824 for killing the mistress who had been unfaithful to him). Created (1925) by Leo Schützendorf.

Wreckers, The (Smyth). Lib. by Harry Brewster; 3 acts; f.p. Leipzig 1906, cond. Richard Hagel.

Cornwall, late 18th cent.: At times of hardship, the people of a small Cornish fishing-village disable the lighthouse and lure ships on to the rocky coast so they can plunder them. The local preacher *Pascoe helps them, but his wife, *Thirza, is revolted by their behaviour. Together with her lover, *Mark (who has abandoned his previous love, *Avis, daughter of the lighthouse keeper, *Lawrence), she warns the ships off. When their actions are discovered, they are captured by the villagers, walled up in a cave and left to drown as the tide rises.

Würfl (Janáček: *The Excursions of Mr Brouček*). Bass. Father of Málinka, he is the publican at whose inn Brouček gets drunk and dreams about life on the Moon. On the Moon, the innkeeper's *alter ego* is the President of the Temple of Arts which Brouček visits. Created (1920) by Václav Novák.

Wurm (Verdi: *Luisa Miller*). Bass. Steward to Count Walter. He is in love with Luisa Miller, but she loves the Count's son Rodolfo. Wurm does his best to win her hand by causing trouble between her and Rodolfo. Rodolfo, having given Luisa and himself poison, realizes the truth and, before he dies, kills Wurm. Created (1849) by Marco Arati.

Xanthe (Strauss: *Die Liebe der Danae*). Sop. Maid to whom Danae tells her dreams of everything she possesses being made of gold. Created (1944) by Irma Handler; (1952) by Anny Felbermayer.

Xenia (Musorgsky: *Boris Godunov*). Sop. Daughter of Boris Godunov, sister of Fyodor. She mourns her fiancé, who died shortly before they were to be married. Created (1874) by Wilhelmina Raab.

Xerxes (Handel: *Serse*). *See* SERSE.

Yamadori, Prince (Puccini: *Madama Butterfly*). Bar. A rich Japanese prince who wants to marry Butterfly and is introduced to her by the marriage-broker Goro. Goro does not believe that her husband, the American naval officer Pinkerton, will return to Nagasaki, and tries to persuade Butterfly to accept Yamadori, who will keep her and her son in comfort. Butterfly is not interested, convinced that Pinkerton will come back to her. Creator (1904) probably Emilio Venturini.

Yaroslavna (Borodin: *Prince Igor*). Sop. Wife of Prince Igor and sister of Prince Galitzky. She awaits her husband's return from leading his army against the Polovtsi. Aria: *Akh, plachu ya, gorka plachu ya* ('I shed tears, shed bitter tears'). Created (1890) by Olga Olghina.

Yeletsky, Prince (Tchaikovsky: *The Queen of Spades*). Bar. He recently became engaged to Lisa, granddaughter of the old Countess, the girl with whom Hermann has fallen in love. When Hermann gambles everything on the Ace of Spades, it is Yeletsky who accepts the bet, determined to destroy Hermann whom he holds responsible for Lisa's suicide. Aria: *Ya vas lyublyu bezmerno* ('I love you beyond measure'). Created (1890) by Leonid Yakovlev.

Yeomen of the Guard, The, or The Merryman and his Maid (Sullivan). Lib. by W. S. Gilbert; 2 acts; f.p. London 1888, cond. Arthur Sullivan.

The Tower of London, 19th cent.: Sergeant *Meryll's daughter Phoebe *Meryll is in love with Col. *Fairfax, who is unjustly imprisoned. She rejects the overtures of the gaoler Wilfred *Shadbolt. Dame *Carruthers is the Tower's housekeeper. Meryll is keen to rescue Fairfax and plans, with Phoebe's help, to free

him and pass him off as her brother, Leonard *Meryll. Fairfax, thinking he is to die, wants to marry in order to have a legal heir. Two strolling players come to the Tower, Jack *Point and Elsie *Maynard. Elsie agrees to be blindfolded and to wed the prisoner. Fairfax is released and when his absence is discovered there is chaos. Elsie now has a husband who is alive, so Jack Point cannot have her. He persuades the gullible Shadbolt to pretend to have shot Fairfax. Elsie, now in love with 'Leonard', vows she will remain faithful to her mysterious husband. As the various threads are untangled, Phoebe has to marry Shadbolt and Serg. Meryll agrees to wed Dame Carruthers. At the last minute, Elsie realizes that the 'Leonard' she loves and her unseen husband are the same man. Jack Point, heartbroken, falls senseless at their feet.

Yevgeny Onegin (Tchaikovsky). *See* Eugene Onegin.

Yniold (Debussy: *Pelléas et Mélisande*). Sop. *Travesti* role (but often sung by boy treble). Young son of Golaud from his first marriage. He is used by his father to spy on his second wife, Mélisande, and report on her relationship with Pelléas, Golaud's half-brother. Yniold sees nothing incriminating to report to his father. Created (1902) by C. Blondin.

Yum-Yum (Sullivan: *The Mikado*). Sop. Sister of Peep-Bo and Pitti-Sing, all wards of Ko-Ko, to whom she is to be married. She is loved by the minstrel Nanki-Poo, son of the Mikado. Their friends conspire to marry Ko-Ko to the elderly Katisha, leaving the lovers free for each other. Aria: *The sun whose rays*; duet (with Nanki-Poo): *Were you not to Ko-Ko plighted*; trio (with her sisters): *Three little* *maids from school.* Created (1885) by Leonora Braham.

Yury, Prince (Rimsky-Korsakov: *The Legend of the Invisible City of Kitezh*). Bass. Ruler of the sacred City of Kitezh, father of Vsevolod who marries Fevronia. In answer to Yury's prayers, the city is saved from destruction by the Tartar enemy by being transported to Paradise. Created (1907) by Ivan Filippov.

Yvonne (Krenek: *Jonny spielt auf*). Sop. A hotel chambermaid, blamed for the theft of a precious violin, actually stolen by the jazz-player Jonny. Created (1927) by Clare Schulthess.

Z

Zaccaria (Verdi: *Nabucco*). Bass. High Priest of Jerusalem. He holds Fenena, Nabucco's daughter, hostage in the temple. After Nabucco regains his sanity, Zaccaria crowns him king. Created (1842) by (Nicholas) Prosper Dérivis.

Zaida (Rossini: *Il turco in Italia*). Mez. A Turkish slave-girl, sentenced to death by the Turkish Prince Selim, to whom she was once engaged, but saved by Albazar. When Selim sees her again, his feelings are rekindled, but he then has to decide between her and Fiorilla, the Italian lady he has met. Created (1814) by Adelaide Carpano.

Zaretsky (Tchaikovsky: *Eugene Onegin*). Bass. Acts as second to Lensky when he meets Onegin to fight a duel. Created (1879) by D. M. Tarkhov.

Zastrow, Frau Elisabeth von (Maw: *The Rising of the Moon*). Mez. Wife of a Prussian Major in Ireland, she is selected as the second conquest for the 'initiation' of a young cornet who wants a commission in the regiment. Created (1970) by Kerstin Meyer.

Zastrow, Major Max von (Maw: *The Rising of the Moon*). Bar. A Prussian major, husband of Elisabeth. Created (1970) by Peter Gottlieb.

Zauberflöte, Die (The Magic Flute) (Mozart). Lib. by Johann Emanuel Schikaneder; 2 acts; f.p. Vienna 1791.
   Ancient Egypt: *Tamino, chased by a snake, falls unconscious. *Three Ladies kill the snake and leave to tell the *Queen of Night what has happened. As Tamino awakes, *Papageno appears, dressed as a bird, and claims *he* killed the serpent. The Three Ladies hear his lie and padlock his mouth. They give Tamino a portrait of *Pamina, the Queen's daughter, and he

falls in love with her. The Queen agrees to their marriage if he rescues Pamina who is a prisoner of *Sarastro. The Ladies give Tamino a magic flute and Papageno a set of magic bells to aid them in their mission. *Three Boys show them the way. Papageno saves Pamina from being tormented by *Monastatos and assures her that rescue is at hand. Tamino plays his flute and wild animals come and listen to him, but he hears Papageno's bells and goes to find him. Papageno rescues Pamina and brings her to join Tamino. They go to meet Sarastro, who tells them they must go through several ordeals before being worthy to join the Temple. Monastatos attempts to seduce Pamina. She is saved by the Queen, who gives her daughter a dagger to kill Sarastro. Two *Armed Men lead Tamino in. He is joined by Pamina to go through his trials by fire and water. Meantime Papageno meets an old crone who turns out to be the beautiful *Papagena who will be his bride. Having come through their trials, Pamina and Tamino are united in Sarastro's presence.

Zdenka (Strauss: *Arabella*). Sop. Younger daughter of Count Waldner and Adelaide, sister of Arabella. She is kept dressed as a boy (Zdenko) to avoid the expense of 'bringing her out'. She is very close to her sister, but is in love with Matteo, a young officer who is in love with Arabella. She writes love-letters to Matteo, signing them as if from Arabella and causes great complications by arranging for Matteo to have the key to Arabella's room and then taking her place in the darkened bedroom. Zdenka is a delightful character, whose efforts to do her selfless best for everyone have disastrous results, sorted out only when she confesses what she has done and is revealed to one and all as a girl, not the boy they have always thought her to be. She is comforted by Arabella and forgiven by them all, as Matteo realizes that this is the person he really loves. Aria: *Sie wollen alle Geld!* ('They all want money!'); (with ens.) *Papa! Mama!* ('Papa! Mama!'). Created (1933) by Margit Bokor. Among notable singers of this role are Trude Eipperle, Lisa Della Casa, Hilde Gueden, Anneliese Rothenberger, Sona Ghazarian, Marie McLaughlin, and Barbara Bonney.

Zerbinetta (Strauss: *Ariadne auf Naxos*). Sop. Leader of the *commedia dell'arte* troupe which has been hired to entertain the guests of one of the richest men in Vienna. His Majordomo informs them that they will perform after the opera, *Ariadne auf Naxos*, has been given. This causes consternation in the opera company, where the Music Master and the Composer, who has written the opera, are upset by the thought of the vulgar antics of the comedians following on their holy art. The Composer finds Zerbinetta attractive, and she tries to explain to him that he has portrayed the character of Ariadne incorrectly—no woman wants to die just because her lover has deserted her. Zerbinetta's motto is: off with the old, on with the new! The Major-domo causes further chaos when his master decides that, in order to finish the entertainment in time for a firework display, the two companies will have to perform simultaneously. The Composer is devastated, but it doesn't really worry Zerbinetta. She feels that there are many dull passages in the opera and the audience will be bored, so she and her company will liven them up. She summons her troupe with a loud whistle. During the performance of the opera, she has a long scene with Ariadne, in which she does her best to prove to her that she must forget about death, and must look for a new love—she succeeds, for Ariadne accepts Bacchus and prepares to leave with him. Arias: *Ein Augenblick ist wenig—ein Blick ist viel* ('A moment is nothing—a look is much'); *Grossmächtige Prinzessin* ('Most gracious Princess'—this very long aria (it lasts over eleven minutes) was shortened and lowered a whole tone by Strauss when he devised the second version of the opera in 1916). Created (1912) by Margarethe Siems, who had created Chrysothemis in *Elektra* and the Marschallin in *Der Rosenkavalier*, (1916) by Selma Kurz.

If the role of Zerbinetta is to be the delight which its composer intended, it requires a coloratura soprano of great accuracy, stamina, and warmth—it is more than a soubrette role. Among notable Zerbinettas have been Hermine Bosetti (a Berlin soprano whom Hofmannsthal wanted for the première, and who sang in the first version), Maria Ivogün, Selma Kurz, Alda Noni, Janine Micheau (the first French Zerbinetta, 1943), Rita Streich, Reri Grist, Mimi Coertse, Sylvia Gestzy, Silvia Greenberg, Edita Gruberova (who for some years made the part her own and sang it all over the world), Ruth Welting, Sumi Jo, Gianna Rolandi, Diana Damrau, and Marlis Petersen.

Zerlina (Mozart: *Don Giovanni*). Sop. A country girl, betrothed to Masetto whom she loves. Flattered by Don Giovanni's amorous attentions, she becomes frightened when he makes it clear he wishes to seduce her. She screams for help and Elvira comes to her aid. (There is a story that Mozart, dissatisfied with the singer's off-stage scream at the first rehearsal, hid in the wings and pinched her leg at the appropriate moment, resulting in a convincing shriek!) She begs Masetto's forgiveness and comforts him after Giovanni has beaten him. Arias: *Batti, batti, o bel Masetto* ('Beat me, beat me, handsome Masetto'); *Vedrai carino* ('You will see, dear little one'); duet (with Giovanni): *Là ci darem la mano* ('There you will give me your hand'). Created (1787) by Teresa Bondoni (whose husband's opera company gave the première).

Zeta, Baron (Lehár: *The Merry Widow*). Bar. The Pontevedrin ambassador in Paris. He is anxious to ensure that Hanna Glawari, the merry widow, marries a Pontevedrian in order to prevent her fortune going to a foreign country. Created (1905) by Siegmund Natzler.

Zia, Principessa La (Puccini: *Suor Angelica*). Cont. Princess and aunt of Angelica. She visits her in the convent and cruelly tells Angelica of the death of her illegitimate child. Created (1918) by Flora Perini.

Zimmer, Elisabeth (Henze: *Elegy for Young Lovers*). Sop. Companion of the poet Mittenhofer. She falls in love with Toni, son of the poet's physician. The young lovers get caught on the mountain in bad weather and realize they will die there. Created (1961) by Ingeborg Bremert.

Zita (Puccini: *Gianni Schicchi*). Cont. Known as *La Vecchia* ('the old one'), she is aged about 60, a cousin of the recently deceased Buoso Donati, and aunt of Rinuccio. Created (1918) by Kathleen Howard.

Živný (Janáček: *Osud*). Ten. A composer. He had an affair with Míla Valková but, because he was not rich, her mother disapproved and they parted. He did not know that Míla was pregnant. They now meet in a spa town and realize that their feelings for each other are as strong as ever. They marry and set up home with their son and Míla's mentally unstable mother. Živny is attacked by her and when Míla tries to intervene the two women are killed. Živny pours his grief into the writing of an opera about these events and years later students rehearse it. During these preparations he hears the dead Míla's voice and collapses, himself dead. Much of this character is thought to be based on Janáček himself. Created (1934, radio) by Zdeněk Knittl; (1958, stage) by Jaroslav Ulrych.

Zorn, Balthasar (Wagner: *Die Meistersinger von Nürnberg*). Ten. One of the *Meistersinger*, a pewter smith by trade. Created (1868) by Herr Weixlstorfer.

Zoroastro (Handel: *Orlando*). Bass. A magician who resolves the complications of the relationships between Orlando and his former love Angelica. Created (1733) by Antonio Montagnan.

Zulma (Rossini: *L'italiana in Algeri*). Cont. Confidante of Elvira, the wife Mustafa no longer loves. Created (1813) by Annunziata Berni Chelli.

Zuniga (Bizet: *Carmen*). Bass. A dragoon Captain under whom Don José serves. He orders Carmen's arrest and when José allows her to escape while escorting her to gaol, Zuniga sends him to prison. Created (1875) by Mons. Dufriché.

Zurga (Bizet: *The Pearl Fishers*). Bar. King of the fishermen. He and his friend Nadir both love Leila. He realizes that she is the person who once saved him from death and he allows her and Nadir to be together. Duet (with Nadir): *Au fond du temple saint* ('From the depths of the holy temple'). Created (1863) by Jean-Vital Ismaël.

Zwerg, Der (*The Dwarf* or *The Birthday of the Infanta*) (Zemlinsky). Lib. by Georg Klaren; 1 act; f.p. Cologne 1922, cond. Otto Klemperer.

For her birthday, Donna Clara, the *Infanta (Princess) has been given as a present a court singer, the *Dwarf. He is unhappy because everyone laughs at him, so he sings only sad songs. He is unaware of his deformity and the mirrors are kept covered. As he and the Infanta play together she tells him, in a childlike way, that she loves him and she gives him a white rose. But he has fallen in love with her—she is the first person not to laugh at him. She orders her maid, *Ghita, to show him a mirror, but the maid refuses. By accident, the Dwarf sees his own reflection. Horrified, he begs Clara to tell him it is not a true likeness. She assures him she will continue to play with him—as one would with an animal. Heartbroken, he dies.

Appendix 1: Biographies of Contributors

Allen, (Sir) Thomas (*b* Seaham Harbour, 1944). Eng. bar. Opera début with WNO 1969 (Figaro in *Il barbiere di Siviglia*). CG début 1971 (Donald in *Billy Budd*). Glyndebourne début 1973 (Papageno in *Die Zauberflöte*); NY Met 1981 (Papageno); La Scala 1987 (Don Giovanni). Fine interpreter of Billy Budd (WNO), of Mozart's Count, Don Giovanni, and Don Alfonso, Janáček's Forester, and of Beckmesser. Sang Ulisse in Henze's realization of Monteverdi's *Il ritorno d'Ulisse in patria*, Salzburg 1985 and title role in f. Brit. stage p. of Busoni's *Doktor Faust*, London (ENO) 1986. CBE 1989. Knighted 1999.

Baker, (Dame) Janet (*b* Hatfield, Doncaster, 1933). Eng. mez. Second prize in the Kathleen Ferrier Competition 1956. Opera début 1956 with Oxford Univ. Opera Club. Leading roles with Handel Opera Society from 1959. Aldeburgh Festival from 1962, creating Kate in Britten's *Owen Wingrave* (TV 1971, CG 1973) and giving f.p. of his *Phaedra*, 1976. NY début 1966 (concert). CG début 1966 (Hermia in *A Midsummer Night's Dream*). Scottish Opera from 1967: Dorabella (*Così fan tutte*), Dido (*Les Troyens*), Octavian (*Der Rosenkavalier*), Composer (*Ariadne auf Naxos*), Gluck's Orpheus (1979). Glyndebourne: Diana (*La Calisto* 1970), Penelope (*Il ritorno d'Ulisse in patria*, 1972). ENO: Poppea (*L'incoronazione di Poppea* 1971), Mary Stuart (Donizetti, 1973), Charlotte (*Werther*, 1977). Last operatic appearance 1982 as Orpheus at Glyndebourne. Equally impressive in operatic parts as in Lieder, English and French song, oratorio, and Mahler. Autobiography *Full Circle* (London, 1982). Hamburg Shakespeare Prize 1971. CBE 1970. DBE 1976. CH 1994.

Brewer, Christine (*b* Springfield, Ill., 1956). Amer. sop. Worked as teacher while singing in chorus at Opera Theatre of St Louis. Won NY Met. Auditions 1989. Opera début St Louis 1989 (Ellen Orford), CG 1994 (Countess in

Figaro), NY Met. 2002 (Ariadne). Acclaimed Isolde (London concert 2002, S. Francisco (stage) 2006). Other roles incl. Donna Anna, Leonora (*Fidelio*), Gloriana (Britten) and Strauss's Ariadne, Helena, and Dyer's Wife. Noted concert and recital artist.

Bullock, Susan (*b* Davenham, Ches., 1958). Eng. sop. Studied RAM and Nat. Op. Studio. Decca Ferrier Prize 1984. Début ENO 1986 (Pamina). Glyndebourne 1995 (Lisa in *Queen of Spades*). NY City Opera 2000 (Butterfly). Brussels 2000 (Elektra, a role she has since sung worldwide). Opera North 2000 (Isolde). Sang first Brünnhilde in *Ring* in Tokyo 2002. CG début 2005 (Marie in *Wozzeck*), Canadian Opera 2007 (Brünnhilde).

DiDonato, Joyce (*b* Prairie Village, Kansas, 1969). Amer. mez. Studied at Academy of Vocal Arts, Philadelphia. 2nd prize Domingo Operalia 1998, won Richard Tucker Award 2002. Santa Fe début 2000 (Cherubino in Mozart's *Figaro*). CG début 2003 (Fox in *Cunning Little Vixen*), Paris Opéra 2003 (Rosina in *Il barbiere di Siviglia*), NY Met 2005 (Cherubino). Created Meg in Mark Adamo's *Little Women*, Houston 1998.

Domingo, Plácido (*b* Madrid, 1941). Spanish ten. and cond. Début as bar. 1957 in zarzuela. Opera début as tenor in Monterrey, Mexico, 1961 (Alfredo in *La traviata*). Member of Israeli Nat. Opera 1962–5. Amer. début (Dallas) 1961 (Arturo in *Lucia di Lammermoor*). NY début 1965 with City Opera (Pinkerton in *Madama Butterfly*). NY Met début 1968 (Maurizio in *Adriana Lecouvreur*), Scala 1969 (Ernani), British début London, 1969, in Verdi's *Requiem*, CG 1971 (Cavaradossi in *Tosca*). Sang his first Otello Hamburg 1975. Salzburg Fest., début 1975 (title-role in *Don Carlos*). Outstanding exponent of lyrical and heroic roles of Italian opera, but also a fine Lohengrin, Parsifal, Walther, and Siegmund—sang Parsifal at La

Scala and NY Met 1991 and at Bayreuth 1993; sang Siegmund in *Die Walküre*, Vienna 1992, CG 1997 and 2005. Has also conducted opera, including *Die Fledermaus* (CG 1983) and *La bohème* (NY Met 1985). He is gen. dir. of Washington National Opera (from 1996) and Los Angeles Opera (from 2000). Autobiography *My First Forty Years* (NY 1983). Hon. KBE 2002.

Douglas, Nigel (*b* Lenham, Kent, 1929). English ten. Début Vienna 1959 (Rodolfo in *La bohème*). Principal tenor Zurich Opera House from 1964; Vienna Volksoper 1964–8, Scottish Opera 1968–71, WNO 1971. Repertoire of over 80 roles, incl. Alwa (*Lulu*), Captain (*Wozzeck*), Loge, Herod, Peter Grimes, Vere, Aschenbach, and the Devil (Rimsky-Korsakov's *Christmas Eve*). Created roles of L'Heureux in Sutermeister's *Madame Bovary* (Zurich 1967), Philip in Gardner's *The Visitors* (Aldeburgh 1972), and Basil in Mathias's *The Servants* (Cardiff 1980). Sang Kent in f. Brit. p. of Reimann's *Lear* (ENO 1989). Expert on Viennese operetta and the only Brit. ten. to sing Danilo at Vienna Volksoper. Frequent broadcaster and author of *Legendary Voices* (1992), *More Legendary Voices* (1994), and *The Joy of Opera* (1996).

Evans, (Dame) Anne (*b* London, 1941). English sop. of Welsh parentage. Principal soprano ENO 1968–78, making début as Mimì and singing Fiordiligi, Violetta, the Marschallin, Ariadne, Elsa, Sieglinde, and Kundry. WNO début as Senta in *Der fliegende Holländer*, Cardiff 1974, and has sung with them Chrysothemis (*Elektra*), Empress and Dyer's Wife (*Die Frau ohne Schatten*), Leonore (*Fidelio*), Brünnhilde (in *Ring* cycle and with WNO at CG), Donna Anna (*Don Giovanni*), and Isolde. Bayreuth début 1983 (Ortlinde and 3rd Norn). Sang Brünnhilde in *Ring* cycles at Bayreuth 1989–92, and has sung role in London (CG), Berlin, Nice, Paris, Turin, and Zurich. NY Met début 1992 (Elisabeth in *Tannhäuser*). DBE 2000.

Hampson, Thomas (*b* Elkhart, Ind., 1955). American bar. Won Lotte Lehmann award 1978 and NY Met auditions 1981. Member Deutsche Oper am Rhein, Dusseldorf, 1981–4, singing Herald in *Lohengrin*, Harlequin in *Ariadne auf Naxos*, etc. Title-role in Henze's

Der Prinz von Homburg, Darmstadt 1982, and Guglielmo in *Così fan tutte*, St Louis 1982. Santa Fe début 1983 (Malatesta in *Don Pasquale*). Recital débuts, London 1983, NY 1985. Débuts NY Met 1986 and Salzburg 1988 (both as Count in *Le nozze di Figaro*). CG début 1993 (Figaro in *Il barbiere di Siviglia*). Fine singer of Amfortas (*Parsifal*) and Anckarstroem (*Un ballo in maschera*) and also of Schubert and Brahms *Lieder* and of Mahler cycles. Co-ed., critical edn. of Mahler songs.

Harewood, George, 7th Earl of (*b* London, 1923). English opera administrator, writer, and ed. Enthusiasm for opera stimulated by his parents and furthered in Italy and Germany while a prisoner of war. Founded magazine *Opera* 1950 (ed. 1950–3). Board of CG 1951–3 and 1969–72, controller of opera planning 1953–60. Dir. of Leeds Fest. 1958–74; Edinburgh Fest. 1961–5; Adelaide Fest. 1988. Managing dir. of SW Opera (ENO) 1972–85, chairman 1986–95. Ed., 8th, 9th, and 10th edns. of *Kobbé's Complete Opera Book*, 1954, 1976, and 1987, and Kobbé's *Illustrated Opera Book* (1989); joint ed. (with Antony Peattie) of *The New Kobbé's Opera Book* (1997); autobiography *The Tongs and the Bones* (1982). KBE 1986.

Isepp, Martin (*b* Vienna, 1930). Austrian-born English pianist and harpsichordist, son of singing-teacher Hélène Isepp. On staff Glyndebourne Opera 1957–93 (chief coach 1973–8, head of music staff 1978–93). Head of opera training, Juilliard School, NY, 1973–7; head of music studies, Nat. Opera Studio 1978–95. Associated with opera training schools in Banff, Alberta, and Ischia. Accompanist to many leading singers. Has conducted Mozart operas at Glyndebourne and at New York Metropolitan Opera.

Johnson, Frank (*b* London, 1943; *d* London, 2007). English journalist. Began his journalistic career as a messenger boy on the *Sunday Express*. On the political staff of the *Sun* 1959–62. He was parliamentary sketch-writer and leader-writer on the *Daily Telegraph* 1972–9, later moving to *The Times*, for which he was also its correspondent in Paris and Bonn. He was associate editor of the *Sunday Telegraph* 1988–93 and its deputy editor 1993–4. Editor of the *Spectator* 1995–9. Opera and ballet were his principal recreations. His interest in opera was stimulated by attending a London school which regularly supplied boy choristers for small parts at Covent Garden. He made his début there in 1955 as a Nibelung dwarf in *Das Rheingold*, later taking part in *Carmen, La bohème, Jenůfa, Otello, The Trojans, The Queen of Spades, Turandot*, and *Tosca*. The peak of his operatic career was as Maria Callas's son in *Norma* at Covent Garden in 1957.

Jurinac, Sena (*b* Travnik, Bosnia, 1921). Austrian sop. of Bosnian birth. Début Zagreb 1942 as Mimì in *La bohème*. Vienna State Opera 1944–83 (début as Cherubino in *Le nozze di Figaro*, farewell as Marschallin in *Der Rosenkavalier*). London début 1947 with Vienna State Opera. Salzburg Fest. 1947–80 (début as Dorabella in *Così fan tutte*). La Scala 1948 (Cherubino in *Le nozze di Figaro*). Glyndebourne 1949–56 (Dorabella at Edinburgh Fest. and Fiordiligi in *Così fan tutte*, Glyndebourne 1950). Memorable in Mozart roles and as Composer in *Ariadne auf Naxos* and Octavian in *Der Rosenkavalier*. San Francisco 1959 (Madama Butterfly), Chicago 1963 (Desdemona in *Otello*). In latter part of her career sang Kostelnička in *Jenůfa*.

Keenlyside, Simon (*b* London, 1959). Eng. baritone. Degree in Zoology, Cambridge Univ., then studied at RNCM with John Cameron. Tauber Prize 1986. Début Hamburg 1987. CG début 1989 (Silvio in *Pagliacci*). ENO 1990 (Guglielmo). S. Francisco 1993 (Olivier in *Capriccio*). La Scala 1995 (Papageno). NY Met 1996 (Belcore in *L'elisir d'amore*). Created Prospero in Adès's *The Tempest* (CG 2004) and Winston Smith in Maazel's *1984* (CG 2005). Outstanding as Papageno, Billy Budd, Don Giovanni, Pelléas. First Wozzeck 2008 (Paris). Notable recitalist (Schubert's *Winterreise*). CBE 2003.

Kennedy, Michael (*b* Manchester, 1926). On the staff of the *Daily Telegraph* 1941–89. Northern Ed. 1960–86 but began writing music criticism for it in 1950. In 1986 he became its joint chief music critic and was music critic of the *Sunday Telegraph* 1989–2005. His books include *The Hallé Tradition* (1960), *The Hallé 1858–1983* (1982), *Portrait of Manchester* (1971), *History of the Royal Manchester College of Music* (1970), *Music Enriches All* (a history of the first 21 years of the RNCM, 1994), and *Barbirolli: Conductor Laureate* (1971). Among his other books are an edn. of Charles Hallé's autobiography (1972); a biography of Sir Adrian Boult; studies of Elgar, Vaughan Williams, Britten, Walton, Strauss and Mahler; and the *Oxford Dictionary of Music* and *Concise Oxford Dictionary of Music*. He is a frequent broadcaster and lecturer. OBE 1981. CBE 1997.

Langridge, Philip (*b* Hawkhurst, Kent, 1939). English ten. Played the violin professionally until 1964 but began singing in 1962. Début Glyndebourne 1964 (Footman in *Capriccio*). Sang Florestan (*Fidelio*) for GTO. Specialist in Britten roles for CG and ENO, having sung Peter Grimes, Captain Vere (*Billy Budd*), Peter Quint (*Turn of the Screw*), and outstanding as Aschenbach (*Death in Venice*). CG début 1983 (Fisherman in *The Nightingale*). Co-created title-role in Birtwistle's *The Mask of Orpheus*, ENO 1986. NY Met début 1985 (Ferrando in *Così fan tutte*), Salzburg Fest. 1987 (Aaron in *Moses und Aron*). Also exponent of Janáček roles and a notable Bénédict in Berlioz's *Béatrice et Bénédict*. CBE 1994.

Leigh, Adèle (*b* London, 1928; *d* London, 2004). English sop. Member of CG co. 1948–56 (début as Xenia in *Boris Godunov*). Created 2 roles in *The Pilgrim's Progress* (CG 1951) and Bella in *The Midsummer Marriage* (CG 1955). USA début Boston 1959 (Musetta in *La bohème*), NY 1960 (Sophie in *Werther*). Zurich Opera from 1961. Prin. sop. Vienna Volksoper 1963–72. Came out of retirement to sing Gabrielle in *La vie parisienne*, Brighton Fest. 1984, and Heidi in Sondheim's *Follies*, London 1987. Taught at RNCM from 1992.

Lott, (Dame) Felicity (*b* Cheltenham, 1947). English sop. Opera début, Unicorn Opera, Abingdon, 1973 (Seleuce in Handel's *Tolomeo*). ENO début 1975 (Pamina in *Die Zauberflöte*), CG 1976 (created Lady 3/Girl 3 in *We Come to the River*), GTO 1976 (Countess in *Capriccio*), Glyndebourne 1977 (Anne in *The Rake's Progress*). Noted singer of Strauss's Octavian (*Der Rosenkavalier*), Countess (*Capriccio*), Christine (*Intermezzo*), and Arabella at Glyndebourne and elsewhere.

USA début (concert in Chicago) 1984, (opera) Chicago (Countess in *Le nozze di Figaro*). Munich 1988 (Christine), NY Met 1990 (Marschallin), Vienna State Opera 1991 (Arabella), Salzburg Fest. 1992 (Countess in *Le nozze di Figaro*). Member of Songmakers' Almanac. CBE 1990. DBE 1996.

Mackerras, (Sir) Charles (*b* Schenectady, NY, 1925). Australian cond. and oboist. Principal oboist in Sydney SO 1943–6. Went to Eng. 1946. Studied conducting 1947–8. Début, SW Opera 1948 (*Die Fledermaus*). Principal conductor BBC Concert Orch. 1954–6. CG début 1963 (*Katerina Ismailova*). Hamburg State Opera 1966–70. Music dir. of SW Opera (ENO from 1974) 1970–8; principal conductor Sydney SO 1982–5. Music dir. WNO 1987–91. Cond. f.p. in England of a Janáček opera, *Katya Kabanová*, SW 1951, following with several other Janáček operas, some of which he has edited. Awarded Janáček Medal, 1978. Arranged music by Sullivan for ballet *Pineapple Poll* and reconstructed his lost cello concerto. Has conducted and edited operas by Handel, J. C. Bach, and Gluck. His *Marriage of Figaro* at SW 1965 was remarkable for addition of 18th-cent. ornamentation. NY Met début 1972 (Gluck's *Orfeo*). Glyndebourne début 1990 (*Falstaff*). CBE 1974. Knighted 1979. CH 2003. Queen's Medal for Music, 2005.

McLaughlin, Marie (*b* Motherwell, 1954). Scottish sop. Won scholarship to London Opera Centre, 1977. Sang Tatyana in *Eugene Onegin*, conducted by Rostropovich, at Snape, 1978. Débuts: London (ENO) 1978 (Anna Gomez in *The Consul*), CG 1980 (Barbarina in *Figaro*), Rome 1982 (Ilia in *Idomenea*), Berlin 1984 (Marzelline in *Fidelio*), Glyndebourne 1985 (Micaëla in *Carmen*), NY Met 1986 (Marzelline), Salzburg Fest. 1987 (Susanna in *Le nozze di Figaro*), La Scala 1988 (Adina in *L'elisir d'amore*). A memorable Violetta (*La traviata*, Glyndebourne 1987). Other roles include Zdenka in *Arabella*, Gilda in *Rigoletto*, and Jenny in Weill's *Mahagonny*.

McNair, Sylvia (*b* Mansfield, Ohio, 1956). American sop. Début in *Messiah*, Indianapolis 1980. Opera début NY 1982 (Sandrina in Haydn's *L'infedeltá delusa*). European début, Schwetzingen 1984 (created title-role in

Kelterborn's *Ophelia*). Sang Pamina in *Die Zauberflöte* at Santa Fe, Ilia in *Idomeneo* and Morgana in *Alcina* in St Louis. Glyndebourne début 1989 (Anne Trulove in *The Rake's Progress*); Salzburg Fest. and CG débuts 1990 (Ilia); NY Met début 1991 (Marzelline in *Fidelio*). Sang with many leading European and Amer. orchestras and with ensembles conducted by Harnoncourt and Gardiner. Won the Marian Anderson Award 1990. More recently has successfully centred her career in 'crossover' light music.

Miller, (Sir) Jonathan (*b* London, 1934). English stage dir. Qualified in medicine, Cambridge University, where he was one of four co-authors and performers in revue *Beyond the Fringe*, 1961. High reputation as producer of Shakespeare and other classics. Opera début 1974, producing the British première of Goehr's *Arden Must Die*, New Opera Company; Glyndebourne 1975 (*The Cunning Little Vixen*). Worked regularly with Kent Opera (*Così fan tutte, La traviata, Falstaff, Eugene Onegin*), and ENO (*The Marriage of Figaro, The Turn of the Screw, Rigoletto* (set in 1950s New York), *The Barber of Seville, Arabella, Otello, Tosca, The Mikado,* and *Der Rosenkavalier*). NY Met début 1991 (*Katya Kabanová*). CG début 1995 (*Così fan tutte*). Has worked with many opera companies in Europe and Amer. and given masterclasses in Ischia, at the RNCM, and on TV. CBE 1983. Knighted 2002.

Porter, Andrew (*b* Cape Town, 1928). English music critic. Taught at All Souls, Oxford, 1973–4, and Univ. of California, Berkeley, 1980–1. Music critic *Manchester Guardian* 1949, *Financial Times* 1953–74, *New Yorker* 1972–92, *Observer* 1992–7. Ed., *Musical Times*, 1960–7. Authority on opera and contributor to many periodicals and dictionaries, especially TLS. Has trans. several operas incl. Verdi's *Otello, Falstaff, Don Carlos,* and *Rigoletto* and Wagner's *Der Ring des Nibelungen* (for ENO). Responsible for rediscovery and subsequent performance of first version of Verdi's *Don Carlos*. Published 5 volumes of his collected *New Yorker* criticisms.

Rodgers, Joan (*b* Whitehaven, 1956). English sop. Studied Russian at Liverpool Univ. and then at RNCM with Joseph Ward, later with

Audrey Langford. Won Ferrier Memorial Scholarship 1981. Sang in RNCM operas. Prof. début Aix-en-Provence 1982 (Pamina in *Die Zauberflöte*). ENO début 1983 (Wood Nymph in *Rusalka*). CG début 1983 (Princess in *L'Enfant et les sortilèges*), Glyndebourne 1989 (Susanna in *Le nozze di Figaro*). Salzburg début 1991 (Mozart Matinée). NY Met début 1995 (Pamina). Concert repertoire includes Mahler, Vaughan Williams, Elgar, Britten, Bruckner, Mozart, Rachmaninov, and Musorgsky. CBE 2001.

Sellars, Peter (*b* Pittsburgh, 1957). Amer. theatre and opera dir. Produced Gogol's *The Inspector General*, Cambridge, Mass., 1980 in modernist style. Produced Handel's *Orlando*, Cambridge, Mass., 1981–2 and *The Mikado* for Chicago Lyric Opera 1982. Dir. of Boston Shakespeare Company 1983, producing f. Amer. p. of Maxwell Davies's *The Lighthouse*. Dir., Amer. Nat. Theatre Co., Washington DC, 1984. At Purchase, NY, produced contemporary Amer. settings of *Così fan tutte* (1986), *Don Giovanni* (1987), and *Le nozze di Figaro* (1988). British début GTO 1987 (f.p. of Osborne's *The Electrification of the Soviet Union*), followed by *Die Zauberflöte*, minus dialogue, Glyndebourne 1990. Produced f.ps. of Adams's *Nixon in China*, Houston 1987, *The Death of Klinghoffer*, Brussels 1991, and *Dr Atomic* (for which he also wrote libretto), San Francisco 2005; *Saint François d'Assise*, Salzburg 1992; *Pelléas et Mélisande*, Amsterdam 1993; Aeschylus' *The Persians*, Salzburg and Edinburgh 1993; *Mathis der Maler*, CG début 1995; *Theodora*, Glyndebourne 1996, *Tristan und Isolde*, Paris 2005.

Tear, Robert (*b* Barry, Glamorgan, 1939). Welsh ten. In 1960 appointed lay vicar, St Paul's Cathedral, and worked with Ambrosian Singers. International chair of vocal studies, RAM 1986–94. Operatic début with Eng. Opera Group 1963 (Quint in *The Turn of the Screw*) and was member of Group 1964–70. CG début 1970 (Lensky in *Eugene Onegin*). Created Dov in *The Knot Garden*, CG 1970, and The Deserter in *We Come to the River*, CG 1976. Has sung with Scottish Opera in Verdi and Mozart. Sang the Painter in f.p. of complete *Lulu*, Paris 1979. Salzburg Fest. début 1985 (Eumeo in Henze's vers. of

Monteverdi's *Il Ritorno d'Ulisse in patria*). GTO 1989 (Aschenbach in *Death in Venice*), Glyndebourne 1992 (Aschenbach). Also a cond. with various British and European orchestras. Autobiography *Tear Here* (1990). CBE 1984.

Terfel, Bryn (*b* Pantglas, N. Wales, 1965). Welsh bass-bar. Won Ferrier Memorial Scholarship 1988, Cardiff Singer of the World Lieder prize 1989. Opera début Cardiff (WNO) 1990 (Guglielmo in *Così fan tutte*). Sang Figaro in *Le nozze di Figaro* WNO and Sante Fe (his USA début) 1991. London (ENO) début 1991 (Figaro in *Figaro's Wedding (The Marriage of Figaro)*). CG début 1992 (Masetto in *Don Giovanni*). Salzburg Festival début 1992 (Spirit Messenger in *Die Frau ohne Schatten* and Jochanaan in *Salome*). Chicago début 1993 (Donner in *Das Rheingold*), Vienna 1993 (Count in *Le nozze di Figaro*), NY Met 1994 (Figaro). First stage Wotan, CG 2004. Concert repertoire includes Elgar, Britten, Vaughan Williams, Handel, Monteverdi, Schubert. CBE 2003. Queen's Medal for Music, 2006.

Tomlinson, (Sir) John (*b* Oswaldtwistle, 1946). English bass. Opera début 1972, GTO (Colline in *La bohème*) and Kent Opera (Leporello in *Don Giovanni*). Sang Reade in f. Eng. p. of Goehr's *Arden Must Die*, London 1974 (New Opera Company). ENO début 1974 (Monk in *Don Carlos*). CG début 1979 (5th Jew in *Salome*). S. Francisco 1983 (Pimen in *Boris Godunov*). Opera North 1986 (Méphistophélès in *Faust*), Scottish Opera 1987 (Claggart in *Billy Budd*). Sang his first Bayreuth Wotan in 1988 and every year for the next twelve years, also at CG, Munich, etc. Salzburg Easter Fest. 1990 (Rocco in *Fidelio*). Created Green Knight in *Gawain*, London (CG) 1991, title-role in *The Minotaur*, (CG) 2008. Sang Hans Sachs (*Die Meistersinger*) at CG 1993. Also a noted Ochs (*Der Rosenkavalier*). CBE 1997. Knighted 2005.

Uppman, Theodor (*b* Pao Alto, San Jose, Calif., 1920; *d* NY, 2005). Amer. bar. Opera début Stanford Univ. 1946 (Papageno in *Die Zauberflöte*). Sang Pelléas (with Maggie Teyte as Mélisande) in concert performance conducted by Pierre Monteux, S. Francisco 1947. S. Francisco Opera 1948, NY City Opera

1948 (Pelléas). Created Billy Budd in Britten's opera, CG 1951. NY Met 1953–77 (début as Pelléas). Sang Billy Budd in f. Amer. stage p., Chicago, 1970. Created Bill in Bernstein's *A Quiet Place*, Houston 1983.

Vaughan Williams, Ursula (*b* Valletta, 1911; *d* London, 2007). English poet and librettist. Married composer Ralph Vaughan Williams 1953. For him wrote texts of masque *The Bridal Day* (1938), *Hymn for St Margaret* (1948), cantata *The Sons of Light* (1950), verses for *The Pilgrim's Progress* (1951), part-song *Silence and Music* (1953), *March of the 3 Kings* in cantata *Hodie* (1954), *Four Last Songs* (1954–8), libretto of unfinished opera *Thomas the Rhymer* (1957–8). Wrote *RVW: A Biography* (1964). Also wrote texts for Maconchy's opera *The Sofa* (1956–7), and for works by Ridout, D. Barlow, Williamson, and others. Author of three novels, five volumes of poetry, and autobiography *Paradise Remembered* (2002).

Walton, Susana (Lady Walton) (*b* Buenos Aires, 1926). Met and married the composer Sir William Walton in 1948 and settled with him on the island of Ischia in the Bay of Naples, where they built their home and one of the world's most beautiful private gardens. After Sir William's death in 1983, she built a recital room next to his study and for ten years held an annual course for young English and Italian singers at which they received three weeks' intensive tuition from first-rate producers and conductors in the art of acting in opera. She also appeared regularly as one of the reciters in Walton's *Façade*. Her biography of Walton, *Behind the Façade*, was published in 1988.

Appendix 2: Composers and Operas

Adamo, Mark (*b* Philadelphia, 1962)
Little Women
Adams, John (*b* Worcester, Mass., 1947)
Death of Klinghoffer, The
Dr Atomic
Nixon in China
Adès, Thomas (*b* London, 1971)
Tempest, The
Albert, Eugen d' (*b* Glasgow, 1864; *d* Riga, 1932)
Tiefland
Balfe, Michael (*b* Dublin, 1808; *d* Rowney Abbey, Herts., 1870)
Bohemian Girl, The
Barber, Samuel (*b* West Chester, Penn., 1910; *d* New York, 1981)
Antony and Cleopatra
Vanessa
Bartók, Béla (*b* Sinnicolau, Rom., 1881; *d* New York, 1945)
Duke Bluebeard's Castle
Beethoven, Ludwig van (*b* Bonn, 1770; *d* Vienna, 1827)
Fidelio
Bellini, Vincenzo (*b* Catania, Sicily, 1801; *d* Paris, 1835)
Capuleti e i Montecchi, I
Norma
pirata, Il
Puritani, I
sonnambula, La
Berg, Alban (*b* Vienna, 1885; *d* Vienna, 1935)
Lulu
Wozzeck
Berlioz, Hector (*b* Isère, 1803; *d* Paris, 1869)
Béatrice et Bénédict
Benvenuto Cellini
Troyens, Les
Bernstein, Leonard (*b* Lawrence, Mass., 1918; *d* New York, 1990)
West Side Story
Birtwistle, (Sir) Harrison (*b* Accrington, 1934)
Gawain
Mask of Orpheus, The
Punch and Judy
Second Mrs Kong, The

Bizet, Georges (*b* Paris, 1838; *d* Paris, 1875)
Carmen
Pearl Fishers, The
Boito, Arrigo (*b* Padua, 1842; *d* Milan, 1918)
Mefistofele
Borodin, Alexander (*b* St Petersburg, 1833; *d* St Petersburg, 1887)
Prince Igor
Britten, Benjamin (Lord Britten of Aldeburgh) (*b* Lowestoft, 1913; *d* Aldeburgh, 1976)
Albert Herring
Billy Budd
Death in Venice
Gloriana
Midsummer Night's Dream, A
Noye's Fludde
Owen Wingrave
Paul Bunyan
Peter Grimes
Rape of Lucretia, The
Turn of the Screw, The
Catalani, Alfredo (*b* Lucca, 1854; *d* Milan, 1893)
Wally, La
Cavalli, Francesco (*b* Crema, 1602; *d* Venice, 1676)
Calisto, La
Egisto, L'
Ormindo, L'
Chabrier, Emmanuel (*b* Ambert, 1841; *d* Paris, 1894)
Étoile, L'
Charpentier, Gustave (*b* Dieuze, 1860; *d* Paris, 1956)
Louise
Cherubini, Luigi (*b* Florence, 1760; *d* Paris, 1842)
Médée
Cilea, Francesco (*b* Palmi, 1866; *d* Varazze, 1950)
Adriana Lecouvreur
Cimarosa, Domenico (*b* Aversa, 1749; *d* Venice, 1801)
matrimonio segreto, Il
Corigliano, John (*b* New York, 1938)
Ghosts of Versailles, The

Debussy, Claude (*b* Saint-Germain-en-Laye,
1862; *d* Paris, 1918)
Pelléas et Mélisande
Delibes, Léo (*b* Saint-Germain du Val, 1836; *d*
Paris, 1891)
Lakmé
Delius, Frederick (*b* Bradford, 1862; *d*
Grez-sur-Loing, 1934)
Fennimore and Gerda
Village Romeo and Juliet, A
Donizetti, Gaetano (*b* Bergamo, 1797; *d*
Bergamo, 1848)
Anna Bolena
Don Pasquale
elisir d'amore, L'
Favorite, La
Fille du régiment, La
Linda di Chamounix
Lucia di Lammermoor
Maria Stuarda
Roberto Devereux
Dove, Jonathan (*b* London, 1959)
Flight
Dvořák, Antonin (*b* Kralupy, 1841; *d* Prague,
1904)
Rusalka
Flotow, Friedrich von (*b* Teutendorf, 1812; *d*
Darmstadt, 1883)
Martha
Floyd, Carlisle (*b* Latta, S. Car., 1926)
Susannah
Gay, John (*b* Barnstaple, 1685; *d* London, 1732)
Beggar's Opera, The
Gershwin, George (*b* Brooklyn, 1898; *d*
Hollywood, 1937)
Porgy and Bess
Giordano, Umberto (*b* Foggia, 1867; *d* Milan,
1948)
Andrea Chénier
Fedora
Glanert, Detlev (*b* Hamburg, 1960)
Caligula
Glass, Philip (*b* Baltimore, 1937)
Akhnaten
Glinka, Mikhail (*b* Novospasskoye (now
Glinka), 1804; *d* Berlin, 1857)
Life for the Tsar, A
Ruslan and Lyudmila
Gluck, Christoph Willibald (*b* Erasbach,
1714; *d* Vienna, 1787)
Alceste
Armide
Iphigénie en Aulide

Iphigénie en Tauride
Orfeo ed Euridice
Gounod, Charles (*b* Paris, 1818; *d* Saint
Cloud, 1893)
Faust
Roméo et Juliette
Halévy, Fromental (*b* Paris, 1799; *d* Nice,
1862)
Juive, La
Handel, George Frideric (*b* Halle, 1685; *d*
London, 1759)
Acis and Galatea
Agrippina
Alcina
Ariodante
Giulio Cesare
Orlando
Rodelinda
Semele
Serse
Tamerlano
Harbison, John (*b* Orange, NJ, 1938)
Great Gatsby, The
Haydn, Joseph (*b* Rohrau, 1732; *d* Vienna,
1809)
fedeltà premiata, La
isola disabitata, L'
mondo della luna, Il
Orfeo ed Euridice
Heggie, Jake (*b* W. Palm Beach, Flor., 1951)
Dead Man Walking
End of the Affair, The
Henze, Hans Werner (*b* Gütersloh, 1926)
Bassarids, The
Elegy for Young Lovers
English Cat, The
Prinz von Homburg, Der
Hindemith, Paul (*b* Hanau, 1895; *d* Frankfurt,
1963)
Mathis der Maler
Holst, Gustav (*b* Cheltenham, 1874; *d*
London, 1934)
Sāvitri
Humperdinck, Engelbert (*b* Siegburg, 1854; *d*
Neustrelitz, 1921)
Hänsel und Gretel
Janáček, Leoš (*b* Hukvaldy, 1854; *d* Ostrava,
1928)
Cunning Little Vixen, The
Excursions of Mr Brouček, The
From the House of the Dead
Jenůfa
Katya Kabanová

Makropulos Case, The
Osud
Josephs, Wilfred (*b* Newcastle upon Tyne,
1927; *d* London, 1997)
Rebecca
Kálmán, Emmerich (*b* Siófok, 1882; *d* Paris,
1953)
Csárdásfürstin, Die
Kern, Jerome (*b* New York, 1885; *d* New York,
1945)
Show Boat
Korngold, Erich (*b* Brno, 1897; *d* Hollywood,
1957)
Tote Stadt, Die
Krenek, Ernst (*b* Vienna, 1900; *d* Palm
Springs, 1991)
Jonny spielt auf
Lehár, Franz (*b* Komáron, 1870; *d* Bad Ischl,
1948)
Land of Smiles, The
Merry Widow, The
Leoncavallo, Ruggero (*b* Naples, 1857; *d*
Montecatini, 1919)
bohème, La
Pagliacci
Ligeti, György (*b* Dicsöszentmáron, 1923)
Grand Macabre, Le
Marschner, Heinrich (*b* Zittau, 1795; *d*
Hanover, 1861)
Hans Heiling
Martinů, Bohuslav (*b* Polička, 1890; *d* Liestal,
Switz., 1959)
Julietta
Mascagni, Pietro (*b* Livorno, 1863; *d* Rome, 1945)
Cavalleria rusticana
Massenet, Jules (*b* Montaud, 1842; *d* Paris, 1912)
Cendrillon
Chérubin
Don Quichotte
Hérodiade
Manon
Werther
Maw, Nicholas (*b* Grantham, 1935)
Rising of the Moon, The
Sophie's Choice
Maxwell Davies, (Sir) Peter (*b* Salford, 1934)
Lighthouse, The
Taverner
Menotti, Gian Carlo (*b* Cadegliano, 1911)
Amahl and the Night Visitors
Consul, The
Medium, The
Telephone, The

Messiaen, Olivier (*b* Avignon, 1908; *d* Paris,
1992)
Saint François d'Assise
Meyerbeer, Giacomo (*b* Vogelsdorf, 1791; *d*
Paris, 1864)
Huguenots, Les
Monteverdi, Claudio (*b* Cremona, 1567; *d*
Venice, 1643)
Incoronazione di Poppea, L'
Orfeo, L'
ritorno d'Ulisse in patria, Il
Mozart, Wolfgang Amadeus (*b* Salzburg,
1756; *d* Vienna, 1791)
Bastien und Bastienne
clemenza di Tito, La
Così fan tutte
Don Giovanni
Entführung aus dem Serail, Die
finta giardiniera, La
Idomeneo
Mitridate, re di Ponte
nozze di Figaro, Le
Zauberflöte, Die
Musorgsky, Modest (*b* Karevo, 1839; *d*
St Petersburg, 1881)
Boris Godunov
Khovanshchina
Nicolai, Otto (*b* Königsberg, Russ., 1810; *d*
Berlin, 1849)
lustige Weiber von Windsor, Die
Offenbach; Jacques (*b* Cologne, 1819; *d* Paris,
1880)
Belle Hélène, La
Contes d'Hoffmann, Les
Grande-Duchesse de Gérolstein, La
Orpheus in the Underworld
Pfitzner, Hans (*b* Moscow, 1869; *d* Salzburg,
1949)
Palestrina
Ponchielli, Amilcare (*b* Paderno
Fasolaro, 1834; *d* Milan,
1886)
Gioconda, La
Poulenc, Francis (*b* Paris, 1899; *d* Paris, 1963)
Dialogues des Carmélites, Les
Voix humaine, La
Previn, André (*b* Berlin, 1929)
Streetcar Named Desire, A
Prokofiev, Sergei (*b* Sontsovka, Ukraine,
1891; *d* Moscow, 1959)
Fiery Angel, The
Love for Three Oranges, The
War and Peace

Puccini, Giacomo (*b* Lucca, 1858; *d* Brussels, 1924)
bohème, La
fanciulla del West, La
Gianni Schicchi (Il trittico)
Madama Butterfly
Manon Lescaut
rondine, La
Suor Angelica (Il trittico)
tabarro, Il (Il trittico)
Tosca
Turandot
Purcell, Henry (*b* London, 1658 or 1659; *d* London, 1695)
Dido and Aeneas
Fairy Queen, The
Rameau, Jean-Philippe (*b* Dijon, 1683; *d* Paris, 1764)
Boréades, Les
Castor et Pollux
Hippolyte et Aricie
Ravel, Maurice (*b* Ciboure, 1875; *d* Paris, 1937)
Enfant et les sortilèges, L'
Heure espagnole, L'
Rimsky-Korsakov, Nikolai (*b* Tikhvin, 1844; *d* Lyubensk, 1908)
Golden Cockerel, The
Legend of the Invisible City of Kitezh and the Maiden Fevronia, The
Rossini, Gioachino (*b* Pesaro, 1792; *d* Paris, 1868)
barbiere di Siviglia, Il
Cenerentola, La
Comte Ory, Le
Ermione
gazza ladra, La
Guillaume Tell
italiana in Algeri, L'
Mosè in Egitto
Otello
Semiramide
turco in Italia, Il
Rubinstein, Anton (*b* Vikhvatinets, 1829; *d* Peterhof, 1894)
Demon, The
Saint-Saëns, Camille (*b* Paris, 1792; *d* Algiers, 1921)
Samson et Dalila
Saariaho, Kaija (*b* Helsinki, 1952)
Amour de loin, L'
Schoenberg, Arnold (*b* Vienna, 1874; *d* Los Angeles, 1951)
Erwartung
Moses und Aron

Shostakovich, Dmitri (*b* St Petersburg, 1906; *d* Moscow, 1975)
Lady Macbeth of the Mtsensk District
Smetana, Bedřich (*b* Litomyšl, Boh., 1824; *d* Prague, 1884)
Bartered Bride, The
Smyth, Ethel (*b* London, 1858; *d* Woking, 1944)
Wreckers, The
Spontini, Gaspare (*b* Maiolati, 1774; *d* Maiolati, 1851)
vestale, La
Strauss II, Johann (*b* Vienna, 1825; *d* Vienna, 1899)
Fledermaus, Die
Strauss, Richard (*b* Munich, 1864; *d* Garmisch-Partenkirchen, 1949)
ägyptische Helena, Die
Arabella
Ariadne auf Naxos
Capriccio
Daphne
Elektra
Frau ohne Schatten, Die
Friedenstag
Intermezzo
Liebe der Danae, Die
Rosenkavalier, Der
Salome
schweigsame Frau, Die
Stravinsky, Igor (*b* Lomonosou, 1882; *d* New York, 1971)
Oedipus Rex
Rake's Progress, The
Sullivan, (Sir) Arthur (*b* London, 1842; *d* London, 1900)
Gondoliers, The
HMS Pinafore
Iolanthe
Mikado, The
Patience
Pirates of Penzance, The
Princess Ida
Ruddigore
Sorcerer, The
Trial by Jury
Yeomen of the Guard, The
Szymanowski, Karol (*b* Tymoszówka, Uk., 1882; *d* Lausanne, 1937)
King Roger
Tchaikovsky, Pyotr (*b* Kamsko-Votkinsk, 1840; *d* St Petersburg, 1893)
Eugene Onegin
Queen of Spades, The

Thomas, Ambroise (*b* Metz, 1811; *d* Paris, 1896)
Hamlet
Mignon
Tippett, (Sir) Michael (*b* London, 1905; *d* London, 1998)
King Priam
Midsummer Marriage, The
Turnage, Mark-Anthony (*b* Corringham, Essex, 1960)
Silver Tassie, The
Ullmann, Viktor (*b* Prague, 1898; *d* Auschwitz concentration camp, 1944)
Kaiser von Atlantis, Der
Vaughan Williams, Ralph (*b* Down Ampney, 1872; *d* London, 1958)
Hugh the Drover
Pilgrim's Progress, The
Riders to the Sea
Verdi, Giuseppe (*b* Roncole, 1813; *d* Milan, 1901)
Aida
Aroldo
ballo in maschera, Un
Don Carlos/Don Carlo
Ernani
Falstaff
forza del destino, La
giorno di regno, Un or *finto Stanislao, Il*
Luisa Miller
Macbeth
Nabucco
Otello
Rigoletto
Simon Boccanegra
Stiffelio
traviata, La
trovatore, Il
Vêpres siciliennes, Les

Wagner, Richard (*b* Leipzig, 1813; *d* Venice, 1883)
fliegende Holländer, Der
Götterdämmerung (*Der Ring des Nibelungen*)
Lohengrin
Meistersinger von Nürnberg, Die
Parsifal
Rheingold, Das (*Der Ring des Nibelungen*)
Rienzi
Siegfried (*Der Ring des Nibelungen*)
Tannhäuser
Tristan und Isolde
Walküre, Die (*Der Ring des Nibelungen*)
Walton, (Sir) William (*b* Oldham, 1902; *d* Ischia, 1983)
Bear, The
Troilus and Cressida
Weber, Carl Maria von (*b* Eutin, 1796; *d* London, 1826)
Euryanthe
Freischütz, Der
Oberon
Weill, Kurt (*b* Dessau, 1900; *d* New York, 1950)
Aufstieg und Fall der Stadt Mahagonny
Threepenny Opera, The
Weir, Judith (*b* Aberdeen, 1954)
Blond Eckbert
Wolf-Ferrari, Ermanno (*b* Venice, 1846; *d* Venice, 1948)
segreto di Susanna, Il
Zemlinsky, Alexander (*b* Vienna, 1871; *d* New York, 1942)
florentinische Tragödie, Eine
Zwerg, Der
Zimmermann, Bernd Alois (*b* Cologne, 1918; *d* Cologne, 1970)
Soldaten, Die

Appendix 3: Some Operas of the Past Ten Years (1998–2008)

Since this book was originally published in 1998, there has been a spate of new operas, especially, but not exclusively, in the United States. A significant—and puzzling—change has taken place geographically. Throughout the Romantic (1830–1900) and late-Romantic (late 19th to early 20th centuries) periods, Italy and Germany, with composers such as Verdi and Puccini, Wagner and Strauss (to name just the greatest) were the founts from which sprang most of the operas which have survived into the 21st century and which will no doubt continue regularly to be seen and loved by audiences worldwide. But since the death of Puccini, no major popular opera composer has emerged from Italy. As the 20th century drew to an end and the 21st century began, the United States of America and Great Britain have been the source of many new operas of note, with Finland and Germany in the picture to a lesser degree.

An interesting feature of these operas has been that most of them have been based on subjects which would already be familiar to the general public: a book; a play; a film; a news story, for instance. One might say 'Twas ever thus'. A surprising number of these operas have had a large degree of popular success, many of then receiving several new productions in their first year. And there has been no shortage of established first-class international singers who have been willing to learn the new roles in order to take part in these productions.

In this appendix I have selected a dozen works from the long lists available and have concentrated on those operas which have, so far, proved popular and successful judging by the number of new productions they have received and the fact that they have travelled to other countries. To introduce these maybe unfamiliar works, rather than concentrating on the characters I have given far more detailed synopses than the standard repertoire received in the rest of the book. I have included the casts who created the roles at the world premières.

I am very grateful to the American mezzo-soprano Joyce DiDonato (*Little Women*) and the English baritone Simon Keenlyside (*The Tempest*) who have been kind enough to find the time in their already overcrowded schedules to write about their experience as creators of one of these roles.

L'amour de loin (*Love from afar*) (Kaija Saariaho, *b* Helsinki, 1952). Comp. 1999–2003; lib. by Amin Maalouf; 5 acts; f.p. Salzburg Festival, 15 August 2000, cond. Kent Nagano; dir. Peter Sellars.

12th cent., Aquitaine, Tripoli, and at sea (the story is based on the life of one of the earliest troubadours, Jaufré, who wrote to a faraway lover in Tripoli): Jaufré Rudel, Prince of Blaye, weary of the pleasures of life, yearns for a different love, but feels that it is unlikely that he will find her. His friends tell him that such a woman does not exist. A Pilgrim, recently arrived from abroad, tells Jaufré that he has met such a woman whereupon Jaufré spends his time thinking only of her. The Pilgrim returns to Tripoli and meets Clémence, Countess of Tripoli, and tells her that a prince-troubadour whom he met in France calls her his 'love from afar' and serenades her in his songs. Clémence begins to dream of this distant lover, wondering if she is worthy of his devotion. When he again returns to Blaye, the Pilgrim tells Jaufré that the lady now knows about him and Jaufré decides that he must go to meet her. But Clémence, unwilling to live constantly waiting, prefers their relationship to remain at a distance. Nothing daunted, Jaufré sets out somewhat apprehensively to meet his 'love from afar'. En route he worries so much about the future and how she will react that he becomes very ill, and by the time his ship arrives in Tripoli, he is dying. When they land, the Pilgrim rushes off to see the countess and tell her that Jaufré has arrived and that he asks to see her, but is close to death. Jaufré is brought to the citadel on a stretcher, and recovers somewhat when he sees Clémence. They confess their love for each other and embrace, then Jaufré dies in Clémence's arms. She feels responsible for his death and enters a convent. Her prayers are ambiguous: is she praying to God or to her 'Love from afar'?

Cast at world première:

Jaufré Rudel, Prince of Blaye, a troubadour	Gerald Finley (bar.)
The Pilgrim	Dagmar Pecková (mez.)
Clémence, Countess of Tripoli	Dawn Upshaw (sop.)

Caligula (Detlev Glanert, *b* Hamburg, 1960). Comp. 2004–06; lib. by Hans-Ulrich Treichel, based on a play by Albert Camus; 4 acts; f.p. Frankfurt, 7 October 2006, cond. Markus Stenz; dir. Christian Pade.

Caligula is a young, good-looking Roman Emperor. The death of his sister Drusilla, who was also his lover, changes his outlook on life, causing a mental and moral collapse. He disappears, returning three days later, depraved and determined to change the order of the entire universe. He is convinced that 'men die and are not happy'. As the Emperor, he has limitless power: he brings in brutal laws and orders Helicon, his former slave, to bring him the moon. His wife, Caesonia, is appalled by his actions, but still loves him. But the senators, observing Caligula's increasingly obvious madness, are conspiring against him. Caligula surprises them at their secret meeting, rapes the wife of one of them and forces another to drink poison. The only one to defy him is the poet Scipio, who is not frightened by Caligula's threats. At a celebration, Caligula appears as Venus, having decided to marry the moon. He forces all his guests to worship him. Helicon has found evidence of conspiracy by the state procurator Chaerea but Caligula destroys the evidence and sets Chaerea free. When Helicon is unable to bring him the moon, Caligula senses his impending death. Suddenly Caligula's death is announced, much to the relief of the senators who have resolved to put an end to the tragedy the Emperor is causing. Then the Emperor reappears—the news was a trick. Caesonia attempts to persuade him to change, and in response he demands her death as the ultimate proof of her love. She consents to be strangled by him. This last act is too much for the senators, who overpower and kill the Emperor.

Cast at world première:

Caligula, Caesar	Ashley Holland (bar.)
Caesonia, Caligula's wife	Michaela Schuster (mez.)
Helicon, Caligula's slave	Martin Wölfel (counterten.)
Cherea, State Procurator	Andreas Hörl (bass)
Scipio, a young patrician	Kristina Wahlin (alto)
Mucius, senator	Alexander Fedin (ten.)
Mereia/Lepidus, Roman nobles	Anthony Sandle/Werner Sindemann (2 bar.)
Livia, Mucius's wife	Katharina Leyhe (sop.)
Four poets	Andrés Felipe Orozco Martinez, David Pichimaler, Robert Z. Milla, Avram Sturz (2 ten., 2 bass)

Dead Man Walking (Jake Heggie, *b* West Palm Beach, Florida, 1961). Comp. 2000; lib. by Terrence McNally, based on the book by Sister Helen Prejean, CSJ; prologue and 2 acts; f.p. San Francisco, 7 October 2000; cond. Patrick Summers; dir. Joe Mantello.

Louisiana in the 1980s: A teenage boy and girl are in their parked car. The De Rocher brothers attack them. Anthony grabs the boy and then shoots him, Joseph rapes the girl and stabs her. Anthony is sentenced to life in prison, Joseph is given the death penalty.

At the mission, Sister Helen tells her colleagues that she has agreed to be spiritual adviser to a prison inmate. At Angola State Prison the prison warden, Father Grenville, tells her that she has bitten off more than she can chew—the man she has agreed to help is remorseless. Warden Benton conducts her to Death Row to meet the prisoner. De Rocher asks her to speak at the board hearing on his behalf. Sister Helen attends the hearing with De Rocher's mother and two younger brothers and pleads with the pardon board. The parents of De Rocher's victims accuse her of not understanding their anguish. The board refuses a pardon. De Rocher is angry with Helen and rejects her suggestion that he confess and ask forgiveness. As she sits in the waiting-room, she hears the voices of the parents, Father Grenville, Warden Benton, and her colleagues, all telling her to stop trying to help De Rocher. De Rocher's execution date is fixed. Helen has nightmares and Sister Rose begs her to stop working with De Rocher. Helen says she cannot. Together they pray for the strength to forgive De Rocher. The night before his execution, Helen visits him. He admits he is frightened. Again she urges him to confess but again he refuses. Mrs. De Rocher and her two younger sons come to visit Joseph, who attempts to apologize, but his mother stops him, preferring to believe he is innocent. She asks Helen to take a last picture of the four of them together. As Joseph is led away his mother, in tears, thanks Helen for all that she has done. Helen goes to speak with the victims' parents. The girl's father, Owen Hart, tells her that he and his wife have separated due to the stress they have felt. He is no longer sure what he wants to happen to his daughter's murderer. Helen and De Rocher meet for the last time. When she again asks him to confess, he breaks down and tells her the entire story. She tells him he will find redemption and that she will be with him when he dies. Guards, inmates, the warden, the parents, the chaplain, and protesters assemble outside the prison and sing the Lord's Prayer. As he prepares for death, Joseph asks forgiveness from the parents of the murdered teenagers. He dies looking at Helen and thanking her for her love.

Cast at world première:

Sister Helen Prejean	Susan Graham (mez.)
Joseph De Rocher, the murderer	John Packard (bar.)
Mrs. Patrick De Rocher, his mother	Frederica von Stade (mez.)
Sister Rose	Theresa Hamm-Smith (sop.)
Boy } the murdered	Sean San Jose
Girl } teenagers	Dawn Walters
Howard Boucher, the boy's father	Gary Rideout (ten.)
Jade Boucher, the boy's mother	Catherine Cook (mez.)
Owen Hart, the girl's father	Robert Orth (bar.)
Kitty Hart, the girl's mother	Nicolle Foland (sop.)
Father Grenville	Jay Hunter Morris (ten.)
Warder George Benton	John Ames (bass)
A Motor Cop/First Prison Guard	David Okerlund (bar.)

Doctor Atomic (John Adams, *b* Worcester, Mass., 1947). Comp. 2004–05; lib. by
Peter Sellars adapted from original sources; 2 acts; f.p. San Francisco, 1 October 2005;
cond. Donald Runnicles; dir. Peter Sellars.

New Mexico, 1945: Germany has surrendered, but the war against Japan continues.
Some of the brightest minds in science are working with Dr J. Robert Oppenheimer to
develop the atom bomb, but many of them are wondering if it is morally right to use it on
the Japanese. General Leslie Groves is the Army commander of the atom bomb project.
Edward Teller finds it difficult to work with other scientists, but he dreams of the success
of this weapon. Teller has had a letter from a Hungarian scientist, Leo Szilard, urging
them all to sign a letter to the US President Truman taking a moral stand, but
Oppenheimer tells them to keep out of politics. A young idealist, Robert Wilson,
organizes a meeting to discuss these moral and social implications. He wants them all to
sign a petition, asking that the Japanese be warned and given the opportunity to
surrender. But Oppenheimer returns from Washington, the decision having been made
to go ahead with the bombing of Japanese cities. Wilson is furious. In their home,
Oppenheimer and his alcoholic wife Kitty discuss the problems of war and love. There is
much pressure on Oppenheimer and Groves to have a successful test of the atom bomb,
so Russia will know the Americans have the bomb. On the night of the test there is a freak
storm and the meteorologist, Frank Hubbard, warns Groves of the dangers of attempting
the test in these conditions. He is supported by the medical officer, Captain James Nolan,
who warns of the dangers of radiation poisoning in the event of an accident. On the night
of 15 July 1945, Kitty Oppenheimer and her maid Pasqualita are at home with the
children. Kitty contemplates the effects of war and death and resurrection. They watch
the rain over the distant mountains. The next night, at the 'Trinity' test site, the bomb is
mounted on its detonating tower and all personnel are cleared from the site. Wilson is at
the top of the tower attaching an instrument and Hubbard is at the bottom measuring
wind velocity. He is anxious that the wind could scatter lethal radioactive material for
miles around. Groves, Oppenheimer and the other scientists are in the observation
bunker, worrying about where this could all end. One of the scientists, Enrico Fermi, has
been taking bets about the outcome. Groves ignores all this and the weather reports and
orders the test launch for 5.30 a.m. The countdown begins, each of them having their
own thoughts: in the house, Kitty waits with the drunken Pasqualita who has visions of
the dead on the march; Oppenheimer, nervous and exhausted, tries to read poetry but
has visions of total destruction and becomes so agitated that Groves fears he will have a
complete nervous breakdown. Suddenly, as the time for the explosion approaches, the
sky clears, warning rockets are fired and a siren sounds. All are still and silent in their
bunkers as the countdown proceeds. Zero minus one. The bomb goes off.

Cast at world première:

Dr J. Robert Oppenheimer, American physicist	Gerald Finley (bar.)
Kitty Oppenheimer, his alcoholic wife	Kristine Jepson (mez.)
Pasqualita, her Pueblo maid	Beth Clayton (cont.)
Gen. Leslie Groves, director of the project	Eric Owens (bass)
Edward Teller, a quantum physicist	Richard Paul Fink (bass)
Robert Wilson, physicist	Thomas Glenn (ten.)
Frank Hubbard, meteorologist	James Maddalena (bar.)
Capt. James Nolan, medical doctor	Jay Hunter Morris (ten.)

End of the Affair (Jake Heggie, *b* West Palm Beach, Florida, 1961). Comp. 2004; lib. by Heather McDonald based on the novel by Graham Greene (which was itself based on an episode in his own life); 2 acts; f.p. Houston 4 March 2004; cond. Patrick Summers; dir. Leonard Foglia.

London during and just after World War II: Sarah Miles, wife of Henry, an important civil servant, and the writer Maurice Bendrix have fallen in love, but he realizes that the affair will end as quickly as it began. He is jealous and frustrated by her refusal to divorce Henry. A bomb blasts Bendrix's flat while he is with Sarah and he nearly dies. She prays that God will save her lover and in return she vows to mend her ways and become a believer. She breaks off the affair with no explanation to Bendrix. Two years later Bendrix is still jealous of Henry, who tells him he suspects Sarah of having a lover. Bendrix engages Parkis, a private detective, to try to discover who this new lover is. It becomes clear that her only secret is her devotion to the Catholic faith and even Parkis has to admire her single-mindedness. Another admirer is the rationalist minister Richard Smythe, who tries to convince Sarah that the God she believes in is a figure of her own making. Bendrix eventually realizes that Sarah made a pact with God when she thought he was dead after the bomb hit his flat. Sarah struggles with her Catholicism, her beliefs slowly increasing. Quite suddenly she develops pneumonia and dies, which totally destroys Bendrix's faith. But he in his turn slowly comes to believe in a God, though not to love him.

Cast at world première:

Sarah Miles	Cheryl Barker (sop.)
Henry Miles, her husband	Peter Coleman-Wright (bar.)
Maurice Bendrix, her lover	Teddy Tahu Rhodes (bar.)
Mr. Parkis, a private detective	Robert Orth (bar.)
Richard Smythe, a rationalist	Joseph Evans (ten.)
Mrs. Bertram, Sarah's mother	Katherine Ciesinski (mez.)
Lancelot, young son	Speaking role

Flight (Jonathan Dove, *b* London, 1959). Comp. 1998; lib. by April de Angelis, based on a real character at a French airport; 3 acts; f.p. Glyndebourne, 24 September 1998; cond. David Parry; dir. Richard Jones.

24 hours in an airport departure lounge. The Controller watches from her tower. The Refugee has no documents, and cannot enter the country legally, so he is unable to leave the airport. The Immigration Officer is looking for the Refugee in order to arrest him. People start to arrive for their flights and get into conversation with each other. The Stewardess and Steward serve the customers, at the same time having a romantic relationship. Bill and Tina are going on holiday to try to rekindle the romance in their rather dull marriage. The Older Woman is on her way to meet a younger man she met on holiday and to whom she is engaged. The highly pregnant Minskwoman and her diplomat husband are emigrating. Their flight is ready, but at the last minute she is afraid to fly, and Minskman leaves without her. She is distressed to be left stranded. The Refugee offers her his magic stone and tries to console her. The Controller makes various announcements which alert the Refugee to the presence of the Immigration Officer, from whom he must hide. The Controller now announces that because of stormy weather, all flights are delayed indefinitely. The passengers attempt to get some sleep. The Refugee talks to them all, giving each of them his supposed magic stone which will cure all ills, and they all make wishes on it. He and the women all drink too much and as they talk they realize that he has fooled them all and they set upon him, knock him unconscious and hide him in a trunk. Bill tries to flirt with the Stewardess, but then goes off with the Steward to look round the control tower. The Controller has left the tower and gone for a walk outside the airport. As dawn breaks the storm clears and a plane lands. It brings back Minskman, who finds himself unable to go without his wife. Tina is angry when she learns of Bill's flirtation. She hits him so much that he loses his memory and greets her as if they have just met. Minskwoman suddenly goes into labour and her baby is born. At the same time, the Refugee awakes from the trunk. The Immigration Officer at last catches up with him. The other characters try, unsuccessfully, to persuade the Officer to 'review the situation'. After The Refugee explains why he has no documentation, the Immigration Officer decides to 'turn a blind eye' and not to arrest him, but he cannot leave the terminal. Having done all they can for him, Minskman and Minskwoman, with their new baby, fly to his new mission. Bill and Tina decide to start afresh and, with the Older Woman, continue to their various departure gates. Only the Refugee and the Flight Controller remain in the terminal.

Cast at world première:

The Flight Controller	Claron McFadden (sop.)
The Refugee	Christopher Robinson (counterten.)
Bill, a passenger	Richard Coxon (ten.)
Tina, his wife	Mary Plazas (sop.)
Older Woman	Nuala Willis (mez.)
Stewardess	Ann Taylor (mez.)
Steward	Garry Magee (bar.)
Minskman	Steven Page (bass-bar.)
Minskwoman	Anne Mason (mez.)
Immigration Officer	Richard Van Allan (bass-bar.)

The Great Gatsby (John Harbison, *b* Orange, NJ, 1938). Comp. 1999; lib. by composer, after the novel by F. Scott Fitzgerald; song lyrics by Murray Horwitz; 2 acts; f.p. Metropolitan Opera, NY, 20 December 1999; cond. James Levine; dir. Mark Lamos.

America, the 1920s: On a visit to Daisy and Tom Buchanan, Nick Carraway meets Jordan Baker. Daisy tells Nick she misses the 'old warm world' of her youth. Tom takes Nick to Wilson's garage to meet George's wife Myrtle. When she talks about Daisy, Tom hits her. At a party given by Jay Gatsby, Gatsby asks Nick to arrange for him to see Daisy. Gatsby later recalls their former love, and swears he will win her back. When they do meet again, there is tension at first, but they quickly relax. Meantime, Nick and Jordan flirt. Gatsby tries to convince Daisy that they can be together again. Tom finds them and invites Gatsby to his house. Daisy and Gatsby leave to go to the Plaza Hotel, much to Tom's annoyance. He later tells Daisy she must make a choice. With great anguish, she decides to stay with Tom who contemptuously suggests that Daisy and Gatsby return together to Long Island. Myrtle Wilson, thinking she has seen Tom outside the house, rushes out to greet him. There is a loud crash: Tom, Nick, and Jordan enter, announcing that Myrtle has been killed. Tom identifies the crashed car as Gatsby's, and Wilson is set on revenge for his wife's death. Gatsby tells Nick that it was Daisy who was driving. But Wilson shoots Gatsby. None of Gatsby's former friends bother to come to his funeral, only Nick and his father.

Cast at world première:

Nick Carraway, a stockbroker	Dwayne Croft (bar.)
Daisy Buchanan, Nick's distant cousin	Dawn Upshaw (sop.)
Tom Buchanan, her husband	Mark Baker (ten.)
Jay Gatsby, Nick's neighbour	Jerry Hadley (ten.)
Jordan Baker, a golfer, Daisy's friend	Susan Graham (mez.)
George Wilson, garage owner	Richard Paul Fink (bass)
Myrtle Wilson, his wife	Lorraine Hunt Lieberson (mez.)
Radio Singer/ Vocalist	Matthew Polenzani (ten.)
Tango Singer	Jennifer Dudley (mez.)
Meyer Wolfshiem, Gatsby's business partner	William Powers (bass-bar.)
Henry Gatz, Jay Gatsby's father	Frederick Burchinal (bar.)
Minister	LeRoy Lehr (bass-bar.)

Little Women (Mark Adamo, *b* Philadelphia, 1962). Comp. 1998; lib. by composer after Louis M. Alcott's novel; 2 acts; f.p. Houston, 13 March 1998; cond. Patrick Summers; dir. Peter Webster.

Set after the American Civil War: In the attic of her childhood home in Concord, Mass., a visit from Laurie, married to her sister Amy, sets Jo on a dreamlike journey through the past.

In that same attic, years earlier, the four March sisters (Meg, Jo, Beth, and Amy) and their friend Laurie are playing. Laurie tells Jo that his tutor, John Brooke, is in love with Meg. Jo cannot believe that Meg would leave home, but when she sees them together in the garden she is upset at their obvious affection for each other. Jo and their wealthy Aunt Cecilia try to dissuade Meg from this marriage, convinced she can do better for herself, but Meg plans to wed the man she loves. The family gathers for the wedding and Meg's parents teach the bride and groom the vows they took at their own wedding. Moved by hearing this, Laurie asks Jo to marry him, but she cannot accept that he loves her and heartbroken he rushes off. Amy follows to console him. Beth collapses in a faint. Jo flees to New York to escape from Laurie and pursue her writing career. She learns in letters from her family that Amy has gone to England where Laurie is studying at Oxford, Beth is very ill, and Meg has twins. In New York Jo has met a German-born professor, Friedrich Bhaer, who takes her to the opera. When they return to her apartment a telegram from home tells Jo that Beth is seriously ill. Jo rushes to the dying Beth's bedside. She later learns from Aunt Cecilia that Amy has married Laurie. Jo is devastated, but Cecilia, believing that wealth will make up for disappointment, makes Jo her heir. Jo retreats to her favourite spot in the attic. The opera ends with Jo back in the attic where she began. She reassures Laurie that they can still be friends, as brother and sister. Left alone remembering the old days, she is brought back to the present by the arrival of an unexpected—but welcome—visitor: Friedrich Bhaer has come to call. *See also* ARTICLE BY JOYCE DIDONATO, p. 347.

Cast at world première:

Jo	}	The	Stephanie Novacek (mez.)
Amy	}	four	Margaret Lloyd (sop.)
Beth	}	March	Stacey Tappan (sop.)
Meg	}	sisters	Joyce DiDonato (mez.)
Alma March, their mother			Gwendolyn Jones (mez.)
Gideon March, her husband			James Maddalena (bar.)
Laurie, Amy's husband-to-be			Chad Shelton (ten.)
John Brooke, in love with Meg			Daniel Belcher (bar.)
Cecilia March, an aunt			Katherine Ciesinski (mez.)
Friedrich Bhaer, friend of Jo			Chen-Ye Yuan (bar.)

MEG   (*Little Women*—Mark Adamo)

by Joyce DiDonato

As the sixth of seven children (the youngest of the five 'Flaherty Girls'), my childhood was replete with quarrels, drama, tears that crushed my heart, and laughter that should have caused permanent lung damage due to its raw, unleashed power! When the Houston Opera Studio announced that we would be premièring Mark Adamo's new opera based on Louisa M. Alcott's novel *Little Women*, I immediately knew that I had the part—after all, *I* was the theatrical one in the family, *I* knew the struggle of the family dynamic and the challenge of letting go, and *I* had walked with my four sisters through thick and thin. There was no question: *I was Jo!*

The casting call came. In fact, I was *not* Jo. I was Meg. 'Oh, great,' I thought: 'the older sister, the pretty one, the *practical one*—NOT the feisty, spirited, rambunctious one—not the passionate rebel. No: *the good girl.*' I could not hide my disappointment in feeling I had lost the role I was born to play, and that my moment to shine in the last season of my training period in Houston was lost. As music trickled in, I looked at *her* music thinking, 'I know how I would play this if I were Jo—what a great character she is!' And I went about the business of dutifully learning Meg's notes, feeling sorry for myself that I wasn't singing the 'other' part.

Then a funny thing began to happen on our journey towards opening night: this group of young artists who had lived through so much together during the years in the Studio, began to grow closer than ever before. Tears began to flow in rehearsal as emotions were laid bare, hairs began to stand up on end as chords were hit perfectly in tune, and we began to enter into this story with all of our efforts. Additional music would trickle in, and it was trying, to say the least—each of us was stretched to our limits and challenged in ways as never before.

As the opening approached, we were struggling still with some of the musical elements ('will the orchestra be finished in time?'); aspects of the staging weren't yet gelling in a convincing way; and tempers began to escalate as the nerves grew more restless. (Late night card sessions seemed to be the remedy of choice for us!) But at the same time, and to my surprise, I was beginning to fall in love with my character—the one that was *not for me*, this 'Meg'. I began to see her as a young woman of immense strength and wisdom, and of real courage for insisting on following her heart. The scene when Meg stands up to her Aunt March's rigid plan for her life, and actually claims ownership of her future, saying she will marry John regardless of what anyone thinks because she loves him, began to take root in me and, before I knew it, I knew that this, in fact, *was* my role.

We were all apprehensive as the curtain rose on our World Première evening—for we still didn't feel 100% secure in the music, or in the vocal challenges asked of us and, perhaps worst of all, we had no idea how the audience would receive our efforts. Premièring a work with no performance history, not to mention no guarantee of success *à la La bohème*, is a truly daunting thing. We all clasped hands and jumped off the proverbial cliff together (secretly thinking that if it was a huge disaster, we'd still meet up for cards afterwards!)

Lights out. (Anxiety) Applause. (Anxiety) Singing. (Anxiety!) And then… laughter. It was spontaneous, sincere laughter, carried generously over the footlights to us on the stage. And then it came again. They were listening! They were laughing! They were GETTING IT! A silent energy began to pass between us all that told us something special was happening—somehow we knew that magic was present. That mystical energy that lifts a performance to the next level can never be planned, can never be rehearsed or forced—it simply arrives unannounced, and sweeps you off your feet. We were swept away that night.

Halfway through Act 1, I stood looking into the tear-filled eyes of Jo (the sublime Stephanie Novacek) and told her, 'Things change, Jo', and in that moment, time stood still. Mark Adamo's stroke of genius in this score was underlining the element of change and the sense of loss that people fear and vainly resist—a perfectly universal trepidation that freezes men and women, young and old. I heard the tears of the audience as they let the impact of those simple words, spun out on the soaring vocal line, touch their heart. It was one of the most powerful moments I've ever had on the stage.

We kept telling our story through the characters' painful realizations of how life marches on: through Beth's hauntingly beautiful death aria, 'Have peace, Jo', to the final quartet of melting harmonies fusing both the unity and separation of the four sisters. We singers *were* four sisters in that moment, but 'one heart', and the audience earnestly took the journey with us every step of the way, letting us bring this new American opera, of the classic American novel, to life. It was indeed a great moment.

The Silver Tassie (Mark-Anthony Turnage, *b* Grays, Essex, 1960). Comp.1997–9; lib. by
Amanda Holden, based on the play by Sean O'Casey; 4 acts; London, 16 February 2000;
cond. Paul Daniel, dir. Bill Bryden.

During World War I, 'somewhere in Britain': In the Heegan home, Harry's parents are
waiting for him to come and collect his kit before returning to the war front. His father
recalls his prowess at sport, his mother is waiting outside, Susie is waiting with them.
From upstairs comes the noise of Mrs Foran being beaten up by her husband. She takes
refuge with the Heegans and her angry husband follows her and they quarrel. Harry
arrives home with his friend Barney and Barney's girlfriend Jessie, who used to go out
with Harry. Harry has scored the winning goal and brings home the trophy—the Silver
Tassie. Harry, Barney and Teddy leave to return to war.

In the trenches The Croucher prophesies doom. A staff officer complains about the
doctors as stretcher-bearers carry the wounded to the Red Cross treatment station. A
Corporal passes round parcels, including a football. The soldiers start to play a game, but
the enemy is advancing and the officer sends them back to battle.

Harry has been wounded. He is back in Britain in hospital, paralysed from the waist
downwards. His neighbour Susie is a nurse. His parents come to visit him, accompanied
by Mrs Foran and Teddy, who has lost his sight. For saving Harry's life, Barney was
awarded the V.C. He and Jessie come to the hospital, but she refuses to come inside to
visit Harry. Released from hospital, Harry, in his wheelchair, is at a football club dance.
He follows Barney and Jessie around the room, deliberately annoying them. Susie dances
with Dr Maxwell, who attends to Harry when he faints. When he recovers, he asks for a
drink in the Silver Tassie. Susie encourages him to sing and play his ukelele. He then
wheels himself out to where Barney and Jessie are making love. He and Barney quarrel
and Harry is thrown from his wheelchair and they fight on the floor. The fight is broken
up by Dr Maxwell and he and Susie lift Harry back into his wheelchair. In sheer
frustration, Harry throws the Tassie to the ground and leaves with his parents and the
blind Teddy.

Cast at world première:

Harry Heegan	Gerald Finley (bar.)
Sylvester, his father	John Graham-Hall (ten.)
Mrs Heegan, Harry's mother	Anne Howells (mez.)
Susie, the girl downstairs	Sarah Connolly (mez.)
Mrs Foran, neighbour	Vivian Tierney (sop.)
Teddy Foran, her husband	David Kempster (bar.)
Barney, Harry's best friend	Leslie John Flanagan (bass-bar.)
Jessie, Harry's girlfriend	Mary Hegarty (sop.)
Dr Maxwell	Mark Le Brocq (ten.)
The Croucher	Gwynne Howell (bass)
Staff Officer	Bardley Daley (ten.)
Corporal	Jozik Koc (bar.)

Sophie's Choice (Nicholas Maw, *b* Grantham, 1935). Comp. 2000–02; lib. by Maw, based on the 1979 novel by William Styron; 4 acts; f.p. London, 7 December 2002; cond. Simon Rattle; dir. Trevor Nunn.

Set in 1947 in America, and in flashbacks to Poland (1938) and Auschwitz-Birkenau concentration camp (1943): In a boarding house, Sophie and Nathan are quarrelling, disturbing Stingo who is writing a novel in the room below. After Nathan storms out, Sophie tells Stingo how she and Nathan first met in a library, where she had fainted and he had cared for her. She told Nathan (a biologist) how she was an immigrant from Poland, where she had been married. Stingo notices a number tattooed on her forearm - she was a prisoner in Auschwitz. Nathan and Stingo become friends. Nathan thinks his Jewish background has influenced his hopes for the future. Sophie tells Stingo how horrified she was when she discovered her father was anti-Semitic and that her husband shared her father's views. They were both shot by the Germans when they invaded Poland.

Back in 1943 Poland, Sophie's friend Wanda tries to persuade her to help the resistance, but she is frightened that if she is caught, her own two young children will suffer. The two friends are arrested and meet on the train to Auschwitz. Wanda tells Sophie to save her children by entering them into the *Lebensborn* programme and having them raised as young Nazis by new parents. Sophie's 8-year-old daughter Eva dies very soon after arrival at the camp. Sophie acts as secretary to the camp Commandant Höss, who tries to attack her sexually, but is interrupted by the Doctor. Höss is being transferred, and Sophie asks him to save her 10-year-old son by putting him in the *Lebensborn* programme. He promises to do so.

In Brooklyn, Sophie tells Stingo she never saw her son again. Nathan arrives and accuses Sophie of being a whore. He becomes violent and demands to know how she saved herself in the camps when so many millions perished. Nathan then disappears. His brother Larry tells Stingo that Nathan is a paranoid schizophrenic and his background story is all fabrication. The landlady at their boarding house, Yetta Zimmerman, has heard from Nathan, who is convinced Stingo and Sophie are having an affair and is set on revenge. Frightened, they leave the house and go to Washington. Stingo wants to marry her and Sophie now tells him the truth about what happened in Auschwitz when she first arrived: she tried to protect both her children, but was forced to choose which one should live and which should die, otherwise they would both be killed. She chose her son to live and her daughter was killed. Stingo loves her, but when he awakens the next morning, she has left and gone to find Nathan. The following day Stingo returns to their boarding house in Brooklyn. Nathan and Sophie have taken cyanide and been found dead together.

Cast at world première:

Narrator	Dale Duesing (bar.)
Stingo, a writer	Gordon Gietz (ten.)
Sophie, ex-Auschwitz prisoner	Angelika Kirchschlager (mez.)
Nathan, her boyfriend	Rodney Gilfry (bar.)
Yetta Zimmerman, their landlady	Frances McCafferty (mez.)
Librarian	Adrian Clarke (bar.)
Zbigniew Bieganski, Sophie's father	Stafford Dean (bass)
Wanda, Sophie's friend	Stephanie Friede (sop.)
Eva } Sophie's	Abigail Browne
Jan } children	Billy Clerkin
Old Woman on train	Gillian Knight (mez.)
Young man on train	Neil Gillespie (bar.)
Rudolph Franz Höss, Camp Commander	Jorma Silvasti (ten.)
Doctor	Alan Opie (bar.)
Bartender	Darren Jeffrey (bass-bar.)
Larry Landau	Quentin Hayes (bar.)

A Streetcar Named Desire (André Previn, *b* Berlin, 1929). Comp.1998; lib. by Philip Littell, based on the play by Tennessee Williams; 3 acts; f.p. San Francisco, 19 September 1998; cond. André Previn; dir. Colin Graham.

New Orleans, after World War II: Blanche Dubois, a teacher, arrives unexpectedly to visit her sister Stella and her husband Stanley Kowalski in their grubby apartment. Blanche is shown in by the upstairs neighbour Eunice. When Stella arrives home, Blanche explains that she has been advised to take time off work for her 'nerves'. She tells Stella that debts have caused her to lose the family home in Laurel, Mississippi, news which upsets Stella. Stanley comes home, bringing his friends—Eunice's husband Steve, and Mitch. There is an immediate attraction between Blanche and Stanley. But Stanley accuses Blanche of cheating him and Stella out of their share of the money from the family home. He ignores her efforts to flirt with him and tells her Stella is pregnant. Blanche expresses her congratulations and the sisters go out together. The men play poker. The sisters return and Blanche now shows an interest in Mitch. She puts on the radio and starts dancing to the music. Stanley, who is drunk, tries to throw the radio out of the window and when Stella intervenes he hits her. The men drag him away, the sisters go upstairs and the other men leave. Stanley calls for Stella and they go to their bedroom.

Some weeks later, Mitch talks about marrying Blanche, who tells how she married when she was 16 and was disgusted when she discovered her husband was a homosexual. He shot himself. A few months later, Stella prepares a party for Blanche's birthday. Stanley has discovered that Blanche was sacked from her teaching job because of her relationship with a 17-year-old pupil. As a 'birthday present', Stanley gives Blanche a ticket back to Laurel. Mitch arrives later that evening, angry with Blanche for deceiving him. She admits she does try to make life look more magical—to make it as she thinks it should be. She confesses her promiscuity and he rejects her. After he leaves, Blanche drinks heavily. Stanley returns from the hospital to find her disorientated and takes her to bed. A few days later, the men are playing cards, and Stella is home with the baby. Blanche has told Stella what happened between her and Stanley. By now Blanche is totally unbalanced and is to be taken to a sanatorium. Stanley tries to comfort Stella and Mitch is upset. Blanche leaves the room with the doctor.

Cast at world première

Blanche Dubois, a teacher	Renée Fleming (sop.)
Stella Kowalski, her sister	Elizabeth Futral (sop.)
Stanley Kowalski, Stella's husband	Rodney Gilfry (bar.)
Harold Mitchell (Mitch), Stanley's friend	Anthony Dean Griffey (ten.)
Eunice Hubbell, a neighbour	Judith Forst (mez.)
Steve Hubbell, her husband	Matthew Lord (ten.)
Pablo Gonzales	Luis Oropeza (silent.)
A Young Collector	Jeffrey Lenz (ten.)
Mexican Woman	Josepha Gayer (mez.)
Doctor	Ray Reinhardt (spoken)
Nurse	Lynne Soffer (spoken)

The Tempest (Thomas Adès, *b* London, 1971). Comp. 2003–04, rev. 2006; lib. by Meredith Oakes after the Shakespeare play; 3 acts; f.p. London, 10 February 2004; cond. Thomas Adès; dir. Tom Cairns.

Miranda is upset that her father Prospero has used magic to whip up a storm which wrecks a ship carrying the Naples Court. Prospero explains that years earlier he was usurped as Duke of Naples by his brother Antonio, helped by the King of Naples (Alonso). Prospero and Miranda were put to sea in a boat. They landed on a small island and survived only because the King's counsellor, the kindly Gonzalo, sent them food and clothing. Prospero sends his daughter to sleep. Caliban, the island's rightful ruler, is being kept from his heritage by Prospero. Caliban lusts after Miranda. Prospero banishes him to his cave. He sends for his spirit Ariel, and orders him to revive the ship's passengers and bring them to the island and bring to him the King's son Ferdinand—he wants to make the King suffer, assuming his son to be drowned. When Miranda awakes, she and Ferdinand fall in love. Prospero is angry with Ferdinand, thinking him unworthy of Miranda. He summons Ariel to help him take revenge on the Naples Court. The King is distressed at the supposed death of his son and Gonzalo tries to console him. Ariel adopts the voice of the King's brother Sebastian and insults the King, starting a furious argument. Ariel's voice is heard, and the courtiers are frightened, thinking there are ghosts on the island. Caliban calms them by describing the good spirits of the island who make him feel he's in paradise. Gonzalo asks everyone to search the island to find Ferdinand. Caliban asks Stefano and Trinculo to help him regain the island for himself. Ferdinand and Miranda again express their love for each other. This breaks Prospero's spell on them.

Stefano and Trinculo approach Prospero, and Caliban can see freedom ahead. The King and his entourage have no food and think they will die. The King disinherits Sebastian and names Gonzalo his heir. Ariel's music lulls everyone to sleep except Antonio and Sebastian, who plot to murder the King and Gonzalo and seize power. Ariel first causes a feast to appear, which they all think is manna from heaven, and then causes the feast to vanish, leaving them miserable. Frightened they will starve to death, the courtiers flee to another part of the island. Prospero is beginning to realize what chaos his magic has caused. He summons Ariel to bless the union of Miranda and Ferdinand, who now discovers that his father is still alive. Ariel feels sorry for the King and Antonio, who are demented with fear. Moved by Ariel's feelings of pity, Prospero decides to be merciful and release him from his service. The King and his courtiers enter, and Alonso is astonished to see Prospero, whom he thought he had killed. He asks forgiveness. Prospero shows him Ferdinand and Miranda, and Alonso is overjoyed that his son is alive and that Naples and Milan are united. The courtiers are delighted to find their prince alive and their ship repaired. Prospero breaks his staff, determined to give up all his magic powers. He pleads with Ariel to stay with him, but the spirit flies away to freedom. They all leave and Caliban is at last alone on his island.

See also ARTICLE BY SIMON KEENLYSIDE, p. 353.

Cast at world première:

Prospero, the rightful Duke of Milan	Simon Keenlyside (bar.)
Miranda, his daughter	Christine Rice (mez.)
Antonio, Prospero's brother	John Daszak (ten.)
Caliban, a deformed and savage slave	Ian Bostridge (ten.)
Ariel, Prospero's airy Spirit	Cyndia Sieden (sop.)
Alonso, King of Naples	Philip Langridge (ten.)
Ferdinand, his son	Toby Spence (ten.)
Sebastian, Alonso's brother	Christopher Maltman (bar.)
Trinculo, a jester	Lawrence Zazzo (counterten.)
Stefano, a drunken butler	Stephen Richardson (bass)
Gonzalo, an old and honest counsellor	Gwynne Howell (bass)

PROSPERO (*The Tempest*—Thomas Adès)

by Simon Keenlyside

Whatever else music theatre is, it occupies the space between the overtly descriptive and literal, and an emotional imaging, an energy, arising from dissonant situations in which people find themselves. What makes music so perfect, is that it so closely resembles life itself: all shadows, no explicit answers, an unreliable plan, a flawed strategy, a dance, a riot.

Tom Adès's *The Tempest* falls within a musical tradition whose roots are bound up in the source material of Shakespeare's plays. To my mind *The Tempest* is wonderfully suited to musical treatment. The play is one long gorgeous exploration of the mind, its feet rarely touching the ground of realism. The endlessly twisting and turning phrases of its metaphor are channelled through a simple story.

It is clear that Tom Adès and his librettist Meredith Oakes chose to do something similar to that which Mozart and Schikaneder had done in *The Magic Flute*, namely to use a relatively plain text as adjunct to the music. Like signposts on a road, these quite simple texts lead us closer to the truth of the matter, where the more complex emotional discussion of the music lies. (Here I hide behind the skirts of Goethe and Beethoven, who both thought much the same thing of *The Magic Flute*.)

Perhaps there is a difference between how Adès's *Tempest* relates to Shakespeare as compared to 19th-century composers who used his plays. Verdi and his librettist Boito were both champions of Shakespeare (and used great tranches of original text in *Falstaff* and *Otello*). The character of Falstaff is, of course, a synthesis of *Henry IV* parts 1 and 2. Nevertheless the drama, tragedy, comedy, and pathos, is all literal and in real time. I feel that in both *Falstaff* and *Otello* there isn't a great deal of character delineation in the orchestral 'discussion' apart from that which supports what is being said on stage by the protagonists.

Tom Adès's music is different. Prospero is more akin to Alban Berg's Wozzeck, in that the character delineations are much more sketchy in the libretto. There isn't the same degree of detail in the verbal depiction as there is with Verdi. Perhaps this is because we are in the 20th/21st centuries, post-Freud and Jung, an age of self-analysis if not introspection and that, as a result of this, orchestral commentary upon the psychological state of the characters is greater than ever it was in 19th-century opera. How fascinating it would be if we could compare a performance of *Hamlet* in the 1830s by the most famous Shakespearean actor of his day, Edmund Kean, with one of his modern counterparts. Would the wonderful introspective investigations by modern actors such as Simon Russell-Beale be anything like the same? Similarly, it is interesting to consider the opera *Hamlet* by Ambroise Thomas, composed in 1868 (not so very far from being contemporary with Kean). Full of melodrama and oratory as it is, nevertheless when I sing it I don't sense, either in the character or the orchestral insinuations underneath, the introspection that I expected to find as a result of my exposure to the play. To me, it is altogether a more declaimed and descriptive piece—or it just may be, as with the great works by Verdi, that the 19th century was a different age, where psychological nuance in the orchestra had yet to develop.

Is Prospero a cruel man? I don't find him so. I don't think I'm being perverse to say that he is not a real man at all. The Four Temperaments, the elements of Earth, Air, Fire, and Water, historically suggest the disparate components fighting to control the make-up of one man. To me, Prospero represents all the elements in one man: undeconstructed, and the cloth unteased-out.

Some of the other characters in *The Tempest* are more obviously representative of one or other element: Ariel—the Air, an untrammelled mind, free to roam to the ends of the Universe and back; Caliban—the Earth, our baser instincts. Prospero himself is like a cracked mirror, looking ever inward, the edges of each shard a different chapter in his life: the Island, Naples, his daughter, brother, Ariel, Caliban, his books etc. —metaphors intended for us all. Prospero is Everyman, if only we have the patience and the wit to notice.

Is Tom Adès's music grateful to sing? It is certainly possible, and serves the drama wonderfully well. The nature of the vocal writing reflects something of the personality of the characters in *The Tempest*. This is most obviously the case with the astonishing music written for Ariel: so arrestingly high and energetic as to be an exquisite miniature painting of the small airborne spirit.

The music for Prospero follows more or less his changing state of mind. In the first half of the opera it is tricky—great angular swipes on the page, awkward leaps in the vocal line, as befits a bitter man (Prospero!) furiously casting around disjointedly, recalling the injustices done to him, railing over his banishment, the usurping of his power, and the loss of his books. In the second half of the opera, Prospero's music becomes progressively more lyrical and easier to sing. Circumstance, fate, his promise to release Ariel, and his daughter's love for another man overwhelm him, ultimately forcing him to break his magic staff and relinquish control on the Island. The music here becomes tender and yearning, uncertain and yet determined, the vocal line simple and hesitant.

Vocally, the arc of the role of Prospero begins with a single word, a dot as it were. One consciousness: one man and his sleeping daughter. The music strains ever upwards, hefting each note laboriously to a great unstable mass of sound and complexity. Time passes and, little by little, the music returns slowly, hesitantly, to that solitary point again—the self, the Ego.

Is he happy at the end? What on earth does that mean? Only an imbecile smiling at the sky is happy all the time. Can Prospero the father be said to be happy as he watches his only child leave his protection and his sphere of influence for ever? There ought to be ten times as many words for happiness as the Eskimos allegedly have for Snow.

No! Acceptance is Prospero's lot at the end of the story. Just as it ought to be at the end of every human life. That was always the deal. Perhaps Shakespeare himself, loosening his miraculous grip on his own wand—the pen—is in this, his last play, alluding to his own mortality?

Appendix 4: Opera Web Links

The internet holds a great deal of information on individual works, composers, and artists, but there are relatively few useful sites for opera in its broadest sense. Of the 'general' opera websites, many are difficult to navigate, are out of date, and have many omissions and inaccuracies. A fair knowledge of the subject is necessary in order to judge which sections are really useful. The web links listed below may be few in number, but do offer some useful information. The major opera magazines give a flavour of what to expect with good samples to whet the appetite. All major opera houses and festivals worldwide have websites. It is usually simpler and more helpful to enter in your search engine the name of a work, an artist, a composer, an opera house, and follow its links to find what you are looking for.

Opera Base is a general opera website, with details for schedules, festivals, opera houses, artists, and cross-references.
www.operabase.com

Opera Glass is quite useful, with access to synopses, librettos, creators, histories, but very many standard repertory operas are not included.
www.opera.stanford.edu

Vocal Images is American based with worldwide listings and reading suggestions.
www.vocalimages.com

Music with Ease is reasonably easy to use and covers many composers (with pictures) and works, but is somewhat arbitrary in content with many omissions—no Britten, no Janáček. Particularly good for synopses.
www.musicwithease.com

Opera magazine is the longest-standing British monthly magazine of high quality, with world-wide cover, articles, information, schedules, reviews of performances, CDs, and books.
www.opera.co.uk

Opera Now includes good articles and information, is British, bimonthly, with world-wide coverage.
www.rhinegold.co.uk

Opera News is the monthly magazine of the NY Metropolitan Opera Guild. Its articles and information are mainly American-based, with some international coverage.
www.metoperafamily.org

Opera lovers forum is a new website organized by people of repute in the opera world. Features, podcasts, reviews, interviews, listings, discussion opportunities. It is too soon to pass judgement on its accuracy and usefulness, but looks promising.
www.operalovers.net